MAKE it WORK!

ELECTRICITY

Wendy Baker & Andrew Haslam

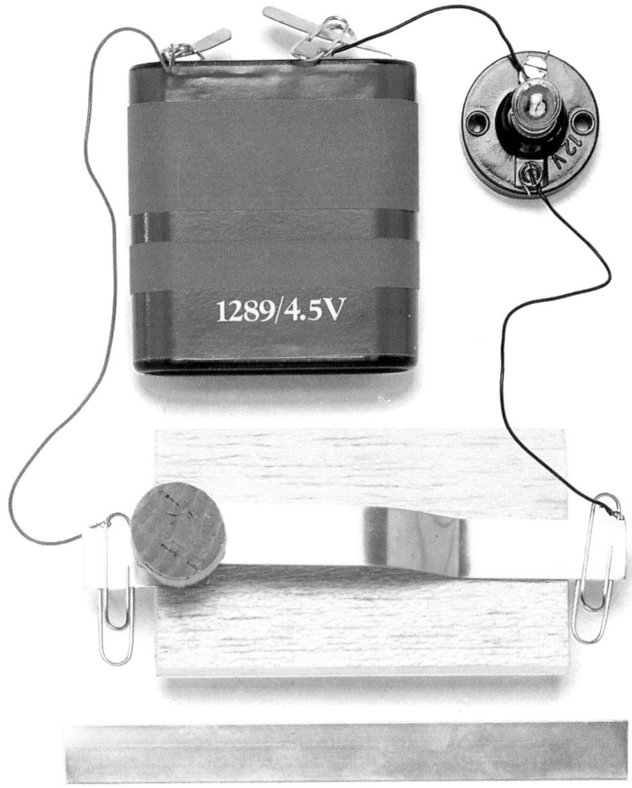

written by
Alexandra Parsons

Photography: Jon Barnes
Series Consultant: John Chaldecott
Science Consultant: Graham Peacock
Lecturer in Science Education at
Sheffield City Polytechnic

Scholastic Canada Ltd.,
123 Newkirk Road, Richmond Hill, Ontario, Canada L4C 3G5

MAKE it WORK!
Other titles

Earth
Sound
Insects
Plants
Machines
Building
Body

Published in Canada in 1994 by
Scholastic Canada Ltd.,
123 Newkirk Road, Richmond Hill, Ontario, Canada L4C 3G5

First published in Great Britain in 1992 by
Two-Can Publishing Ltd
346 Old Street
London EC1V 9NQ

Printed in Hong Kong

2 4 6 8 10 9 7 5 3 1

Canadian Cataloguing in Publication Data

Baker, Wendy
    Electricity

(Make it work!)
Includes index.
ISBN 0-590-74521-2 (bound) ISBN 590-24404-3 (pbk.)

1. Electricity – Juvenile literature.
2. Electricity – Experiments – Juvenile literature.
I. Haslam, Andrew. II. Parsons, Alexandra.
III. Barnes, Jon. IV. Title. V. Series.

QC527.2.B34 1992 j537 C92-094883-9

Editor: Mike Hirst
Illustrators: Diana Leadbetter and Michael Ogden
Additional design: Belinda Webster

Additional thanks to: Albert Baker, Catherine Bee, Tony Ellis,
Elaine Gardner, Nick Hawkins, Claudia Sebire and everyone at Plough Studios

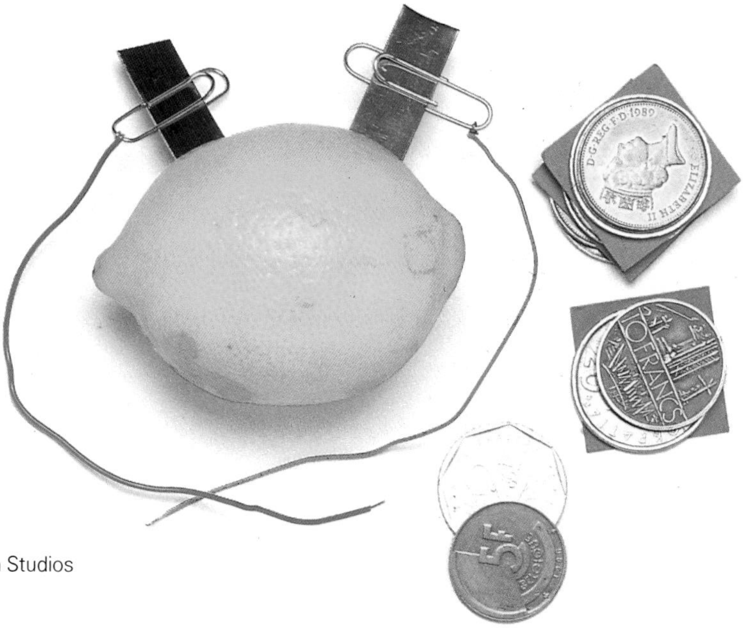

Contents

Be Careful! Electricity can be very dangerous. All the activities in this book use batteries as the power source. You should **never** experiment with any electricity, plugs, or sockets in your home.

Words marked in **bold** are explained in the glossary.

Being a Scientist

Scientists study the world around them and the way it works. They ask themselves questions and then work out systematic methods for answering those questions. Scientists usually start out with a **theory,** which they test by doing **experiments**. Then they observe and record the results.

Investigating electricity is part of the science of **physics**. Physicists study **energy** and **matter**, and find out how to put the forces of nature to work on our behalf. For instance, physicists discovered how to make **hydroelectricity** and **atomic** power.

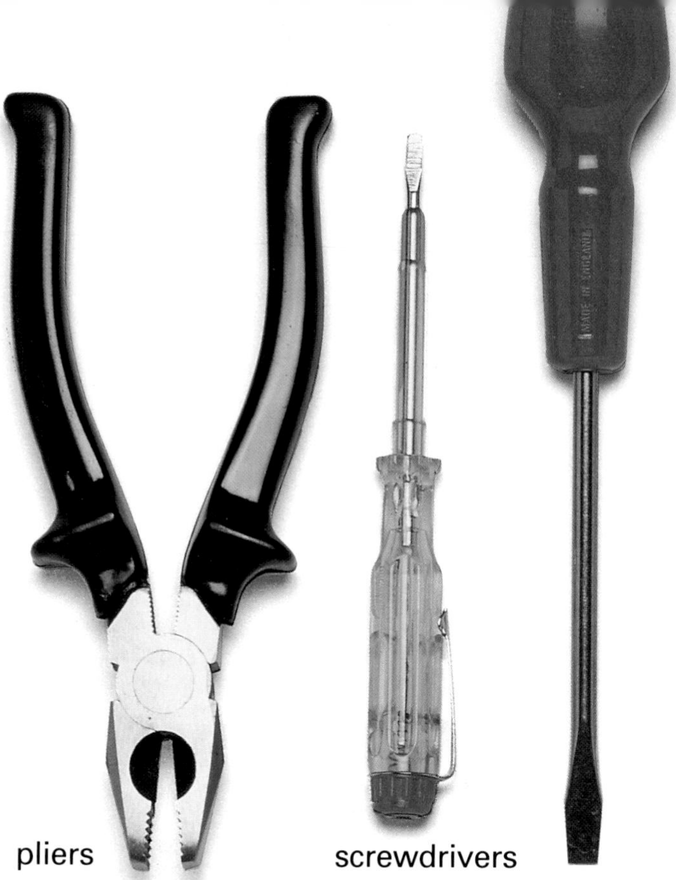

pliers

screwdrivers

MAKE it WORK!

This book is all about electricity. As you do the projects, you will be investigating the science of physics for yourself. It is important to use scientific methods. Draw pictures as accurately as you can, or take photographs. Write down clearly what you have done and observed.

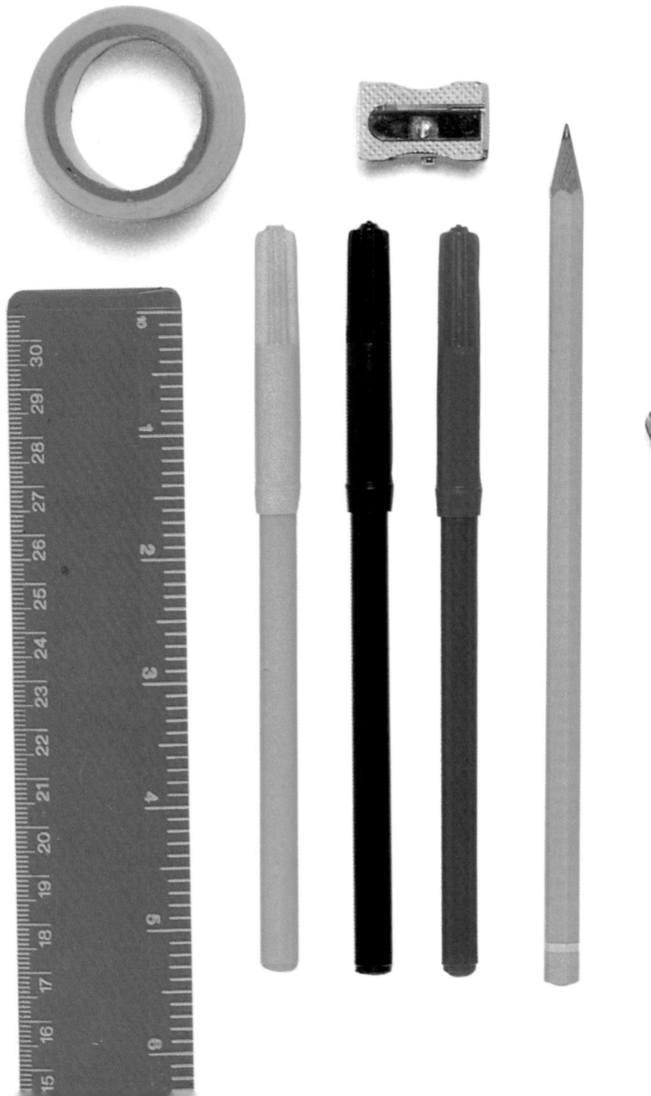

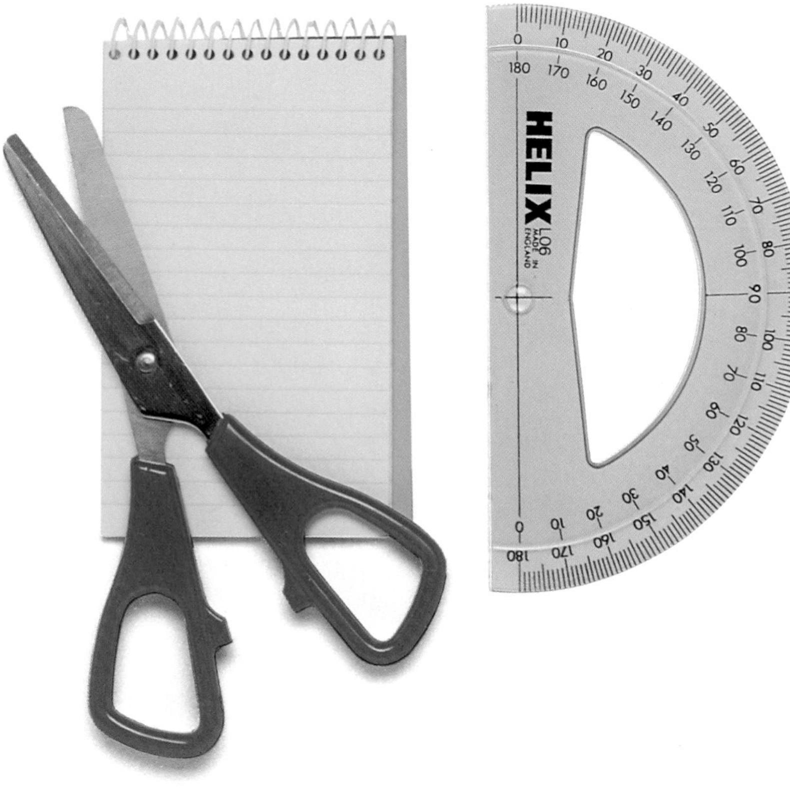

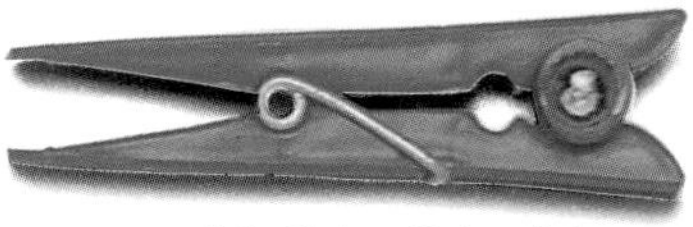
peg and foil bulbholder

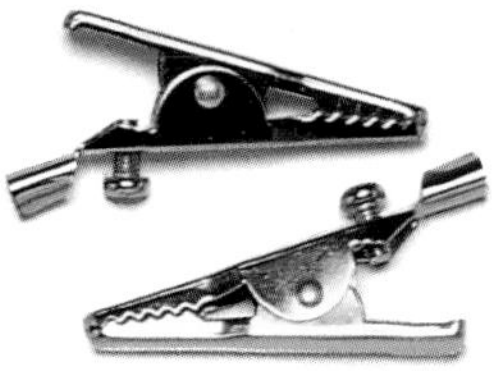

LED bulb

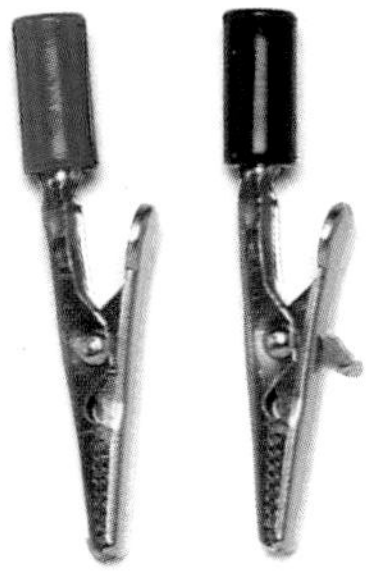

small bulbs

crocodile clips

bulbholders

You will need
Notebooks, pens, and pencils, tape, ruler, scissors and a protractor. Specialist equipment needed for the projects can be bought from any electrical goods or hobby shop.

Wire cutters and **pliers** Special wire cutters are best. You can use an old pair of scissors, but the wire will make them blunt.

Screwdrivers You will need a small, insulated electrical screwdriver and a larger one for screwing pieces of wood together.

horseshoe magnet

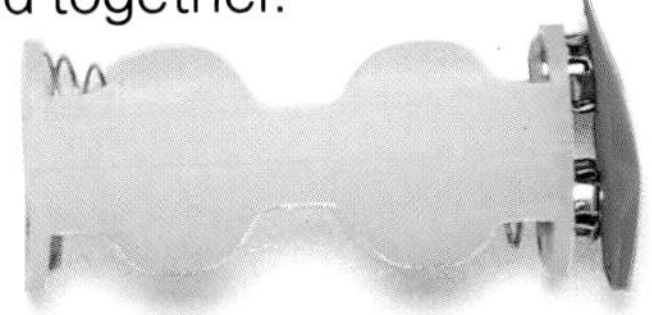
battery holder

crocodile clips

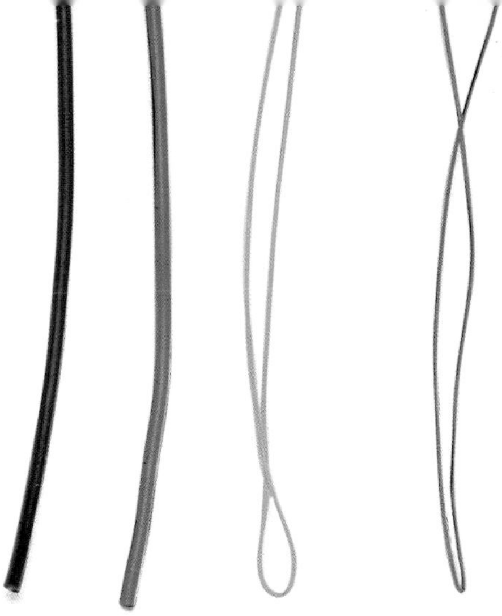
single coil wire

paper fasteners

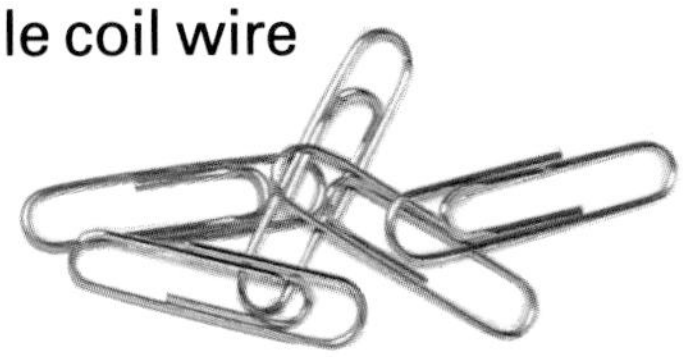
paper clips

electric motors

Bulbs and bulbholders Use 6-volt bulbs and matching bulbholders. A square of aluminum foil held in place by a peg makes a good substitute bulbholder.

Wire Use single-core, plastic-coated wire.

Clips Buy crocodile clips for connecting wires to one another or to batteries. You can also use ordinary paper clips or paper fasterers.

Small electric motors These come from hobby shops in a variety of shapes and sizes. Use 3-volt or 6-volt motors.

Buzzers and **magnets** These are sold in model shops and hardware stores.

Batteries Most of the activities in this book use simple 6-volt or 4.5-volt flat batteries.
Be careful! Never touch car batteries and never plug anything into the sockets in your home. Electric circuits and large batteries are extremely dangerous!

6 Static Electricity

Have you ever noticed that when you brush your hair, it sometimes sticks to the comb? That happens because of **static elecricity**.

Every single thing is made up of tiny particles called **atoms**. Normally atoms have no electrical activity, but when two things rub together, like hair and a comb, the outer layer of **electrons** on the atoms of the hair are rubbed off. They stick to the atoms on the comb. When atoms lose electrons we say they become positively charged. When they gain electrons they are negatively charged. Two like charges repel one another – and different charges attract.

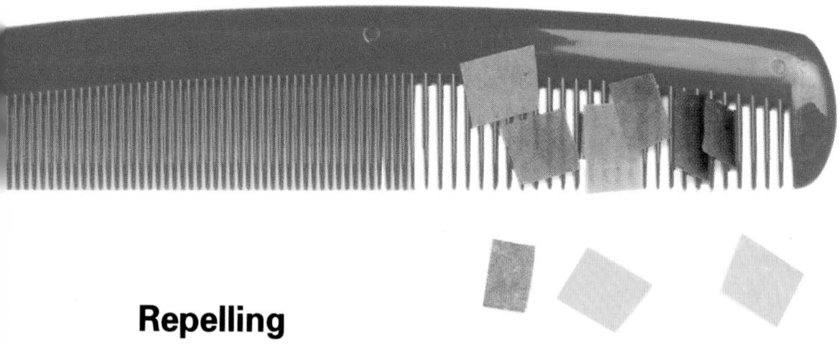

Repelling

Rub a balloon against your clothes and ask a friend to rub one too. Tie the balloons to a stick, with the rubbed sides facing each other. Because both balloons have the same charge, they swing away from one another.

MAKE it WORK!

With an **electroscope** you can measure the strength of static electricity.

You will need

bare wire
aluminum foil
a glass jar with a plastic lid
foil from a candy wrapper
a plastic pen or ruler

Ask an adult to help you push a piece of wire through the lid of a jam jar. Bend up one end and drape a thin piece of foil from a candy wrapper over it. Crumple a ball of aluminum foil around the other end. Rub a plastic pen with a piece of silk or wool, and then hold it over the foil ball. If the pen is charged, then the candy wrapper will move.

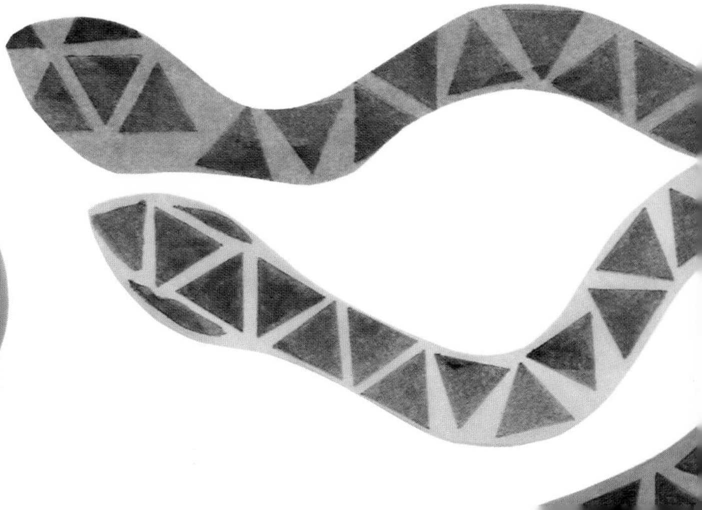

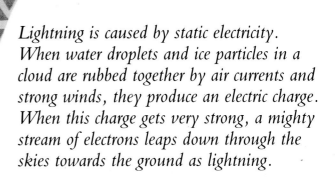

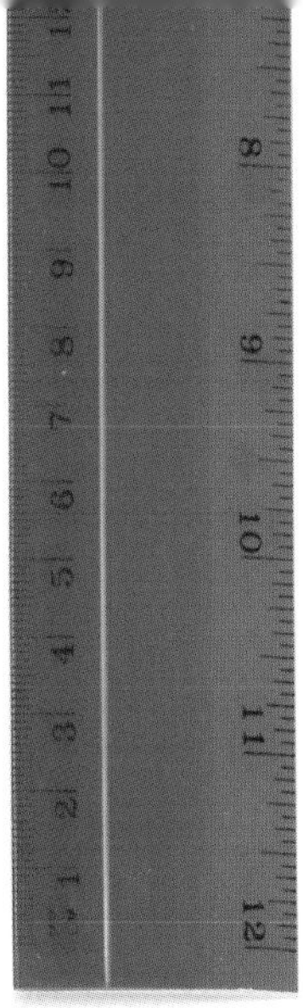

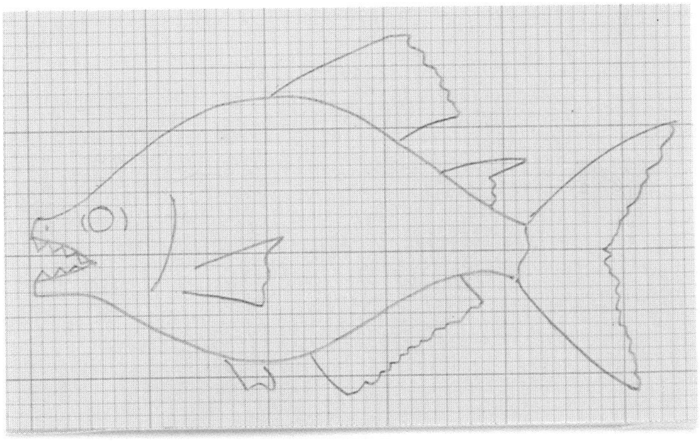

Attracting

Make some piranha fish like the ones above. Using the graph paper shape as a guide, cut out the fish from a single layer of coloured tissue paper. Place them on a flat surface. Rub a plastic ruler on a piece of silk or wool to get the ruler's electrons moving. Now pass the ruler over the fish and watch them jump up, attracted by the electric charge.

▼ Make some curly tissue-paper snakes and decorate them using stencils or felt-tip pens. (Be careful because tissue paper tears easily.) Pass a charged ruler over them – and watch them wiggle and wriggle!

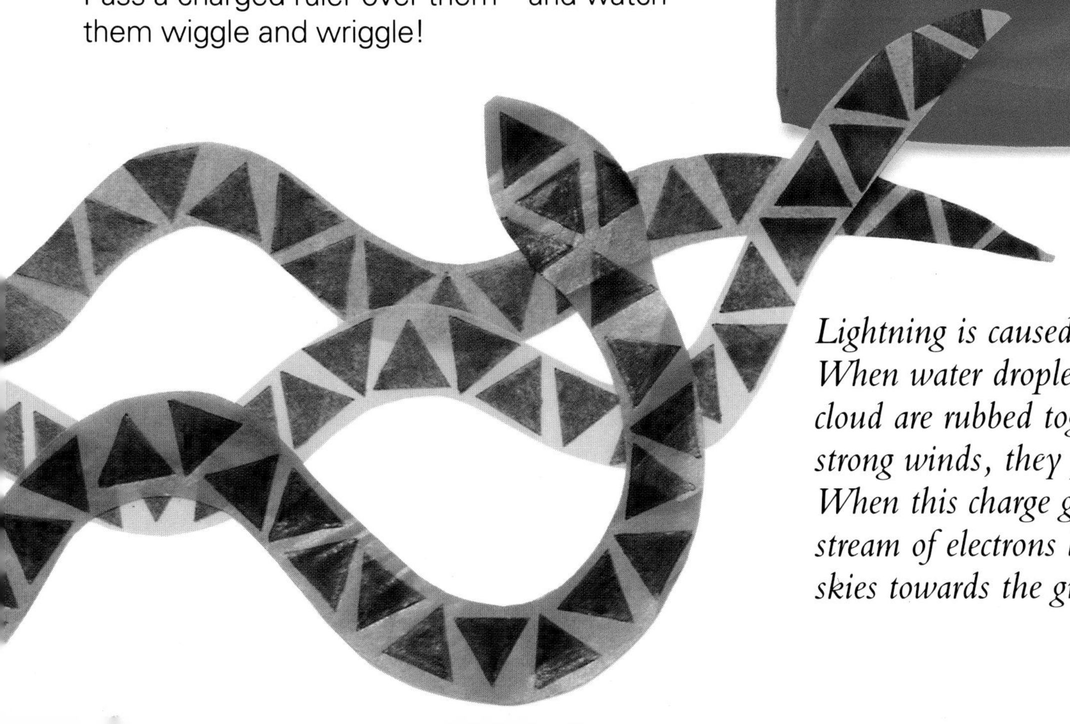

Lightning is caused by static electricity. When water droplets and ice particles in a cloud are rubbed together by air currents and strong winds, they produce an electric charge. When this charge gets very strong, a mighty stream of electrons leaps down through the skies towards the ground as lightning.

8 Simple Circuits

Static electricity itself is not very useful to us – we have to harness electricity before it can be used. The power that we actually use in our homes is called **current electricity** and is made up of millions of moving electrons.

An electric current is formed when the electrons in a substance, such as a piece of wire, are all made to move in the same direction. To provide us with electrical energy, the electrons must flow in an uninterrupted loop, called an electrical **circuit**.

battery

▲ All the projects and activities in this book use batteries as the source of power.

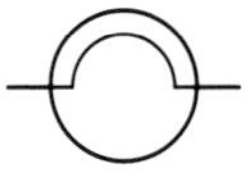

bulbs

bulbholder

▲ Scientists and electrical engineers use special symbols when they are drawing or designing a circuit. This symbol is a bulb inside a bulbholder. A drawing of a whole circuit is called a circuit diagram.

MAKE it WORK!

Try making a simple circuit for yourself. It is very easy, but you must check carefully that all your connections are properly made.

You will need

a battery
wire
a bulb and bulbholder
paper clips/crocodile clips
a collection of household objects

1 Cut two pieces of wire about 15cm long. Remove the plastic coating from the ends of the wire, without breaking the wire itself.

2 Attach one piece of wire under each of the connecting screws on your bulbholder.

3 Attach the other ends of the wires to the battery **terminals**. If all your connections are made properly, the bulb should light.

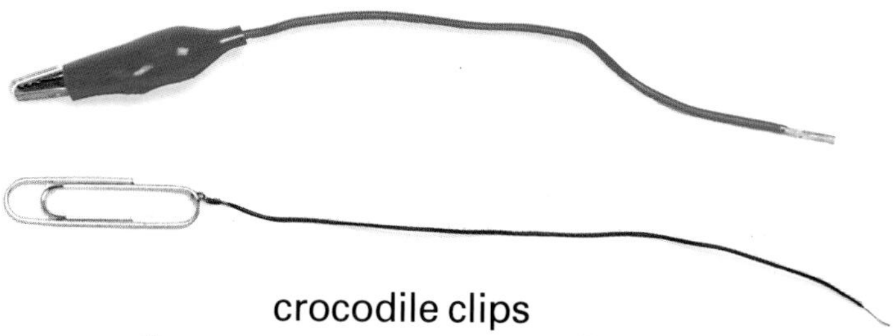

crocodile clips

Anything that electricity can flow through, such as metal, is called a ***conductor****. Materials such as plastic, rubber and glass that do not allow electricity to pass through them are called* ***insulators****. Electrical circuits make use of both conductors and insulators. The conductors, in this case the metal in the wires, allow the current to flow around the circuit. The insulators, such as the plastic around the wires and on bulbholders, stop the current from passing into any metal objects that the circuit is touching.*

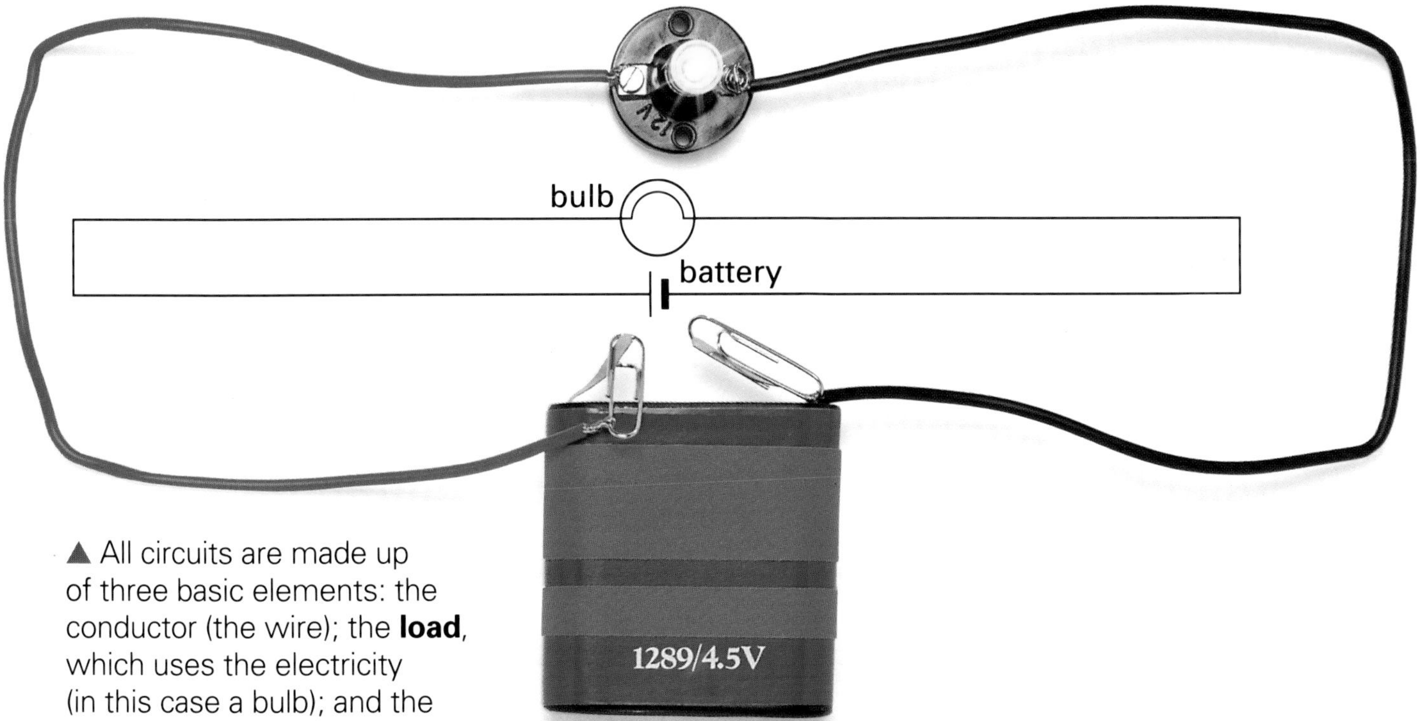

▲ All circuits are made up of three basic elements: the conductor (the wire); the **load**, which uses the electricity (in this case a bulb); and the energy source (the battery).

Conductor test

Test some household objects to see if they are conductors or insulators. Make a simple circuit with a gap in it, like the one below. Touch an object with both wires. If the bulb lights up, you know that electricity must be passing through in order to complete the circuit, so the object must be a conductor.

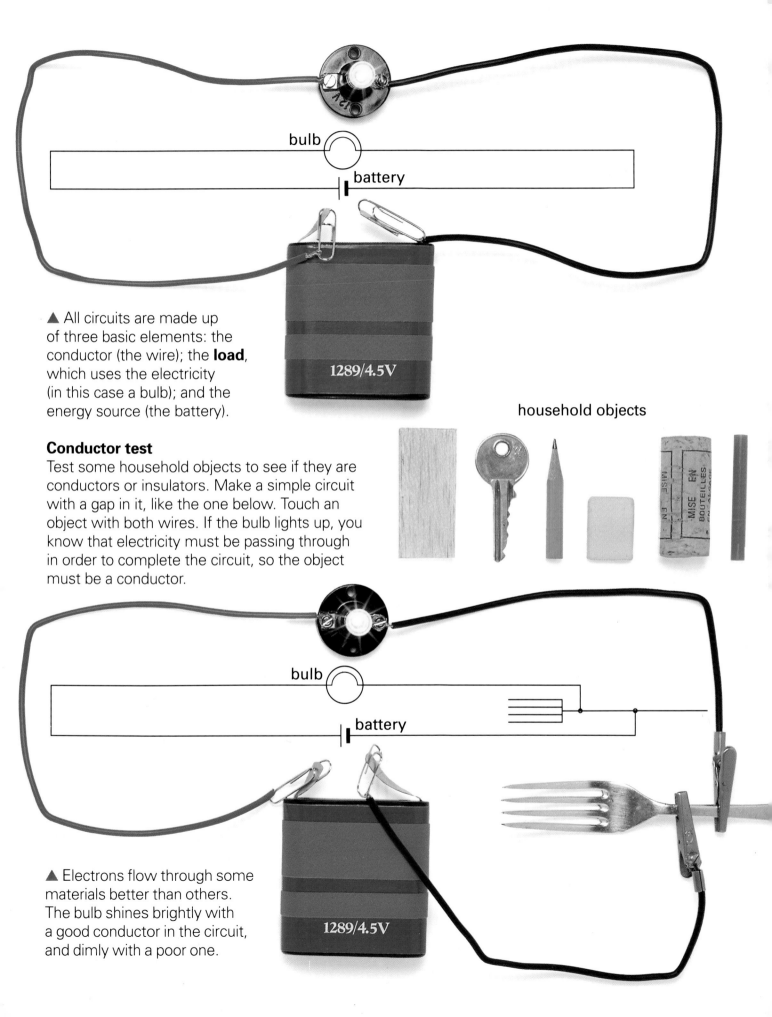

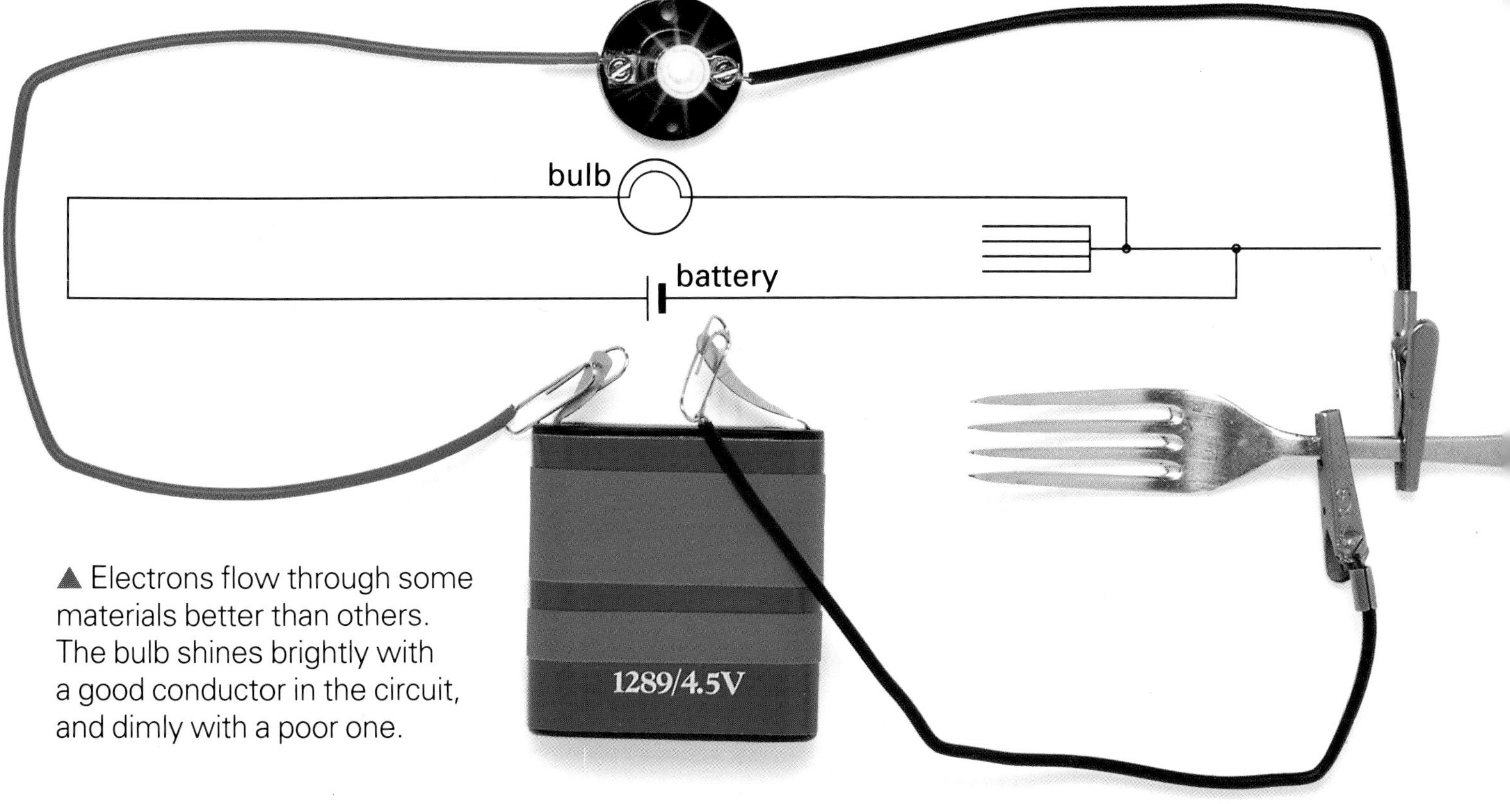

▲ Electrons flow through some materials better than others. The bulb shines brightly with a good conductor in the circuit, and dimly with a poor one.

10 Batteries

Batteries produce electricity from chemical energy. Usually, two metals, called electrodes, are placed in an **acid** solution called an **electrolyte**. A chemical reaction takes place and creates electric power.

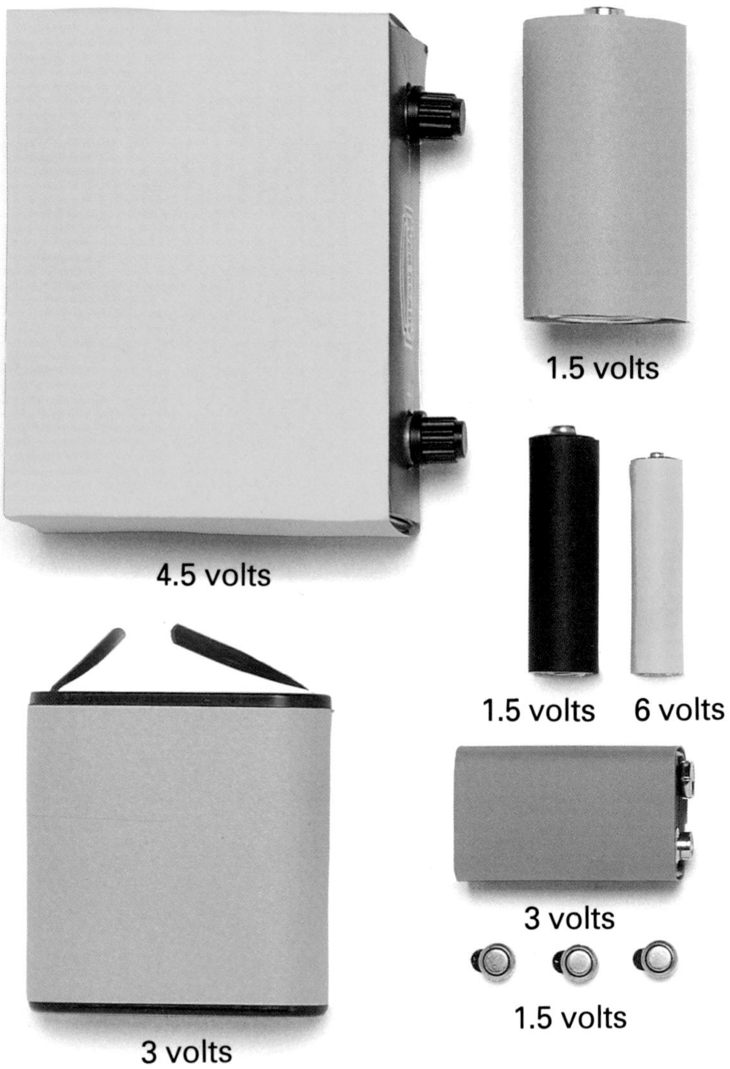

Positive and negative

An electric current needs a destination in order to keep it moving. In a battery, two metals, zinc and copper, are used to make a current. When they are put into acid, negative electrons move from the copper to the zinc through the liquid. From the zinc, they move back down the wire to the copper, causing an electric flow.

MAKE it WORK!

There are many different kinds of battery. Wet batteries have metal plates in a liquid acid. In dry batteries, a chemical paste separates a carbon rod from the zinc case. Other batteries contain the metals nickel and cadmium, and an **alkaline** substance instead of an acid.

To make a wet battery you will need

a glass jar
wire
a strip of zinc
a light emitting diode (LED)
white vinegar
crocodile clips/paper clips
a piece of copper pipe

1 Put the strips of metal in the jar and fill it with vinegar. (Vinegar is a kind of acid.)

2 Attach clips and wires as shown, and the bulb will light up. However, LEDs only work when wired up the right way round. If yours doesn't light first time, reverse the connections.

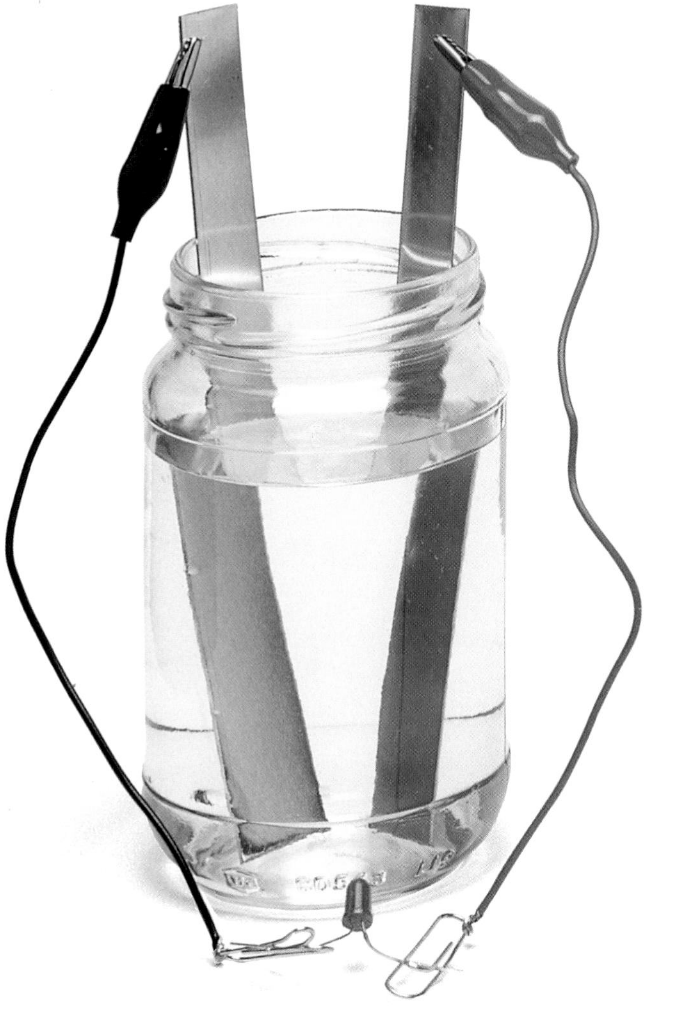

The first battery was invented by an Italian count, Alessandro Volta, in the 1790s. It used silver and zinc discs, rather like our coin battery.

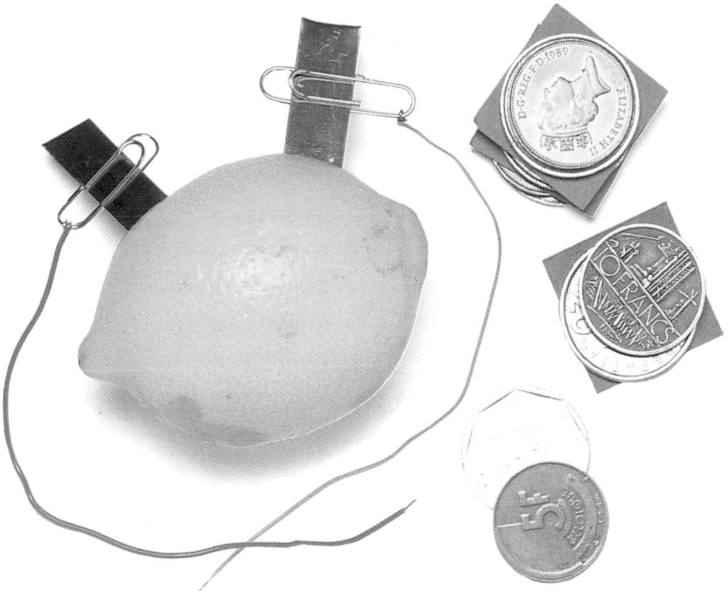

To make a battery tester you will need

balsa wood	card
insulated copper wire	a compass
screws and washers	wire and clips

1 Wrap the compass and the backing card in copper wire, attaching the ends to screws on the wooden base as shown.

2 To test a battery, clip wires from the battery terminals to the screws. The compass needle will move. Try this experiment with a brand new battery and a battery that has been used a lot. Can you notice a difference?

▲ **Mini-batteries** You can make a coin battery using silver and copper coins. Pair up the coins, and separate each pair with a square of blotting paper soaked in salty water. Attach a wire to the bottom coin of the pile, and a wire to the top coin. Don't let the wires touch each other, but clip them to your battery tester and see what happens. The current won't be very strong, but the tester should make some reaction.

You can also make a low-voltage mini-battery by pushing copper and zinc strips into a lemon.

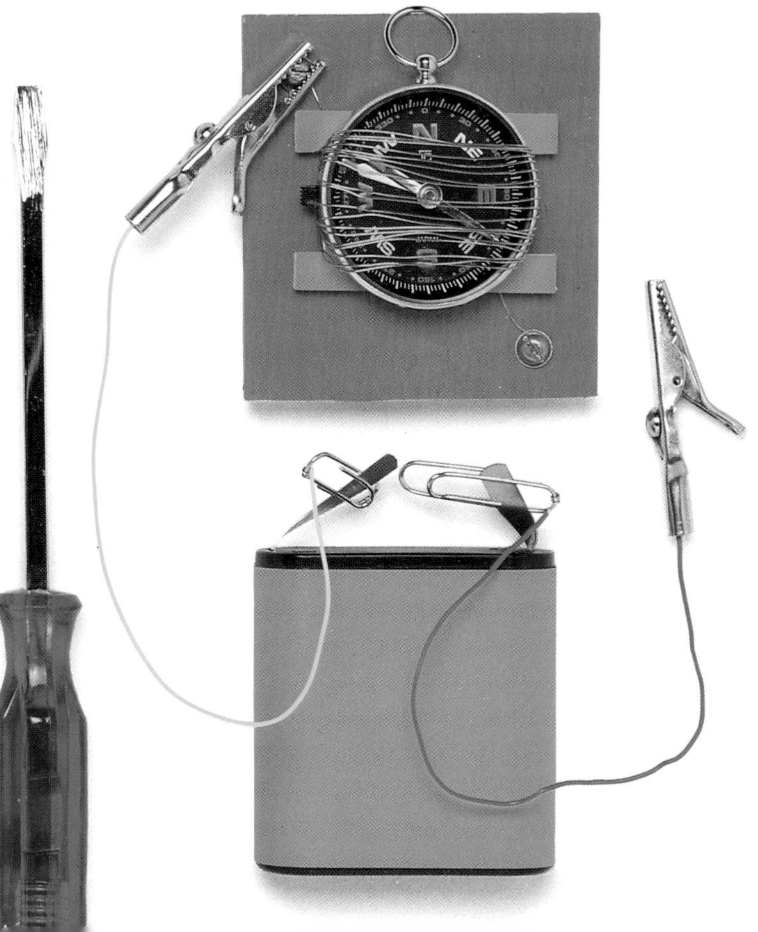

12 Lighthouse

Electricity has many uses – in homes, factories and schools. It is produced in power stations by burning coal or oil fuels to power electricity **generators**. It can also be produced from nuclear fuel or in hydroelectric turbines.

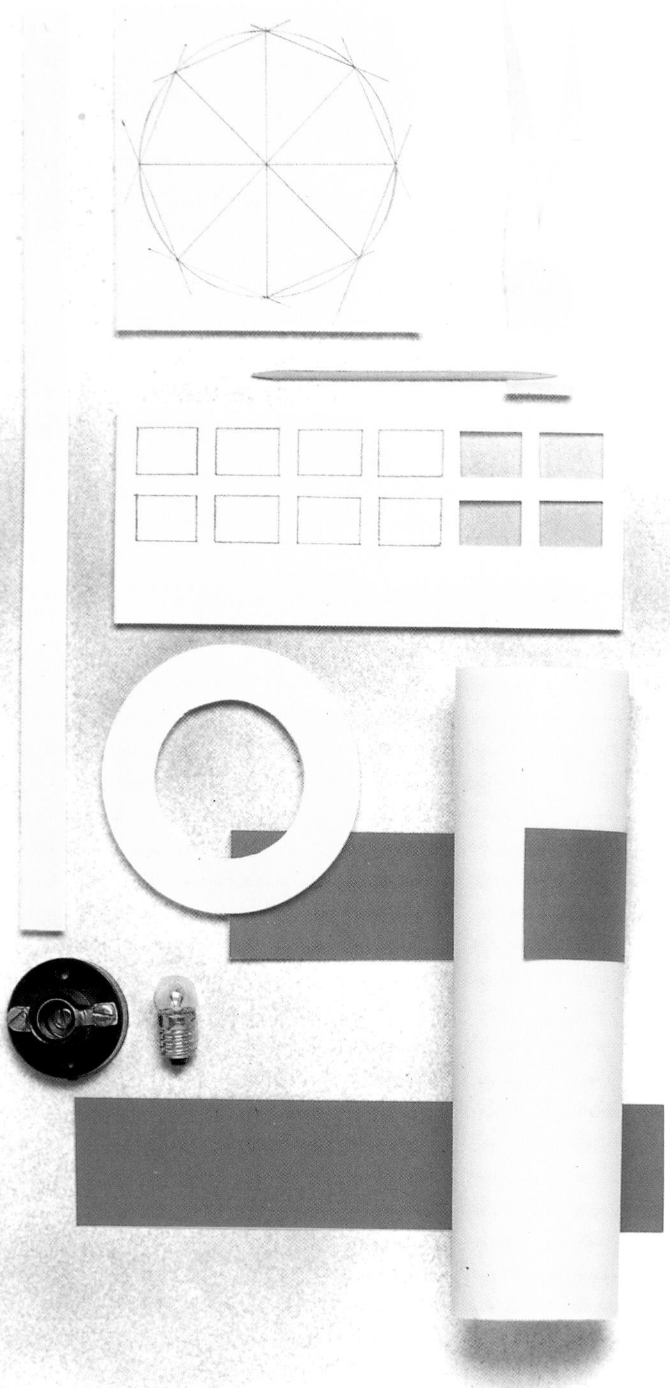

MAKE it WORK!

Lighthouses were among the first users of electric power. Put your circuit-building know-how to good use and make a battery-operated mini-lighthouse for your bedroom.

You will need

thin card
a craft knife/scissors
a bulb and bulbholder
crocodile clips/paper clips
glue and sticky tape
wire
a battery

1 Make a round tube from a piece of white card and decorate it with red stripes. You could also use the cardboard tube from a toilet roll and cover it with white paper.

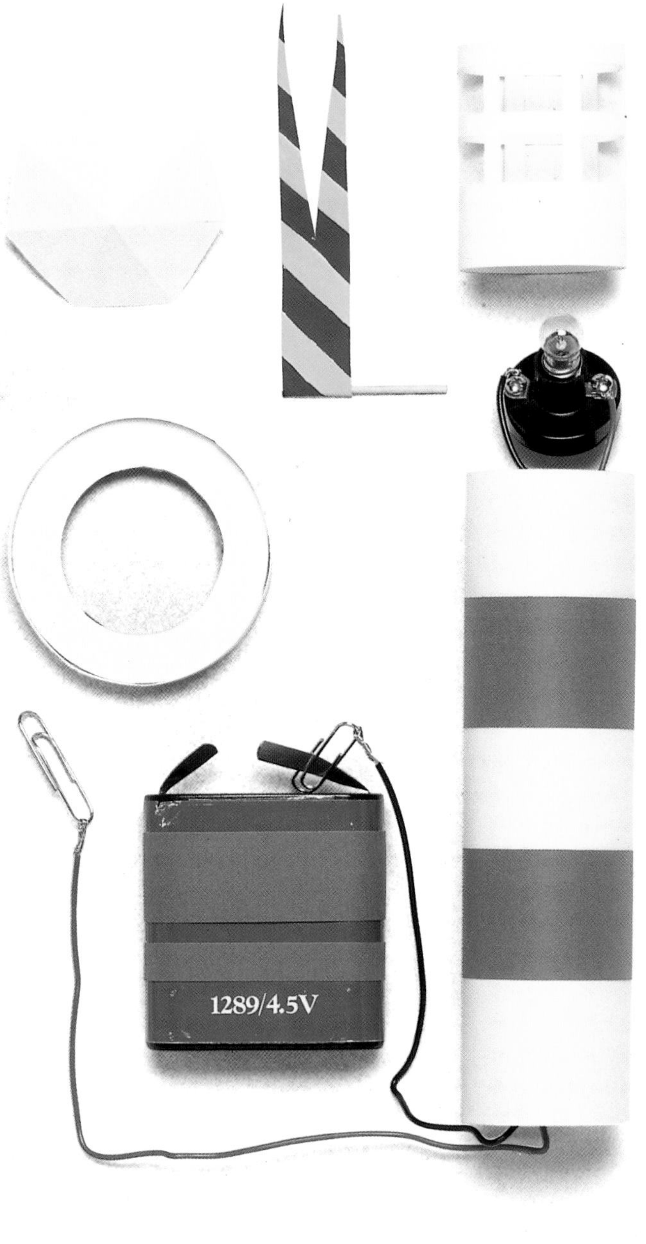

2 Cut out a circle of card for the balcony, make a hole in the centre, and glue or tape it to the top of the tube. Glue a strip of card around the edge of the balcony to make the rail.

3 Attach two long wires to a bulbholder and tape the bulbholder into place at the top of the tube. Push the wires down through the tube and out at the bottom.

4 Take a strip of card to make the windows at the top of the lighthouse. Cut out small squares with a craft knife or scissors, using the picture on the left as a guide. Then bend the card round to make a cylinder shape and glue it in position on the balcony.

5 To make the roof, draw a circle. Make two cuts close together from the rim to the centre and cut out a small segment. Fold and glue the circle to form a cone. Make a flag from paper and a cocktail stick.

6 Attach the ends of the wires to a battery and the bulb in your lighthouse will light up.

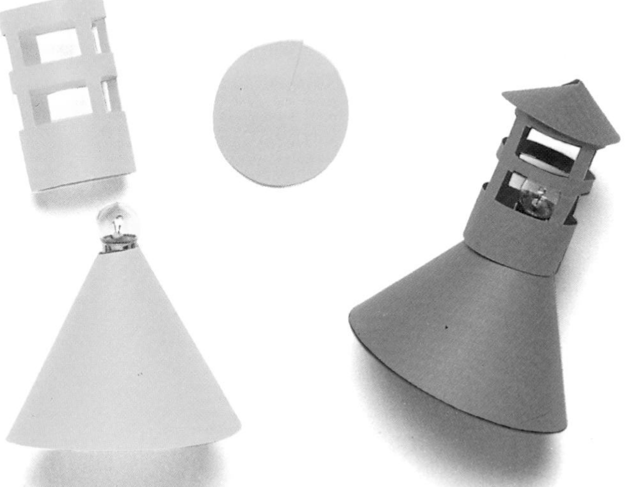

The first people to build lighthouses were probably the Ancient Egyptians. They began by lighting bonfires on hilltops to guide their ships. During the third century BC, *they built the tallest ever lighthouse, the Pharos of Alexandria, which was over 122 m (400 ft) high.*

Scientists measure electricity with two separate units called volts and watts. Volts measure electrical force, the amount of power produced by a source of electricity, such as a battery. Watts measure the electrical power at the point where it is actually used – in an electric fire or bulb, for instance.

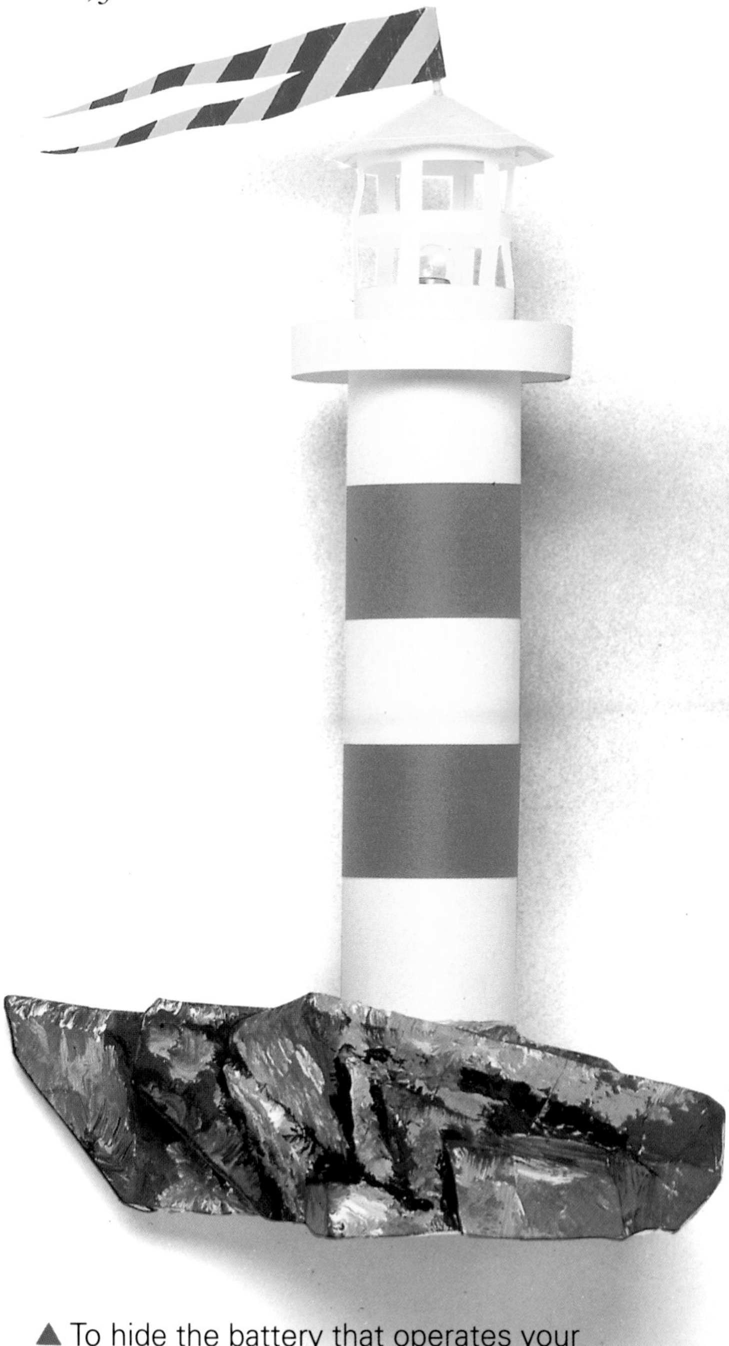

▲ To hide the battery that operates your lighthouse, make a 'rock' out of pieces of old cardboard, stuck together in a jagged shape and painted. Around the lighthouse, put a series of buoys like those on the next page.

14 Complex Circuits

In an electrical circuit, all the parts must be joined up to one another, so that the current can flow. There are basically two ways of wiring a circuit with more than one **component** (or part) – in series or in parallel.

MAKE it WORK!

In a series circuit, the electric current flows along a single path, going through each of the components in turn. If one component is removed, or breaks (when the filament in a bulb burns out, for instance), all the other components will stop working too.

In a parallel circuit, each of the components is connected to the battery on its own branch of the main circuit. Even if one of the bulbs in a parallel circuit burns out, the other bulbs will continue to shine, because their own branches of the circuit remain complete.

You will need

card or thick paper
wire
batteries
crocodile clips/paper clips
scissors/a craft knife
glue and sticky tape
bulbs and bulbholders

1 You are going to make a string of buoys like the ones used to mark out shipping lanes. For each buoy you will need to cut out the shapes you see below from thin card: a semicircle for the body, a strip with windows for the lantern and a circle with a slit in it for the cone-shaped top. Use a craft knife to cut out the windows.

2 Assemble the buoys as shown below, fitting a bulbholder firmly into the body of each buoy with sticky tape.

3 Wire up the series circuit as shown on the left-hand side of the opposite page. Take a wire from bulbholder to bulbholder, completing the circuit from the last buoy back to the battery. You could put a switch in this section if you wish to.

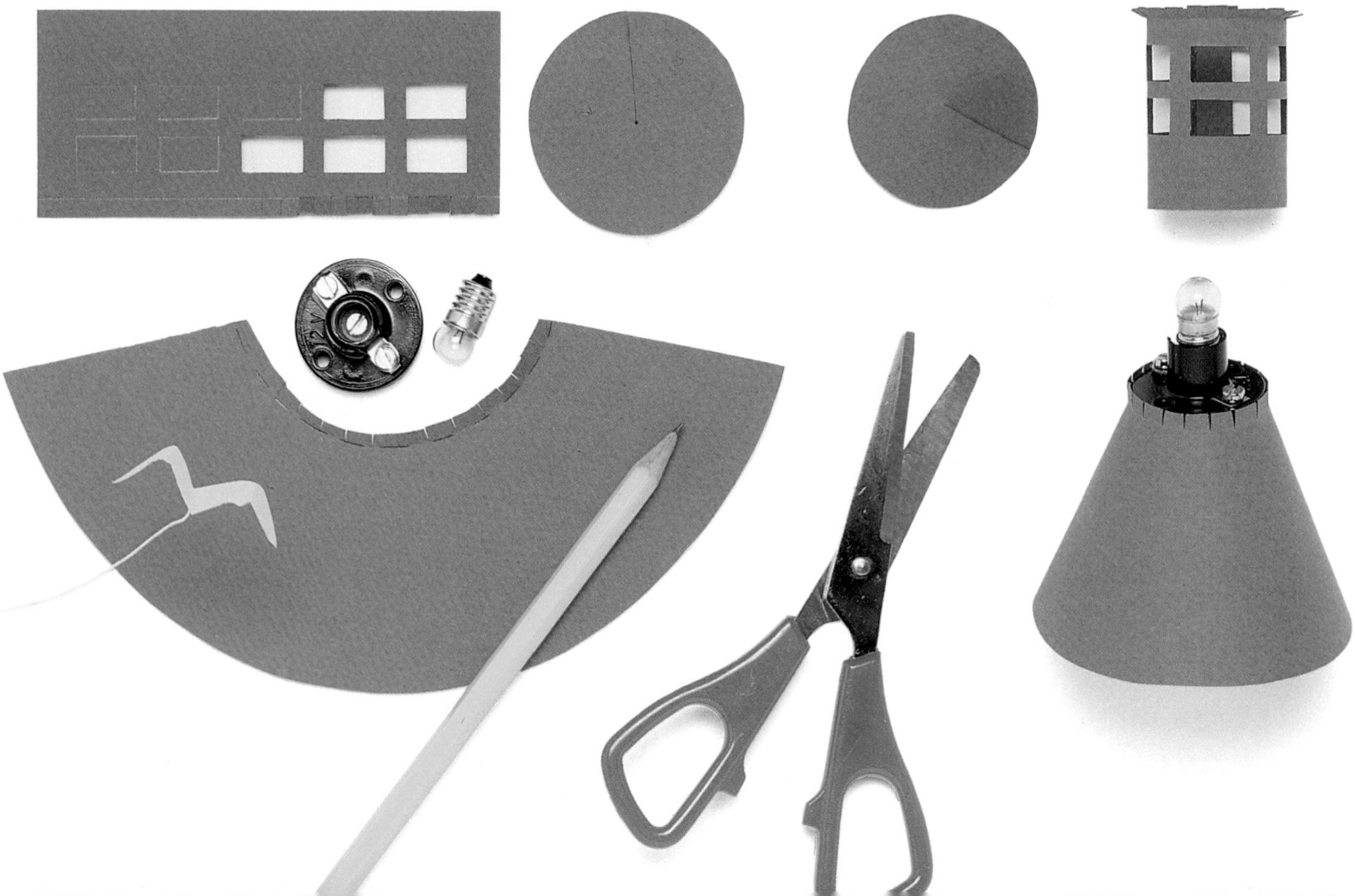

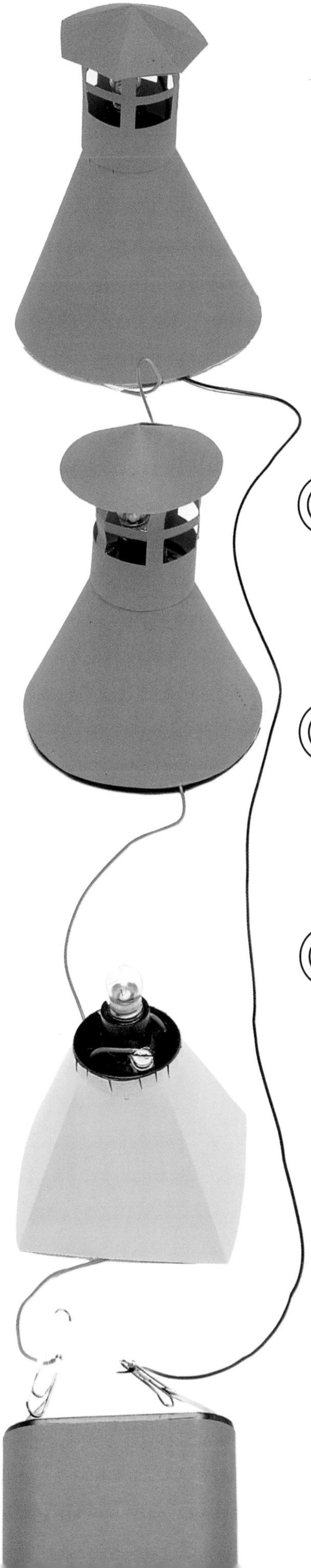

4 Wire up the parallel circuit as shown below on the right. Take two wires, one from each battery terminal, to the two terminals on the first bulbholder. Then connect that bulbholder to the next one with two more wires. Add any other bulbholders to the circuit in the same way.

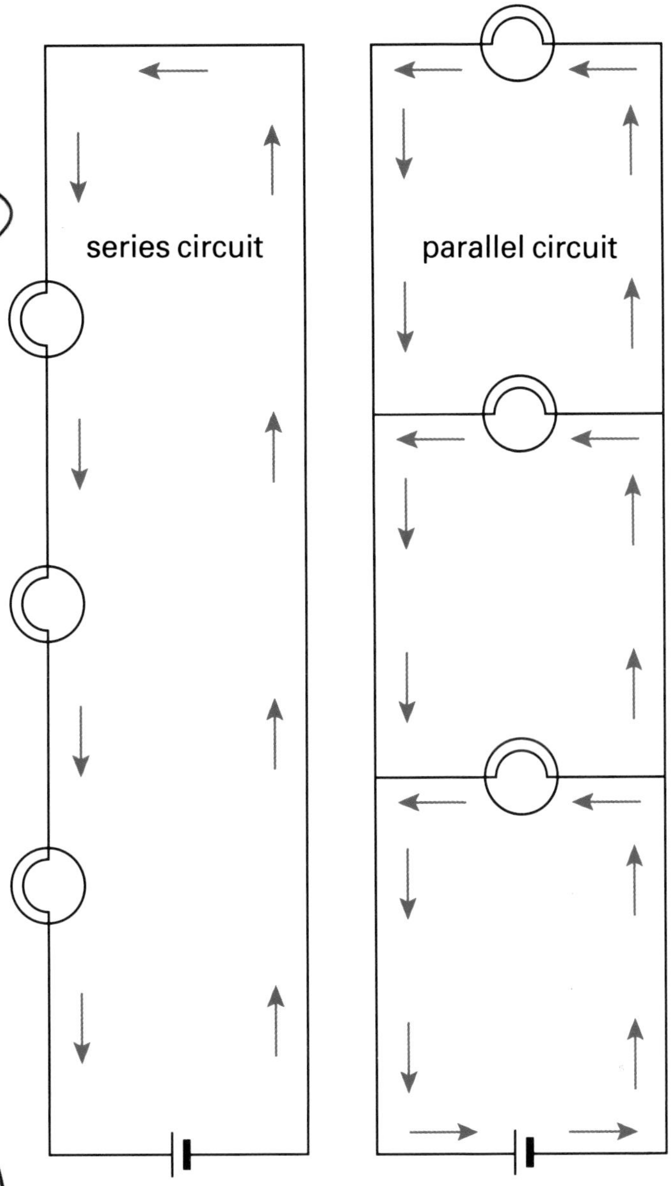

▲ Try taking the middle bulb out of each circuit and watch what happens.

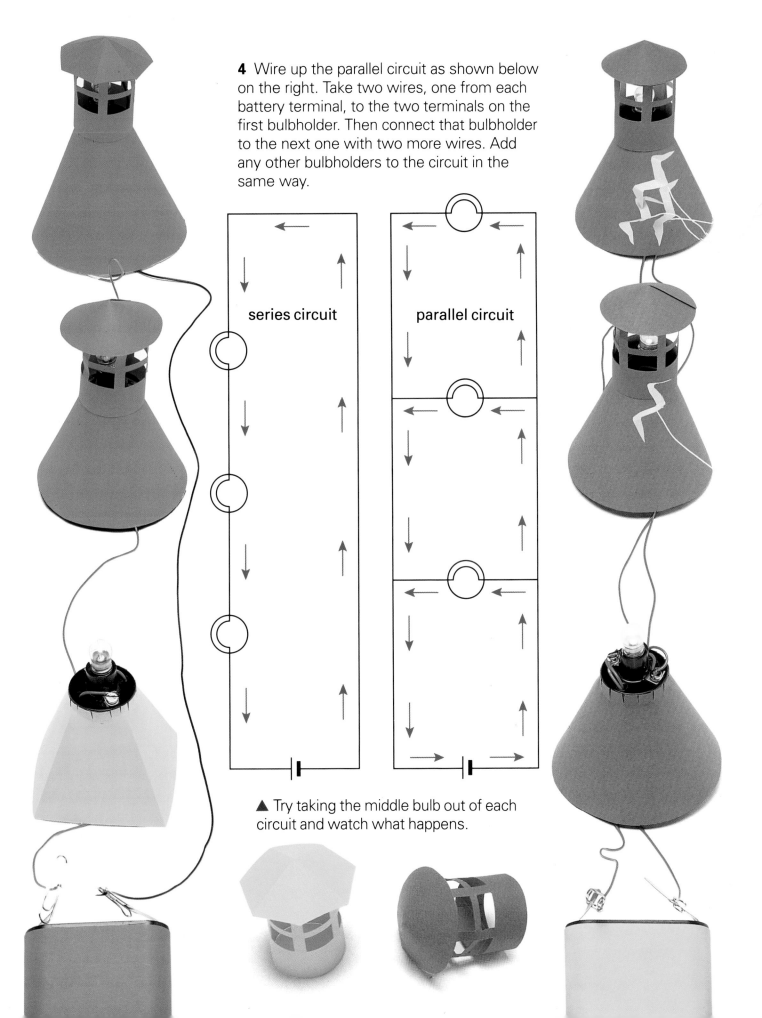

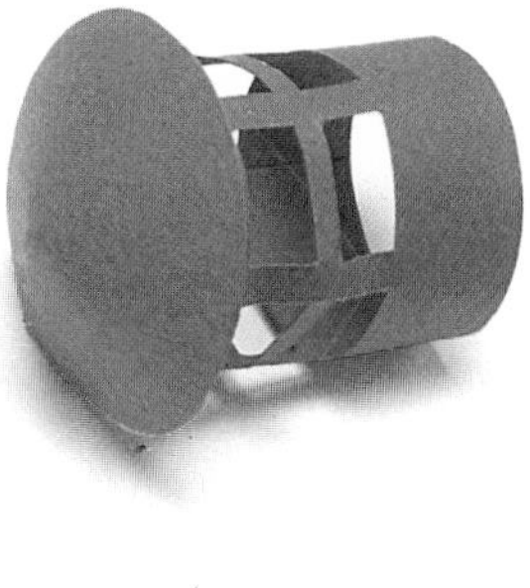

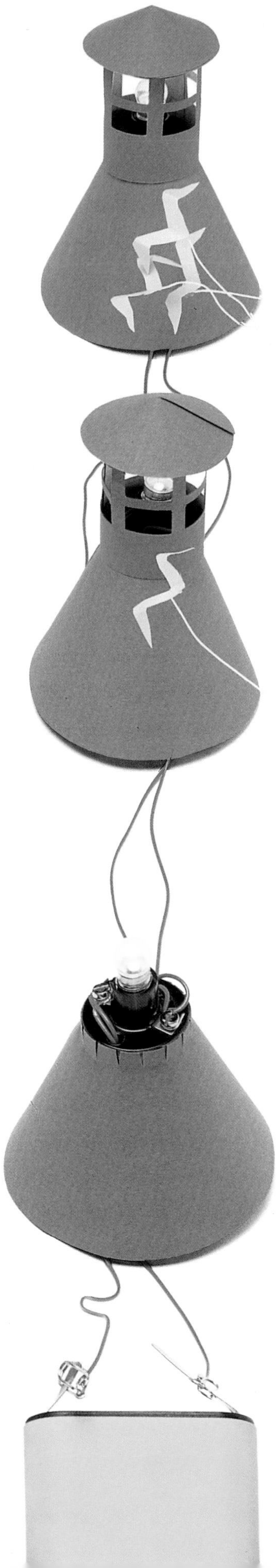

16 Light Bulbs

Light bulbs are used to produce light from electricity. The bulb contains a thin metal thread called a **filament**. When an electric current forces its way through this thin part of the circuit, the filament glows a bright white colour and the bulb gives off light.

You will need

a collection of old light bulbs
a craft knife
glue or tape
card
a ruler

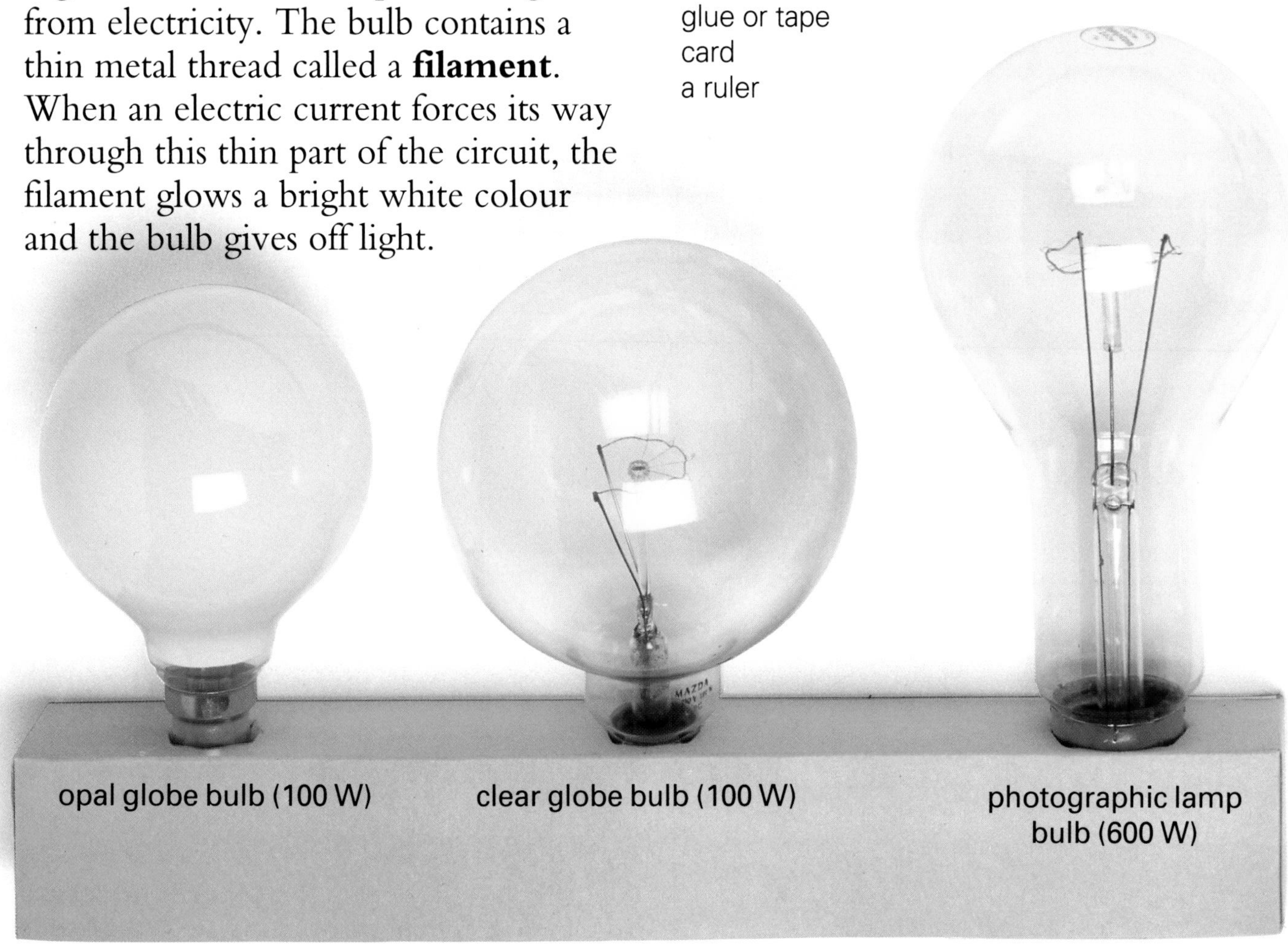

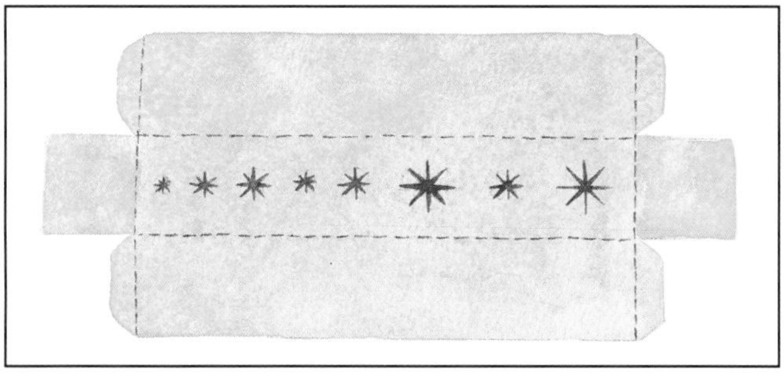

MAKE it WORK!

Light bulbs come in all shapes and sizes. Make a collection of different light bulbs, with a special box to display and store your collection. New bulbs are expensive, so just collect those which do not work any more. Handle light bulbs carefully, as the glass is delicate.

1 Work out what size you want your box. Then cut out a flat shape like the one on the left.

2 Fold up the sides of the box. Tuck in the corner flaps and glue or tape them in place.

3 Carefully cut the card along the top of the box so that you make spaces where you can stick the ends of the bulbs. Make sure that the bulbs fit in firmly.

4 Try to label your collection. Mark the different types of bulb (whether they have a filament or a fluorescent tube) and also how bright they are. You can tell the brightness of a bulb from the number of watts (W) of power that it uses.

The light bulb was invented in 1879 by an American called Thomas Edison. His first bulb used a piece of scorched thread as a filament.

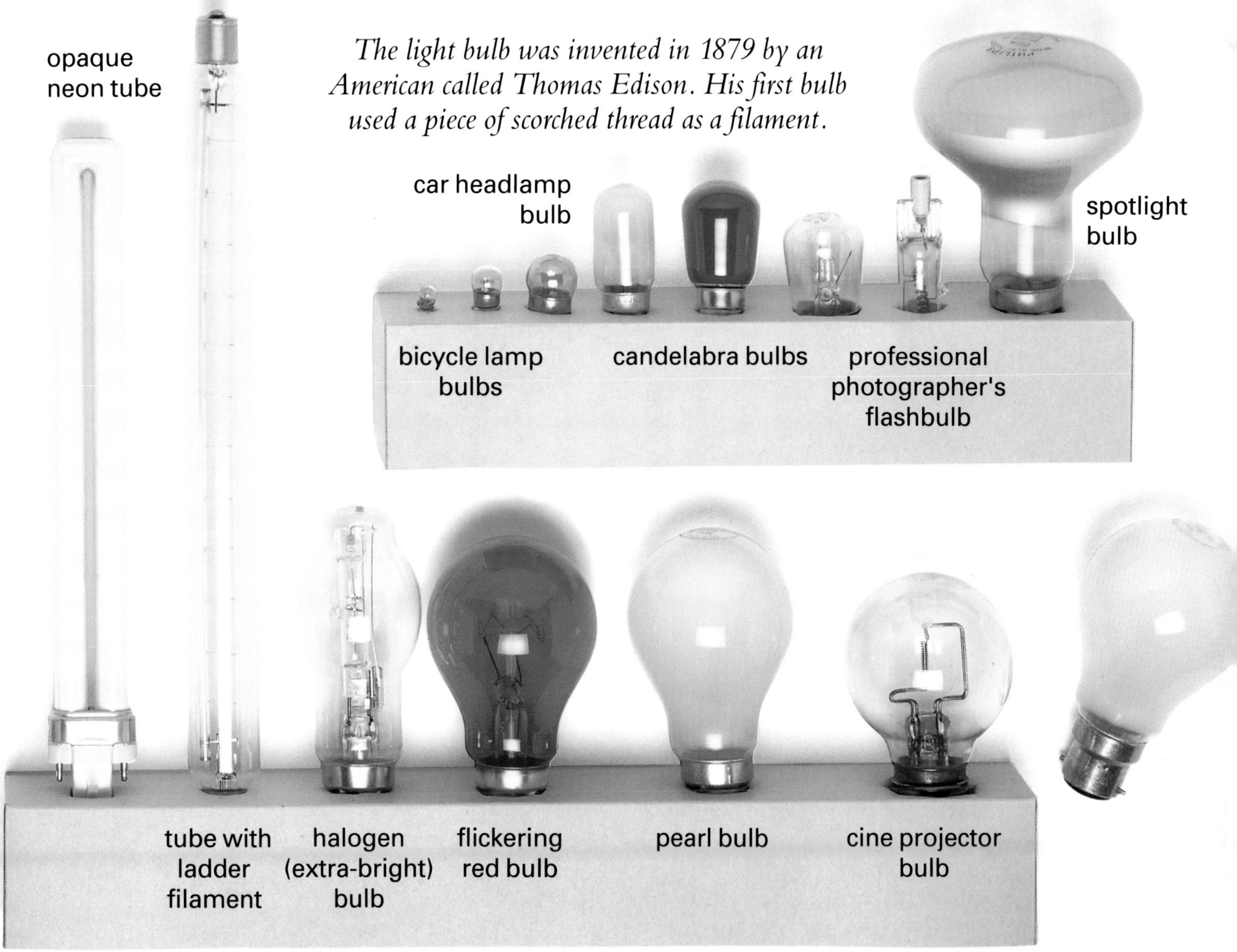

A bulb is a sealed unit filled with the gases nitrogen or argon. It contains no oxygen, the gas in the air that substances need to burn. Nitrogen or argon lets the filament glow, but doesn't allow it to catch fire.

Fluorescent bulbs have no glowing filament. Electricity is passed through a gas contained under pressure in the bulb. The gas gives off light, but the bulbs don't get very hot.

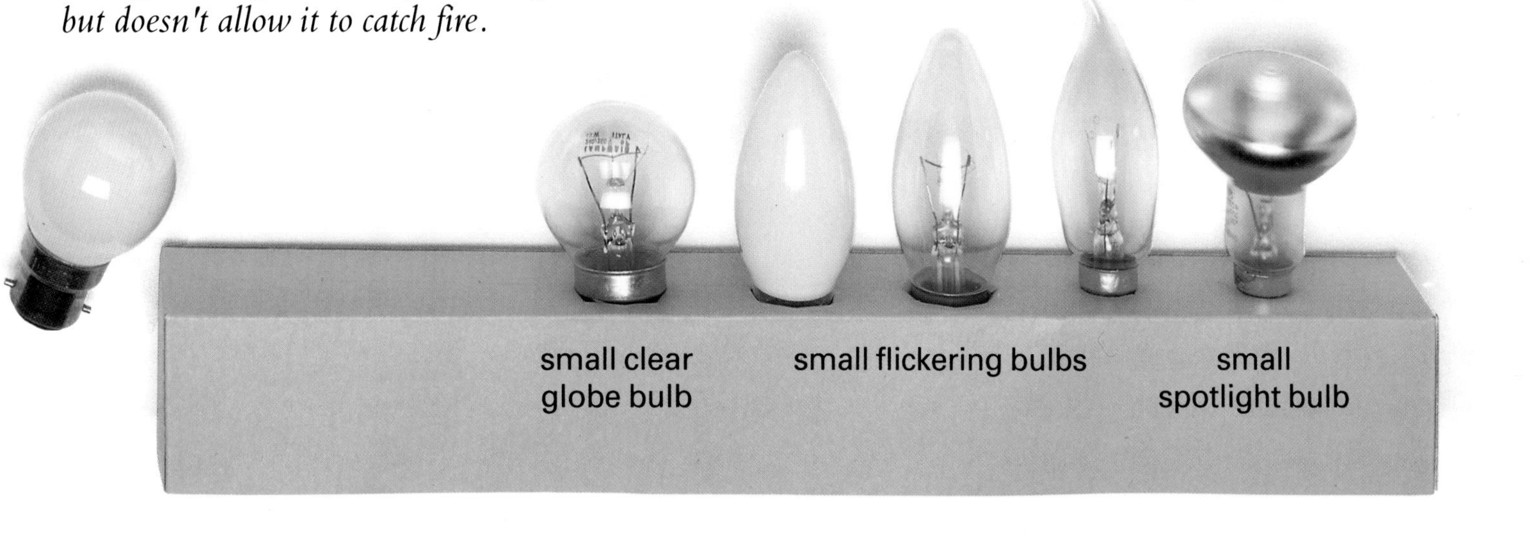

18 Circuit Game

An electric current must always flow through a complete circuit. No current can flow in a broken circuit, because electrons have to keep moving in a continuous stream.

MAKE it WORK!
Test how steady your hand is with this circuit game. At the start of the game, the circuit is broken, so the light is off. If your hand shakes as you move the playing stick along, the loop touches the wire, the circuit is completed and the bulb lights up!

You will need

- a battery
- a bulb and bulbholder
- crocodile clips/paper clips
- an old wire coathanger
- screw eyes, large and small
- balsa wood and wood glue, or a shoe box
- wire
- dowel
- coloured tape

Most coathangers are lacquered with a thin layer of clear plastic to stop them marking cloth. You should rub away the plastic with a piece of sandpaper – otherwise the plastic will insulate the wire and the circuit won't work.

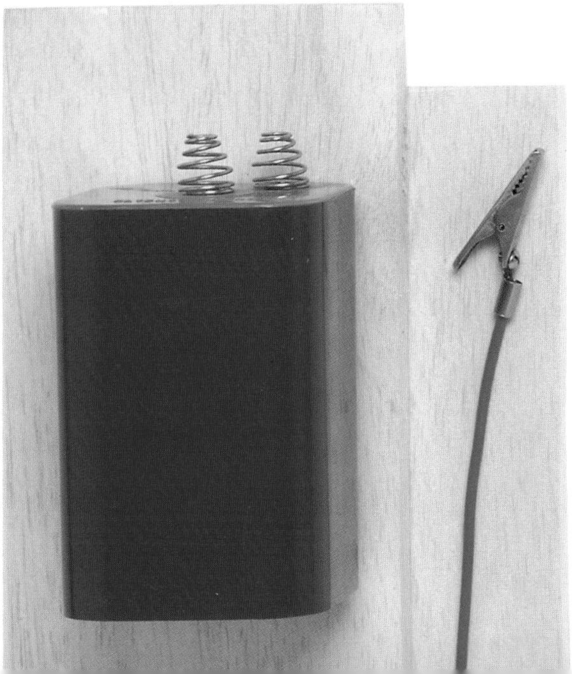

1 Make the playing stick by screwing a large screw eye into the end of the dowel. Connect a long piece of wire to the eye, and tape it down the length of the playing stick.

2 Make a box by gluing together pieces of wood, or use a shoe box. Paint the box, then divide it into sections with coloured tape.

3 Position the bulbholder at one end of the box, wire it up and push the wires through the top of the box.

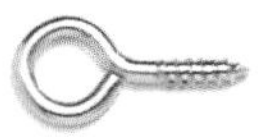

screw eye

dowel

wire

4 Twist a small screw eye onto each end of the box. If you are using a shoe box, you may have to tape them in place. Bend and twist the coathanger wire to make the top part of the game. Slip the eye on the handle over the wire. Then connect the ends of the coathanger wire to the screw eyes on the box.

5 Beneath the box, connect one of the wires from the bulbholder to the battery. Put a crocodile clip on the other bulbholder wire and attach it to one end of the bent coathanger.

6 Connect the wire from the playing stick to the free battery terminal. Now you are ready to play the game!

circuit diagram of the circuit game

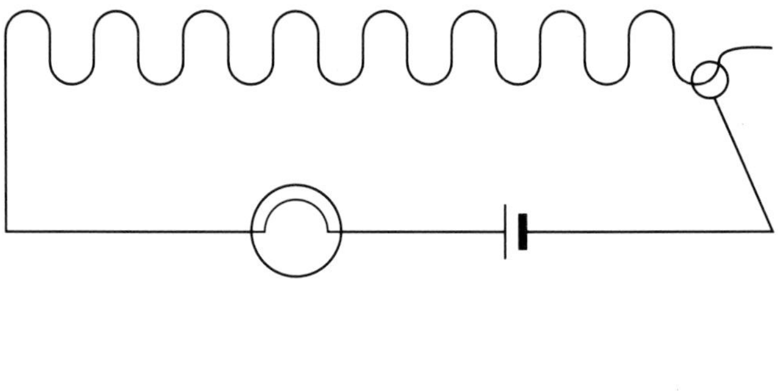

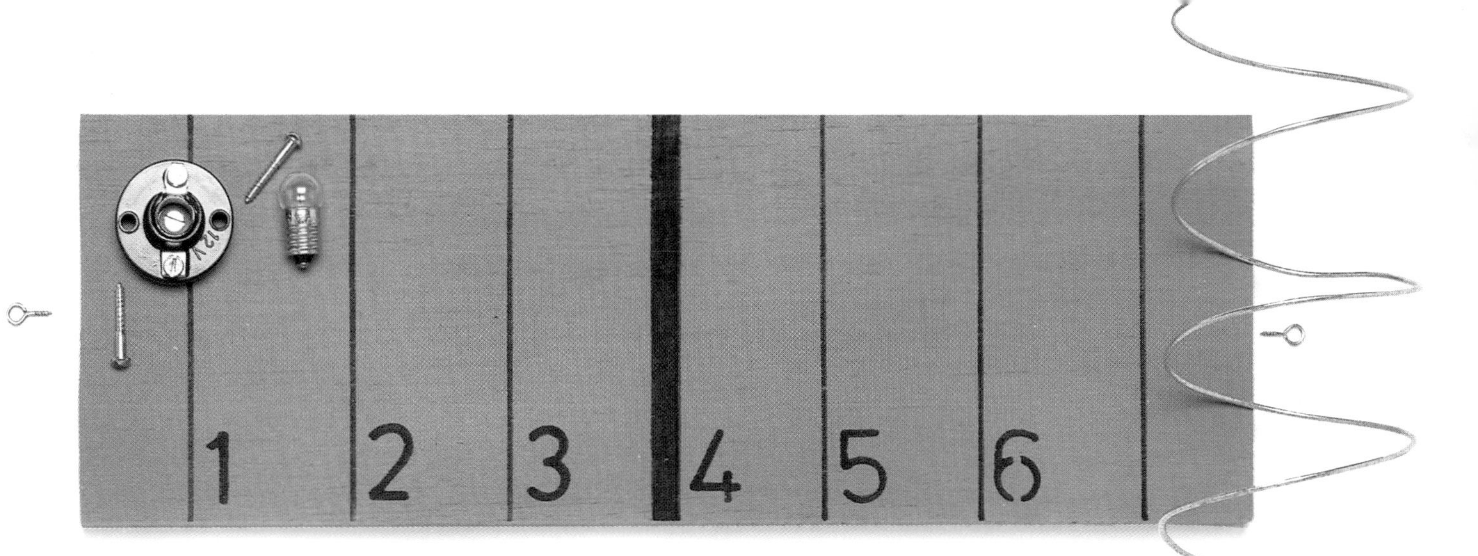

Playing the game
Hold the handle and move the loop along the wire without touching it. If your hand slips, the bulb will light up. Challenge your friends and see who can get furthest along the wire without the bulb lighting up.

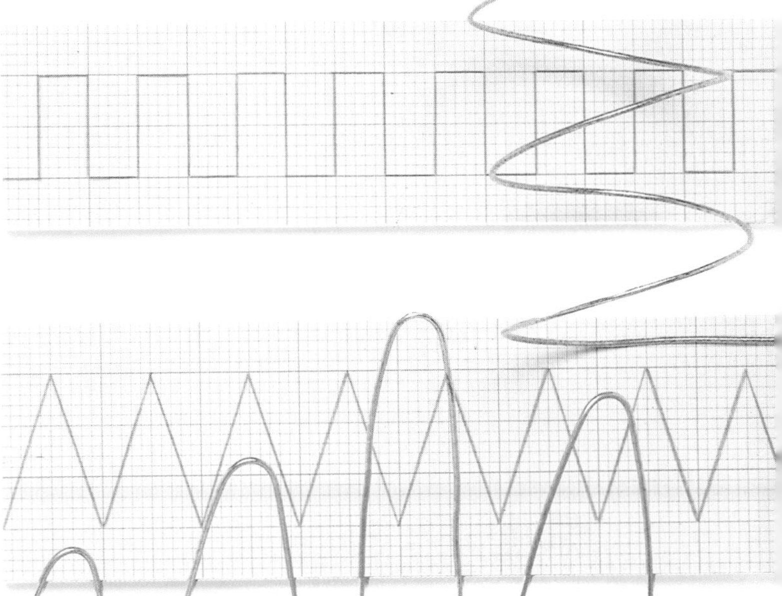

▼ Make some different wire shapes to attach to your box. Try to make both easy and hard shapes. You will find that coathanger wire is quite stiff and you might need a pair of pliers to help you bend it, especially if you are attempting right angles.

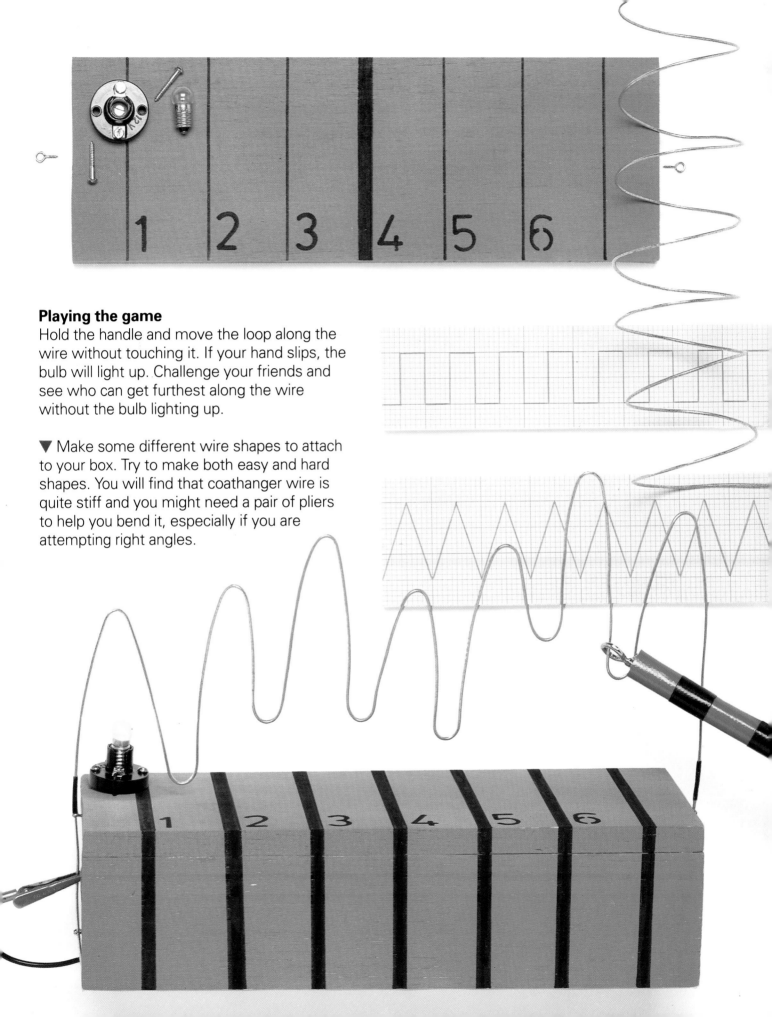

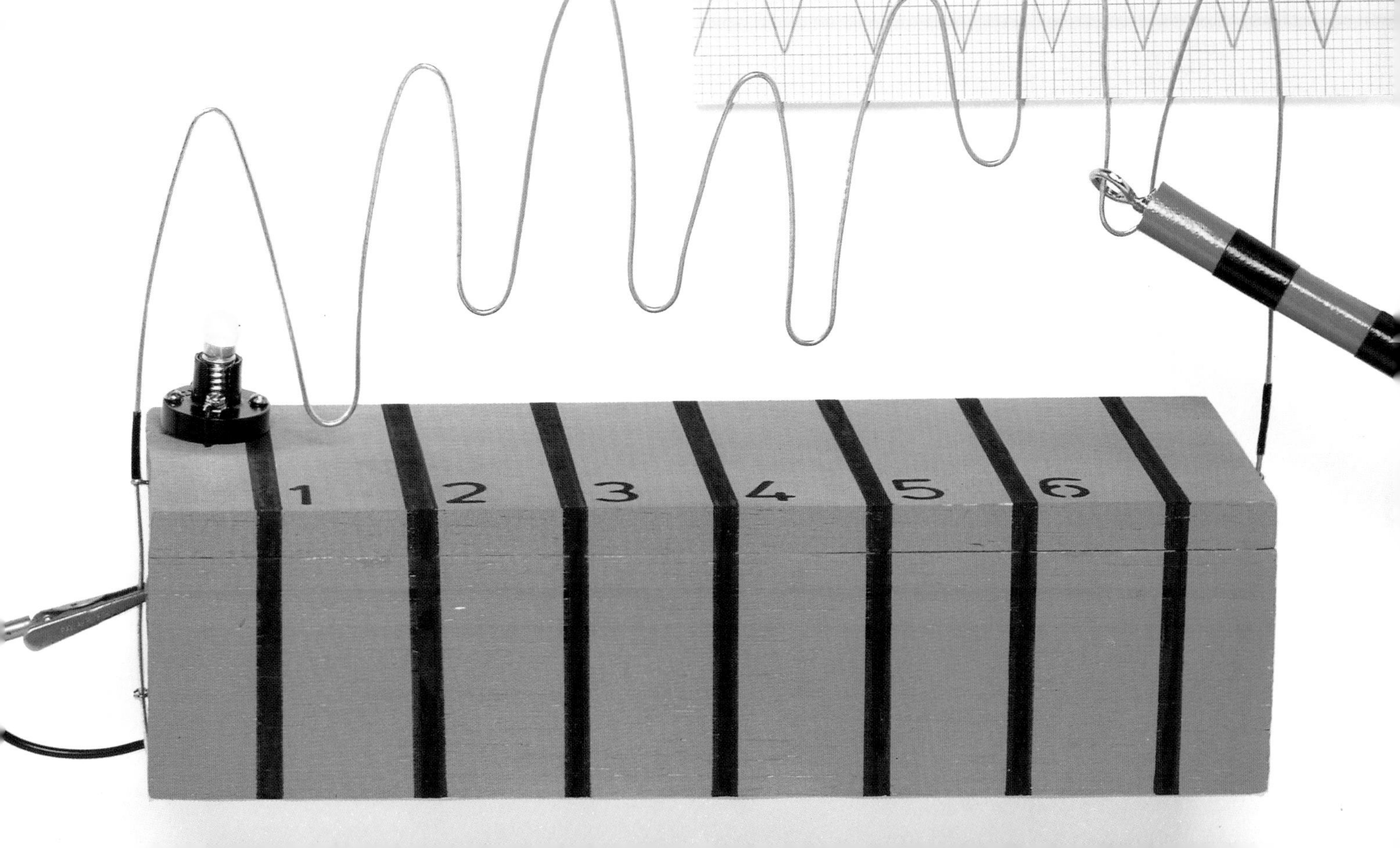

20 Switches

Switches are used to turn electrical circuits on and off. When they are switched off, they break the circuit so that electricity cannot flow around it. When they are switched on, they complete the circuit, allowing the electricity to flow through.

MAKE it WORK!
Switches can be made to work in lots of different ways. For instance, you may not want a light to go out completely but just to be a little less bright. Or you may need a switch that can turn a buzzer on and off very quickly, to make a special pattern of signals. Here are four different types of switch for you to try.

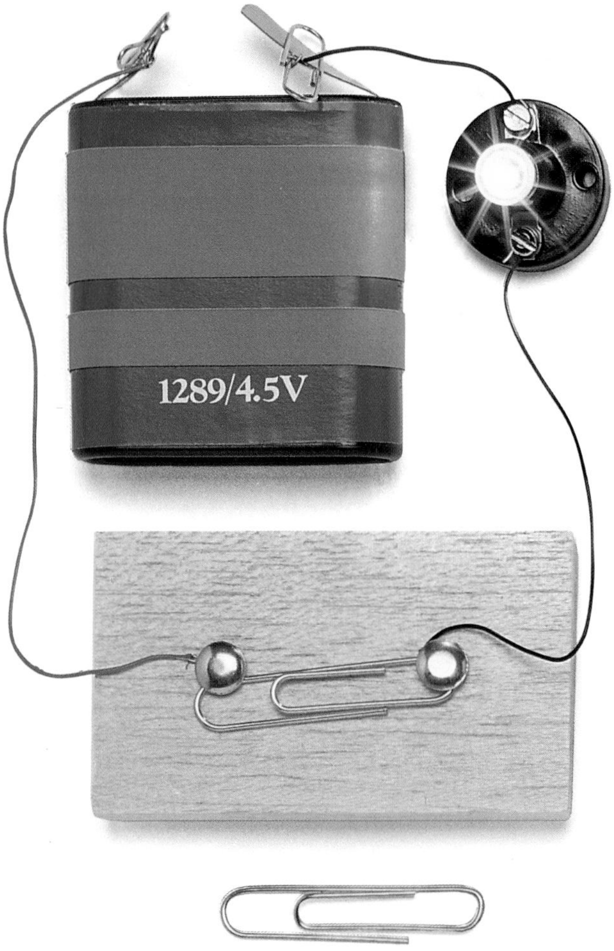

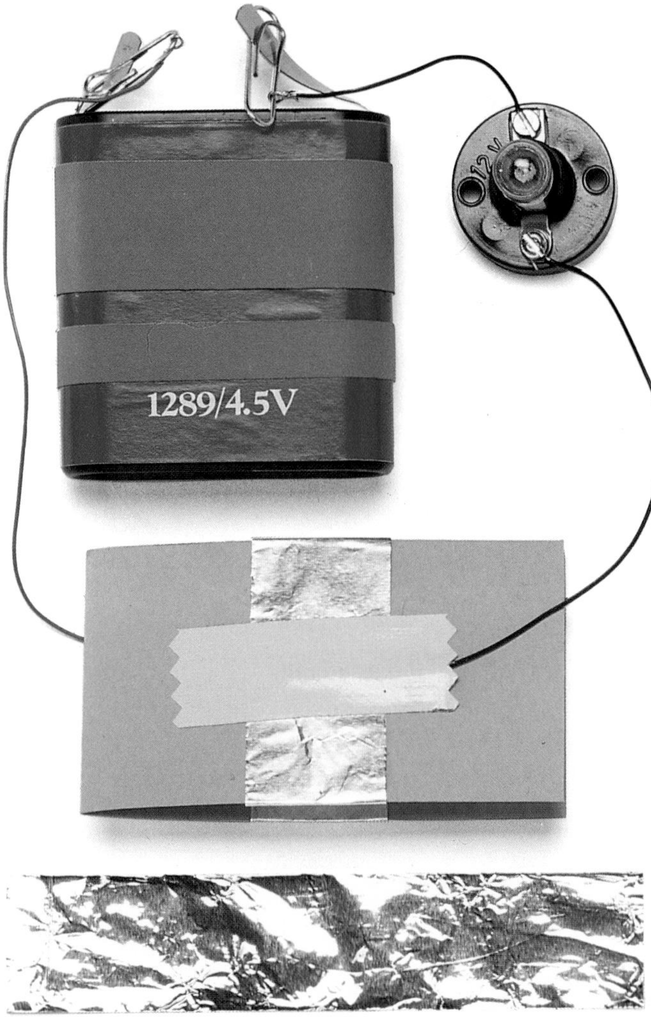

Simple switch
This is a simple on/off switch. When it is on, the current flows through the circuit; when it is off, the current stops. Wire up a simple circuit, like the one on page 8, but leave a break in the wires. Make a switch as shown above, using a block of balsa wood, a paper clip, and two metal thumbtacks. When the clip touches both thumbtacks, the switch is on.

Pressure switch
This is the type of switch that can be used to make a doorbell ring when someone steps on a doormat. Wire up a circuit as before. Fold a piece of card in half. Wrap strips of foil around each half of the card so that they touch when pressed together. Tape the wires to the foil on the outside of each side of the card. When the two strips of foil touch, the switch is on.

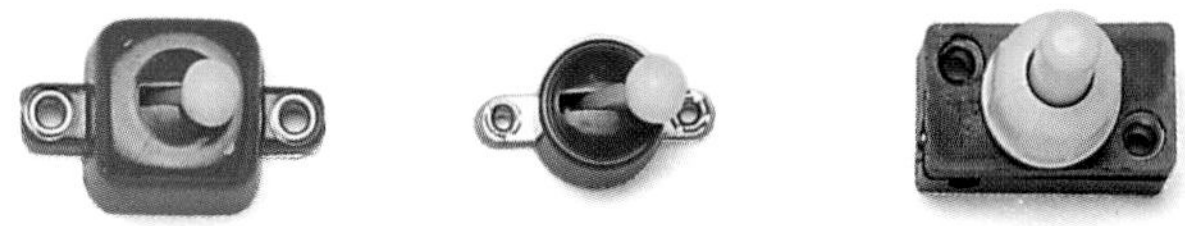

◀ These are low-voltage switches from a model shop. You can include them in any of the circuits shown in this book.

You will need

batteries
bulbholders
balsa wood
paper clips
thumbtacks
aluminum foil
strips of thin copper
wire
bulbs
card
tape
cork
a pencil
a crocodile clip

Dimmer switch

Electricity can pass through the **graphite** in a pencil, but it is hard work. Graphite is called a **resistor**, because it offers resistance to the electric current. You can use a graphite pencil resistor to make a dimmer switch. The longer your pencil lead, the more resistance there is and the dimmer your light will be.

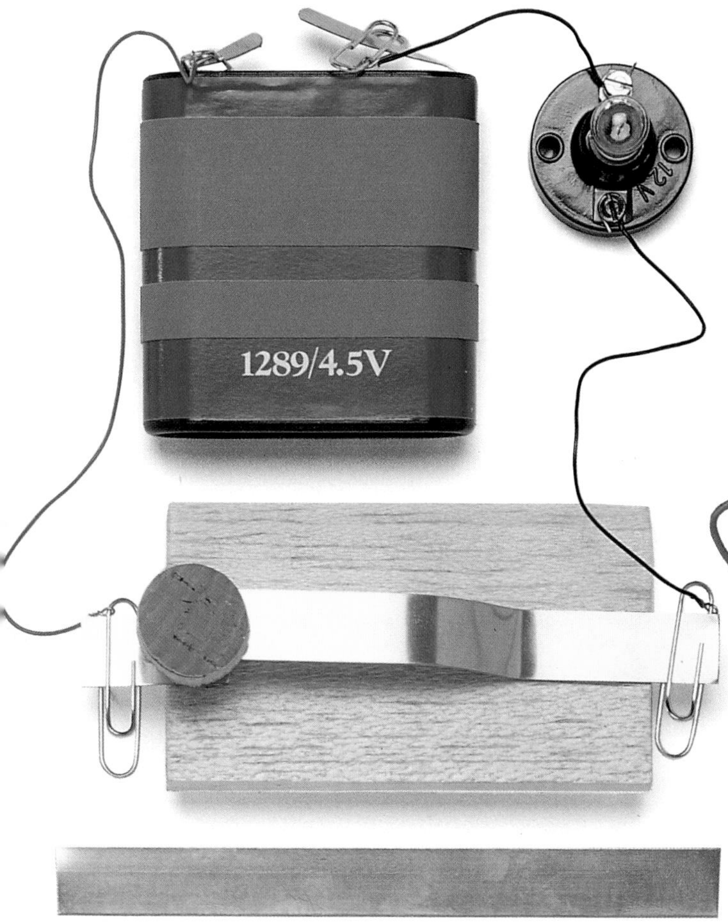

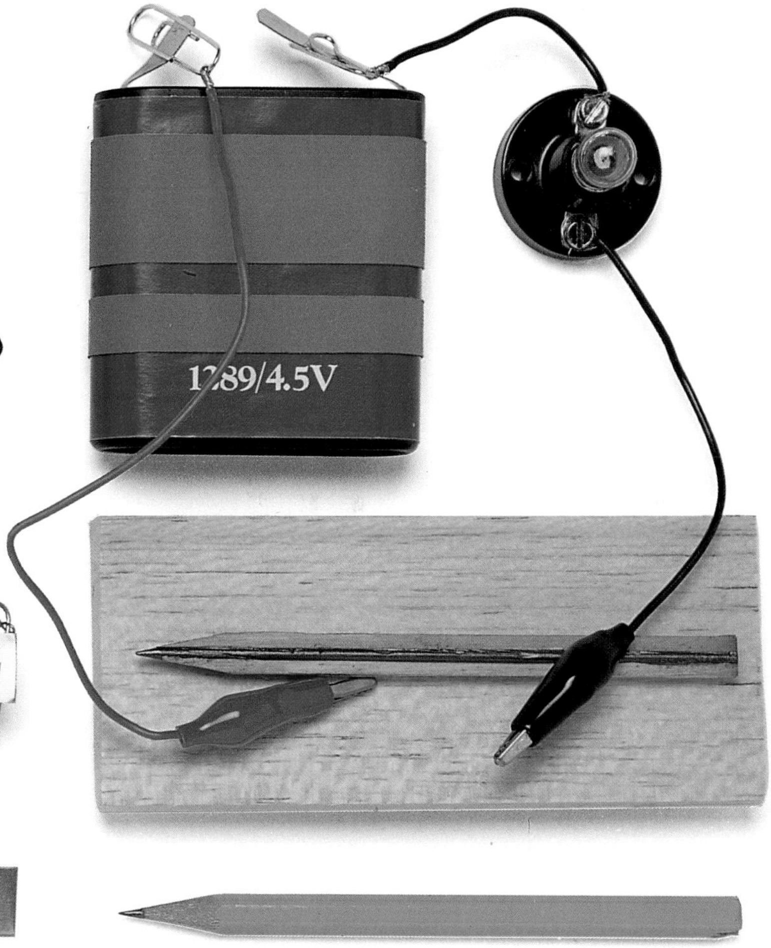

Tapper switch

This switch is used by Morse code operators. It gives the operator total control over the length of time the circuit is complete or broken. The switch is on when the two strips of copper are pressed together. It returns automatically to the 'off' position when not in use. The full instructions for how to make a Morse code tapper are given over the page.

Make a simple circuit as before, but fit crocodile clips to the free ends of the wire. Soak a pencil in water and then ask an adult to slice it open down the middle.
(**Be careful!** You should not try to cut the pencil yourself.) Attach the crocodile clips to opposite ends of the pencil lead, and then gradually slide one clip towards the other. What happens?

Morse Code

Morse code was invented in 1840 by the American painter and inventor, Samuel Morse. Each letter of the alphabet is represented by a simple combination of short and long electrical signals which can easily be transmitted down a single wire. The code is written down on paper as dots, dashes and spaces. Before the days of **communications satellites** and fax machines, all international newspaper reports and messages were sent flashing and buzzing down telegraph wires by Morse code operators.

MAKE it WORK!
Make a pair of Morse code tappers for sending and receiving secret messages.

You will need

- two pieces of wood
- two bulbs and bulbholders
- two strips of copper
- two slices of cork
- two batteries
- wire
- paper clips
- glue and screws

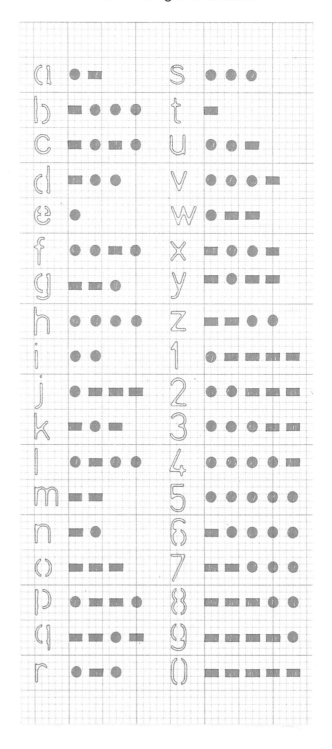

▼ International Morse code
These are the Morse code symbols. As you can see, they are made up of dots, dashes and spaces. A dot is transmitted by pressing and instantly releasing the transmitter key. To send a dash, hold the key down twice as long as you did for the dot. A space between letters is the same length as a dot, and a space between words is the same length as a dash.

a	• −	s	• • •
b	− • • •	t	−
c	− • − •	u	• • −
d	− • •	v	• • • −
e	•	w	• − −
f	• • − •	x	− • • −
g	− − •	y	− • − −
h	• • • •	z	− − • •
i	• •	1	• − − − −
j	• − − −	2	• • − − −
k	− • −	3	• • • − −
l	• − • •	4	• • • • −
m	− −	5	• • • • •
n	− •	6	− • • • •
o	− − −	7	− − • • •
p	• − − •	8	− − − • •
q	− − • −	9	− − − − •
r	• − •	0	− − − − −

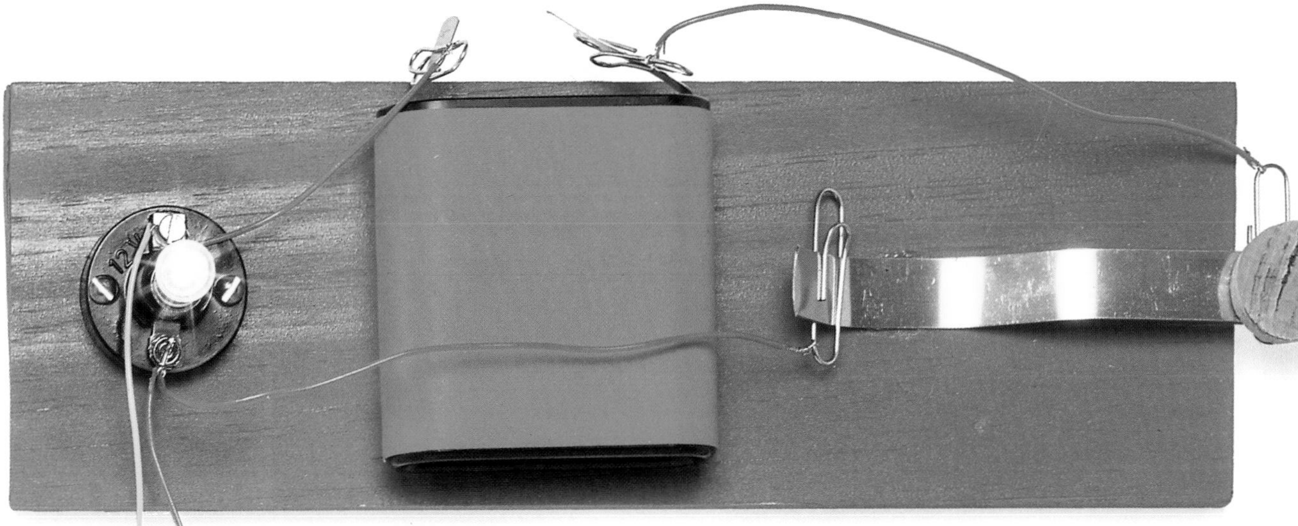

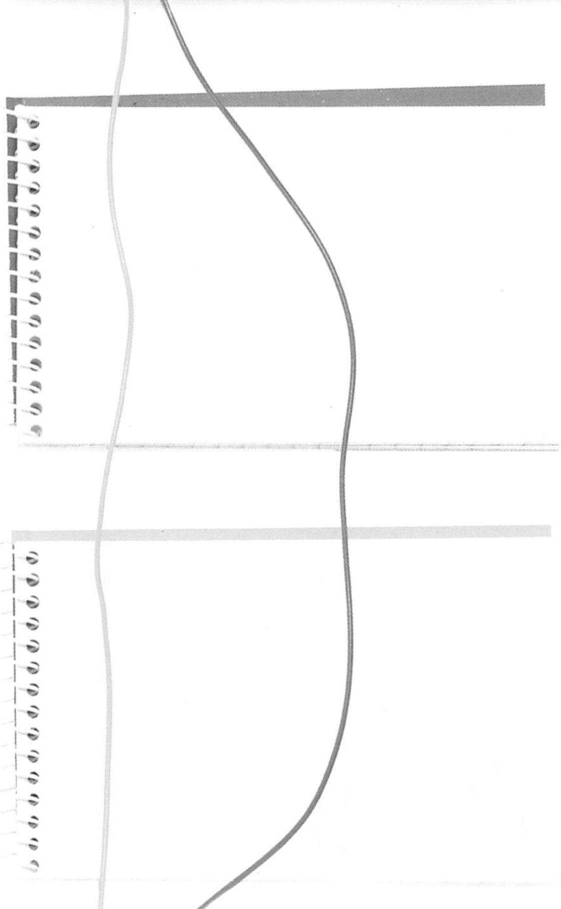

1 Glue the batteries to the boards and screw the bulbholders into position as shown.

2 Ask an adult to cut the copper strips into four pieces – two long and two short. Glue one small piece to the end of each board, making sure that they stick out a little. These are the bottom parts of the transmitter keys. To make the top parts of the keys, bend the long pieces of copper and fix them securely to the board, copying the shape in the diagram below.

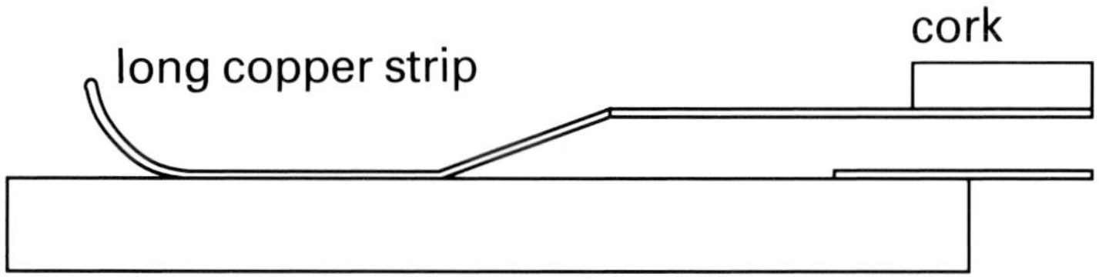

3 Glue a slice of cork onto each transmitter key and wire up the keys as shown in the photograph. When you press the cork end, the long copper strip should touch the short one underneath and both bulbs will light up.

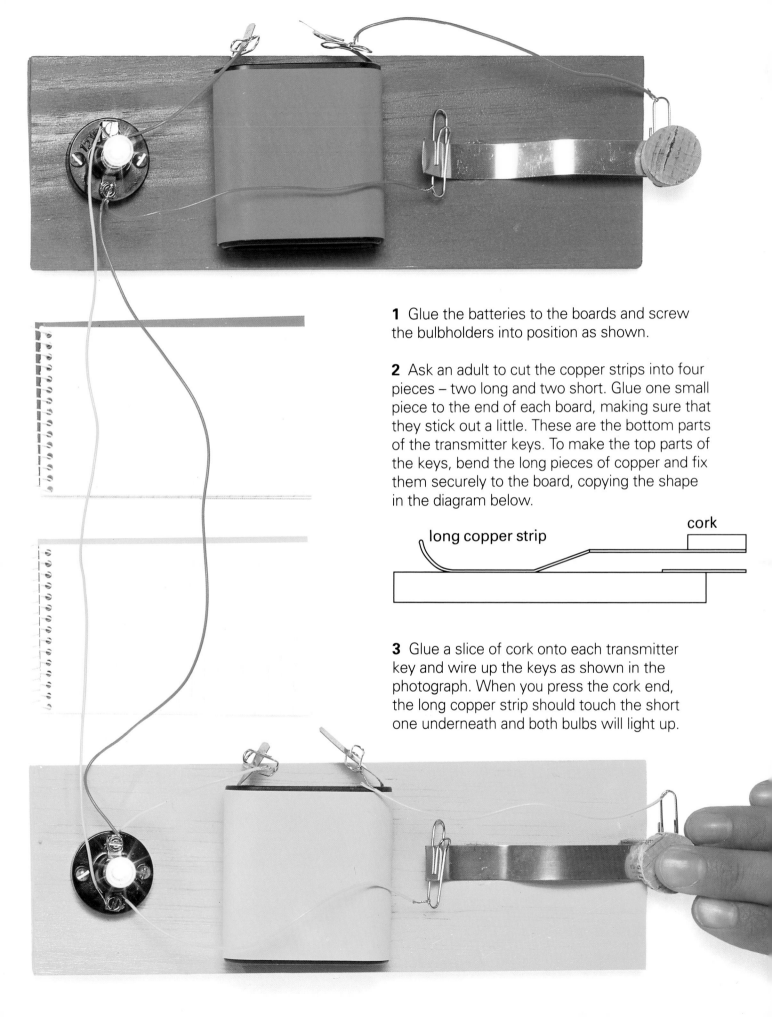

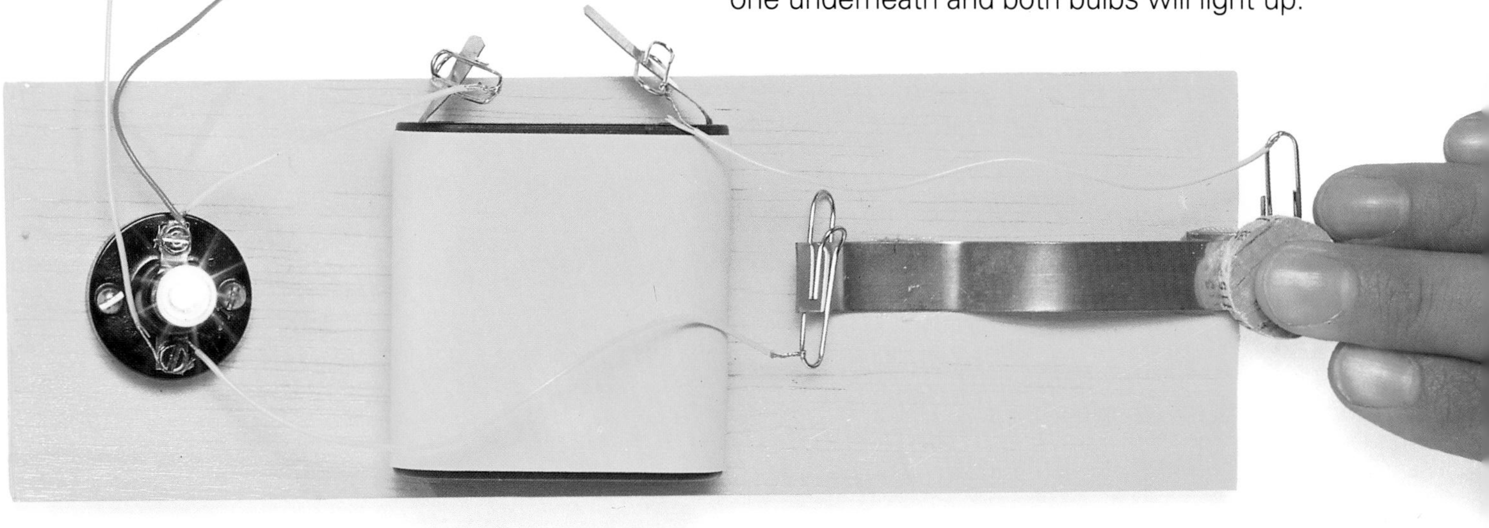

24 Circuit Quiz

Some circuits are made up of lots of different connections, which act together to perform complex tasks. In electrical equipment such as radios, where many tiny circuits are needed, the circuits themselves may not be made as wires, but tiny strips of metal printed on a sheet. In computers, thousands of microscopic circuits are crammed onto one **silicon chip**.

MAKE it WORK!

Most circuits are made on a circuit board. All the wires are spaced out so they cannot accidentally touch one another. This question and answer game shows you what a simple circuit board looks like. Each connection, when correctly made, will complete a circuit and the bulb will light up.

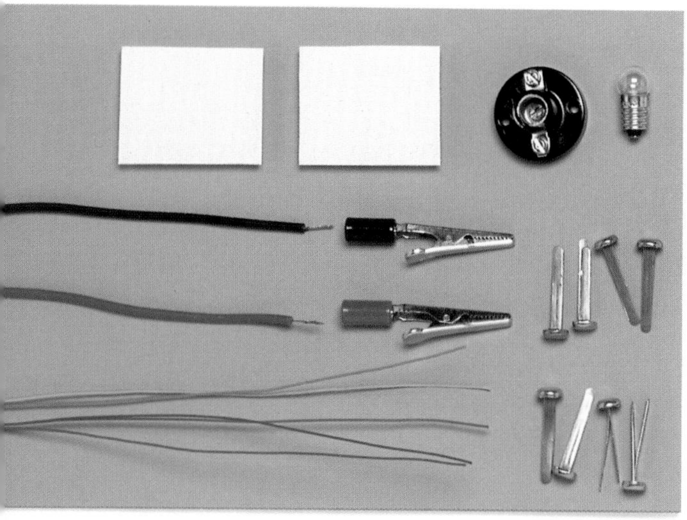

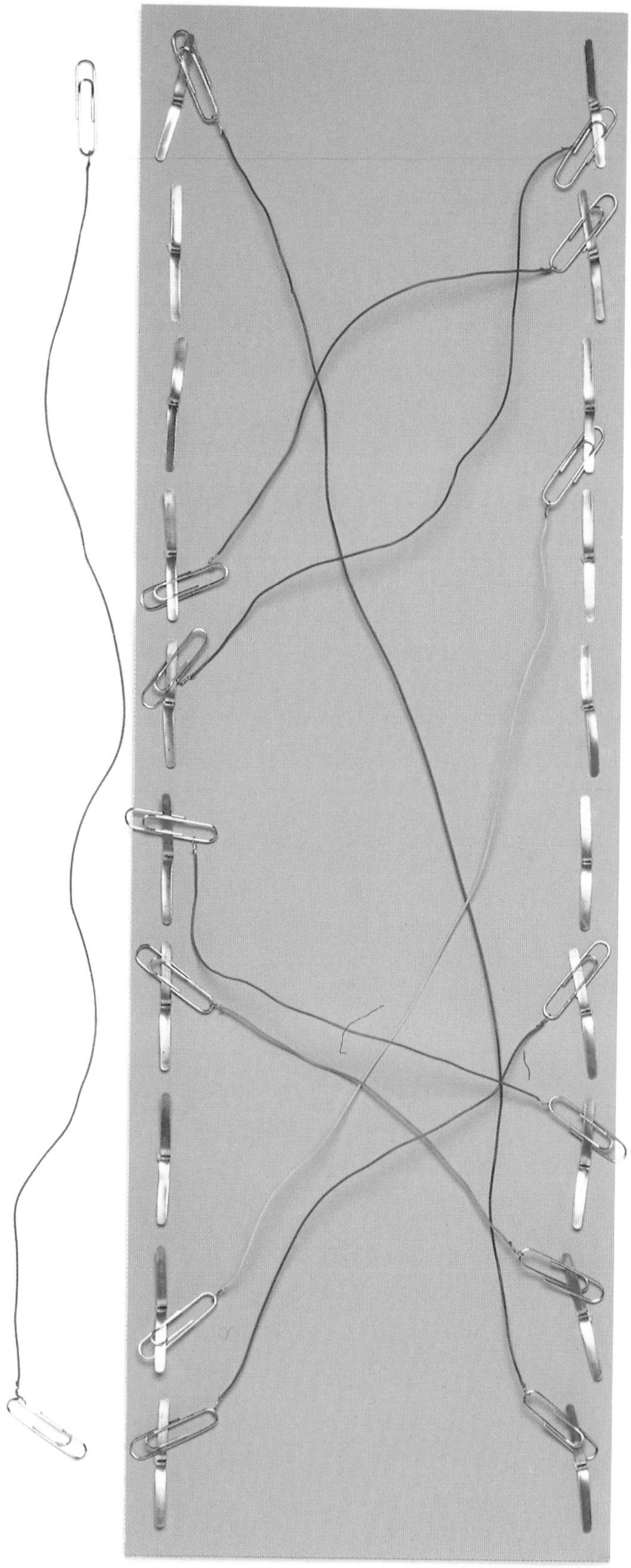

You will need

wire
a battery
a bulb and bulbholder
stick-on Velcro tape
crocodile clips/paper clips
card
paper fasteners
a buzzer
coloured pens

1 Cut out a piece of card for your quiz board. Down each side of the card, push through a row of paper fasteners. On the front of the card, stick strips of Velcro backing tape next to each paper fastener.

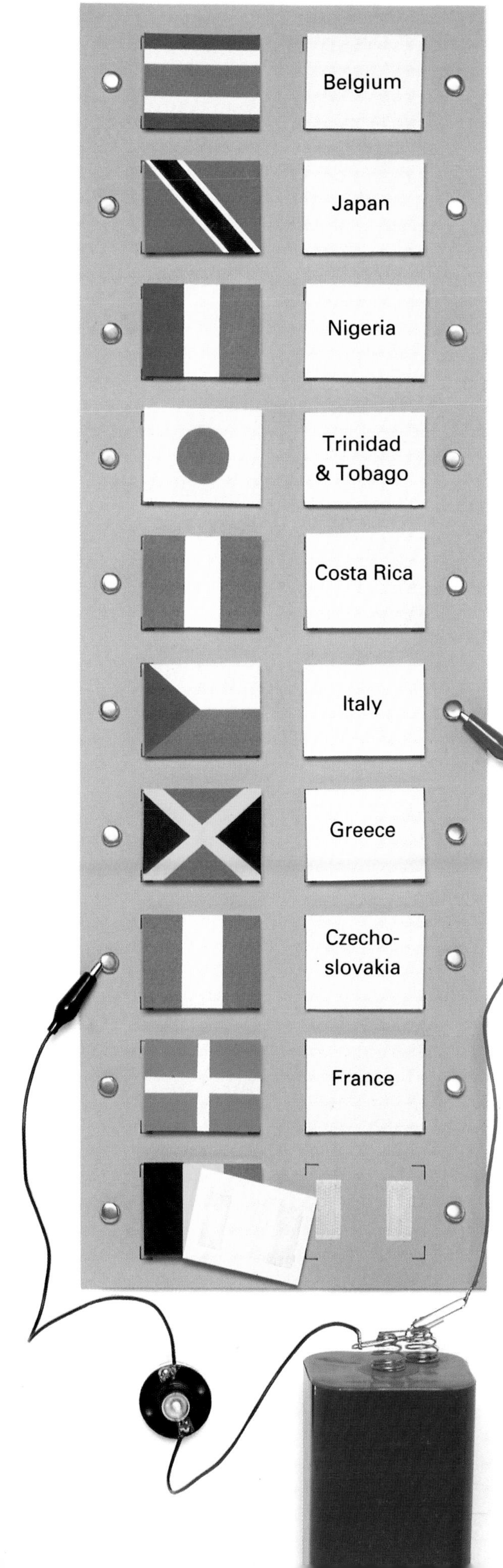

2 Make question and answer cards. Back them with Velcro and stick them down in random order. On the back of the board, wire up the questions to the correct answers.

3 Set up your testing kit of battery, bulb, wires and clips as shown.

4 Touch one of the paper fasteners on the question side with one of the testing wires. Then match it up with an answer on the other side. If you have picked the correct answer, the electrical circuit will be completed and the bulb will light up.

▲ Make raised shapes for your quiz board and replace the light bulb with a buzzer. Now you can play blindfold!

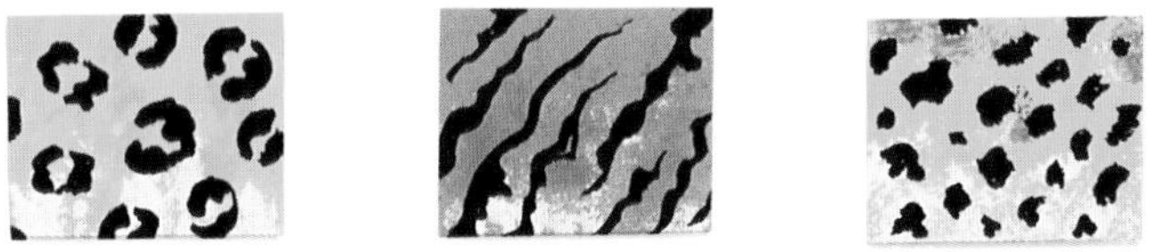

▲▼ Think up different quizzes for your board. What about animals, or tennis players?

Always check your connections carefully before you start to play. The game will not work if any of the wires become loose.

Magnetism

Just like static electricity, magnetism is a natural, invisible force. It was discovered over 2,000 years ago, when the Ancient Greeks first noticed that certain stones would jump together or move apart depending on which way they were facing.

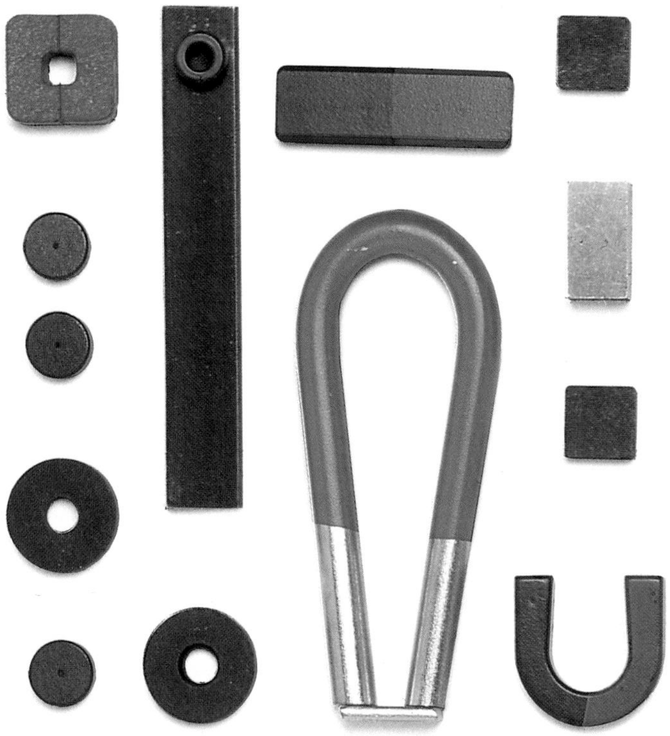

What is a magnet?
A magnet is a piece of iron or steel that attracts or repels certain other pieces of iron or steel. Like all other substances, metals are made up of the tiny particles we call **molecules** which, in turn, are made up of atoms. Normally, all the molecules in a piece of iron are facing in different directions. However, if we can rearrange the molecules and get them all facing the same way, they will act together as a magnet, making a powerful force.

MAKE it WORK!
You can watch the power of magnets at work with this fishing game. The object is to 'catch' as many high-scoring fish as possible. Players take it in turns to fish, and the winner is the player with the highest score.

1 Using the shape above, cut out large, medium and small versions of the fish from different colours of card.

2 Draw in the eye, gill and mouth using a thick black marker.

3 To get a fish-scale effect, stipple paint onto the fish using a stencil brush and a piece of wire mesh. Use a lighter coloured paint on the belly. Give each fish a score number.

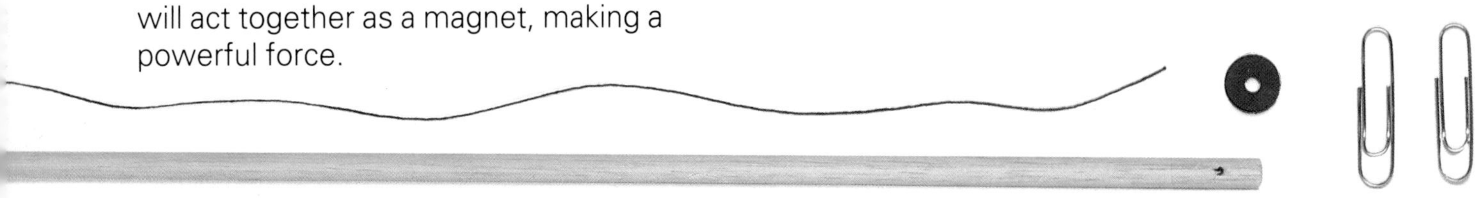

You will need

- thin card
- thin wire mesh
- a craft knife
- paint and paint brushes
- dowels and string
- paper clips
- a small magnet with a hole in the centre

4 Make fishing lines by tying the magnet to the string. Attach the other end of the string to a dowel rod as shown.

5 Attach paper clips to the fishes' noses.

6 Make a sea from a cardboard box covered in blue card. Put in the fish and start fishing.

28 Magnetic Power

Around a magnet is an area called a **force field**, where the pull or push of metal and magnet is at its strongest. The force field is strong enough to pass through wood or glass. The ends of a magnet, where most of the energy is directed, are much more powerful than the middle.

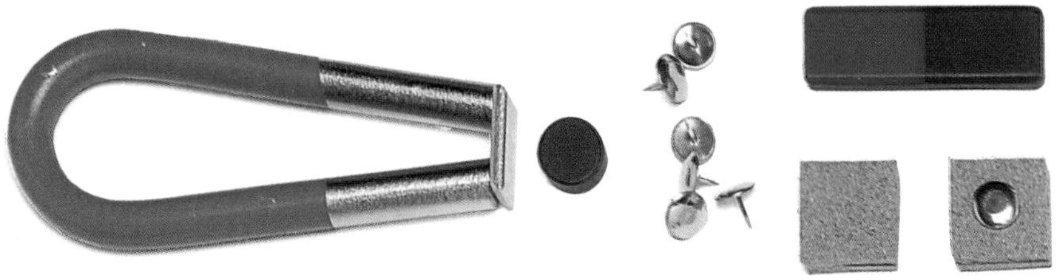

For the insects you will need

card
slices of cork
metal thumbtacks
glue
paint and paint brushes
a horseshoe magnet

MAKE it WORK!
The more powerful the magnet, the larger and stronger its force field. See how a small magnet works through card, and how the force field of a strong steel magnet can even pass through a wooden door.

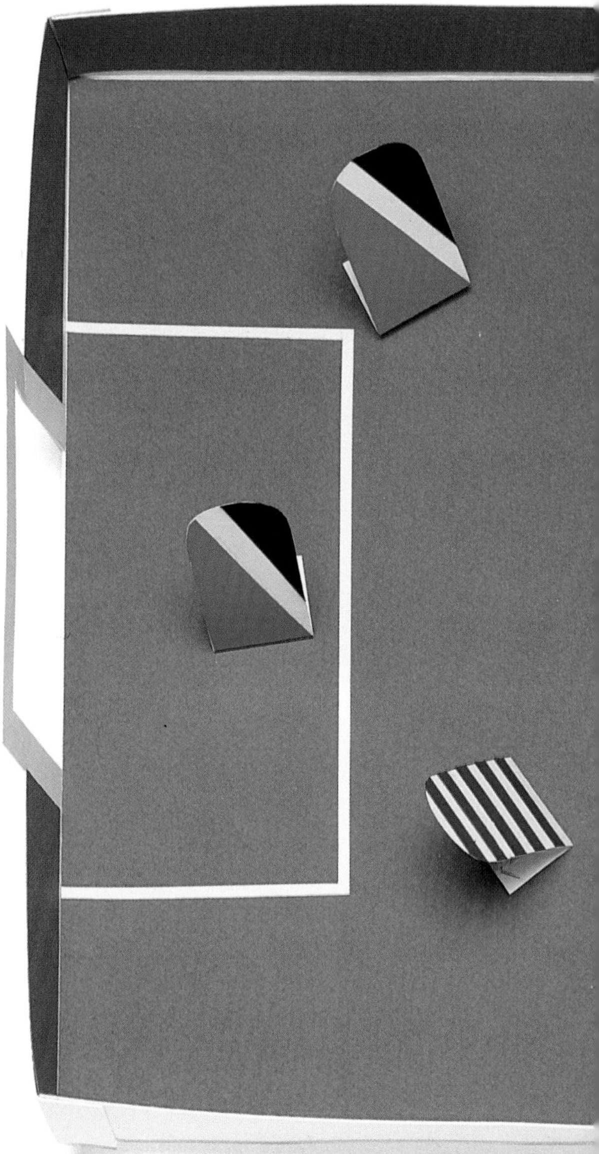

Magnetic insects
Using a craft knife, cut out insect shapes from thin card and paint them carefully. Stick each insect onto a small square of cork into which you have pushed a thumbtack. Use a strong horseshoe magnet to make the insects move from the other side of a door.

For the soccer game you will need

- white card
- a craft knife
- metal thumbtacks
- small magnets
- a table soccer ball
- green card
- cork
- dowels
- glue
- paints or crayons

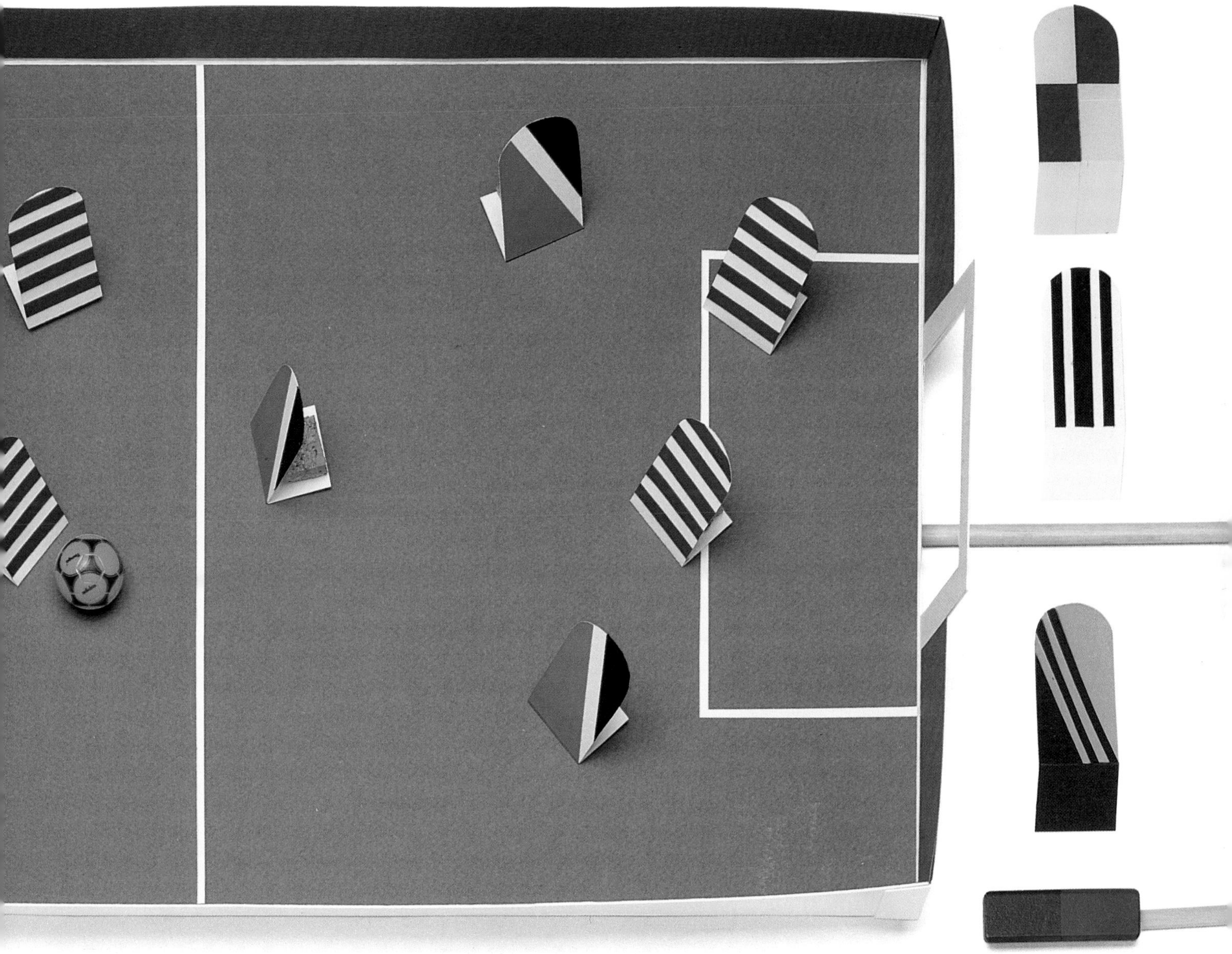

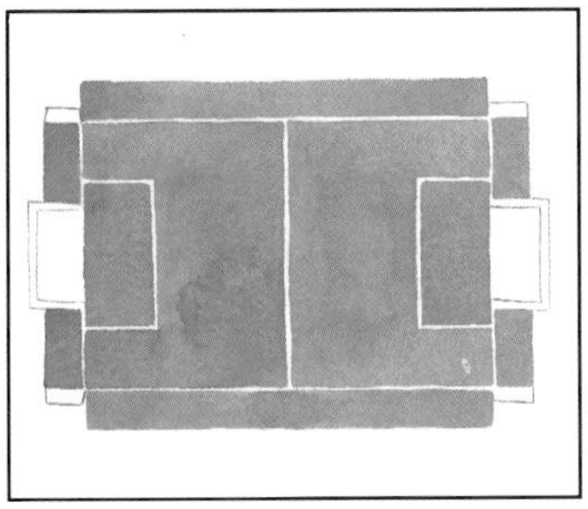

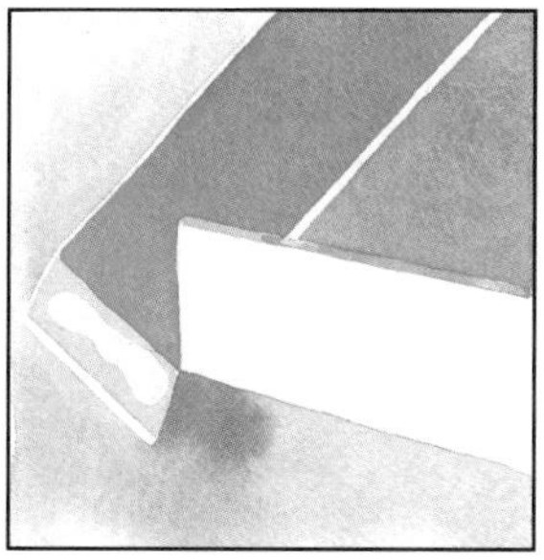

Table soccer

Make a box out of green card, folding and gluing the corners as shown. Mark out the lines of the soccer field in white. Make cardboard players with a piece of cork glued to the inside of each base. Stick a thumbtack through from the outside. The players are moved from under the field by magnets attached to dowels.

30 Magnetic Boats

The force fields of magnets can pass through many different substances. The magnetic insects and magnetic soccer on the previous pages work because magnets can attract through wood and cardboard. A magnetic force field can also pass through water.

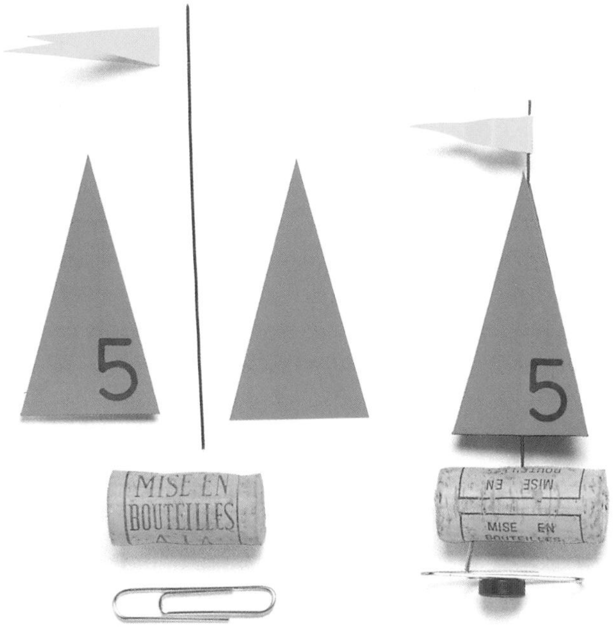

MAKE it WORK!

There are two different kinds of magnetic boat to make. The cork boats work by magnet to magnet attraction. The boat magnets are close to the bottom of the water container, so the boats can be pulled around by a small bar magnet attached to the end of a stick. The balsa-wood boat has thumbtacks pushed into its keel and needs a stronger magnet with a force field that will attract through shallow water.

Even though the Ancient Greeks knew of magnets, for hundreds of years people did not know how to make magnets for themselves. It was not until the nineteenth century that magnetism, and its close connection to electricity, was properly understood.

You will need

thin, coloured card
corks
door magnets
dowels
balsa wood
metal thumbtacks
wire
paper clips
glue
strong magnets
a wooden skewer
a glass tank

To make the cork boats

1 Make the sails out of coloured card. You can make one triangular sail by cutting out two triangles and sticking them back to back with the mast in the middle.

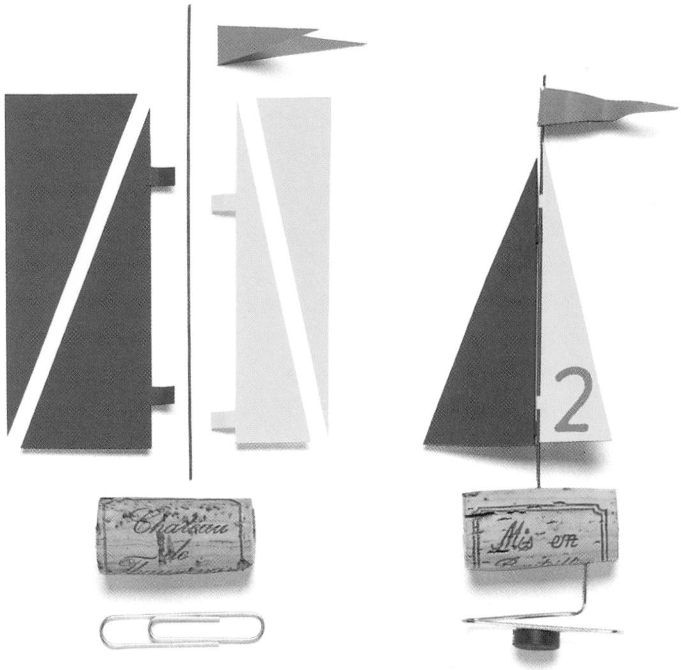

2 You can also make a more complex rig of a mainsail and jib. Cut a rectangle of card diagonally, leaving enough card on the straight edge to make two tabs. With these tabs, attach the sail to a piece of wire.

3 Push the wire mast into a cork. **Be very careful!** Do not stab yourself with the wire. Top the mast with a flag made from a folded strip of card of a contrasting colour.

4 Unbend a paper clip as shown above. Push one end into the underside of the cork and glue a small door magnet onto the other end, using waterproof glue.

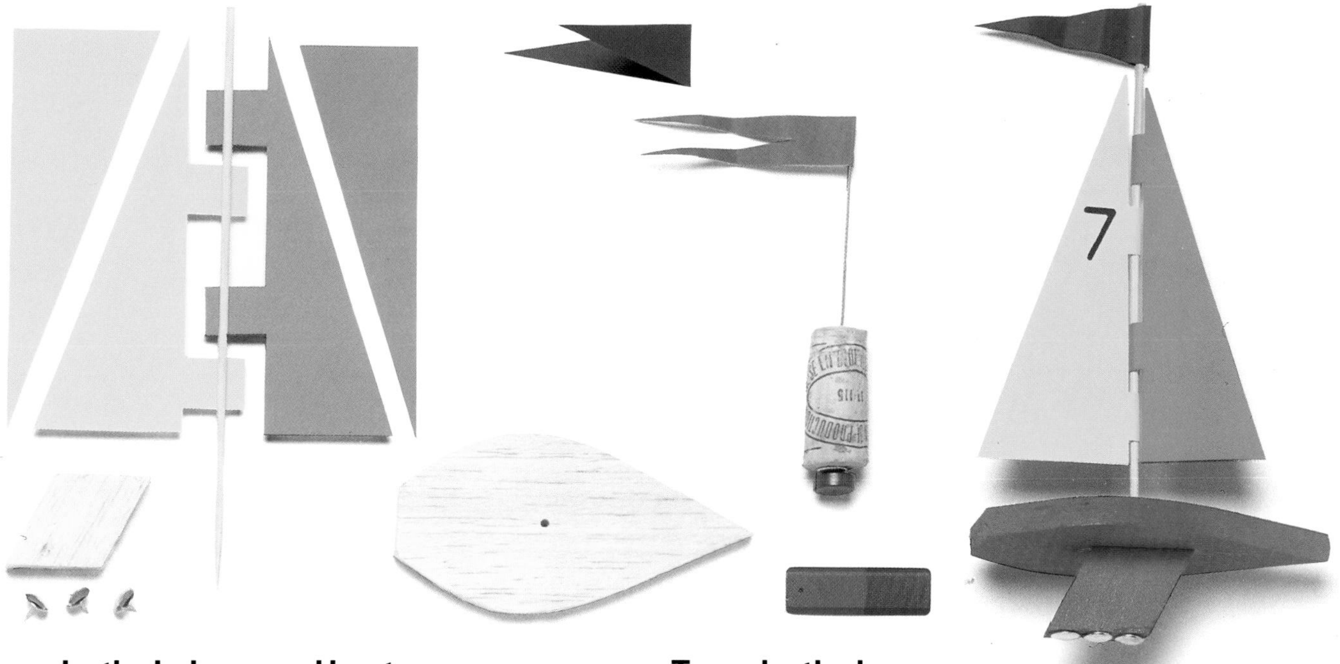

To make the balsa-wood boat

1 Ask an adult to help you cut a deck and keel out of balsa wood as shown above.

2 Stick a wooden skewer into the centre of the deck to make a mast.

3 Make sails and flags as for the cork boats, but in a larger size.

4 Glue the boat together with waterproof glue and paint it. Push three thumbtacks into the bottom of the keel.

To make the buoys

Put a short piece of wire into a cork and top it with a coloured flag. Stick a door magnet to the bottom of the cork with waterproof glue.

The ancient Greeks had a mythical story about an island of magnetic mountains, which pulled the iron nails out of passing ships!

32 Magnetic Earth

The Earth itself is a giant magnet and, like any other magnet, its strongest points are at the North Pole and the South Pole. No one really knows why the Earth is a magnet, but its force field extends thousands of miles into space. Any magnet on Earth allowed to swing freely will always point to the north – which is very handy if you need to find out where you are.

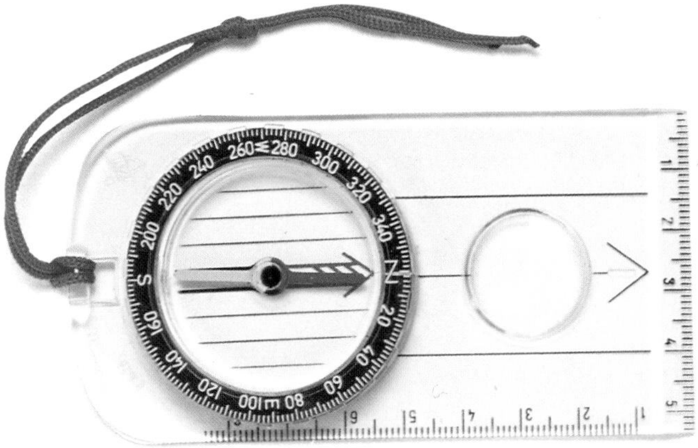

MAKE it WORK!
Because magnets always line up with magnet Earth, the end of a magnet that points north is called the north pole and the end that points to the south is called the south pole. Compasses are used to find directions, and they come in many varieties. Some are marked off with all 180 degrees of a circle. These compasses give a very accurate reading, but even the simplest compass will let you know if you are heading in the right direction. All you need is a magnetized needle that can swing freely.

To make a water compass you will need

an old yoghurt pot	a magnet
a needle	a slice of cork
card	a protractor

1 Cut out a circle of card and make a hole in the centre just smaller than the diameter of the yoghurt pot.

2 Using a protractor, divide the circle into accurate quarters and mark on the four compass points: north, south, east and west.

3 Make the needle magnetic by stroking it with one end of a magnet about twenty times. Always stroke in the same direction. Tape the needle onto a thin slice of cork.

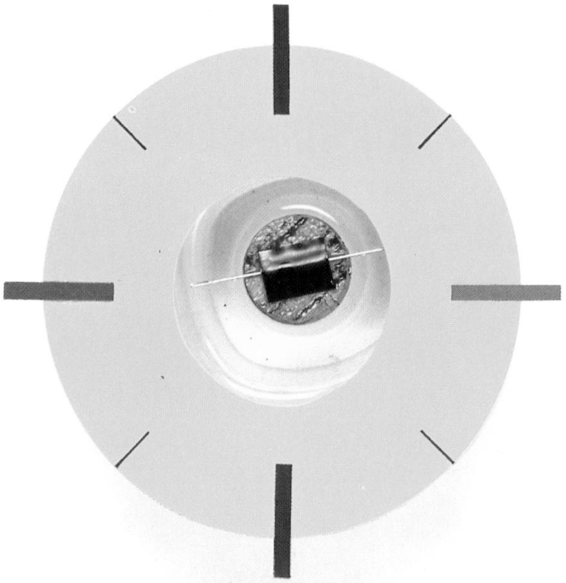

4 Fill the yoghurt pot with water and float the cork in it. When the needle has settled to the north, tape the ring of card onto the pot. Check your readings against a real compass.

The poles of magnets react to one another just like the two kinds of electric charge. Opposite poles attract – and like poles repel.

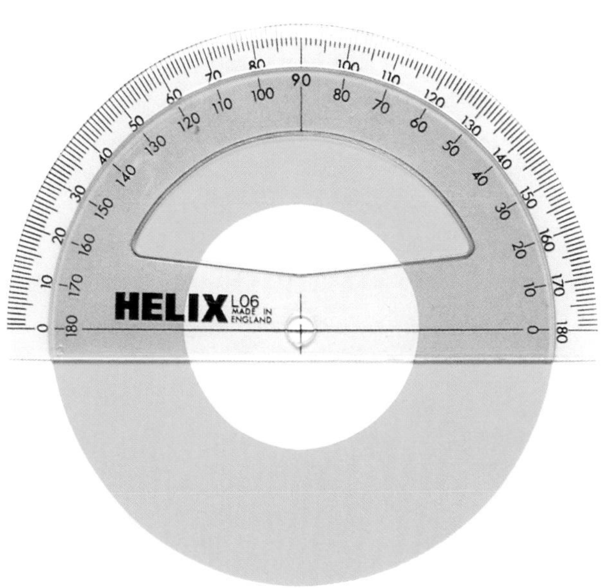

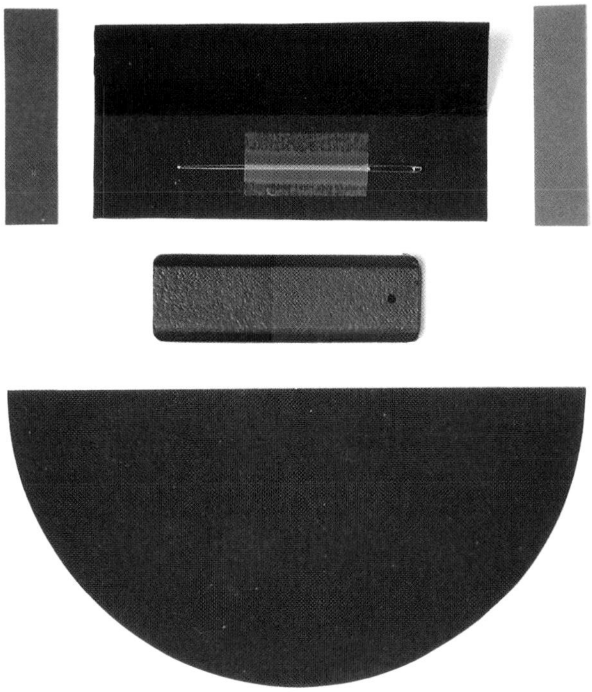

For two simple compasses you will need

card
a magnet
needles
tape

Fold a strip of card and tape a magnetized needle on it.

◀ Balancing compass
Make a cone from a semicircle of card. Fix a wooden skewer or cocktail stick into the top of the cone and balance the compass strip on the end. This is strictly an indoor model!

Jar compass
Suspend the compass strip in a glass jar using a straw or a pencil and some thread. This compass will work out of doors because the jar protects the needle from the wind.

34 Magnetic Fields

You can actually see the force field that surrounds a magnet by sprinkling iron filings onto a piece of paper and then putting a magnet wrapped in paper down amongst them. The filings will rearrange themselves according to the magnet's force field, clustering around the north and south poles where the force is at its greatest.

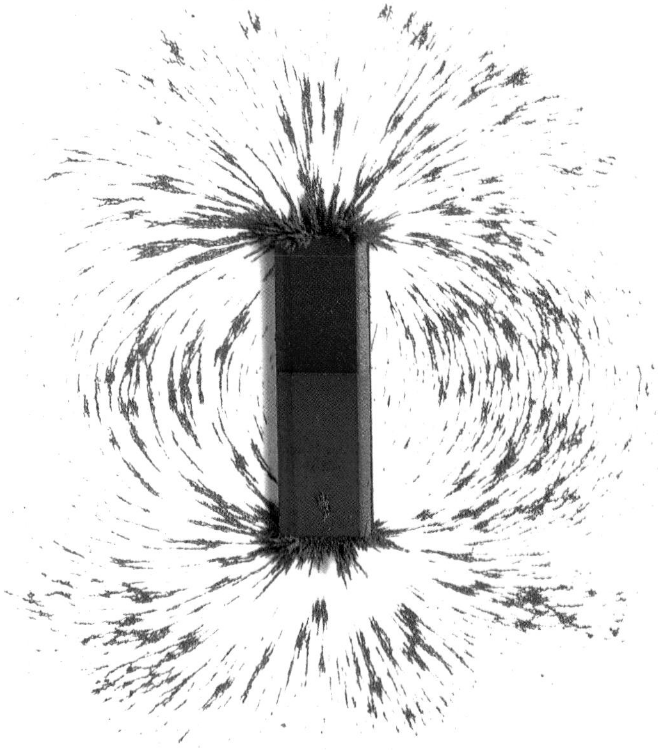

▲ Here you can see the force field at work. The iron filings form a pattern of lines running from pole to pole. These lines are called lines of force, and they show up the invisible force field of the magnet.

MAKE it WORK!
Use the power of magnetism to draw pictures with iron filings.

You will need

- card
- rubber bands
- scissors
- clear acetate sheets
- iron filings and a magnet
- clear sticky tape

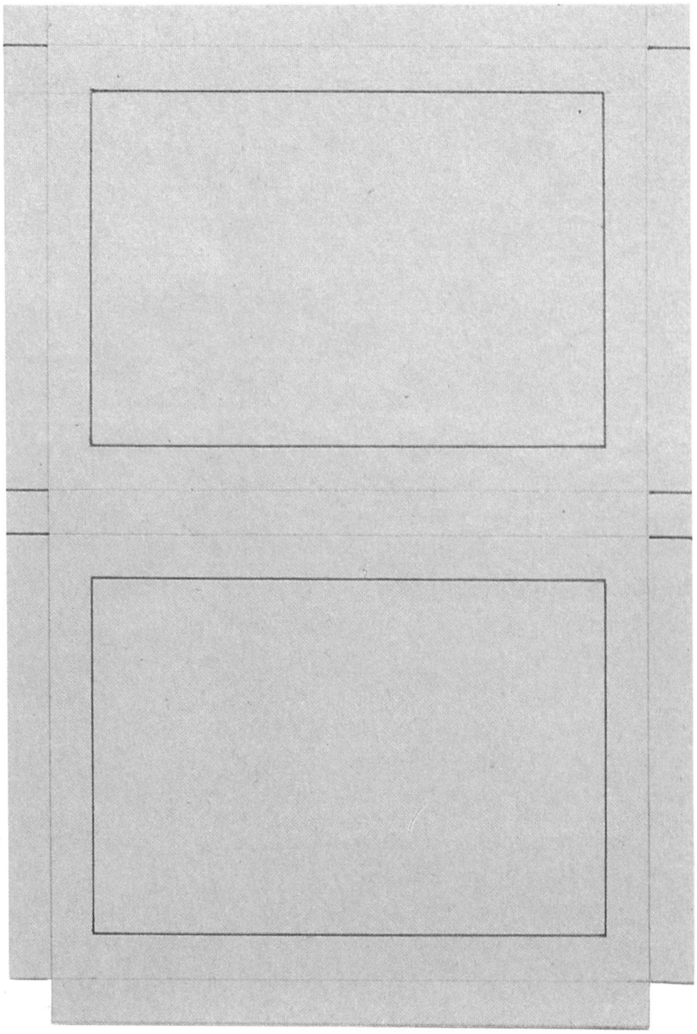

Be careful! Iron filings are dangerous. Don't breathe them in or swallow any, and don't lick your fingers after touching them.

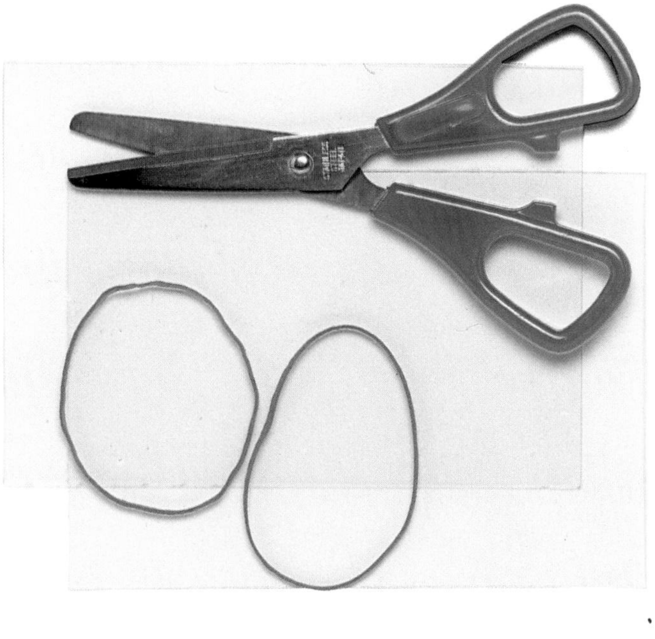

1 Cut out a rectangle of card and mark it as shown. Cut along the red lines and fold and glue along the pencil lines to make a box.

2 Take two pieces of clear acetate and cut them slightly bigger than the windows of the drawing box. Tape them in place with clear sticky tape.

3 Draw some faces on sheets of white card, leaving out the hair.

4 Put a face card inside the box and shake iron filings on top of the card. Snap the box shut with the elastic bands. Put the drawing box on a flat surface. Now you can 'draw' the hair on your face using a magnet.

*A new kind of experimental train in Japan runs on the principle of magnetic levitation. Both the track and parts of the train are magnetic. It works on the pull and push of magnets that repel and attract. The train floats above the track because the train and the track repel one another. There are no wheels and tracks to wear out, and no **friction** to slow the train down.*

36 Electromagnetism

We have seen that electricity and magnetism are closely related to each other. In fact, every electric current has its own magnetic field. This magnetic force in electricity is very handy. We can use electricity to make powerful electromagnets that can be turned on and off at the flick of a switch.

MAKE it WORK!

This crane uses an electromagnetic coil. The magnetic field produced by a single wire is not very strong, but when electricity flows through a wire coiled around a nail, the coil becomes a powerful magnet.

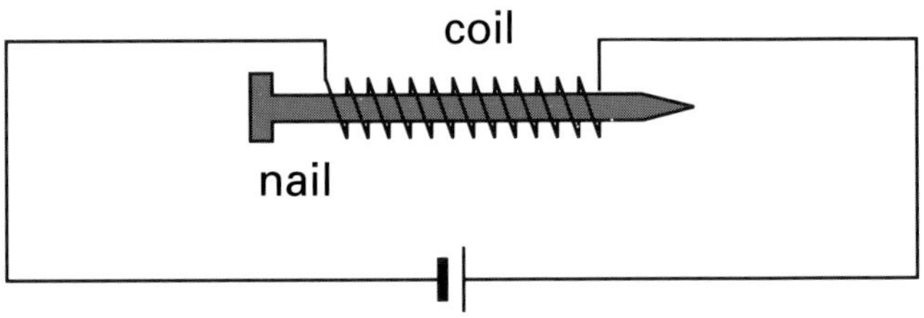

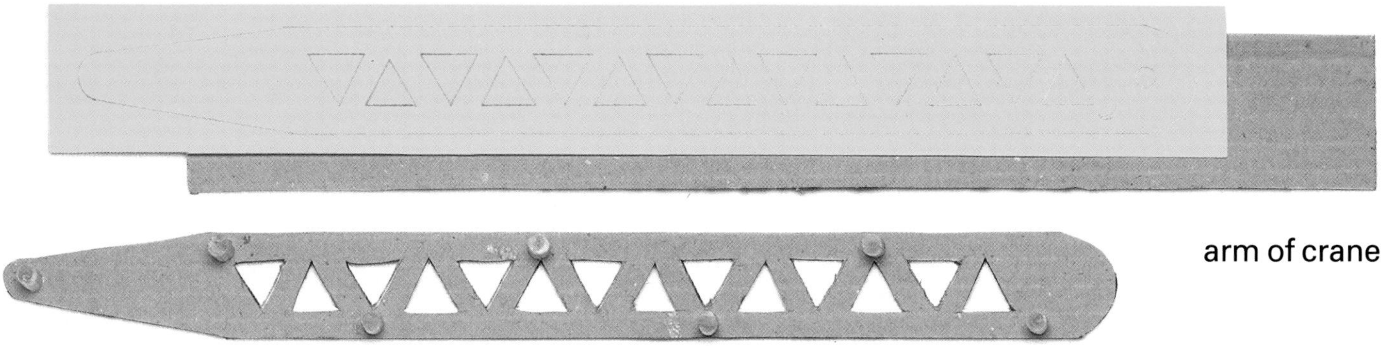

arm of crane

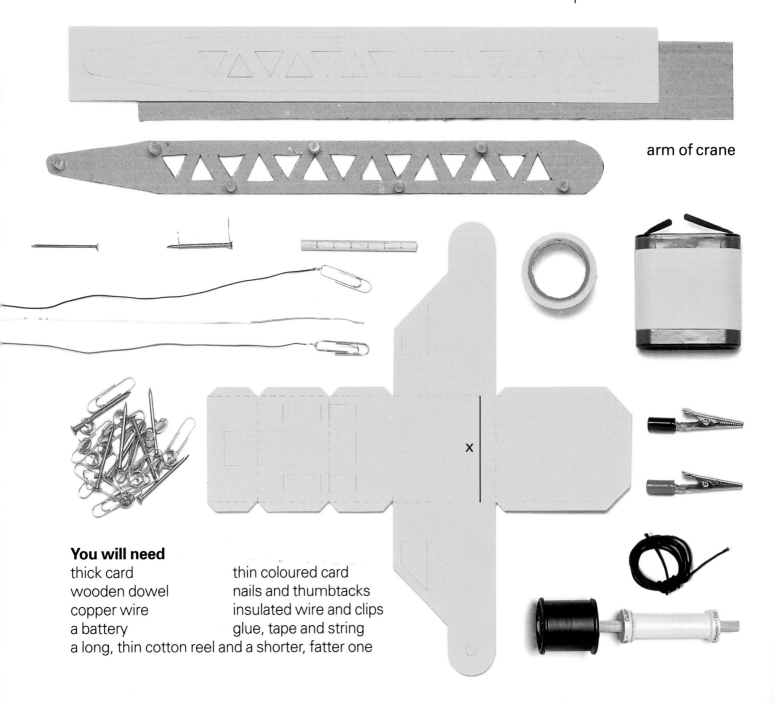

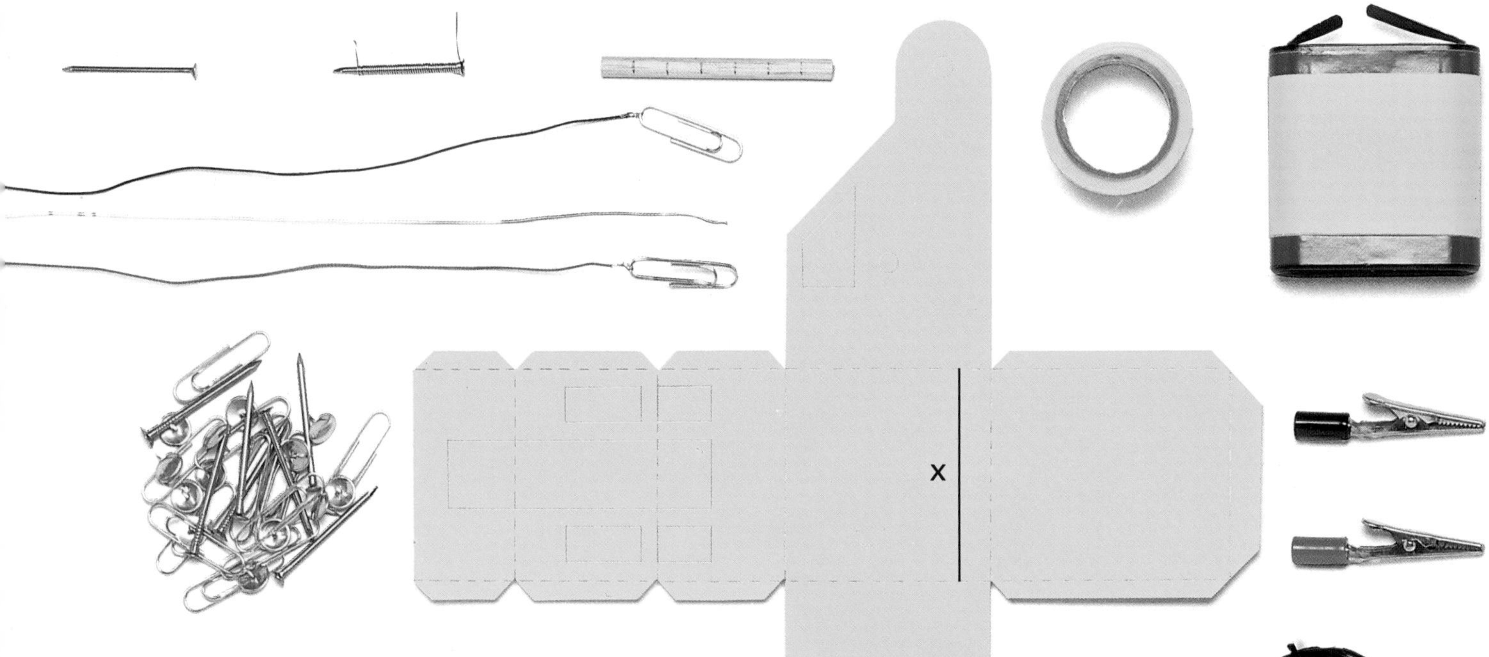

You will need

thick card
wooden dowel
copper wire
a battery
thin coloured card
nails and thumbtacks
insulated wire and clips
glue, tape and string
a long, thin cotton reel and a shorter, fatter one

1 Draw shapes shown below onto the thick and thin card. Make sure that the line marked 'x' is the same length as the long, thin cotton reel.

2 Cut along the solid lines and fold along the dotted ones to assemble the body of the crane. Glue the thick card inside the body structure to make it stronger.

3 Assemble winch as shown below, using the two spools, dowels, and string. Attach the other end of the string to the dowel at the tip of the crane arm.

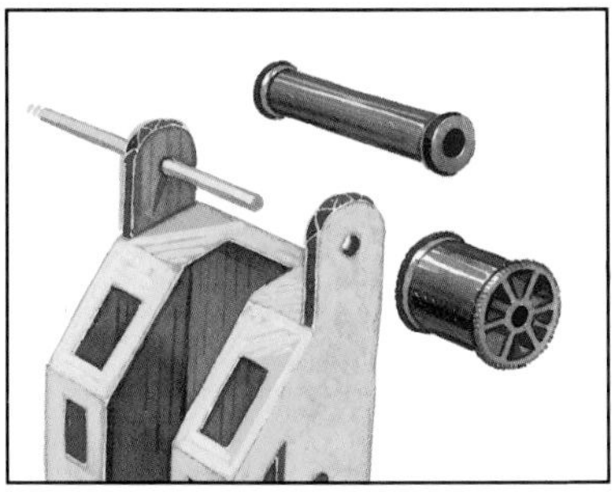

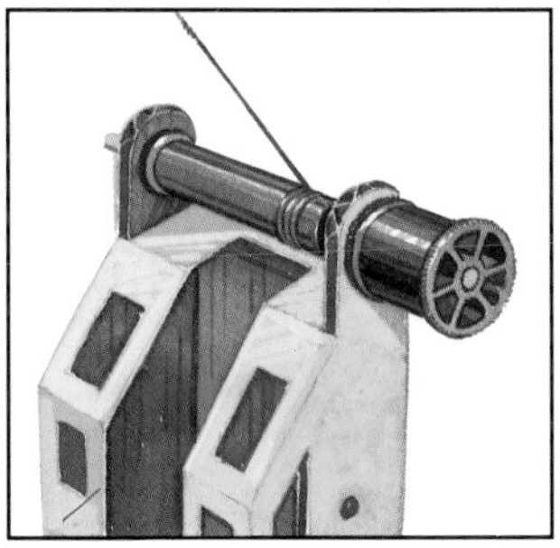

reinforcing card

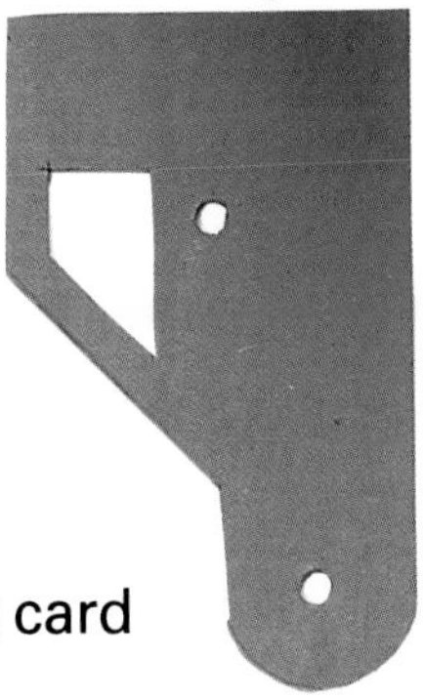

reinforcing card

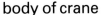

base support

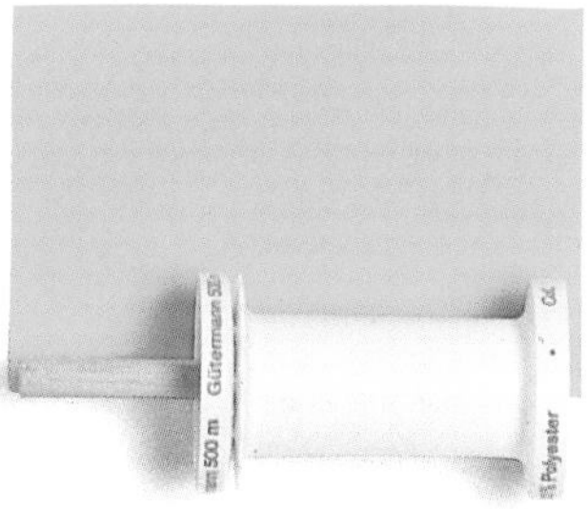

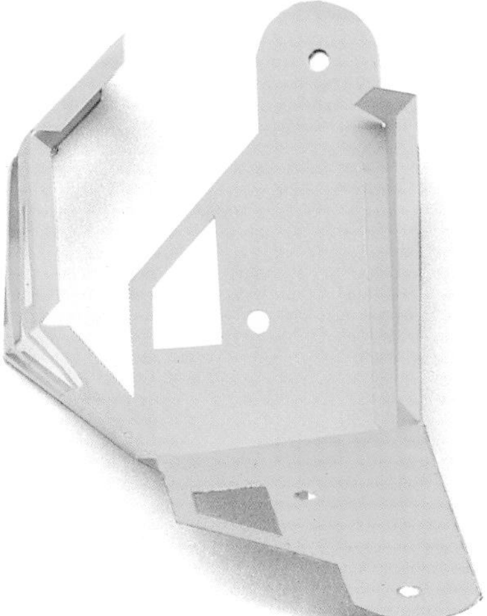

body of crane

4 Wrap copper wire around an iron nail to make an electromagnet. Then connect it to the battery with insulated wire, run over the top of the crane arm.

5 Tape the battery to the back of the crane. Check the circuit diagram to make sure the crane is correctly wired. When the leads and battery are connected the nail will become magnetized and you can pick up a load of thumbtacks. Disconnect and the tacks will fall to the ground.

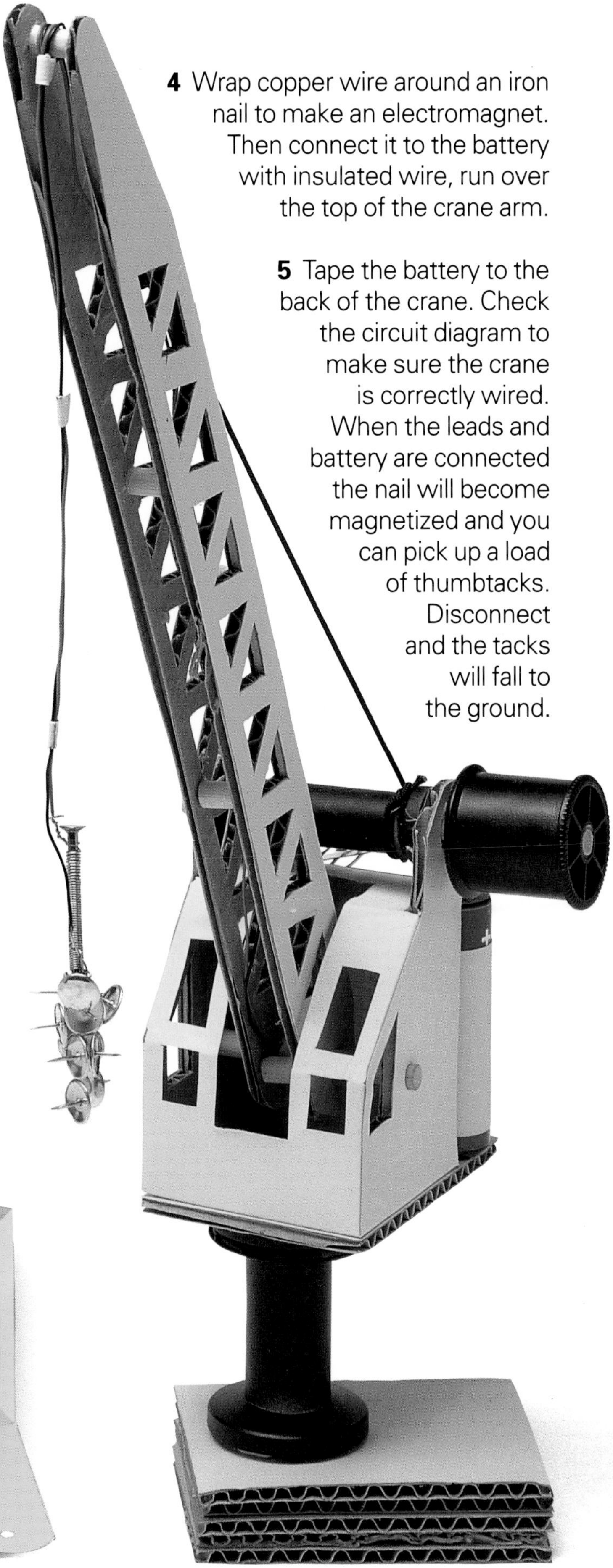

38 Making a Motor

Electrical energy can be converted into mechanical energy, that is, energy that can pull and push and make things go. When electricity flows through the wires inside the motor, it makes them magnetic. The coil of wires becomes an electromagnet. It is attracted to fixed magnets inside the motor, which sets it off spinning around and around.

MAKE it WORK!

In this electric motor, a copper coil (the electromagnet) is connected to a battery by a clever little device called a **commutator**. The commutator brushes up against the wire leads of the electromagnetic coil, so that the electric current passes through; but the connections are loose enough to allow the coil to rotate freely.

As the coil turns, the connections of the commutator switch from side to side, so the direction of the electric current keeps changing. As the direction of the current changes, the poles of the electromagnet change sides too. The electromagnet is always attracted to the furthest fixed magnet and so it keeps on spinning and spinning.

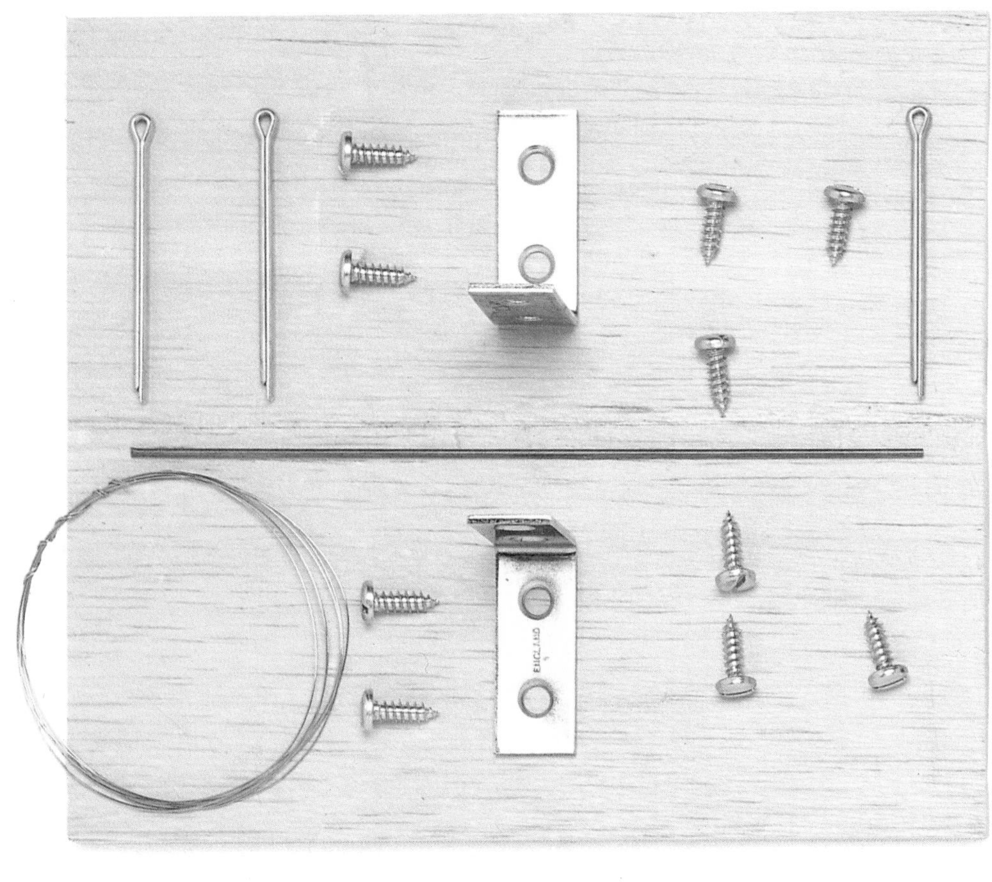

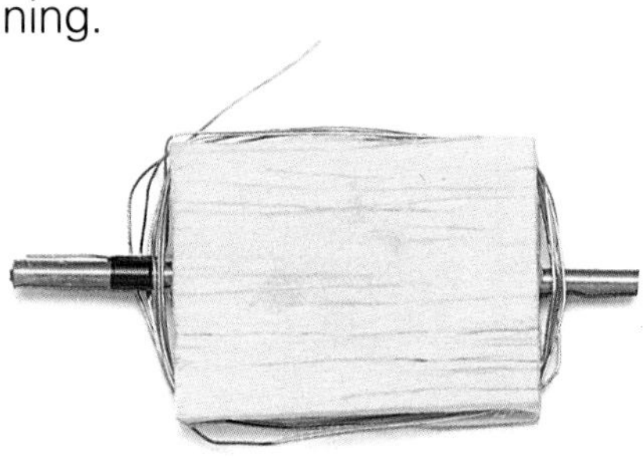

coil (electromagnet)

You will need

wood for the base
two angle brackets
thin copper tube
screws
split-pin clips
a metal spindle
copper wire
balsa-wood block
crocodile clips/paper clips
two strong magnets
insulating tape
a battery

1 Cut the base board out of a piece of balsa wood, or find a piece of soft wood. You could paint it a bright colour.

2 Ask an adult to drill a hole through the length of a small block of balsa wood. The hole should be wide enough in diameter for the copper tube to fit through.

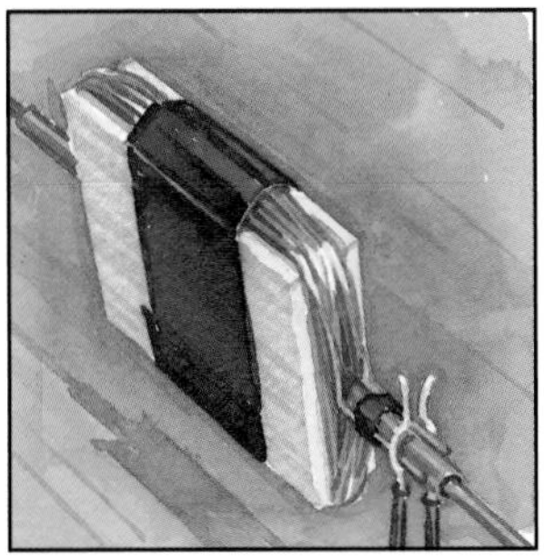

4 Screw the angle brackets to the base board. Stick on the magnets and position them so that they attract one another. Ask an adult to drill three holes along the centre of the board for the split pins to stand up in.

5 Thread the metal spindle through the split pins and the balsa-wood block so that the coil is suspended and can turn easily.

6 Now make the commutator. You have to get the wires from the battery to touch the ends of the wire from the electromagnetic coil without stopping the coil spinning round and round. You should strip some of the casing from the ends of the wires and bend them inwards. Follow the illustration on the left.

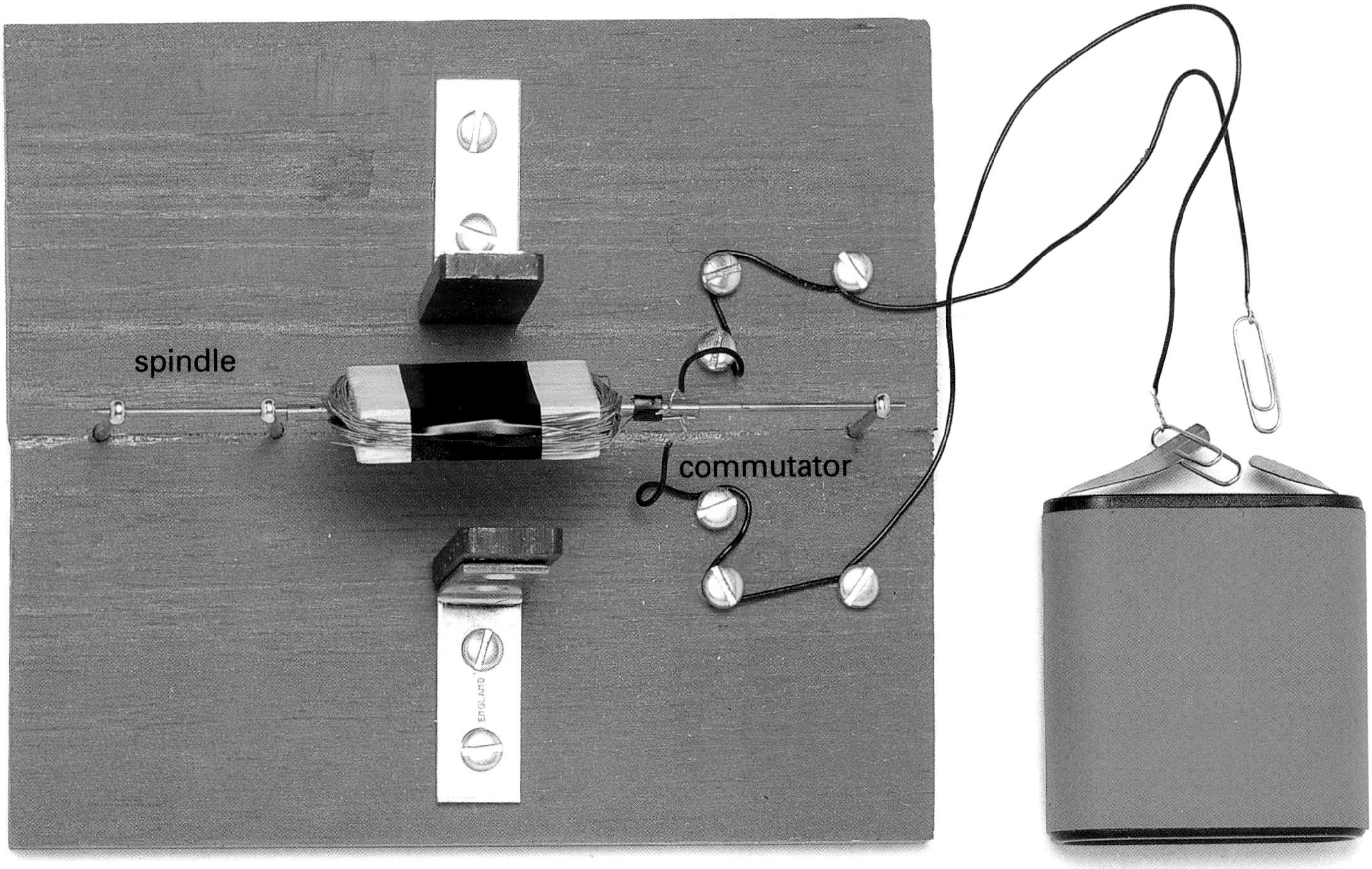

3 Cut grooves along two edges of the balsa-wood block and wrap copper wire tightly round the block. Insulate one end of the copper tube with clear sticky tape and fix the two ends of the coil wire in place with insulating tape as shown.

7 Screw the electrical wires into position so that the commutator connection is firmly fixed in place and cannot move. You may have to experiment a bit to get the screws positioned in the right place.

40 Working Motor

A simple electric motor turns a spindle round and round. One of the most direct and efficient ways of using this energy is to fix a propeller to the spindle. Boats are often driven by propellers in this way.

MAKE it WORK!
This propeller-driven boat makes good use of energy. It is designed with a propeller that drives through air rather than water because air is thinner than water and easier to move.

1 Make a balsa-wood framework for the hull and deck as shown on the right. Ask an adult to drill holes for the dowelling struts and glue them in place with a waterproof glue. Screw the electric motor in position. Paint the hull and deck with gloss paint.

2 Glue the battery onto the upper deck and wire up the circuit for the motor.

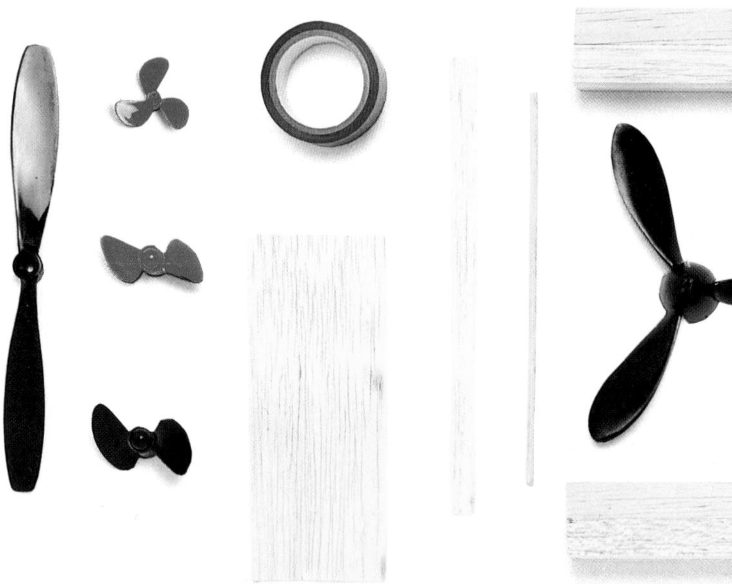

You will need
balsa wood	thin dowels
an electric motor	wire and clips
screws and nails	tape and glue
thin card	a propeller

To make the buoys
You can follow the instructions on page 15 to make marker buoys for your propeller boat.

3 Make the framework for the rudder, drilling shallow holes for the dowel to sit in so that it can turn freely from side to side. Glue and nail the balsa-wood support into position on the upper deck. Cut a rectangle of card for the rudder and tape it into place on the dowel as shown below.

4 Glue the propeller to the motor spindle, clip the leads onto the battery and watch your boat go! Turn the rudder to make it change direction.

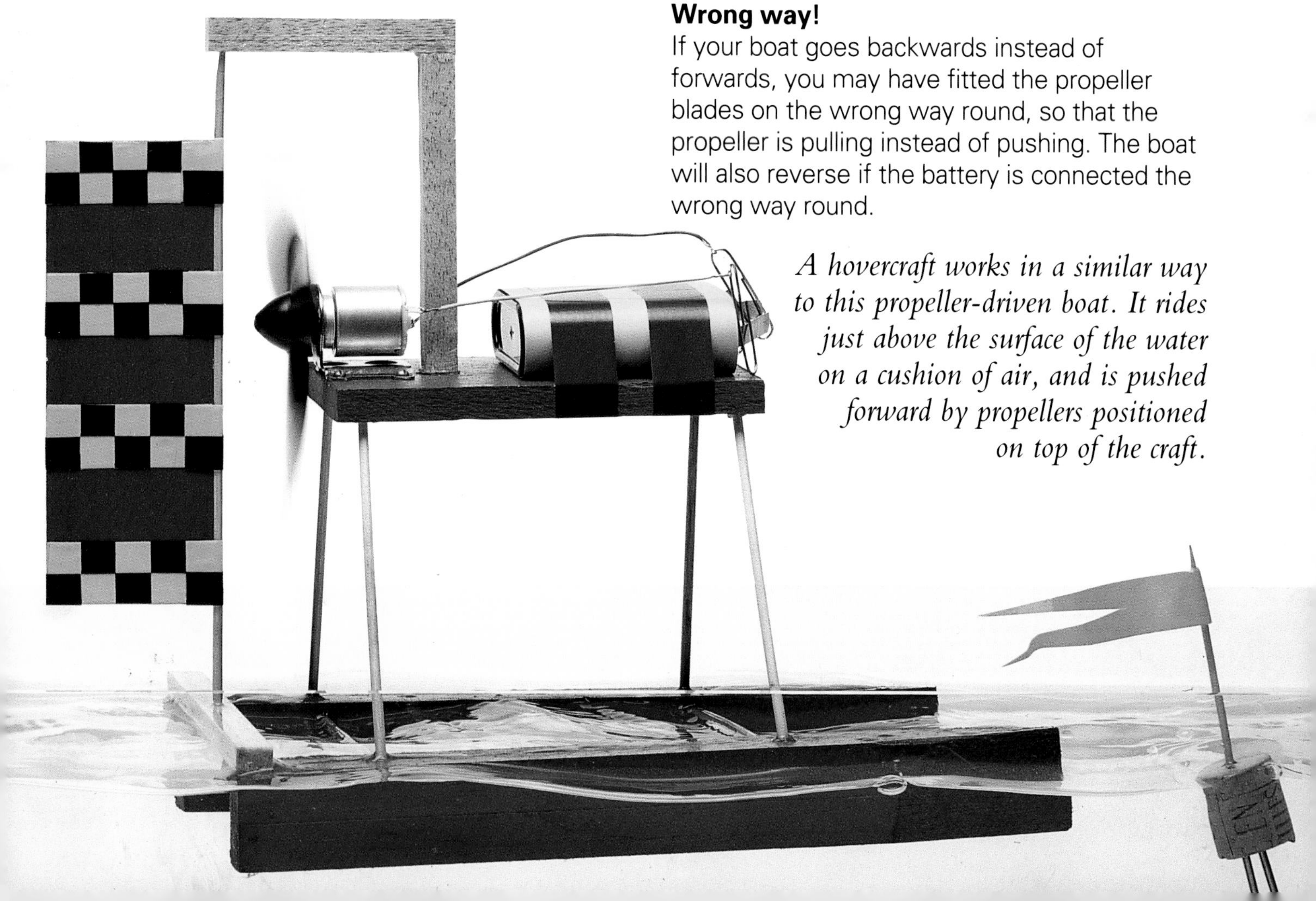

Wrong way!
If your boat goes backwards instead of forwards, you may have fitted the propeller blades on the wrong way round, so that the propeller is pulling instead of pushing. The boat will also reverse if the battery is connected the wrong way round.

A hovercraft works in a similar way to this propeller-driven boat. It rides just above the surface of the water on a cushion of air, and is pushed forward by propellers positioned on top of the craft.

42 Electric Train

Modern high-speed electric trains are run by large electric motors. They take their power supply from overhead wires or electrified tracks. Not having to carry fuel increases their efficiency.

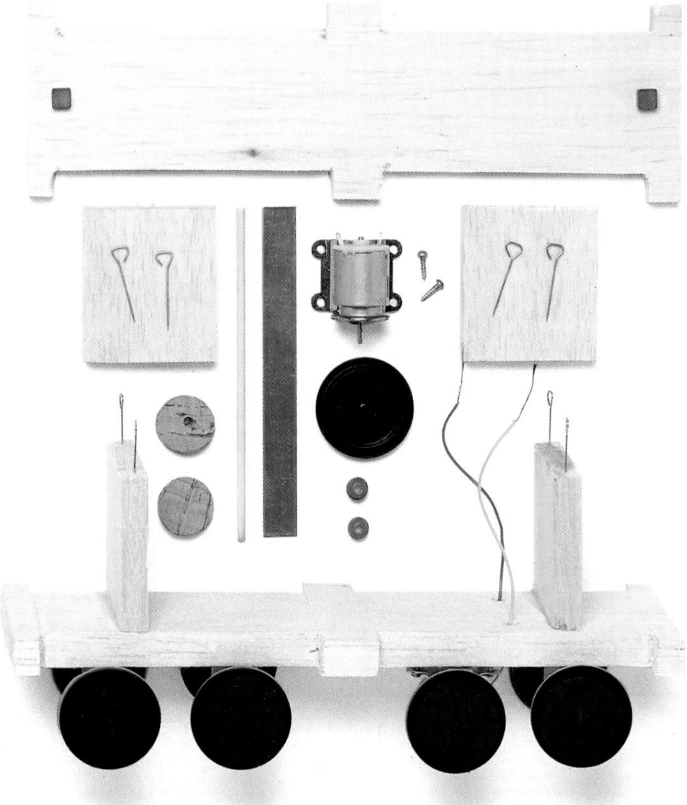

You will need

- thin card
- wooden dowelling
- an electric motor
- a battery
- copper wire
- screws, thin nails and glue
- seven plastic bottle tops
- three thin copper strips
- balsa wood
- beads
- paper clips
- slices of cork
- upholstery pins

1 Ask an adult to help you cut out the balsa-wood base of the engine. Then glue and nail the two roof supports into position as shown. Stick the upholstery pins into the supports.

MAKE it WORK!
This model electric train works just like the real thing. The motor is on board but the power is supplied through power lines overhead and is passed down to the motor through the upholstery pins.

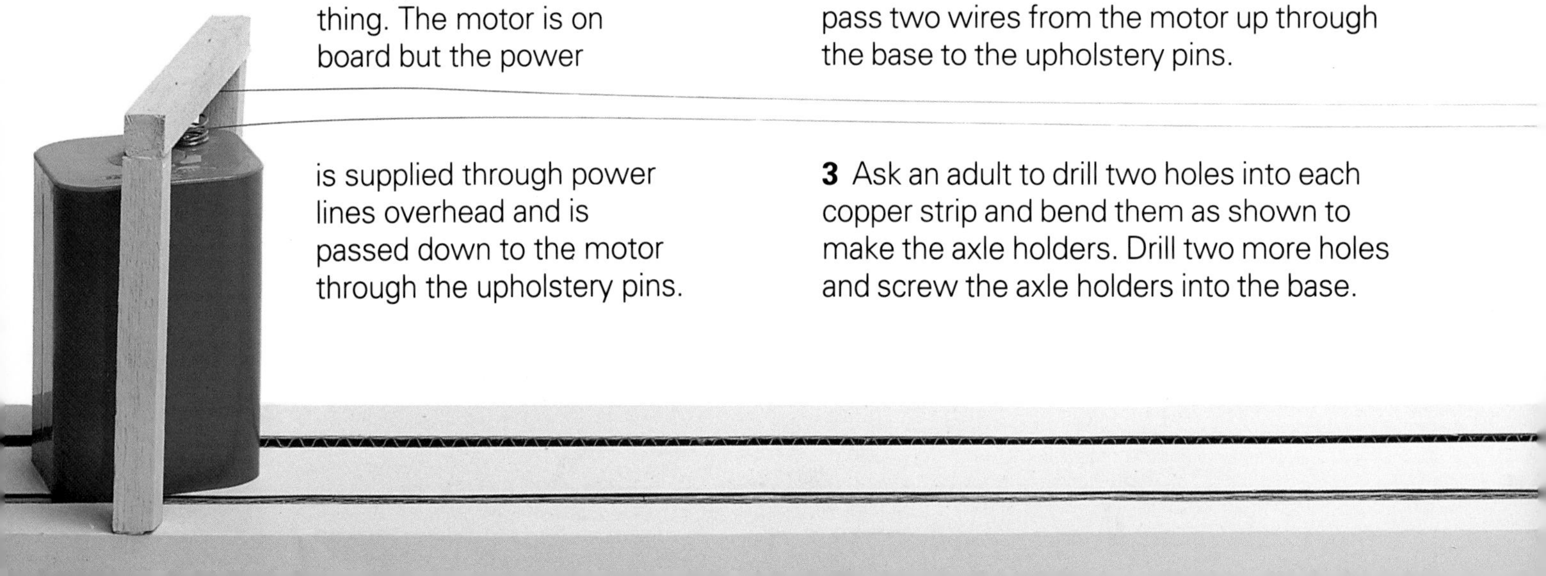

2 Glue a plastic bottle top to the spindle of the electric motor to make a wheel. Screw the motor to the base of the train, and then pass two wires from the motor up through the base to the upholstery pins.

3 Ask an adult to drill two holes into each copper strip and bend them as shown to make the axle holders. Drill two more holes and screw the axle holders into the base.

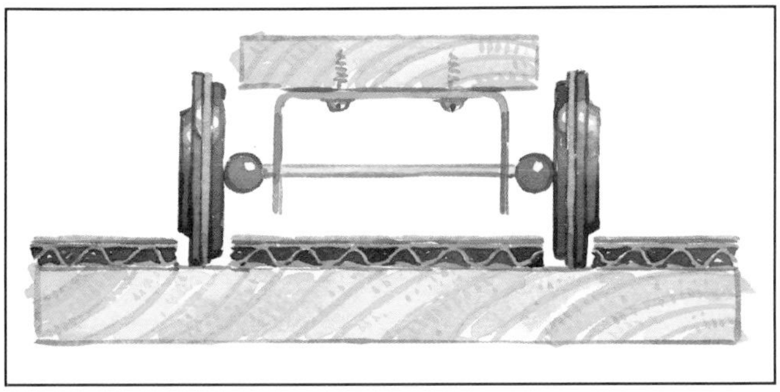

4 Make the axles by feeding the dowels through the axle holders. Then glue the beads and bottle tops to the ends of the axles to make the wheels.

6 Lay down three long strips of card to make two grooves for your train to run along. Add balsa-wood pylons overhead and fix a length of wire between them, threading it through the upholstery pins. Connect the overhead wires to the battery and watch your train go!

Extra carriages
Experiment making different kinds of carriages for your train. They do not need motors or wires, but you can make wheels and bases in the same way as for the engine. Join them up with small door magnets behind cork buffers.

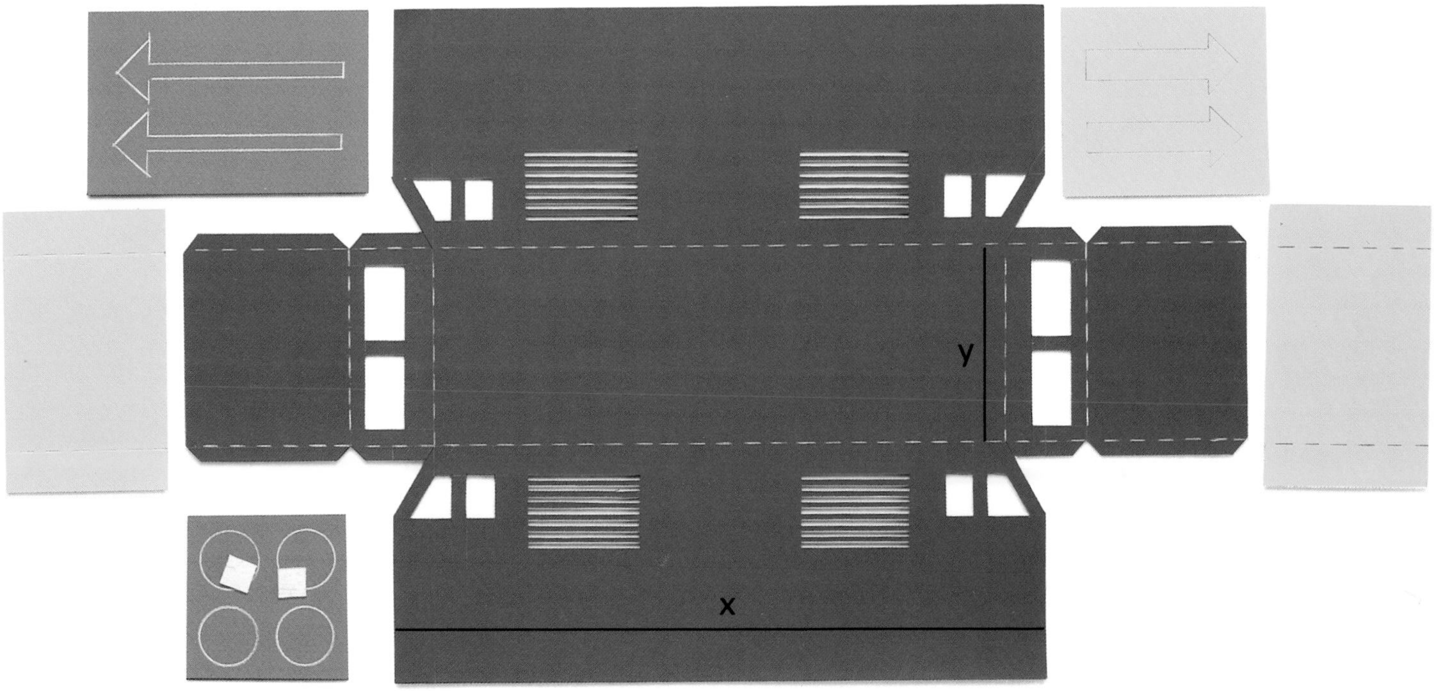

5 Mark out coloured card as shown, making sure that line 'x' is as long as the balsa-wood base and line 'y' is the same width. Assemble the body of the train and fit it over the base.

Running backwards and forwards
To make your train run the opposite way, just reverse the connections on the battery.

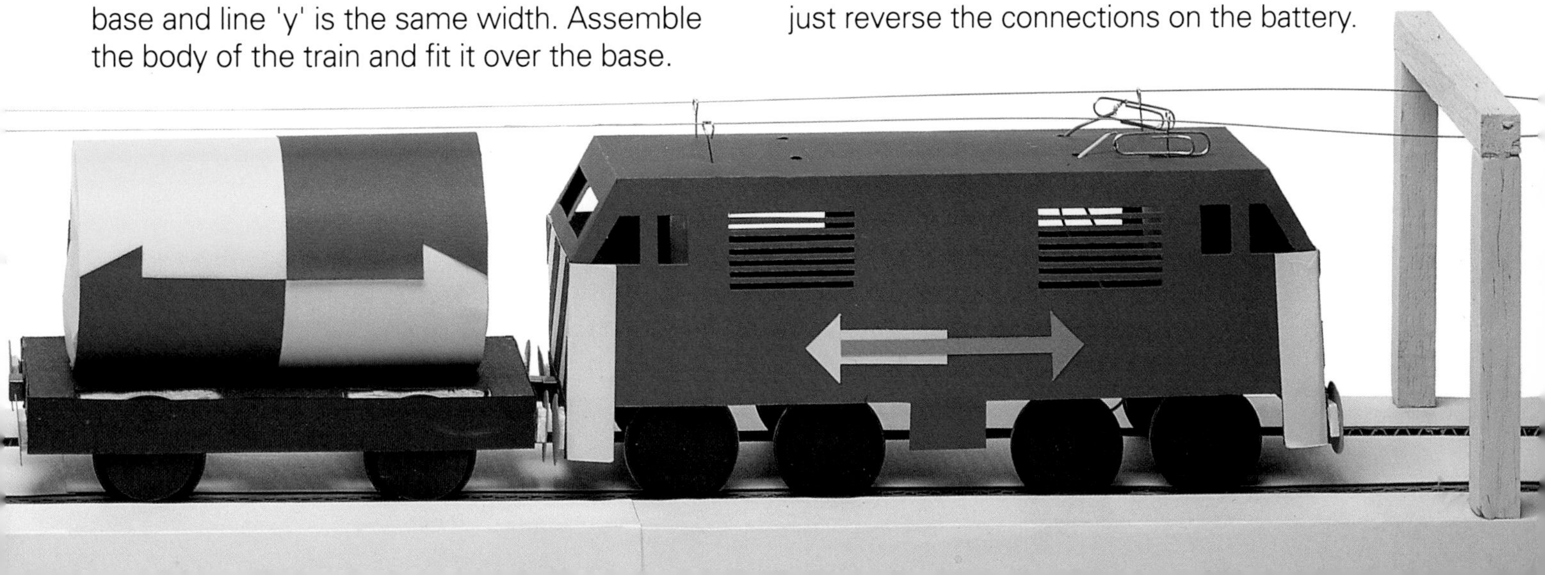

Boosting Power

Electric motors range from the very small to the enormous. There are small battery-operated motors in model trains and clocks; but some electric motors in factories need a power supply so strong that it has to come directly from the power station.

MAKE it WORK!
See for yourself what happens if you double the power supply to an electric motor. Build a Spin-o-Matico to make colourful patterns with paint. Compare the different results you get with one battery and with two.

1 Glue the two tubs together, bottom to bottom, so you have two open ends. The top tub will be the paint tub and the bottom one will hold the motor and batteries.

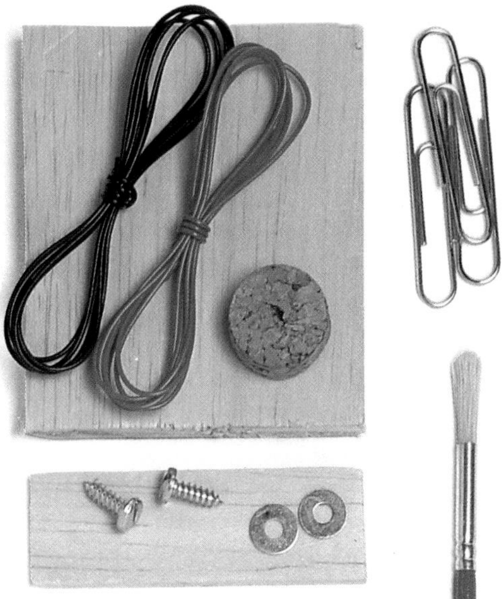

You will need

two old margarine tubs
two 4.5-volt batteries
screws and washers
a slice of cork
poster paint
an electric motor
paper clips
wire
wood
card

2 Poke the spindle of the electric motor through the centre of the bottom tub (the motor tub) so it pokes up through the bottom of the top tub (the paint tub). Screw the electric motor down onto a small piece of wood to hold it in place, and glue the wood into position.

3 Glue the batteries firmly to the bottom of the motor tub as shown. Then connect the two positive terminals and the two negative terminals with paper clips.

4 Make an on/off switch like the one shown on page 20, using a paper clip and two screws. Wire the batteries up to the motor, including the on/off switch in the circuit. Fix the on/off switch to the outside of the margarine tub, strengthening it on the back with a small piece of balsa wood.

5 Turn the margarine tubs over. Put a slice of cork over the top of the electric spindle that is poking up through the bottom of the top tub. Test to see if the motor is working and the cork whizzes around when you switch on.

6 Take a piece of card and stick it onto the cork using a dab of rubber glue.

7 Switch on the motor and dribble paint onto the whirling card to make a pattern. You can also use a paint brush if you want to.

full power

half power

▲ Try doing some paintings using half the power. Move the paper clips so they touch the terminals of just one of the batteries instead of both of them. How does the reduced power affect your finished painting?

When something is spinning very fast, the outside spins much faster than the inside. The force that seems to push everything towards the outside is called centrifugal force.

Acid A certain kind of chemical. Foods that contain acids, such as lemons, taste sour or sharp. Very strong acids are dangerous, and can burn holes in wood or cloth.

Alkaline A word used by chemists to describe a chemical property of certain substances. In chemistry, an alkali is the opposite of an acid. One common kind of alkali is magnesia, the white liquid or powder we take to cure an upset stomach. Caustic soda is an example of a very strong, dangerous alkali.

Atomic power Energy that comes from making changes to the centre of an atom. By splitting atoms, an enormous amount of heat is created. This heat is used to boil water, making steam to drive turbines and produce electricity.

Atoms Tiny particles, over a million times smaller than the thickness of a human hair. Everything around us is made up of atoms – they are like building blocks, and by combining different atoms in different ways, different substances are created.

Circuit A loop-shaped path along which electricity can flow.

Communications satellite A spacecraft that goes round and round the Earth and is used to relay telephone conversations, fax messages and television pictures from one part of the globe to another.

Commutator A special kind of electrical connection, used in an electric motor. A commutator makes the direction of the electric current change at regular intervals.

Component In electronics, a component is one single part of a whole circuit. For example, a switch or a battery is a component in an electrical circuit.

Conductor In electronics, a conductor is any substance that an electric current can pass through.

Current electricity Current electricity is the electricity we use in homes, offices and factories. It is produced in power stations, and is then distributed around the country through wires, pylons and transformers.

Electrolyte A liquid solution that is able to conduct electricity. Batteries use electrolytes to make electricity.

Electromagnets When an electric current passes through a metal, such as a piece of iron or copper, it always produces a magnetic field. Electromagnets are especially useful because their magnetism can be switched on and off with the electric current.

Electrons Tiny particles of atoms. Each electron carries an electrical charge.

Electroscope A scientific instrument used to measure the strength of an electrical charge.

Energy Energy is needed to do any kind of job or action. Motors and engines use energy, and our bodies do too. The food we eat, or the electricity that powers an electric motor, are called energy sources.

Experiments Scientists do experiments to test out their theories about how the world works.

Filament A thin coil of wire, usually made from a substance called tungsten, inside a light bulb. The electricity has to work so hard to push its way through the tungsten that the coil glows and gives off light.

Force field The area around a source of energy (such as a magnet) where the energy works.

Friction Friction happens when one object moves side by side to another one. Friction produces heat (like when you rub yourself to keep warm) and makes the two objects stick together (like tires gripping the road).

Generator A machine that turns heat or movement into an electrical current.

Graphite The substance that pencil leads are made out of. Pencils used to contain actual lead until people discovered that graphite was better for writing with.

Hydroelectricity Electricity that is produced by the movement of water through a generator.

Insulators Materials that do not conduct electricity. Rubber and plastic are both good insulators.

Load The part of an electric circuit that uses the electric power. In a lighting circuit, the load is the light bulb.

Matter All the different substances in the universe are matter. There are three forms: solids, liquids, or gases.

Molecule A tiny particle of a substance. Every molecule is made up of two or more atoms joined together.

Physics The study of energy and matter.

Resistor A substance which offers resistance to an electric current. The current has to work very hard to get through a resistor, so resistors are put into circuits to reduce the voltage of the current.

Scientist Someone who studies the world in a systematic way, to try and understand how it works.

Silicon chip A tiny, wafer-thin slice of the substance silicon, which has a whole electronic circuit on it, in miniature. Silicon chips are an especially important part of modern computers.

Static electricity Static electricity is an electrical charge, produced naturally when two things rub together. Lightning is the best-known example of static electricity.

Terminals The points in an electrical circuit where the electric current leaves or enters the circuit.

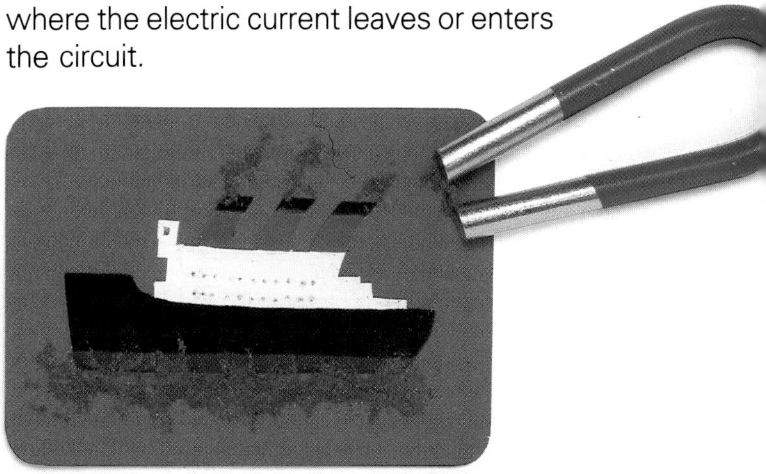

Theory An idea which tries to explain something. Scientific theories usually have to be proved by experiments before they are said to be true.

Index

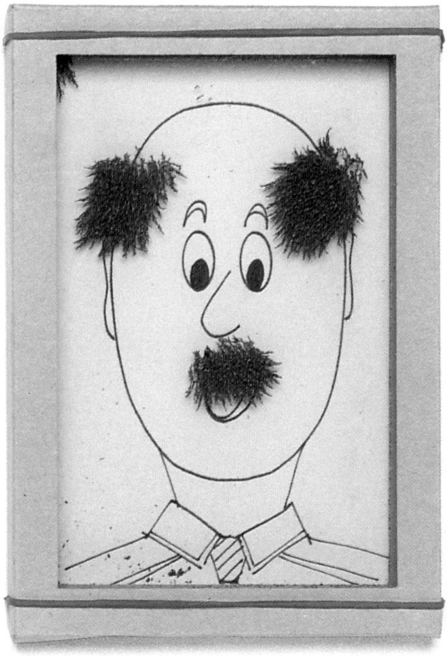

PHYSICAL CHEMISTRY USING MATHCAD®

Joseph H. Noggle

Department of Chemistry & Biochemistry
University of Delaware

Pike Creek Publishing Company
Newark, Delaware

Corrections and additional material will be posted at:

http://www.udel.edu/noggle/mcadlist.htm

I would like to thank Mary Wirth for talking me into trying the program, Donald Sands for his careful reading of the manuscript and many valuable suggestions, and Ed Adams of MathSoft for his patience and support. The support of the Camille and Henry Dreyfus Foundation is gratefully acknowledged.

Joseph H. Noggle, Newark, Delaware

http://www.udel.edu/noggle/noggle.htm

Table of Contents

INTRODUCTION

The basic operations of Mathcad are very easy to learn, and the result on the screen looks pretty much like normal mathematics as you would type it. The catch is that what you see on the screen is not always what you type to achieve that result. Nonetheless, what you need to know is quickly learned, and this is our first objective. In the following, it is presumed that you are running Mathcad, are looking at the screen, and entering text as described, and, it is hoped, trying out your own ideas. It is assumed that you are familiar with the user interface of the operating system (Windows or MacIntosh) that you are using.

After starting the program, look around the screen. At the top you will see a series of menus — click on each to see what commands appear. You will also see a series of buttons. If you move the mouse cursor over one of them, a descriptions will appear shortly. The buttons (in version 6) are divided into three groups: the operations palette bar, the tool bar, and the font bar. The font bar is relatively unimportant at present and you may want to hide it (you do this on the Window menu).

Getting Started

The first thing you must learn is how to enter equations into Mathcad; this is actually more difficult to explain in words than it is to do. Unfortunately a book has only words, and you may find that a few moments with an experienced user are more beneficial than the several pages of explanation that follow. Furthermore, this text is intended to be read while looking at the program; otherwise is will appear to be much more complicated than it really is.

When you start Mathcad, you are presented with a blank document (or worksheet) on which you do your calculations. You may create other documents with File-menu, New. You may have several documents open at the same time, but these do not share information. After you have done a significant amount of work, save the document with File-menu, Save, providing a file name with extension .mcd.

In this book, what you type into the document will be shown in quotes; *do not type the quotes* (unless explicitly told to do so) but what is inside. For example, use the mouse to place a cursor in the document and type "`22.3+4.5/14.5=`". (Note that there are no spaces in a Mathcad entries; sometimes we may include spaces for clarity, but you do not type them.) The entry can be terminated in several ways; the simplest is to use the mouse to click elsewhere in the document. If the program is in automatic mode you will see the result below.

If you do not see this result, look under the Math menu to be sure Automatic mode is on (a check mark should be next to Automatic Mode); if not click there to turn it on. Normally you want Automatic on, but there are times that it may be beneficial to turn it off, for example, when doing extensive editing on a lengthy or complicated document.

$$22.3 + \frac{4.5}{14.5} = 22.61$$

$$\frac{22.3 + 4.5}{14.5} = 1.848$$

Next, put the cursor elsewhere in the document and type "`22.3+4.5↑↑/14.5=`" (↑ denotes the up-arrow key); you should see the expression in box. When you press the up arrow key you surround portions of the expression with a *selection box*; the box determines the level of the expression to which the next operation (divide, in this case) applies. The number of times to press the arrow key depends on the situation; you will be able to tell by observing the screen when you have the correct level. (The down arrow does the opposite — it moves the selection box to a lower level.) The spacebar does much the same as up arrow, but typically moves several levels at once. The priority of operations (add, multiply, divide) in Mathcad is somewhat different from that in most programs, but it matters less since you see on the screen exactly what is going to happen.

Numbers can be assigned to symbols that represent names of constants or mathematical variables. Place a cursor anywhere in the document and type "`a:1.234`". The result in Mathcad will be displayed as shown in the box. Note that you typed a colon, but "`:=` " was the result. This assigns a number to the variable *a*.[1] Some symbols are predefined; for example, click elsewhere and type "p"; then hold down the control key (ctrl) and press "g" (instructions for typing control keystrokes will be displayed as, "ctrl+g"; this should not be typed literally but interpreted as "type g while pressing the ctrl key"). Then (while still editing the expression) type "=".

$$a := 1.234$$

Now your document should look as in box to right. This is the value of π to 4 figures; double click on the number — a box labeled "displayed precision" appears — type "6" and click on the "OK" button.

$$a := 1.234 \qquad \pi = 3.142$$

$$a := 1.234 \qquad \pi = 3.141593$$

Now you should see the result shown in box left. The results of a calculation are displayed with "="; click elsewhere in the document and type this: "`15*p ctrl+g =`" (spaces are for clarity and are not to be typed, "ctrl+g" means to type "g" while holding down the control key). The display should be as shown below.

$$a := 1.234 \qquad \pi = 3.142 \qquad 15\cdot\pi = 47.124$$

Editing Mathcad statements is fairly simple; for example to change 15 to 1.5 click between the numerals and type a period (decimal); when you move the cursor from on the edited statement, your screen should look as below:

$$a := 1.234 \qquad \pi = 3.142 \qquad 1.5\cdot\pi = 4.712$$

[1] Typographical conventions dictate that variable names be displayed in italic while units (kg, m, sec, ...) and functions (log, sin, cos, ...) are displayed in Roman. While it is possible to make variables italic in Mathcad, this action will also italicize units and functions which should be Roman. Therefore we shall use Roman symbols for variables in Mathcad, but show them as italic in text.

Characters can be removed with either the Delete (character after) or Backspace (character before) key and inserted by simply typing at the cursor. Mathcad is case sensitive so a variable named *A* is different from a variable named *a*.

The symbol π is more easily inserted by clicking a button on the Greek-letters palette, or by pressing ctrl+p; the ctrl+g method also works for other Greek letters. (The palette-bar names used here are for version 6; in earlier versions they are numbered.)

As you probably noticed, Mathcad statements can be entered at any place in the document. However the location may be critical since statements are executed from top to bottom and left to right. Somewhere below the statement defining *a*, type "`a/3=`".

A statement can be selected for moving by clicking nearby (outside the statement box[2]) and dragging into the statement; it will then be surrounded by dotted lines. Multiple statements can be selected in this manner by simply dragging over them. While the statements are so marked you can (from the Edit menu or tool bar) delete or copy the contents. You can also move them by simply placing the mouse cursor inside the box and dragging it.

Select for move, and drag the "a:= 1.234" statement to a position below the "a/3" statement. After moving, in the "a/3" statement the "a" is highlighted in reverse video indicating that it is an undefined variable. In Mathcad, *all variables must be assigned a numeric value prior to use* (that is, above or to the left of the place where it is used); there are two exceptions (functions and symbolic calculations), discussed later.

Mathematical Functions

Mathcad knows most of the usual functions such as **log** (base 10 logarithm) **ln** (base e logarithm), **sin**, **cos**, and so forth. The arguments are enclosed in parentheses.

$\log(100) = 2 \qquad \ln(100) = 4.60517 \qquad \exp(4.60517) = 100$

To display 6 decimals as in the second statement, double-click on the number (originally 4.605) to bring up the Numerical format menu: enter 5 for the displayed precision and click the OK button. The last statement demonstrates the exponential function: the inverse of the natural logarithm, **ln**.

A power is made using the caret (^). To get the display below, type "`2.456^4.333 -2.111 ↑↑↑-17=`"; note how the level of expression to which the next operation applies changes as you press the up arrow; it must be done 3 times so the second subtraction applies to the whole expression and not to the exponent. This is what you should see:

$$2.456^{4.333-2.111} - 17 = -9.636$$

Trigonometric functions require units in radians, but the symbol deg is built in—

---

[2] Each statement occupies a box which, ordinarily, is invisible. You can see the box when the statement is selected, or display all such boxes with Edit-menu, Regions, View. When viewing the regions, Mathcad shows, with a dot, the nominal position of the statement: this quantity is used to determine the relative position of statements in the document which, in turn, determines the order of execution.

$$\mathrm{deg} = 0.017453293 \qquad \frac{\pi}{180} = 0.017453293$$

The first of the following expressions calculates the sine of 45 (radians, not degrees); the second provides the argument as 45° in radians; the third enters the argument as "`45*deg`" and, as you can see, Mathcad interprets it correctly.

$$\sin(45) = 0.851 \qquad \sin\left(\frac{\pi}{4}\right) = 0.707 \qquad \sin(45\cdot \mathrm{deg}) = 0.707$$

There are many other built-in functions, which will be explained as needed.

On-line Help

You have no doubt noticed that there is a help menu at the top of the screen and a question-mark button, either of which can be used to access the on-line help of the program. If you allow the cursor to linger over any button, a help balloon appears.

Less obviously, if you press shift+F1, the cursor turns into a question mark: by clicking with this cursor on any button or command on the screen, you can get context-sensitive help. Press Esc to return to the normal cursor. This feature is, perhaps, the most useful one in Mathcad, but it is easy to forget about it — it's a shame it is not more prominently featured.

Labeling Worksheets with Text

Mathcad permits two types of text field: full width and free form. The full-width text band can be created from the text menu by clicking a button on the tool bar (create a text paragraph) or pressing ctrl+t. The free-form band can be started anywhere simply by typing a quotation mark (there is a button and menu command as well); this band can be of any width (up to first return) and length. In either case, you complete text-entry by clicking back in the math area, and edit it again by clicking in the text area.

Examples

In this section a number of sample calculations are presented, primarily as vehicles for learning to use Mathcad. You may either start a new worksheet to continue with the one you have been using.

Example 1: Unit conversion.

Mathcad is very good at handling units and dimensions. Start a new document (File-menu, New) and open Math-menu, Units. Select Math-menu, Units, Change System of Units and make sure that the mks system is selected.

$$\mathrm{gal} = 0.004\cdot \mathrm{m}^3$$

Return to the document and type "`gal=`"; you should see the display to the right. When no unit is selected, the default system (mks) is used. To get other units, click in the space just after the unit (or delete the unit by clicking in it and backspacing); a unit placeholder appears as a solid square. Click on the placeholder and type in the unit you want. You can always type ctrl+u or click the unit button to see a selection of units, or double-click on a placeholder to see a selection of appropriate units (for volume, in this case).

$gal = 3.785 \cdot liter$

If you select liter as the unit for this calculation, you should see the value in liters (box to right). After the first unit selection, you can change unit by erasing the old unit, or double-clicking on the unit to see an appropriate selection.

$gal = 231 \cdot in^3$

For volume, you can also enter the cube of any length. Click at the end of liter and backspace until the placeholder reappears. Type "`in^3`" to see the value shown in box to left.

Units in Mathcad are a mixed bag of abbreviations and spelled-out words; for example, milliliter is mL, but liter is not L. Some units, like coul for coulomb, are partially spelled. This may seem confusion at first, but you will get the hang of it, and on-line help is always available. It knows most common conversions (box right). (Some versions have an incorrect value for the calorie — it should be 4.184 joule. What does your version give?)

$coul \cdot volt = 1 \cdot kg \cdot m^2 \cdot sec^{-2}$

$joule = 1 \cdot kg \cdot m^2 \cdot sec^{-2}$

$cal = 4.187 \cdot kg \cdot m^2 \cdot sec^{-2}$

$BTU = 1.055 \cdot 10^3 \cdot kg \cdot m^2 \cdot sec^{-2}$

Mathcad supports some unit multiples such as cm and km, but not all (which could get confusing). But you may define any you like; for example, bond lengths are often given in Angstroms (Å, we denote this as *A* in Mathcad), picometers (pm) or nanometers (nm). Define these and display the bond length of H_2 — 0.7417 Å — in a variety of units. The first equation in the box below is entered as "`nm:10^-9↑↑↑*m`"; the up arrows are so the multiplication by the unit is not entered in the exponent (do not type quotes). The others are entered similarly.

$nm := 10^{-9} \cdot m$ $\qquad pm := 10^{-12} \cdot m$ $\qquad A := 10^{-8} \cdot cm$

$R := 0.7417 \cdot A$ $\qquad R = 74.17 \cdot pm$ $\qquad R = 0.074 \cdot nm$

You may also use the predefined symbols for other purposes since any definition you give overrides the built-in definition. In fact, we have already done so: *R* is used as the symbol for the Rankine degree if it is not redefined.

Example 2: Ideal gas law.

The ideal gas law is:

$$PV = nRT$$

$R := 8.31451 \cdot \frac{joule}{K \cdot mole}$

To do a calculation, you must solve for the desired variable (Mathcad can do this for you, but it is not worth the trouble for such a simple calculation). Before doing any calculation in Mathcad, you must enter values for the constants. For the gas constant, type "`R:8.31451*joule/K*mole`" (see box).

Mathcad knows about the most common units; the only problem is in guessing which are abbreviated and which are spelled out.[3] Here we see that joule and mole are spelled out but kelvin (K) is abbreviated. To calculate the pressure we must enter values for the number of moles, the kelvin temperature and the pressure. You can use any unit that Mathcad supports, or define your own as desired. Enter the following:

$R := 8.31451 \cdot \frac{\text{joule}}{\text{K} \cdot \text{mole}}$ $\quad n := 1 \cdot \text{mole}$ $\quad P := 1 \cdot \text{atm}$ $\quad T := 273.15 \cdot \text{K}$

$V := \frac{n \cdot R \cdot T}{P}$ $\quad V = 22.414 \cdot \text{liter}$ $\quad V = 5.921 \cdot \text{gal}$

The middle two statements (first line) are entered as "`n:1*mole`" and "`P:1*atm`". The volume calculation could be entered as "`V:n*R*T/P`" but you would get an unattractive display (but not an incorrect one). Instead, press up arrow before slash until the whole numerator is boxed: "`V:n*R*T↑↑/P`". The value of *V*, displayed with "`V=`", must be exactly to the right or below the calculation. It can be difficult to enter statements exactly side-by-side and to get them even. So, after they are typed, click outside one of the end statements and drag across them all. Now they should all be enclosed in dotted frames. You can align them by selecting Edit-menu, Align Regions, Align Horizontal. Click elsewhere to resume normal operation.

There is a catch to this calculation: Mathcad does not really treat "mole" as a unit. Type "`mole=`" and see what happens. This symbol is simply equal to 1, which means it can be placed anywhere in a definition or answer without effect. It is only a label; Mathcad does not keep track of or cancel it. You may use it to label your input or answers, but the responsibility for its being correct is yours alone. If you enter nonsense (for example a pressure as atm/mole or temperature as K/mole), Mathcad will not contradict you.

Example 3: Square roots.

Click the arithmetic palette to open it. Among others, there is a button for a square root. Click the square root button or type a backslash (\). All Mathcad operations are available as both a button on one of the palettes or by a keystroke. Obviously the button method is easier to learn, but the keystroke is easier to use and you will eventually learn the common ones. Keystrokes for operations are listed in the Appendix and can be found in the on-line help of the program. Directions will often be given for the keystroke method since it is easier to explain.

Type "`\5=`"; you should see the result in the box to the right.

$\sqrt{5} = 2.236$

$\sqrt{5-2} = 1.732$

The box to the left demonstrates what happens if you type "`\5-2=`".

But what if you wanted the subtraction after the root? After typing "`\5`" press the up-arrow key twice so the entire radical is framed; then continue with "`-2=`". You should get the result shown to the right.

$\sqrt{5} - 2 = 0.236$

[3] Be careful — the symbol "R" has a default as the Rankine-scale degree. If you did a calculation of this type and forgot to define *R*, Mathcad would not flag is as an undefined variable but assume that it meant degree Rankine, which can lead to some interesting confusions.

How would you calculate $\sqrt{\sqrt{5}-2}$? Click the square root button (or type \) twice; type "5" and then use the up-arrow key to until the inner radical is selected; then type "-2="; you should see the result to the right. (This is the *Gillen number.*) The number of displayed decimals has been increased in the manner described earlier: double click on the number and type in the number of decimals required.

$$\sqrt{\sqrt{5}-2} = 0.485868$$

Example 4: Functions and graphs.

We have seen a few examples of built-in functions. You can define your own functions by placing the arguments in parentheses following a variable name. Type "`f(x):x*sin(4*ctrl+p *x)*exp(-x)`" (do not type spaces, and remember that "ctrl+p" means to type "p" while pressing the control key):

$$f(x) := x\cdot\sin(4\cdot\pi\cdot x)\cdot\exp(-x) \qquad f(0.5352) = 0.134$$

The argument can be replaced by a number to display the value of the function as shown to the right in the box above. The argument of the function (x in this example) is a *dummy argument*, and can be replaced by a number of any legal variable name, as shown in the next box.

$$\text{number} := 0.552 \qquad f(\text{number}) = 0.193 \qquad f(0.552) = 0.193$$

You can use multiple arguments in functions by separating them with commas; for example, the function *rad* calculates the distance from the origin to the point (x, y, z):

$$\text{rad}(x,y,z) := \sqrt{x^2+y^2+z^2} \qquad \text{rad}(1,2,3) = 3.742$$

It is very easy to make graphs with Mathcad. We will use the function defined above, *f(x)*, as an example. Before making a graph it is necessary to enter numerical values for the range of the independent variable, which we shall call x. Do this by typing "x:0,0.01;10"; this defines x as a series of numbers between 0 and 10 by steps of 0.01 (1001 numbers). You can see what the x values are by typing "x=", but the list is so long you certainly will want to delete it immediately.

In defining a Mathcad range, the second number is not (directly) the increment; rather, the increment is the difference between the first and second. For example, the range "`x:1.05, 1.06;10`" gives a range from 1.05 to 10 with increment 0.01.

Click into an open area of the worksheet (below the function and range definitions) and select Graphics-menu, Create X-Y Plot (or type @). A frame appears with 6 place holders. Those in the center of each axis are the ones of immediate interest: click on the one in the center of the x axis and type "x". Click on the placeholder in the middle of the y axis and type "f(x)". Click anywhere outside the graph to display it (box below).

To move or size the graphic, drag the mouse cursor in from outside until the dotted frame appears. You can size by pulling the lower or right sides of the box, or move it by clicking anywhere in the box and dragging.

$f(x) := x \cdot \sin(4 \cdot \pi \cdot x) \cdot \exp(-x)$ $\qquad x := 0, .01 .. 10$

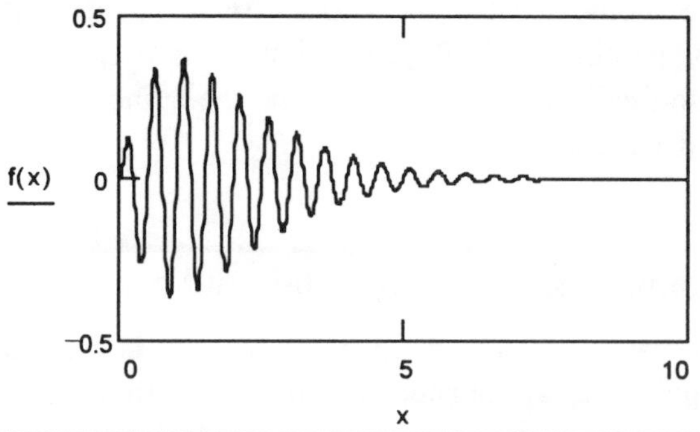

When you click inside a graphic (that is not selected for size/move — that is, not surrounded by a dotted line) a solid frame appears. Additional numbers appear at the corners, showing the actual limits for the numbers being plotted. If you prefer to show a different part of the graph, click on any of these additional numbers and backspace. When the number disappears, a placeholder appears and you can type in the limit you want for that axis.

$f(x) := x \cdot \sin(4 \cdot \pi \cdot x) \cdot \exp(-x)$ $\qquad x := 0, .01 .. 10$

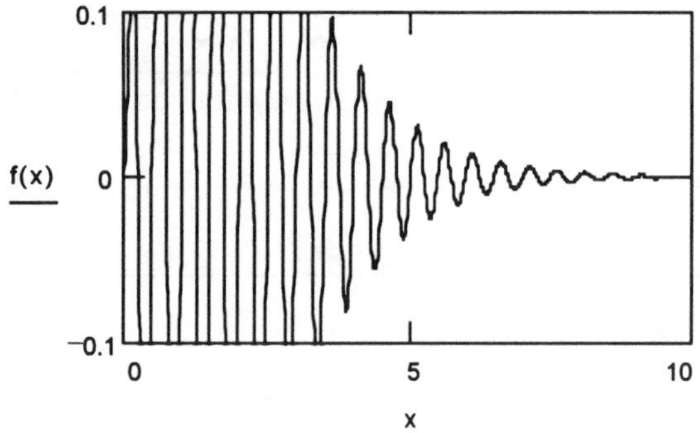

Display your graph with *y*-limits 0.1 to -0.1 (as in box to left). To change the *x*-limits, it is usually simplest to change the definition of the *x* range, but you can also type in limits (as for *y*).

You can plot several functions on the same graphs (called "traces" by Mathcad); just enter several functions in the *y* placeholder, separated by commas. The example below illustrates the plotting of several variables.

$f(x) := \sin(8 \cdot \pi \cdot x)$ $\qquad g(x) := \cos(2 \cdot \pi \cdot x)$ $\qquad x := 0, 0.01 .. 1$

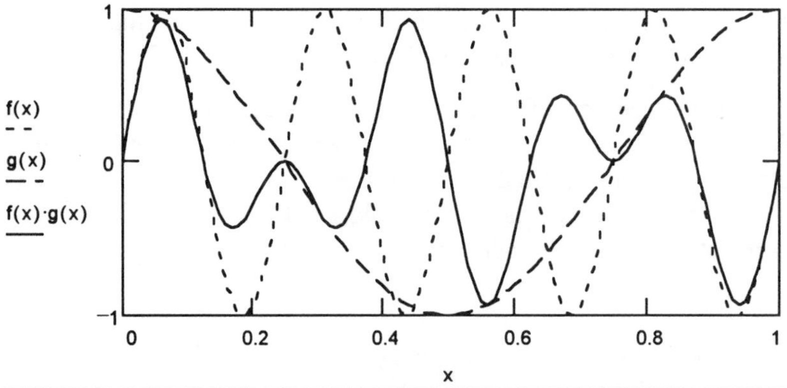

Double-click the graphic to display the Graph-Format menu. Select the characteristics (line-type, color, etc.) for the various traces by clicking on them and selecting from the drop-down menus. The line types shown above are dot (*f*), dashed (*g*) and solid (for the product, *fg*). (Colors are a better way to distinguish among the curves, but they cannot be shown in this text.)

Example 5: Entering and graphing data.

Few operations are more basic to physical chemistry than data analysis. In Mathcad, data are entered into subscripted arrays (vectors), so first we must discuss subscripts. Mathcad supports two types of subscripts. One of these is purely a label: type "P.new:1*atm"; the result shown in the box below.

$$P_{new} := 1 \cdot atm$$

True subscripts, which label positions (indices) of an array (vector or matrix), must be numerical (either a number or a symbol previously defined as a number or range); they are created using the left bracket ([ ). Type the following: "`j:0;4`"; this defines a range of numbers from 0 to 4 that can be used to index an array (note that they are displayed differently from the way you typed them). We will use this to enter 5 sets of data points, x_j and y_j. Type this: "`x[j:1,2,3,4,5`"; the *y* data are entered in a similar fashion (see box, below right).

$j := 0 .. 4$

$x_j :=$	$y_j :=$
1	2.01
2	2.98
3	4.04
4	4.97
5	6.03

It is very easy to edit these numbers — just click in its box and delete or type as desired. (In this particular case we could have entered the *x* values as a range (the way we did for *j*) since they are integers and evenly spaced; however the method used here is more generally useful.) Why didn't we index these 5 numbers 1 to 5? This is certainly more logical, but for certain operations Mathcad assumes that arrays are numbered starting at zero (the *origin*), and you risk error by not following their preferred method.

To make a graph of these numbers, place the cursor in an open area (to the right or below the definitions) and select Graphics-menu, Create X-Y plot. Click on the *y*-axis place holder and type "`y[j`"; for the *x*-axis type "`x[j`". Click anywhere outside the graph to display it.

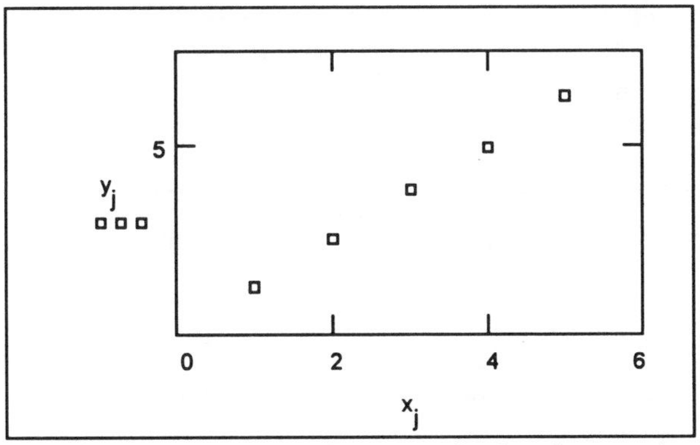

To see the graph as it appears to the left, double click on it to bring up the formatting screen. Select traces and click on trace 1 and select symbol = box, line = points. The default plot limits for this example were not well chosen by Mathcad, so the limits shown were entered manually as described before (for both axes).

We have seen examples of plotting lines and points. You can display lines and points on the same graph by simply selecting different trace types. We shall see many examples of this technique.

Example 6: Mean and standard deviation.

Nearly any operation in Mathcad can be carried out on the elements of a list; however since Mathcad treats such lists as vectors, most operations do not distribute across the elements. This is not a problem (once you are aware of it) because the index variable can be used to carry out any operation for all members of the array: once a range variable (such a *j* in the previous example) is defined, any reference to it applies to all values. We illustrate it with a set of numbers for which we want to calculate a mean and standard deviation. (Mathcad has a functions **mean** and **stdev,** which are used later, but we ignore them for now because this example has important lessons applicable in other areas.) First, let's look at how you manipulate lists of numbers in Mathcad.

$N := 4 \qquad i := 0 .. N-1$

$x_i :=$	$\frac{1}{x_i}$	$\log(x_i)$	$\exp(x_i)$	$\sqrt{x_i}$
1.234	0.81	0.091	3.435	1.111
5.678	0.176	0.754	292.364	2.383
9.000	0.111	0.954	$8.103 \cdot 10^3$	3
0.100	10	-1	1.105	0.316

Using the method described previously, enter the set of 4 numbers x_i shown in box to left. Type "`N:4`" to define *N*, the number of points. Define the range for the index variable *i* with "`i:0;N-1`". (Note that the index numbers begin at 0; this is the default method in Mathcad.) The numbers x_i use real (i.e. indexing) subscripts, so the numbers are entered as "`x[i:1.234,`", continuing with the remainder of the numbers, separated by commas. Because *x* is a vector, we cannot enter "`1/x=`" to display the reciprocals (try it an see what happens). However, we can enter "`1/x[i=`" for this operation are (box above). Any operation containing the index *i* is repeated for all values assigned to that variable (0 to 3 in this case). Other examples of operations are shown, and are implemented in the usual fashion (the last one is, for example, "`\x[i=`").

$N := 4$

$i := 0 .. N - 1$

$x_i :=$

1.234
1.322
1.411
1.111

Next we will calculate the mean and standard deviation of a set of numbers. Start a new worksheet and enter the numbers in the box to left. Open the calculus palette; you will see two summation operations, denoted as Σ. Enter "`sum:`" and then click on the summation symbol with one placeholder (below Σ). Two placeholders appear; type the summation variable (*i*) into the placeholder below the summation and "`x[i`" into the other. The calculation of the mean is as shown below.

$$sum := \sum_i x_i \qquad sum = 5.078 \qquad mean := \frac{sum}{N} \qquad mean = 1.2695$$

$$ssq := \sum_i (x_i)^2 \qquad ssq = 6.496 \qquad msq := \frac{ssq}{N} \qquad msq = 1.624$$

The calculation of the sum of squares (*ssq*, see box) and mean square (*msq*) is scarcely more complicated — for the argument of the summation, type "`x[i↑↑^2`".

There are actually three summation symbols in Mathcad; two on the Calculus palette and one on the Vector and Matrices palette. For the most general (on the Calculus palette) you must specify the index and the upper and lower limits (box to right). For the one used above you specify only the index, and the summation is done over the full range of the index subscript (0 to 3 in this case). The operation on the Vector and Matrices palette (box to left) is the simplest to use but also the most easily misused since, if you don't have a clear idea of the extent of the vector being summed, you may get an unexpected answer. (But you can always find out the extent by displaying the vector, with "x=". Try it!)

$$\sum_{i=0}^{3} x_i = 5.078$$

$$\sum x = 5.078$$

The calculation of the standard deviation (mean square deviation from the mean) is demonstrated next.

$$\sigma := \sqrt{\frac{1}{N} \cdot \left[\sum_i \left(x_i - \text{mean}\right)^2\right]}$$

Standard deviation, σ

$\sigma = 0.110861$

Alternative method: $\sqrt{\text{msq} - \text{mean}^2} = 0.110861$

The expression for σ is entered as "`s ctrl+g :1/N↑↑*`" (do not type spaces or quotes); at this point, click on the summation button and enter "`(x[i↑↑-mean)^2`"; then press spacebar or up arrow until the entire right-hand side of the expression is selected, then click on the square root button (or type \). After entering the summation variable (*i*), click outside the expression and display the result. The box above also shows another method for calculating σ —

$$\sigma = \sqrt{<x^2> - <x>^2}$$

— where $<x>$ and $<x^2>$ denote the averages of *x* and *x*-squared respectively. This method of calculation is somewhat more susceptible to roundoff error than the direct summation method; in this case they give identical answers to 6 significant figures.

An alternative definition of the standard error (*s*, below) is frequently used for small data sets.

$$s := \sqrt{\frac{1}{N-1} \cdot \left[\sum_i \left(x_i - \text{mean}\right)^2\right]}$$

$\sigma = 0.110861$

$s = 0.128012$

This task is, of course, much easier with Mathcad's built-in functions, **mean** and **stdev**. Unfortunately it is difficult to illustrate the former in the current worksheet because we have used a variable named *mean*; the box to left shows what you may get. This illustrates the danger of using function names as variable names; unfortunately this problem is difficult to avoid since you may not remember all of the functions built into Mathcad. Having discovered such an error, it is easy to correct: Select Edit-menu, Replace, and change "mean" to "ave". Then the function **mean** should work.

mean(x) =   stdev(x) = 0.111

illegal function name

Other Features

Mathcad has a variety of mathematical capabilities; this section demonstrates a few mostly to acquaint you with the possibilities; you actually have all you need to proceed with the rest of the book and this section can be skipped without harm. Others will be introduced as needed and explained when needed. Start a new document for the exercises to follow.

Calculus

Looking at the calculus palette you will see symbols representing integration and differentiation. What may not be obvious is that these are usually numerical procedures. Mathcad can do symbolic integration and differentiation but these operations are separate from its primary operations and are found on the Symbolic menu at the top of the screen.

We illustrate the numeric integration and differentiation with a quadratic function. After entering the constants and *f(x)*, click the integral button on the calculus palette. Fill the placeholders as shown below.

$a := 3 \qquad b := 22 \qquad c := 13 \qquad f(x) := a\cdot x^2 + b\cdot x + c \qquad \int_0^5 f(x)\,dx = 465$

$df(x) := \frac{d}{dx}f(x) \qquad df(2) = 34$

Then type "`df(x):`" and click the derivative button (*d/dx*); fill the placeholders as shown above. The differentiation shown on the operator palette is normally a numerical procedure, so the operation *df/dx* can be done only if *x* has a numeric value. Here we define it as a function so any value can be calculated or plotted.

The symbolic capabilities of Mathcad are a subset of the symbolic-algebra program *Maple*™[4] and operates pretty much independent of the remainder of the program. (In version 4 you must load the symbolic processor: select Symbolic-menu, Load Symbolic Processor.) Continuing on the same worksheet, copy the right-hand side of the *f(x)* definition and paste it several times below the preceding definitions. To get your output looking like that below, select Symbolic-menu, format, click boxes for horizontal and show comments. Returning to the worksheet, place the cursor next to an *x* in the first copy and select Symbolic-menu, Integrate. Then put the cursor on an *x* in the second copy and select Symbolic-menu, Differentiate. On a third copy, place the cursor next to *x* and select Symbolic-menu, Solve. You should get:

$a\cdot x^2 + b\cdot x + c$ by integration, yields $\frac{1}{3}\cdot a\cdot x^3 + \frac{1}{2}\cdot b\cdot x^2 + c\cdot x$

$a\cdot x^2 + b\cdot x + c$ by differentiation, yields $2\cdot a\cdot x + b$

$a\cdot x^2 + b\cdot x + c$ has solution(s) $\begin{bmatrix} \frac{1}{(2\cdot a)}\cdot\left(-b + \sqrt{b^2 - 4\cdot a\cdot c}\right) \\ \frac{1}{(2\cdot a)}\cdot\left(-b - \sqrt{b^2 - 4\cdot a\cdot c}\right) \end{bmatrix}$

Note that the numeric values of *a*, *b*, and *c* (entered earlier) have been ignored. To use these derived results for computation, you must copy and paste them into a normal Mathcad expression.

---

[4] Waterloo Maple Software, Waterloo, Ontario, Canada.

To demonstrate this, copy the solutions (above) into the clipboard, and paste them elsewhere in the document. The click in the expressions and press space or up arrow until a selection box (solid) surrounds the whole statement; then press equals (box right). Now the definitions for *a, b* and *c* are recognized and used.

$$\begin{bmatrix} \frac{1}{(2\cdot a)}\cdot\left(-b+\sqrt{b^2-4\cdot a\cdot c}\right) \\ \frac{1}{(2\cdot a)}\cdot\left(-b-\sqrt{b^2-4\cdot a\cdot c}\right) \end{bmatrix} = \begin{pmatrix} -0.648 \\ -6.685 \end{pmatrix}$$

In the PLUS version of Mathcad 6.0, there is another way to do symbolic integrals, shown in the box to the right. Select the indefinite integral from the calculus palette no placeholders for the limits), and enter *f(x)* into the argument placeholder and *x* for the integration variable. Press ctrl+period (effectively, control >) and click outside the box. This integral is symbolic, but the previously assigned values of the constants are used.

$$\int f(x)\,dx \rightarrow x^3 + 11\cdot x^2 + 13\cdot x$$

A final example uses the function:

$$g(x) = \exp(-x^2)$$

This is called the *Gaussian* function; it arises in many contexts in physical chemistry, mathematics, and many other areas of science and engineering. Click on the integral with limits (calculus palette), enter the expression and limits of negative infinity and infinity (ctrl+z for infinity, or use button on the arithmetic palette).

$$g(x) := \exp\left(-x^2\right) \qquad \int_{-\infty}^{\infty} g(x)\,dx \rightarrow \sqrt{\pi} \qquad \int_{-1}^{1} g(x)\,dx \rightarrow \sqrt{\pi}\cdot \mathrm{erf}(1)$$

$$\mathrm{erf}(1) = 0.843$$

Also, calculate (as shown) the integral from -1 to 1. Integrals of the Gaussian function between finite limits cannot be done symbolically; they can only be done numerically. However this integral is so common that many programs including Mathcad provide a special function for it: the *error function*, erf. The last statement (above) shows that Mathcad provides a numerical value for erf(*x*) when asked.

Solving Equations

Mathcad provides several ways for solving equations for a variable. Symbolic solutions can be found using the symbolic processor; load the symbolic processor and enter the following equation as "`a+b ctrl+= c/d`" (box below); as usual ctrl+= means to type = while holding down the ctrl key, and you do not type quotes or spaces. The symbolic equals entered with ctrl+= is shown as **bold** by Mathcad.

Place the cursor next to *d* and select Symbolic-menu, Solve; this gives the result shown in box to the right.

$$a + b \mathbf{=} \frac{c}{d} \quad \text{has solution(s)} \quad \frac{c}{(a+b)}$$

Mathcad can also solve polynomial equations; for example type "`4*x^2↑↑+22*x -5`"; place the cursor next to one of the *x* and select Symbolic-menu, Solve. This is what you should see:

$$4\cdot x^2 + 22\cdot x - 5 \quad \text{has solution(s)} \quad \begin{bmatrix} \frac{-11}{4} + \frac{1}{4}\cdot\sqrt{141} \\ \frac{-11}{4} - \frac{1}{4}\cdot\sqrt{141} \end{bmatrix}$$

If you prefer a decimal solution, select Symbolic-menu, evaluation, floating-point (select number of digits) (box below).

$$\begin{bmatrix} \frac{-11}{4} + \frac{1}{4}\cdot\sqrt{141} \\ \frac{-11}{4} - \frac{1}{4}\cdot\sqrt{141} \end{bmatrix} \quad \text{floating point evaluation yields} \quad \begin{pmatrix} .21858 \\ -5.71858 \end{pmatrix}$$

If you need to use the results provided by the symbolic processor in normal Mathcad expressions, you must copy and paste them.

$$c := \begin{pmatrix} -5 \\ 22 \\ 4 \end{pmatrix} \qquad \text{polyroots}(c) = \begin{pmatrix} -5.719 \\ 0.219 \end{pmatrix}$$

If you only want numeric solutions to a polynomial, the Mathcad function **polyroots** is best. For this function you need to place the coefficients of the polynomial in a vector. Type "c:"; then Select Matrix palette, Matrix or Vector, to create an array with 1 column and 3 rows. Into the 3 placeholders, type the coefficients of the polynomial terms, from lowest power to highest (box, above left). The roots are calculated as shown. (To display 5 decimals as for the previous calculation, double-click on the answer to get the numeric-format menu, and enter 5 for displayed precision)

$$f(x) := 4\cdot x^2 + 22\cdot x - 5$$
$$xg := 0.5$$
$$xr := \text{root}(f(xg), xg)$$
$$xr = 0.219$$

Often we will be interested in obtaining a single numeric root, usually with a value in a well-defined region. The function **root** is demonstrated in the box to the left. First, define a function whose root is to be found (same as above). Next, enter an estimated value for the root (*xg*); when several roots are possible (as in this example), this estimate determines which root will be found. For this example, the answer is assigned to the variable *xr*.

$$f(x) := 4\cdot x^2 + 22\cdot x - 5$$
$$xg := 0.5$$
Given
$$xg > 0$$
$$f(xg) = 0$$
$$\text{Find}(xg) = 0.219$$

Another method for doing such problems is the **Given ... Find** (solve) block. This method can do the same thing as **root** but is somewhat more flexible. The function **Given** (no arguments) begins a block of statements that ends with **Find**, whose argument names the variable or variables whose value is sought. Between these statements are a series of equations or conditions that tell Mathcad how to solve for the unknowns. As for **root** an initial value (*xg*) must be provided for the unknown quantity. The box to the right illustrates the method (with *f(x)* as before). The *f(x)*=0 statement is entered using ctrl+= to create the symbolic equals (displayed as bold by Mathcad). The additional flexibility of solve blocks consists of the ability to enter multiple expressions between **Given** and **Find,** which allows this construct to handle more complicated situations than **root** (the condition $xg > 0$ is not necessary in this case, but is included here to illustrate the possibility). Display more figures for the root by double clicking on the number (0.219) and increasing the "Displayed Precision". How does it compare with the symbolic solutions given above?

One utility of **Given ... Find** for solving simultaneous equations. Consider the pair of equations:

$$xy = 1;\ x + y = 2$$

This may seem like an easy problem — you can probably do it in your head — but it is actually quite difficult for a computer. The reason is that there are a lot of "almost correct" answers such as:

$x := 1.001 \quad y := 0.999 \quad x + y = 2 \quad x \cdot y = 1$

That these are not the exact solution can be demonstrated by changing the numerical format to display more figures (select Math-menu, Numerical Format).

Mathcad does a very good job on this system, as demonstrated by the solution shown in the box to the right. Type the lines shown in the box, remembering that ctrl+= is used to enter the logical equals (bold). (In the last line, use a normal = to display the result.) By changing the numerical format, you can demonstrate that these are accurate to at least 7 significant figures. In this case, the mandatory initial values (for x and y) do not affect the answer, but in more complicated cases they may. Both **root** and **Given ... Find** are numerical procedures, but this is usually what we will want, even when symbolic solutions are possible.

$x := 5 \qquad y := 10$

Given

$x + y \mathbf{=} 2$

$x \cdot y \mathbf{=} 1$

$$\text{Find}(x, y) = \begin{pmatrix} 1 \\ 1 \end{pmatrix}$$

Any computer program that calculates numerical solutions for equations may, in some circumstances, give incorrect answers. It is simply impossible to define a set of conditions defining "finished: problem solved" to fit all occasions. You, as the user, must carefully check and verify the solutions that the computer provides.

Curve Fitting

Given a set of paired data $\{x_i\}$, $\{y_i\}$, *linear regression* refers to finding the coefficients c_i of the equation

$$y = \sum_i c_i\, f_i(x)$$

where the $f_i(x)$ are arbitrary functions of x, so as to minimize the sum of squares of the deviations of the calculated and observed y. A more restricted sense of the term refers to fitting data to a linear function:

$$y = a + bx$$

Mathcad supports both types of linear regression, the general type uses the function **linfit**. Fitting data to a straight line is the most common type of linear regression and is supported more fully by Mathcad; it is illustrated in the example that follows. General linear regression is explained in Section 4.2.

Another method, interpolation, which serves many of the same purposes as curve fitting, is illustrated in Example 8.

Example 7: Fitting data to a straight line.

There are many applications in physical chemistry that require finding the best straight line to fit a set of data, and this example can serve as a template for these. We begin by specifying the number of points (N) and defining a range variable: "`i:0;N-1`". The data are entered as described earlier: "`x[i:-1,0,`" and so forth, separating values by commas. The slope and intercept are calculated with the Mathcad functions **slope** and **intercept** as "`a:intercept(x,y)`" "`b:slope(x,y)`". The straight-line function, y_{fit} is defined as "`y.fit(x):a+b*x`".

$N := 7 \qquad i := 0..N-1$ **Linear regression**

$x_i :=$	$y_i :=$
-1	2.95
0	4.25
1	5.43
2	6.64
3	7.92
4	9.15
5	10.32

$a := \text{intercept}(x, y) \qquad a = 4.209$

$b := \text{slope}(x, y) \qquad b = 1.229 \qquad y_{fit}(x) := a + b \cdot x$

$r := \text{corr}(x, y)$

$r = 0.9999324$

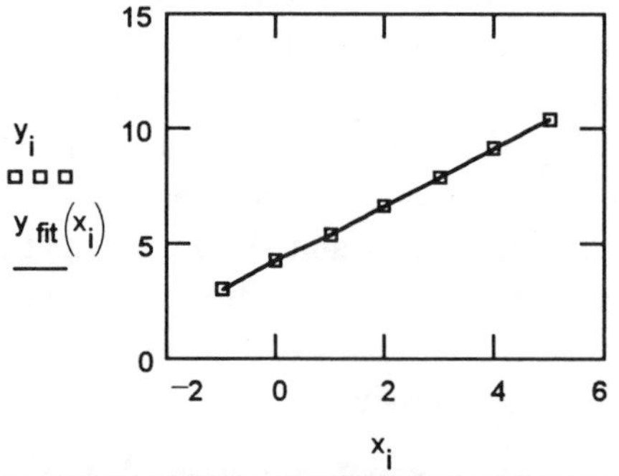

The function $y_{fit}(x)$ is used to calculate the fitted line, which is compared to the data with a graph. To make this graph, select Graphics-menu, Create X-Y plot; enter "`x[i`" in the x-axis placeholder and "`y[i↑↑,y.fit(x[i)`" in the y-axis placeholder. Then double-click in the center of the graph to bring up the Graph-Format menu, and set the first trace as type = point, Symbol = box, and the second as a solid line. The correlation factor (r, calculated using **corr**) will initially display as 1; double-click that number to bring up the numerical-format menu, and set Displayed Precision = 7. Correlation factors should always be displayed with at least 2 figures shown after the 9s stop.

$$\text{resid}_i := y_i - y_{fit}(x_i) \qquad \sigma := \sqrt{\sum_i \frac{(\text{resid}_i)^2}{N-2}}$$

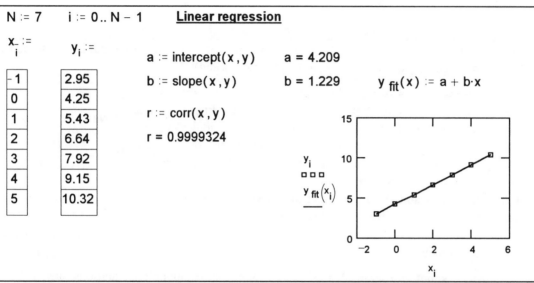

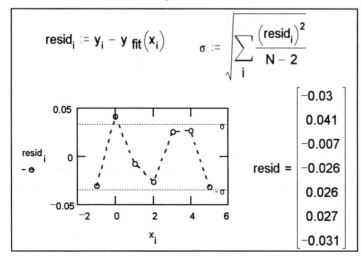

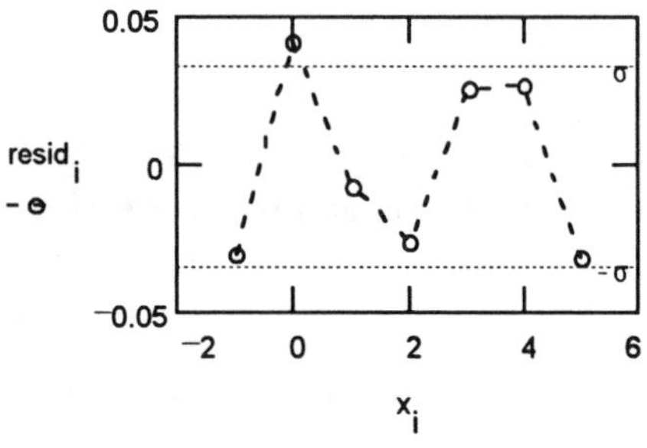

$$\text{resid} = \begin{bmatrix} -0.03 \\ 0.041 \\ -0.007 \\ -0.026 \\ 0.026 \\ 0.027 \\ -0.031 \end{bmatrix}$$

How good is our fit? The graph above looks very good, and the correlation factor, which is ideally equal to plus or minus one, seems close enough to perfection, but these criteria are often deceptive. The box to the left shows how to calculate the residuals (*resid*); these are displayed and graphed. The residuals should scatter randomly about 0, showing no pattern or trend. The *standard deviation of the fit* (σ) is also calculated and displayed on the graph. (The Greek letter σ is made with "`s ctrl+g`" or selected from the Greek-letters palette.). Approximately 2/3 of the points should lie within ±σ and 90% within ±2σ. Points that deviate by more than 2σ are considered as candidates for deletion (or, at least, for careful checking — for example, see if you typed it wrong, or if there was a problem with the experiment). To display the values of ±σ on the graph, double-click on the graph to bring up the graph-format menu. Then, under the *x-y* axes tab, click Show Markers for the *y* axis. When you exit the menu, two additional placeholders will appear; type +σ in one and -σ in the other.

Very often the object of such an analysis is to determine the value of the slope or intercept, which has some physical significance. The box to the right demonstrates how to calculate the standard errors for these parameters. The parameter σ_a measures the uncertainty of the calculated intercept, and σ_b does the same for the slope. The standard deviation of the fit measures the reliability of the model for predicting values of *y* for a given *x*. Any or all of these may be the principal criterion for quality of fit, depending on the objective of the analysis and the physical context. Although we have used the correlation coefficient for calculating the errors of the slope and intercept, it usually does not, by itself, give a very good indication of the quality of the fit.

$$sxx := \sum_i (x_i)^2 \qquad \sigma_b := \frac{b}{r}\cdot\sqrt{\frac{1-r^2}{N-2}} \qquad \sigma_a := \sigma_b \cdot \sqrt{\frac{sxx}{N}}$$

Results

intercept: $a = 4.209$ $\sigma_a = 0.018$

slope: $b = 1.229$ $\sigma_b = 0.006$

standard deviation of fit: $\sigma = 0.034$

Example 8: Interpolation

A set of data, {*x, y*} such as you might measure in an experiment measuring some property (*y*) as a the independent variable (*x*) is varied, gives you, for the points measured, values of a function $y = f(x)$ that represents how the property *y* varies with *x*. Often it is necessary to find out the form of that function. With a form for the function you can do further operations such as interpolation (finding the value of *y* for values of *x* not measured), integration or differentiation. One way to do this is by curve fitting, of which fitting to a straight line is an example (see above). A more flexible method is to use interpolation. A disadvantage to interpolation is that it does no smoothing on the data (as when we found the *best* straight line passing near most points, as opposed to a line that passed exactly through all points). Thus interpolation is suitable only for data sets that are relatively error-free; that is, data that does not contain a lot of random scatter due to experimental errors.

Interpolation in Mathcad requires two functions. The first, which may be **cspline**, **pspline,** or **lspline**, creates a numeric table for interpolation. The second, **interp**, does the interpolation. Enter the data as shown in the box below.

$j := 0..9$ $r_j :=$ $h_j :=$

r_j	h_j
1	0.0000
2	0.0012
3	0.0291
4	0.2521
5	0.8043
6	0.9438
7	0.4075
8	0.0647
9	0.0038
10	0.0001

Interpolation

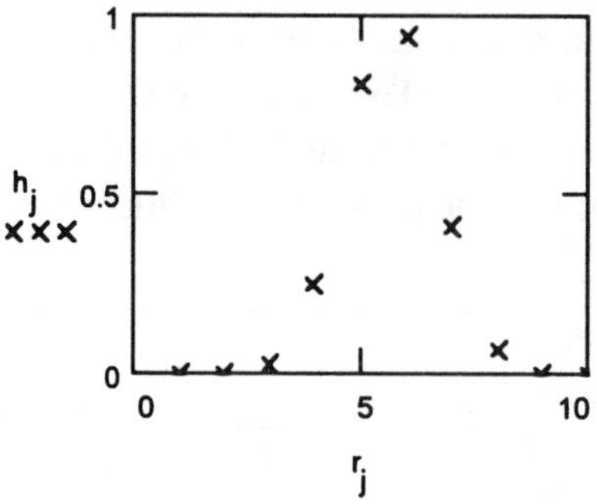

$vs := cspline(r, h)$

$f(x) := interp(vs, r, h, x)$

The graph shows the data. These are typical "peaked" data such as you might obtain from a chromatography or spectroscopy experiment. The objectives typically are to find position of the peak and the area. The box above also shows how to do the interpolation: the variable *cs* contains the interpolation table that is used to define *f(x)* with **interp**

The box below shows a graph of the interpolated function together with the original data. Interpolated functions are reliable only within the range of the experiment; that is, between the smallest and largest *x* for which the dependent variable (*y*, *h* in this example) is measured. Try a wider range for the graph; is the function realistic outside the range $x = 1$ to 9?

$xp := 1, 1.02..9$

$$\int_1^{10} f(x)\,dx = 2.513$$

(actual 2.505)

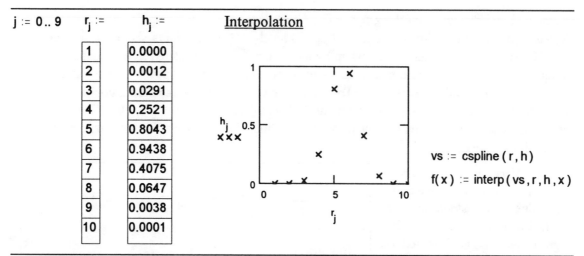

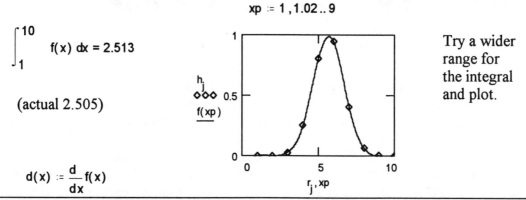

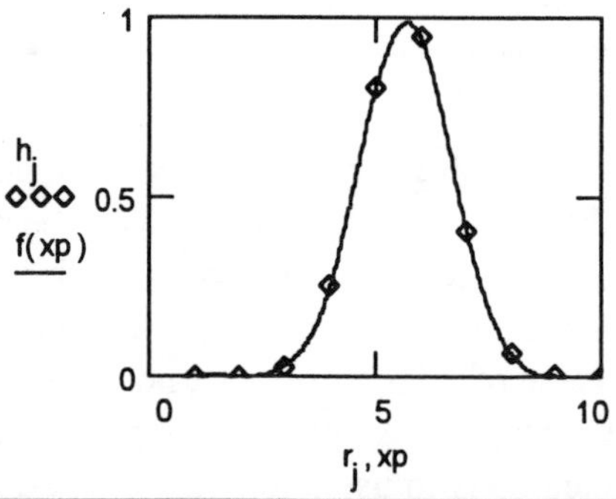

Try a wider range for the integral and plot.

$$d(x) := \frac{d}{dx} f(x)$$

The box above also demonstrates the measurement of the area, approximated as the integral from 1 to 9. The actual area (calculated from the function used to generate the "data" points) is shown for comparison. There are two sources of error here: the truncation of the integral to the region 1 to 9 and the approximation of the interpolation. In this example, the second problem is the more serious; you could improve the area measurement by increasing the number of measured points.

The box above also defines a function (*d*) for the derivative of the function. This is used (below) to find the maximum.

xg := 5 guess

xr := root(d(xg), xg)

xr = 5.698 (actual 5.660)

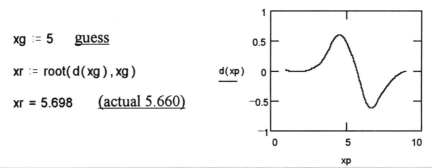

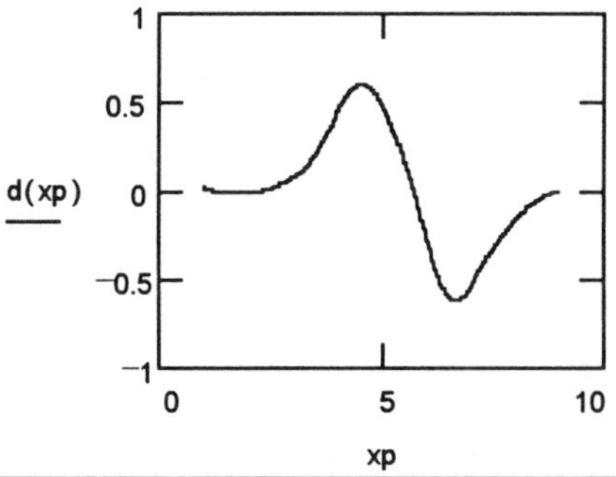

For this example, note the distinction between the maximum of the function and the maximum value measured. In doing such a measurement, it would be fortuitous if you hit the maximum exactly. To find the maximum intensity (value of h at the maximum), enter "`f(xr)=`". (Answer: 0.985)

Pitfalls and Precautions

Mathcad has a number of built-in variables and defaults, and you must be aware of them. A few of the more important ones are discussed below.

Numerical Formatting

In a new document, select Math-menu, Numerical Format. Several defaults are displayed; the most important for us are the Displayed Precision, which determines the number of figures displayed after the decimal, the Exponential Threshold, which determines how large or small a number can become before the program switches to exponential notation, and the Zero Tolerance, which determines the size of a number that will be displayed as zero. Without making any changes, return to the document and enter the value for Planck's constant (SI, but without units); type "`h:6.626075*10^-34`". Display the number by typing "`h=`". It displays as zero because it is smaller than 10^{-15}, the smallest nonzero number when Zero Tolerance is 15. Open the Numerical-Format menu (under the Math menu) and change the zero tolerance to 99 (307 is the maximum value in some versions). Now it should be displayed correctly. Define the cube of h with "`h3:h^3`" and display this number. You see zero: Mathcad cannot display a number less than 10^{-99}. Has it rounded the value to zero? Type "`10^10↑↑*h3=`"; the result demonstrates that Mathcad does know the value. This is what you should see now:

$h := 6.626075 \cdot 10^{-34}$	$h = 6.626075000 \cdot 10^{-34}$	Displayed precision 9, trailing zeros on, zero tolerance, 99.
$h3 := h^3$	$h3 = 0.000000000$	$10^{10} \cdot h3 = 2.909169609 \cdot 10^{-90}$

Also, on the Numerical-Format screen, note the "trailing zeros" box; with this box checked, a number 0.990122 will, with Displayed Precision 3, be displayed as 0.990; when this box is not checked, this number is displayed as 0.99. Although you usually would want to show trailing zeros on decimal numbers, its not a good idea to make it the default; if you do, integers such as 5 will be displayed as 5.000.

The largest value possible for zero tolerance is 307. Whereas zero tolerance represents only how numbers are displayed, 307 has a deeper significance: the largest number that can be represented in Mathcad is 10^{307} and the smallest is 10^{-307}. If a calculation gives a result smaller than 10^{-307}, it will be replaced by zero; results larger than 10^{307} will receive an error indication. While there are no physical constants (an probably, no quantity at all) larger than the maximum or smaller than the minimum, there may be calculations where intermediate answers may cross these limits. In such cases you may have to change the order of evaluation to maintain accuracy. All finite computational devices (computers, calculators) have such a limit (99 is common for calculators); 307 is sufficiently generous that you will rarely have a problem.

Built-in Variables

Select Math-menu, Built-in Variables. The most important quantities here are *TOL*, which determines the accuracy of many numerical procedures and *ORIGIN*, which determines the index number for the first element of an array. The default origin (zero) is a bit of a nuisance, but we shall keep it since making a mistake about this quantity is a serious error. The default value for *TOL* is a bit large for most of the problems we will be solving, but don't change it (permanently) since there is no "always correct" value, and you will be better served by learning how to recognize when it needs to be changed.

Common Errors

Normally if you type the name of a variable or command incorrectly, Mathcad will stop, highlight the unknown symbol in reverse video, and wait for you to fix it. However since there are built-in symbols complications sometimes arise. Some common problems likely to arise in physical chemistry calculations are:

- The symbol *R* is by default the Rankine-scale degree and if you want it to be the gas constant you must define it so. Failure to do so may give bizarre results and often an "inconsistent units" error message.
- The symbol *g* is the default for the acceleration of gravity, *not* gram. The symbol for gram is gm. This is a very dangerous error since it can cause serious errors that are not immediately apparent.
- The symbol for second is *sec* not *s* as you would find in most modern texts. However *s* has no default value so this error will be flagged.
- The symbol for meter is *m*. Like other simple symbols, it is common to inadvertently use this symbol for another purpose, which is not an error, but may give bizarre results if you are using units at the same time. Avoid using the names of the base units (m, sec, gm, K, etc.) for variables wherever possible.
- The symbol for Kelvin temperature is K, but this symbol is also commonly used to denote and equilibrium constant. If you are doing an equilibrium problem with units, and define K to be an equilibrium constant, you will get some very confusing errors.
- Remember that Mathcad evaluates from left to right, top to bottom. When multiple definitions of a symbol are given, the closest one to the left or above is used. If a variable is redefined, the new definition applies from there downward and not to previous work.
- You may have a number of worksheets open at one time, but symbols defined in one do not apply to the others. Each sheet is completely independent of the others.

- The default numbering system for subscripts begins with 0 (zero) so a set of three numbers named x is accessed as x_0, x_1 and x_2. This is also a dangerous error since you can get incorrect answers without an error indication.

A cautionary example.

The last point above is worth amplification since it is the source of the most insidious error you can make in Mathcad. Suppose you have a list of numbers and want to calculate the mean. Mathcad has a function **mean** that will do this for you.

Let's do an easy problem — the average of the 3 numbers 2, 4 and 6 — which you should be able to do without a computer. The Mathcad calculation is shown in the box to the right and would appear logical to nearly anyone. But is this the correct answer? What is wrong with this picture?

$$j := 1..3 \qquad x_j := \begin{array}{|c|}\hline 4 \\ \hline 5 \\ \hline 6 \\ \hline \end{array} \qquad \text{mean}(x) = 3.75$$

$$x = \begin{bmatrix} 0 \\ 4 \\ 5 \\ 6 \end{bmatrix}$$

The list of numbers x_i constitute a vector (**x**) which can be displayed using "x="; this display is shown in the box to the left. Mathcad has done something sneaky — it added a zero to our list, and that is why the calculated mean is not what we expected. No error message, no warning, just did it. With a longer list of numbers, and numbers with more significant figures, we might not notice this error, which is why it is so insidious. This problem will also occur with other array operations including those involved in linear regression.

$$i := 0..4 \qquad x_i := \begin{array}{|c|}\hline 1 \\ \hline 2 \\ \hline 3 \\ \hline 4 \\ \hline 5 \\ \hline \end{array} \qquad \text{mean}(x) = 3 \qquad \text{length}(x) = 5 \qquad \frac{1}{\text{length}(x)} \cdot \left(\sum_i x_i\right) = 3$$

There is a related problem that can cause errors. Suppose you did the calculation shown in the box to left; having avoided the previous error, the answer is correct. Now, later in the same worksheet, you do another calculation and use the same name for the array (x), but, this time, the array is shorter (box below right). As you can see, the answers are now incorrect. The 4th and 5th elements are still there, even though the index variable has been shortened Demonstrate this by displaying the whole vector with "x=". This error can be avoided by setting the variable to equal to zero between the two uses; try this by entering "x:0" between these two calculations. Again, this is an error that could be hard to detect when using large lists of numbers with more digits.

$$i := 0..2 \qquad x_i := \begin{array}{|c|}\hline 1.111 \\ \hline 2.222 \\ \hline 3.333 \\ \hline \end{array} \qquad \text{mean}(x) = 3.133 \qquad \text{length}(x) = 5 \qquad \frac{1}{\text{length}(x)} \cdot \left(\sum_i x_i\right) = 1.333$$

You now know enough about Mathcad to proceed with the chapters on physical chemistry. There is, of course, much more to be learned, but it is best to do so in the context of solving problems.

CHAPTER 1

PROPERTIES OF GASES

1.1 Equations of State

In this section we discuss PVT calculations using two gas laws: the traditional van der Waals equation and the Redlich-Kwong equation, a law which is nearly as simple as van der Waals and often more effective. We do this by defining a pressure function for *P(V, T)* containing 3 constants, *a*, *b* and the gas constant *R*. Remember that, in Mathcad, all constants must be entered before they are used in formulas. We shall use SI (mks) units throughout, taking advantage of Mathcad's unit feature to enter data or display answers in other units as desired.

The van der Waals Equation

The first step in any gas-law calculation is to enter the value of the gas constant and any subsidiary units; we choose to define the MPa = 10^6 Pa and to give *R* in SI units:

$$\mathrm{MPa} := 10^{6}\cdot\mathrm{Pa} \qquad R := 8.31451\cdot\frac{\mathrm{joule}}{\mathrm{K}\cdot\mathrm{mole}}$$

Before entering the gas law you must enter values for the constants: *a* and *b* for the van der Waals (vdw) equation of state. Older references are likely to give these constants for liter-atm units; such values are perfectly usable with *R* in SI since Mathcad knows these units and will convert all to SI. Newer references give the gas constants in SI. We will start by entering the constants in the older units to illustrate the flexibility of Mathcad. The constants for ethane are:

$$a := \frac{5.489\cdot\mathrm{liter}^{2}\cdot\mathrm{atm}}{\mathrm{mole}^{2}} \qquad b := 0.0638\cdot\frac{\mathrm{liter}}{\mathrm{mole}}$$

When you display the value of these constants (with "a=" for example) they will be shown in the default unit system, which should be SI. (In older versions of Mathcad they would be displayed with dimensions only until you supplied a unit; in version 6 this is an option but not the default.)

$$a = 0.556\cdot\mathrm{kg}\cdot\mathrm{m}^{5}\cdot\mathrm{sec}^{-2} \qquad b = 6.38\cdot10^{-5}\cdot\mathrm{m}^{3}$$

Instead, let's replace the preceding with the SI values (e.g. from Table 1.1, Noggle); you can either delete the old values, or just enter the new ones below them on the work sheet.

$$a := 0.5581\cdot\mathrm{Pa}\cdot\mathrm{m}^{6}\cdot\mathrm{mole}^{-2} \qquad b := 65.14\cdot10^{-6}\cdot\mathrm{m}^{3}\cdot\mathrm{mole}^{-1}$$

These differ slightly from the preceding values; it is not unusual to find such variations in data from different sources, nor is it a matter for great concern. (It's not a concern because the equation is not exact and using "exact" constants will not make it so.)

Generally we will prefer to enter the critical constants and to calculate the a and b constants from these; this is, indeed, the source of most van der Waals constants found in reference books. For the van der Waals equation, we would do the following:

$T_c := 305.33 \cdot K \quad P_c := 4.871 \cdot MPa \quad mw := 30.070 \cdot gm$ *ethane*

$$a := \frac{27 \cdot R^2 \cdot T_c^{\ 2}}{64 \cdot P_c} \qquad b := \frac{R \cdot T_c}{8 \cdot P_c} \qquad a = 0.558 \cdot kg \cdot m^5 \cdot sec^{-2}$$

$$b = 6.515 \cdot 10^{-5} \cdot m^3$$

$$P(V_m, T) := \frac{R \cdot T}{V_m - b} - \frac{a}{V_m^{\ 2}}$$

After numerical values are entered for the constants you can enter the gas law (box left). It is convenient to do this as a function: $P(V_m, T)$ with V_m the molar volume. Do some sample calculations illustrating the use of a variety of units; for example, type "`P( 22.414*liter,273.15*K)=`". When the number appears, type the desired unit in the unit placeholder (black square after the unit).

$P(22.414 \cdot liter, 273.15 \cdot K) = 0.992 \cdot atm \qquad P(1 \cdot liter, 355 \cdot K) = 2.599 \cdot MPa$

$P(456 \cdot mL, 800 \cdot K) = 14.334 \cdot MPa \qquad P(1 \cdot m^3, 400 \cdot K) = 24.943 \cdot torr$

The first calculation, with the STP volume of an ideal gas (22.414 liter) is a good place to start since you know that the answer must be near 1 atm; however since that calculation is very near the ideal-gas value, it may not reflect some errors (in typing constants, for example); for that reason its a good idea to try more extreme, nonideal, conditions.

Example 1.1 Pressure of a gas using the van der Waals equation.

Calculate the pressure exerted by 256 g of ethane in a 1.50 liter container at 25° C. First, enter the data and calculate the molecular weight (*mw*).

$$mass := 256 \cdot gm \qquad mw := (2 \cdot 12.011 + 6 \cdot 1.00794) \cdot \frac{gm}{mole} \qquad V := 1.50 \cdot liter$$

Next, calculate and display the number of moles (n) and the molar volume:

$$n := \frac{mass}{mw} \qquad n = 8.514 \qquad V_m := \frac{V}{n} \qquad V_m = 0.176 \cdot liter$$

Note that n has no unit: Mathcad does not keep track of the unit "mole" (it just has a value 1) so you must do so; you can enter it at the unit placeholder if you like, but this has no effect on any subsequent calculation. Finally, the pressure calculation is very simple:

$$P(V_m, 298.15 \cdot K) = 4.345 \cdot 10^6 \cdot Pa \qquad P(V_m, 298.15 \cdot K) = 42.879 \cdot atm$$

You will want to save this worksheet to use as a starting point for other van der Waals calculations.

Example 1.2 Graph isotherms using the vdw equation.

Continuing with the previous example (ethane), we demonstrate how to make P vs. V graphs at constant temperature: isotherms. First we must enter a range of values for the volumes (which we denote *vp*). Before doing this we must be aware of the value of the b constant — since the gas law has a division by V_m - b we do not want to graph values smaller than b. If the value of b is no longer visible on your screen, just display it again with "b=" (mL = milliliter = cm^3).

b = 65.14 ·mL vp := 70·mL , 75·mL .. 500·mL

Selecting an appropriate range for *vp* is pretty much trial and error. The quantities graphed must be unitless, so we will make the y coordinate P/MPa and the x coordinate *vp*/mL.

Try a temperature of 300 K (box right). This graph is rather uninformative: it does show how much pressure rises at small volume, but obscures some interesting details. Click on the graph and replace the upper limit of pressure with 10 MPa (knowing that the critical pressure of ethane is 4.871 MPa helps us determine an appropriate value for this limit) and the lower limit with 0 (zero); on the x axis (volume), set limits to 0 and 500 (box below).

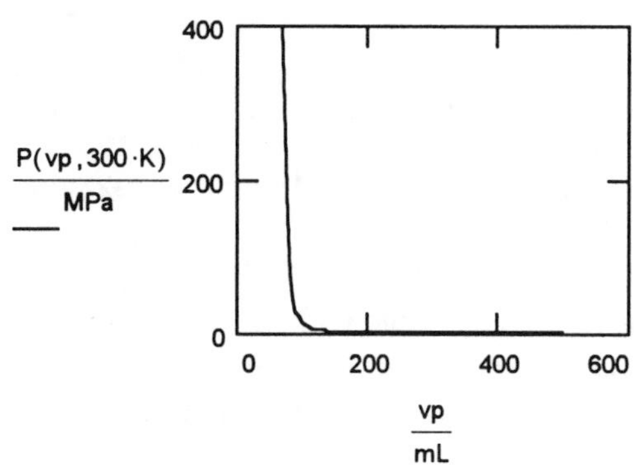

b = 65.14 ·mL vp := 70·mL, 75·mL .. 500·mL

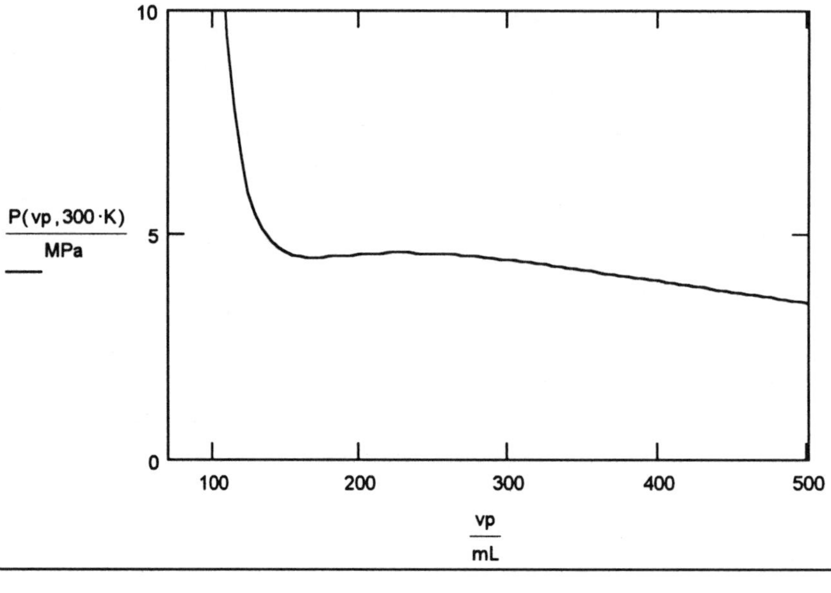

Note that there is a slight undulation in the isotherm: this is because the temperature is below the critical temperature of ethane (305.33 K). Try other temperatures in the general range 250 to 350 K, including the critical temperature. For the higher temperatures you may want to increase the volume range, which can be done by editing the line defining *vp*. Scales can be expanded by editing the placeholders for the axes limits. For example, try to reproduce this magnification of the critical isotherm:

b = 65.14·mL   vp := 70·mL, 75·mL.. 500·mL

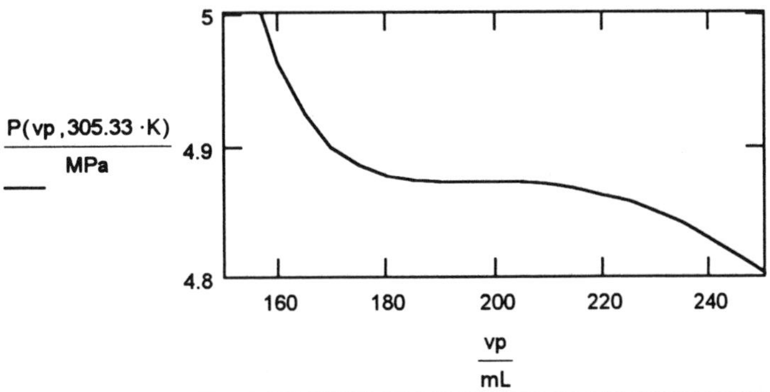

The critical pressure (the pressure of the inflection point) can be seen to be approximately 4.87 MPa — this is the correct value, but it is no more than a self-fulfilling prophecy since the critical temperature and pressure were used to calculate the *a* and *b* constants used in the computation. The critical volume, which can be seen to be approximately 190 mL, is an independent test of the accuracy of the gas law; it is very different from the experimental value: 148 mL. As you can see, the horizontal inflection makes it difficult to determine the critical volume accurately, which is why the it is generally the least accurate of the critical constants.

Below is an example of how to plot several isotherms on the same graph. To make this graph, type the functions to be plotted, *P(V, T)*, with different temperatures, separated by commas.

b = 65.14·mL   vp := 70·mL, 75·mL .. 500·mL

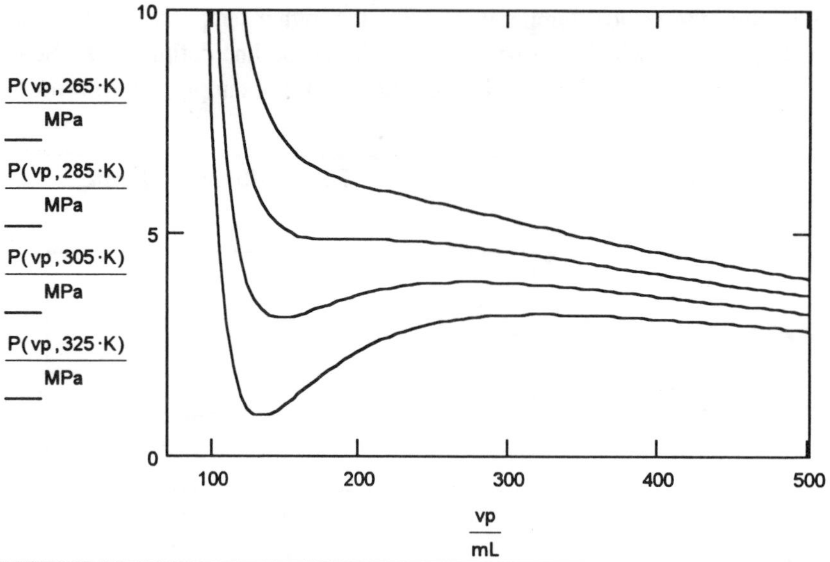

The picture above is not very clear because it is not in color. On your screen, the isotherms will be distinguished by color and this graph will be clearer. You can select the colors and line types from the Graph-Format menu, Traces section. You can also distinguish lines by using various combinations of dotted and dashed lines, but this presentation is not especially clear or attractive.

Example 1.3 Volume and density of a gas using the van der Waals equation.

The van der Waals equation, like many other equations of state (including Redlich-Kwong) is cubic in volume and so, for any temperature and pressure, has 3 solutions for volume. Above the critical temperature, only one of these roots is real, but below the critical temperature (as illustrated by the undulations seen on the isotherms of the preceding section) there may be three real roots (volumes). When there are three real roots for the equation of state, there may be a phase separation, in which case the smaller molar volume (larger density) is that for the liquid phase and the larger is for the gas phase. (The middle root does not represent a thermodynamically stable phase.) In this chapter we shall focus on the single-phase region, reserving the discussion of liquid-vapor equilibrium to Chapter 4. Also, in Chapter 4 (section 4.4), the topic of volume-calculation is treated more thoroughly.

We solve this equation by finding the numeric roots with either a solve block (**Given ... Find**) or **root**; the former procedure is preferred: it nearly always gives either a correct answer or no answer, whereas the latter (**root**) has occasionally given incorrect answers. We will develop a procedure for calculating the molar volume since, knowing that, you can calculate related properties such as volume (moles times molar volume), specific volume (molar volume divided by molecular weight) and density (as explained below).

Begin as before by defining the gas constants, *R*, *a* and *b* and the gas law. You can copy and paste these from the previous worksheet, but change the constants to those for methane (CH_4).

$MPa := 10^6 \cdot Pa$ $\qquad R := 8.31451 \cdot \frac{joule}{K \cdot mole}$

$a := 0.2283 \cdot Pa \cdot m^6 \cdot mole^{-2}$ $\qquad b := 42.69 \cdot 10^{-6} \cdot m^3 \cdot mole^{-1}$ $\qquad P(V_m, T) := \frac{R \cdot T}{V_m - b} - \frac{a}{V_m^{\ 2}}$

$P(22.414 \cdot liter, 273.15 \cdot K) = 0.997 \cdot atm$ $\qquad P(1 \cdot liter, 300 \cdot K) = 23.462 \cdot atm$

The pressure calculations are for testing and can be deleted once confirmed.

For finding a numeric root, you must first provide an estimate for the volume: this is conveniently done using the ideal gas law. We will calculate the molar volume of methane at 335 K, 20 atm. We use **Given** ... **Find** to calculate the root; recall that a logical equals (bold =, in the box below, only the equation immediately following **Given** uses the logical =) is made with ctrl+= and the equation to be solved must be below or directly to the right of **Given** and above **Find**. We must use a different symbol for the pressure and the pressure function, *P(V,T)* above. Mathcad variables are case sensitive, so we can use *p* for the pressure and *P* for the function.

$T := 335 \cdot K$ $\qquad p := 20 \cdot atm$ $\qquad V_g := \frac{R \cdot T}{p}$ $\qquad V_g = 1.374 \cdot liter$

Given $\qquad$ TOL = 0.001

$P(V_g, T) = p$

$V_m := Find(V_g)$ $\qquad V_m = 1.335 \cdot liter$ $\qquad P(V_m, T) = 20 \cdot atm$

Here we display the value of the built-in variable *TOL* which determines the accuracy of the calculated root; this is the default value, which can be reset using Math-menu, Built-in Variables. The last calculation above recalculates the pressure to check the accuracy of the volume calculation.

Calculate the density of the gas. Density calculations could be set up the same way as the volume calculation above, but since density = mass/volume it is also equal to (molar mass)/(molar volume) and, thus, the calculation of the molar volume as illustrated above is sufficient. For the same example, calculate the molecular weight and, from it, the density.

$mw := (12.011 + 4 \cdot 1.00794) \cdot \frac{gm}{mole}$ $\qquad density := \frac{mw}{V_m}$ $\qquad density = 12.013 \cdot \frac{gm}{liter}$

Remember that gram is abbreviated "gm" by Mathcad; by default, "g" denotes the acceleration of gravity.

The Redlich-Kwong Equation

Although it is generally more accurate, the Redlich-Kwong (RK) equation of state is less widely used than van der Waals and its constants are more difficult to find. Therefore we shall enter equations to calculate them from the critical temperature and pressure of the gas; these are called T_c and P_c respectively in the box below. The "c" is a labeling subscript, entered into Mathcad as (for example) "`T.c:305.22*K`" (do not type quotes). As always, we must begin by entering the constants. Next, we enter the equations for calculating *a* and *b* (shown in box below). Finally, we can enter the gas law as *P(V, T)*:

$$R := 8.31451 \cdot \frac{joule}{K \cdot mole} \qquad MPa := 10^6 \cdot Pa \qquad T_c := 305.33 \cdot K \quad P_c := 4.871 \cdot MPa \quad \textbf{ethane}$$

$$a := \frac{0.42748 \cdot R^2 \cdot T_c^{2.5}}{P_c} \qquad b := \frac{0.086640 \cdot R \cdot T_c}{P_c} \qquad P(V_m, T) := \frac{R \cdot T}{V_m - b} - \frac{a}{\sqrt{T} \cdot V_m \cdot (V_m + b)}$$

Be sure to save your work at this point: the equations given (changing T_c and P_c as needed) form the start of all RK calculations. In fact, you ought to save it under a special name — something easy to remember (like *rk.mcd*); then it can be inserted (File-menu, Insert) into any document that needs the RK law. Make some test calculations for pressure:

$$P(22.414 \cdot liter, 273.15 \cdot K) = 0.990 \cdot atm \qquad P(255 \cdot mL, 355 \cdot K) = 7.213 \cdot MPa$$

To show the trailing zero on the first calculation you must double-click on the number to bring up the numerical format menu and, on that menu, click the "trailing zeros" box.

Example 1.4 Pressure of a gas using the RK law.

Calculate the pressure when 60 g ethane is placed in a 250 mL container at 20° C:

$$mw := (2 \cdot 12.011 + 6 \cdot 1.00794) \cdot \frac{gm}{mole} \qquad V := 250 \cdot mL \qquad mass := 60 \cdot gm$$

$$n := \frac{mass}{mw} \qquad V_m := \frac{V}{n} \qquad V_m = 125.29 \cdot mL \qquad T := (20 + 273.15) \cdot K$$

$$P(V_m, T) = 3.386 \cdot MPa$$

The unit of V_m is, of course, volume per mole, but Mathcad does not carry mole as a unit.

The next calculation will be for nitrogen; if you want to keep the ethane calculation, the simplest thing to do is to save the file (File-menu, Save) and then save it again under a new name (File-menu Save As); then edit the new file to change the constants and save again.

Example 1.5 Density of a gas using the RK law.

The calculation of volumes and density is exactly as for van der Waals, except, of course, we need the pressure function for RK as above. We will calculate the density of nitrogen gas. You can use all of the definitions above, but replace the critical constants and molecular weight with:

$$P_c := 3.394 \cdot MPa \qquad T_c := 126 \cdot K \qquad mw := (2 \cdot 14.0067) \cdot \frac{gm}{mole}$$

Make a few pressure calculations for testing (compare to the results for ethane, above):

$$P(22.414 \cdot liter, 273.15 \cdot K) = 0.999 \cdot atm \qquad P(255 \cdot mL, 355 \cdot K) = 11.785 \cdot MPa$$

Calculate the density of nitrogen gas at 130.2 °C and 2000 psi pressure. Enter the data and display the pressure in SI units (again we use *p* for the pressure, since *P* denotes the pressure function).

$T := (273.15 + 130.2)\cdot K$ $\quad$ $p := 2000\cdot psi$ $\quad$ $p = 13.79\cdot MPa$

$V_x := \frac{R\cdot T}{p}$ $\quad$ $V_x = 0.243\cdot liter$ $\quad$ $\frac{mw}{V_x} = 115.185\cdot\frac{gm}{liter}$

The last line calculates the ideal gas law estimate for the molar volume; this is needed for use by **Given** ... **Find**, below. The ideal gas density, calculated as before as (molar mass) / (molar volume), is displayed for comparison to the RK value calculated below. The RK volume and density are calculated as:

Given $\quad P(V_x, T) = p$

$V_m := \text{Find}(V_x)$

$V_m = 0.252\cdot liter$ $\quad$ $density := \frac{mw}{V_m}$ $\quad$ $density = 111.174\cdot\frac{gm}{liter}$

(The equal sign just after **Given** is a logical equals, typed as ctrl+=).

1.2 The Virial Series

The virial series is an expansion of the compressibility factor (*z*) —

$$z = \frac{PV_m}{RT} \tag{1.1}$$

— as a power series in concentration: $c = n/V = 1/V_m$.

$$z = 1 + B(T)c + C(T)c^2 + \cdots \tag{1.2}$$

B(T) is the second virial coefficient; *C(T)* is the third virial coefficient (and so forth). These coefficients are, in general, functions of temperature.

Example 1.6 Virial coefficients from compressibility data.

Data on compressibility factors (*z*) of gases are typically available as a function of pressure. The molar volume can be calculated from Eq. (1.1) as $V_m = zRT/P$ and the concentration is the reciprocal of this quantity. Thus:

$$c \equiv \frac{n}{V} = \frac{P}{zRT} \tag{1.3}$$

The following are data for ethane at 315 K (pressure in bar):

Data for ethane at 315 K

$N := 5$ $\quad i := 0..N-1$ $\quad T := 315 \cdot K$ $\quad R := 8.31451 \cdot \frac{joule}{K}$ $\quad bar := 10^5 \cdot Pa$

$P_i :=$ $\quad z_i :=$ $\quad c_i := \frac{P_i \cdot bar}{z_i \cdot R \cdot T}$ $\quad c_i$

P_i	z_i	c_i
1	.9937	$38.424 \cdot m^{-3}$
5	.9681	$197.198 \cdot m^{-3}$
10	.9346	$408.533 \cdot m^{-3}$
15	.8993	$636.853 \cdot m^{-3}$
20	.8620	$885.881 \cdot m^{-3}$

Since the pressures were entered as unitless numbers, the unit must be supplied when concentration is calculated. Concentration has unit mole/m^3, but mole is not included in Mathcad's display, as usual.

The calculation of the first two virial coefficients (B and C) is a linear-analysis problem since the first term of the virial series (1) is known. Rearrange Eq. (1.2) to give:

$$\frac{z-1}{c} = B + C\,c \tag{1.4}$$

This is an equation of a straight line $y = (z\text{-}1)/c$ vs. $x = c$ with intercept B and slope C. The slope and intercept are calculated with the Mathcad functions **slope and intercept**.

$y_i := \frac{z_i - 1}{c_i}$ $\quad B := \text{intercept}(c, y)$ $\quad C := \text{slope}(c, y)$ $\quad \text{zfit}(c) := 1 + B \cdot c + C \cdot c^2$

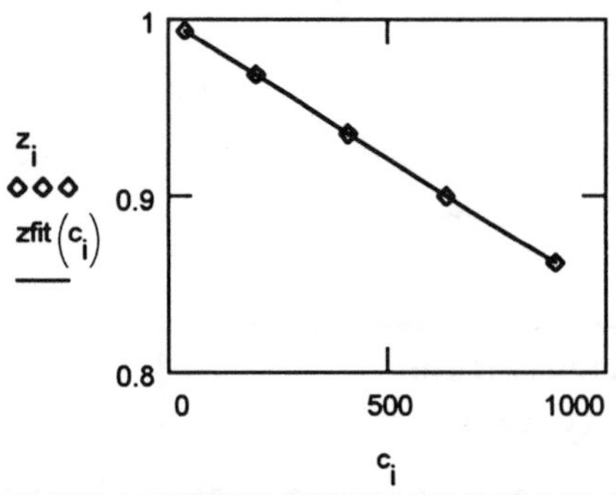

$B = -0.164 \cdot liter$

$C = 0.009 \cdot liter^2$

(The unit for B is actually liter/mol; for C it is liter^2/mol^2.) The graph above shows the calculated compressibility (*zfit*, solid line) and data (points) vs. concentration (mole/m^3).

The fitted line above is scarcely distinguishable from a straight line; for a better view, make a graph of the fitted function (*fit*) and data (*y*) —box to right. The deviations of the two lowest points are surely due to limited accuracy of the data: when z = 0.9937, 1 - z only has two significant figures. There is no clear indication of curvature, so fitting higher virial coefficients is not justified by these data (to determine higher virial coefficients, you need data for higher pressures). If more terms were needed, we would have to use the Mathcad function **linfit**; this topic is discussed in Chapter 4 of this book.

$$\mathrm{fit}(c) := B + C \cdot c$$

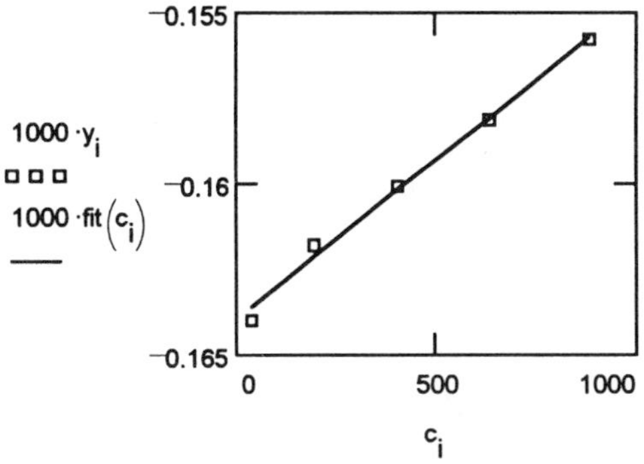

Example 1.7 Derive the virial coefficients of a van der Waals gas.

Next we seek a relationship between the traditional equations of state (such as vdw or RK) and the virial series. The van der Waals pressure,

$$P = \frac{RT}{V_m - b} - \frac{a}{V_m^2}$$

is multiplied by V_m/RT to give

$$z = \frac{V_m}{V_m - b} - \frac{a}{RT}\frac{1}{V_m}$$

In Mathcad, load the symbolic processor and enter the two expressions to right. (For simplicity, we use V to represent molar volume.) We need to do an expansion in concentration, $c = 1/V_m$, and thus must change V in the first expression to $1/c$. Select the expression to the right ($1/c$) and copy it to the clipboard. Then place the cursor on the first expression, next to one of the V symbols; select Symbolic-menu Substitute. You should get the expression below (left).

$$\frac{V}{V-b} - \frac{a}{R \cdot T} \cdot \frac{1}{V} \qquad \frac{1}{c}$$

$$\frac{1}{\left[c \cdot \left(\frac{1}{c} - b\right)\right]} - \frac{a}{(R \cdot T)} \cdot c \quad \textbf{which simplifies to} \quad \frac{1}{(1 - b \cdot c)} - \frac{a}{(R \cdot T)} \cdot c$$

You may want to simplify this expression (although this is not necessary). If you simplify the whole expression it actually becomes more complicated; instead, place the cursor in the denominator of the first term and press the up arrow until the entire denominator is selected; then select Symbolic-menu, Simplify. You should get the result shown above (right). To match this expression to the virial series we must expand it in a power series in c. Place the cursor on a c

and select Symbolic-menu, Expand-to-Series; enter 3 for the "order of approximation" when requested. The result is shown below (box below left).

$$1+\left[b-\frac{a}{(R\cdot T)}\right]\cdot c+b^2\cdot c^2+O\left(c^3\right)$$

The last term of this result indicates that terms of order c^3 are being neglected. Comparing this result to the virial series, Eq. (1.2), we identify the virial coefficients as:

$$B=b-\frac{a}{RT};\quad C=b^2 \tag{1.5}$$

These approximate formulas are useful for qualitative explanations of gas behavior but virtually useless for quantitative calculation. The examples to follow discuss several more accurate methods for estimating virial coefficients.

Example 1.8 Derive the virial coefficients of an RK gas.

The procedure for the determining the virial coefficients from the RK equation is scarcely more complicated than for van der Waals. Start with the RK equation,

$$P=\frac{RT}{V_m-b}-\frac{a}{\sqrt{T}V_m(V_m+b)}$$

and multiply by V_m/RT to get:

$$z=\frac{V_m}{V_m-b}-\frac{a}{RT^{3/2}(V_m+b)}$$

Enter the right-hand side of this equation into Mathcad (below, V denotes molar volume). As before, copy $1/c$ to the clipboard and substitute it for V.

$$\frac{V}{V-b}-\frac{a}{R\cdot T^{1.5}}\cdot\frac{1}{V+b} \qquad \frac{1}{c}$$

$$\frac{1}{\left[c\cdot\left(\frac{1}{c}-b\right)\right]}-\frac{a}{\left[R\cdot\left[T^{1.5}\cdot\left(\frac{1}{c}+b\right)\right]\right]}$$

To simplify, you would have to do each term individually (in two steps), but this is not necessary. Click on any c and select Symbolic-menu, Expand-to-Series to give:

$$1+\left[1.\cdot b-1.\cdot\frac{a}{\left(R\cdot T^{1.5}\right)}\right]\cdot c+\left[1.\cdot b^2+1.\cdot\frac{a}{\left(R\cdot T^{1.5}\right)}\cdot b\right]\cdot c^2+O\left(c^3\right)$$

Once again the virial coefficients can be identified as the coefficients of the powers of c, namely:

$$B=b-\frac{a}{RT^{1.5}};\quad C=b^2+\frac{ab}{RT^{1.5}} \tag{1.6}$$

Second Virial Coefficient and Boyle Temperature

The Boyle temperature is the temperature at which the second virial coefficient is equal to zero. We will use this and experimental values for *B* to test a variety of formulas for calculating second virial coefficients.

Example 1.9 Second virial coefficient and Boyle temperature using the van der Waals equation.

Start a new worksheet and enter values for the constants of nitrogen and the vdw equation for the second virial coefficient.

$R := 8.31451 \cdot \frac{\text{joule}}{\text{K} \cdot \text{mole}}$ $a := 0.1364 \cdot \text{Pa} \cdot \text{m}^6 \cdot \text{mole}^{-2}$ $b := 38.58 \cdot 10^{-6} \cdot \text{m}^3 \cdot \text{mole}^{-1}$

$B(T) := b - \frac{a}{R \cdot T}$ $B(300 \cdot \text{K}) = -16.104 \cdot \text{cm}^3$

The last calculation is for testing, and shows the unit for *B* (which is, strictly, volume/mole). The graph (below) demonstrates that this result is qualitatively correct, but the van der Waals formula for *B* cannot usually be relied upon for quantitative calculation as is demonstrated by the sample calculations (below).

$T := 150 \cdot \text{K}, 151 \cdot \text{K} .. 2000 \cdot \text{K}$

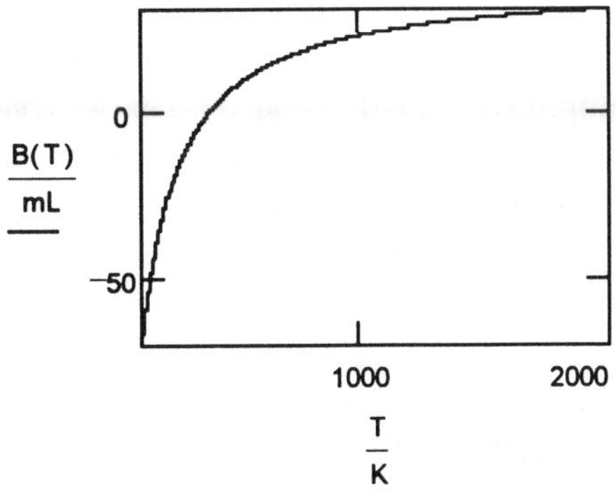

$B(90 \cdot \text{K}) = -143.698 \cdot \text{mL}$ *obs. -200*

$B(273 \cdot \text{K}) = -21.512 \cdot \text{mL}$ *obs -10*

$B(673 \cdot \text{K}) = 14.204 \cdot \text{mL}$ *obs 24*

The "obs" numbers (which are text fields) give the experimental values of *B* at the temperatures indicated; these will be repeated as we try and compare various methods for estimating *B*.

For van der Waals, the algebra for solving *B(T)* = 0 is simple enough for you to do without a computer.

$T_B := \frac{a}{b \cdot R}$ $T_B = 425.222 \cdot \text{K}$ *obs 324 K*

It is instructive to try it to solve the same problem using **root**.

$\text{TOL} = 0.001$ $T_B := 300 \cdot \text{K}$

$T_B := \text{root}(B(T_B), T_B)$ $T_B = 388.434 \cdot \text{K}$ $B(T_B) = -3.654 \cdot 10^{-6} \cdot \text{m}^3$

This is not the correct answer and the value of B at T_B is not zero but -3.654 mL. On the other hand, in the native SI unit (as shown above) it *is* a small number, and this is the criterion that Mathcad uses. Like most programs that do numerical roots, Mathcad uses an absolute criterion for when a function is equal to zero which, as in this case, is often the wrong thing to do. You could improve the accuracy by resetting the built-in variable *TOL*, but a better solution is to find the root of a quantity whose magnitude is (ordinarily) greater than 1; for example, B expressed in mL. Try this:

$$TOL = 0.001 \qquad T_B := 300 \cdot K$$

$$T_B := \mathrm{root}\left(\frac{B(T_B)}{mL}, T_B\right) \qquad T_B = 425.222 \cdot K \qquad B(T_B) = -4.741 \cdot 10^{-6} \cdot mL$$

Now the root is correct, and the value of the function $B(T_B)$ is indeed small. Of course, the answer for the Boyle temperature is, by either method, still the wrong answer! The van der Waals form for the second virial coefficient has the virtue of simplicity, but little else to recommend it.

The lessons of the preceding example are important, and extend far beyond what Mathcad is doing (which, indeed, is not unusual for programs of this type):

- Never trust a computer implicitly — always check the answer, especially an answer obtained by a numerical procedure.
- When calculating roots, try to use a function whose value (away from the root) is of magnitude 1; this can always be done by scaling (for the example above, we simply changed the unit of the calculation).

A mathematical expression such as $f(x) = 0$ can, as we learned in algebra, be multiplied or divided by any large but finite number with no effect. But on a computer, or a calculator, or any computational device with finite precision, multiplication or division by a large constant does have an effect. The reason is that such a device cannot represent an arbitrarily small or large number, and the smallest number that it can represent is equivalent to zero. This number depends on the program more than the computer (since the program can use any reasonable number of bits to represent a number); for Mathcad, the smallest possible nonzero number is approximately 10^{-307}. More important than this effect is that the programmer, when writing a root-finding procedure, must decide what constitutes zero in a practical sense; in Mathcad, this quantity is determined by the variable *TOL* (Math-menu, Built-in variables). The programmer clearly cannot know what problem you are solving, so you are the only one who can provide a sensible answer to the question "what is zero?".[1]

[1] Actually, a more sensible criterion for deciding whether a root problem $f(x) = 0$ has converged to a correct answer is that the value of the root (x) has reached a reproducible value to some degree of precision rather than that the function is equal to zero, but Mathcad, like most other such programs, does not use this criterion and, in any case, even it this method is not totally foolproof.

Example 1.10 Second virial coefficient and Boyle temperature using the RK equation.

For calculating the RK second virial coefficient, we enter formulas for calculating *a* and *b* (these can be copied from previous work). Then enter the formula and make a graph (which qualitatively resembles that for van der Waals, above).

constants for nitrogen

$R := 8.31451 \cdot \frac{joule}{K \cdot mole}$ $MPa := 10^6 \cdot Pa$ $T_c := 126 \cdot K$ $P_c := 3.394 \cdot MPa$

$a := \frac{0.42748 \cdot R^2 \cdot T_c^{2.5}}{P_c}$ $b := \frac{0.086640 \cdot R \cdot T_c}{P_c}$ $B(T) := b - \frac{a}{R \cdot T^{1.5}}$

The Boyle temperature is slightly better than the van der Waals estimate, as are the three calculated values (box below).

$T_B := \left(\frac{a}{b \cdot R}\right)^{\frac{2}{3}}$ *obs 324* $T_B = 365.176 \cdot K$

$B(90 \cdot K) = -191.833 \cdot mL$ *obs. -200*

$B(273 \cdot K) = -14.63 \cdot mL$ *obs -10*

$B(673 \cdot K) = 16.054 \cdot mL$ *obs 24*

For this application, the RK equation is nearly always better than the van der Waals law.

Example 1.11 Second virial coefficient and Boyle temperature using Berthelot formula.

The Berthelot formula for the second virial coefficient (box below) is very simple to use, especially since we have already entered the critical constants. Continuing with nitrogen:

$B(T) := \frac{9 \cdot R \cdot T_c}{128 \cdot P_c} \cdot \left(1 - \frac{6 \cdot T_c^2}{T^2}\right)$

$B(90 \cdot K) = -233.529 \cdot mL$ *obs. -200*

$B(273 \cdot K) = -6.036 \cdot mL$ *obs -10*

$B(673 \cdot K) = 17.139 \cdot mL$ *obs 24*

Solve this for the Boyle temperature; you should get 308.636 K, somewhat better than the RK estimate. The Berthelot equation for *B* is not always better than the RK equation; both are generally reliable with moderate accuracy.

Example 1.12 Second virial coefficient and Boyle temperature using the Beattie-Bridgeman formula.

The Beattie-Bridgeman equations for the virial coefficients (e.g. Noggle, Tables 1.2 and 1.3) are generally very reliable, but constants are available for only a few gases. We will compare calculations for nitrogen to the same test data.

Beattie-Bridgeman $R := 0.08206 \cdot \text{liter} \cdot \text{atm} \cdot K^{-1} \cdot \text{mole}^{-1}$ constants for nitrogen

$A_0 := 1.3455 \cdot \text{liter}^2 \cdot \text{atm} \cdot \text{mole}^{-1}$ $B_0 := 0.05046 \cdot \frac{\text{liter}}{\text{mole}}$ $c := 4.20 \cdot 10^4 \cdot \text{liter} \cdot K^3$

$$B(T) := B_0 - \frac{A_0}{R \cdot T} - \frac{c}{T^3}$$

$B(90 \cdot K) = -189.337 \cdot mL$ obs. -200

$B(273 \cdot K) = -11.665 \cdot mL$ obs -10

$B(673 \cdot K) = 25.959 \cdot mL$ obs 24

These calculations are much closer than any of the preceding ones.

Estimate $T_B := 300 \cdot K$

$T_B := \text{root}\left(\frac{B(T_B)}{mL}, T_B\right)$ *T_B observed = 324 K*

$T_B = 332.468 \cdot K$ $B(T_B) = -5.917 \cdot 10^{-4} \cdot mL$

The calculation of the Boyle temperature (box right) requires solving a cubic equation, which is best done numerically. The value calculated for the Boyle temperature is the best so far.

Table 1.3, Noggle, gives the Beattie-Bridgeman constants without units, indicating only that the liter-atm system is used. However you can deduce the units knowing that *B*, and every term in its equation, must have unit liter/mol. Similarly, *C* must have unit (liter/mol)^2. With Mathcad, this easier than it appears to be: if you get it wrong, Mathcad flags the error as "inconsistent units".

1.3 Kinetic Theory

In addition to the usual traps (the internal definition of *R* must be replaced by the gas constant, and the symbol for gram is "gm" rather than "g"), in this section we must be aware that Mathcad abbreviates the second as "sec" rather than the usual "s".

Example 1.13 Average, rms and most probable molecular speeds.

In assessing how fast the molecules of a gas are moving, we can calculate the rms speed (v_{rms}), the average speed (v_{ave}) or the most probable velocity (v_{mp}). The equations, derived in most texts, are displayed below. Note that the ratio of Boltzmann's constant to the molecular mass, k_b/m, is equal to the ratio of the gas constant to the molar mass, *R/M*. As before, we denote the molar mass *M* as *mw*. For nitrogen:

$$R := 8.31451 \cdot \frac{joule}{K \cdot mole} \qquad mw := 2 \cdot 14.0067 \cdot \frac{gm}{mole} \qquad T := 298.15 \cdot K$$

$$v_{rms} := \sqrt{\frac{3 \cdot R \cdot T}{mw}} \qquad v_{rms} = 515.245 \cdot m \cdot sec^{-1}$$

$$v_{ave} := \sqrt{\frac{8 \cdot R \cdot T}{\pi \cdot mw}} \qquad v_{ave} = 474.704 \cdot m \cdot sec^{-1}$$

$$v_{mp} := \sqrt{\frac{2 \cdot R \cdot T}{mw}} \qquad v_{mp} = 420.695 \cdot m \cdot sec^{-1}$$

Try other temperatures and molecules. Display the speeds in other units; for example, the rms speed for the example above is 1153 mph.

Example 1.14 Average molecular weight of air and the number of collisions with a wall.

Calculate the number of collisions of a gas with a wall, per unit area per unit time (Z_{wall}) for air, using the average molecular weight. First, calculate this the average molecular weight of air at 20°C, 0.01 torr, assuming average composition. First we calculate the average molecular weight of air.

$$mwN2 := 2 \cdot 14.0067 \cdot \frac{gm}{mole} \qquad mwO2 := 2 \cdot 15.9994 \cdot \frac{gm}{mole} \qquad mwAr := 39.948 \cdot \frac{gm}{mole}$$

$$mwCO2 := (12.001 + 2 \cdot 15.9994) \cdot \frac{gm}{mole}$$

$$mwAir := 0.7809 \cdot mwN2 + 0.2095 \cdot mwO2 + 0.0093 \cdot mwAr + 0.0003 \cdot mwCO2$$

$$mwAir = 0.028964 \cdot kg$$

Use this number to calculate Z_{wall}. In the following, L denotes Avogadro's number, and *ns* denotes the number density, $n^* \equiv N/V$, which is calculated from the ideal gas law as $n^* = PL/RT$; this quantity is denoted as *ns* below.

$$mw := 28.964 \cdot \frac{gm}{mole} \qquad R := 8.31451 \cdot \frac{joule}{K \cdot mole} \qquad L := 6.022137 \cdot 10^{23} \cdot mole^{-1}$$

$$P := .01 \cdot torr \qquad T := 293 \cdot K \qquad ns := \frac{P \cdot L}{R \cdot T} \qquad Z_{wall} := ns \cdot \sqrt{\frac{R \cdot T}{2 \cdot \pi \cdot mw}}$$

$$ns = 3.296 \cdot 10^{20} \cdot m^{-3} \qquad Z_{wall} = 3.813 \cdot 10^{22} \cdot m^{-2} \cdot sec^{-1}$$

Try other conditions, varying pressure in particular. Demonstrate that, at 1 atm, 40 °C, the collision frequency is 3 moles per square inch per second.

Example 1.15 Pumping rate of a vacuum system as limited by Knudsen flow.

When attempting to achieve high vacuums in the laboratory, the pumping rate at low pressures becomes limited by the collision rate of the residual gas with the orifice to the pump; this is called *Knudsen flow*. It is the ratio of this pumping rate to the rate of leakage that limits the quality of vacuum that can be achieved in a particular system. Calculate the pumping rate in a vacuum of 10^{-9} torr in a system with an exit orifice of 22 cm^2.

$mw := 28.964 \cdot \frac{gm}{mole}$ $R := 8.31451 \cdot \frac{joule}{K \cdot mole}$ $L := 6.022137 \cdot 10^{23} \cdot mole^{-1}$

$P := 10^{-9} \cdot torr$ $T := 300 \cdot K$ $ns := \frac{P \cdot L}{R \cdot T}$

$Z_{wall} := ns \cdot \sqrt{\frac{R \cdot T}{2 \cdot \pi \cdot mw}}$ $Z_{wall} = 3.768 \cdot 10^{15} \cdot m^{-2} \cdot sec^{-1}$

$area := 22 \cdot cm^2$ $\frac{area \cdot Z_{wall}}{L} = 1.377 \cdot 10^{-11} \cdot \frac{mole}{sec}$

Note: zero tolerance set to 99

When you to this, you may find that the number density in moles (*ns/L*) is displayed as zero; one of the built-in variables of Mathcad is the "zero tolerance" which determines the size of numbers that should be assumed to be zero. This can be reset (for the entire worksheet) with Math-menu, Numerical Format. Change the number in the box labeled "zero tolerance" to 99.

Example 1.16 Vapor pressure of a material by the Knudsen method.

In the Knudsen method for measuring vapor pressure a material is placed in a container with a small hole, and the assembly is placed in a vacuum. The rate of escape of the material through the hole is (if the size of the hole is small compared to the mean free path) proportional to Z_{wall} times the area of the hole. The pressure is calculated as

$$P = \mu \sqrt{\frac{2\pi RT}{M}} \tag{1.7}$$

where μ is the mass loss per unit area per unit time. An organic material with molecular weight 409 g/mole is placed into a container with a circular hole of radius 0.032 mm. After 180 minutes at 450 K, the sample was weighed and found to have lost 0.452 mg. Calculate the vapor pressure.

$R := 8.31451 \cdot \frac{joule}{K \cdot mole}$ $mass := 0.452 \cdot mg$ $T := 450 \cdot K$ $time := 180 \cdot min$

$radius := 0.032 \cdot mm$ $area := \pi \cdot radius^2$ $area = 3.217 \cdot 10^{-5} \cdot cm^2$

$\mu := \frac{mass}{area \cdot time}$ $mw := 409 \cdot \frac{gm}{mole}$ $\mu = 0.013 \cdot \frac{kg}{m^2 \cdot sec}$

$P := \mu \cdot \sqrt{\frac{2 \cdot \pi \cdot R \cdot T}{mw}}$ $P = 3.119 \cdot Pa$ $P = 0.023 \cdot torr$

The Greek letter μ (mu) is made in Mathcad by " `m ctrl+g` "; it is also on the Greek-letter palette.

Distribution Function for Speed

The Maxwell-Boltzmann distribution function $F(v)dv$ gives the fraction of molecules having a velocity in the range v to $v + dv$. Derivations, such as those for the average speed are rather awkward for Mathcad, so here we shall focus on graphing and the calculation of the fraction of molecules having speeds in a finite range.

Example 1.17 Graphing the Maxwell-Boltzmann Distribution

In order to enter the formula into Mathcad we must first define symbols for all constants including the temperature (T), Avogadro's number (L), molar mass (usually called molecular weight, denoted mw below but as M in most texts), and the gas constant R. The mass of one molecule (usually denotes as m but as ma below — m denotes meter in Mathcad), is calculated by dividing mw by L. Likewise, Boltzmann's constant (k_b) is calculated from R. In order to display numbers as small as the molecular mass and Boltzmann's constant, you must reset the zero-tolerance using Math-menu, Numerical Format.

$$T := 3000 \cdot K \qquad L := \frac{6.022137 \cdot 10^{23}}{mole} \qquad mw := (2 \cdot 14.0067) \cdot \frac{gm}{mole} \qquad R := 8.31451 \cdot \frac{joule}{K}$$

$$ma := \frac{mw}{L} \qquad ma = 4.652 \cdot 10^{-26} \cdot kg \qquad k_b := \frac{R}{L} \qquad k_b = 1.381 \cdot 10^{-23} \cdot \frac{joule}{K}$$

$$F(v) := 4 \cdot \pi \cdot \left(\frac{ma}{2 \cdot \pi \cdot k_b \cdot T}\right)^{1.5} \cdot \exp\left(\frac{-ma \cdot v^2}{2 \cdot k_b \cdot T}\right) \cdot v^2 \qquad F\left(1000 \cdot \frac{m}{sec}\right) = 5.416 \cdot 10^{-4} \cdot \frac{sec}{m}$$

The sample calculation is shown only for testing: it has no meaning of itself: it is a probability for an infinitesimal velocity interval and is meaningful only when summed over a finite interval.

$$velocity := 1, 11 .. 5000$$

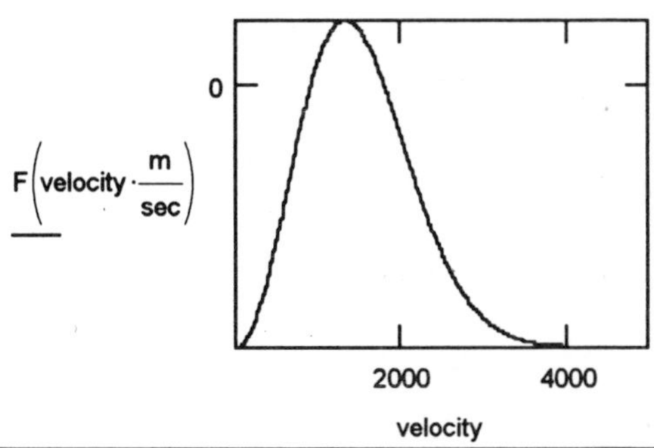

Make a graph for nitrogen at 3000 K (box to left). This is a fine opportunity to explore, so make other graphs, trying different temperatures, different plot ranges, and different molecules (i.e. molecular weight, the only quantity here that characterizes the molecule itself). Observe how the width, height and position of maximum for the distribution changes with temperature and molecular weight.

Example 1.18 Fraction of molecules in a gas moving faster than some speed.

To calculate the fraction of molecules that are traveling faster than 1000 m/s, we need to calculate the integral:

$$\int_{1000}^{\infty} F(v)\,dv$$

We cannot use infinity as a limit for a numerical integral, but examination of the graph demonstrates that the function drops off rapidly at high velocity, so there is some suitably large velocity that can be used instead.[2] We need the definitions from the preceding example, and the calculations below are for nitrogen at 3000 K.

$v1 := 1000 \cdot \frac{m}{sec}$ $\quad$ $v2 := 50000 \cdot \frac{m}{sec}$ $\quad$ $\int_{v1}^{v2} F(v)\,dv = 77.151 \cdot \%$

$mw = 28.013 \cdot \frac{gm}{mole}$ $\quad$ $T = 3 \cdot 10^3 \cdot K$

The meaning of this calculation is the 77% of the molecules are traveling 1000 m/s or faster. (To display the answer as a percent, type % in the unit placeholder.) How can we be sure the upper limit is high enough? Change it and see if the answer changes significantly. But there is a better method: since the total area under the distribution function is 1 (demonstrate this by making the lower limit zero) we can get the result by calculating the fraction with speeds less than 1000 m/s and subtracting this result from 1:

$v1 := 0 \cdot \frac{m}{sec}$ $\quad$ $v2 := 1000 \cdot \frac{m}{sec}$ $\quad$ $P_{in} := \int_{v1}^{v2} F(v)\,dv$

$P_{in} = 0.228$ $\quad$ $1 - P_{in} = 0.772$

Repeat these calculations for other temperatures and other molecules. What is the effect of mass?

Another method for such calculations is to rewrite the Maxwell-Boltzmann distribution function in terms of a unitless variable (w) as:

$$f(w) = \frac{4}{\sqrt{\pi}} \exp(-w^2) w^2 \tag{1.8}$$

where $w = v/v_{mp}$ and v_{mp} is the most-probable velocity

$$v_{mp} = \sqrt{2k_b T / m} = \sqrt{2RT/M} \tag{1.9}$$

---

[2] There are, in any case, no molecules traveling at infinite speed; the extension of kinetic-theory integrals to infinity is just a mathematical convenience.

(m is the mass of one molecule, M is the molar mass, $k_b = R/L$ is Boltzmann's constant). This way it is possible to enter the function without specifying in advance the mass or temperature.

Make a graph of the function to see what it looks like (box to right). There is not much area (i.e. probability) above 3, which means that very few molecules have speeds greater than 3 times v_p.. To see this, revise the graph to plot w from 2 to 6. Calculate the area under $f(w)$ between $w = 1$ and 2 (box below); this is the fraction of molecules having speeds in that range.

$$f(w) := \frac{4}{\sqrt{\pi}} \cdot \exp\left(-w^2\right) \cdot w^2 \qquad w := 0, 0.1 .. 5$$

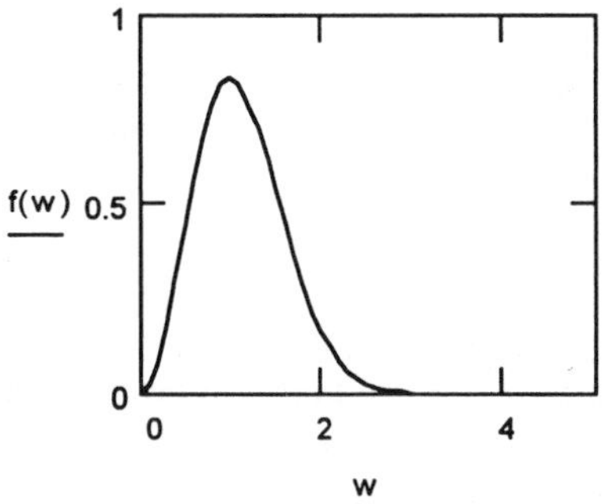

$$\int_1^2 f(w)\, dw = 0.526395$$

Calculate the fraction of molecules in nitrogen gas at 600 K that are traveling faster than 2000 mph. You can enter the lower velocity as "`v1:2000*mph`" and Mathcad will convert it to SI units. You cannot make the upper limit infinity for a numerical integration, but, as we have seen, the function $f(w)$ drops off rapidly so some value and order of magnitude greater than $v1$ will be sufficient. The box below shows the complete calculation.

$$f(w) := \frac{4}{\sqrt{\pi}} \cdot \exp\left(-w^2\right) \cdot w^2 \qquad R := 8.31451 \cdot \frac{\text{joule}}{\text{K} \cdot \text{mole}} \qquad T := 600 \cdot \text{K} \qquad mw := 2 \cdot 14.0067 \cdot \frac{\text{gm}}{\text{mole}}$$

$$v_{mp} := \sqrt{\frac{2 \cdot R \cdot T}{mw}} \qquad v_{mp} = 596.796 \cdot \frac{\text{m}}{\text{sec}} \qquad v1 := 2000 \cdot \text{mph} \qquad v1 = 894.08 \cdot \frac{\text{m}}{\text{sec}}$$

$$w1 := \frac{v1}{v_{mp}} \qquad w1 = 1.498 \qquad \int_{w1}^{15} f(w)\, dw = 21.329 \cdot \%$$

Example 1.19 Fraction of molecules having kinetic energy less than k_bT.

Calculate the fraction of molecules in methane (CH_4) at 500 K having a kinetic energy less than k_bT. The previous example can be used as a starting point. Note that k_bT is RT per mole and the symbol ke (below) is actually the kinetic energy per mole; the velocity calculated from it is correct because mw is the mass per mole (molecular weight).

$$f(w) := \frac{4}{\sqrt{\pi}} \cdot \exp\left(-w^2\right) \cdot w^2 \qquad R := 8.31451 \cdot \frac{joule}{K \cdot mole} \qquad T := 500 \cdot K$$

$$mw := (12.011 + 4 \cdot 1.00794) \cdot \frac{gm}{mole} \qquad v_{mp} := \sqrt{\frac{2 \cdot R \cdot T}{mw}} \qquad v_{mp} = 719.911 \cdot \frac{m}{sec}$$

$$ke := R \cdot T \qquad v2 := \sqrt{\frac{2 \cdot ke}{mw}} \qquad v2 = 719.911 \cdot \frac{m}{sec} \qquad v1 := 0 \cdot \frac{m}{sec}$$

$$w1 := \frac{v1}{v_{mp}} \qquad w2 := \frac{v2}{v_{mp}} \qquad \int_{w1}^{w2} f(w)\, dw = 42.759 \cdot \%$$

This fraction *does not* depend on temperature, which you can easily prove by changing the temperature definition. However, unless you do the work to algebraically eliminate T and reformulate the problem, you must supply a value for T; this is certainly the simplest thing to do.

Problems

1.1 Calculate the pressure when 500 gm of carbon dioxide is confined to a 5 liter volume at 50 °C using the van der Waals equation.

1.2 Calculate the density of carbon dioxide at 75 °C, 50 atm, using the van der Waals equation.

1.3 Use the Redlich-Kwong gas law to graph the isotherm of silicon tetrafluoride at 25 °C. Plot volumes from just above b to 10 liter, and use units MPa vs. liter. Calculate the molar volume for volumes of 10, 5, 1, 0.1 liter/mol.

1.4 Calculate the density of silicon tetrafluoride at 298.15 K, and pressure 500 psi.

1.5 Calculate the compressibility factor (z) of silicon tetrafluoride in the preceding problem.

1.6 For krypton, using the RK law, calculate the second and third virial coefficients at 300 K, and the Boyle temperature. Make graphs of B and C vs. temperature (range 250 to 1000 K).

1.7 Use the pressure series $PV_m = RT + \beta P + \gamma P^2$ with the RK virial coefficients for krypton to calculate the volume as a function to temperature for P = 100 atm. Make a graph of volume vs. T from 250 to 500 K, comparing the results of this equation with the ideal gas law. Calculate the volume at 250, 300 and 400 K with both this equation and the ideal gas law. Note: $\beta(T) = B(T)$ and. $\gamma = (C - B^2)/RT$.

1.8 For propane (molecular weigh, 44.097 gm/mol), graph the Maxwell-Boltzmann distribution at 300, 500 and 1000 K. For 300 K, calculate the fraction of molecules having velocities in 300 m/sec intervals: 0-300, 300-600, etc., until the fraction is less than 0.1%.

1.9 Benzanthrone (mw = 230.266 gm/mol) has a vapor pressure of 1 torr at 225.0 C. This material is placed in a container, under vacuum, at that temperature. The container has a hole with radius 0.15 mm. Calculate the mass loss in 1 hour.

Answers

1.1: 4.878 MPa

1.2: molar volume = 0.477 liter/mol, density = 92.4 gm/liter

1.3: 0.244, 0.481, 2.137 and 16.655 MPa

1.4: 189 gm/liter

1.5: $z = 0.767$

1.6: $B = -52.54\ \text{cm}^3/\text{mol}$, $C = 2978\ \text{cm}^6/\text{mol}$, $T_B = 610$ K.

1.7: V_m for 250, 300 and 400 K (all liter/mole, ideal in parentheses): 0.116 (0.205), 0.195 (0.246), 0.309 (0.328)

1.8: 33.858%, 56.624%, 9.267%, 0.249%, 0.001%.

1.9: 100.9 mg

CHAPTER 2

THE FIRST LAW OF THERMODYNAMICS

2.1 Heat Capacity

There are theoretical formulas for the heat capacity of, at least, simple molecular gases, and we shall explore these in Chapter 5. For this chapter we shall generally use empirical formulas such as those found in Tables 2.2 and 2.3 of Noggle. Such empirical formulas are generally valid for some specific temperature range, typically 300-2000 K. (Many of those in Noggle are valid to 3000 K.)

Example 2.1 Graphing heat capacity.

Just looking at formulas gives one little feeling for how the function behaves, so the easy-to-use graphing capabilities of Mathcad are very useful. Also, we learn here a way to enter such equations that is simple to do and easy to change, and this will be used for the remainder of the book. There are 4 coefficients that we enter as a data list: type "`j:1;4`" and then "`c[j:`" followed by the coefficients separated by commas (when coefficients are missing, enter zero).

$j := 1..4$ $\qquad c_j :=$ $\qquad$ ***Data for acetylene - C_2H_2***

47.18
$25.91\cdot 10^{-3}$
$-4.23\cdot 10^{-6}$
$-9.37\cdot 10^{5}$

$$C_{pm}(T) := \left[c_1 + c_2\cdot\frac{T}{K} + c_3\cdot\left(\frac{T}{K}\right)^2 + c_4\cdot\left(\frac{T}{K}\right)^{-2}\right]\cdot\frac{\text{joule}}{\text{K}\cdot\text{mole}}$$

$$C_{pm}(300\cdot K) = 44.161\cdot\frac{\text{joule}}{\text{K}\cdot\text{mole}} \qquad C_{pm}(1000\cdot K) = 67.923\cdot\frac{\text{joule}}{\text{K}\cdot\text{mole}}$$

These coefficients are used to define a function for the heat capacity, $C_{pm}(T)$. For this definition we use both types of subscripts supported by Mathcad: the labeling subscript used for C_{pm} is entered as "`C.pm:`" and the indexing subscript used for the coefficients is entered as (for example) "`c[2`". Rather than giving units to the coefficients, we add the unit at the end of the definition and enter the temperature as T/K. Also, the 4th term has been entered as a negative 2 power rather than $1/T^2$ to facilitate changing the formula other forms, for example, that used in

Example 2.10. The sample calculations given should be done to check for errors; do some other temperatures (for 300 to 3000 K, the range for which the function is valid) demonstrating how much the heat capacity varies with temperature for this gas.

Make a graph (box right). To get your graph looking like this one you must enter the axis limits manually. Graphing from 0 up on the y axis extends gives a better perspective on the variation with temperature.

$T := 300\cdot K, 310\cdot K .. 3000\cdot K$

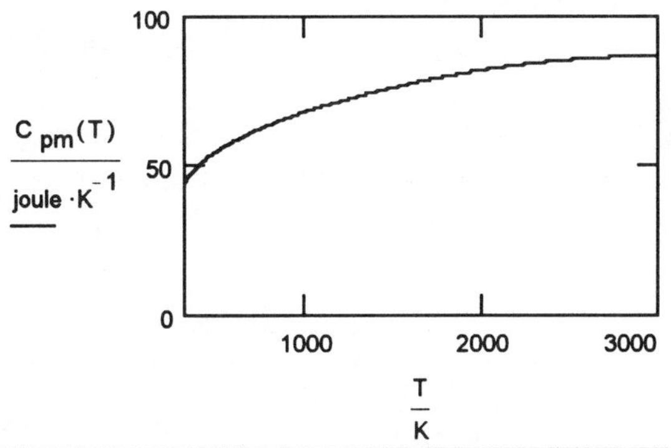

Try other gases, observing the variation in magnitude of C_p and the degree to which the heat capacity changes with temperature. How this related to molecular size and complexity? Try other ranges, including ranges outside the range of validity of the formulas (typically 300-2000, but 300-3000 for many of those on Table 2.2, Noggle). To use cubic formulas such as those in Table 2.3 Noggle you must edit the heat capacity function; otherwise the procedure is identical.

2.2 Energy and Enthalpy vs. Temperature

The variation of the internal energy, U, with temperature and volume is given by the equation of state:

$$dU = C_v\,dT + \left[T\left(\frac{\partial P}{\partial T}\right)_V - P\right]dV \tag{2.1}$$

The second term can be ignored for constant-volume processes, and is rigorously zero for an ideal gas. The equation of state for enthalpy (H) is:

$$dH = C_p\,dT + \left[V - T\left(\frac{\partial V}{\partial T}\right)_P\right]dP \tag{2.2}$$

The second term is zero for an ideal gas or for any process at constant pressure.

Integration of Heat Capacity Formulas

In this section we shall illustrate the evaluation of the first terms of Eqs. (2.1) and (2.2) for the variation of H or U with temperature. The procedure illustrated in the preceding section for entering heat capacity formulas is used.

Example 2.2 ΔH and ΔU for heating HI (ideal gas).

The heat-capacity formula and coefficient array created above is easily altered for another gas; save your work and enter the coefficients for HI (hydrogen iodide) as below:

$j := 1..4$ $\quad c_j :=$ **Data hydrogen iodide (gas)**

25.89
$8.43 \cdot 10^{-3}$
$-1.49 \cdot 10^{-6}$
$0.73 \cdot 10^{5}$

$$C_{pm}(T) := \left[c_1 + c_2 \cdot \frac{T}{K} + c_3 \cdot \left(\frac{T}{K}\right)^2 + c_4 \cdot \left(\frac{T}{K}\right)^{-2}\right] \cdot \frac{joule}{K \cdot mole}$$

$$C_{pm}(300 \cdot K) = 29.096 \cdot \frac{joule}{K \cdot mole} \qquad C_{pm}(2000 \cdot K) = 36.808 \cdot \frac{joule}{K \cdot mole}$$

The test data will help to detect errors in entering the coefficients. Most heat-capacity formulas of this type are for the constant-pressure heat capacity. For C_v for an ideal gas we use:

$$C_{vm} = C_{pm} - R \tag{2.3}$$

Calculate ΔU and ΔH for heating one mole HI (ideal gas) from 500 to 1500 K.

$$R := 8.31451 \cdot \frac{joule}{K \cdot mole} \qquad C_{vm}(T) := C_{pm}(T) - R \qquad kJ := 1000 \cdot joule$$

$$\Delta U := \int_{500 \cdot K}^{1500 \cdot K} C_{vm}(T)\, dT \qquad \Delta H := \int_{500 \cdot K}^{1500 \cdot K} C_{pm}(T)\, dT$$

$$\Delta U = 24.489 \cdot kJ$$

$$\Delta H = 32.803 \cdot kJ$$

Note that the unit for temperature has to be included in the integration limits. Also, we have defined the kilojoule for this problem. (Delta, Δ, is made by typing D ctrl+g.)

Example 2.3 $\quad$ **ΔH for cooling graphite (constant P).**

The calculation of ΔH for constant-pressure heating of a solid is done in the same manner; calculate the enthalpy change for cooling graphite from 2000 to 300 K.

$j := 1..4$ $\quad c_j :=$ $\quad$ Graphite (solid) $\quad$ $kJ := 1000 \cdot joule$

14.22
$9.22 \cdot 10^{-3}$
$-1.87 \cdot 10^{-6}$
$-7.51 \cdot 10^{5}$

$$C_{pm}(T) := \left[c_1 + c_2 \cdot \frac{T}{K} + c_3 \cdot \left(\frac{T}{K}\right)^2 + c_4 \cdot \left(\frac{T}{K}\right)^{-2}\right] \cdot \frac{joule}{K \cdot mole}$$

$$\Delta H := \int_{2000 \cdot K}^{300 \cdot K} C_{pm}(T)\, dT \qquad \Delta H = -35.101 \cdot kJ$$

For a solid the calculation of ΔU is more difficult because the relationship of C_p to C_v is more complicated and is, therefore, omitted here. (Constant-volume processes with condensed phases are rare in any case.)

Integration of Heat Capacity Data

The empirical formulas we have been using come, of course, from heat capacity data. When you have the data rather than the formula, there are two choices: use curve fitting to find a formula or interpolate the data. Mathcad excels in the latter method, using the superior cubic spline method. Interpolation starts with two indexed arrays, x and y, with corresponding points (that is, x_3 is the x-value corresponding to y_3, and so forth). (Interpolation is an effective method for fitting data that contain little noise, that is, random error.) The equation-fitting method is also possible with version 6, but we will not use it here; it is explained in Chapter 4.

Interpolation in Mathcad consists of two steps: (1) create an interpolation table using **cspline** and (2) define a function using **interp**. These are illustrated in the following example.

Example 2.4 ΔH by numerical integration.

The heat-capacity data used in this example have unit cal K^{-1} mol^{-1}. Mathcad has "cal" as a defined unit, but there are several definitions for the calorie. To find out which one you have, enter "`cal=`" and note the answer. The most common value used in thermodynamics is the *thermochemical calorie*, cal = 4.184 J (exactly); if this is not the definition in your version of Mathcad, you must replace it as below.

$$J := joule \quad kJ := 10^3 \cdot J \quad R := 8.31451 \cdot \frac{J}{K \cdot mole} \quad cal := 4.184 \cdot J$$

When entering data, you must use index subscripts (invoked with [ ), and define a range variable for the index in advance; in this case, we use 7 data points and so begin with "`i:0;6`". The data (below) are entered, for example, as "`Tx[i:298, 500, 1000`" and so forth, separating each number with a comma (do not type quotes or spaces). The heat capacities are constant-pressure values (C_p) in cal/K. It is simplest to enter the numbers without units and add units later. To add units, we create two new arrays (*Txu* and *Cpu*) as below.

$i := 0..6 \qquad J := joule$

$Tx_i :=$	$Cpx_i :=$
298	9.918
500	11.688
1000	13.621
1500	14.390
2000	14.770
2500	15.002
3000	15.167

$$Cpu_i := Cpx_i \cdot \frac{cal}{K \cdot mole}$$

$$Txu_i := Tx_i \cdot K$$

$$vs := cspline(Txu, Cpu)$$

$$Cpi(T) := interp(vs, Txu, Cpu, T)$$

$$Cpi(1500 \cdot K) = 14.39 \cdot \frac{cal}{K \cdot mole}$$

$$Cpi(850 \cdot K) = 55.549 \cdot \frac{J}{K \cdot mole}$$

The technique for creating the interpolation table (*vs*) and interpolation function (*Cpi*) are demonstrated in the box to the left. The function so defined can be used for any purpose that you could use a normal function for, including the calculation of values and integration. The sample calculations illustrate how to obtain numerical interpolations. The first calculation is given in cal to demonstrate that interpolation will (and must) exactly reproduce the input data; there is no possibility of smoothing as there is for curve fitting.

It is always a good idea to make a graph (box right) to be sure the function you have created is reasonable.

The interpolation functions can, of course, be used for other purposes including differentiation and integration. In this case we want to integrate to obtain the enthalpy change. Calculate the enthalpy change for heating 1 kg of OCS from 500 to 1200 K. This is the heat required if the process is done at constant pressure.

T := 200, 205.. 3000

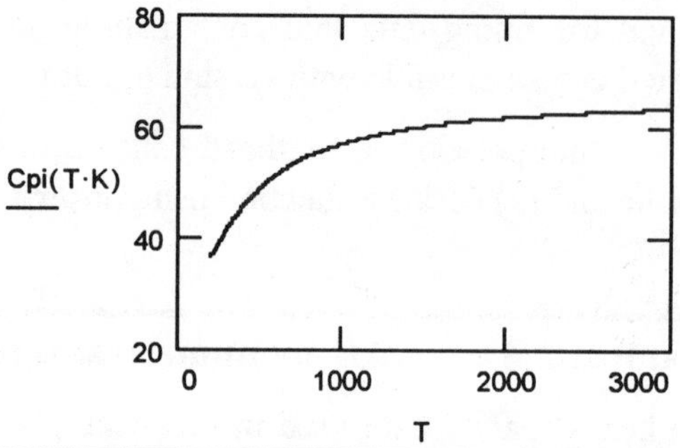

$mw := (15.9994 + 12.011 + 32.066)\cdot\frac{gm}{mole}$ $\quad n := \frac{1\cdot kg}{mw}$ $\quad T_1 := 500\cdot K$ $\quad T_2 := 1200\cdot K$

$\Delta H := n\cdot\int_{T_1}^{T_2} Cpi(T)\, dT \qquad \Delta H = 640.015\cdot kJ$

The method used makes it very easy to change the amount and temperatures. Demonstrate this by finding ΔH for heating 1 pound (symbol lb in Mathcad) of OCS between the same temperatures (ANSWER: 290.3 kJ).

Save these calculations (*cp-ocs.mcd*) for later use.

2.3 Variation of *U* and *H* With Pressure

The second term of the internal-energy equation of state, Eq. (2.1) is called the *internal pressure*:

$$\left(\frac{\partial U}{\partial V}\right)_T = T\left(\frac{\partial P}{\partial T}\right)_V - P \qquad (2.4)$$

This can be evaluated symbolically from an equation of state, but here we shall only illustrate how Mathcad evaluates such expressions numerically.

Example 2.5 Internal pressure of an RK Gas

For the RK equation of state, which you should be able to insert from earlier work (*rk.mcd*), and data for nitrogen:

$R := 8.31451 \cdot \frac{joule}{K \cdot mole}$ $MPa := 10^6 \cdot Pa$ ***Constants for nitrogen***

$T_c := 126 \cdot K$ $P_c := 3.394 \cdot MPa$ $mw := (2 \cdot 14.0067) \cdot \frac{g}{mole}$

$a := \frac{0.42748 \cdot R^2 \cdot T_c^{2.5}}{P_c}$ $b := \frac{0.08664 \cdot R \cdot T_c}{P_c}$ $P(V,T) := \frac{R \cdot T}{V - b} - \frac{a}{\sqrt{T} \cdot V \cdot (V + b)}$

$bar := 10^5 \cdot Pa$

$ip(V,T) := T \cdot \frac{d}{dT} P(V,T) - P(V,T)$

$ip(1 \cdot liter, 300 \cdot K) = 1.309 \cdot bar$

$ip(100 \cdot mL, 100 \cdot K) = 183.641 \cdot bar$

Define and test a function (*ip*) for the internal pressure, Eq. (2.4) (box to left). (Recall that the derivative operator, *d/dT*, is implemented with a button on the Calculus Palette, not typed as such.)

$b = 26.743 \cdot mL$ $T := 100 \cdot K$

$vol := 30 \cdot mL, 40 \cdot mL .. 500 \cdot mL$

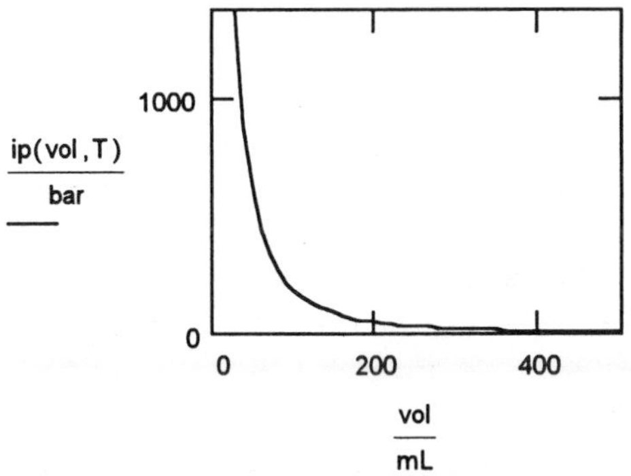

Make a graph of internal pressure vs. volume at constant temperature (box to right). Note how sharply the internal pressure increases as volume is decreased, reflecting an increasing nonideality as the molecules are forced closer and closer to each other.

Make a graph showing the temperature dependence of the internal pressure for 50 to 300 K and volumes around 100 mL. Note that the critical volume of nitrogen is 90 mL and the critical temperature is 126 K, so you are getting into the region where the material is a liquid. There is a rise at low temperature, but it is not as sharp as the rise with volume seen above.

Example 2.6 Internal pressure of benzene liquid.

For condensed phases (solid or liquid) it is often simpler to work with the coefficient of thermal expansion (α) and isothermal compressibility (κ_T) It can be shown that:

$$\left(\frac{\partial P}{\partial T}\right)_V = \frac{\alpha}{\kappa_T} \tag{2.5}$$

Thus the internal pressure is, from Eq. (2.4):

$$\left(\frac{\partial U}{\partial V}\right)_T = T\frac{\alpha}{\kappa_T} - P \tag{2.6}$$

(Values of α and κ_T are given in, for example, Table 1.8, Noggle.) For benzene (liquid):

$\alpha := 1.237 \cdot 10^{-3} \cdot K^{-1}$ $\kappa_T := 63.5 \cdot 10^{-6} \cdot atm^{-1}$ $T := 293.15 \cdot K$

$MPa := 10^6 \cdot Pa$ $P := 1 \cdot atm$ $T \cdot \frac{\alpha}{\kappa_T} - P = 578.531 \cdot MPa$

This is notably higher than the values we found for nitrogen gas, but comparable to those for which nitrogen was approaching liquefaction. Try some other materials to get a feeling for the magnitude of the internal pressure. For example, calculate the internal pressure of mercury. (ANSWER: 1371 MPa.)

Example 2.7 ΔH with pressure for a condensed phase.

Changes in enthalpy with pressure are usually quite small for condensed phases, but they can be significant under extreme pressure. For condensed phases, Eq. (2.2) is conveniently written in terms of the coefficient of thermal expansion (α)

$$\alpha = \frac{1}{V}\left(\frac{\partial V}{\partial T}\right)_P \tag{2.7}$$

as

$$dH = C_p dT + V(1 - \alpha T)dP \tag{2.8}$$

It is often sufficient to assume that the material is incompressible so V is independent of P, but you can also use the isothermal compressibility (κ_T) with

$$V = V_0(1 - \kappa_T P) \tag{2.9}$$

where V_0 is the volume at low pressure (P_0, which is neglected here). We shall do the calculation with data from Table 1.8, Noggle for mercury (Hg, liquid). The data in the table are for 20 °C, and we will assume a pressure of 1000 atm.

$T := 293.15 \cdot K$ $\alpha := 0.0567 \cdot 10^{-3} \cdot K^{-1}$ $\kappa_T := 3.9 \cdot 10^{-6} \cdot atm^{-1}$

$V_0 := 14.8 \cdot \frac{cm^3}{mole}$ $MPa := 10^6 \cdot Pa$ $kJ := 1000 \cdot joule$

$\Delta H(P) := \int_{1 \cdot atm}^{P} V_0 \cdot (1 - \kappa_T \cdot P) \cdot (1 - \alpha \cdot T)\, dP$ $\Delta H(1000 \cdot atm) = 1.47 \cdot kJ$

One thousand atmospheres is a large pressure, about 100 MPa or 15000 pounds per square inch, and the enthalpy change is far from negligible. This calculation makes several questionable assumptions: that α and κ_T do not change with pressure, and that the pressure causes no phase change in the mercury (for example, it could solidify).

2.4 Variation of Heat Capacity with *P* and *V*

One of the problems with integrating Eqs. (2.1) and (2.2) for a general change (T, V and P all changing) is that the P/V terms depend on temperature and the heat capacity terms depend on pressure and volume (at constant T). We have seen how the internal pressure varies with temperature; in this section we explore how heat capacity varies with pressure or volume. It can be shown:

$$\left(\frac{\partial C_v}{\partial V}\right)_T = T\left(\frac{\partial^2 P}{\partial T^2}\right)_V \text{; and } \left(\frac{\partial C_p}{\partial P}\right)_T = -T\left(\frac{\partial^2 V}{\partial T^2}\right)_P \qquad (2.10)$$

We shall evaluate the first expression for the constant-volume heat capacity.

Example 2.8 Heat capacity (C_v) of ethane at 5 MPa.

We will now calculate the constant-volume heat capacity of ethane at 5 MPa from its low-pressure heat capacity using the RK equation of state. Insert *rk.mcd* or enter the RK equations as below. Enter data for ethane.

$R := 8.31451 \cdot \frac{\text{joule}}{\text{K} \cdot \text{mole}}$ $\quad \text{MPa} := 10^6 \cdot \text{Pa}$ $\quad$ ***Constants for ethane***

$T_c := 305.33 \cdot \text{K}$ $\quad P_c := 4.871 \cdot \text{MPa}$ $\quad \text{mw} := (2 \cdot 12.011 + 6 \cdot 1.00794) \cdot \frac{\text{gm}}{\text{mole}}$

$a := \frac{0.42748 \cdot R^2 \cdot T_c^{\,2.5}}{P_c}$ $\quad b := \frac{0.08664 \cdot R \cdot T_c}{P_c}$ $\quad P(V,T) := \frac{R \cdot T}{V - b} - \frac{a}{\sqrt{T} \cdot V \cdot (V + b)}$

Note that V denotes the molar volume: all calculations will be for one mole.

Next you need an expression for $(\partial^2 P/\partial T^2)$. Mathcad can do this for you: copy the right-hand side of the pressure function into the clipboard: place a cursor in the expression and press the up arrow until the entire right-hand side is boxed; then select Edit-menu, Copy. Open a new document and paste it there (Edit-menu, Paste).[1] Load the symbolic processor (Symbolic-menu, Load). Place the cursor in the expression next to a T and select Symbolic-menu, Differentiate. Do the same to the result of this operation; to simplify the second result, place the whole expression in a selection box and use Symbolic-menu, Simplify. Now copy the final result to the clipboard and return to the first document. Type "`cvv(V,T):`" and paste the clipboard contents (the second derivative of P with respect to T); edit the expression to insert the T required by Eq. (2.10). The function *cvv* represents $(\partial C_v/\partial V)_T$.

$\text{cvv}(V,T) := \frac{-3}{4} \cdot \frac{a \cdot T}{\left[T^{\left(\frac{5}{2}\right)} \cdot (V \cdot (V + b))\right]}$ $\quad T := 350 \cdot \text{K}$

$\text{cvv}(1 \cdot \text{liter}, T) = -1.083 \cdot \frac{\text{joule}}{\text{K} \cdot \text{liter}}$

[1] Here, and elsewhere, I use different documents for derivations and calculations; I find this convenient, but this is not really essential.

Test the function as above as a check.

Next, we enter the pressures and calculate the volumes (box below).

$P_1 := 0.1 \cdot MPa$ $\quad V_1 := \frac{R \cdot T}{P_1}$ $\quad V_1 := root(P(V_1, T) - P_1, V_1)$

$P_2 := 5 \cdot MPa$ $\quad V_2 := \frac{R \cdot T}{P_2}$ $\quad V_2 := root(P(V_2, T) - P_2, V_2)$

$P(V_2, T) = 5 \cdot MPa$ $\quad P(V_1, T) = 0.1 \cdot MPa$ $\quad$ ***Back calculate as a check***

Next we enter data C_{v1} and C_{v2}:

$C_{v1} := mw \cdot \left(1.687 \cdot \frac{joule}{K \cdot gm}\right)$ $\quad C_{v2} := mw \cdot \left(1.824 \cdot \frac{joule}{K \cdot gm}\right)$ $\quad$ ***Data for C_v***

These are the experimental values at P_1 and P_2 respectively, entered as specific heats and multiplied by the molecular weight to get molar heat capacity. The first of these heat capacities is used to calculate the value at 5 MPa, which is then compared to the second value (C_{v2}).

Now we are ready to calculate the heat capacity as a function of volume:

$$C_v(V_2) = C_v(V_1) + \int_{V_1}^{V_2} \left(\frac{\partial C_v}{\partial V}\right) dV$$

The calculation is shown in the box to the right. The result is moderately good (much better than you would get from van der Waals), but it is worse for lower temperature or higher pressure. The RK is much better for ethane than for most gases, and usually works better than this. The problem is probably the second derivative: any approximate expression tends to lose accuracy when differentiated — even more on second differentiation.

$C_{vm} := C_{v1} + \int_{V_1}^{V_2} cvv(V, T)\, dV$ $\quad V_1 = 28.964 \cdot liter$ $\quad V_2 = 0.427 \cdot liter$

$C_{vm} = 53.208 \cdot \frac{joule}{K}$ $\quad$ compare $\quad C_{v2} = 54.847 \cdot \frac{joule}{K}$

The dependence of C_p on pressure, Eq. (2.10), is more difficult to calculate since derivatives of volume are not easy to do with equations of state, like RK or vdw, that are explicit in pressure, and, even so, the problem of integrating Eq. (2.2) for a general process (T and P both changing) remains. A much better method is to use gas imperfection functions, as explained in the next section.

2.5 Standard State and Gas Imperfections

For an ideal gas, $(\partial U/\partial V)_T = 0$, meaning that the internal energy of an ideal gas depends on temperature only. For real gases, it is convenient to divide the internal energy into two parts: the value it would have if it were an ideal gas at the same temperature and an *imperfection*, the difference between the energy of the gas and of an ideal gas at the same temperature. The latter quantity is called the *standard* internal energy: U° The internal energy imperfection, U_i, is calculated as:

$$U_i = \int_{\infty}^{V} \left[T\left(\frac{\partial P}{\partial T}\right)_V - P \right] dV \tag{2.11}$$

The change in U from state 1 (T_1, V_1) to state 2 (T_2, V_2) is:

$$\Delta U = \int_{T_1}^{T_2} C_v^\circ \, dT + U_i(V_2, T_2) - U_i(V_1, T_1) \tag{2.12}$$

Here, C_v° is the ideal-gas heat capacity (the heat capacity of the real gas in the low-pressure limit).

It is usually simplest to calculate enthalpy from $H = U + PV$ which, for the ideal gas standard state, becomes $H^\circ = U^\circ + RT$. Thus the enthalpy imperfection is:

$$H_i = U_i + PV - RT \tag{2.13}$$

Calculations are usually done for one mole (and multiplied by the number of moles when necessary) so V in these expressions is the molar volume. The enthalpy change for a change from state 1 (T_1, V_1) to state 2 (T_2, V_2) is:

$$\Delta H = \int_{T_1}^{T_2} C_p^\circ \, dT + H_i(V_2, T_2) - H_i(V_1, T_1) \tag{2.14}$$

The development of the internal energy and enthalpy imperfections is discussed in Section 2.8 Noggle. There the van der Waals formulas are generally done as examples and the RK formulas are done in the problems. Table 3.3, Noggle summarizes the results for RK. The symbolic derivation required for the RK law are illustrated in the next example.

Example 2.9 Derive imperfection formulas for RK

The key derivation is for U_i, Eq. (2.11). This is quite simple for van der Waals (see Noggle Examples 2.3 and 2.14) and slightly more challenging for RK; for other gas laws it can be quite difficult. We illustrate the procedure with the RK law.

First, start a new document and insert (File-Menu, Insert) the file *rk.mcd*. Enter constants for nitrogen:

$\mathrm{MPa} := 10^6 \cdot \mathrm{Pa}$ **constants for nitrogen**

$T_c := 126 \cdot \mathrm{K}$ $P_c := 3.394 \cdot \mathrm{MPa}$ $\mathrm{mw} := (2 \cdot 14.0067) \cdot \frac{\mathrm{gm}}{\mathrm{mole}}$

Copy the right-hand side of the pressure function to the clipboard (place the cursor on it and press the up arrow until it is selected, then copy). Open a new document (File-menu, New) and paste it. Then place the cursor on the expression next to a T and select Symbolic-menu Differentiate.

$$\frac{R \cdot T}{V-b} - \frac{a}{\sqrt{T} \cdot V \cdot (V+b)}$$

by differentiation, yields

$$\frac{R}{(V-b)} + \frac{1}{2} \cdot \frac{a}{\left[T^{\left(\frac{3}{2}\right)} \cdot (V \cdot (V+b))\right]}$$

You now have an expression for ($\partial P/\partial T$); copy it to the clipboard. Now type "`T*()`" and paste the derivative expression into the placeholder inside the parentheses. Then select the whole expression and type "-" (minus).

At this point you must select the expression for P and copy it to the clipboard; return to the placeholder and paste. Now select the whole expression and select Symbolic-menu Simplify (box to right). You should now have an expression representing the integrand of Eq. (2.11).

simplifies to

$$\frac{3}{2} \cdot \frac{a}{\left[\sqrt{T} \cdot (V \cdot (V+b))\right]}$$

by integration, yields

$$\frac{3}{2} \cdot \frac{a}{\left(\sqrt{T} \cdot b\right)} \cdot \ln(V) - \frac{3}{2} \cdot \frac{a}{\left(\sqrt{T} \cdot b\right)} \cdot \ln(V+b)$$

To calculate the energy imperfection, place the cursor in this expression next to V and select Symbolic-menu Integrate (box to left). This expression is not usable without combining the log terms, and Mathcad will not do it for you. Edit (or just retype) the expression until you get:

$$\frac{3a}{2\sqrt{T}\,b} \ln\left(\frac{V}{V+b}\right)$$

We actually needed the integral from V to infinity; in this form it may be apparent that the limit as V goes to infinity is (since b is finite), ln(1) = 0. Therefore the expression derived is the internal-energy imperfection, U_i of Eq. (2.11). Copy this result into the original document (with the RK equations) and the right-hand side of a function $U_i(V,T)$. With the internal-energy imperfection in hand, calculating the enthalpy imperfection with Eq. (2.13) is simple. Enter and test the functions shown in the box below.

$$U_i(V,T) := \frac{3}{2} \cdot \frac{a}{\sqrt{T} \cdot b} \cdot \ln\left(\frac{V}{V+b}\right) \qquad H_i(V,T) := U_i(V,T) + P(V,T) \cdot V - R \cdot T$$

$$U_i(1 \cdot \text{liter}, 200 \cdot K) = -162.419 \cdot \text{joule} \qquad H_i(1 \cdot \text{liter}, 200 \cdot K) = -223.588 \cdot \text{joule}$$

Save this file (*rkimp.mcd*). These functions are used in the next example.

Example 2.10 Internal energy and enthalpy imperfection.

Start a new document and insert the worksheet (*rkimp.mcd*) developed in the preceding example (or just enter the equations as given). Change the constants to those for SO_2:

Redlich-Kwong Equation of State $MPa := 10^6 \cdot Pa$ $J := joule$ $kJ := 10^3 \cdot J$

$R := 8.31451 \cdot \frac{joule}{K \cdot mole}$ $T_c := 430 \cdot K$ $P_c := 7.873 \cdot MPa$ **Data for SO_2**

$mw := (32.0662 + 2 \cdot 15.9994) \cdot \frac{gm}{mole}$ $\Delta Hvap := 24.92 \cdot kJ$ $T_b := 263.13 \cdot K$

$$a := \frac{0.42748 \cdot R^2 \cdot T_c^{2.5}}{P_c} \qquad b := \frac{0.08664 \cdot R \cdot T_c}{P_c} \qquad P(V,T) := \frac{R \cdot T}{V - b} - \frac{a}{\sqrt{T} \cdot V \cdot (V + b)}$$

(In this example, J is defined as the symbol for joule and kJ for 1000 of them.) Next, enter heat capacity data for SO_2; this too can be done by inserting and editing earlier work, but since we are using a cubic expression (below), some editing is needed. Note that you must change both the exponent of the 4th coefficient and the power in the 4th term of the equation.

$j := 1 .. 4$ $c_j :=$ **Data for SO_2**

25.72
$57.923 \cdot 10^{-3}$
$-38.09 \cdot 10^{-6}$
$8.606 \cdot 10^{-9}$

$$C_{pm}(T) := \left[c_1 + c_2 \cdot \frac{T}{K} + c_3 \cdot \left(\frac{T}{K}\right)^2 + c_4 \cdot \left(\frac{T}{K}\right)^3 \right] \cdot \frac{joule}{K \cdot mole}$$

The equations for the energy and enthalpy imperfections should be present from the previous example, but if they are not, enter them as shown below.

$$U_i(V,T) := \frac{3 \cdot a}{2 \cdot b \cdot \sqrt{T}} \cdot \ln\left(\frac{V}{V + b}\right) \qquad H_i(V,T) := U_i(V,T) + P(V,T) \cdot V - R \cdot T$$

$U_i(22.4 \cdot liter, 273 \cdot K) = -58.277 \cdot J$ $H_i(22.4 \cdot liter, 273 \cdot K) = -93.101 \cdot J$

$H_i(50 \cdot mL, 263 \cdot K) = -21.498 \cdot kJ$ **Compare enthalpy of vaporization: 24.92 kJ/mol**

The last sample calculation is interesting: the temperature is the normal boiling point of SO_2 and the volume is, approximately, the molar volume of the liquid at that temperature. We see that the enthalpy imperfection is comparable in magnitude to the enthalpy of vaporization. We shall explore this topic more thoroughly in Chapter 4; for now we note that gas imperfections are related to liquefaction and heats of vaporization. Save this document (as *so2rk.mcd*) for future use.

Example 2.11 ΔH using the RK equation of state.

Calculate ΔH for heating SO_2 from 300 to 500 K at a constant volume of 12 liter. Earlier we noted that, for an ideal gas, the enthalpy change depended only on temperature, so constant-volume and constant-pressure expansions gave the same result. To compare, we calculate the two terms of Eq. (2.14) separately.

The calculation in the box to the right is a continuation of previous example (for SO_2). The ideal-gas value is denoted ΔH_1 and the difference (ideal to real) as ΔH_2. The latter quantity is small for these conditions, but try some other numbers: the difference is not always small.

$T1 := 300\cdot K \quad V1 := 12\cdot liter \quad P(V1,T1) = 2.001\cdot atm$

$T2 := 500\cdot K \quad V2 := 12\cdot liter \quad P(V2,T2) = 3.386\cdot atm$

$\Delta H_1 := \int_{T1}^{T2} C_{pm}(T)\, dT \qquad \Delta H_1 = 8.651\cdot kJ$

$\Delta H_2 := H_i(V2,T2) - H_i(V1,T1) \qquad \Delta H_2 = 0.044\cdot kJ$

$\Delta H_1 + \Delta H_2 = 8.695\cdot kJ$

What happens if you choose the second volume to keep the pressure constant ($V2$ = 20.39 liter for the initial volume and temperatures given above)? It may seem odd that there is any difference at all since the second term of Eq. (2.2) is zero for a constant-pressure process. The reason is that the heat capacity of a real gas is different from an ideal gas — this is the heat capacity imperfection. The method of calculation we are using avoids this complication because the first term of Eq. (2.14) uses the standard heat capacity, C_p° — that is, the heat capacity of the ideal gas.

Save this work for we shall use it again later in this chapter (Joule-Thomson expansion, below, page 60).

2.6 Expansions of Gases

Adiabatic Reversible Expansion

The temperature and volume in an adiabatic reversible expansion of an ideal gas are related as:

$$\int_{T_1}^{T_2} \frac{C_{vm}}{T} dT = -R\ln\left[\frac{V_2}{V_1}\right] \qquad (2.15)$$

Sometimes the formula explicit in pressure is more convenient:

$$\int_{T_1}^{T_2} \frac{C_{pm}}{T} dT = R\ln\left[\frac{P_2}{P_1}\right] \qquad (2.16)$$

Example 2.12 Temperature change on adiabatic reversible expansion.

Calculate the final temperature when methane, initially at 580 K, is expanded to increase its volume 15-fold. First we must enter data and formulas for the heat capacity of methane:

$j := 1..4$ ***Data for methane (gas)*** $R := 8.31451 \cdot \frac{joule}{K \cdot mole}$

$c_j :=$

24.87
$55.8 \cdot 10^{-3}$
$-10.24 \cdot 10^{-6}$
$-4.87 \cdot 10^{5}$

$$C_{pm}(T) := \left[c_1 + c_2 \cdot \frac{T}{K} + c_3 \cdot \left(\frac{T}{K}\right)^2 + c_4 \cdot \left(\frac{T}{K}\right)^{-2} \right] \cdot \frac{joule}{K \cdot mole}$$

$$C_{vm}(T) := C_{pm}(T) - R \qquad C_{pm}(300 \cdot K) = 35.277 \cdot \frac{joule}{K \cdot mole}$$

$V_1 := 1 \cdot liter \quad V_2 := 15 \cdot liter \quad T_1 := 580 \cdot K$

$$f(T_2) := \int_{T_1}^{T_2} \frac{C_{vm}(T)}{T} \, dT + R \cdot \ln\left(\frac{V_2}{V_1}\right)$$

Next, enter the initial conditions (the actual volumes do not matter since only the ratio is used), and Eq. (2.15) in the form *f(T)* whose value is zero at the correct final temperature (box to left).

Try to locate root

$test := 900, 700 .. 300$

test	$\frac{f(test \cdot K)}{joule \cdot K^{-1}}$
900	44.798
700	31.312
500	16.287
300	-0.779

Next, we need to find an approximate location for the root; this is easily done by calculating *f(T)* for a range of temperatures (*test*, box to left). The list displays are made by typing `"test="` and `"f(test*K) /joule*K^-1="` respectively; dividing by the unit makes the display a great deal simpler. Observing the values of *f* it appears that the root is near 300 K; this value is used as a guess for the **root** function (box below).

$T_2 := 300 \cdot K$ ***estimate***

$T_2 := root(f(T_2), T_2)$

$T_2 = 308.665 \cdot K$

The procedure for the equation explicit in pressure is very similar. Calculate the final temperature when methane at 300 K, 1 atm, is compressed adiabatically and reversibly to 50 atm.

$P_1 := 1 \cdot atm \quad P_2 := 50 \cdot atm \quad T_1 := 300 \cdot K$

$$f(T_2) := \int_{T_1}^{T_2} \frac{C_{pm}(T)}{T} \, dT - R \cdot \ln\left(\frac{P_2}{P_1}\right)$$

$T_2 := 500 \cdot K$

$T_2 := root(f(T_2), T_2) \qquad T_2 = 622.24 \cdot K$

$test := 300, 500 .. 900$

test	$\frac{f(test \cdot K)}{joule \cdot K^{-1}}$
300	-32.527
500	-11.213
700	6.609
900	22.185

Example 2.13 Adiabatic lapse rate. Celsius to Fahrenheit conversion.

The pressure and temperature in the atmosphere vary with altitude (h), as any pilot can testify. The variation of pressure is given by

$$\frac{dP}{dh} = -g\rho \tag{2.17}$$

where ρ is the density and g is the acceleration of gravity. For an adiabatic process in an ideal gas, the temperature and pressure are related as

$$C_{pm}\frac{dT}{T} = R\frac{dP}{P} \tag{2.18}$$

Combining Eqs. (2.17) and (2.18) and using the ideal gas formula for density, $\rho = PM/RT$ (M is the molecular weight, denoted as *mw* in Mathcad), gives:

$$\frac{dT}{dh} = \frac{-gM}{C_{pm}} \tag{2.19}$$

This is the adiabatic lapse rate.

Most Americans are still accustomed to thinking of temperature on the Fahrenheit scale (including scientists who regularly use Celsius in the laboratory). Mathcad can only do multiplicative unit conversions, so we must write our own functions to convert between Fahrenheit and Celsius. The Rankine degree (R) is related to Fahrenheit as the Kelvin degree is related to Celsius. To get labels correct, we define symbols for C and F as equal to K and R respectively (which should not be understood to imply that these scales are equal, but only that the degree size is the same). Then we define the functions (box above right). Note that when *degF* is used, the numerical value is displayed in K, and this number is incorrect. To get the correct number, enter F in the unit placeholder.

$C := K$ $F := R$ ice point $273.15 \cdot K = 491.67 \cdot R$

$$\mathrm{degC}(t) := \left[\left(\frac{t}{F} + 40\right)\cdot\frac{5}{9} - 40\right]\cdot K$$

$$\mathrm{degF}(t) := \left[\left(\frac{t}{C} + 40\right)\cdot\frac{9}{5} - 40\right]\cdot R$$

$\mathrm{degF}(0\cdot C) = 32\cdot F$ $\mathrm{degC}(32\cdot F) = 0\cdot C$

$\mathrm{degF}(100\cdot C) = 212\cdot F$ $\mathrm{degC}(98.6\cdot F) = 37\cdot C$

F/R answers wrong unless correct unit used in placeholder

$$mw := (0.79 \cdot 28 + 0.21 \cdot 32) \cdot gm$$

$$C_{pm} := 29.1 \cdot joule \cdot K^{-1}$$

$$lapse\_rate := \frac{mw \cdot g}{C_{pm}}$$

$$lapse\_rate = 9.719 \cdot \frac{C}{km}$$

$$lapse\_rate = 28.154 \cdot \frac{F}{mi}$$

$$lapse\_rate = 5.332 \cdot \frac{F}{1000 \cdot ft}$$

Calculate the lapse rate for air (box to left). The heat capacities of nitrogen and oxygen are nearly the same, so we can presume that, for air, the heat capacity is approximately 29.1 J K^{-1} mol^{-1}; this quantity does not vary much with temperature at and below room temperature, so we presume it to be constant. The acceleration of gravity is represented by *g* in Mathcad.

The calculated lapse rate is presented in a number of units. Aviation manuals gives the lapse rate for dry air as 5.5 to 5.6 °F per 1000 feet, which is in substantial agreement with our result. This is affected by moisture content; the value for "normal air" is given as 3.5 °F per 1000 feet, and the value for moist air is smaller.

When a wind blows across a mountain, the air cools as it climbs the slope and this often results in fog or clouds on the windward side. When the air descends on the leeward side, it warms again and the weather is often clear. Adiabatic cooling and warming thus accounts for the fact that, on the Pacific coast of North America, the westward slopes of the mountains are moist and green while the eastern slopes are dry.

On the rim of the mile-deep Grand Canyon, the day is warm and pleasant, 80 °F, so you decide to hike to the bottom. The calculation (box to right) suggests that you should carry a lot of water.

$$T_{top} := degC(80 \cdot F) \quad T_{top} = 26.667 \cdot C$$

$$T_{bot} := T_{top} - lapse\_rate \cdot (-1 \cdot mi)$$

$$T_{bot} = 42.308 \cdot C \quad degF(T_{bot}) = 108.154 \cdot F$$

Joule Expansion

A Joule expansion is the expansion of a gas adiabatically into a vacuum; since no work is done, and there is no heat transferred into or out of the gas, the internal energy is constant: $\Delta U = 0$. The change of U with V and T is:

$$\Delta U = \int_{T_1}^{T_2} C_v \, dT + \int_{V_1}^{V_1} \left[\frac{\partial U}{\partial V} \right]_T dV \qquad (2.20)$$

For a van der Waals gas

$$\left[\frac{\partial U}{\partial V} \right]_T = \frac{a}{V_m^2} \qquad (2.21)$$

is independent of temperature. This implies that C_v is independent of V (at constant T) and, hence, the calculation is very simple.

Example 2.14 Final temperature of a Joule expansion.

Enter data for the heat capacity of methane (above) and its van der Waals *a* constant.

Data for methane

$a := 0.2283 \cdot Pa \cdot m^6 \cdot mole^{-2}$ $\quad R := 8.31451 \cdot \frac{joule}{K \cdot mole}$

$j := 1..4$

$c_j :=$

24.87
$55.8 \cdot 10^{-3}$
$-10.24 \cdot 10^{-6}$
$-4.87 \cdot 10^{5}$

$$C_{pm}(T) := \left[c_1 + c_2 \cdot \frac{T}{K} + c_3 \cdot \left(\frac{T}{K}\right)^2 + c_4 \cdot \left(\frac{T}{K}\right)^{-2}\right] \cdot \frac{joule}{K \cdot mole}$$

$$C_{vm}(T) := C_{pm}(T) - R \qquad C_{pm}(300 \cdot K) = 35.277 \cdot \frac{joule}{K \cdot mole}$$

We shall do a calculation for the same expansion as for adiabatic reversible example (above) for comparison. The procedure is similar: enter the volumes and initial temperature and then set up and expression for ΔU as a function of temperature (box to right). Then provide a guess for the final temperature and use **root** to find the temperature for which $\Delta U = 0$. The temperature drop is much smaller because no work is done in the expansion: it is due solely to the attractive forces of the molecules.

$V_1 := 1 \cdot liter \qquad V_2 := 15 \cdot liter \qquad T_1 := 580 \cdot K$

$$\Delta U(T) := \int_{T_1}^{T} C_{vm}(T)\, dT + \int_{V_1}^{V_2} \frac{a}{V^2}\, dV$$

$T_{guess} := 300 \cdot K$

$T_2 := root(\Delta U(T_{guess}), T_{guess})$

$T_2 = 575.147 \cdot K \qquad T_2 - T_1 = -4.853 \cdot K$

Joule-Thomson Expansion

The Joule-Thomson expansion is of considerable practical interest, being the operating principle of nearly all refrigeration equipment, as well as the effect generally used to liquefy gases. In this process, a gas is expanded through a throttle valve; the drop in pressure (usually) causes a drop in temperature. For this expansion, the enthalpy is constant: $\Delta H = 0$.

Example 2.15 Joule-Thomson inversion temperature.

Gases do not always cool when subjected to a Joule-Thomson expansion: if the Joule-Thomson coefficient (μ) is negative, the temperature will rise. The Joule-Thomson coefficient can be calculated as:

$$\mu = \frac{T\left(\frac{\partial V}{\partial T}\right)_P - V}{C_p} \tag{2.22}$$

This equation is difficult to evaluate for gas laws (such as vdw and RK) that are explicit in pressure, so we shall use the pressure virial series

$$V_m = \frac{RT}{P} + \beta + \gamma P + \cdots \tag{2.23}$$

(truncating to just that number of terms). These coefficients are related to the usual virial coefficients as:

$$\beta = B; \ \gamma = \frac{C - B^2}{RT} \tag{2.24}$$

Furthermore we shall use the RK forms for the virial coefficients.

Start a new document and recover the earlier results with File-menu Insert (*so2rk.mcd*). You should have definitions for the critical and heat-capacity constants for SO_2 as well as the RK gas law, the formulas for calculating a and b, etc. Enter the formulas for the virial coefficients and volume and test them.

$B(T) := b - \frac{a}{R \cdot T^{1.5}}$ $\quad C(T) := b^2 + \frac{a \cdot b}{R \cdot T^{1.5}}$ $\quad \gamma(T) := \frac{C(T) - B(T)^2}{R \cdot T}$

$B(300 \cdot K) = -0.294 \cdot liter$ $\quad C(300 \cdot K) = 0.015 \cdot liter^2$ $\quad \gamma(300 \cdot K) = -0.00291 \cdot \frac{liter}{atm}$

$V(P,T) := \frac{R \cdot T}{P} + B(T) + \gamma(T) \cdot P$ $\quad V(1 \cdot atm, 273.15 \cdot K) = 22.065 \cdot liter$

$V(10 \cdot atm, 500 \cdot K) = 3.986 \cdot liter$

Next we enter Eq. (2.22) for the Joule-Thomson coefficient and test it:

$$\mu(T,P) := \frac{T \cdot \frac{d}{dT} V(P,T) - V(P,T)}{C_{pm}(T)}$$

$\mu(300 \cdot K, 1 \cdot atm) = 2.058 \cdot \frac{K}{atm}$

$\mu(300 \cdot K, 20 \cdot atm) = 2.876 \cdot \frac{K}{atm}$

$\mu(2500 \cdot K, 1 \cdot atm) = -0.007 \cdot \frac{K}{atm}$

$T_{guess} := 2000 \cdot K$ $\quad T_{inv} := root\left(\mu\left(T_{guess}, 1 \cdot atm\right), T_{guess}\right)$ $\quad T_{inv} = 2240 \cdot K$

It should be evident that there is a change in sign above 2000 K; above this temperature, the gas will become warmer on expansion. The temperature where $\mu = 0$ is called the *inversion temperature*. Find this value using **root** (as shown in preceding box). The guess used does not quite yield the correct root, but it is close. Change T_{guess} to 2240 and the answer will be given as 2293; entering this value as a guess gives 2294. (If you check the value of μ at these temperatures you will see that it is quite small at 2240, but even smaller at 2294. The root would have been correct the first time if the value of *TOL* had been smaller.) At room temperature, there are only two gases with negative Joule-Thomson coefficients: H_2 and He. Clearly inversion is not a problem one need worry about with an ordinary refrigerator.

Example 2.16 Temperature drop on Joule-Thomson.

Sulfur dioxide is used as a refrigerant, but not usually in home refrigerators since it is quite noxious (you don't want it in your kitchen). First you must recover or re-enter the data for SO_2, and the formulas for the imperfection of an RK gas used earlier (page 54); if you saved the document you can recover it with File-menu Insert (file name: *so2rk.mcd*). We will calculate the final temperature for an expansion from 2.2 liter to 22 liter (per mole), starting at 30°C. After entering the initial data, set up an expression for $\Delta H(T)$, which will be equal to zero at the correct final temperature. Then provide a guess for the final temperature and use **root** to calculate it.

Joule-Thomson Expansion of SO_2 $T_{ice} := 273.15 \cdot K$ $C := K$

$T_1 := T_{ice} + 30 \cdot C$ $V_1 := 2.2 \cdot liter$ $V_2 := 22 \cdot liter$ $P(V_1, T_1) = 9.857 \cdot atm$

$$\Delta H(T_2) := \int_{T_1}^{T_2} C_{pm}(T)\,dT + H_i(V_2, T_2) - H_i(V_1, T_1)$$

$\Delta H(350 \cdot K) = 2.714 \cdot kJ$ $\Delta H(250 \cdot K) = -1.291 \cdot kJ$ $T_2 := 300 \cdot K$ ***estimate***

$T_2 := root(\Delta H(T_2), T_2)$ $T_2 = 283.248 \cdot K$ $P(V_2, T_2) = 1.041 \cdot atm$

$T_1 - T_{ice} = 30 \cdot C$ $T_2 - T_{ice} = 10.098 \cdot C$

The pressure calculations given are to demonstrate the magnitudes of pressure required for this degree of cooling, which is important for design, affecting the wall thickness of the tubing and the power of the compressor, and so forth. A symbol C is established as equal to K so temperatures in degrees Celsius can be labeled correctly, which does not mean or require that the Kelvin and Celsius temperatures are equal, only that the size of the degree is the same. This is a respectable temperature drop for a refrigerant; a smaller initial volume (greater compression), of course, would give a larger temperature drop (try it). After the fluid passes through the refrigerator, gaining heat in the process so as to cool the contents, it is compressed. Compression, of course, warms the gas considerably. Then it is cooled in heat exchange coils in contact with the room air. When cooled, it is expanded again for return to the refrigerator.

It is simple to alter the preceding calculation for other materials, and you should use this opportunity to explore what characteristics make a good refrigerant. The box below illustrates such a calculation for HCFC-22 ($CHClF_2$), another common refrigerant. (In the first line of this example we use the symbol R in its original meaning, degree Rankine, and later (3rd line) define it to be the gas constant. If it were necessary to use both symbols at the same time, we would have to use another symbol.)

$CHClF_2$ (HCFC-22)

$sph := 0.152 \cdot \frac{BTU}{lb \cdot R}$ ***at 30 C, 1 atm*** $T_c := (96.0 + 273.15) \cdot K$

$mw := 86.48 \cdot \frac{gm}{mole}$ $C_p := mw \cdot sph$ $C_p = 55.035 \cdot \frac{joule}{K}$ $P_c := 48.7 \cdot atm$

$R := 8.31451 \cdot \frac{joule}{K \cdot mole}$ $Tb := (273.15 - 48.8) \cdot K$ $DHv := mw \cdot 100.66 \cdot \frac{BTU}{lb}$

$kJ := 10^3 \cdot joule$ $DHv = 20.248 \cdot kJ$

Redlich-Kwong Equation of State

$$a := \frac{0.42748 \cdot R^2 \cdot T_c^{2.5}}{P_c} \qquad b := \frac{0.08664 \cdot R \cdot T_c}{P_c} \qquad P(V,T) := \frac{R \cdot T}{V - b} - \frac{a}{\sqrt{T} \cdot V \cdot (V + b)}$$

$$U_i(V,T) := \frac{3 \cdot a}{2 \cdot b \cdot \sqrt{T}} \cdot \ln\left(\frac{V}{V + b}\right) \qquad H_i(V,T) := U_i(V,T) + P(V,T) \cdot V - R \cdot T$$

Joule-Thomson Expansion $T_{ice} := 273.15 \cdot K$ $C := K$

$T_1 := T_{ice} + 30 \cdot C$ $V_1 := 2.2 \cdot liter$ $V_2 := 22 \cdot liter$ $P(V_1, T_1) = 9.799 \cdot atm$

$\Delta H(T_2) := C_p \cdot (T_2 - T_1) + H_i(V_2, T_2) - H_i(V_1, T_1)$ $T_e := 300 \cdot K$ ***estimate***

$T_2 := root(\Delta H(T_e), T_e)$ $T_2 = 287.816 \cdot K$ $P(V_2, T_2) = 1.057 \cdot atm$

$T_2 - T_1 = -15.334 \cdot K$ $T_2 - T_{ice} = 14.666 \cdot C$

In this case we used a constant value for the heat capacity (for 30 °C) since that is all that was available. However, for the small temperature range of this calculation this approximation should not cause too much error (on the other hand, we could not get a good value for the inversion temperature with only this value).

Chlorofluorocarbons (CFCs) have long been used as safe and effective refrigerants in the home and in vehicles. However, they are being phased out because they appear to do harm to the Earth's ozone layer. HCFCs, such as the one in this example, are being used as replacements. The data for this example were taken from an old reference (the 1961 Matheson Gas Data Book) with some quaint units (like BTU per lb per degree F for heat capacity); note that Mathcad has no problem with these units.

Problems

2.1 Make a graph of the heat capacity of carbon dioxide (Table 2.2, Noggle). Calculate ΔH for heating 5 kg of carbon dioxide from 300 K to 1500 K at constant pressure.

2.2 Use interpolation with the heat capacities (table) for titanium dioxide to calculate ΔH for heating 500 gm from 300 K to 2300 K (constant pressure). Make a graph of the interpolated heat capacity and data. Remember cal = 4.184 J.

Heat capacity of TiO_2	
T/K	C_{pm}/(cal/K)
200	10.053
300	13.191
500	15.429
1000	17.5
1500	18.99
2000	20.293
2500	21.771

2.3 One hundred grams of titanium dioxide has a temperature of 600 K. What would be the new temperature if 25 kJ of heat were removed? Use the interpolated heat capacity from the preceding problem.

2.4 Calculate the pressure and internal pressure of ethylene (C_2H_4) when 100 gm is placed in a 1-liter container at 300 K (use the RK gas law). Make a graph showing these quantities for 300 K (volumes from 0.1 to 1.9 liter).

2.5 For ethylene (C_2H_4), using the RK gas law, make a graph of the internal energy imperfection vs. volume at 300 K (volume range as in preceding problem). Calculate this quantity for volumes 0.1, 1.0 and 10 liter/mol.

2.6 Calculate ΔH when one mole of ethylene is heated and expanded from 300 K, 5 liter to 900 K, 15 liter assuming ideal gas and using the RK gas law. Calculate the pressures for the initial and final states. Note that if this were an ideal gas, the pressure would be constant.

2.7 Ethylene at 1 atm, 300 K, is compressed adiabatically and reversibly until the final pressure is 15 atm. Assuming ideal gas, calculate the final temperature.

2.8 Ethylene at 500 mL/mol, 500 K, undergoes a Joule-Thomson expansion to 39.4 liter/mol. Use the RK gas law to calculate the final temperature. Also, calculate the initial and final pressures.

Answers

2.1: 6967 kJ

2.2: 952 kJ

2.3: 278 K

2.4: 5.389 MPa, 7.440 MPa

2.5: -5.63, -0.655, -0.067 kJ/mol

2.6: $P_1 = 4.788$ atm, $P_2 = 4.925$ atm, $\Delta H = 41.873$ kJ (ideal), 42.052 kJ (RK)

2.7: 460 K

2.8: 480.33 K, 76.479 atm, 0.999 atm

Chapter 3

The Second and Third Laws of Thermodynamics

3.1 Entropy Change with Temperature

The change in entropy on changing temperature at constant pressure is given by

$$\Delta S = \int_{T_1}^{T_2} \frac{C_p}{T} dT \tag{3.1}$$

This calculation assumes that there is no phase change in the temperature interval. If there is a phase change, Eq. (3.1) is used up to the transition temperature, the entropy of the phase transition

$$\Delta S = \frac{\Delta H}{T} \tag{3.2}$$

is added, and the calculation using Eq. (3.1) is continued (using now the heat capacity of the new phase).

Example 3.1 ΔS and ΔH for melting 1 kg of aluminum.

We will calculate the change in enthalpy and entropy for melting aluminum, starting at room temperature. This problem might be of interest should you decide to go into the scrap-metal business. Because there is a phase transition, for both H and S we must calculate the change up to the melting temperature and then add the appropriate amounts for fusion.

Using the format developed in Chapter 2, enter the heat capacity constants for aluminum (solid) as shown.

Data for aluminum $C_{pm}(T) := \left(20.67 + 12.38 \cdot 10^{-3} \cdot \frac{T}{K}\right) \cdot \frac{joule}{K \cdot mole}$

$C_{pm}(500 \cdot K) = 26.86 \cdot \frac{joule}{K \cdot mole}$

Next enter the heat of fusion (given as 96 cal/g by a reference book) and the melting temperature (933.5 K). If the value for calorie is incorrect in your version of Mathcad, you must enter the new one.

$cal := 4.184 \cdot joule$ $\quad \Delta H_{fus} := 96 \cdot \frac{cal}{gm}$ $\quad n := \frac{1 \cdot kg}{26.98154 \cdot gm \cdot mole^{-1}}$

$kJ := 1000 \cdot joule$ $\quad T1 := 300 \cdot K$ $\quad T2 := 933.5 \cdot K$

$$\Delta H := n \cdot \int_{T1}^{T2} C_{pm}(T)\, dT + 1 \cdot kg \cdot \Delta H_{fus} \qquad \Delta H = 1.066 \cdot 10^{3} \cdot kJ$$

$$\Delta S := n \cdot \int_{T1}^{T2} \frac{C_{pm}(T)}{T}\, dT + \frac{1 \cdot kg \cdot \Delta H_{fus}}{T2} \qquad \Delta S = 1.591 \cdot 10^{3} \cdot \frac{joule}{K}$$

This example illustrates how to use data for different quantities (per mole and per gram). Remember that "mole" is not a true unit in Mathcad, so if you do this incorrectly you will get an incorrect answer without an error indication by the program.

Example 3.2 **ΔS for heating CO_2 at constant *V* or *P*.**

For heating at constant volume,

$$\Delta S = \int_{T_1}^{T_2} \frac{C_v}{T} dT \tag{3.3}$$

Enter coefficients for the heat capacity given below:

Data for carbon dioxide

$j := 1 .. 4$ $\quad c_j :=$

41.58
$15.6 \cdot 10^{-3}$
$-2.95 \cdot 10^{-6}$
$-7.97 \cdot 10^{5}$

$C_{pm}(T) := \left[c_1 + c_2 \cdot \frac{T}{K} + c_3 \cdot \left(\frac{T}{K}\right)^2 + c_4 \cdot \left(\frac{T}{K}\right)^{-2}\right] \cdot \frac{joule}{K \cdot mole}$

$C_{pm}(500 \cdot K) = 45.454 \cdot \frac{joule}{K \cdot mole}$

The calculation is as follows:

$kJ := 1000 \cdot joule \qquad T1 := 300 \cdot K \qquad T2 := 1200 \cdot K \qquad n := 1$

$R := 8.31451 \cdot \frac{joule}{K} \qquad C_{vm}(T) := C_{pm}(T) - R$

$\Delta Sv := n \cdot \int_{T1}^{T2} \frac{C_{vm}(T)}{T} \, dT \qquad \Delta Sv = 54.013 \cdot \frac{joule}{K}$ ***constant volume***

$\Delta Sp := n \cdot \int_{T1}^{T2} \frac{C_{pm}(T)}{T} \, dT \qquad \Delta Sp = 65.54 \cdot \frac{joule}{K}$ ***constant pressure***

As before, we use $C_{vm} = C_{pm} - R$ for an ideal gas.

Example 3.3 ΔS for heating OCS by data interpolation.

In Example 2.4 it was shown how heat capacity data could be integrated by interpolation. Recover or re-enter the data for OCS (file: *cp-ocs.mcd*). There are two approaches we could use: either make a new array for C_p/T for interpolation, or use the interpolation function for C_p made already. Since interpolation is more effective for smoothly varying functions, the choice may rest on which, C_p or C_p/T, is smoother. Look at the graphs (using the interpolation function, *Cpi*, as defined in Example 2.2):

$T := 300, 305 .. 3005$ ***Heat capacity of OCS (gas)***

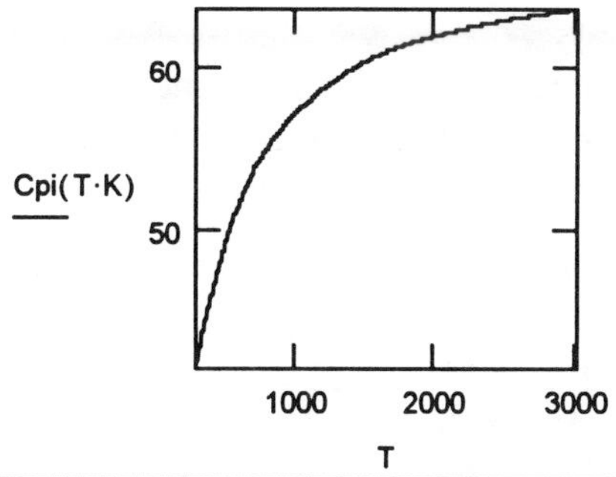

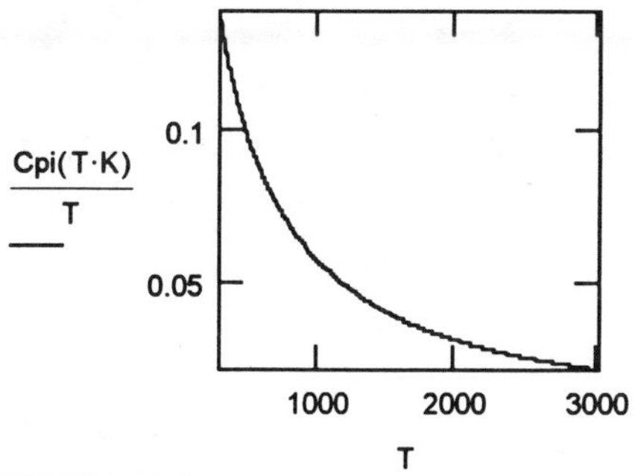

(Since the plot-range variable T is unitless, the argument for *Cpi* must include the unit.) There doesn't seem to be a big difference in this case, so we proceed with the *Cpi* function already made. The entropy change for heating at constant pressure is:

$$T_1 := 500 \cdot K \qquad T_2 := 1200 \cdot K \qquad n := \frac{1 \cdot kg}{mw}$$

$$\Delta H := n \cdot \int_{T_1}^{T_2} Cpi(T)\, dT \qquad \Delta H = 640.015 \cdot kJ$$

$$\Delta S := n \cdot \int_{T_1}^{T_2} \frac{Cpi(T)}{T}\, dT \qquad \Delta S = 790.515 \cdot \frac{J}{K}$$

constant pressure

For a constant-volume calculation, we must make some sort of assumption. Since these are low-pressure (i.e. ideal gas) heat capacities, we assume ideal gas and:

$$Cvi(T) := Cpi(T) - R$$

$$\Delta S := n \cdot \int_{T_1}^{T_2} \frac{Cvi(T)}{T}\, dT \qquad \Delta S = 669.351 \cdot \frac{J}{K}$$

constant V (ideal gas)

Both calculations are, of course, for 1 kg of the material.

3.2 Entropy of an Ideal Gas

The general formulas for the change in entropy with T and V or P are:

$$dS = \frac{C_v}{T}dT + \left(\frac{\partial P}{\partial T}\right)_V dV \quad \text{or} \quad dS = \frac{C_P}{T}dT - \left(\frac{\partial V}{\partial T}\right)_P dP \tag{3.4}$$

Either equation can be used, the choice being largely a matter of convenience. For example, in the previous section we used the first form for constant-volume heating and the second for constant-pressure heating, since then the second terms are zero in each case.

For an ideal gas (one mole) the required derivatives are:

$$\left(\frac{\partial P}{\partial T}\right)_V = \frac{R}{V} \quad \text{and} \quad \left(\frac{\partial V}{\partial T}\right)_V = \frac{R}{P}$$

These give two completely equivalent equations for the entropy change between state 1 (T_1, P_1, V_1) and state 2 (T_2, P_2, V_2) as:

$$\Delta S = \int_{T_1}^{T_2} \frac{C_v}{T}dT + R\ln\left[\frac{V_2}{V_1}\right] = \int_{T_1}^{T_2} \frac{C_P}{T}dT - R\ln\left[\frac{P_2}{P_1}\right] \tag{3.5}$$

The evaluation of Eq. (3.4) is much more difficult for real gases and this situation is best handled through the gas-imperfection method described below (Section 3.4).

Example 3.4 Entropy change of a monatomic ideal gas with *T* and *P*.

Calculations of entropy when none of the variables PVT are constant can be complicated. Here we consider a monatomic ideal gas for which these complications are minimal.

Calculate the change of entropy for a monatomic ideal gas when it is heated from 300 to 700 K while being compressed from 23 liter/mol to 6 liter/mol. Monatomic ideal gases (with closed electronic shells) all have heat capacity $C_{vm} = {}^3/_2 R$, independent of temperature. Thus the integration of Eq. (3.5) is very simple, and we will use the integrated formulas. The following gives the parameters for this example:

$T_1 := 300 \cdot K \quad T_2 := 700 \cdot K \quad n := 1 \cdot mole \quad V_1 := 23 \cdot liter \quad V_2 := 6 \cdot liter$

$R := 8.31451 \cdot \frac{joule}{K \cdot mole} \quad P_1 := \frac{n \cdot R \cdot T_1}{V_1} \quad P_2 := \frac{n \cdot R \cdot T_2}{V_2}$

$C_{vm} := 1.5 \cdot R$

$C_{pm} := C_{vm} + R \quad P_1 = 1.07 \cdot atm \quad P_2 = 9.573 \cdot atm$

The pressure is calculated for information and to compare the methods. We calculate the two terms of Eq. (3.5) separately to show their size.

$\Delta S_1 := C_{vm} \cdot \ln\left(\frac{T_2}{T_1}\right) \quad \Delta S_2 := R \cdot \ln\left(\frac{V_2}{V_1}\right)$

$\Delta S_1 = 10.567 \cdot \frac{joule}{K} \quad \Delta S_2 = -11.172 \cdot \frac{joule}{K} \quad \Delta S_1 + \Delta S_2 = -0.605 \cdot \frac{joule}{K}$

$C_{pm} \cdot \ln\left(\frac{T_2}{T_1}\right) - R \cdot \ln\left(\frac{P_2}{P_1}\right) = -0.605 \cdot \frac{joule}{K}$

The last calculation demonstrates that the second form of Eq. (3.5) gives the same answer. This is the same value as before. For an ideal gas it doesn't matter which form of Eq. (3.4) is used, but for condensed phases and real gases one is usually more convenient than the other.

There is considerable cancellation in this calculation and the net entropy change is very nearly zero. For an *adiabatic reversible expansion* (Section 2.6) $\Delta S = 0$. For the same temperature change, what would be the new volume if the process were adiabatic and reversible? The calculated value (box to right) is quite close to the one we used.

Given

$C_{vm} \cdot \ln\left(\frac{T_2}{T_1}\right) + R \cdot \ln\left(\frac{V_2}{V_1}\right) = 0$

$\text{Find}(V_2) = 6.453 \cdot liter$

3.3 Third Law Entropy

Unlike internal energy and enthalpy, absolute values of entropy can be determined either by integration of heat capacity from 0 kelvin (3rd law entropy) or by statistical calculation (Chapter 5). Such entropies are generally given for the standard state. For gases, the standard state is the ideal gas at the standard pressure, P^o = 1 bar. For solids and liquids, the standard state is the material at 1 bar (not significantly different from the older standard state, 1 atm).

Example 3.5 Entropy of benzene. Importing data.

In this example we shall determine the standard entropy of benzene (C_6H_6, liquid) at 298.15 K from measured heat capacities and the third law of thermodynamics. The example also explains how to import data from disk files and spreadsheets.

The data on Table 3.1 are for C_p of solid benzene (unit: cal K^{-1} mol^{-1}); the value at 0 K is, of course, not measured; it is the theoretical value. In addition we have the heat of fusion at the melting point T_m = 278.69 K which is $\Delta_f H$ = 2358.1 cal/mol, and the heat capacity of the liquid: 31.52 cal K^{-1} mol^{-1} at 278.69 K and 32.52 cal K^{-1} mol^{-1} at 298.15 K.

Table 3.1 Heat capacity of benzene (solid) vs. temperature. Unit: cal K^{-1} mol^{-1}.

T/K	C_{pm}	*T*/K	C_{pm}	*T*/K	C_{pm}
0	0	40	6.340	140	14.70
13	0.685	50	7.885	160	16.23
14	0.830	60	9.065	180	18.02
15	0.996	70	9.975	200	20.01
20	2.000	80	10.75	220	22.32
25	3.145	90	11.43	240	24.88
30	4.300	100	12.05	260	27.76
35	5.385	120	13.31	278.69	30.76

Data can be imported from a text file, which you can prepare from the data on the table. This can be done with any text editor — Windows Notepad is a good one to use. (If you use a word processor, be sure to save it as a text file, thus omitting the formatting information all word processors include in their files.). Enter the data with one *T*, C_p pair per line, separated by commas or spaces. To read these data into Mathcad from a text file, type:

```
M:READPRN(bdata)
```

Here *bdata* is either the name of a disk file (with extension .PRN) or it is the name of a Mathcad variable that, for the moment, has no meaning. If *bdata* is not the name of a .PRN file in the current directory, you must execute File-menu, Associate. Type the name of the variable (*bdata*) in the box at the top; then click on the file containing the data, or type its name into the File-Name box; click "OK" to return to the document. To confirm that the data have been read correctly, type "`M=`"; the display takes a lot of space so you may want to delete it after confirming that the data are correct.

To import data directly from a compatible spreadsheet (the current Windows versions of Lotus 123, QuattroPro or Excel should work), in the spreadsheet program, place the data in side-by-side columns; select these columns and copy into the clipboard. In Mathcad, type "`M:`"; then, while the cursor is in the placeholder, select Edit-menu, Paste Special. The name of your spreadsheet should be in the box (if not, this may not work), but you want to select Numerical. Click on Paste. You should see the data displayed on the screen. (Alternatively you could import the *x*- and *y*-data separately, making the procedure in the next paragraph unnecessary.)

By either method, the data are now in a matrix having 2 columns and 24 rows. The columns of a matrix are specified using ctrl+6 (that is, control caret). Type "`M ctrl+6 0=`" and "`M ctrl+6 1=`" (do not type quotes, spaces or plus; Mathcad displays these as $M^{<0>}$ and

$M^{<1>}$). Because the data arrays for this problem are very large, a simple example is given to illustrate the point:

$$M := \begin{bmatrix} 1 & 5.6 \\ 2 & 7.8 \\ 3 & 8.9 \\ 4 & 11.1 \end{bmatrix} \qquad M^{<0>} = \begin{bmatrix} 1 \\ 2 \\ 3 \\ 4 \end{bmatrix} \qquad M^{<1>} = \begin{bmatrix} 5.6 \\ 7.8 \\ 8.9 \\ 11.1 \end{bmatrix}$$

$M_{0,0} = 1 \qquad M_{0,1} = 5.6 \qquad M_{1,0} = 2 \qquad M_{3,1} = 11.1$ Indices for row, column

The last line shows how to address individual elements of the matrix: type "`M[0,0=`" for the first example; the subscripts are for row and column in that order. At the moment, we are only interested in separating the columns since these from the *xy* data for our example.

The absolute entropy is calculated by evaluating the integral

$$\Delta S_1 = \int_0^{T_m} \frac{C_p}{T} dT \tag{3.6}$$

up to the melting point (T_m). Then the entropy of fusion is added:

$$\Delta S_2 = \frac{\Delta_f H}{T_m} \tag{3.7}$$

Finally the entropy change for heating the liquid to 298.15 K is added (ΔS_3), calculated with Eq. (3.6). If the material were a gas at the final temperature, you would need to add the enthalpy of vaporization and a correction to the ideal-gas standard state.

Heat-capacity measurements cannot, of course, be made down to 0 K. Traditionally, the region between 0 K and the lowest temperature (T^*) at which the heat capacity was measured is evaluated using the Debye *T*-cube law, which states that, at low temperature, the heat capacity is proportional to the cube of the Kelvin temperature —

$$C_p = aT^3 \tag{3.8}$$

(*a* is a constant of proportionality). If the Debye law is obeyed, the entropy at T^* is just 1/3 of the heat capacity at that temperature:

$$S(T^*) = \tfrac{1}{3} C_p{}^* \tag{3.9}$$

where $C_p{}^*$ is the heat capacity at T^*. We shall use an alternative method: Using the theoretical result that C_p and C_p/T are zero at $T = 0$, we shall evaluate the integral of Eq. (3.6) directly by interpolation. There is one small problem: we have data for C_p and T, but the ratio of the first two points is 0/0 — indeterminate to the computer. As it happens, Mathcad (unlike most other such programs) simply evaluates 0/0 as 0, so the problem is taken care of.

$M := \text{READPRN}(bdata) \qquad J := \text{joule} \qquad cal := 4.184 \cdot J$

$Tx := M^{<0>} \qquad Cpx := M^{<1>} \qquad li := \text{last}(Tx)$

$T_m := Tx_{li} \qquad T_m = 278.69$

First, enter the data as given above, and separate the columns for temperature (*Tx*) and heat capacity (*Cpx*) (box left). We also define units, but we will not use them until after the main calculation is done. The last statement of the 2nd line uses the Mathcad function **last** to determine the index number (*li*) for the last element of the index array, and the last line uses that index to extract the melting temperature (T_m) from that array. Note that T_m uses a literal subscript while Tx_i has an index subscript; thus the first statement on the last line is typed "`T.m:Tx[li`".

Mathcad does not permit division of arrays (an operation not defined in vector algebra) so we must do it element by element (box to right); use the last-index variable (*li*) to define a range variable *i*, create the vector **vy**. (All subscripts here are index subscripts, created with the left bracket: "[".) The interpolation array (*vs*) can be made using either **cspline**, **pspline** or **lspline**, which use different methods to interpolate the end-points of the cubic spline (*cubic*, *parabolic* and *linear* respectively). You should try them all, comparing the results.

$i := 0 .. li$

$$vy_i := \frac{Cpx_i}{Tx_i} \qquad vs := \text{pspline}(Tx, vy)$$

Choices
cspline
pspline
lspline

$$f(T) := \text{interp}(vs, Tx, vy, T)$$

It is very important to examine the low-temperature range of the interpolated function. For some data sets and interpolation methods, you may find peculiar behavior — and irregular curve, or a curve that dips into the negative region (heat capacity is never negative and an integral evaluated with such a function will be incorrect). This curve (box to right) is very acceptable. If it were not, then the *T*-cube law should be used to calculate the entropy up to the first measured temperature (13 K in this case), and the interpolated function used to calculate the entropy above that temperature. Next, look at the interpolated function for the entire range.

$T := 0, 1 .. 30$

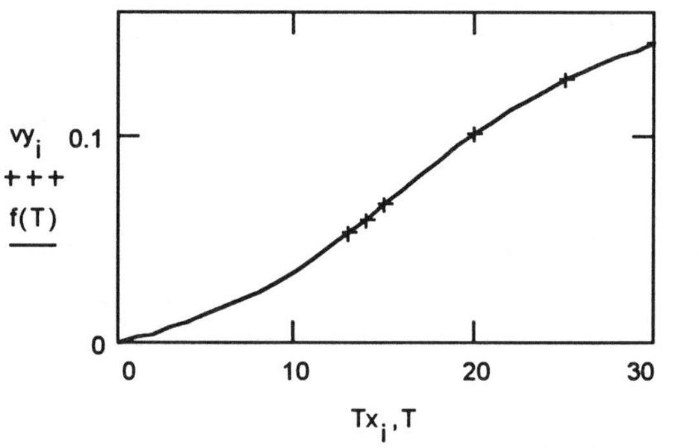

$T := 0, 1 .. T_m$

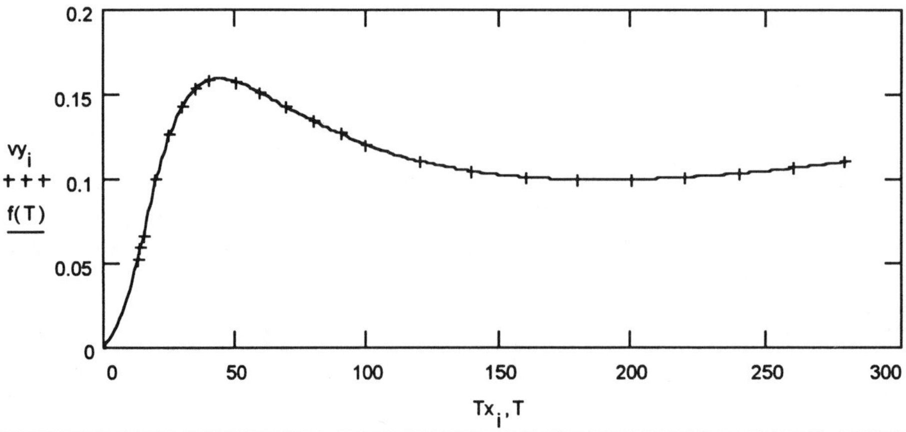

Since interpolation does no smoothing, if there were a lot of random error (noise) in the data you might see an irregular curve. In this case, the interpolated curve is smooth and realistic.

The entropy up to the melting point is calculated with Eq. (3.6) using the interpolated function *f*. The entropy of fusion is calculated with Eq. (3.7). Since there are only two data for the heat capacity of the liquid, we cannot do better than to use the mean-value theorem

$$\Delta S_3 = \overline{C_p}\,\ln\left[\frac{298.15}{T_m}\right]$$

where $\overline{C_p}$ is the mean of the two values given. The box following shows all of these calculations.

$$\Delta S_1 := \int_0^{T_m} f(T)\,dT \qquad \Delta S_1 = 30.845 \qquad \Delta S_2 := \frac{2358.1}{T_m} \qquad \Delta S_1 = 30.845$$

$$\Delta S_2 = 8.461$$

$$\Delta S_3 := \frac{32.52 + 31.52}{2}\cdot\ln\left(\frac{298.15}{T_m}\right) \qquad \Delta S_3 = 2.161$$

$$S := \left(\Delta S_1 + \Delta S_2 + \Delta S_3\right)\cdot\frac{cal}{K} \qquad S = 173.500\cdot\frac{J}{K}$$

The observed value for the standard entropy at 298.15 K is 173 J K^{-1} mol^{-1}. Demonstrate that the other methods of interpolation give for these data: **cspline** 173.613, **lspline** 173.573.

$$\frac{Cpx_1}{3} = 0.228$$

$$\int_0^{13} f(T)\,dT = 0.278$$

Compare the result up to the first measured temperature (13 K) to the Debye *T*-cubed law prediction of Eq. (3.9) (box to left). If we had used the *T*-cube law, the entropy would have been 0.05 cal/K (0.21 J/K) lower; slightly closer to the given value, but not significantly so. The smoothness of the extrapolation, and the fact that the *T*-cube law is not strictly applicable to this material (it is derived for atomic crystals), inclines us to accept the current, interpolated result.

Mathcad also has commands **WRITEPRN** to write data to files (in the format used by **READPRN**), and **READ** and **WRITE** for simple lists of numbers. The latter two are illustrated in the box to the right For this example, the disk file will be named "test.dat". Multicolumn data (such as we used above) is saved with **WRITEPRN** and read (as we have seen) with **READPRN**. The default extension then is ".prn". For more detail, see the Mathcad manual or help screens.

$j := 0..5$

$A_j :=$ 1.2, 2.3, 4.5, 5.6, 6.7, 7.8

$WRITE(test) := A$

$B_j := READ(test)$

$$B = \begin{bmatrix} 1.2 \\ 2.3 \\ 4.5 \\ 5.6 \\ 6.7 \\ 7.8 \end{bmatrix}$$

Example 3.6 Standard entropy of silver at 850 K.

Standard entropies are commonly tabulated for a particular temperature (T_{ref}), typically 298.15 K. Calculating this quantity at another temperature involves a calculation using Eq. (3.1) since standard state implies a specific pressure, $P^o = 1$ bar, so we are calculating a change at constant pressure. We start with the usual formula for heat capacity (here with constants from Table 2.2):

$j := 1..4$ Data for silver, Ag(solid)

$$c_j := \begin{bmatrix} 21.3 \\ 8.54\cdot 10^{-3} \\ 0\cdot 10^{-6} \\ -1.5\cdot 10^{5} \end{bmatrix}$$

$$C_{pm}(T) := \left[c_1 + c_2\cdot\frac{T}{K} + c_3\cdot\left(\frac{T}{K}\right)^2 + c_4\cdot\left(\frac{T}{K}\right)^{-2}\right]\cdot\frac{joule}{K\cdot mole}$$

$$C_{pm}(300\cdot K) = 22.195\cdot\frac{joule}{K\cdot mole} \qquad C_{pm}(1000\cdot K) = 29.69\cdot\frac{joule}{K\cdot mole}$$

The calculation of the standard entropy at 850 K (box to right) is very similar to the calculation of Examples 3.1 and 3.2, except that the entropy at the lower limit is known. Formulas for constant-pressure heating are used because standard state implies a particular pressure (1 bar). These are all standard entropies (S^o is a symbol not possible in Mathcad).

$$S_{ref} := 42.55\cdot\frac{joule}{K\cdot mole} \qquad T_{ref} := 298.15\cdot K \qquad T := 850\cdot K$$

$$S := S_{ref} + \int_{T_{ref}}^{T}\frac{C_{pm}(T)}{T}\,dT \qquad S = 68.838\cdot\frac{joule}{K\cdot mole}$$

Entropy Change With Pressure

The standard entropy is the entropy of the material at 1 bar. In this section we explore how to determine entropies in other states from the standard entropy, for ideal gases and condensed phases.

Example 3.7 Entropy change with pressure for an ideal gas.

For an ideal gas, using Eq. (3.4) it is readily shown that the entropy relative to the standard entropy is:

$$S(P,T) = S^0(T) - R\ln\frac{P}{P^o} \tag{3.10}$$

The following example is for argon, a monatomic gas, but the only difference for a polyatomic ideal gas would be the necessity to use temperature-dependent heat capacity and to integrate the (C_p/T) term.

Calculate the molar entropy of Ar at 578 K under a pressure of 1000 psi. Tables (such as those in Noggle) typically give the standard entropy at 298.15 K: this value (called S_{ref}, below) is 154.853 J/(K mol). We must calculate the change in entropy due to the change in temperature, Eq. (3.1) and pressure, Eq. (3.10), and add these two.

$bar := 10^5 \cdot Pa$ $\quad R := 8.31451 \cdot \frac{joule}{K \cdot mole}$ $\quad T_{ref} := 298.15 \cdot K$

$C_{pm} := 2.5 \cdot R$ $\quad S_{ref} := 154.853 \cdot joule \cdot K^{-1} \cdot mole^{-1}$

$P_{std} := 1 \cdot bar$ $\quad P := 1000 \cdot psi$ $\quad T := 578 \cdot K$

$S := S_{ref} + C_{pm} \cdot \ln\left(\frac{T}{T_{ref}}\right) - R \cdot \ln\left(\frac{P}{P_{std}}\right)$ $\quad S = 133.415 \cdot \frac{joule}{K \cdot mole}$

A similar calculation for a polyatomic ideal gas would need to take into account the temperature dependence of the heat capacity.

Example 3.8 Entropy change with pressure, condensed phase (Hg).

For condensed phases it is convenient to use the coefficient of thermal expansion (α) and:

$$\left(\frac{\partial S}{\partial P}\right)_T = -\left(\frac{\partial V}{\partial T}\right)_P = -V\alpha \tag{3.11}$$

For moderate pressures it is often accurate enough to assume that the material is incompressible and, hence, V is independent of pressure. However, using Mathcad, if the isothermal compressibility of the material is known, it is only slightly more trouble to assume

$$V = V_0(1 - \kappa_T P) \tag{3.12}$$

where V_0 is the volume at low pressure (assumed negligible in Eq. (3.12)).

Calculate the entropy of mercury (Hg, liquid) at 298.15 K under a pressure of 18 ton per square inch. (The ton = 2000 lb is recognized by Mathcad; it also has the metric ton, tonne = 1000 kg). Enter data as below:

$S_{ref} := 76.02 \cdot \frac{joule}{K \cdot mole}$ $\quad \alpha := 0.0567 \cdot 10^{-3} \cdot K^{-1}$ $\quad \kappa_T := 3.9 \cdot 10^{-6} \cdot atm^{-1}$

$V_0 := 14.8 \cdot \frac{cm^3}{mole}$ $\quad bar := 10^5 \cdot Pa$ $\quad P_{std} := 1 \cdot bar$

Define a function for entropy as a function of pressure, then calculate the new pressure and entropy (g is the acceleration of gravity).

$mass := 18 \cdot ton$

$area := 1 \cdot in^2$

$S(P) := S_{ref} - \alpha \cdot V_0 \cdot \int_{P_{std}}^{P} (1 - \kappa_T P)\, dP$

$P := \frac{mass \cdot g}{area}$ $\quad P = 2.482 \cdot 10^3 \cdot bar$ $\quad S(P) = 75.813 \cdot \frac{joule}{K \cdot mole}$

Comparing to the standard entropy (76.02), the change is quite modest for such a large pressure. It is not unreasonable to assume that the entropy (and enthalpy as well) of condensed phases is independent of pressure for moderate changes.

3.4 Entropy of Real Gases

The entropy of a gas relative to the ideal-gas standard state is:

$$S(P,T) = S^0(T) - R\ln\left[\frac{P}{P^o}\right] + S_i(P,T) \qquad (3.13)$$

The first two terms on the right-hand side should be recognizable as the ideal gas case (Example 3.4, above); S_i is the *entropy imperfection* which is calculated as:

$$S_i(P,T) = \int_0^P \left[\frac{R}{P} - \left(\frac{\partial V}{\partial T}\right)_P\right] dP \qquad (3.14)$$

(Derivation in Noggle, Section 3.7.) Since derivatives of V are difficult to handle for some gas laws, equations with V as the independent variable are often more convenient:

$$S(V,T) = S^0(T) + R\ln\left[\frac{P^o V_m}{RT}\right] + S_i(V,T) \qquad (3.15)$$

For this equation we must use the imperfection formula:

$$S_i(V,T) = \int_\infty^V \left[\left(\frac{\partial P}{\partial T}\right)_V - \frac{R}{V}\right] dV \qquad (3.16)$$

The entropy imperfection for a virial series and the van der Waals equation of state are worked out in Noggle, Examples 3.23 and 3.25. The results for RK are given in Table 3.3, Noggle. Since RK usually works better for such calculations than van der Waals, we shall use it for most of the calculations.

Example 3.9 Entropy imperfection using the RK law.

Enter (or recover) the formulas for the RK law (*rkimp.mcd*, developed in Chapter 2), and add unit definitions and data for ammonia (NH_3).

$J := \text{joule} \quad kJ := 10^3 \cdot J \quad bar := 10^5 \cdot Pa \quad MPa := 10^6 \cdot Pa$

$T_{ref} := 298.15 \cdot K \quad P_{std} := 1 \cdot bar \quad R := 8.31451 \cdot \frac{J}{K \cdot mole}$

$T_c := 405.3 \cdot K \quad P_c := 11.30 \cdot MPa \quad S_{ref} := 192.45 \cdot \frac{J}{K \cdot mole}$ ***Data for ammonia***

$a := \frac{0.42748 \cdot R^2 \cdot T_c^{2.5}}{P_c} \quad b := \frac{0.08664 \cdot R \cdot T_c}{P_c} \quad P(V,T) := \frac{R \cdot T}{V - b} - \frac{a}{\sqrt{T} \cdot V \cdot (V + b)}$

S_{ref} is the standard entropy at the reference temperature, 298.15 K in this case. Next, enter the formula for the RK entropy imperfection and calculate some test values.

$$S_i(V,T) := \frac{a}{2 \cdot b \cdot T^{1.5}} \cdot \ln\left(\frac{V}{V + b}\right) - R \cdot \ln\left(\frac{V}{V - b}\right)$$

$S_i(22.4 \cdot liter, 273 \cdot K) = -0.052 \cdot \frac{J}{K \cdot mole} \qquad S_i(1 \cdot liter, 500 \cdot K) = -0.600 \cdot \frac{J}{K \cdot mole}$

$S_i(1 \cdot liter, 250 \cdot K) = -1.298 \cdot \frac{J}{K \cdot mole} \qquad S_i(5 \cdot liter, 1500 \cdot K) = -0.058 \cdot \frac{J}{K \cdot mole}$

After testing, save the file as *rkimp.mcd* for use in Chapter 4.

Now we can obtain a formula for the entropy as a function of volume and temperature. First we need the heat capacity formula for ammonia:

$j := 1..4 \quad c_j :=$ ***Data for ammonia***

29.75
$25.10 \cdot 10^{-3}$
$0 \cdot 10^{-6}$
$-1.55 \cdot 10^5$

$$C_{pm}(T) := \left[c_1 + c_2 \cdot \frac{T}{K} + c_3 \cdot \left(\frac{T}{K}\right)^2 + c_4 \cdot \left(\frac{T}{K}\right)^{-2}\right] \cdot \frac{J}{K \cdot mole}$$

$$C_{vm}(T) := C_{pm}(T) - R$$

$$S(V,T) := S_{ref} + \int_{T_{ref}}^{T} \frac{C_{pm}(T)}{T}\, dT + R \cdot \ln\left(\frac{P_{std} \cdot V}{R \cdot T}\right) + S_i(V,T)$$

Save this file under another name (File-menu, Save as). Calculate the entropy at 1 bar, 298.15 K. Why is it different from the reference entropy?

$Px := P_{std} \qquad T := T_{ref} \qquad V_{id} := \frac{R \cdot T}{Px}$

$V := root\left(P\left(V_{id}, T\right) - Px, V_{id}\right) \qquad V = 24.612 \cdot liter$

$S(V,T) - S_{ref} = -0.103 \cdot \frac{J}{K \cdot mole} \qquad S_i(V,T) = -0.043 \cdot \frac{J}{K \cdot mole}$

This differs from the standard entropy because the gas is not ideal, but the difference is small. Note that the imperfection, S_i, accounts for only part of the difference: there is also a difference because the V in the second term of Eq. (3.15) is not the ideal-gas volume. For this reason, you must be careful to distinguish between Eqs. (3.14) and (3.16) for S_i — they are not interchangeable and have a different relationship to S, given by Eqs. (3.13) and (3.15) respectively.

The use of **root** for solving for volume, as illustrated above and elsewhere, occasionally fails to give correct answers. If you have a problem, use the **Given ... Find** method illustrated below; it seems to be generally more robust than **root**. In some cases you may need a more accurate estimate than that given by the ideal-gas volume, and for high pressures a guess slightly larger than the b constant may work better.

Calculate the entropy of ammonia at 500 bar, 450 K and compare to the ideal-gas prediction.

$Px := 500 \cdot bar \qquad T := 450 \cdot K \qquad V_{id} := \frac{R \cdot T}{Px}$

Given $\quad P\left(V_{id}, T\right) = Px \qquad V := Find\left(V_{id}\right) \qquad V = 49.111 \cdot mL$

$S(V,T) = 139.225 \cdot \frac{J}{K \cdot mole} \qquad S_i(V,T) = -13.621 \cdot \frac{J}{K \cdot mole}$

Ideal gas

$$S_{ref} + \int_{T_{ref}}^{T} \frac{C_{pm}(T)}{T} \, dT - R \cdot \ln\left(\frac{Px}{P_{std}}\right) = 156.348 \cdot \frac{J}{K \cdot mole}$$

The last line shows how far off the ideal-gas equation is for this example; again the entropy imperfection (S_i) accounts for only part of the difference. Save this work (*rknh3.mcd*).

Example 3.10 Adiabatic reversible expansion of a real gas.

For an adiabatic reversible expansion, $\Delta S = 0$. In Chapter 2 we learned how to make this calculation for an ideal gas. Now we have the tools to do it for a real gas.

Recover the file from the preceding example (*rknh3.mcd*). For an adiabatic reversible expansion starting at 700 K, 1 liter/mole and expanding to 25 liter/mole, we make a guess for the final temperature of 300 K. First, do the calculation for an ideal gas. Then, calculate for the real gas by setting the entropy function for the two states equal (box to right).

In this example the ideal-gas estimate is fairly accurate; this is likely to be the case so long at the gas does not approach liquefaction. (Pressures are calculated for information only.) (The equal signs inside **Given ... Find** are logical equals: ctrl+=.)

Adiabatic Reversible Expansion

$V_1 := 1\cdot \text{liter}$ $T_1 := 700\cdot K$

$V_2 := 25\cdot \text{liter}$ $T_2 := 300\cdot K$ ***(guess)***

Given $$\int_{T_1}^{T_2} \frac{C_{vm}(T)}{T}\, dT = -R\cdot \ln\left(\frac{V_2}{V_1}\right)$$

$\text{Find}(T_2) = 308.17\cdot K$ ***Ideal gas***

Given $S(V_1, T_1) = S(V_2, T_2)$ ***RK gas***

$T_{ad} := \text{Find}(T_2)$ $T_{ad} = 303.636\cdot K$

$P(V_2, T_{ad}) = 1.003\cdot \text{bar}$

Problems

3.1 Calculate the change in entropy when 7.6 moles of carbon dioxide is heated from 300 to 1200 K (a) at constant pressure and (b) at constant volume. Use formula for C_{pm} as on Table 2.2, Noggle.

3.2 Lead melts at 600.58 K, with an enthalpy of fusion 1151 cal/mol (cal = 4.184 J). The table to the right gives the heat capacities solid and liquid Pb. Calculate ΔH and $\Delta \underline{S}$ for heating 1 kg Pb from 298.15 to 1000 K.

Heat capacity of Pb (solid) cal/(K mol)		Heat Capacity of Pb (liquid) cal/(K mol)	
T	C_{pm}	T	C_{pm}
298.15	6.414	600	7.322
400	6.626	700	7.250
500	6.821	800	7.174
600	7.028	1000	7.026

3.3 Use data from the table for the heat capacity of KCl (table, below) to calculate the entropy of KCl at 298.15 K.

3.4 The standard entropy of Pb at 298.15 K is 64.81 J/(K mol). Calculate the standard entropy of liquid Pb at its melting point. Use data from problem 3.2

3.5 The standard entropy of chlorine is 223.066 J/(K mol) at 298.15 K. Use the RK gas law and heat capacity formula (e.g. Table 2.2, Noggle) to calculate the entropy of this gas at 500 K, V_m = 4 liter/mol. What is the pressure?

3.6 Chlorine at 300 K, 3.81 liter/mol is compressed adiabatically and reversibly until the volume is 0.6 liter/mol. Calculate the final temperature using (a) ideal gas and (b) RK. (c) Calculate the initial and final pressures using the RK law.

Heat capacity of KCl in cal/(K mol)					
T	C_{pm}	T	C_{pm}	T	C_{pm}
0	0	17.09	0.458	116.47	10.03
2.345	0.000936	21.21	0.842	158.02	11.06
3.52	0.00338	32.41	2.36	205.23	11.64
5.14	0.0101	44.25	4.189	246.41	11.98
7.89	0.039	69.92	7.365	273.34	12.16
10.06	0.0838	89.28	8.844	284.68	12.23
14.73	0.31				

Answers

3.1: (a) 498.1 (b) 410.5 J/K

3.2: 122.15 kJ, 207.25 J/K

3.3: 82.653 J/(K mol)

3.4: 92.42 J/(K mol)

3.5: 221.564 J/(K mol), 9.986 atm

3.6: (ideal) 530.1 K (RK) 549.1 K; RK pressures 6.00 atm, 62.3 atm

CHAPTER 4

PHASE EQUILIBRIUM

4.1 The Clausius-Clapeyron Equation

The Clausius-Clapeyron equation gives a relationship between P and T for two phases in equilibrium, when one of the phases is a gas:

$$\frac{d(\ln P)}{dT} = \frac{\Delta H}{RT^2} \tag{4.1}$$

ΔH is the enthalpy of vaporization (or sublimation, if the condensed phase is a solid). This equation can be integrated easily by assuming that the enthalpy of vaporization is constant (independent of temperature):

$$\ln\left[\frac{P_2}{P_1}\right] = \frac{-\Delta H}{R}\left[\frac{1}{T_2} - \frac{1}{T_1}\right] \tag{4.2}$$

This equation is very useful for interpolating vapor pressures and, if used cautiously (for ΔH is not constant with temperature), for extrapolation.

Example 4.1 Estimate vapor pressure from boiling-point data.

Many texts and reference books have tables (like Table 4.2, Noggle) which list the normal (1-atm) boiling temperature and enthalpy of vaporization for a number of liquids. We will use data of that sort to estimate the vapor pressure of $CClF_3$ at 150 K. The known quantities are T_1 (the 1-atm boiling point), P_1 (1 atm) and the enthalpy of vaporization. You must provide either of the other two quantities, T_2 in this case, and solve for the other.

It is easy enough to solve the Eq. (4.2) algebraically for the unknown, but we will solve for it numerically using a **Given ... Find** block (box to right). This procedure has the advantage that it can be adapted to other such problems with minimal changes. The "estimate" for the final pressure is mandatory because a numerical procedure is being used, but any guess within reason should work. If in doubt, substitute the found value (last line) for the guess and see if you get the same answer again.

$J := joule \quad kJ := 1000 \cdot J \quad R := 8.31451 \cdot \frac{J}{K}$

$T_1 := 191.8 \cdot K \quad P_1 := 1 \cdot atm \quad \Delta H := 15.50 \cdot kJ$

$T_2 := 150 \cdot K \quad P_2 := 1 \cdot atm$ ***estimate***

Given

$$\ln\left(\frac{P_2}{P_1}\right) = \frac{-\Delta H}{R} \cdot \left(\frac{1}{T_2} - \frac{1}{T_1}\right)$$

$\mathrm{Find}(P_2) = 50.643 \cdot torr$

Example 4.2 Interpolation and extrapolation of vapor-pressure data.

Reference books usually list boiling points for a particular series of pressures so, if you need a boiling point at a different pressure, or want to find the pressure that gives a particular temperature, you must interpolate the data on the table. In this example, we calculate values that are found on the table in order to check the accuracy of Eq. (4.2) for such calculations.

The following are data for chloroform ($CHCl_3$). Since temperatures are given in Celsius, we define a symbol C as equal (in size) to K; this is done only so numbers can be added and labeled correctly, and should not be read to imply that the Celsius and Kelvin scales are identical.

$T_{ice} := 273.15 \cdot K \quad C := K \quad J := joule \quad kJ := 1000 \cdot J$

$P_1 := 20 \cdot torr \quad T_1 := T_{ice} - 19.0 \cdot C \quad R := 8.31451 \cdot \frac{J}{K}$

$P_2 := 60 \cdot torr \quad T_2 := T_{ice} + 0.5 \cdot C$

We use the same procedure as in Example 4.1 to calculate the enthalpy of vaporization (although the algebra to solve for it is trivial), but because we are using a numerical procedure we must supply a starting value (see box to right).

$\Delta H := 5 \cdot kJ$ ***need any starting value***

Given

$$\ln\left(\frac{P_2}{P_1}\right) = \frac{-\Delta H}{R} \cdot \left(\frac{1}{T_2} - \frac{1}{T_1}\right)$$

$\Delta H := \mathrm{Find}(\Delta H) \quad \Delta H = 32.579 \cdot kJ$

$P_2 := 40 \cdot torr$

Given

$$\ln\left(\frac{P_2}{P_1}\right) = \frac{-\Delta H}{R} \cdot \left(\frac{1}{T_2} - \frac{1}{T_1}\right)$$

$T_2 := Find(T_2)$ ***observed value***

$T_2 = 266.114 \cdot K$ $\quad T_{ice} - 7.1 \cdot C = 266.05 \cdot K$

With this we can calculate the boiling temperature for 40 torr; indeed, you will find it simplest to copy, paste and edit the previous work (box to left). As you can see, the accuracy is very good, demonstrating that Eq. (4.2) is effective for interpolation (but provided the two points given are sufficiently close to each other).

Estimate the boiling point for 1 atm (box to right). This is an extrapolation because the point calculated is not between the 2 known points. Extrapolation is much riskier than interpolation because the assumption that the enthalpy of vaporization is independent of temperature is bound to break down eventually. Depending on the accuracy required, this may still be a perfectly acceptable estimate.

$P_2 := 1 \cdot atm$

Given

$$\ln\left(\frac{P_2}{P_1}\right) = \frac{-\Delta H}{R} \cdot \left(\frac{1}{T_2} - \frac{1}{T_1}\right)$$

$T_2 := Find(T_2)$

observed value

$T_2 = 332.633 \cdot K$ $\quad T_{ice} + 61.3 \cdot C = 334.45 \cdot K$

Example 4.3 Temperature dependence of the enthalpy of vaporization.

A better relationship between T and P in a vaporization equilibrium can be obtained by considering the explicit dependence of ΔH on temperature in Eq. (4.1). For the vaporization of liquid nitrogen, the enthalpy is approximately represented by a linear equation (given in box below). We use this in Eq. (4.1), integrating from a known point (in this case, the normal boiling point of nitrogen) to an indefinite temperature. For simplicity, we do this example without units, so we must be careful to get them right. For example, since ΔH is in J, we must use R in J/K. If the first pressure ($P1$) is in atm, the final pressure is also in that unit.

$\Delta H(T) := 8070 - 32.07 \cdot T$ $\quad R := 8.31451$

$T1 := 77.33$ $\quad P1 := 1$ ***P in atm***

$$lnp(T) := \ln(P1) + \int_{T1}^{T} \frac{\Delta H(T)}{R \cdot T^2}\, dT$$

$lnp(80) = 0.288$

Vapor pressure in atm = $\exp(lnp(80)) = 1.334$

(The unit of ΔH is J/mol with T in K).

Make a graph of ln(*P*) (the function we call *lnp* in Mathcad) vs. reciprocal temperature (box to right). (This is the graph that, elsewhere, we assume to be a straight line.) Using 1000/*T* for the *x* axis gives a better looking graph than does using 1/*T* (try it and see). Making such a graph is no problem at all: simply type "1000/T" in the *x*-axis placeholder.

T := 60 .. 120

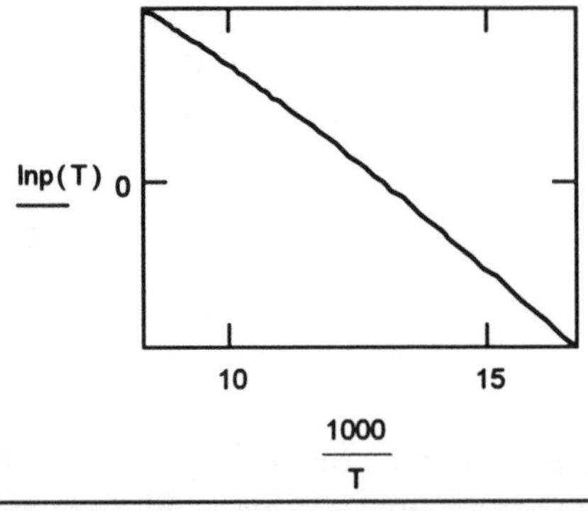

T := T1

Given

$$\mathrm{lnp}(T1) = \ln\left(\frac{100}{760}\right)$$

T2 := Find(T1)   T2 = 63.199

760·exp(lnp(T2)) = 100

Calculate the temperature at which nitrogen would boil under a reduced pressure of 100 torr (box to left). The last calculation is for the vapor pressure at the calculated temperature (in torr) and is made to confirm the calculated temperature and to demonstrate the use of the function (*lnp*) for calculating vapor pressures.

Graphs of ln(*P*) vs. *T* or (more so) 1/*T* give a misleading impression of how fast vapor pressures increase with temperature. Making graphs in Mathcad is very easy, and you should not neglect any opportunity to use this facility to look at data and equations from a different point of view. The current example will serve this purpose nicely.

P(T) := exp(lnp(T))   T := 60 .. 120

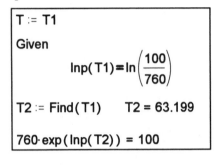

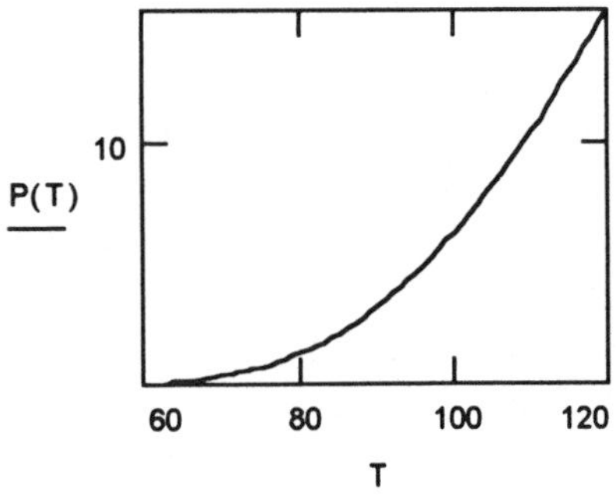

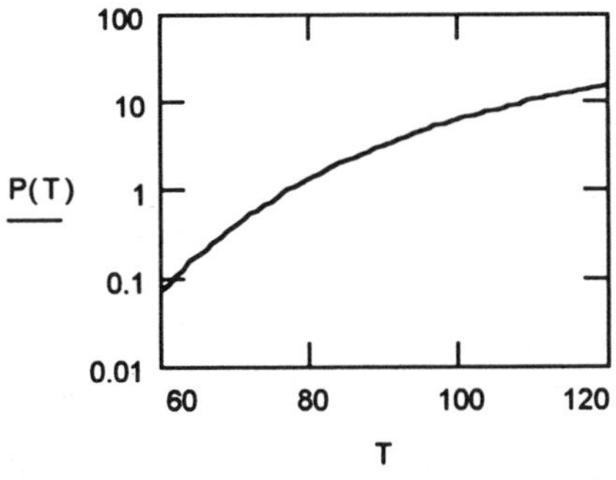

The second graph is given with a log scale on *y*, but this is done using the Mathcad log-scale feature (Graph-Plot-Format menu) which labels the axes with the original numbers (pressure, in this case). Such a graph gives as good if not better impression of how fast vapor pressure increases with temperature.

4.2 Curve Fitting

Fitting data to a model equation to derive values for physical parameters is one of the most fundamental operations in physical chemistry or any other experimental science. In this section we learn how to fit data by linear regression, which is very easy to do with Mathcad.

The Clausius-Clapeyron equation, Eq. (4.1), can be written as:

$$\frac{d(\ln P)}{d(1/T)} = \frac{-\Delta H}{R} \tag{4.3}$$

This demonstrates that the enthalpy of vaporization is related to the slope of a ln(P) vs. $1/T$ plot. This does not imply that the plot is linear (constant slope) but such plots are often close to linear (which is the assumption made in deriving Eq. (4.2)).

Example 4.4 Enthalpy of vaporization by linear regression of vapor pressure vs. temperature data.

Table 4.1 gives data for the vapor pressure of carbon dioxide. To enter these data into Mathcad, you can use the disk-file method described in Example 3.4 or just enter them directly. To enter the data directly into Mathcad, type "`i:0;16`" and "`Tx[i:`" followed by the temperatures, separated by commas. Then "`vp[i:`" followed by the vapor pressures.

Table 4.1 Vapor pressure of carbon dioxide (liquid).

T/K	P/atm	T/K	P/atm	T/K	P/atm
216.55	5.1102	249.83	17.5082	283.16	44.4747
222.05	6.4439	255.38	20.7880	288.72	50.9390
227.61	8.0430	260.94	24.5101	294.27	58.0702
233.16	9.9211	266.49	28.7017	299.83	65.9159
238.73	12.0985	272.05	33.3968	304.16	72.7681
244.27	14.6230	277.61	38.6364		

The code below presumes that these data have been entered into a matrix **M**, either directly, read from a disk file, or pasted from a spread sheet. Enter the data in any manner you find convenient.

$Tx := M^{<0>}$ $\quad vp := M^{<1>}$ $\quad li := \text{last}(Tx)$ $\quad i := 0..li$ $\quad R := 8.31451$

$x_i := \frac{1}{Tx_i}$ $\quad y_i := \ln(vp_i)$ $\quad DF := \text{length}(Tx) - 2$ $\quad kJ := 1000$

Here we use the Mathcad function **last**, which returns the index of the last element in the vector (li); this is used to define a range variable (i) for carrying out operations that must be made on the list. The last line creates the arrays for the x variable ($1/T$) and the y variable, ln(P). DF is the degree of freedom needed for error estimation (below). Note that R is not given units, and kJ is defined solely for the purpose of labeling the answer.

The slope and intercept of a straight line are calculated with the Mathcad functions **slope and intercept**; the correlation factor (r) is calculated with **corr**.

$a := \text{intercept}(x, y)$ $\quad b := \text{slope}(x, y)$ $\quad r := \text{corr}(x, y)$

$a = 10.822$ $\quad b = -1.989 \cdot 10^3$ $\quad r = -0.99999447$

With the default Displayed Precision, r is displayed as 1, implying a perfect fit. Since, as we shall see shortly, the significant quantity is $(1-r^2)^{1/2}$, the significant part of r does not begin until the 9s end. Double-click on the number to bring up the Numerical Format menu and set the displayed precision to show as least 3 figures after the 9s end.

Next we calculate ΔH from Eq. (4.2) and calculate the standard deviation of the slope (σ_H):

$\Delta H := -R \cdot b$ $\Delta H = 16.538 \cdot kJ$

$t_c := 1.75$ ***t_c for 90% confidence*** $\sigma_H := \frac{R \cdot b}{r} \cdot \sqrt{\frac{1 - r^2}{DF}}$

enthalpy of vaporization $\Delta H = 16.538 \cdot kJ$ ***error*** $t_c \cdot \sigma_H = 0.025 \cdot kJ$

The standard deviation is a very conservative estimate for the error. Instead, we obtain the value for the critical-t factor (t_c, for example, from Table AI.1 Noggle) and calculate the 90% confidence limits. The conclusion is:

$$\Delta H = (16.538 \pm 0.025)\ \text{kJ / mol}$$

$lnp(T) := a + \frac{b}{T}$

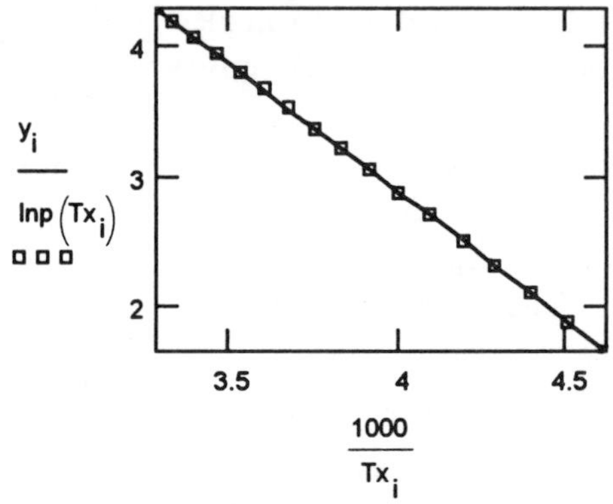

$rs_i := y_i - lnp(Tx_i)$

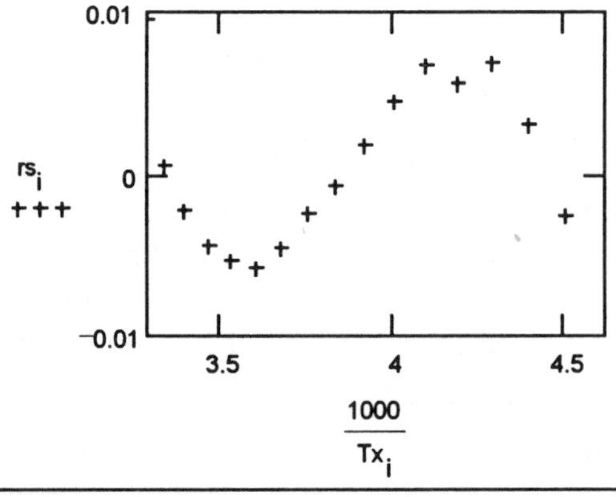

This is clearly very good accuracy, but we should check the graph in any case (inspection of the graph is essential for any regression or curve-fitting procedure). First, we need to make a function for the fitted ln(*P*) as a function of *T*; we call it *lnp*. Comparing the data to the fitted line (box to right), there is no apparent cause for concern.

Normally, when we plot a function (such as *lnp*, above), we would need to supply a range variable; in this case, since the function is a straight line (for which two points are adequate) we can use the temperature vector, **Tx**. When there is more than one variable on the *y* axis, and only one on the *x* axis, the *x*-axis variable is used for all *y*-axis variables.

The box to the right also shows a graph of the residuals — the observed values of the *y* coordinate, ln(*P*), minus the value calculated with the model. Clearly there is a systematic deviation, although small. This could be an error in the experiment, but is more likely a deficiency in the model. Although our analysis gave very good results (with $r = -0.999994$!), it is not the best possible. The next example demonstrates a more general method for treating such data. (The residual graph is also a good way to spot mistyped data; but remember that when plotting vs. $1/T$, the data points are in the opposite order — the first point is the right-most one.)

$P(T) := \exp(lnp(T)) \cdot atm$

$P(300) = 66.145 \cdot atm$

The box to the left demonstrates how to create a function (*P*) for the vapor pressure. The pressure at 300 K is clearly very large. Carbon dioxide is most commonly seen as a solid — dry ice (which sublimes at 194.65 K under 1 atm). The liquid form is observed only under high pressure. (Save your work before proceeding.)

Example 4.5 General linear regression.

Better models for vapor pressure, which take into account the variation of ΔH with temperature, are available (see Example 4.3, page 83). For example, if ΔH is assumed to be a polynomial in T, then Eq. (4.1) integrates to

$$\ln P = c_0 + \frac{c_1}{T} + c_2 \ln T + c_3 T + c_4 T^2 + \cdots \quad (4.4)$$

where c_0 c_1, ... are constants to be determined. This equation can be fit by Mathcad using the function **linfit**.

We will be continuing with the same data as for Example 4.4, which you should have saved; if so, recover it and save it under another name (File-menu, Save As). All lines after those that enter the data and define the vectors **y** and **Tx** can be deleted (we no longer need **x**).

First we must define a vector of functions (**F** below). Type "`F(T):`" and select Math-menu, Matrices; specify 4 rows and 1 column; click the create button and close the matrix window. Then enter the functions in the placeholders; for a constant term, enter 1 (one). (Why did we choose 4 functions? Two was almost enough, and it's easier to switch from 4 to 3 than vice versa. It can be shown that using 5 functions does not improve the fit, but this is not easy to do with Mathcad.) Next we use **linfit** to create a vector of coefficients.

$$F(T) := \begin{bmatrix} 1 \\ \frac{1}{T} \\ \ln(T) \\ T \end{bmatrix} \qquad \text{ans} := \text{linfit}(Tx, y, F) \qquad \text{ans} = \begin{bmatrix} 111.684 \\ -4.327\cdot 10^3 \\ -18.159 \\ 0.035 \end{bmatrix}$$

$$\text{lnp}(T) := \text{ans}\cdot F(T)$$

We denoted the vector of coefficients, the c_i of Eq. (4.4), as **ans**; the numbers are displayed at the right. A function for ln(P) is created by multiplying the functions times the coefficients; since they are both vectors, we need a dot product. The dot product in Mathcad is just an ordinary multiplication (*) between vectors. The last line of the box above is obtained by typing: "`lnp(T): ans*F(T)`". The graph looks no better than before.

$Tp := 220, 225..\, 320$ $\qquad$ $rs_i := y_i - \text{lnp}(Tx_i)$

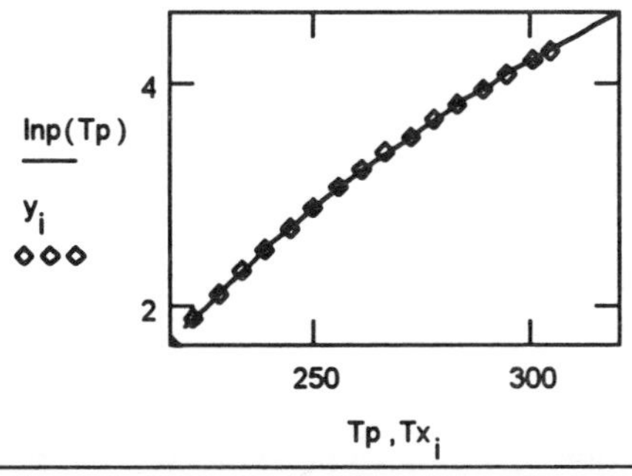

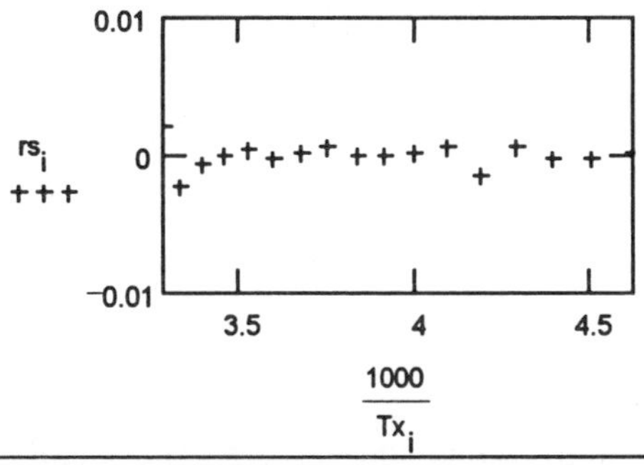

The residual graph is much improved, showing a random scatter with no systematic trend or pattern. This is exactly what you want from a good data analysis. (The leftmost graph above uses different x-range variables, which correspond in order to the y-axis variables. This permits us to show a range extended beyond the data span, and a finer grid for x to draw a smooth curve.)

Why didn't we use a three-term equation? After all, the two term equation was very close to a perfect fit. You can try this by editing the function vector, replacing the last term (T) by a zero. Usually in such problems, one additional term is sufficient, but in this case, two are needed to get rid of the systematic deviations.

The enthalpy of vaporization is a function of temperature, so we must calculate it using Eq. (4.1).

$\Delta H(T) := R \cdot T^2 \cdot \frac{d}{dT} \ln p(T)$ $\Delta H(Tx_0) = 16.939 \cdot kJ$ $\Delta H(Tx_{li}) = 16.999 \cdot kJ$

The calculations shown are for the lowest and highest temperatures in the data array, and they demonstrate that the variation of the enthalpy is quite small (40 J/mol). On the other hand, the difference is larger than the 90% confidence limit for the two-term fit (0.025 kJ/mol), so it is significant.

Be careful: with a sufficient number of terms, Eq. (4.4) can fit vapor pressures nearly up to the critical temperature, but Eq. (4.1) is derived presuming that the volume of the gas phase is much greater than the volume of the liquid and this is not true near the critical point. In other words, your pressure function would be correct, but the enthalpy of vaporization calculated as in the box just above would not be correct — you will get an answer, but it is not the enthalpy of vaporization.

In such analyses, never make the number of functions greater than the number of data points. In fact, the degree of freedom — the number of data points minus the number of coefficients determined — should never be less than 2 (preferably, more). A problem with using too many terms would normally be revealed by an increase in the uncertainties of the coefficients, but Mathcad does not calculate these for you. In general, use the smallest number of terms that gives a good random scatter for the residuals.

4.3 Condensed-Phase Equilibria

Two phases are in equilibrium when their chemical potentials are equal: $\mu_1 = \mu_2$. The variation of free energy with pressure at constant temperature is given by $dG = VdP$; for the chemical potential, this becomes $d\mu = V_m dP$. For a phase change 1 to 2, the free energy change (ΔG) can be measured relative to the standard free energy, $\Delta G^o = \mu_2^o - \mu_1^o$ with

$$\mu_i = \mu_i^o + \int_{P^o}^{P} V_{mi} dP$$

(for $i = 1$ and 2). Thus for the phase change

$$\Delta G = \Delta G^o + \int_{P^o}^{P} \Delta V \, dP \tag{4.5}$$

is equal to zero at equilibrium. The equilibrium condition can also be expressed by the Clapeyron equation:

$$\frac{dP}{dT} = \frac{\Delta H}{T\Delta V} \tag{4.6}$$

Example 4.6 Variation of the melting point of water with pressure.

Ice is unusual in that the change in volume on fusion

$$\Delta V = V_{\text{water}} - V_{\text{ice}}$$

is negative — that is, ice is less dense than water at 0°C, 1 atm (as demonstrated by the fact that ice floats in water). The effect of a negative ΔV in Eq. (4.6) is that the melting point decreases with pressure. The melting point of ice decreases to -22.0°C at 2040 atm; at this pressure it changes to another (and denser) crystal structure called ice III. The melting point of ice III increases with pressure, so -22.0°C is the minimum melting point of ice.

Separating variables in Eq. (4.6) gives:

$$\int_{T_1}^{T_2} \frac{dT}{T} = \ln\left[\frac{T_2}{T_1}\right] = \int_{P_1}^{P_2} \frac{\Delta V}{\Delta H} dP$$

The simplest thing to do is to assume that the phases are incompressible, that ΔV does not change with P, and that ΔH is constant. These assumptions give the first estimate of the freezing point at 2040 atm as shown in the box below. For data we use the densities (D) of the phases to calculate the change in the molar volume (ΔV).

$D_{ice} := 0.915 \cdot \frac{gm}{cm^3}$ $\quad D_{water} := 0.999841 \cdot \frac{gm}{cm^3}$ $\quad \Delta H := 6010 \cdot \frac{joule}{mole}$

$mw := 18.01 \cdot \frac{gm}{mole}$ $\quad T_1 := 273.15 \cdot K$ $\quad P_1 := 1 \cdot atm$

$\Delta V := \frac{mw}{D_{water}} - \frac{mw}{D_{ice}}$ $\quad \Delta V = -1.67 \cdot \frac{cm^3}{mole}$ $\quad P_2 := 2040 \cdot atm$

$T_2 := T_1 \cdot \exp\left[\frac{\Delta V \cdot (P_2 - P_1)}{\Delta H}\right]$ $\quad T_2 = 257.909 \cdot K$

$T_2 - T_1 = -15.241 \cdot K$

To get a more accurate answer, we might consider the volume to be a function of pressure as

$$V(P) = V_0(1 - \kappa_T P) \tag{4.7}$$

where κ_T is the isothermal compressibility (Table 1.8 Noggle). The isothermal compressibility of ice is not available, but it seems reasonable to assume that it is less compressible than water and, thus, neglect it. The calculation including the compressibility of water is shown in the box below; DV denotes ΔV as a function of P.

$\kappa := 47 \cdot 10^{-6} \cdot atm^{-1}$ $DV(P) := \frac{mw}{D_{water}} \cdot (1 - \kappa \cdot P) - \frac{mw}{D_{ice}}$

Given

$$\ln\left(\frac{T_2}{T_1}\right) = \int_{P_1}^{P_2} \frac{DV(P)}{\Delta H} \, dP$$

$T_2 := Find(T_2)$ $T_2 = 250.362 \cdot K$ $T_2 - T_1 = -22.788 \cdot K$

This is very close to the observed temperature (-22.0 °C), which may be due as much to good luck as good management. We are still making approximations: neglecting the compressibility of ice and the effect of pressure on the enthalpy of fusion.

Example 4.7   Changing graphite to diamond.

Diamond is unstable relative to graphite at ordinary pressures, but diamonds, presumably made from graphite at high pressure, are stable essentially forever. Given the difference in price between graphite and even industrial-grade diamonds, the phase transition

$$C(\text{solid, graphite}) \rightarrow C(\text{solid, diamond})$$

has obvious interest. The equilibrium between graphite and diamond can be treated using Eq. (4.5), for which we need the standard free energy change for the process. The difference between the enthalpies of diamond and graphite can be determined from heats of combustion (Chapter 6), and the entropies can be measured using the 3rd law of thermodynamics (Chapter 3). Thence we can calculate $\Delta G° = \Delta H° - T\Delta S°$. Data for standard enthalpies, free energies and entropies may be found in many places (e.g. Table 6.1, Noggle) usually for 298.15 K. (The changes for the standard state are denoted below as *ΔHs*, *ΔGs* and *ΔSs* respectively, since the standard-state superscript cannot be implemented in Mathcad.)

$D_{graphite} := 2.260 \cdot \frac{gm}{cm^3}$ $D_{diamond} := 3.513 \cdot \frac{gm}{cm^3}$ $mw := 12.011 \cdot \frac{gm}{mole}$

$\Delta Gs := 2.900 \cdot 10^3 \cdot \frac{joule}{mole}$ $\Delta Ss := (2.377 - 5.740) \cdot \frac{joule}{K \cdot mole}$ $bar := 10^5 \cdot Pa$

$\Delta Hs := 1.895 \cdot 10^3 \cdot \frac{joule}{mole}$ $T_1 := 298.15$ $P_1 := 1 \cdot bar$ $kbar := 1000 \cdot bar$

$\Delta V := \frac{mw}{D_{diamond}} - \frac{mw}{D_{graphite}}$ $\Delta V = -1.896 \cdot cm^3$

$DG(P) := \Delta Gs + \Delta V \cdot (P - P_1)$

starting value

$P_2 := 1000 \cdot bar$

Given

$$DG(P_2) = 0$$

$P_2 := Find(P_2)$ $P_2 = 15.3 \cdot kbar$

At 15 thousand bar one might well worry about the variation of volume with pressure, at least for graphite if not diamond. Below, find the calculation using Eq. (4.7) for the volume as a function of pressure.

$$\kappa_g := 3.03\cdot 10^{-6}\cdot \text{bar}^{-1} \qquad \kappa_d := 0.18\cdot 10^{-6}\cdot \text{bar}^{-1}$$

$$DV(P) := \frac{mw}{D_{diamond}}\cdot\left(1-\kappa_d\cdot P\right) - \frac{mw}{D_{graphite}}\cdot\left(1-\kappa_g\cdot P\right)$$

$$DG(P) := \Delta Gs + \int_{P_1}^{P} DV(P)\, dP$$

Given

$$DG(P_2) = 0$$

$$P_2 := \text{Find}(P_2) \qquad P_2 = 16.398\cdot \text{kbar}$$

This is not too far from the original answer, which gives us some confidence in the result.

For kinetic reasons, the conversion of graphite to diamond is usually carried out at high temperature. We use $\Delta G^\circ = \Delta H^\circ - T\Delta S^\circ$ and assume that the enthalpy and entropy do not change with temperature.

$$T := 1000\,K$$

$$DG(P) := \Delta Hs - T\cdot\Delta Ss + \int_{P_1}^{P} DV(P)\, dP$$

Given

$$DG(P_2) = 0$$

$$\text{Find}(P_2) = 31.895\cdot \text{kbar}$$

The pressure required at 1000 K is significantly greater than at room temperature.

4.4 Calculating Vapor Pressure From Gas Laws.

Equations of state such as van der Waals and Redlich-Kwong that show an undulation of the isotherm for temperatures below the critical temperature, can be used to calculate vapor pressures. The procedure can be illustrated with the graph below (calculated using the Peng-Robinson gas law..

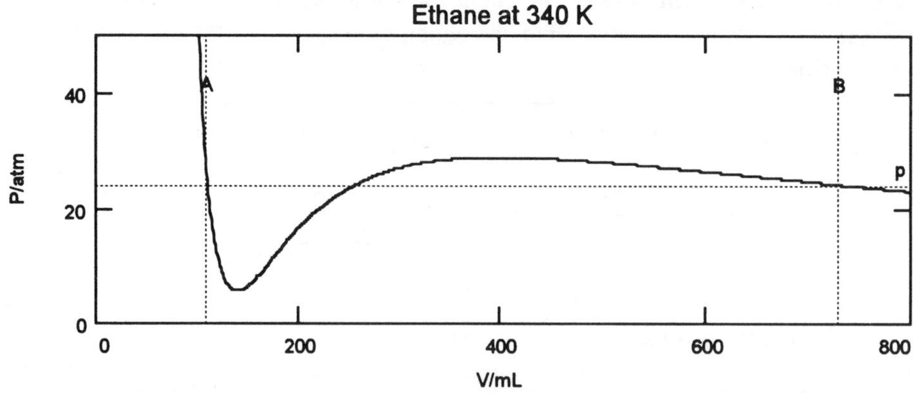

For the pressure represented by the horizontal dashed line (p), there are three roots — that is, for that temperature and pressure, there are three volumes that fit the equation of state. The middle root can be shown to represent an unstable state. The smaller root (A) is the volume of the liquid phase while the larger root (B) is that of the gas.

In order to have an equilibrium between the liquid and gas phases, the chemical potentials (Gibbs free energy per mole) must be equal: $\mu_A = \mu_B$. The variation of free energy at constant temperature is given by $dG = VdP$, or (per mole) $d\mu = V_m\, dP$. This can be integrated by parts to give:

$$\Delta G = \int_A^B V\,dP = PV_B - PV_A - \int_A^B P(V)\,dV$$

But $\Delta G = 0$ at equilibrium, so:

$$P(V_B - V_A) = \int_{V_A}^{V_B} P(V)\,dV \qquad (4.8)$$

Of course, there is still a problem: we must know the pressure to calculate the volumes and we must know the volumes to calculate the pressure. However, this can be overcome with successive approximations and good initial estimates.

How do we obtain the initial estimate for the vapor pressure? First, the estimate must be in the region where there are three real roots for volume: that is, between the maximum and minimum of the undulation of the isotherm (see above, page 91). Second, it can be shown that the equilibrium vapor pressure is that pressure for which the area of the undulation above that pressure is equal to the area below: that is, look for a horizontal line for which the area of the undulation above is equal to the area below. The second criterion would seem to be definitive, but unfortunately it is not always possible to make a graph in which the positive and negative swings can both be seen clearly.

Example 4.8 Calculate volume in the 2-phase region.

Before calculating the vapor pressure, let's examine the problem of calculating volume in the two-phase region. Equations of state like RK and van der Waals are cubic in volume. This means that, for a given pressure, there are 3 roots — values of the volume that satisfy the equation of state. Above the critical temperature, two roots are complex, and the calculation discussed in Chapter 1, starting with an ideal-gas estimate for the volume, will nearly always converge to the one real root. Below the critical temperature, there are three real roots. The smaller root is the volume of the liquid, the larger is the volume of the gas, and the middle root represents an unstable state.

Mathcad can solve a cubic equation (or any other polynomial) with the function **polyroots**. To use this function, the equation of state must be rearranged into the standard polynomial form. Rearrange the equation of state by placing all terms on one side (which is, then, equal to zero); for van der Waals, this could be:

$$\left[P+\frac{a}{V_m^2}\right]\left[V_m-b\right]-RT$$

Then multiply by some factor to clear volume from the denominator; for van der Waals, you would multiply by $V_m^{\,2}$. Enter this expression as shown below. (Here, and henceforth, V denotes the molar volume.)

$$\left[\left(P+\frac{a}{V^2}\right)\cdot(V-b)-R\cdot T\right]\cdot V^2$$ by collecting terms, yields $$V^3\cdot P+(-P\cdot b-R\cdot T)\cdot V^2+V\cdot a-a\cdot b$$

Place the cursor on V and select Symbolic-menu, Collect, to get the result above. As you can see, the equation is in standard form. More to the point is to select (from the same expression, placing the cursor on V) Symbolic-menu, Polynomial Coefficients, which yields:

$$\left[\left(P+\frac{a}{V^2}\right)\cdot(V-b)-R\cdot T\right]\cdot V^2 \quad \text{has coefficients} \quad \begin{bmatrix}-a\cdot b\\ a\\ -P\cdot b-R\cdot T\\ P\end{bmatrix}$$

This gives the polynomial coefficients as a vector in exactly the form required by **polyroots**. One problem remains: all of the polynomial coefficients must have the same units and the vector must be unitless; then the roots (the volumes) will similarly be unitless. We get around this by introducing a volume unit (*vu*) which is multiplies the coefficients as required, and then a polynomial unit (*pu*) to divide the resulting vector, making it unitless. First, we need the van der Waals law and definitions for the constants:

$$R := 8.31451\cdot\frac{\text{joule}}{K} \qquad MPa := 10^6\cdot Pa \qquad bar := 10^5\cdot Pa \qquad kPa := 10^3\cdot Pa$$

$$Tc := 126\cdot K \qquad Pc := 3.394\cdot MPa$$ constants for nitrogen

$$a := \frac{27\cdot R^2\cdot Tc^2}{64\cdot Pc} \qquad b := \frac{R\cdot Tc}{8\cdot Pc} \qquad P(V,T) := \frac{R\cdot T}{(V-b)}-\frac{a}{V^2}$$

Next, copy and edit the vector of coefficients to give the vector function **vc** (below). The display of the vector (for 1 atm, 300 K) is to confirm that it is unitless. (Initially this display was used to find out what *pu* had to be.)

$$vc(P,T) := \begin{bmatrix} -a\cdot b \\ a\cdot vu \\ (-P\cdot b - R\cdot T)\cdot vu^2 \\ P\cdot vu^3 \end{bmatrix}\cdot\frac{1}{pu} \qquad vu := liter \qquad pu := kg\cdot m^8\cdot sec^{-2}$$

$$vc(1\cdot atm, 300\cdot K) = \begin{bmatrix} -5.264\cdot 10^{-6} \\ 1.364\cdot 10^{-4} \\ -0.002 \\ 1.013\cdot 10^{-4} \end{bmatrix}$$

$$vf(P,T) := polyroots(vc(P,T))\cdot vu$$

The last line defines a function *vf* for the volume. Its use is shown in the next box.

$$vf(1\cdot atm, 273.15\cdot K) = \begin{pmatrix} 0.03 - 0.038i \\ 0.03 + 0.038i \\ 22.393 \end{pmatrix}\cdot liter \qquad vf(1\cdot atm, 77.33\cdot K) = \begin{pmatrix} 50.653 \\ 166.296 \\ 6.167\cdot 10^3 \end{pmatrix}\cdot mL$$

Here we see clearly what was stated earlier: Above the critical temperature, there is only one real root, which is the molar volume of the gas. Below the critical temperature there are 3 real roots; the larger one is the molar volume of the gas, the smaller one is the molar volume of the liquid, and the middle root is for the unstable state (just ignore it).

The procedure for the RK equation is similar. Enter the equation of state as shown below.

$$\left[\left[P + \frac{1}{\sqrt{T}\cdot V\cdot(V+b)}\right]\cdot(V-b) - R\cdot T\right]\cdot V\cdot(V+b)$$

Place the cursor in the expression and press up arrow until the whole expression is selected. Then select Symbolic-menu, Simplify. In the resulting expression, place the cursor next to *V* and select Symbolic-menu, Collect. Now you should have the polynomial in *V* shown below.

$$P\cdot V^3 - R\cdot T\cdot V^2 + \frac{\left[-R\cdot T^{\left(\frac{3}{2}\right)}\cdot b - P\cdot b^2\cdot\sqrt{T} + 1\right]}{\sqrt{T}}\cdot V - \frac{1}{\sqrt{T}}\cdot b \quad \textbf{has coefficients} \quad \begin{bmatrix} \frac{-1}{\sqrt{T}}\cdot b \\ -P\cdot b^2 + \frac{1}{\sqrt{T}} - R\cdot T\cdot b \\ -R\cdot T \\ P \end{bmatrix}$$

Obtain the coefficient vector (above, right) as before.

Next, enter the RK equation for pressure with constants for argon (below).

$$R := 8.31451\cdot\frac{joule}{K} \qquad MPa := 10^6\cdot Pa \qquad bar := 10^5\cdot Pa \qquad kPa := 1000\cdot Pa$$

$$Tc := 151\cdot K \qquad Pc := 4.955\cdot MPa \qquad \textbf{constants for argon}$$

$$a := \frac{0.42748\cdot R^2\cdot Tc^{2.5}}{Pc} \qquad b := \frac{0.086640\cdot R\cdot Tc}{Pc} \qquad P(V,T) := \frac{R\cdot T}{V-b} - \frac{a}{\sqrt{T}\cdot V\cdot(V+b)}$$

Now copy and edit the coefficient vector to give:

$$vc(P,T) := \begin{bmatrix} \dfrac{-a}{\sqrt{T}}\cdot b \\ \left(-P\cdot b^2 + \dfrac{a}{\sqrt{T}} - R\cdot T\cdot b\right)\cdot vu \\ -R\cdot T\cdot vu^2 \\ P\cdot vu^3 \end{bmatrix}\cdot\frac{1}{pu}$$

$vu := liter \qquad pu := kg\cdot m^8\cdot sec^{-2}$

$vf(P,T) := polyroots(vc(P,T))\cdot vu$

Do the following calculations to check your work.

$$vf(1\cdot atm, 273.15\cdot K) = \begin{pmatrix} 0.011 + 0.029i \\ 0.011 - 0.029i \\ 22.392 \end{pmatrix}\cdot liter \qquad vf(11.5\cdot atm, 120\cdot K) = \begin{pmatrix} 34.511 \\ 118.398 \\ 703.347 \end{pmatrix}\cdot mL$$

An alternate method for calculating volume is to use a numerical iteration (such as a solve block), controlling which root is found by the initial estimate. This is the method we used in Chapter 1; to use it in the 2-phase region, you must provide two initial guesses that will converge to the two desired roots — liquid and gas. We will repeat the calculation (above) for argon at 120 K, 11.5 atm.

$T := 120\cdot K \qquad px := 11.5\cdot atm$

$V_b := \dfrac{R\cdot T}{px}$

Given $\quad px = P(V_b, T)$

$V_b := Find(V_b)$

$V_b = 703.347\cdot mL$

The box to the left shows the calculation beginning with the ideal-gas volume as an estimate. The answer is the volume of the gas phase for these conditions.

The calculation of the liquid volume is more problematical. We know that the minimum volume is b, so an estimate a bit greater than that often works (as illustrated in the box to the right). However, for temperatures closer to the critical temperature than this one, the calculation may not converge with this estimate. In this case, you must plot the isotherm and obtain a better initial estimate from the graph.

$V_a := 1.1\cdot b$

Given $\quad px = P(V_a, T)$

$V_a := Find(V_a)$

$V_a = 34.511\cdot mL$

To see what we have done, graph the isotherm for this temperature (box below). For making the graph, we define a volume range (*vol*) to begin slightly above b (displayed here for information only), and go to a value somewhat greater than the gas volume calculated above. For making the graph, we define a volume range (*vol*) to begin slightly above b (displayed here for information only), and go to a value somewhat greater than the gas volume calculated above. We also define *v2, v1* and *pp* as unitless versions of the volumes and pressure for reasons to become apparent shortly. You will need to set the y-axis limits manually to get the display shown.

This graph is clearer with a log scale for volume: this is set by clicking the Log-scale box in the X-Y Axes part of the graph-format menu. For the x axis, autoscaling has been turned off and 4 entered for "No. of Grids".

The graph displays dashed lines for the volumes ($v1$ and $v2$) and pressure (pp). To accomplish this, from the graph-format menu, X-Y Axes, click the Show Markers boxes. When you return to the graph, 4 new placeholders appear. On the y axis, type "pp" into one of the y-axis placeholders (leave the other one blank). On the x axis, type "v1" and "v2" into the placeholders.

$b = 21.953 \cdot mL \qquad vol := 25 \cdot mL, 30 \cdot mL .. 2 \cdot liter$

$$v2 := \frac{V_a}{mL} \qquad v1 := \frac{V_b}{mL} \qquad pp := \frac{px}{atm}$$

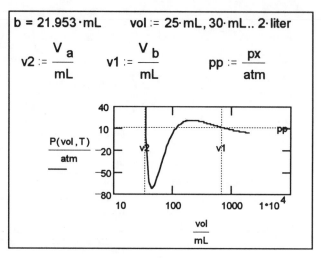

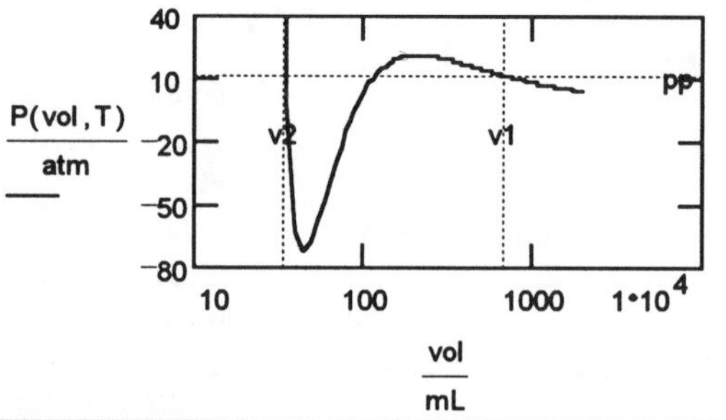

Is this calculation meaningful? Generally, depending on pressure, one or the other of the phases is the stable one, and this calculation does not tell us which. (We need to calculate the free energy to determine which is stable.) There is one pressure at which both phases are stable: the equilibrium vapor pressure. If px is the correct vapor pressure (as predicted by the RK law) then Eq. (4.8) should be obeyed. Calculate the pressure using Eq. (4.8) and these volumes (box below).

$$pxx := \frac{1}{\left(V_b - V_a\right)} \cdot \int_{V_a}^{V_b} P(V,T)\, dV$$

$px = 11.5 \cdot atm$

$pxx = 11.469 \cdot atm$

The pressure we used was quite close to the vapor pressure. (This was not just a lucky guess — it was calculated in the manner explained in the next example.)

Save this file as *rkvol.mcd*.

Example 4.9 Free energy and volume.

It has been stated that, of the three volumes (roots of the equation of state), the middle volume represents an unstable state, and the stable volume (liquid or gas) is determined by the free energy. We will demonstrate this by calculating the free energy for each of these volumes.

Since they are at the same temperature and pressure, we can determine the relative free energy by calculating G - $G°$ which, in turn, can be calculated from the enthalpy and entropy as:

$$G - G^\circ = (H - H^\circ) - T(S - S^\circ) \tag{4.9}$$

Recover the earlier work for the imperfection quantities of an RK gas (*rkimp.mcd*). The enthalpy imperfection (Chapter 2) is $H_i = H - H^\circ$. In Section 3.4, we introduced a function for the entropy imperfection, $S_i(V, T)$ which should be in *rkimp.mcd*. We now need:

$$S - S^\circ = R\ln\left[\frac{P^oV_m}{RT}\right] + S_i(V,T) \qquad (4.10)$$

We will call this function $S_v = S - S^o$. Add the following functions as necessary.

$$U_i(V,T) := \frac{3\cdot a}{2\cdot b\cdot\sqrt{T}}\cdot\ln\left(\frac{V}{V+b}\right) \qquad H_i(V,T) := U_i(V,T) + P(V,T)\cdot V - R\cdot T$$

$$S_i(V,T) := \frac{a}{2\cdot b\cdot T^{1.5}}\cdot\ln\left(\frac{V}{V+b}\right) - R\cdot\ln\left(\frac{V}{V-b}\right) \qquad S_v(V,T) := R\cdot\ln\left(\frac{V\cdot bar}{R\cdot T}\right) + S_i(V,T)$$

Also, add the volume function developed above to *rkimp.mcd* and save it (it is needed in Chapter 6).

These can be used to create a function (G_v) for G - $G°$ as shown below (results are for argon, with constants as given above).

$T := 100\cdot K \qquad px := 2.630\cdot atm \qquad vol := vf(px, T)$

$$vol = \begin{pmatrix} 0.029 \\ 0.159 \\ 2.931 \end{pmatrix}\cdot liter$$

$j := 0..2 \qquad G_v(V,T) := H_i(V,T) - T\cdot S_v(V,T)$

The index variable *j* permits us to specify each of the 3 elements of the vector **vol**, which can be used to calculate the free energy as shown in the box to right. The temperature and pressure used were deliberately chosen to make the first and last values (for liquid and gas respectively) equal. Try higher or lower pressures. Try higher or lower temperatures for this pressure. The minimum free energy tells you which volume represents the equilibrium state. This will never be the middle volume. Which is more stable is determined by the temperature and pressure used.

$\frac{G_v(vol_j, T)}{kJ}$
0.766
1.640
0.766

This example demonstrates clearly how we can use gas laws such as RK to find the equilibrium vapor pressure or boiling temperature of a gas, but there is a more direct method that is explained in the next section.

The Redlich-Kwong Equation of State

The RK law is generally much more effective for such calculations than van der Waals, so we demonstrate it first.

Example 4.10 Vapor pressure of nitrogen at 77 K.

Enter or paste the RK equation into a new worksheet and enter the critical constants for nitrogen.

$\mathrm{MPa} := 10^{6}\cdot \mathrm{Pa}$ $\quad$ $\mathrm{kJ} := 1000\cdot \mathrm{joule}$ $\quad$ $R := 8.31451\cdot \mathrm{joule}\cdot K^{-1}$

$\mathrm{Tc} := 126.0\cdot K$ $\quad$ $\mathrm{Pc} := 3.394\cdot \mathrm{MPa}$ $\quad$ $\mathrm{mw} := 2\cdot 14.0067\cdot \mathrm{gm}$ $\quad$ ***Data for nitogen***

$$a := \frac{0.42748\cdot R^{2}\cdot \mathrm{Tc}^{2.5}}{\mathrm{Pc}} \qquad b := 0.086640\cdot R\cdot \frac{\mathrm{Tc}}{\mathrm{Pc}} \qquad P(V,T) := \frac{R\cdot T}{(V-b)} - \frac{a}{\sqrt{T}\cdot (V+b)\cdot V}$$

For repeated numerical calculation, the integral of Eq. (4.8) may be a bit slow. For that reason we do it symbolically (the function *pi* below). To derive the expression for the integral of *PdV*, copy the right-hand side of the pressure definition to the clipboard. Open a new document and paste it.[1] Place the cursor next to a V and select Symbolic-Menu Integrate. Copy the result to the clipboard for creating a function (*pi*) for the integral of the pressure over volume (see box above for what you should get). Because you cannot take the logarithm of a number with units, the arguments of the logarithms must be divided by some volume unit. Edit the expression you derived to divide the argument of each logarithm by liter (it doesn't matter which volume unit you use; they cancel in the actual calculation). The box below shows the function you need; it also gives the equation for energy and enthalpy imperfection (used in Chapter 2); these are used later.

pi is the Integral PdV

$$\mathrm{pi}(V,T) := \ln\left(\frac{V-b}{\mathrm{liter}}\right)\cdot R\cdot T + \frac{a}{\left(\sqrt{T}\cdot b\right)}\cdot \ln\left(\frac{V+b}{\mathrm{liter}}\right) - \frac{a}{\left(\sqrt{T}\cdot b\right)}\cdot \ln\left(\frac{V}{\mathrm{liter}}\right)$$

$$U_i(V,T) := \frac{3\cdot a}{2\cdot b\cdot \sqrt{T}}\cdot \ln\left(\frac{V}{V+b}\right) \qquad H_i(V,T) := U_i(V,T) + P(V,T)\cdot V - R\cdot T$$

Do some sample calculations to be certain that there are no errors so far (see box, below, left).

$P(1\cdot \mathrm{liter}, 200\cdot K) = 15.808\cdot \mathrm{atm}$

$\mathrm{pi}(1\cdot \mathrm{liter}, 200\cdot K) = 63.202\cdot \mathrm{joule}$

$U_i(1\cdot \mathrm{liter}, 200\cdot K) = -162.419\cdot \mathrm{joule}$

$H_i(1\cdot \mathrm{liter}, 200\cdot K) = -223.588\cdot \mathrm{joule}$

We will demonstrate the method by calculating the vapor pressure of nitrogen at 77.33 K. This is the normal boiling point of nitrogen, so the correct answer is 1 atm. To make things more difficult for Mathcad, we will use a poor initial guess (*px*) of 3 atm.

First we need to plot and inspect the isotherm in order to obtain an estimate of the root. To do this we need to define a range variable (*vol*) for volume. The lower limit of this range must be greater than *b* (whose value is displayed below for information); the upper limit of the volume scale is somewhat more speculative and you will need to experiment. A straightforward plot is rather uninformative:

[1] It is not really necessary to start a new document, but it keeps the original document clearer to put such side calculations in a different one.

$T := 77.33 \cdot K \quad b = 26.743 \cdot mL \quad vol := 30 \cdot mL, 35 \cdot mL .. 4 \cdot liter$

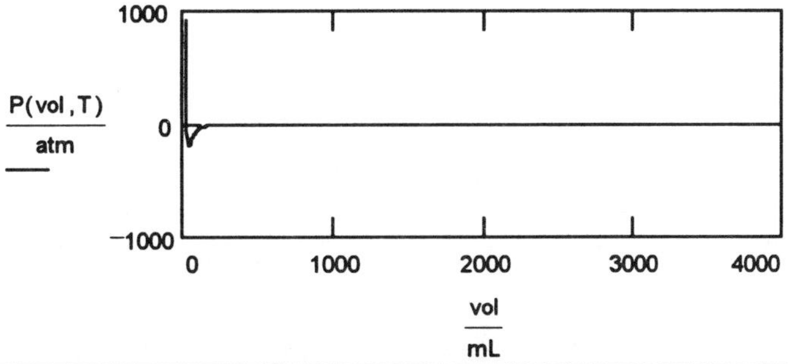

It requires a lot of trial and error to find the proper plot ranges (they are different for each case). Among other things you will need to do is to set the *y* axis limits manually. The graph below shows what you are seeking. (The volume axis has been displayed with a logarithmic scale; to do this, double-click on the graphic and, under X-Y axes, click the box for Log Scale.)

$px := 3 \cdot atm$ *(pressure estimate)*

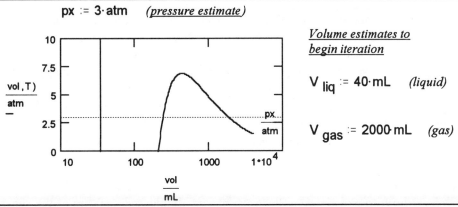

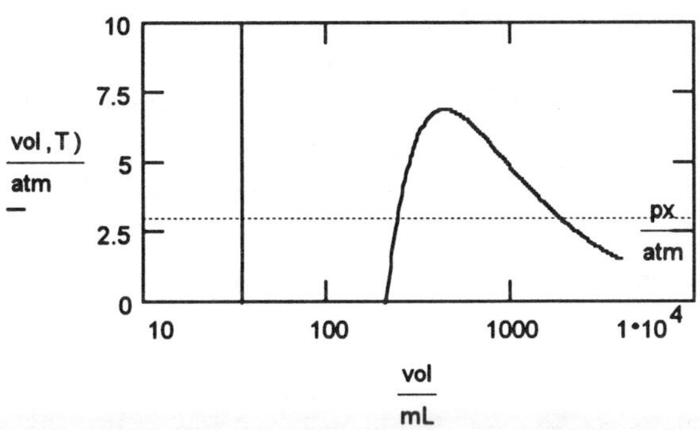

Volume estimates to begin iteration

$V_{liq} := 40 \cdot mL$ *(liquid)*

$V_{gas} := 2000 \cdot mL$ *(gas)*

From this graph we must obtain estimates for the molar volumes of the gas and liquid and the vapor pressure. The "equal area" rule mentioned above is of little help in this case. At this temperature, any graph scale for which you can see the entire undulation would obscure other things you need to see (in any case, the areas are not equal when a log scale is used for volume). What we do know is that the pressure (*px*) must be greater than 0 and less than the pressure at the top of the undulation (about 7 atm). The horizontal dashed line marks the location of the 3-atm pressure estimate — this guess is too high, but, as we shall see, it is close enough to give convergence.

The left- and rightmost intersections of the pressure line (*px*) with the isotherm give us estimates of the liquid and gas volumes respectively. It is hard to read the log scale, but anything reasonable will work (remember that the smaller volume must be larger than *b*). We estimate the volumes as 40 mL and 2000 mL (entered in box above). As we saw in Example, 4.8, the volume estimate controls the root found when solving for volume; the 40 mL estimate should converge to the liquid volume while the 2000 mL estimate should converge to the gas volume. Now we must solve 3 equations simultaneously and iteratively:

- Molar volume of the liquid:

$$px = P\left(V_{liq}, T\right)$$

- Molar volume of the gas:

$$px = P(V_{gas}, T)$$

- Vapor pressure (*px*, Eq. (4.8)):

$$px \cdot (V_{gas} - V_{liq}) = pi(V_{gas}, T) - pi(V_{liq}, T)$$

Mathcad can do this in a single solve block as illustrated below.

Given $\quad px = P(V_{liq}, T) \qquad px = P(V_{gas}, T)$

$$px \cdot (V_{gas} - V_{liq}) = pi(V_{gas}, T) - pi(V_{liq}, T)$$

$$\begin{pmatrix} px \\ V_{gas} \\ V_{liq} \end{pmatrix} := Find(px, V_{gas}, V_{liq}) \qquad px = 0.866 \cdot atm$$

(The vector on the left-hand side of the **Find** statement is created with the Vector and Matrices palette, Matrix or Vector button or Math-menu, Matrices. Also, remember that the logical equals, those used in the 3 equation just below **Given**, are made with ctrl+=.) To obtain convergence in this calculation, good initial guesses are very important. If the calculation does not give a reasonable answer, or does not converge, try different estimates for the pressure (*px*) and volumes (V_{gas} and V_{liq}). This particular calculation should converge for any reasonable estimate of the pressure (*px*). The answer, 0.866 atm, is, of course, not the experimental value (1 atm), but it is the "correct" answer in the sense that it is the value predicted by the RK equation of state. That is, the problem is in the model, not the calculation.

Once we have a valid calculation for the vapor pressure, we can calculate properties of the gas for comparison to experiment. Since the phases (liquid and gas) are at the same temperature, the enthalpy of vaporization is the difference between the enthalpy imperfections of the two phases. (The equations for the imperfection should have been entered earlier.) Also, we calculate the density and molar volume.

$T = 77.33 \cdot K \qquad px = 0.866 \cdot atm$ *(obs. 1 atm)*

$V_{liq} = 34.399 \cdot mL$ *(obs. 34.8 mL)* *Density* $\dfrac{mw}{V_{liq}} = 814.367 \cdot \dfrac{gm}{liter}$ *(obs. 807)*

$V_{gas} = 7.068 \cdot liter$ *(obs. 6.19 liter)* *Density* $\dfrac{mw}{V_{gas}} = 3.963 \cdot \dfrac{gm}{liter}$ *(obs. 4.526)*

Enthalpy of vaporization $\Delta H := H_i(V_{gas}, T) - H_i(V_{liq}, T) \qquad \Delta H = 6.273 \cdot kJ$ *(obs. 5.577 kJ)*

The calculated vapor pressure, 0.866 atm, and heat of vaporization are about 13% low. This is considerably better than the comparable calculation for van der Waals (which gives 3.382 atm, 3.192 kJ), but not as good as you could achieve with the Peng-Robinson equation (which is optimized for this type of calculation).

Example 4.11 Vapor pressure of nitrogen at 110 K.

The method of calculation given in the previous example works at temperatures other than the boiling point. The bad news is that, for temperatures closer to the critical temperature, you need much more accurate estimates for *px* and the volumes. The good news is that, at higher temperatures, the full undulation of the isotherm can be displayed and the equal-area rule for vapor pressure is usable.

The box below shows the isotherm for 110 K. The markers indicate the pressure estimate (*px*) and the estimated volumes.

$T := 110 \cdot K$ $px := 15 \cdot atm$ $b = 26.743 \cdot mL$ $V_{liq} := 45 \cdot mL$

$b = 26.743 \cdot mL$ $vol := 30 \cdot mL, 35 \cdot mL .. 590 \cdot mL$ $V_{gas} := 500 \cdot mL$

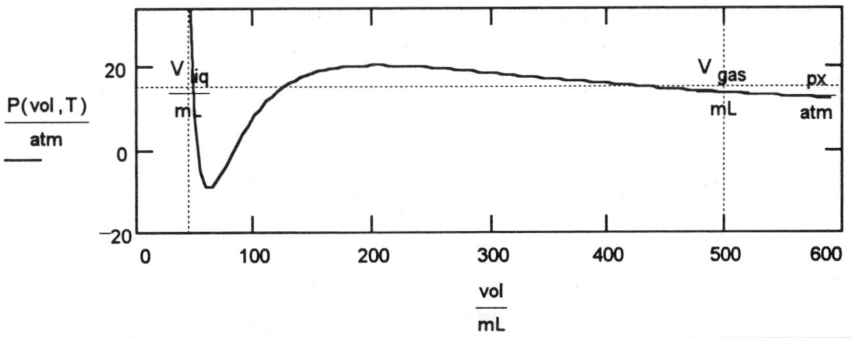

This graph and the numbers that go into it did not just appear in a dream. How was it created? Start by just plotting the isotherm, then replot a number of times to get the scale and range correct. Then you try a guess for *px*, displaying it with Show Markers; look for a *px* with equal areas between it and the isotherm above and below. Then read the volumes from the leftmost (for liquid) and rightmost intersections of the horizontal line (*px*) with the isotherm. Display the volumes with Show Markers.

Next, use a solve block as before to calculate the pressure and volumes. The results are given below.

$T = 110 \cdot K$ $px = 14.865 \cdot atm$ $V_{gas} = 433.875 \cdot mL$ $V_{liq} = 48.482 \cdot mL$

$\frac{mw}{V_{gas}} = 64.566 \cdot \frac{gm}{liter}$ $\frac{mw}{V_{liq}} = 577.813 \cdot \frac{gm}{liter}$ $\Delta H := H_i(V_{gas}, T) - H_i(V_{liq}, T)$

$\Delta H = 3.729 \cdot kJ$

Note that the enthalpy of vaporization is smaller than before (at 77 K) and the gas and liquid volumes are closer to each other. This is what happens as you approach the critical temperature (126 K); at the critical temperature, the volumes are equal and the enthalpy of vaporization is zero. The box above below the isotherms with the calculated volumes and pressure (dashed lines).

$$v1 := \frac{V_{liq}}{mL} \qquad v2 := \frac{V_{gas}}{mL} \qquad pp := \frac{px}{atm}$$

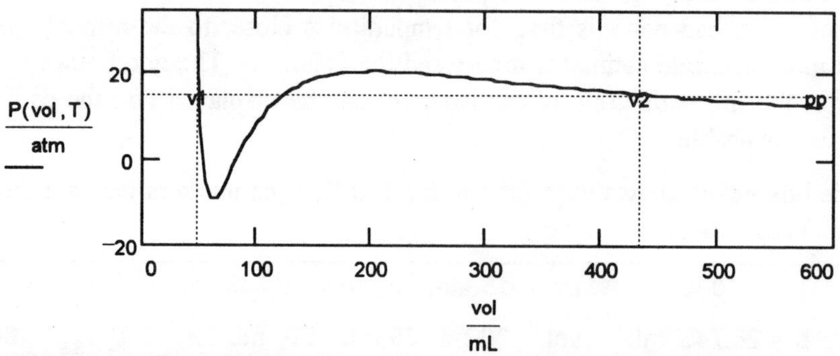

To make the display simpler, unitless variables (*v1, v2* and *pp*) are defined for the markers. This demonstrates what you were looking for earlier. Does it look as if the areas between the horizontal dashed line and the undulation are the same above and below? Even here it is difficult to visually confirm the equal-area rule, but it is helpful for obtaining initial estimates.

Example 4.12 Calculate the boiling temperature of a gas.

In this example we attempt to calculate the boiling point of nitrogen at 1 atm and compare it to the observed value (77.33 K). The procedure for calculating boiling points is very similar to that for vapor pressure except you keep the pressure fixed and vary the temperature. Given that the predicted vapor pressure at 77.33 K was a bit low, we expect the boiling point at 1 atm to be a bit higher than the actual value. However, to try to push the limits of the calculation, we use a starting value of 100 K, a lot higher than the observed value.

$$px := 1\cdot atm \qquad T := 100\cdot K$$

$$V_{liq} := 1.1\cdot b \qquad V_{gas} := \frac{R\cdot T}{px}$$

Given

$$px = P\left(V_{liq}, T\right) \qquad px = P\left(V_{gas}, T\right)$$

$$px\cdot\left(V_{gas} - V_{liq}\right) = pi\left(V_{gas}, T\right) - pi\left(V_{liq}, T\right)$$

$$\begin{pmatrix} T \\ V_{gas} \\ V_{liq} \end{pmatrix} := Find\left(T, V_{gas}, V_{liq}\right) \qquad T = 78.441\cdot K$$

The calculation is shown in box to left. For this case, the volume estimates are calculated as in Example 4.8 (this method usually works for temperatures well below the critical temperature).

The RK equation predicts a 1-atm boiling point of 78.44 K for nitrogen compared to the experimental 77.33 K. This may seen like a more accurate calculation than the preceding one for vapor pressure, which was 13% in error, but this is deceiving. Vapor pressure increases almost exponentially with temperature (see page 84) so the vapor pressure is likely to be more sensitive to approximations than temperature.

The van der Waals Equation of State

The van der Waals equation of state is much simpler than RK (or any other reasonable gas law), but it is much less accurate in many applications, as the example following demonstrates.

Example 4.13 Calculate the boiling point of nitrogen using vdw.

It is not too difficult to adapt the above procedure to the van der Waals equation of state. First, save the file, and then save it under another name with File-menu Save As (give a different name, for example, *vpvdw.mcd*). Then replace the pressure function and the constants (the *a* and *b* constants could be calculated or entered directly). You must also replace the pressure-integral function (*pi*) and the formula for the energy imperfection. For van der Waals, the energy imperfection is:

$$U_i = \frac{-a}{V_m} \tag{4.11}$$

The enthalpy imperfection is calculated from this as before.

Enter the equations for van der Waals with data for nitrogen. (The pressure integral, *pi*, is, of course, different; it can be calculated as before.)

$kJ := 10^3 \cdot joule$ $\quad MPa := 10^6 \cdot Pa$ $\quad R := 8.31451 \cdot \frac{joule}{K}$

$Tc := 126.0 \cdot K$ $\quad Pc := 3.394 \cdot MPa$ $\quad mw := 2 \cdot 14.0067 \cdot gm$ ***data for nitrogen***

$a := \frac{27 \cdot R^2 \cdot Tc^2}{64 \cdot Pc}$ $\quad b := \frac{R \cdot Tc}{8 \cdot Pc}$ $\quad P(V,T) := \frac{R \cdot T}{(V-b)} - \frac{a}{V^2}$ $\quad U_i(V,T) := -\frac{a}{V}$

$pi(V,T) := \ln\left(\frac{V-b}{liter}\right) \cdot R \cdot T + \frac{a}{V}$ $\quad H_i(V,T) := U_i(V,T) + P(V,T) \cdot V - R \cdot T$

The calculation is just as before (with volume estimates as in Example 4.8; any temperature estimate in the vicinity of the actual boiling point, 77 K, should work). The box below shows the results you should get.

$px = 1 \cdot atm$ $\quad T = 63.674 \cdot K$

$V_{liq} = 0.047 \cdot liter$ $\quad V_{gas} = 4.996 \cdot liter$ $\quad \Delta H := H_i(V_{gas}, T) - H_i(V_{liq}, T)$

$\frac{mw}{V_{liq}} = 593.204 \cdot \frac{gm}{liter}$ $\quad \frac{mw}{V_{gas}} = 5.607 \cdot \frac{gm}{liter}$ $\quad \Delta H = 3.363 \cdot kJ$

Compare these to the experimental values and RK calculations given earlier; note how poor the accuracy of this calculation is. Of dozens of gases tested by me and my students, there were only two for which van der Waals was better: Hg (for which both were abysmal) and He (for which van der Waals appeared to be somewhat better). Students (and their teachers) generally have an exaggerated opinion of this venerable equation. These examples demonstrate that the RK equation, while only slightly more complicated is greatly superior in most respects.

Problems

4.1 Aluminum has a vapor pressure of 1 torr at 1284 °C and 10 torr at 1487 °C. (a) Calculate the enthalpy of vaporization. (b) Calculate the temperature at which the vapor pressure is 5 torr.

Vapor pressure of CCl_4.	
t/C	*P*/torr
30	142.3
50	314.4
70	621.1
100	1463

4.2 Use the vapor pressures of carbon tetrachloride (table) with linear regression to calculate the enthalpy of vaporization. Estimate the error for 90% confidence. Calculate the normal (760 torr) boiling point.

4.3 Use data for the vapor pressure of difluorodichloromethane (table) to determine the enthalpy of vaporization by (a) fitting ln(*P*) vs. 1/*T* and (b) using the formula

$$\ln(P) = A + B/T + C\ln(T) + DT$$

For (b), do the calculation for 150, 200 and 250 K. (c) Using the formula for method (b), estimate the vapor pressure of this material at -78 °C.

Vapor pressure of CCl_2F_2			
P/torr	*t*/C	*P*/torr	*t*/C
1	-118.3	60	-76.1
5	-104.6	100	-68.6
10	-97.8	200	-57
20	-90.1	400	-43.9
40	-81.6	760	-29.8

4.4 Use the RK gas law to calculate the normal (1 atm) boiling point and enthalpy of vaporization of ethane. Compare your answers to experimental. Calculate the densities of the gas and liquid phases.

4.5 Repeat the preceding calculation for ethane using the van der Waals equation.

4.6 You have a tank of SF_6 with volume is 500 mL and weight 3.422 kg when empty. (a) Calculate the vapor pressure and enthalpy of vaporization of SF_6 at 300 K. The tank (at 300 K) is found to weigh 3.671 kg. Calculate the volumes of the gas and liquid phases inside the tank.

4.7 You have a gas grill with a 10 gal tank. (a) If it is filled with propane at 60 °F, use the RK gas law to calculate the gauge pressure (psig) and weight of the tank. (b) Repeat this calculation for 90 °F. (c) Assuming that the dealer's tank and meter are at ambient temperature, how much less propane would you get on a 90 °F day compared to 60 °F? (HINT: gauges measure the difference between the pressure in the tank and outside; you may assume that the outside pressure is 1 atm.)

Answers

4.1: (a) 258.486 kJ/mol (b) 1421 °C

4.2: ΔH = 31.3 kJ/mol, error = 0.9 kJ/mol, 76.86 °C.

4.3: (a) 23.41 kJ (b) 26.62, 22.81, 20.63 kJ (c) 52.23 torr

4.4: T = 183.47 K (obs 184.52), ΔH = 15.45 kJ (obs 14.72) (gas) 2.058 gm/liter (liq) 523 gm/liter.

4.5: T = 146.4 K, ΔH = 8.22 kJ, density = 382 gm/liter, 2.59 gm/liter

4.6: (a) 26.21 atm, 6.515 kJ/mol (b) 358 mL, 142 mL

4.7: (a) At 90 °F, weight = 35.57 lb, gauge pressure = 174.4 psig. (b) At 60 °F, weight = 38.17 lb, gauge pressure = 112.4 psig. (c) 7% less by weight.

CHAPTER 5

STATISTICAL THERMODYNAMICS

Statistical mechanics provides the connection between the mechanical properties of atoms and molecules and their macroscopic properties — that is, the properties of matter in bulk. This chapter demonstrates the calculation of the thermodynamic properties introduced in Chapters 2 and 3 for ideal gases (standard-state properties).

Atoms and molecules obey the laws of quantum mechanics. For the purposes of this chapter, the only thing you need to know about quantum mechanics is its most important conclusion, that energy is quantized. That is, a molecule may have only certain values for its energy: the *energy levels* of the system. This is actually known experimentally (from spectroscopy) and quantum mechanics merely provides an explanation for the phenomenon. Furthermore, the energy levels of a molecule can be measured experimentally, and that is all that is needed to calculate its thermodynamic properties.

5.1 Configurations and Entropy

The connection between the states of individual atoms and molecules and thermodynamics is provided by Boltzmann's formula for entropy

$$S = k_b \ln W \tag{5.1}$$

where W is the number of equivalent configurations possible for the system.

Example 5.1 Probability for coin flips.

The basis of statistical mechanics is that molecules, in large quantities, can be treated using the laws of probability. In this example we explore probability and randomness with a simple example: the flipping of coins. A direct application can be made to the distribution of molecules between two connected equal-volume containers. The distribution of the molecules between the containers is, presumably, determined by a coin flip: heads, put it in box 1; tails, put it in box 2.

The probability (P) for getting p heads in N tosses is given by:

$$P(N,p) = \frac{1}{2^n}\frac{N!}{p!(N-p)!} \tag{5.2}$$

The calculation of factorials with Mathcad could not be easier:

$0! = 1 \qquad 4! = 24 \qquad 10! = 3.629\cdot 10^{6} \qquad 100! = 9.333\cdot 10^{157}$

The calculation of the probabilities using Eq. (5.2) is illustrated in the box below.

$C(N,p) := \dfrac{N!}{p!\cdot(N-p)!} \qquad N := 6 \qquad j := 0..N$

$prob_j := \dfrac{C(N,j)}{2^N} \qquad \sum_j prob_j = 1$

$$prob = \begin{bmatrix} 0.016 \\ 0.094 \\ 0.234 \\ 0.313 \\ 0.234 \\ 0.094 \\ 0.016 \end{bmatrix}$$

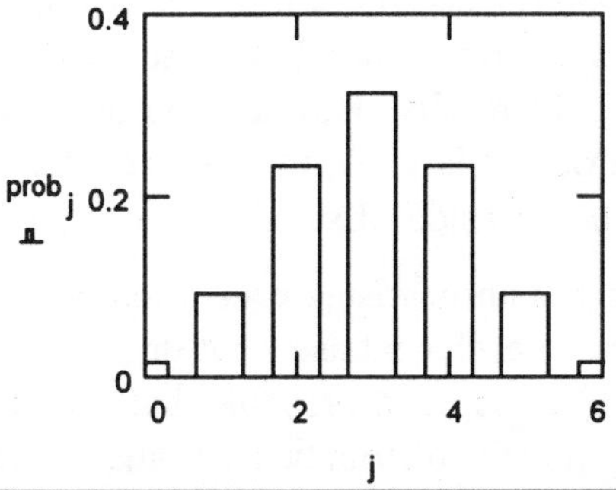

The create the bar graph, open the graph-format menu (double click on the graph) and select trace-type bar for trace 1. Note the sum of the probabilities is 1, as it should be, and most probable result is half heads and half tails. The latter conclusion is not surprising, but you may be surprised that the probability of getting exactly half each is rather small. Repeat the calculation for increasing number (N); you will see that for larger numbers, the probability of getting exactly half each gets smaller, but (looking at the graph) the probability tends to clump in the middle: that is, the probability of getting close to one half is getting larger — it becomes overwhelming for really big numbers, but this is difficult to illustrate by this method since the large-number factorials cause numeric overflow.

The box below illustrates the calculation that p (the number or heads, or the number of molecules in one of the equal-volume containers) is within ±20% of the mean.

$N := 20 \qquad j := 0..N \qquad prob_j := \dfrac{C(N,j)}{2^N} \qquad n1 := 0.4\cdot N \qquad n1 = 8$

$n2 := 0.6\cdot N \qquad n2 = 12$

$$\sum_{j=n1}^{n2} prob_j = 0.737$$

Repeat the calculation, increasing N. (It is necessary that the numbers $n1$ and $n2$ are integers, for which it suffices that N be a multiple of 5.) At what number does the probability become greater than 99%? At what number is the calculation halted by numeric overflow?

Given that there are $N/2$ particles in each container, what is the likely fluctuation from that mean? The theory of random walks (Noggle, Chapter 9) demonstrates that fluctuations for

N particles are a normal error distribution with standard deviation of $\sqrt{N}$. In this case, there are *N*/2 in each container, so most fluctuations should fall between ($N \pm \sqrt{N}$)/2; this can be demonstrated with a calculation.

$$C(n,p) := \frac{n!}{p!\cdot(n-p)!} \qquad \text{Try N = 16, 36, 64, 100, 144}$$

$$N := 64 \qquad j := 0..N \qquad prob_j := \frac{C(N,j)}{2^N} \qquad n1 := \frac{N-\sqrt{N}}{2} \qquad n1 = 28$$

$$\sum_{j=n1}^{n2} prob_j = 0.740 \qquad n2 := \frac{N+\sqrt{N}}{2} \qquad n2 = 36$$

The nature of the calculation restricts us to values of *N* that are squares of even numbers, and numbers of this ilk greater than 144 cause overflow. Do the calculation for *N* = 16, 36, 64, 100 and 144, noting the results. How do your numbers compare? What is the trend? (It is proven in Chapter 9 that, for large *N*, the standard deviation is the square root of *N*. Recall that the probability of being inside ±1 standard deviation for a normal error distribution is 0.683.)

The rather unsurprising conclusion is that the most probable result is that half of the particles will be in each container; but this is not the only thing that can happen. For *N* = 64, for example, 32-32 is most probable, but 30-34 is also quite possible. As you go to larger numbers, however, the distribution becomes relatively narrower, and the probability of being *close* to the most probable result (half in each) becomes very large. With very large numbers, the distribution becomes narrow enough that it is not too far from wrong to assume that the most probable result is the only possibility. But fluctuations from the mean do occur, and account for some interesting facts — like that blue color of the sky.

To deal with larger numbers, we need a better way to calculate factorials, which is the subject of the next example.

Example 5.2 Stirling's approximation.

As the preceding example illustrates, factorials grow very rapidly and cause numeric overflow for large numbers. For large numbers, factorials can be approximated by Stirling's formula given in the box below, which also compares the exact and approximate calculations.

$$\text{lnW}(n) := 0.5\cdot\ln(2\cdot\pi) + (n + .5)\cdot\ln(n) - n + \frac{1}{12\cdot n} - \frac{1}{360\cdot n^3}$$ Stirling's Formula

$\ln(20!) = 42.336$ $\qquad$ $\text{lnW}(20) = 42.336$

$\ln(100!) = 363.739$ $\qquad$ $\text{lnW}(100) = 363.739$

$\ln(1000!) =$ overflow $\qquad$ $\text{lnW}(1000) = 5.912\cdot 10^3$ $\qquad$ $\sum_{m=1}^{1000} \ln(m) = 5.912\cdot 10^3$

$1000\cdot\ln(1000) - 1000 = 5.908\cdot 10^3$

Even for 20 the approximation is quite good, and it gets better for larger numbers. For 1000, the exact number cannot be calculated directly because of numeric overflow, but it can be calculated exactly as the sum of the logarithms. The last line tests the approximate formula:

$$\ln(N!) = N\ln(N) - N \tag{5.3}$$

which can be seen to be fairly good even for $N = 1000$. For the gigantic number of molecules in even a microscopic bit of matter, the approximation of Eq. (5.3) is good enough, and it is used to derive many of the formulas of statistical mechanics (for example, Boltzmann's law, illustrated below).

Example 5.3 The mass distribution and entropy of isotopic mixing.

The formula for entropy of mixing is:

$$\Delta_{\text{mix}}S = -R\sum_i n_i \ln(X_i) \tag{5.4}$$

Chlorine consists of two isotopes, 75.53% ^{35}Cl and 24.47% ^{37}Cl. Chloroform, CCl_3H (ignoring the isotopes of carbon and hydrogen) consists of molecules with 4 different masses, with 0 to 4 mass-35 chlorine atoms (the remainder mass 37). The fraction with all mass-35 is $(0.7553)^3$; the fraction with 2 mass-35 and 1 mass-37 is $3(0.7553)^2(0.2447)$ (times 3 because there are three ways to choose the mass-37 atom), and so forth. The full calculation is shown in the box below.

$pa := .7553$ $\qquad$ $pb := 1 - pa$ $\qquad$ $i := 0..3$ $\qquad$ $R := 8.31451$

$$X := \begin{bmatrix} pa^3 \\ 3\cdot pa^2\cdot pb \\ 3\cdot pa\cdot pb^2 \\ pb^3 \end{bmatrix} \qquad X = \begin{bmatrix} 0.431 \\ 0.419 \\ 0.136 \\ 0.015 \end{bmatrix} \qquad \sum_i X_i = 1 \qquad \Delta S := -R\cdot\sum_i X_i\cdot\ln(X_i)$$

$\Delta S = 8.815$

We have assumed one mole total so n_i in Eq. (5.4) is equal to the mole fraction X_i. (The unit for ΔS is the unit of R: J K^{-1}mol^{-1}.) The calculated distribution vector would be observed in the mass spectroscopy as a pattern of peaks separated by mass 2, with an intensity distribution given by **X**.

				1		1				
			1		2		1			
		1		3		3		1		
	1		4		6		4		1	
1		5		10		10		5		1

The coefficients used in **X**, (1, 3, 3, 1) give the number of combinations that result can be made at random. For example (A = ^{35}Cl, B = ^{37}Cl), the second result can be made as AAB, ABA or BAA. (These are also the binomial coefficients.) There is a formula for the number of combinations, but the simplest method for generating them is Pascal's triangle (table to left). Each additional row is formed by adding the adjacent two numbers in the row above.

The most serious error in this calculation is the neglect of ^{13}C, which is 1.1% in natural abundance. Show that, when this is included, the entropy of mixing is $\Delta S = 9.318$ and the fractions are {0.426, 0.414, 0.134, 0.014, 0.005, 0.005, 0.001, 1.612×10^{-4}} (the first 4 for ^{12}C and the last 4 for ^{13}C, with the chlorine-numbers in the order as before). (A possible error here, if you do this problem as an extension of the previous one, is to forget to change the index (*i*) for the new vector of mole fractions — that is, be sure to sum over *all* of the elements of **X**.)

5.2 Boltzmann's Law

The number of distinguishable permutations of N objects consisting of N_1 objects of type 1, N_2 objects of type 2 and so forth is given by

$$W(N,\{N_i\}) = \frac{N!}{\prod_i N_i!} \tag{5.5}$$

where Π denotes a product and N is the sum of the set of numbers $\{N_i\}$. The product operation in Mathcad is on the calculus palette. Try these examples, which illustrate the product operator.

$1^1 \cdot 2^2 \cdot 3^2 \cdot 4^2 = 576$ $\quad i := 1..4 \quad$ $\prod_i i^2 = 576$ $\quad (4!)^2 = 576$

Example 5.4 Permutations of the letters of a word.

We illustrate Eq. (5.5) by calculating the number of permutations of the letters in the word MISSISSIPPI. For the calculation (box right), a vector with 6 elements is used to represent the 4 distinct letters of the word; the excess elements cause no harm (since 0! = 1) (the next example, for which this is a template, requires 6 numbers). The entropy (S) is calculated with Eq. (5.1) using R in place of Boltzmann's constant (effectively, the entropy of a mole

$R := 8.31451$

mississippi

$p := \begin{bmatrix} 1 \\ 4 \\ 4 \\ 2 \\ 0 \\ 0 \end{bmatrix}$ $\quad n_t := \sum p \quad n_t = 11$

$i := 0..\mathrm{last}(p) \quad W := \frac{n_t!}{\prod_i p_i!}$

$W = 3.465\cdot10^4 \quad S := R\cdot\ln(W) \quad S = 86.912$

of words "MISSISSIPPI")

Now generalize the example to a set of 11 objects distributed among 6 boxes. (The analogy is an 11-letter word, made from varying numbers of 6 distinct letters.) The objects are distinguished only by the box they are in. One possible distribution is {1, 4, 4, 2, 0, 0} as in the box above. What distribution has the maximum entropy? It is clear that we need to make the denominator of Eq. (5.5) as small as possible, and this can be done by distributing the particles as evenly as possible; the distribution {2, 2, 2, 2, 2, 1} has S = 116.707, and this is the maximum.

Example 5.5 Distribution of identical particles among a set of energy levels.

Now, following up on the preceding example, suppose that what distinguishes the boxes is the energy of the objects within. Thus, they may represent the energy levels of some system. We choose a new example as shown in the box below.

$$e := \begin{bmatrix} 0 \\ 1 \\ 2 \\ 3 \\ 4 \\ 5 \end{bmatrix} \quad p := \begin{bmatrix} 32 \\ 16 \\ 8 \\ 4 \\ 2 \\ 1 \end{bmatrix}$$

$R := 8.31451$

$n_t := \sum p \qquad n_t = 63 \qquad i := 0 .. \mathrm{last}(p)$

$E := e \cdot p \qquad E = 57 \qquad W := \dfrac{n_t!}{\prod_i p_i!} \qquad W = 1.861 \cdot 10^{32}$

$S := R \cdot \ln(W) \qquad S = 617.799$

We use 6 states with energy 0 to 5 (arbitrary units). The total energy

$$E = \sum_i p_i e_i$$

is calculated by making a dot product between the vector of energies (**e**) and the vector of population (**p**). This example also demonstrates the vector sum (Σ with no summation index, used for the population vector, above); it is available on the Matrices palette.

Starting with this example, vary the populations keeping the total number of objects (63) and total energy (57) constant. Here is another example:

$$e := \begin{bmatrix} 0 \\ 1 \\ 2 \\ 3 \\ 4 \\ 5 \end{bmatrix} \quad p := \begin{bmatrix} 33 \\ 14 \\ 9 \\ 4 \\ 2 \\ 1 \end{bmatrix}$$

$R := 8.31451$ Keep N=63 and E=57

$n_t := \sum p \qquad n_t = 63 \qquad i := 0 .. \mathrm{last}(p)$

$E := e \cdot p \qquad E = 57 \qquad W := \dfrac{n_t!}{\prod_i p_i!} \qquad W = 1.504 \cdot 10^{32}$

$S := R \cdot \ln(W) \qquad S = 616.027$

This has a smaller probability and entropy than the original. Here is an example with a very small entropy.

$$e := \begin{bmatrix} 0 \\ 1 \\ 2 \\ 3 \\ 4 \\ 5 \end{bmatrix} \quad p := \begin{bmatrix} 45 \\ 3 \\ 5 \\ 2 \\ 2 \\ 6 \end{bmatrix}$$

R := 8.31451   Keep N=63 and E=57

$n_t := \sum p$ $n_t = 63$ $i := 0..\,\mathrm{last}(p)$

$E := e \cdot p$ $E = 57$ $W := \dfrac{n_t!}{\prod_i p_i!}$ $W = 7.993 \cdot 10^{24}$

$S := R \cdot \ln(W)$ $S = 476.759$

The original distribution (above) is the one having the maximum probability (maximum entropy) for the same energy and number of particles. The Boltzmann distribution is the distribution with maximum probability (maximum entropy) for a given fixed energy and number of systems. The population of a set of energy levels with energy ε_i at temperature T is:

$$p_i = \frac{N_i}{N} = \frac{e^{-\varepsilon_i/k_b T}}{z} \quad \text{with } z = \sum_{\text{all } j} e^{-\varepsilon_j/k_b T} \tag{5.6}$$

From this, it is readily shown that the ratio of two levels separated by $\Delta\varepsilon$ is proportional to $\exp(\Delta\varepsilon/k_b T)$; for a set of levels with constant $\Delta\varepsilon$, the ratio of populations is constant, which is the case for the original distribution of this example. Equation (5.6) is called Boltzmann's law; Eq. (5.7) (below) is a more general statement of this law.

Example 5.6 Boltzmann distribution for a 2-level system.

For practical use we will rewrite Eq. (5.6) with the energy in kelvin — $\theta_i = \varepsilon_i/k_b$ — and including the possibility of a degeneracy g_i for the levels:

$$p_i = \frac{N_i}{N} = \frac{g_i\, e^{-\theta_i/T}}{z} \quad \text{with } z = \sum_{\text{all } j} g_j\, e^{-\theta_j/T} \tag{5.7}$$

The energy in K (θ) will be denoted as e in Mathcad, since that is easier to type.

A lot about the Boltzmann distribution can be understood by examining the simplest possible energy-level system: 2 levels.

$j := 0..1$

$e_j :=$	$g_j :=$
0	1
100	1

$$z(T) := \sum_j g_j \cdot \exp\left(-\frac{e_j}{T}\right) \qquad \mathrm{pop}(j,T) := \frac{1}{z(T)} \cdot \left(g_j \cdot \exp\left(-\frac{e_j}{T}\right)\right)$$

R := 8.31451

The calculation has been set up in such a way that it is easy to extend it to other examples (with more levels). Sample calculations for the partition function (z) and populations (p, called *pop* in Mathcad).

z(20) = 1.007 z(100) = 1.368 z(500) = 1.819 z(5000) = 1.98

pop(j,20)	pop(j,100)	pop(j,500)	pop(j,5000)
0.993	0.731	0.55	0.505
0.007	0.269	0.45	0.495

The average energy (E) is for a mole (L particles) is calculated as:

$$E = L\sum_i p_i \varepsilon_i = R\sum_i p_i \theta_i \tag{5.8}$$

(Unit: J/mol) The average energy is also the internal energy referenced to 0 K (where all particles are in the ground state: $E = U - U_0$ (U_0 is the internal energy at 0 K).

$$E(T) := R\cdot\left(\sum_j e_j \cdot pop(j,T)\right)$$

$$T := 10, 20 .. 600$$

$$C_v(T) := \frac{d}{dT}E(T)$$

$$S(T) := R\cdot\ln(z(T)) + \frac{E(T)}{T}$$

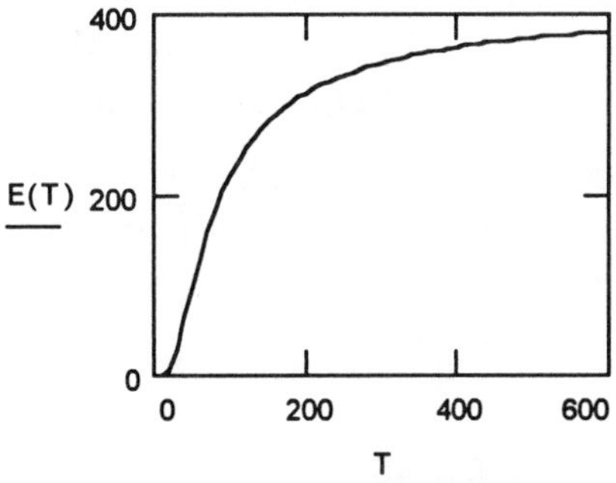

(unit: J) The heat capacity (at constant volume) is the derivative of the internal energy; in Mathcad, this derivative is calculated numerically. The graphs for heat capacity and entropy are shown in the box below.

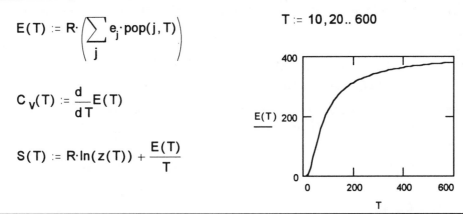

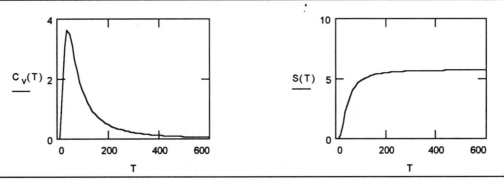

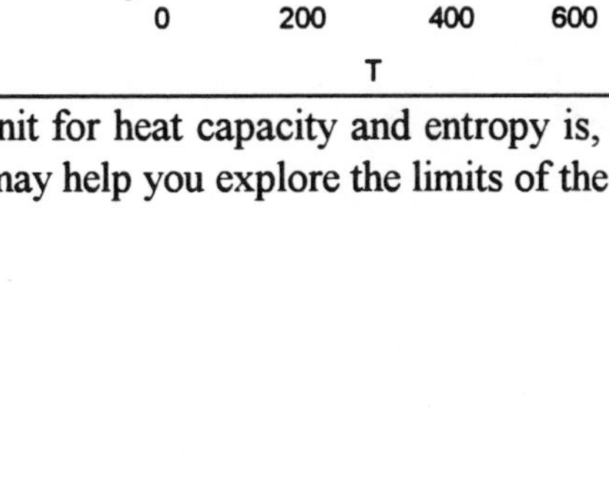

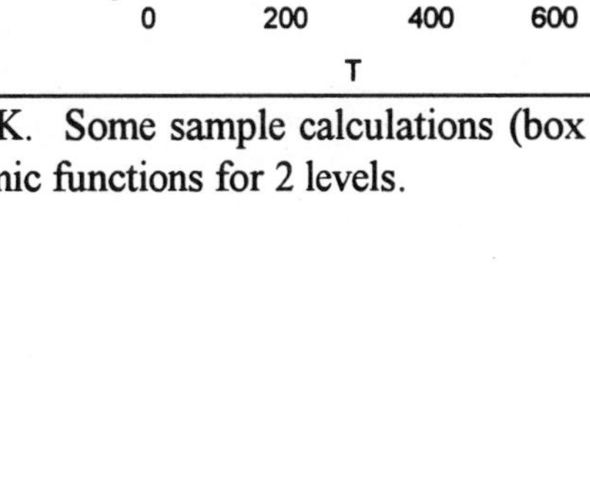

The unit for heat capacity and entropy is, of course, J/K. Some sample calculations (box below) may help you explore the limits of the thermodynamic functions for 2 levels.

$T := 100, 500 .. 2100$

E(T)	$C_V(T)$	S(T)
223.612	1.635	4.841
374.291	0.082	5.722
392.653	0.026	5.75
399.744	0.012	5.757
403.502	0.007	5.76
405.829	0.005	5.761

$\frac{100 \cdot R}{2} = 415.726$ $R \cdot \ln(2) = 5.763$

What is the significance of the calculations in the lower corners, and how would they change if the original system changed (in energy or degeneracy)?

Modify this example for larger numbers of levels and for other degeneracy patterns. Never miss an opportunity to use Mathcad and models of this sort to explore and learn.

Example 5.7 Boltzmann distribution for a series of equally spaced levels.

For a series of equally spaced levels, it is simpler to use a formula to calculate the energy and degeneracy vectors than to type them in.

$j := 0 .. 25$ $e_j := j \cdot 100$ $g_j := 1$ $z(T) := \sum_j g_j \cdot \exp\left(-\frac{e_j}{T}\right)$

$R := 8.31451$ $pop(j, T) := \frac{1}{z(T)} \cdot \left(g_j \cdot \exp\left(-\frac{e_j}{T}\right)\right)$

A bar graph of the populations is interesting and informative:

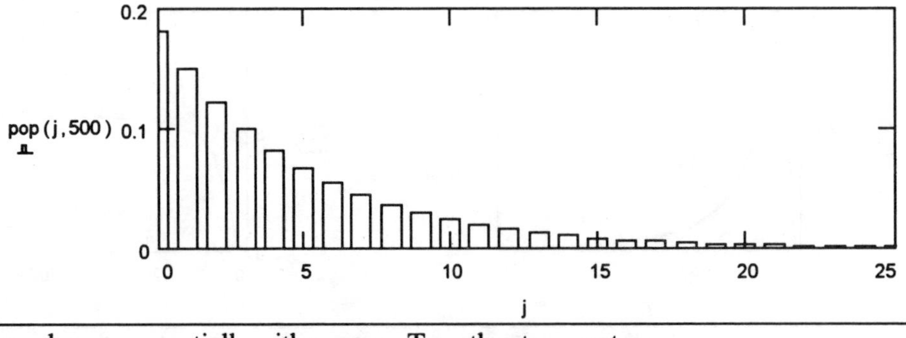

Populations drop exponentially with energy. Try other temperatures.

Calculations of energy and heat capacity can be quite slow with so many levels, but try them anyway. The slowness is primarily in taking the derivative for the heat capacity. Unfortunately, this system is most interesting for a very large (effectively infinite) number of levels, in which case it represents a harmonic oscillator (representing, approximately, the effect of molecular vibration). The infinite sum required for the harmonic oscillator is evaluated in most texts; the result is given and explored in the next example.

$$E(T) := R\cdot\left(\sum_j e_j\cdot pop(j,T)\right) \qquad C_v(T) := \frac{d}{dT}E(T)$$

$n := 0..4$

$T_n :=$	$E(T_n)$	$C_v(T_n)$
20	5.64	1.42
50	130.137	6.02
100	483.885	7.655
300	$2.098\cdot10^3$	8.13
500	$3.635\cdot10^3$	7.033

Example 5.8 Boltzmann distribution and thermodynamics of a harmonic oscillator.

The vibration of a chemical bond can be approximated as a harmonic oscillator — a spring obeying Hooke's law. The partition function for this system is:

$$z_{vib} = \frac{1}{1-\exp(-\theta_v / T)} \tag{5.9}$$

where θ_v is the vibrational constant (e.g. Table 5.1 Noggle), representing the stiffness of the bond-spring. From this (or any partition function) the energy and entropy are calculated as:

$$U - U_0 = RT^2\frac{d\ln(z)}{T} = \frac{RT^2}{z}\frac{dz}{dT}$$
$$S = R\ln(z) + \frac{U-U_0}{T} \tag{5.10}$$

(We will assume $U_0 = 0$.)

For carbon monoxide the vibrational constant (denoted *thv*) is 3122 K.

thv := 3122 for CO, carbon monoxide $\qquad$ R := 8.31451

$$z(T) := \frac{1}{1-\exp\left(-\frac{thv}{T}\right)} \qquad U(T) := \frac{R\cdot T^2}{z(T)}\cdot\frac{d}{dT}z(T) \qquad S(T) := R\cdot\ln(z(T)) + \frac{U(T)}{T}$$

We can graph or calculate any of these quantities.

$T := 50, 100..6000$

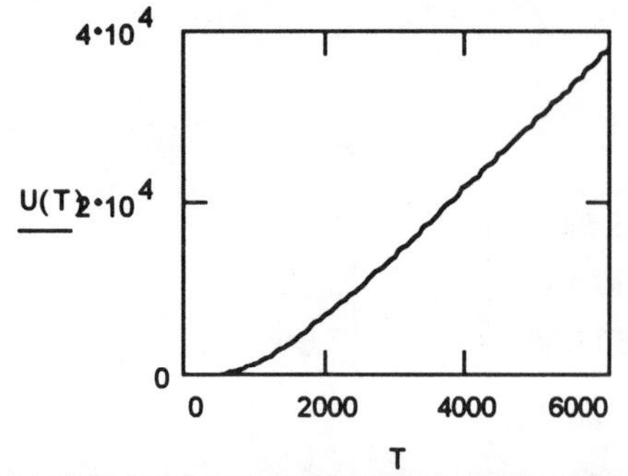

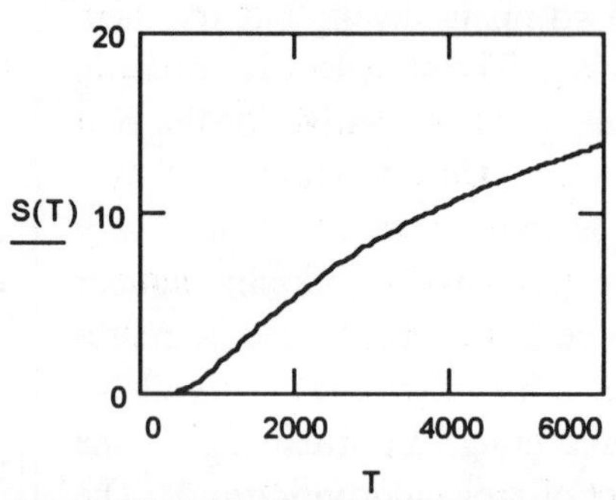

The heat capacity is problematical because of the derivatives (which are done numerically by Mathcad, unless you go to the trouble to do them symbolically). Errors are quite possible as the example following may demonstrate (the problem may be corrected in your version, so your results may not be identical to these).

$C_V(T) := \frac{d}{dT}U(T)$ $\quad C_V(200) = 8.315 \quad C_V(500) = 0.632 \quad C_V(5000) = 8.05$

$U(198) = 0.004$

$\frac{U(202) - U(198)}{4} = 3.376 \cdot 10^{-4}$

$U(202) = 0.005$

The answer at 200 K is completely incorrect, as the finite-difference of the last line demonstrates. You may find this to be different in your calculation, but the lesson is still valid: numerical differentiation is a troublesome procedure that can and will fail in certain circumstances no matter how good the algorithm is. What is needed, for both speed and accuracy, are the symbolic formulas derived in most texts. (Although the symbolic capabilities of Mathcad can be helpful in these derivations, we shall simply use the results. Mathcad's contribution here, and it is an important one, is to enable facile calculation and graphing.)

The box to the right shows the exact calculation at 200 K using the symbolic formula for heat capacity.

$u := \frac{thv}{200} \qquad \frac{R \cdot u^2 \cdot \exp(u)}{(\exp(u) - 1)^2} = 3.367 \cdot 10^{-4}$

5.3 Calculating Thermodynamic Properties

In many cases, particularly for small molecules at high temperature (and if the temperature is high enough, small molecules are all you are likely to have), statistical calculation of thermodynamic properties is the method of choice. Practical calculations are done by direct summation in the manner illustrated above, but this method is not practical with a program such as Mathcad (it would be very slow, as Example 5.8 illustrates). The formulas derived in texts (e.g. Noggle, Table 5.3) make approximations but are reasonably accurate. They are easy to use (with Mathcad or any similar program) and illustrate the patterns and nature of thermodynamic properties for simple molecules. This section presents calculations for stable molecules that obey Lewis pairing — that is, they have no low-lying electronic states (exceptions are discussed in the next section).

Example 5.9 Translational partition function and entropy.

The energy for translation is very simple, $U_{tr} = {}^3/_2RT$, and its calculation needs no help from a computer, but the partition function (below) and entropy are more involved and help is appreciated.

$$mw := 39.948 \cdot \frac{gm}{mole} \quad R := 8.31451 \cdot \frac{joule}{K \cdot mole} \quad L := \frac{6.022137 \cdot 10^{23}}{mole}$$

$$k_b := \frac{R}{L} \qquad m := \frac{mw}{L} \qquad h := 6.626075 \cdot 10^{-34} \cdot joule \cdot sec$$

$$Ps := 10^5 \cdot Pa \quad \text{standard pressure} \qquad V(T) := \frac{R \cdot T}{Ps}$$

$$z_{tr}(T) := \frac{\left(2 \cdot \pi \cdot m \cdot k_b \cdot T\right)^{1.5} \cdot V(T)}{h^3}$$

$$z_{tr}(100 \cdot K) = 3.945 \cdot 10^{29} \qquad z_{tr}(300 \cdot K) = 6.15 \cdot 10^{30}$$

We do the calculation for a monatomic gas, argon, since it has no other contributions to its properties. The calculation of the translational partition function is shown in the box to the left. We use the standard pressure (1 bar) and, since the formulas assume ideal gas (they neglect intermolecular interactions), the quantity calculated is the standard-state partition function. The entropy is calculated using Eq. (5.33), Noggle (see below — this equation is different from Eq. (5.10), above; see box below). The calculated entropy is very close to the value observed.

$$T := 298.15 \cdot K \qquad U := 1.5 \cdot R \cdot T \qquad S_{tr} := R \cdot \ln\left(\frac{z_{tr}(T)}{L}\right) + R + \frac{U}{T} \qquad \text{Eq. (5.33), TEXT}$$

$$S_{tr} = 154.847 \cdot \frac{joule}{K} \qquad \underline{\text{obs } 154.853 \text{ J/K}}$$

$$1.5 \cdot R \cdot \ln\left(\frac{mw}{gm}\right) + 2.5 \cdot R \cdot \ln\left(\frac{T}{K}\right) - 1.15167 \cdot R = 154.847 \cdot \frac{joule}{K}$$

The last calculation above uses Eq. (5.35) Noggle, which is a simplification of the translational entropy formula, with values substituted for all constants. As you can see, it gives the same answer with far less trouble, so we shall use it from now on.

Example 5.10 Entropy and heat capacity of a diatomic molecule.

For a diatomic molecule with no low-lying electronic states, we need to add contributions for molecular rotation and vibration to that of translation. We use carbon monoxide (CO) as an example. The box below gives data for CO (*sigma* denotes the symmetry number, $\sigma = 1$, *thv* denotes the vibrational constant, θ_v, and *thr* denotes the rotational constant, θ_r).

$thv := 3122.43$ $\quad thr := 2.7788$ $\quad sigma := 1$ $\quad mw := 12.011 + 15.9994$

$$C_v(T) := 1.5 \cdot R + R + \frac{R \cdot \left(\frac{thv}{T}\right)^2 \cdot \exp\left(\frac{thv}{T}\right)}{\left(\exp\left(\frac{thv}{T}\right) - 1\right)^2}$$

$R := 8.31451$ $\quad cal := 4.184$

$T := 100, 110 .. 3000$

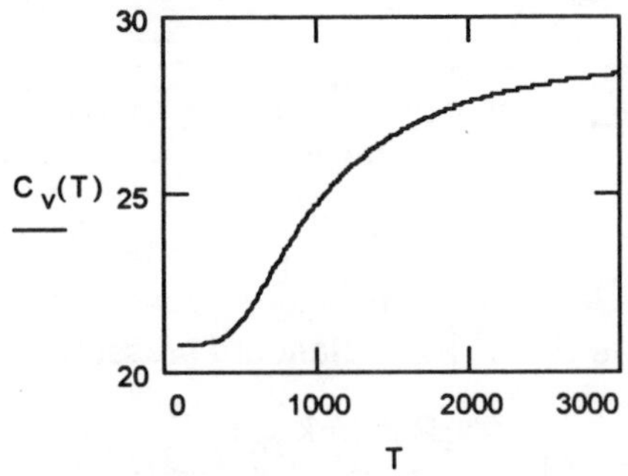

$C_p(T) := C_v(T) + R$

$C_p(298.15) = 29.127$ $\quad$ obs 29.142

(unit J/K, for one mole)

The graph shows the characteristic behavior of the heat capacity of a diatomic molecule vs. temperature: increasing slowly at low temperature, rising rapidly, and leveling off at high temperature. Other diatomics exhibit the same behavior, differing only in the temperature at which the rapid rise occurs, which is determined by the value of *thv*.

Because of the approximations made, the heat capacity at high temperature is a more critical test of the formula; comparisons are shown below.

$C_p(1000) = 33.008$ $\quad$ JANAF gives $7.931 \cdot cal = 33.183$

$C_p(2000) = 35.914$ $\quad$ JANAF gives $8.664 \cdot cal = 36.250$

$C_p(3000) = 36.704$ $\quad$ JANAF gives $8.895 \cdot cal = 37.217$

Even at 3000 K, the error is not too serious, and most of this error can be corrected by a simple remedy described below (Example 5.14).

The entropy calculation is illustrated in the box below. Because the formula is so long, the translation, rotational and vibrational contributions are calculated separately; this also affords us an opportunity to compare their relative contributions.

$$Str(T) := 1.5 \cdot R \cdot \ln(mw) + 2.5 \cdot R \cdot \ln(T) - 1.15167 \cdot R \qquad Srot(T) := R + R \cdot \ln\left(\frac{T}{sigma \cdot thr}\right)$$

$$Svib(T) := \frac{R \cdot \left(\frac{thv}{T}\right)}{\exp\left(\frac{thv}{T}\right) - 1} - R \cdot \ln\left(1 - \exp\left(-\frac{thv}{T}\right)\right) \qquad S(T) := Str(T) + Srot(T) + Svib(T)$$

Some results, compared to experiment, are shown next. Note how much the various motions contribute the entropy.

S(298.15) = 197.612	obs 197.674	Str(298.15) = 150.419
		Srot(298.15) = 47.19
		Svib(298.15) = 0.003

S(1000) = 234.396   JANAF gives 56.026·cal = 234.413

S(2000) = 258.403   JANAF gives 61.807·cal = 258.600   vibration only (below)

S(3000) = 273.143   JANAF gives 65.370·cal = 273.508   Svib(3000) = 8.347

The accuracy is good even at 3000 K; the vibrational contribution is relatively small even at that temperature.

Having set up one problem, it is duck soup to try others — all you have to do is vary the constants. In particular, try various molecules to see how the heat capacity varies from one to the other and with temperature. Try some homonuclear diatomics ($\sigma = 2$). What is the effect of σ? Again, use Mathcad to explore and learn; the first problem is always the hardest.

Example 5.11 Entropy and heat capacity of a polyatomic molecule.

We take our example for a nonlinear molecule, methane (CH_4). Methane has $N = 5$ atoms and, hence, 15 degrees of freedom; of these, 3 are translational, 3 are rotational and $3N - 6 = 9$ are vibrational. Hence, there are 9 vibrational constants of which some are degenerate: there are only 4 distinct constants. These are given in the list *thv* below. For rotation, the product of the three rotational temperatures, $\theta_a\theta_b\theta_c$, is denoted *thr3*.

sigma := 12   thr3 := 435.6   mw := 12.011 + 4·1.00794

j := 0 .. 8   R := 8.31451   cal := 4.184

$$thv_j := \begin{pmatrix} 4193 \\ 2196 \\ 2196 \\ 4345 \\ 4345 \\ 4345 \\ 1879 \\ 1879 \\ 1879 \end{pmatrix}$$

$$C_v(T) := 1.5\cdot R + 1.5\cdot R + \sum_j \frac{R\cdot\left(\frac{thv_j}{T}\right)^2\cdot\exp\left(\frac{thv_j}{T}\right)}{\left(\exp\left(\frac{thv_j}{T}\right) - 1\right)^2}$$

$$C_p(T) := C_v(T) + R$$

T := 200, 220 .. 3000

$C_p(298.15) = 35.655$

compare 35.309

$C_p(3000) = 101.397$

compare 24.233·cal = 101.391

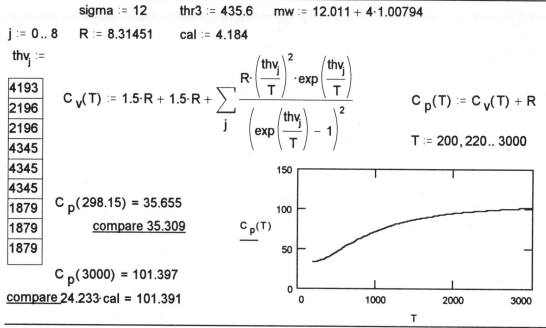

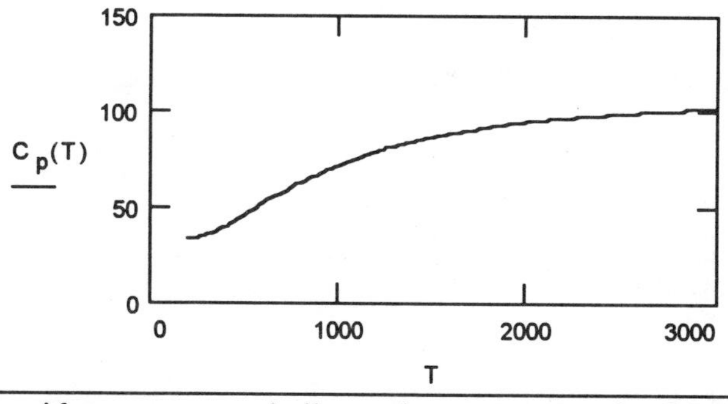

Methane exhibits a rise in heat capacity with temperature similar to the one we saw for CO, but both larger and more gradual; it is more gradual because it has several vibrational constants and the different vibrational terms of the heat capacity begin their rise at different temperatures, thus smearing out the effect.

The entropy calculation is shown next (the molecular weight, *mw*, in the formula for translational entropy must be in grams).

$$\mathrm{Str}(T) := 1.5\cdot R\cdot \ln(mw) + 2.5\cdot R\cdot \ln(T) - 1.15167\cdot R \qquad \mathrm{Srot}(T) := 1.5\cdot R + R\cdot \ln\left(\frac{\sqrt{\pi}\cdot T^{1.5}}{sigma\cdot\sqrt{thr3}}\right)$$

$$\mathrm{Svib}(T) := \sum_j \left[\frac{R\cdot\left(\frac{thv_j}{T}\right)}{\exp\left(\frac{thv_j}{T}\right)-1} - R\cdot\ln\left(1-\exp\left(-\frac{thv_j}{T}\right)\right)\right] \qquad S(T) := \mathrm{Str}(T) + \mathrm{Srot}(T) + \mathrm{Svib}(T)$$

$S(298.15) = 186.258$ compare 186.264 $\mathrm{Svib}(298.15) = 0.423$

The accuracy is excellent. The vibrational contribution, although small, is significant.

The calculation for linear polyatomics has much in common with that for diatomics (Example 5.10), except that there are now $3N - 5$ vibrations. We take carbon dioxide (CO_2, with 3 atoms and 4 vibrations) as the example.

$j := 0..3 \quad sigma := 2 \quad thr := 0.56166 \quad mw := 12.011 + 2\cdot 15.9994$

$R := 8.31451 \quad cal := 4.184$

$thv_j :=$

1997
960
960
3380

$$C_v(T) := 1.5\cdot R + R + \sum_j \frac{R\cdot\left(\frac{thv_j}{T}\right)^2\cdot\exp\left(\frac{thv_j}{T}\right)}{\left(\exp\left(\frac{thv_j}{T}\right)-1\right)^2} \qquad C_p(T) := C_v(T) + R$$

$T := 200, 220..3000$

The heat capacity:

$C_p(298.15) = 37.049$

compare 37.11

$C_p(3000) = 61.091$

compare $14.873\cdot cal = 62.229$

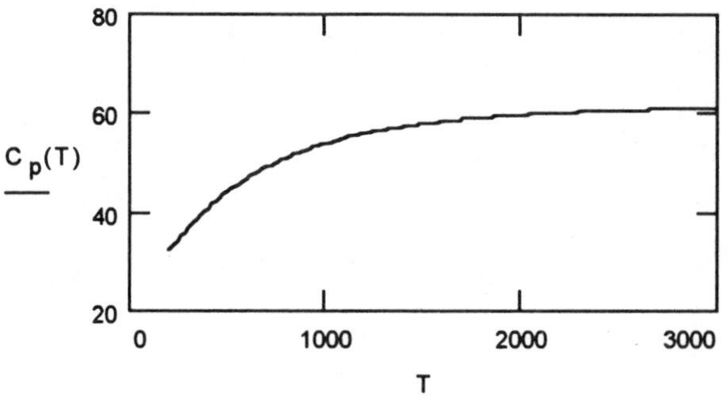

The entropy:

$$\mathrm{Str}(T) := 1.5 \cdot R \cdot \ln(mw) + 2.5 \cdot R \cdot \ln(T) - 1.15167 \cdot R \qquad \mathrm{Srot}(T) := R + R \cdot \ln\left(\frac{T}{sigma \cdot thr}\right)$$

$$\mathrm{Svib}(T) := \sum_j \left[\frac{R \cdot \left(\frac{thv_j}{T}\right)}{\exp\left(\frac{thv_j}{T}\right) - 1} - R \cdot \ln\left(1 - \exp\left(-\frac{thv_j}{T}\right)\right)\right] \qquad S(T) := \mathrm{Str}(T) + \mathrm{Srot}(T) + \mathrm{Svib}(T)$$

$S(298.15) = 213.762$ compare 213.74 $\mathrm{Svib}(298.15) = 2.987$

It is simple and instructive to repeat these calculations for other molecules, but avoid those with a ground-state degeneracy or low-lying excited electronic states, since these have additional contributions as explained in the next section.

5.4 Excited Electronic States

If you have not studied quantum mechanics, the only excited electronic states with which you are likely to be familiar are those of the hydrogen atom, which has a 1*s* ground state and excited states 2*s*, 2*p*, 3*d* and so forth. All atoms and molecules have such excited states, but there are no simple formulas for calculating their energies. However, the electronic energy can be measured with spectroscopy and, from the measured energies, the contribution to thermodynamic properties can be calculated.

There is a very large (perhaps infinite) number of electronic states, and summing over all of them is impossible. However, you only need to sum over those with a significant population, as determined by Boltzmann's law, Eq. (5.7). An electronic state with energy ε, expressed in temperature units as $\theta = \varepsilon / k_b$, can be ignored if $\theta >> T$ for the highest temperature to be calculated. In chemistry, we are rarely interested in temperatures higher than 5000 K (the temperature of an acetylene-oxygen flame is 3300 K), so we will never consider excited states above 50000 K.

Stable molecules generally have closed electronic shells, with all electrons paired. Such molecules rarely have excited states below 50000 K and, thus, electronic contributions to thermodynamic properties are negligible; these include the cases we studied in the preceding sections. Notable exceptions to this rule include oxygen (O_2, which as two unpaired electrons in the ground state) and odd-electron species such as NO and NO_2.

Molecules with open electronic shells are, of course, unstable, or at least very reactive. Nonetheless, we may be interested in their properties since they may participate in chemical reactions, or be found at high temperature. The statistical calculation is doubly valuable for such calculations since traditional thermochemical methods are difficult to use on unstable species or species that are present only at very high temperatures.

Since there are no simple formulas for electronic energies, there are no formulas equivalent to those we used for vibration and rotation (above) for the electronic heat capacity, entropy, and so forth. However, since there are often only a few contributing states, the direct method of calculation illustrated in Examples 5.6 and 5.7 is very practical. We begin with the partition function:

$$z_{\mathrm{elec}} = g_0 + g_1 \exp(-\theta_1 / T) + g_2 \exp(-\theta_2 / T) + \cdots \tag{5.11}$$

The internal energy U (as before we assume $U_0 = 0$) is the average energy; for one mole:

$$U = L\sum p_i\varepsilon_i = R\sum p_i\theta_i \tag{5.12}$$

Here, p_i is the Boltzmann population of Eq. (5.7). The heat capacity will be calculated as the derivative of U: $C_v = (\partial U/\partial T)_V$. Recalling that Mathcad does these derivatives numerically, and that numerical differentiation is always problematical, we must be alert to anomalous results that may indicate a computational error. (A computational method that avoids numerical differentiation is discussed on page 125.) The entropy is calculated using Eq. (5.10).

Example 5.12 Heat capacity of open-shell atoms.

One of the verities that students learn is that "the heat capacity of an ideal gas is $C_{vm} = {}^3/_2R$"; this is entirely false, as illustrated by the calculations of this Chapter (not to mention those of Chapters 2 and 3). All of these calculations were for ideal gases, and this value applied only for argon. An improved version is "the heat capacity of *monatomic* ideal gases is $C_{vm} = {}^3/_2R$"; this is much more accurate, but still must be limited to those monatomic species with closed electronic shells. We shall illustrate this with two examples, the Na and Cl atoms.

Atomic sodium has an electronic configuration $[Ne](3s)^1$; because the electron can be either spin-up or spin-down, this state has a degeneracy $g_0 = 2$. The first excited electron states occur when the outer electron is promoted to the $(3p)$ orbital; because the different ways of arranging the electrons in a p orbital, there are actually two energies, $\theta = 24396$ K (g= 2) and θ = 24420 K (g = 4). The box below illustrates the calculation of the electronic partition function and energy of this atom.

Sodium Atom $\quad i := 0..2 \quad R := 8.31451$

$g_i :=$	$\theta_i :=$
2	0
2	24396
4	24420

$$z_{elec}(T) := \sum_i g_i\cdot\exp\left(-\frac{\theta_i}{T}\right) \qquad U_{elec}(T) := R\cdot\sum_i \frac{\theta_i\cdot g_i\cdot\exp\left(-\frac{\theta_i}{T}\right)}{z_{elec}(T)}$$

$z_{elec}(300) = 2 \qquad U_{elec}(300) = 0 \qquad$ adds to S = $R\cdot\ln(2) = 5.763$

$z_{elec}(3000) = 2.002 \qquad U_{elec}(3000) = 177.903$ (unit: J/mol)

adds to S, $R\cdot\ln(2.002) + \dfrac{177.9}{3000} = 5.831$

At 300 K, the electronic energy is effectively zero, and the electronic contribution to the entropy is essentially R ln(2) (the ground-state degeneracy is $g_0 = 2$). At 3000 K, the excited-state electronic contributions to U and S are significant, but still relatively small (the translation entropy is 195.952 J $K^{-1}mol^{-1}$ at 3000 K).

$$C_v(T) := 1.5 \cdot R + \frac{d}{dT} U_{elec}(T)$$

$C_v(300) = 12.472$ $\quad$ $C_v(3000) = 12.954$

$T := 300, 350 .. 3000$ $\quad$ compare $1.5 \cdot R = 12.472$

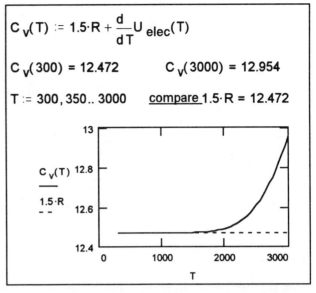

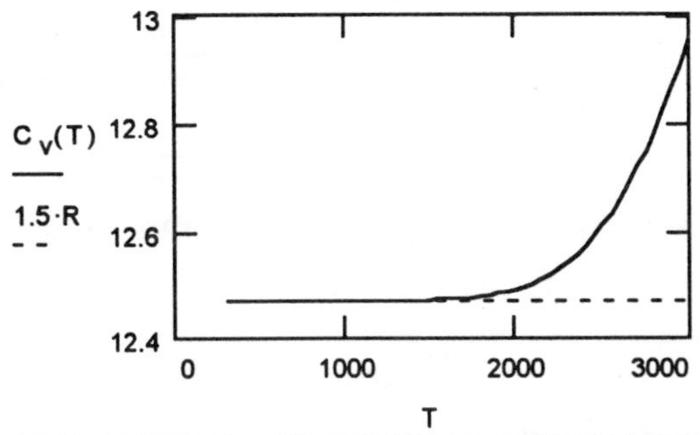

The heat capacity is very interesting (box to right). For atoms, the only other contribution to the heat capacity (and other properties) is that for translation: $1.5R$. At 300 K, the electronic contribution is essentially zero, but at 3000 K, it is becoming significant. Note how we graphed the translational contribution ($1.5\,R$), a constant, for comparison.

The chlorine atom is quite a different story. Its ground-state electronic structure is $[Ne](3s)^2(3p)^5$; because there are several different ways to arrange the 5 electrons in a p orbital, and not all of these have the same energy, this atom can have electronic excitation without promoting the electron to a higher orbital. Thus, Cl has a low-lying excited state (1269.5 K). The next higher states involve promotion of an electron to the $n = 4$ shell ($4s$, $4p$ and so forth), or to the $3d$ orbital, and have very high energy; there are none less than 100,000 K, so we will ignore them.

The calculation (below) is a slight modification of the preceding one; you can either edit the Na calculation, or copy it and edit.

Chlorine Atom $\quad$ $i := 0 .. 1$ $\quad$ $R := 8.31451$

$g_i :=$	$\theta_i :=$
4	0
2	1269.5

next excited states above 100,000 K

$$z_{elec}(T) := \sum_i g_i \cdot \exp\left(-\frac{\theta_i}{T}\right) \qquad U_{elec}(T) := R \cdot \sum_i \frac{\theta_i \cdot g_i \cdot \exp\left(-\frac{\theta_i}{T}\right)}{z_{elec}(T)}$$

$z_{elec}(300) = 4.029$

$z_{elec}(3000) = 5.31$ $\quad$ $U_{elec}(300) = 76.121$

$z_{elec}(6000) = 5.619$ $\quad$ $U_{elec}(3000) = 2.604 \cdot 10^3$

Even at room temperature there electronic some energy, and at 3000 K it is considerable.

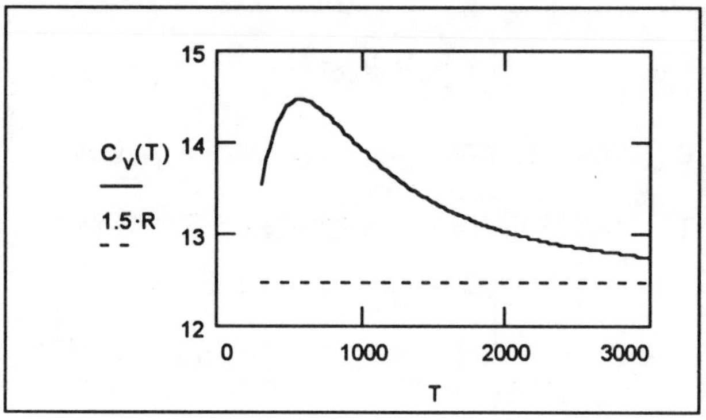

The heat capacity of the chlorine atom (calculated as before, see box to left) contrasts vividly with that for sodium. The electronic contribution is considerable at room temperature, but drops off at higher temperature; this is because the upper level is becoming saturated, approaching the maximum population allowed at equilibrium (recall the 2-level example, page 112). Some details are omitted from this calculation, but they are the same as for the preceding one.

Example 5.13 Heat capacity of NO

Calculations for the electronic states of molecules follows the same pattern as for atoms except, of course, we must include the effect of rotation and vibration. The odd-electron molecule NO has a very low-lying excited electronic state, at 174.2 K, and this has an interesting effect in its heat capacity. The data for the vibrational constant (*thv*) and electronic levels of NO are:

$R := 8.31451 \quad i := 0..1$

$cal := 4.184 \quad thv := 2739$

$mw := 14.0067 + 15.9994$

$$g_i := \begin{pmatrix} 2 \\ 2 \end{pmatrix} \qquad \theta_i := \begin{pmatrix} 0 \\ 174.2 \end{pmatrix}$$

$$z_{elec}(T) := \sum_i g_i \cdot \exp\left(-\frac{\theta_i}{T}\right)$$

The total heat capacity includes contributions from translation, rotation, vibration and electronic (in that order).

$$U_{elec}(T) := R \cdot \sum_i \frac{\theta_i \cdot g_i \cdot \exp\left(-\frac{\theta_i}{T}\right)}{z_{elec}(T)}$$

$U_{elec}(300) = 519.651$

$$C_{elec}(T) := \frac{d}{dT} U_{elec}(T)$$

$$C_v(T) := 1.5 \cdot R + R + \frac{R \cdot \left(\frac{thv}{T}\right)^2 \cdot \exp\left(\frac{thv}{T}\right)}{\left(\exp\left(\frac{thv}{T}\right) - 1\right)^2} + C_{elec}(T)$$

$C_{elec}(300) = 0.645$

$C_p(T) := C_v(T) + R$ $\qquad T := 10, 20 .. 5000$

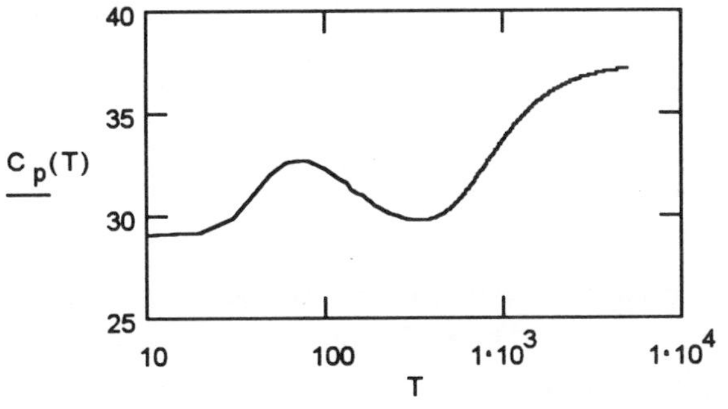

The heat-capacity graph (box to left, note log- scale for temperature) shows a maximum in the heat capacity around 100 K due to the low-lying electronic state. The rise at temperatures above 500 K is due to the vibration. Note the use of a logarithmic scale for T, which displays the effect better (this option is selected on the Graph-Format menu). The need to use a numeric derivative for the heat capacity makes this calculation relatively slow; the method described in the next section circumvents this problem.

5.5 Alternate Computational Method

As we have seen in the preceding examples, the need to take numerical derivatives to calculate heat capacity makes such computations very slow and error-prone. There is an alternate method that is particularly suited for programs like Mathcad. Given a set of energy levels $\{\varepsilon_i\}$ — in kelvin units, $\{\theta_i\}$ — with degeneracies $\{g_i\}$, three sums suffice to calculate all thermodynamic properties. The sums are:

$$z = \sum g_i \exp(-\theta_i / T)$$
$$< u > = \frac{1}{z} \sum (\theta_i / T)\, g_i \exp(-\theta_i / T) \qquad (5.13)$$
$$< u^2 > = \frac{1}{z} \sum (\theta_i / T)^2\, g_i \exp(-\theta_i / T)$$

($u = \theta / T$). From these we calculate:

$$U = RT < u >; \qquad S = R \ln(z) + R < u >; \qquad C_v = R\left[< u^2 > - < u >^2\right] \qquad (5.14)$$

The box below shows such a calculation, and can serve as a template for others. The energy levels (θ, but denoted e, unit kelvin) and corresponding degeneracies (g) are entered as a list, but could equally well be generated by a formula, as the example following demonstrates.

$i := 0 .. 2$ $\qquad R := 8.31451$

$e_i :=$	$g_i :=$
0	4
500	2
1500	1

$$z(T) := \sum_i g_i \cdot \exp\left(-\frac{e_i}{T}\right)$$

$$uave(T) := \frac{1}{z(T)} \cdot \left[\sum_i \left(\frac{e_i}{T}\right) \cdot g_i \cdot \exp\left(-\frac{e_i}{T}\right)\right]$$

$$u2ave(T) := \frac{1}{z(T)} \cdot \left[\sum_i \left(\frac{e_i}{T}\right)^2 \cdot g_i \cdot \exp\left(-\frac{e_i}{T}\right)\right]$$

$U(T) := R \cdot T \cdot uave(T)$

$S(T) := R \cdot \ln(z(T)) + R \cdot uave(T)$

$Cv(T) := R \cdot u2ave(T) - R \cdot uave(T)^2$

Try the sample calculations in the box to the right, and, when they are correct, save your work for future use.

T := 100	U(T) = 13.96	z(T) = 4.013
	S(T) = 11.694	u2ave(T) = 0.084
	Cv(T) = 0.696	uave(T) = 0.017

Example 5.14 The anharmonic oscillator

You may have noted that the calculated heat capacities of Section 5.4 tended to underestimate the heat capacity at high temperature. There are a number of approximations that entered the derivations of the formulas used including the neglect of vibrational anharmonicity, the vibration-rotation interaction and centrifugal distortion. Anharmonicity accounts for about half of the error, and it is this topic that we now explore.

To see why a vibration may not be harmonic, we must first look at what a harmonic vibration is. Suppose you had a weight attached to the ceiling with a spring or a rubber band. If you tugged at it slightly and released it, it vibrates up and down. The position oscillates sinusoidally in time: this is a harmonic oscillator. Harmonic vibrations can be shown to be the result if the spring obeys Hooke's law: restoring force is proportional to displacement. All elastic materials obey Hooke's law for small displacements. If you tug harder on the weight, resulting is larger-amplitude vibrations, deviations from the harmonic-sinusoidal vibration will be observed: no material obeys Hooke's law for large displacements. If you tug hard enough, two very unharmonic things may happen: the weight may approach the ceiling, and be repelled by the compressed spring, or the spring may break.

The vibration of a chemical bond can be approximated reasonably by a spring. For low levels of vibrational excitation, the motion is reasonably harmonic, as demonstrated by the success of the harmonic oscillator model in calculating thermodynamic properties. However, as temperature rises, and more energy is placed into the vibration, it becomes anharmonic. For large amplitude swings, the bond may compress sufficiently that the inner electronic shells of the atoms begin to overlap: this results in a strong repulsion comparable to that of the compressed spring when the weight approaches the ceiling. (An important part of this repulsion is the Coulombic interaction between the like-charged nuclei.) If sufficient energy is placed into the bond, it will break, resulting in dissociative processes such as

$$Cl_2 \rightarrow Cl + Cl$$

The harmonic oscillator model for bond vibration predicts that the vibration gains energy through series of equally spaced steps (energy levels) —

$$\frac{\varepsilon_n}{k_b} = (n + \tfrac{1}{2})\theta_v \tag{5.15}$$

for $n = 0, 1, 2 \ldots \infty$. Compared to reality, this is wrong on at least two counts: the vibrational energy levels are not equally spaced and you cannot put an infinite amount of energy into a bond without breaking it. The *anharmonic oscillator* model approximates this energy as

$$\frac{\varepsilon_n}{k_b} = (n + \tfrac{1}{2})\theta_v - (n + \tfrac{1}{2})^2\,\theta_a \tag{5.16}$$

where θ_a is the anharmonicity constant (θ_v is the same vibrational constant as before. It can be shown that the maximum value for the index (quantum number) n is:

$$n_{max} = \frac{\theta_v}{2\theta_a} \tag{5.17}$$

(Energies higher than that given by Eq. (5.16) with $n = n_{max}$ result in dissociation.)

Next, we examine how to use this model to calculate the heat capacity of a diatomic molecule, using chlorine as an example.

Anharmonic Oscillator: chlorine, Cl_2 $\quad R := 8.31451 \quad \theta_v := 812.78 \quad \theta_a := 5.76$

$$max := \frac{\theta_v}{2 \cdot \theta_a} \qquad max = 70.554 \qquad n := 0..70$$

Harmonic oscillator: $C_{ho}(T)$

$$e_n := \left[\left(n + \frac{1}{2}\right)\cdot\theta_v - \left(n + \frac{1}{2}\right)^2\cdot\theta_a\right] \qquad g_n := 1$$

$$C_{ho}(T) := \frac{\left(\frac{\theta_v}{T}\right)^2\cdot\exp\left(\frac{\theta_v}{T}\right)\cdot R}{\left(\exp\left(\frac{\theta_v}{T}\right) - 1\right)^2} + 2.5\cdot R$$

Although the vibrational energy levels are not degenerate (all $g = 1$), we have included a degeneracy list g_n so we can use the template developed above. Also we have included the formula for the constant-volume heat capacity for the harmonic model (C_{ho}) for purposes of comparison. The maximum value for the vibrational quantum number (*max*) is truncated to the next lower integer, since this quantum number must be an integer. We did this by simply retyping the number, but Mathcad has functions **floor** and **ceil** for such purposes.

$$x := 70.544 \qquad floor(x) = 70 \qquad ceil(x) = 71$$

The following formulas can be copied from earlier work and modified accordingly (you can replace the index i with n by Edit-menu, Replace). For C_v we must add the contributions from translation and vibration.

$$z(T) := \sum_n g_n\cdot\exp\left(-\frac{e_n}{T}\right) \qquad uave(T) := \frac{1}{z(T)}\cdot\left[\sum_n \left(\frac{e_n}{T}\right)\cdot g_n\cdot\exp\left(-\frac{e_n}{T}\right)\right]$$

$$u2ave(T) := \frac{1}{z(T)}\cdot\left[\sum_n \left(\frac{e_n}{T}\right)^2\cdot g_n\cdot\exp\left(-\frac{e_n}{T}\right)\right] \qquad C_v(T) := 1.5\cdot R + R + R\cdot u2ave(T) - R\cdot uave(T)^2$$

$$C_v(300) = 25.564 \qquad C_{ho}(300) = 25.45 \qquad C_v(3000) = 30.725 \qquad C_{ho}(3000) = 29.05$$

$i := 1..7$

$Tx_i :=$	$Cx_i :=$	$C_{ho}(Tx_i)$	$C_v(Tx_i)$
298.15	25.53	25.419	25.532
400	26.99	26.746	26.883
600	28.29	27.938	28.133
800	28.89	28.421	28.684
1000	29.19	28.658	28.996
1500	29.69	28.9	29.455
2000	29.99	28.987	29.821

The sample calculations above compare the harmonic and anharmonic models. At 300 K, the difference is minor, but at 3000 K (where more higher levels are occupied), the difference is significant. The box to the left shows a comparison to experimental data (list *Cx*) for various temperatures (list *Tx*). You can see that the anharmonic model (C_v) is substantially closer to reality than the harmonic model.

The comparison is made more persuasively with a graph — see box below (dashed line for the harmonic approximation, and solid line for the anharmonic calculation).

$T := 300, 310..2000$ $eq := 3.5 \cdot R$ $eq = 29.101$

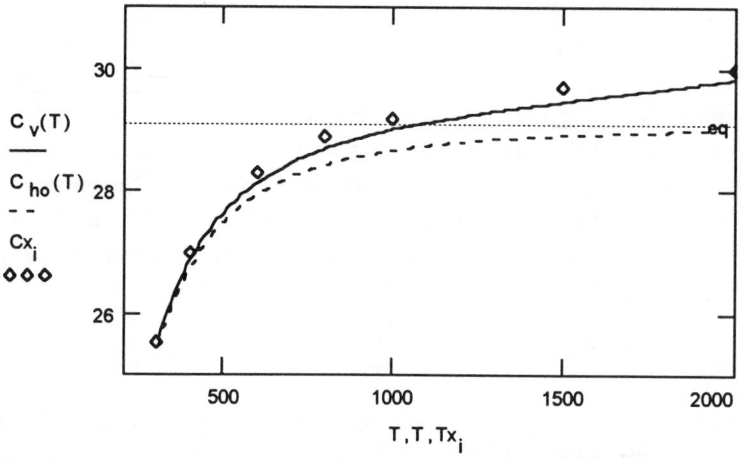

According to equipartition theory, the heat capacity of a diatomic molecule should be $C_v = {}^7/_2R$; this value is shown on the graph as *eq*; you can see that the harmonic-oscillator model approaches the equipartition value at high temperature, but the experimental values and the anharmonic model exceed it. Making the graph above is still slow, but it is still faster than if the heat capacity were calculated by a numerical derivative.

Problems

5.1 Make a bar graph of the probabilities for various outcomes on flipping a coin 36 times. Calculate the probability that the number of heads is between 12 and 24 (inclusive).

5.2 A sample of methane is enriched to 78% in deuterium. Assuming the deuteriums are randomly distributed, calculate the probabilities for the various isotopes -- CD_4, CD_3H etc. -- and the entropy of mixing.

5.3 For a system of 4 equally spaced energy levels with energy-spacing 250 K and degeneracies 1, 3, 3, 1, (a) calculate the populations at 300 K. (b) Calculate the average energy

5.4 Calculate the constant-volume heat capacity of HF. Make a graph for temperatures between 300 and 3000 K, and report values for 300, 500,1000, 2000 and 3000 K.

5.5 Calculate the constant-volume heat capacity of OCS, making a graph for $T = 300$ to 3000 K and reporting values for 300, 500, 1000, 2000 and 3000 K.

5.6 Calculate the constant-volume heat capacity of SO_2, making a graph for $T = 300$ to 3000 K and reporting values for 300, 500, 1000, 2000 and 3000 K. (Note: this molecule is not linear.)

5.7 For the C atom, calculate the electronic partition function and populations of the lowest 4 electronic levels at 1000 K. Calculate the average energy at this temperature.

5.8 Make a graph of the constant-volume heat capacity of Br atoms from 300 to 4000 K. Report values at 300, 2000 and 4000 K.

5.9 Calculate the constant-volume heat capacity of HF using the anharmonic oscillator model. Use $\theta_v = 5994.5$ K and $\theta_a = 129.6$ K. Make a graph of C_{vm} from 300 to 3000 K, comparing the harmonic and anharmonic models. Report values for $T = 300$ and 3000 K.

Answers

5.1 97.118%

5.2 0.370, 0.418, 0.177, 0.033, 0.002; 9.695 J/(K mol)

5.3 (a) 33.87%, 44.16%, 19.19%, 2.78% (b) 227.2 K = 1.889 kJ/mol

5.4 20.786, 20.794, 21.555, 24.954, 26.835 J/(K mol).

5.5 33.272, 40.486, 48.163, 52.216, 53.194 J/(K mol)

5.6 31.524, 38.071, 45.623, 48.697, 49.347 J/(K mol)

5.7 $z = 8.627$; populations 0.116, 0.340, 0.544, 2.5×10^{-7}; energy = 42.016 K = 349.34 J/mol.

5.8 12.472, 14.396, 13.984 J/(K mol)

5.9 (HO) 300 K, 20.786 (20.786); 3000 K, 27.288 (26.810)

CHAPTER 6

CHEMICAL REACTIONS

6.1 Enthalpy of Reaction

Most texts have tables (e.g. Table 6.1, Noggle) which list enthalpies for the formation reactions of compounds. The formation reaction is rarely a practical reaction, but these quantities can be calculated from other reactions as demonstrated in the example below. With these formation enthalpies, enthalpies of any reaction can be calculated as:

$$\Delta_{rxn} H = \sum_i \nu_i \, \Delta_f H(i) \tag{6.1}$$

where ν_i is the stoichiometric coefficient of the reaction (negative for reactants, positive for products).

Example 6.1 Enthalpy of formation from the heat of combustion.

The heat of combustion for sucrose is -5643.8 kJ/mol; the combustion reaction is:

$$C_{12}H_{22}O_{11}(s) + 12\ O_2(g) = 12\ CO_2(g) + 11\ H_2O(liq)$$

The calculation is made from the enthalpies of formation for CO_2 and H_2O. From Eq. (6.1) we have the enthalpy of the combustion reaction as:

$$\Delta_c H = 12\,\Delta_f H(CO_2) + 11\,\Delta_f H(H_2O, liq) - \Delta_f H(\text{sucrose})$$

$\Delta H_c := -5643.8$ $\quad DHf_{CO2} := -393.509$ $\quad DHf_{H2Oliq} := -285.830$

$DHf_{sucrose} := 12 \cdot DHf_{CO2} + 11 \cdot DHf_{H2Oliq} - \Delta H_c$ $\quad DHf_{sucrose} = -2.222 \cdot 10^3$

Here we have denoted the standard enthalpy of formation as *DHf*. For problems of this type, Mathcad is only slightly more effective than a calculator, the sole advantage being in the ability to proofread and edit the input data.

Change of Reaction Enthalpy with Temperature

Tables of thermodynamic data typically give values for 298.15 K; we will call these values the *reference values* and the temperature T_{ref}. While it is often reasonable to assume that enthalpies of reaction are constant, when a more accurate calculation is needed the enthalpy of reaction at another temperature is calculated as:

$$\Delta H_T = \Delta H_{ref} + \int_{T_{ref}}^{T} \Delta C_p \, dT \tag{6.2}$$

For such a calculation, it is best to have formulas giving C_p as a function of temperature , but such data must be available for all reactants and products. If such data are not available, values for the heat capacities at some temperature (e.g. as given on Tables 6.1 or 2.1 of Noggle) may be used, assuming them to be constant.

Example 6.2 Enthalpy of reaction vs. T

Coal is an abundant fuel, but not nearly as useful as liquid and gaseous fuels. The Fischer-Tropsch process makes liquid and gaseous hydrocarbons from coal by using the carbon monoxide, produced by burning coal in limited oxygen, and hydrogen produced by reduction of water with hot coal. One of the reactions in this process is

$$4\ H_2(g) + 2\ CO(g) = C_2H_4(g) + 2\ H_2O(g)$$

Calculate the enthalpy of this reaction for temperatures up to 800 K.

Data for this reaction are given below. Since units can be a bit of a nuisance in such calculations, we define the symbols J and K to be equal to 1. This permits us to label input data and answers without actually using units.

$J := 1 \quad K := 1 \quad kJ := 10^3 \cdot J \quad R := 8.31451 \cdot \frac{J}{K} \quad T_{ref} := 298.15 \cdot K$

$DH_{ref} := (2 \cdot (-241.818) + 52.26 - 4 \cdot (0) - 2 \cdot (-110.525)) \cdot kJ \quad DH_{ref} = -210.326 \cdot kJ$

$DC_{ref} := (2 \cdot 33.577 + 43.56 - 4 \cdot 28.824 - 2 \cdot 29.142) \cdot \frac{J}{K} \quad DC_{ref} = -62.866 \cdot J \cdot K^{-1}$

Equation (6.2) is easily integrated if we assume that the heat capacity difference is constant at the value given (above, at 298.15 K). The result of this calculation is displayed in the box to the right. How accurate is this calculation? We can do better by using temperature-dependent heat capacity formulas for the evaluation of Eq. (6.2) (box below).

$\Delta H(T) := DH_{ref} + DC_{ref} \left(T - T_{ref}\right)$

$\Delta H(500) = -223.016 \cdot kJ$

$\Delta H(800) = -241.875 \cdot kJ$

$$C_{pH2O}(T) := 26.06 + 17.7\cdot 10^{-3}\cdot T - 2.63\cdot 10^{-6}\cdot T^2 + \frac{2.2\cdot 10^5}{T^2}$$

$$C_{pC2H4}(T) := 44.28 + 60.1\cdot 10^{-3}\cdot T - 11.1\cdot 10^{-6}\cdot T^2 - \frac{16.8\cdot 10^5}{T^2}$$

$$C_{pCO}(T) := 26.28 + 8.055\cdot 10^{-3}\cdot T - 1.49\cdot 10^{-6}\cdot T^2 + \frac{0.45\cdot 10^5}{T^2}$$

$$C_{pH2}(T) := 26.36 + 4.35\cdot 10^{-3}\cdot T - .245\cdot 10^{-6}\cdot T^2 + \frac{1.15\cdot 10^5}{T^2}$$

Empirical heat capacities such as these are valid only for the range of temperature over which the data were fitted, and it is very dangerous to use such formulas outside the range for which the coefficients were determined. Those above are valid from 300 to 3000 K, but many texts give formulas and constants useful only to 2000 K.

The ΔC_p for this reaction is:

$$\Delta C_p(T) := 2\cdot C_{pH2O}(T) + C_{pC2H4}(T) - 2\cdot C_{pCO}(T) - 4\cdot C_{pH2}(T)$$

$\Delta C_p(T_{ref}) = -64.356$ $\quad$ $DC_{ref} = -62.866$ $\quad$ $\Delta C_p(500) = -40.865$

The calculation at 298.15 K is not what Table 6.1 gives, but the difference is small and to be expected with data from different sources. Calculate the test values as a check for errors in entering the formulas. We can also see from these calculations that ΔC_p of this reaction does change significantly with temperature. Next we evaluate Eq. (6.2) with the heat-capacity function.

$$\Delta Hx(T) := DH_{ref} + \int_{T_{ref}}^{T} \Delta C_p(T)\, dT$$

$DH_{ref} = -210.326\cdot kJ$

$\Delta H(500) = -223.016\cdot kJ$

$\Delta Hx(500) = -220.597\cdot kJ$

$T := 300, 310 .. 800$

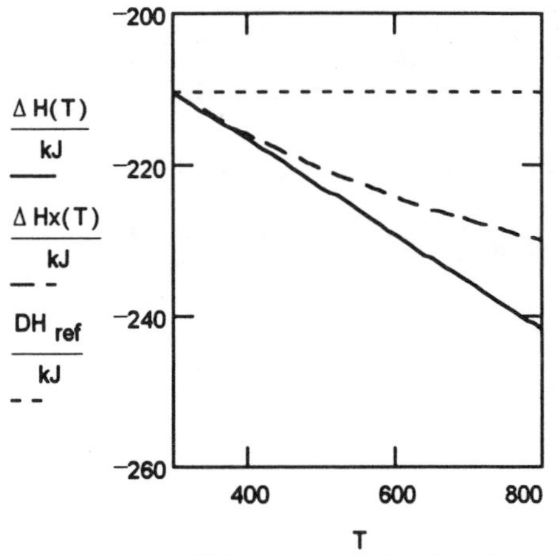

The calculations at 500 K (above) demonstrate reasonable accuracy for the constant-heat-capacity method, but at 800 K you will find that this method has significantly overestimated the change. The graph (box to left) shows this effect clearly. The constant-heat-capacity approximation is adequate for small changes in temperature, but tends to overestimate the change. At some point it may be less accurate than the simpler approximation: that the enthalpy of reaction is constant (try extending the range of the plot to 2000 K). In any case, note that the change in ΔH is relatively small: about 10% over a 500° range in this case.

6.2 Adiabatic Flame Temperature

The temperature of an adiabatic reaction can be calculated from

$$\Delta H + \int_{T_1}^{T_2} C_p^{\text{prod}}\, dT = 0 \tag{6.3}$$

where ΔH is the heat of reaction and C_p^{prod} is the heat capacity of the reaction products. This calculation neglects dissociation of products and, therefore, is useful only for combustions in air, for which the final temperature usually does not exceed 3000 K.

Combustions in air (flames) typically have adiabatic temperatures in the range 2000-3000 K, so the assumption of constant heat capacity for evaluating Eq. (6.3) is not likely to be accurate. Fortunately, combustion products usually contain only three materials: carbon dioxide, water (gas) and nitrogen (from the air). You must enter the heat-capacity formulas, but that is the majority of the work. (You need formulas valid to 3000 K, at least, such as those from Table 2.2 Noggle.)

$$C_{pN2}(T) := 25.79 + 8.09\cdot 10^{-3}\cdot T - 1.46\cdot 10^{-6}\cdot T^2 + \frac{0.88\cdot 10^5}{T^2}$$

$$C_{pCO2}(T) := 41.58 + 15.6\cdot 10^{-3}\cdot T - 2.95\cdot 10^{-6}\cdot T^2 - \frac{7.97\cdot 10^5}{T^2}$$

$$C_{pH2O}(T) := 26.06 + 17.7\cdot 10^{-3}\cdot T - 2.63\cdot 10^{-6}\cdot T^2 + \frac{2.20\cdot 10^5}{T^2}$$

$kJ := 1000 \qquad \Delta H_{vap} := (-241.818 + 285.830)\cdot kJ$

We have included the enthalpy of vaporization for water because heats of combustion (such as those in Table 6.2, Noggle) are usually for 25 °C with H_2O(liquid) as a product, but in a flame the product with be H_2O(gas). Therefore the enthalpy for vaporizing the water must be added to the heat of combustion. The heat-capacity formulas are valid to 3000 K, and can be used for most combustions in *air* (see page 135 for a discussion of the problems encountered in calculating flame temperatures in pure oxygen).

Example 6.3 Flame temperature of butane in air.

The combustion reaction of butane in air is

$$C_4H_{10} + 6.5\ O_2 + 26\ N_2 = 4\ CO_2(\text{gas}) + 5\ H_2O(\text{liq}) + 26\ N_2(\text{gas})$$

For simplicity, we approximate the amount of nitrogen as 4 times the amount of oxygen. In the flame, of course, the product will be H_2O(gas), so we must add 5 times the heat of vaporization:

combustion	$C_4H_{10} + 6.5\ O_2 + 26\ N_2 = 4\ CO_2(\text{gas}) + 5\ H_2O(\text{liq}) + 26\ N_2(\text{gas})$	ΔH_c
vaporization	$5\ H_2O(\text{liq}) = 5\ H_2O(\text{gas})$	$+5\ \Delta H_v$
flame reaction	$C_4H_{10} + 6.5\ O_2 + 26\ N_2 = 4\ CO_2(\text{gas}) + 5\ H_2O(\text{gas}) + 26\ N_2(\text{gas})$	ΔH_x

Using data for the heat of combustion and the heat capacities above gives:

$C_{prod}(T) := 4 \cdot C_{pCO2}(T) + 5 \cdot C_{pH2O}(T) + 26 \cdot C_{pN2}(T) \qquad T := 300, 310 .. 3000$

$\Delta H_c := -2878.5 \cdot kJ$

$\Delta H_x := \Delta H_c + 5 \cdot \Delta H_{vap}$

$\Delta H_x = -2.658 \cdot 10^3 \cdot kJ$

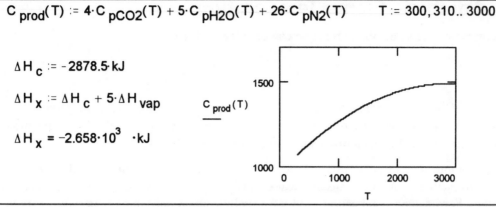

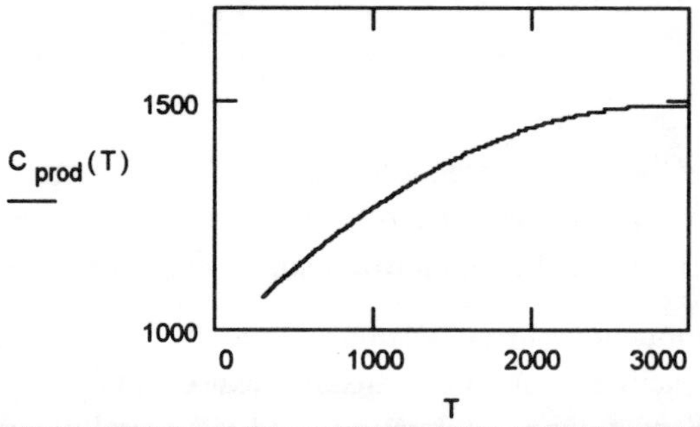

ΔH_c is the heat of combustion to H_2O(liquid), to which we add the heat for vaporizing 5 moles of water to get the heat of reaction, ΔH_x.

The graph of the product heat capacity (C_{prod} above) demonstrates that this quantity varies a lot with temperature and cannot be considered constant for this calculation. However, this is no problem for Mathcad, and the calculation of the final temperature is simple (box to right). As always with a **Given ... Find** block, we must provide an initial estimate; this quantity is not too critical, but we know that flames are hot, so guesses like 200 K are unrealistic. (Remember that the equals inside a solve block is a logical equality, ctrl+=.)

$T_1 := 298.15 \qquad T_2 := 1000$

Given

$$\Delta H_x + \int_{T_1}^{T_2} C_{prod}(T)\, dT = 0$$

$T_{ad} := \text{Find}(T_2) \qquad T_{ad} = 2325$

Temperatures calculated in this manner represent the maximum temperature of the flame. They assume a stoichiometric amount of air and no heat loss. An efficient flame, as in a Bunsen burner, may have this temperature in the hottest portion.

Example 6.4 Flame temperature of acetylene in air.

The combustion reaction for acetylene is

$$C_2H_2 + 2.5\ O_2 + 10\ N_2 = 2\ CO_2 + H_2O + 10\ N_2$$

The enthalpy of reaction can be calculated from enthalpies of formation (e.g. Table 6.1, Noggle). Since we know that the water will be a gas, it is simplest to just calculate for that as a product. The calculation for ΔH_x below uses these in order H_2O(gas), CO_2 and C_2H_2.

$\Delta H_x := (-241.818 - 2\cdot 393.509 - 226.73)\cdot kJ \qquad \Delta H_x = -1.256\cdot 10^6$

$C_{prod}(T) := 2\cdot C_{pCO2}(T) + C_{pH2O}(T) + 10\cdot C_{pN2}(T)$

$T_1 := 298.15 \qquad T_2 := 2000$

Given

$$\Delta H_x + \int_{T_1}^{T_2} C_{prod}(T)\, dT = 0$$

$T_{ad} := \mathrm{Find}(T_2) \qquad T_{ad} = 2808$

This is a higher temperature than for butane because acetylene is a more energetic compound and its products have a smaller heat capacity.

Calculations for combustion in oxygen are easy enough — just change the coefficient for nitrogen in C_p^{prod} to zero. However, such a calculation would grossly overestimate the flame temperature because it ignores the dissociation of products (answers too high by several thousand degrees are common).

6.3 Calculating Equilibrium Constants

The basic equation for calculating equilibrium constants from thermodynamic data is:

$$K = \exp\left(\frac{-\Delta G^o}{RT}\right) \tag{6.4}$$

Of course, the free energy of reaction, ΔG^o, must be for the temperature used in the calculation, but data tables like Table 6.1, Noggle, give such data only for one temperature (usually 298.15 K). If you need to calculate an equilibrium constant at another temperature, you must either find data for another temperature or make an approximation. One simple approximation is to use $\Delta G^o = \Delta H^o - T\Delta S^o$, and assume that the enthalpy and entropy of reaction are constant (independent of temperature). This gives:

$$K = \exp\left(\frac{\Delta S^o}{R} - \frac{\Delta H^o}{RT}\right) \tag{6.5}$$

This equation is useful for approximations over a moderate temperature range.

A more accurate calculation is possible if heat capacities are available for all reactants and products, permitting the calculation of ΔC_p of the reaction. Then:

$$\begin{aligned} \Delta H(T) &= \Delta H_{ref} + \int_{T_{ref}}^{T} \Delta C_p\, dT \\ \ln(K_T) &= \ln(K_{ref}) + \int_{T_{ref}}^{T} \frac{\Delta H}{RT^2}\, dT \end{aligned} \tag{6.6}$$

Another type of data from which equilibrium constants can be calculated are the free-energy functions (for example, Tables 6.4 and 6.5, Noggle). These are given for a variety of temperatures (up to 2000 K) and are especially useful for high-temperature calculations. The equations for the equilibrium constants from free-energy functions are:

$$\ln K = \frac{\Delta\phi^\circ}{R} - \frac{\Delta H_0^\circ}{RT} = \frac{\Delta\phi'}{R} - \frac{\Delta H_{298}^\circ}{RT} \qquad (6.7)$$

(ϕ° is the 0-K-based function and ϕ' is the 298-K-based function.)

If you are doing an equilibrium problem with units, remember that K cannot be used as the symbol for the equilibrium constant — it is used by Mathcad for the kelvin degree.

Example 6.5 Equilibrium constant of the Boudouard reaction.

The Boudouard reaction refers to the reduction of carbon dioxide by carbon:

$$CO_2(g) + C(\text{solid, graphite}) = 2\ CO(g)$$

Do the calculations in the box below.

$T_{ref} := 298.15\cdot K$ $\quad J := \text{joule}$ $\quad kJ := 10^3\cdot J$ $\quad R := 8.31451\cdot\frac{J}{K}$

$\Delta H := 2\cdot(-110.525\cdot kJ) - (-393.509\cdot kJ) - 0$ $\qquad \Delta H = 172.459\cdot kJ$

$\Delta G := 2\cdot(-137.168\cdot kJ) - (-394.359\cdot kJ) - 0$ $\qquad \Delta G = 120.023\cdot kJ$

$\Delta S := (2\cdot 197.674 - 213.74 - 5.740)\cdot\frac{J}{K}$ $\qquad \Delta S = 175.868\cdot\frac{J}{K}$

$\Delta C_p := (2\cdot 29.142 - 37.11 - 8.527)\cdot\frac{J}{K}$ $\qquad \Delta C_p = 12.647\cdot\frac{J}{K}$

(These are all standard-state properties; it is difficult to show the full subtlety of the notation in Mathcad.) The equilibrium constant at 298.15 K is very unfavorable.

$\exp\left(-\frac{\Delta G}{R\cdot T_{ref}}\right) = 9.397\cdot 10^{-22}$ $\qquad \Delta H - T_{ref}\Delta S = 120.024\cdot kJ$

The right-most calculation in the box above for $\Delta G^\circ = \Delta H^\circ - T\Delta S^\circ$, demonstrates that there is a slight inconsistency in the data, but this is not unusual nor is it worrisome.

To find out how the equilibrium constant varies with temperature, we use Eq. (6.5), assuming that the enthalpy and entropy of the reaction are constant. This is shown in the box to the right. This is a pretty big temperature range for this approximation, but it has given us, if not exact equilibrium constants, valuable information: the equilibrium shifts to the right with increasing temperature and becomes favorable around 1000 K.

$K1(T) := \exp\left(\frac{\Delta S}{R} - \frac{\Delta H}{R\cdot T}\right)$

$K1(500\cdot K) = 1.479\cdot 10^{-9}$

$K1(1000\cdot K) = 1.507$

$K1(1500\cdot K) = 1.516\cdot 10^{3}$

As a next step, we can use the numerical value for ΔC_p calculated above (for 298.15 K, assumed to be independent of temperature) to evaluate Eq. (6.6).

$$DH(T) := \Delta H + \int_{T_{ref}}^{T} \Delta C_p \, dT \qquad lnK(T) := -\frac{\Delta G}{R \cdot T_{ref}} + \int_{T_{ref}}^{T} \frac{DH(T)}{R \cdot T^2} \, dT$$

$$DH(1000 \cdot K) = 181.335 \cdot kJ \qquad exp(lnK(1000 \cdot K)) = 3.266$$

The difference between these two values is not very great as equilibrium constants go, but this agreement may be due to a cancellation of error, an event upon which it is unwise to depend.

$$\Delta H_0 := (-2 \cdot 113.81 + 393.17) \cdot kJ$$

$$Dphi := (2 \cdot 204.1 - 11.6 - 224.7) \cdot \frac{J}{K}$$

$$exp\left(\frac{Dphi}{R} - \frac{\Delta H_0}{R \cdot 1000 \cdot K}\right) = 2.146$$

The free-energy function data for this reaction for the temperature required are in Table 6.4, Noggle. This permits us to use Eq. (6.7) for this calculation (and to check the accuracy of the previous calculation): see box to left. This value lies between the constant-H/S and the constant-C_p estimates, suggesting that perhaps the latter may have overcorrected. But, again, these are very small differences for an equilibrium constant.

An alternative method would be to evaluate Eq. (6.6) with temperature-dependent heat-capacity functions. The calculated equilibrium constant for 1000 K is, by this method, 1.697. (You might also be concerned that the Table 6.1 data are for 1 bar while the data of Tables 6.4 and 6.5 are for 1 atm, but this is only a 1% correction and is negligible compared to other sources of error.)

Example 6.6 Interpolating the free-energy function.

Free-energy-function data such as those on Tables 6.4 and 6.5 Noggle provide accurate calculations of equilibrium constants for the temperatures given, but also provide good values at other temperatures by interpolation. We will do the calculation for the dissociation of phosgene:

$$COCl_2(g) = CO(g) + Cl_2(g)$$

Data for the reactants and product are found on Table 6.4, Noggle. To do calculations for 5 temperatures, enter the data as vectors. Type "`Tx:`" and then, from the Vectors and Matrices palette, select Matrix or Vector; specify 5 rows and 1 column, and click the Create button. Then type the temperatures into the 5 placeholders. (To get the unit, it is simplest to multiply the whole vector by K) For the free-energy function (vector **phix**) you proceed similarly. I found it to be convenient to type in all numbers for one of the molecules and then edit each entry to add or subtract the others, one at a time. This way you read across a row of the table rather than looking up the 3 compounds 5 separate times. You should end up as shown in the box below.

These vectors can be used for interpolation as described in earlier chapters. The graph (box below) demonstrates that the numbers vary smoothly, so interpolation is apt to be reliable.

$J := joule \qquad kJ := 1000 \cdot J \qquad R := 8.31451 \cdot \frac{J}{K}$

$\Delta H_0 := 0 + (-113.81 \cdot kJ) - (-217.8 \cdot kJ) \qquad \Delta H_0 = 103.99 \cdot kJ$

$$Tx := \begin{bmatrix} 298.15 \\ 500 \\ 1000 \\ 1500 \\ 2000 \end{bmatrix} \cdot K \qquad phix := \begin{bmatrix} 192.2 + 168.4 - 240.6 \\ 208.6 + 183.5 - 266.2 \\ 231.9 + 204.1 - 304.6 \\ 246.2 + 216.6 - 331.1 \\ 256.6 + 225.9 - 351.1 \end{bmatrix} \cdot \frac{J}{K}$$

$i := 0 .. \mathrm{last}(Tx)$

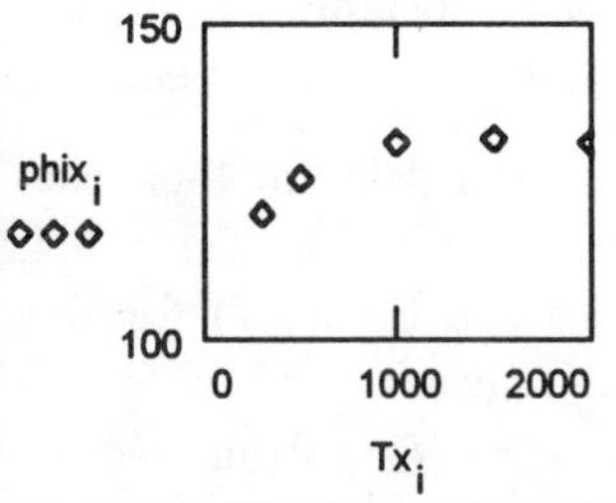

The interpolation is shown in the next box. We use **cspline** to create an interpolation table using with the cubic spline method, and **interp** to define a function for the logarithm of the equilibrium constant vs. temperature.

$vs := \mathrm{cspline}(Tx, phix) \qquad phi(T) := \mathrm{interp}(vs, Tx, phix, T) \qquad phi(760 \cdot K) = 129.942 \cdot \frac{J}{K}$

$lnK(T) := \frac{phi(T)}{R} - \frac{\Delta H_0}{R \cdot T} \qquad Ka(T) := \exp(lnK(T))$

The graph below shows the variation of the equilibrium constant between 300 and 2000 K. (Be cautious about using this function for extrapolation outside the data range since the accuracy is unpredictable.)

$T := 300 \cdot K, 350 \cdot K .. 2000 \cdot K \qquad j := 0 .. 4$

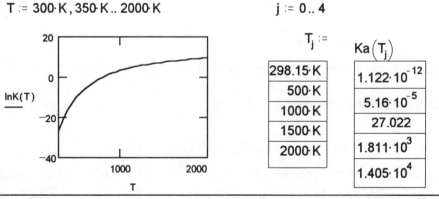

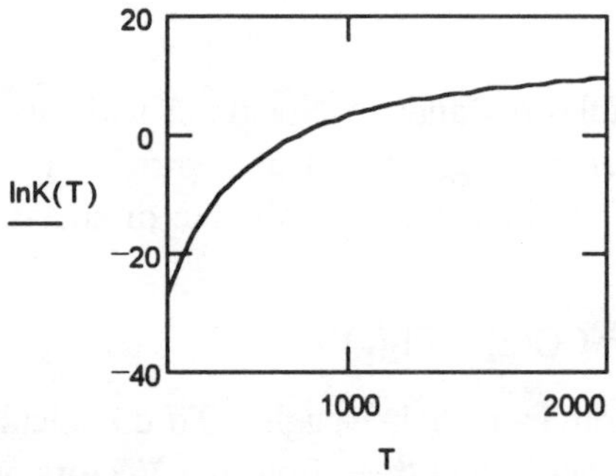

$T_j :=$	$Ka(T_j)$
298.15·K	$1.122 \cdot 10^{-12}$
500·K	$5.16 \cdot 10^{-5}$
1000·K	27.022
1500·K	$1.811 \cdot 10^{3}$
2000·K	$1.405 \cdot 10^{4}$

The advantage of this method over that used in the preceding example (which was, effectively, an extrapolation, although based on physical facts) is that the errors are limited. Therefore, the answer will never be too far from wrong. Save these results (*phosgene.mcd*) for later use.

6.4 Fugacity of a Gas

The fugacity of a real gas is related to its partial pressure as:

$$f_i = \phi P_i \tag{6.8}$$

The fugacity coefficient (ϕ) at some pressure P can be calculated from compressibility factors (z) as:

$$\ln\phi = \int_0^P \left[\frac{z-1}{P}\right] dP \qquad (6.9)$$

Example 6.7 Fugacity from compressibility factors.

Table 6.1 gives values for the compressibility factor (z) of ethane at 400 K vs. pressure (in MPa). Enter these data into Mathcad by whatever method you prefer, placing them in vectors named **px** for pressure and **zx** for compressibility. Enter the data in any method you find convenient; the box below assumes it is in the matrix **M**.

$$R := 8.31451 \qquad MPa := 10^6$$

$$px := M^{<0>} \cdot MPa$$

$$zx := M^{<1>} \qquad j := 0..\,last(px)$$

Table 6.1 Compressibility factors for ethane at 400 K.

P/MPa	z	P/MPa	z	P/MPa	z
0.1	0.9970	8	0.7657	25	0.7574
0.5	0.9851	10	0.7123	30	0.8364
1	0.9703	12	0.6800	35	0.9189
2	0.9405	15	0.6586	40	1.0023
3	0.9107	18	0.6705	50	1.1679
4	0.8810	20	0.6899	60	1.3304
6	0.8221	22	0.7146	70	1.4899
				80	1.6468

To evaluate the integral we need some sort of curve fitting, the likely choices being polynomial regression or interpolation. The function to be fit,

$$y = \frac{z-1}{P}$$

often varies too sharply for a polynomial fit to be effective, especially for temperatures just above the critical temperature (below the critical temperature, it is discontinuous — we exclude such cases here). Alternatively you could fit (z - 1) as a polynomial (this is just the virial series, Chapter 1), but then you have a problem at $P = 0$ (where y is 0/0, indeterminate). The zero-pressure problem could probably be overcome by integrating to some small but finite pressure, but any error in the fitted function is exaggerated by division by P at low pressure.

Interpolation has none of these problems, but it has one of its own. Unlike regression, there is no smoothing of the data so errors in z become a problem. This is especially true at low pressure: if $z = 0.9954$, with 4 significant figures, 1 - z has only two significant figures, and the error is exaggerated by division by a small P. Thus interpolation is best for relatively smooth data, but that is the case for our example so we shall use this method. (See page 141 for alternatives.)

The box below shows how to create an interpolation function. As before, we use **cspline** to set up an interpolation table (using cubic spline) and **interp** to interpolate it.

$$y_j := \frac{zx_j - 1}{px_j}$$

$vs := \text{cspline}(px, y)$

$f(p) := \text{interp}(vs, px, y, p)$

$p := 0, 0.5\cdot\text{MPa} .. 80\cdot\text{MPa}$

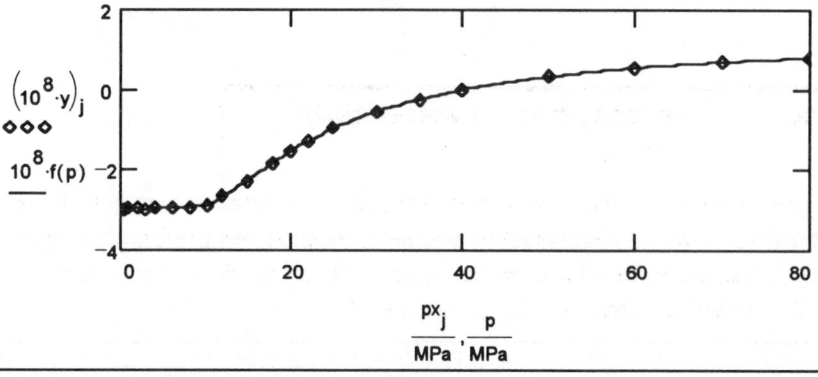

As always, a close examination of the graph is important. There is some irregularity in the data at low pressure (which you can see more clearly by graphing only that portion), but these are not too serious and will be smoothed out by the integration. (If we had to differentiate the data, this scatter would be very serious, if not debilitating.)

The box below displays a graph and some sample calculations. (Because the numerical integral must be repeated for each point, the calculation of the graph may be rather slow.)

$\text{lng}(P) := \int_0^P f(p)\,dp \qquad \text{phi}(P) := \exp(\text{lng}(P)) \qquad k := 0 .. 4$

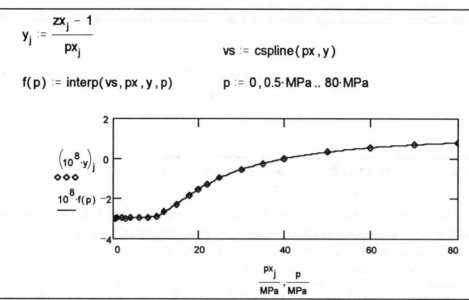

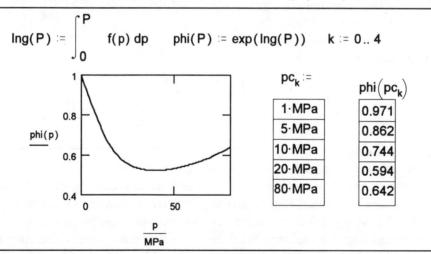

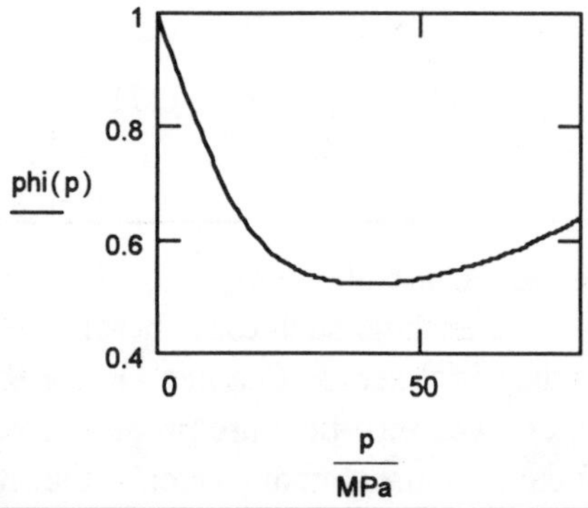

$pc_k :=$	$\text{phi}(pc_k)$
1·MPa	0.971
5·MPa	0.862
10·MPa	0.744
20·MPa	0.594
80·MPa	0.642

As has happened so often, in this problem the data entry was the most trouble. Yet the calculations that Mathcad did for you would be quite formidable if you tried them with a calculator.

If data are too noisy for interpolation, and the curve not suited to polynomial regression (as this one probably is not), the only alternative is to make a trapezoidal-rule integration of the data. This method has two severe limitations: you can only integrate to one of the base points (one of the pressures in the data set) and you must somehow estimate the area from $P = 0$ to the lowest pressure measured . The last can be difficult because $(z - 1)/P$ is indeterminate at $P = 0$; however, it has a finite limit as the graph above demonstrates.

$$\text{last}(y) = 21 \qquad N := 12 \qquad px_N = 20\cdot\text{MPa}$$

$$\text{area} := \sum_{j=0}^{N-1} \frac{y_{j+1}+y_j}{2}\cdot\left(px_{j+1}-px_j\right) + y_0\cdot px_0$$

$$\text{area} = -0.520 \qquad \int_0^{px_N} f(x)\,dx = -0.521$$

The box to the left demonstrates the trapezoidal-rule integration up to 20 MPa. The second term of *area* is an approximation of the area of the sliver between 0 and 0.1 MPa. To estimate that area, we assume that $y(0) = y(0.1)$ (the first datum) which, as inspection of the graph above shows, is not too unreasonable. The area calculated in this instance is quite close to that obtained from interpolation. Regardless, the flexibility of interpolation makes it the method of choice wherever possible.

Example 6.8 Fugacity from the RK law.

The fugacity is related to the chemical potential (μ) as:

$$f = f^\circ \exp\left[\frac{\mu - \mu^\circ}{RT}\right] \tag{6.10}$$

f° is the standard fugacity, 1 bar. The chemical potential μ - μ° is, effectively, G - G° for one mole, which can be calculated (as in Example 4.9) from:

$$G - G^\circ = (H - H^\circ) - T(S - S^\circ) \tag{6.11}$$

You should have functions for these in *rkimp.mcd* — U_i, H_i, S_i, S_v — as developed in Example 4.9. Recover these and enter constants for ethane. The first term on the right-hand side of Eq. (6.11) is H_i and the second is the function we called S_v. We will call the left-hand side of Eq. (6.11):

$$G_v = H_i - T\,S_v$$

You will also need the volume function *vf* from Chapter 4 (box below).

$$vc(p,T) := \begin{bmatrix} \dfrac{-a}{\sqrt{T}}\cdot b \\ \left(-p\cdot b^2 + \dfrac{a}{\sqrt{T}} - R\cdot T\cdot b\right)\cdot vu \\ -R\cdot T\cdot vu^2 \\ p\cdot vu^3 \end{bmatrix}\cdot\frac{1}{pu}$$

$$vu := \text{liter} \qquad pu := \text{kg}\cdot\text{m}^8\cdot\text{sec}^{-2}$$

$$vf(P,T) := \text{polyroots}(vc(P,T))\cdot vu$$

The imperfection functions are used to define a function for μ - μ° (G_v) and fugacity (*fug*).

$$G_v(V,T) := H_i(V,T) - T\cdot S_v(V,T) \qquad fug(V,T) := (bar)\cdot \exp\left(\frac{G_v(V,T)}{R\cdot T}\right)$$

$$V := 1\cdot liter \quad T := 300\cdot K \qquad G_v(V,T) = 7.153\cdot kJ \qquad S_i(V,T) = -1.314\cdot J\cdot K^{-1}$$

$$U_i(V,T) = -0.837\cdot kJ \qquad H_i(V,T) = -1.265\cdot kJ \qquad S_v(V,T) = -28.059\cdot J\cdot K^{-1}$$

(The sample calculations are for testing your work.) Now, the, calculation of fugacity coefficients is simple (box below).

$$T := 400\cdot K \qquad px := 80\cdot MPa \qquad vol := vf(px, T)$$

$$\phi := \frac{fug(vol_2, T)}{px} \qquad \phi = 0.643 \qquad vol = \begin{pmatrix} -13.356 + 62.501i \\ -13.356 - 62.501i \\ 68.284 \end{pmatrix}\cdot mL$$

Do this for other pressures and compare to the results of Example 6.7. The agreement is excellent — better than we would normally expect from the RK law. (RK seems to be better for ethane than for most other gases.)

6.5 Calculating the Extent of Reaction

Students often find calculating the extent of reaction from an equilibrium constant to be difficult. The difficulty generally arises from the setup, which depends on understanding chemical reactions and the nature of equilibrium, and, for this, Mathcad (or any computer program) cannot help you. Once the problem is set up, the solution is relatively easy using a computer. For some reason, equilibrium problems are, numerically, very difficult for computer programs. Apparently the mixture of additive conditions (the material balance equations) and multiplicative relationships (the equilibrium constants) cause the problem since the first requires good absolute accuracy while the second requires good relative accuracy. Whatever the reason it is important, after any numerical solution of an equilibrium problem, to recalculate the original equations to ensure that the answer is correct.

Example 6.9 Dissociation of phosgene.

Actually, dissociation problems gain little from Mathcad, but we shall use the results of Example 6.6 to determine the degree of dissociation as a function of temperature, which would be a lot of work without Mathcad.

We begin by writing the equilibrium constant in terms of the activities, partial pressures and mole fractions:

$$K_a = \frac{a_{CO}a_{Cl_2}}{a_{COCl_2}} \approx \frac{P_{CO}P_{Cl_2}}{P_{COCl_2}P^o} = \frac{X_{CO}X_{Cl_2}}{X_{COCl_2}}\frac{P}{P^o}$$

P^o is the standard pressure; we can omit this factor by simply using P in the same unit: bar or atm (depending on the standard state for the data used). The material balance is:

	$COCl_2$	=	CO	+	Cl_2
moles	$1-\alpha$		α		α
mole fraction	$\frac{1-\alpha}{1+\alpha}$		$\frac{\alpha}{1+\alpha}$		$\frac{\alpha}{1+\alpha}$

The mole fraction is calculated by adding the moles (to give $1 + \alpha$), and dividing that into the number of moles. Substituting into the expression for K_a gives (after some simplification):

$$K_a = \frac{\alpha^2 P}{1-\alpha^2}$$

$$Ka = \frac{\alpha^2 \cdot P}{1-\alpha^2} \text{ has solution(s) } \begin{bmatrix} \frac{1}{\sqrt{Ka+P}} \cdot \sqrt{Ka} \\ \frac{-1}{\sqrt{Ka+P}} \cdot \sqrt{Ka} \end{bmatrix}$$

This is easily solved for the degree of dissociation (α). To get Mathcad to do the algebra for you, enter the equation using a logical equals (ctrl+=) (box to left). Place the cursor next to α and select Symbolic-menu, Solve. The positive root is clearly the one we want. It can be copied, pasted and edited to give the function below.

Before creating $\alpha(T, P)$ (box to right), insert the results for the equilibrium constant vs. T, *Ka(T)* saved earlier (*phosgene.mcd*).

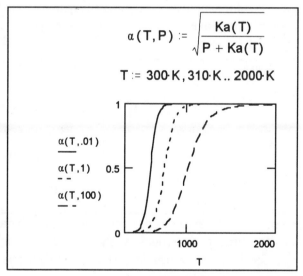

The box to the right shows the calculation of the degree of dissociation as a function of T and P (pressure in atm). As you can see, the degree of dissociation rises over a fairly narrow range of temperature, especially at low pressure (curve to left). At room temperature, phosgene is effectively undissociated. By 1300 K, it is nearly all dissociated unless the pressure is high.

$$\alpha(T,P) := \sqrt{\frac{Ka(T)}{P + Ka(T)}}$$

$$T := 300 \cdot K, 310 \cdot K .. 2000 \cdot K$$

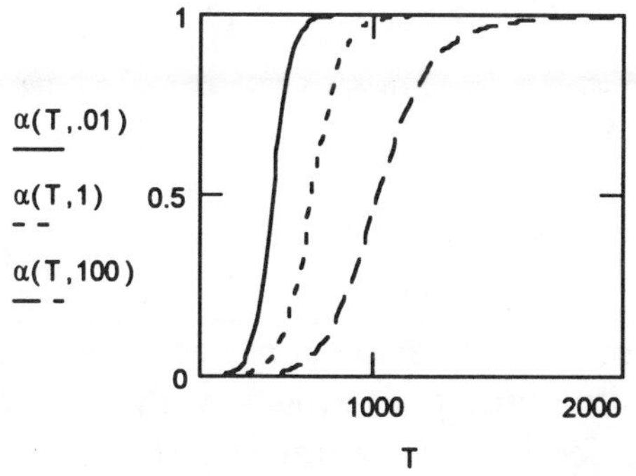

Phosgene is very poisonous, and was used as a weapon during World War I. Both of its dissociation products are also poisonous, so dissociation does not affect this unfortunate property.

Example 6.10 The Haber synthesis.

Nitrogen is an essential nutrient for plants, but most plants cannot directly use the most plentiful source, the nitrogen of the air. Ammonia, which is soluble in water, can be used as a fertilizer, or in the synthesis of other nitrogen compounds. The Haber synthesis

$$\tfrac{1}{2}N_2(g) + \tfrac{3}{2}H_2(g) = NH_3(g)$$

does just what is required. At 723 K, 1000 atm, the equilibrium constant is:

$$K_p = \frac{P_{\mathrm{NH_3}}}{P_{\mathrm{N_2}}^{1/2} P_{\mathrm{H_2}}^{3/2}} = 0.02496\,\mathrm{atm}^{-1}$$

(At this pressure, K_p is very different from K_a because the gases are not ideal; we do not need to be concerned about this since it is K_p that we need.) For purposes of calculation, it is best to remove fractional coefficients by doubling the reaction

$$N_2(g) + 3\,H_2(g) = 2\,NH_3(g)$$

and squaring the equilibrium constant, to give:

$$K_p = \frac{P_{\mathrm{NH_3}}^2}{P_{\mathrm{N_2}} P_{\mathrm{H_2}}^3} = \frac{X_{\mathrm{NH_3}}^2}{X_{\mathrm{N_2}} X_{\mathrm{H_2}}^3 P^2}$$

The material balance is:

	$N_2(g)$ +	$3\,H_2(g)$ =	$2\,NH_3(g)$
moles =	$n_{N2} - \xi$	$n_{H2} - 3\xi$	2ξ

(n denotes the initial moles, and ξ is the extent of reaction.) We will let Mathcad do rest. (The extent-of-reaction variable ξ is made using x ctrl+g, or selected from the Greek-letter palette, or just use x for simplicity.) Assume an equimolar mixture of ammonia and nitrogen; since equilibrium is intensive, we can arbitrarily take one mole each (try some other number to see what happens).

---

molN2(ξ) := 1 − ξ   molH2(ξ) := 1 − 3·ξ   molNH3(ξ) := 2·ξ

molT(ξ) := molN2(ξ) + molH2(ξ) + molNH3(ξ)

$$XH2(\xi) := \frac{molH2(\xi)}{molT(\xi)} \qquad XN2(\xi) := \frac{molN2(\xi)}{molT(\xi)} \qquad XNH3(\xi) := \frac{molNH3(\xi)}{molT(\xi)}$$

$$K_p := \left(\frac{0.02496}{atm}\right)^2 \qquad P := 1000\cdot atm \qquad T := 723\cdot K$$

To solve for the extent of reaction, it is best to rearrange the equilibrium expression by clearing the denominator of fractions, as shown in the box below. We also must provide an initial estimate for the extent of reaction, which must lie between $0 < \xi < {}^1/_3$ (none of the variables representing moles can be negative).

$$f(\xi) := K_p \cdot P^2 \cdot XN2(\xi) \cdot XH2(\xi)^3 - XNH3(\xi)^2$$

xg := 0.1 Guess for answer   TOL := 10^{-8} Tolerance for answer.

Given

$xg > 0$ $xg < \frac{1}{3}$ f(xg)=0   Solve block works better than Root.

ξ := Find(xg)   ξ = 0.294575

The box above also sets the system variable *TOL*, which determines the accuracy of the answer. For this problem (and many others) a solve block seems to work better than **root**. Also, being able to put in inequalities to limit the range for the root decreases the likelihood of getting an incorrect root.

Equilibrium problems are, numerically, very difficult and error-prone so it is essential to recalculate the equilibrium constant and compare it to the input value.

$\xi = 0.294575$ $\qquad$ $XNH3(\xi) = 0.418$

$f(\xi) = 0$ $\qquad$ $\dfrac{XNH3(\xi)^2}{XN2(\xi)\cdot XH2(\xi)^3\cdot P^2} = 1.000000\cdot K_p$

Recheck: to be sure the answer is correct, recalculate the original equilibrium expression.

The box above demonstrates a useful trick: type K_p ("K.p") into the unit placeholder for its calculation, thus displaying the answer as a multiple of K_p. The multiple should, of course, be exactly 1; the numerical-format menu was used in this example to display more significant figures than is usual (also, click the trailing-zeros box).

The box to right illustrates a more direct way to do this problem. The method is a bit touchier than the previous one (it gave an incorrect answer with this initial guess but without the inequalities, whereas the previous method worked fine that way), but it is much more convenient. The important thing is not so much how you solve equilibrium problems, but that you check the answer; errors are endemic in this type of calculation.

$K_{pf}(\xi) := \dfrac{XNH3(\xi)^2}{P^2\cdot XN2(\xi)\cdot XH2(\xi)^3}$ $\qquad$ $xg := 0.1$

Given

$K_p = K_{pf}(xg)$ $\qquad$ $xg > 0$ $\qquad$ $xg < \dfrac{1}{3}$

$\xi := \text{Find}(xg)$ $\qquad$ $\xi = 0.294575$

$K_{pf}(\xi) = 1.000000\cdot K_p$

Example 6.11 Multiple equilibria: Fischer-Tropsch.

Many important processes, including the Fischer-Tropsch process for the production of liquid fuels from coal, consist of a group of simultaneous reactions. Such problems can be very difficult to solve, particularly when there are a lot of reactions with equilibrium constants differing greatly in magnitude. We illustrate the method by solving two reactions of this process (at 700 K):

$$CO + 3\,H_2 = CH_4 + H_2O \qquad K_1 = 3.88\times10^3$$

$$CO + H_2O = H_2 + CO_2 \qquad K_2 = 9.32$$

The symbolic equilibrium constant are, assuming ideal gas and pressure with unit bar (so P^o = 1):

$$K_1 = \frac{P_{CH_4}P_{H_2O}}{P_{CO}P_{H_2}^3} = \frac{X_{CH_4}X_{H_2O}}{X_{CO}X_{H_2}^3}\frac{1}{P^2} = \frac{n_{CH_4}n_{H_2O}}{n_{CO}n_{H_2}^3}\frac{n_{total}^2}{P^2}$$

$$K_2 = \frac{P_{H_2}P_{CO_2}}{P_{CO}P_{H_2O}} = \frac{X_{H_2}X_{CO_2}}{X_{CO}X_{H_2O}} = \frac{n_{H_2}n_{CO_2}}{n_{CO}n_{H_2O}}$$

The box below sets up the calculation. The temperature is for information only, and bar is defined as 1 so we can label the pressure appropriately. We need extent-of-reaction variables for each equation; we call them *x* and *y* for reactions 1 and 2 respectively.

---

1. $CO + 3\,H_2 = CH_4 + H_2O$ $\quad K_1 := 3.88 \cdot 10^3$ $\quad bar := 1$
2. $CO + H_2O = H_2 + CO_2$ $\quad K_2 := 9.32$ $\quad T := 700 \cdot K$

$CO_{init} := 2 \quad W_{init} := 1 \quad H2_{init} := 1 \quad CO2_{init} := 0$

$n_{CO}(x,y) := CO_{init} - x - y \qquad n_{H2}(x,y) := H2_{init} - 3 \cdot x + y$

$n_{H2O}(x,y) := W_{init} + x - y \qquad n_{CO2}(x,y) := CO2_{init} + y \qquad n_{CH4}(x,y) := x$

$total(x,y) := n_{CO}(x,y) + n_{H2}(x,y) + n_{H2O}(x,y) + n_{CO2}(x,y) + n_{CH4}(x,y)$

Economics argues for starting with water and CO (since H_2 is more expensive than water), but the problem is difficult to solve for these conditions.

To solve the problem we must enter a value for the pressure and initial estimates for the extents of reaction. We also set *TOL*, which determines the accuracy of the solutions.

$P := 20 \cdot bar \quad x := 0.4 \quad y := 1.2$ initial estimates $\quad TOL := 10^{-6}$

Given

$n_{CO}(x,y) + n_{CH4}(x,y) + n_{CO2}(x,y) = CO_{init} + CO2_{init}$ carbon balance

$total(x,y) > 0 \qquad x > 0 \qquad y > 0$

$K_1 \cdot P^2 \cdot \left(n_{CO}(x,y) \cdot n_{H2}(x,y)^3\right) = n_{CH4}(x,y) \cdot n_{H2O}(x,y) \cdot total(x,y)^2$

$K_2 \cdot \left(n_{CO}(x,y) \cdot n_{H2O}(x,y)\right) = n_{H2}(x,y) \cdot n_{CO2}(x,y)$

$\begin{pmatrix} x \\ y \end{pmatrix} := Find(x,y) \qquad x = 0.735 \qquad y = 1.252 \qquad ERR = 1.114 \cdot 10^{-14}$

With only two unknowns, the equilibrium equations are by themselves sufficient, but we have added other conditions including carbon balance and the requirement that *x*, *y* and the total moles (*total*) must be positive. In this case, the extra conditions are not necessary, but in more difficult cases could prevent the solution process from wandering too far from reality. There are other conditions that could be included, for example that all of the mole variables must be positive. If you have difficulty getting a solution, you might try replacing **Find** with **minerr**; then it is more likely that an answer will be displayed. Even a wrong answer is better than no answer since it may help you decide which direction to go. The equilibrium expressions themselves have been cleared of fractions, which facilitates the solution considerably. In the last line, the answer is displayed together with *ERR*, which indicates the accuracy of the solution.

Next we calculate the mole fractions of the gases at equilibrium.

$$\frac{n_{CH4}(x,y)}{total(x,y)} = 0.29 \qquad \frac{n_{CO}(x,y)}{total(x,y)} = 0.005 \qquad \frac{n_{CO2}(x,y)}{total(x,y)} = 0.495$$

$$total(x,y) = 2.531 \qquad \frac{n_{H2}(x,y)}{total(x,y)} = 0.019 \qquad \frac{n_{H2O}(x,y)}{total(x,y)} = 0.191$$

$$\frac{n_{CH4}(x,y)}{CO_{init}} = 36.735 \cdot \%$$

If any of the mole fractions are negative, the solution is not correct. The last calculation shows the percent of carbon converted to methane.

Finally, and most important, we check the values of the equilibrium constants to be sure the solution is correct. As before, we use the value as "units" for the comparison: that is, the symbols K_1 and K_2 are typed into the unit placeholders of the first two equalities. Double-click on the number to increase the number of displayed digits (also, we have selected "trailing zeros" to get this display).

$$\frac{n_{CH4}(x,y) \cdot n_{H2O}(x,y)}{n_{CO}(x,y) \cdot n_{H2}(x,y)^3} \cdot \frac{total(x,y)^2}{P^2} = 1.000000 \cdot K_1$$

$$\frac{n_{CO2}(x,y) \cdot n_{H2}(x,y)}{n_{CO}(x,y) \cdot n_{H2O}(x,y)} = 1.000000 \cdot K_2$$

$$n_{CO}(x,y) + n_{CH4}(x,y) + n_{CO2}(x,y) = 1.000000 \cdot \left(CO_{init} + CO2_{init}\right)$$

The last line shows the carbon balance. There are also material balance equations for hydrogen and oxygen, but these are more complicated and probably unnecessary.

Explore this system, varying the initial reactant mixture and pressure. You will probably find it easy to generate erroneous solutions. If the solution is close, you may be able to improve it by setting the initial estimates for x and y closer to the calculated values. What is the effect of a CO/H_2 mixture with no water? What conditions optimize the CO to CH_4 conversion?

Problems

6.1 Propane is commonly used for heating and in applications like gas grills. Calculate the maximum temperature of propane burning in air from its heat of combustion: -2220.0 kJ/mol.

6.2 Alcohol burners are a safe and convenient as a small heat source; at one time they were used in "chemistry sets" provided for children. Calculate the adiabatic flame temperature of ethanol burning in air from its heat of combustion: -1367 kJ/mol

6.3 For the dissociation $N_2O_4(g) = 2\ NO_2(g)$, use enthalpies of formation and entropies (assumed constant) to calculate the equilibrium constant as a function of temperature. (a) Make a graph of K vs. T from 300 to 600 K. Calculate K at 350, 450 and 550 K. (b) Calculate the degree of dissociation at 500 K, 2600 psi. (c) Make a graph of α vs. P (1 to

1000 atm) at 300, 400 and 500 K (same graph). (d) At what temperature is the degree of dissociation equal to 0.5 at $P = 1$ atm?

6.4 Nitrogen and oxygen are, ordinarily, considered unreactive with each other (they coexist peaceably in the atmosphere), but in engines they react forming a variety of oxides (collectively known as NO_x). For the reaction $N_2 + O_2 = 2\ NO$, use free-energy functions (as on Noggle, Table 6.4) to interpolate the equilibrium constant between 298 and 2000 K. (a) Make a graph of K vs. T and report values at 1700 and 1900 K. (b) Calculate the mole percent NO in a reacting mixture (containing equal amounts of oxygen and nitrogen) at 1800 K.

6.5 Use data from the table to calculate the fugacity coefficients of CO_2 at 373.15 K. Make a graph of the coefficients vs. pressure, and report values at 200, 400, 600, 800 and 1000 atm.

6.6 Use the RK gas law to calculate the fugacity coefficients of CO_2 at 373.15 K. (a) Report values at 200, 400, 600, 800 and 1000 atm. Compare to results of previous problem. Make a graph showing the experimental values and the RK calculations. (In this case, "experimental" will be a solid curve, calculated with the interpolation function of the previous problem, and the theoretical will be the 5 points calculated for these pressures.)

Compressibility of carbon dioxide vs. pressure at 373.15 K.

P/atm	z	P/atm	z
1	0.9975	400	0.7551
50	0.8772	500	0.8729
100	0.7489	600	0.9928
150	0.6384	700	1.1113
200	0.5922	800	1.2280
250	0.6075	900	1.3422
300	0.6471	1000	1.4534

6.7 Sulfur in the gas phase can take many forms. Considering only the reaction $4S_2 = S_8$, calculate the mole fraction of S_2 at 1000 K and pressures of 5, 15 and 25 atm. Use $K_a = 1.923\times10^{-3}$.

6.8 For the equilibrium

$$4\ HCl(g) + O_2(g) = 2\ Cl_2(g) + 2\ H_2O(g)$$

calculate the mole fraction and partial pressure of Cl_2 for a (total) equilibrium pressure of 6, 12, and 22 atm when a 1:1 mixture of the reactants is used. This is the Deacon process which was once used for the commercial production of chlorine. Use $K_p = 23.14\ atm^{-1}$ for .723 K.

6.9 For the equilibrium H_2(gas) + I_2(solid) = 2HI(gas) (at 50 °C). $K_a = 1.348$. Calculate mole fraction HI at 1, 10 and 100 atm total pressure. (Assume ideal gas for the gases and unit activity for the solid.)

6.10 For the Fischer-Tropsch reaction at 700 K (Example 6.11), calculate the mass of methane formed if 5 moles CO, 5 moles water and 5 moles CO_2 (no H_2) are reacted at 50 bar. What percent of the total carbon present is converted to methane?

Answers

6.1 2320 K

6.2 2227 K

6.3 (a) 5.060, 399.2, 6.432×10^3 (b) 0.848 (d) 328 K

6.4 (a) 5.806×10^{-5},2.232×10^{-4} (b) 0.5408%

6.5 0.617, 0.482, 0.457, 0.471, 0.507

6.6 0.597, 0.473, 0.452, 0.469, 0.507 (calculating V from RK)

0.597, 0.505, 0.488, 0.504, 0.556 (calculating V from z)

6.7 X_{S2} = 0.862, 0.517, 0.376

6.8 P_{Cl2} = 1.423, 2.925, 5.476 atm; X_{Cl2} = 0.237, 0.244, 0.249

6.9 0.666, 0.304, 0.109

6.10 19.464 gm, 12.133%

CHAPTER 7

SOLUTIONS

7.1 Raoult's Law

The calculations involved with Raoult's law gain little from Mathcad, so we choose our single example to take advantage of the programs ability to do a series of calculations from lists of data.

Example 7.1 Activity coefficients from vapor pressures.

The data in the box below give the vapor pressures of isopropanol, n-decane solutions together with the mole fractions (component 2, n-decane) in the liquid (X_2) and gas phases (Y_2). The variables *pz1* and *pz2* (denote P^* in text) are the vapor pressures of the pure liquids at the same temperature.

$i := 0..3$ $P_i :=$ $X2_i :=$ $Y2_i :=$

P_i	$X2_i$	$Y2_i$
942.6	.1312	.0243
883.9	.2714	.0342
830.2	.4425	.0411
758.7	.6036	.0489

1 = isopropanol
2 = n-decane

$X1 := 1 - X2$

$Y1 := 1 - Y2$

$pz1 := 1008$

$pz2 := 48.3$

pz: vapor pressure of pure material

The box below shows the calculations of the partial pressures of the components using Dalton's law, $P_i = Y_i P$, and the Raoult's-law (RL) activity, $a_i = P_i/P_i^*$.

$p1_i := p_i \cdot Y1_i$ $\quad a1_i := \dfrac{p1_i}{pz1}$ $\quad p2_i := p_i \cdot Y2_i$ $\quad a2_i := \dfrac{p2_i}{pz2}$

$$p1 = \begin{bmatrix} 919.695 \\ 853.671 \\ 796.079 \\ 721.6 \end{bmatrix} \quad a1 = \begin{bmatrix} 0.912 \\ 0.847 \\ 0.79 \\ 0.716 \end{bmatrix} \quad p2 = \begin{bmatrix} 22.905 \\ 30.229 \\ 34.121 \\ 37.1 \end{bmatrix} \quad a2 = \begin{bmatrix} 0.474 \\ 0.626 \\ 0.706 \\ 0.768 \end{bmatrix}$$

The RL activity coefficients calculated below measure how far the solution is from ideal (γ = 1).

$$\gamma 1_i := \frac{a1_i}{X1_i} \quad \gamma 1 = \begin{bmatrix} 1.05 \\ 1.162 \\ 1.417 \\ 1.806 \end{bmatrix} \quad \gamma 2_i := \frac{a2_i}{X2_i} \quad \gamma 2 = \begin{bmatrix} 3.615 \\ 2.306 \\ 1.596 \\ 1.273 \end{bmatrix}$$

RL activity coefficients should approach 1 (ideal) as the mole fraction approaches 1 (pure liquid); this can be seen for isopropanol (X_1 = 1 - 0.1312 = 0.8688 for the first solution), but not for the n-decane, whose maximum concentration (0.6036) is too far from pure liquid for the limit to apply.

7.2 Henry's Law

The Henry's law constant k_X (mole-fraction scale) and k_m (molality scale) can be determined from vapor pressures of volatile components in dilute solution as the dilute-solution limit:

$$k_X = \lim_{X_2 \to 0}\left[\frac{P_2}{X_2}\right] \qquad k_m = \lim_{m \to 0}\left[\frac{P_2}{m}\right] \tag{7.1}$$

Example 7.2 Henry's law constant for bromine in carbon tetrachloride.

The box below gives vapor pressures of bromine (vector **p**, in torr) vs. mole fraction (**X**) for solutions in carbon tetrachloride at 298.15 K. First we calculate $y_i = P_i / X_i$; for an ideal solution, these numbers would all be equal to the Henry's law constant. According to Eq. (7.1), the dilute-solution limit of these numbers is that constant, so be make a linear extrapolation using the Mathcad function **intercept**.

$i := 0..7$

$N := 8$

$X_i :=$	$p_i :=$
0.00394	1.52
0.00420	1.60
0.00599	2.39
0.0102	4.27
0.0130	5.43
0.0236	9.57
0.0238	9.83
0.0250	10.27

$y_i := \frac{p_i}{X_i}$ pressure in torr

$k_X := \text{intercept}(X, y)$ $k_X = 390.863$

$b := \text{slope}(X, y)$ $b = 952.228$

$r := \text{corr}(X, y)$ $r = 0.612$

$y_{fit}(x) := k_X + b \cdot x$ $x := 0, .01 .. .03$

The correlation coefficient for this analysis is not encouraging; it is far from the ideal value (-1 or, in this case +1), but does this have anything to do with the accuracy of our determination? The answer to this question lies in the standard deviation of the constant determined (the intercept); this calculation is shown in the box below.

$sxx := \sum_i (X_i)^2$

$\sigma_b := \frac{b}{r} \cdot \sqrt{\frac{1 - r^2}{N - 2}}$

$\sigma_a := \sigma_b \cdot \sqrt{\frac{sxx}{N}}$

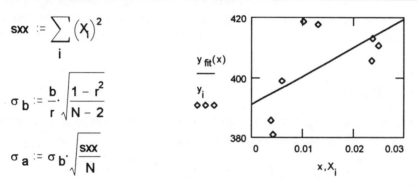

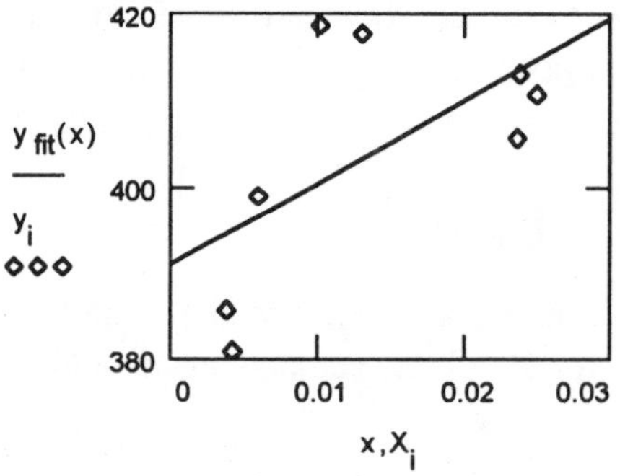

Henry's law (HL:X) constant: $k_X = 390.863$ torr standard error: $\sigma_a = 8.13$ torr

In fact, although the graph has a lot of scatter (as predicted by *r*), the value of the Henry's law constant is reasonably good, with a standard deviation of about 2% of the value.

$k_X + \sigma_a = 398.993$
$\text{mean}(y) = 403.924$
$k_X - \sigma_a = 382.733$

In fact, most of the deviation of the points from Henry's law is due to experimental error rather than solution nonideality. The box to the left demonstrates that, if we assumed Henry's law and just averaged the determinations of the constants (using the Mathcad function **mean**), we get an answer only a little outside one standard deviation from the mean. Nonetheless, the extrapolation is the correct procedure and, at higher concentrations (less ideal solutions), the difference between the methods would be greater.

The determination of the molality-scale Henry's law constant is shown in the box below (*mw1* is the molecular weight of the solvent, CCl_4).

$$mw1 := 12.011 + 4\cdot 35.453 \qquad molality_i := \frac{1000\cdot X_1}{mw1\cdot(1 - X_1)} \qquad y_i := \frac{P_i}{molality_i}$$

$$k_m := intercept(molality, y) \qquad k_m = 60.156 \quad \text{(unit torr)}$$

$$molality = \begin{bmatrix} 0.026 \\ 0.027 \\ 0.039 \\ 0.067 \\ 0.086 \\ 0.157 \\ 0.158 \\ 0.167 \end{bmatrix} \qquad activity_i := \frac{P_i}{k_m} \qquad \gamma_i := \frac{activity_i}{molality_i} \qquad \gamma = \begin{bmatrix} 0.983 \\ 0.97 \\ 1.014 \\ 1.06 \\ 1.054 \\ 1.012 \\ 1.031 \\ 1.024 \end{bmatrix}$$

The Henry's law (HL) activity is the ratio of the vapor pressure to the Henry's law constant: $a_2 = P_2/m$ (these would be equal to 1 if Henry's law were exact). The calculation for the HL activity coefficient (γ) demonstrates that these solutions are very near ideal: the limit of this quantity as $m \to 0$ is 1, and you can see that the lowest-concentration value deviates as much from 1 as the highest. Thus, these deviations are largely random error rather than actual deviations from ideality.

7.3 Gibbs-Duhem Equation

Henry's law (HL) activity coefficients of nonvolatile solutes must be determined from solvent activity using the Gibbs-Duhem equation. Solvent activity can be determined by measuring the vapor pressure, freezing-point depression, or any other colligative property.

Example 7.3 Activity coefficients from freezing-point depression.

The box below gives the freezing-point depressions (θ) as a function of molality for solutions of ethanol in water. From these data the osmotic coefficient (*phi*) is calculated using the freezing-point constants from Table 7.6, Noggle.

$i := 0..8$

$N := 9$

$m_i :=$

$\theta_i :=$

m_i	θ_i
.009815	.01833
.01879	.03493
.03503	.06522
.07423	.13706
.13477	.24821
.18263	.33535
.3092	.5666
.4150	.7579
.5160	.9396

$K_f := 1.860 \qquad b := 4.8 \cdot 10^{-4}$

$$\phi_i := \frac{\theta_i}{K_f m_i} \cdot \left(1 + b \cdot \theta_i\right)$$

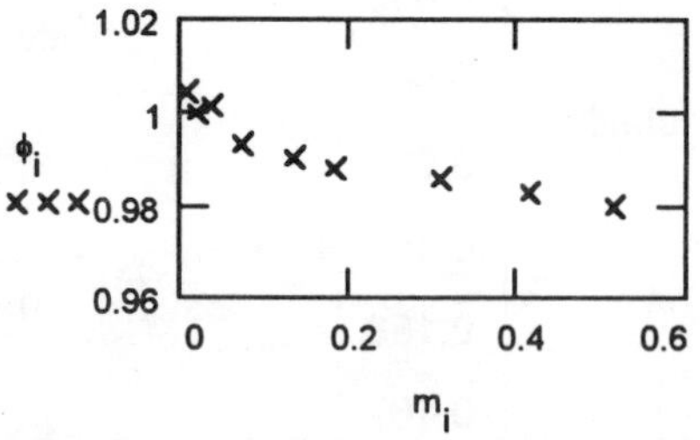

The graph of *phi* vs. *m* shows that these data should be fit by a low-order polynomial. The Greek letter θ (theta) is made by typing "`q ctrl+g`".

For the vector of functions (**F**) required by **linfit**, we set up a matrix with 3 rows (1 column) using the button on the Matrices and Vectors palette. Initially this was set to do the three terms of a cubic equation, but then the 3rd term was eliminated by making it zero (example below, you should also try it with m^3 in that spot).

$$F(m) := \begin{pmatrix} m \\ m^2 \\ 0 \end{pmatrix} \qquad ans := \text{linfit}(m, \phi - 1, F) \qquad ff(m) := ans \cdot F(m)$$

$$ans = \begin{pmatrix} -0.073 \\ 0.067 \\ 0 \end{pmatrix}$$

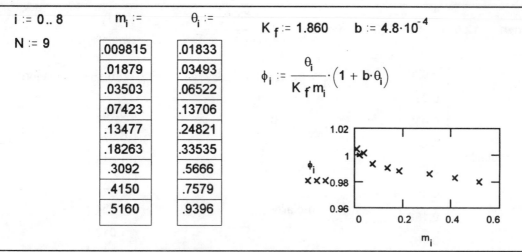

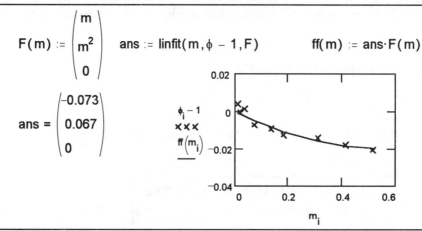

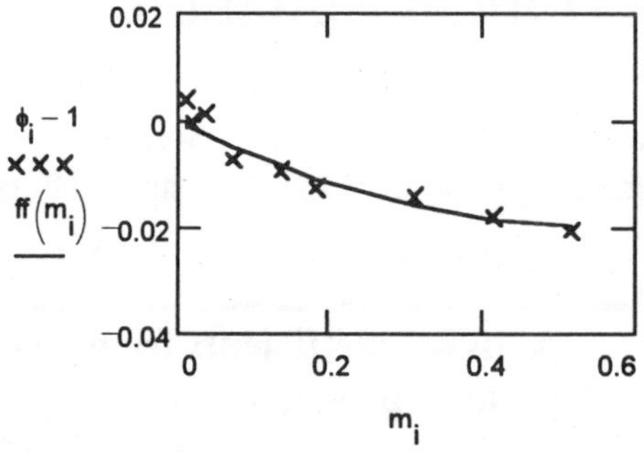

The fitted function (*ff*) for (ϕ - 1) with 2 terms does well enough considering the scatter of the data; an additional term is hard to justify.

The box below demonstrates the calculation of the activity coefficient (γ):

$$\gamma(m) := \exp\left(ff(m) + \int_0^m \frac{ff(mv)}{mv}\,dmv\right)$$

$\gamma(m_i)$	m_i	$m_i \cdot \gamma(m_i)$
0.999	0.01	0.01
0.997	0.019	0.019
0.995	0.035	0.035
0.99	0.074	0.073
0.982	0.135	0.132
0.977	0.183	0.178
0.965	0.309	0.299
0.958	0.415	0.398
0.953	0.516	0.492

molality := 0, .01 .. 0.49

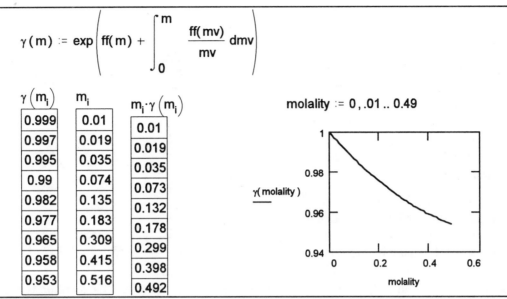

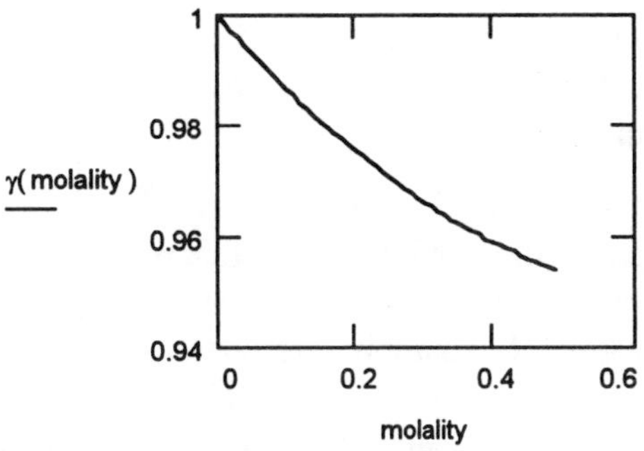

The calculations show that, up to 0.5 mol/kg, the deviations from ideality are not great. The third column of numbers displays the activity, $a_2 = \gamma m$, demonstrating that the activity and molality are nearly equal: an assumption we make in the next section for dilute solutions.

7.4 Equilibrium in Solution

The most interesting problems regarding equilibrium in solution involve ions and, thus, are discussed in Chapter 8. Here we give two simple examples involving solubility, contrasting solids and gases.

Example 7.4 Solubility of iodine in water.

For the equilibrium

$$I_2(\text{solid}) = I_2(\text{ao})$$

we use thermodynamic data (e.g. Tables 8.3 and 3.2, Noggle) to calculate ΔH°, ΔG°, and ΔS°. Because the standard-state symbol cannot be displayed in Mathcad (which does not support label-type superscripts), these quantities (for the reference temperature, 298.15) are denoted *DHref*, *DGref* and *DSref* respectively.

$R := 8.31451$ $\quad kJ := 1000$ $\quad T_{ref} := 298.15$

$DHref := (22.6 - 0)\cdot kJ$ $\quad DGref := (16.40 - 0)\cdot kJ$ $\quad DSref := 137.2 - 116.135$

$DHref - T_{ref} DSref = 16.319\cdot kJ$ $\quad DHref = 22.6\cdot kJ$

Iodine solid, is, of course, an element so its formation enthalpy and free energy are equal to zero. We note that there is a slight difference between ΔG° and $\Delta H^\circ - T\Delta S^\circ$ reflecting a slight inconsistency in the data; this is neither uncommon nor worrisome, and reflects an uncertainty in the data and the calculation. The equilibrium constant for this process is:

$$K_a = \frac{a_{I_2,ao}}{a_{I_2,solid}} \approx m$$

For the approximation, we have set the activity of the solid to 1 and approximated the activity of the dissolved iodine (ao) with its HL ideal-solution value, the molality. Since this is the molality of a saturated solution (solid is present), it is also the solubility.

$$sol(T) := \exp\left(\frac{DSref}{R} - \frac{DHref}{R \cdot T}\right) \qquad T := 273..373$$

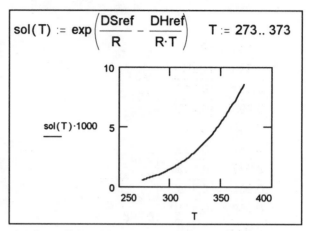

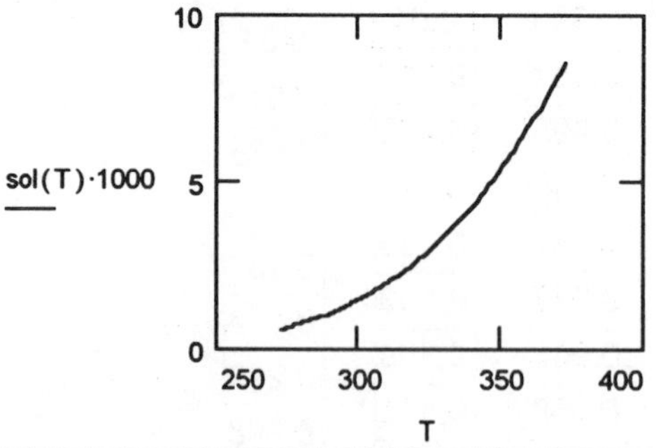

The box to the right displays the calculation of the solubility as a function of temperature, assuming that the enthalpy and entropy of solution are constant (independent of temperature). The increase in solubility with temperature is common for solids. Also note that the solution is sufficiently dilute that our assumption of HL ideal solution (activity coefficient = 1) is justified.

Example 7.5 Solubility of carbon dioxide in water.

For the solubility of a gas such as carbon dioxide, we consider the equilibrium

$$CO_2(g, P) = CO_2(ao, m)$$

for which the equilibrium constant is:

$$K_a = \frac{a_{CO_2,ao}}{a_{CO_2,gas}} \approx \frac{m}{P / P^o}$$

For the approximation, we have assumed ideal gas and HL ideal solution. The data needed are found, for example, in Noggle Table 6.1 (for the gas) and Table 8.3 (ao). We will use pressure in bar so the standard pressure is just 1; also, we set the symbol *bar* equal to 1 in Mathcad so data can be labeled correctly without the bother of units.

$R := 8.31451 \qquad kJ := 1000 \qquad T_{ref} := 298.15 \qquad bar := 1$

$DHref := (-413.80 + 393.509) \cdot kJ \qquad DHref = -20.291 \cdot kJ$

$DGref := (-385.98 + 394.359) \cdot kJ \qquad DGref = 8.379 \cdot kJ$

$DSref := 117.6 - 213.74 \qquad DSref = -96.14$

$$\mathrm{sol}(T,P) := P\cdot \exp\left(\frac{DSref}{R} - \frac{DHref}{R\cdot T}\right) \qquad T := 273..373$$

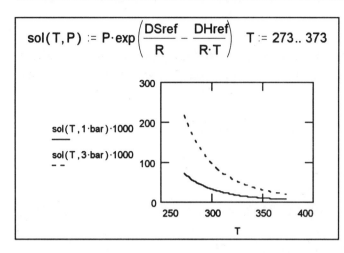

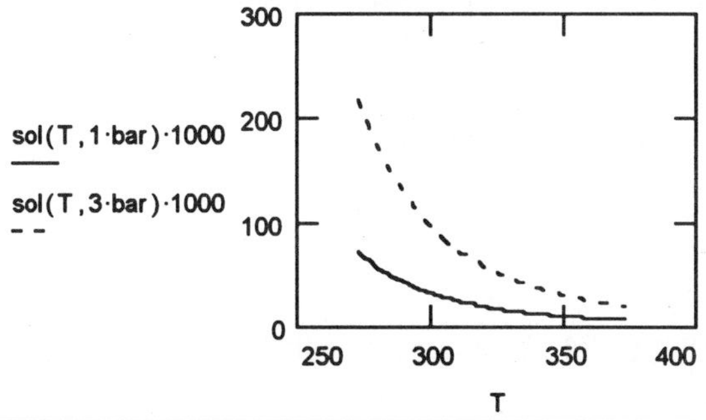

Compare the enthalpy of solution to that for the previous example.

The calculation is shown in the box to the left. Solubility depends, of course on pressure (Henry's law), but it also decreases with increasing temperature. You can observe this phenomenon by taking a glass of cold water and letting it sit at room temperature; as it warms, bubble appear as the dissolved air comes out of solution. When you open a bottle of soda water (carbon dioxide in water), you see bubbles; this is because the release of the pressure in the bottle has decreased the solubility.

The distinction between a thermodynamic property and its standard-state value, as between ΔG and ΔG°, is very important, especially for free energy and entropy (less so for enthalpy, which does not vary much with moderate changes in pressure). It is difficult to make that distinction with the notations available in Mathcad, but you should keep it in mind at all times.

Problems

7.1 Use the data on the table for the vapor pressure vs. composition of carbon tetrachloride (1) in acetonitrile (2) (at 45 °C) to calculate the activity coefficients. The vapor pressures of the pure components at the temperature are 0.3405 atm for CCl_4 and 0.2742 atm for CH_3CN.

7.2 Calculate the Henry's law constant for 1-butene in benzyl alcohol (0 °C) from the solubil-

Carbon tetrachloride (1) in acetonitrile (2) at 40 °C			Solubility vs. *P* for 1-butene in benzyl alcohol (0° C).		Osmotic coefficients of sucrose in water at 25 °C.			
X_1	Y_1	P/atm	P/torr	X_2	m	ϕ	m	ϕ
0.0347	0.1801	0.3263	200	0.040	0	1	3	1.288
0.1914	0.4603	0.4421	400	0.087	0.4	1.033	3.5	1.334
0.3752	0.5429	0.4797	600	0.151	0.8	1.068	4.0	1.375
0.4790	0.5684	0.4863	700	0.193	1.0	1.088	4.5	1.414
0.6049	0.5936	0.4882	760	0.226	1.4	1.129	5.0	1.450
0.8069	0.6470	0.4773			1.8	1.169	5.5	1.482
0.9609	0.8001	0.4136			2	1.189	6.0	1.511
					2.5	1.24		

ity data given in the Table.

7.3 Use the osmotic coefficients of sucrose in water at 25 °C (table) to calculate the activity coefficients of sucrose at 0.1, 0.5, 1, 3 and 6 mole/kg. Use interpolation to fit $\phi(m)$ and the Gibbs-Duhem equation:

$$\ln(\gamma_{2m}) = (\phi - 1) + \int_0^m \frac{(\phi - 1)}{m'} dm'$$

Answers

7.1 γ_1 = 4.974, 3.122, 2.038, 1.695, 1.407, 1.124, 1.011, γ_2 = 1.011, 1.076, 1.28, 1.469, 1.831, 3.182, 7.712

7.2 5355 torr

7.3 γ_{2m} = 1.017, 1.086, 1.187, 1.75, 2.879

CHAPTER 8

IONIC SOLUTIONS

8.1 Equilibrium in Solution

Ions in solution are usually referenced to the HL:*m* standard state discussed in Chapter 7. The critical difference between dilute solutions of ions and nonionic solutes is that it is rarely accurate to assume ideal solution for ions. Therefore we begin by learning how to estimate the activity coefficients of ions in solution.

Example 8.1 Mean ionic activity coefficient.

For calculations in ionic solutions we use the Debye-Hückel-Guggenheim (DHG) equation for the mean ionic activity coefficient ($\gamma_\pm$, *gpm* in Mathcad):

$$\ln\gamma_\pm = \frac{-\alpha_{DH}|z_+z_-|\sqrt{I}}{1+\sqrt{I}} \tag{8.1}$$

where I is the ionic strength:

$$I = \tfrac{1}{2}\sum m_i z_i^2 \tag{8.2}$$

The charge product, $|z_+z_-|$, is denoted as *zz* in Mathcad. The constants α_{DH} are listed in Table 8.2 Noggle. In order to be able to handle various temperatures, we use some of these values to interpolate for any temperature between 0 and 100 °C.

Enter the data and equations shown in the box below.

$i := 0..3$

$tc_i :=$	$adh_i :=$
0	1.133
25	1.177
40	1.207
100	1.372

$vs := \mathrm{cspline}(tc, adh)$

$\alpha_{DH}(t) := \mathrm{interp}(vs, tc, adh, t)$

$$gpm(I, zz, t) := \exp\left(\frac{-\alpha_{DH}(t)\cdot zz\cdot\sqrt{I}}{1+\sqrt{I}}\right)$$

This function is be used in several examples, so, after testing, it should be saved (*gpm.mcd*) for inclusion or insertion into other worksheets. To include a worksheet in another, both must be open. Then, in the object worksheet, select Edit-menu, Include. A list of open files appears, from which you select the name of the file to be included. The included file has to be open when included, but does not have to be open for subsequent use.

The following tests will check your work and demonstrate the limitations of the DHG formula.

gpm(0.01,1,25) = 0.899	compare KCl 0.901, NaCl 0.904, HCl 0.904
gpm(0.03,2,25) = 0.706	compare $ZnCl_2$ 0.708, $CaCl_2$ 0.723
gpm(0.04,4,25) = 0.456	compare $CdSO_4$ 0.383, $ZnSO_4$ 0.387, $CuSO_4$ 0.41
gpm(0.1,1,25) = 0.754	compare KCl 0.769, NaCl 0.778, HCl 0.796

As you can see (comparing to the experimental values shown to right) the DHG equation is effective for 1:1 electrolytes up to 0.1 mol/kg, but significantly less effective for more highly charged electrolytes. As a general rule, this formula should never be used for ionic strengths greater than 0.1 mol/kg.

Solubility of Salts

Example 8.2 Solubility of silver sulfate.

The solubility of silver sulfate

$$Ag_2SO_4(s) = 2\,Ag^+(ao) + SO_4^{2-}(ao)$$

has an equilibrium constant:

$$K_a = \frac{a^2_{Ag^+} a_{SO_4^{2-}}}{a_{solid}} = m_+^2 m_- \gamma_\pm^3$$

In the case that all of the silver and sulfate ions come from the solubility of the salt, $m_+ = 2S$ and $m_- = S$, where S is the solubility (moles salt dissolved per 1 kg water). Then:

$$K_a = 4m^3\gamma_\pm^3$$

Start a new worksheet and include or insert *gpm.mcd*. Then enter the following data:

$Ag_2SO_4(s) = 2\,Ag^+(ao) + SO_4^{2-}(ao)$ Tref := 298.15 kJ := 1000 R := 8.31451

DHref := (2·105.579 + (-909.27) - (-715.88))·kJ DHref = 17.768·kJ

DGref := (2·77.107 - 744.53 - (-618.41))·kJ DGref = 28.094·kJ

DSref := 2·72.68 + 20.1 - 200.4 DSref = -34.94

$\mathrm{Kref} := \exp\left(-\frac{\mathrm{DGref}}{\mathrm{R}\cdot\mathrm{Tref}}\right)$ $\mathrm{Kref} = 1.197\cdot 10^{-5}$ $\left(\frac{\mathrm{Kref}}{4}\right)^{\frac{1}{3}} = 0.014$

Here, *DHref* (and so forth) denotes the change in the standard enthalpy, free energy, or entropy of the reaction at the reference temperature (298.15 K). The last line shows the calculation of the equilibrium constant and ideal solubility at the reference temperature. This is a rather high ionic strength to expect DHG to be very accurate (the ionic strength for a 2:1 electrolyte is 3 times the molality), especially (as we saw in Example 8.1) for high-charge ions. In order to do other temperatures, we use:

$$K_a = \exp\left[\frac{\Delta S^o}{R} - \frac{\Delta H^o}{RT}\right] \tag{8.3}$$

assuming the enthalpy and entropy are independent of temperature (therefore equal to the reference values calculated above).

In the following calculation we allow for the possibility that some other salt contributes ix to the ionic strength; this salt must contain neither common ions nor form an insoluble salt or a complex with silver ion or sulfate ($NaNO_3$ would be OK).

$Ka(T) := \exp\left(\frac{DSref}{R} - \frac{DHref}{R \cdot T}\right)$ ix and t set at bottom of worksheet $ix = 0$ $t = 0$

$T := 273.15 + t$

$S := S_{id}$ $S_{id} := \left(\frac{Ka(T)}{4}\right)^{\frac{1}{3}}$ $S_{id} = 0.011$ $TOL := 10^{-8}$

Given

$$Ka(T) = 4 \cdot S^3 \cdot gpm(3 \cdot S + ix, 2, t)^3$$

$S := Find(S)$

$S = 0.017$ ionic strength = $3 \cdot S + ix = 0.052$ $gpm(3 \cdot S + ix, 2, t) = 0.656$

$4 \cdot S^3 \cdot gpm(3 \cdot S + ix, 2, t)^3 = 1.000000 \cdot Ka(T)$

For this calculation, *ix* and *t* (the Celsius temperature) are set later in the worksheet — they are only displayed in the box above. Since Mathcad requires that all definitions precede use, how is this done? Any assignment using the global definition "≡" (which is selected from the Evaluation and Boolean palette) is valid globally — in any part of the worksheet. The reason for placing these assignments later is so they can be altered while watching the results. (As a practical matter, they were initially placed above the solve block, then moved after everything was working.) The next to last line of the box above displays the ionic strength (which should not exceed 0.1 for accuracy) and the calculated mean ionic activity coefficient for this solution. The last line recalculates the equilibrium constant, a wise precaution. (You don't have to retype the expression, just copy it from the right-hand side of the expression in the solve block.) The comparison is facilitated by entering "`Ka(T)`" into the unit placeholder of the calculated equilibrium constant.

The box below shows the results together with some literature values.

$mw := 2\cdot 107.87 + 32.066 + 4\cdot 15.9994$ $t \equiv 0$ $ix \equiv 0$

solubility in grams per kg water obs 5.7 g/liter at 0 C

$S_{id}\cdot mw = 3.567$ $S\cdot mw = 5.439$ obs 14.1 g/liter at 100 C

The agreement of the calculated and literature values is fairly good. Part of the discrepancy is the distinction between *molality* (mole solute per kg solvent) and *concentration* (mole solute per liter, a.k.a. *molarity*), but the most important effect is probably the approximation in the DHG equation. Even with the DHG approximation, this estimate is much better than the one that assumed ideal-solution (S_{id}). How accurate is the calculation at 100 °C? What is the effect of the other salt (*ix*) on solubility?

Example 8.3 The common-ion effect on the solubility of a salt.

Continuing the same worksheet as for the preceding example (solubility of Ag_2SO_4), we explore the effect of adding some other salt with a common ion: Na_2SO_4 for example, with molality *mx*. Now the molalities of the cation and anion are $m_+ = 2S$ and $m_- = S + mx$, and the equilibrium expression is as shown in the box below.

$mx := 0.018$ $S := 0$ $t := 0$ mx for added Na_2SO_4

Given

$$Ka(T) = 4\cdot S^2\cdot(S + mx)\cdot gpm(3\cdot S + 3\cdot mx, 2, t)^3$$

$S := Find(S)$

$S = 0.0152$ ionic strength = $3\cdot S + 3\cdot mx = 0.100$ $gpm(3\cdot S + 3\cdot mx, 2, t) = 0.581$

$mw\cdot S = 4.732$ grams of salt per kg water $TOL = 1\cdot 10^{-8}$ $ERR = 0$

$4\cdot S^2\cdot(S + mx)\cdot gpm(3\cdot S + 3\cdot mx, 2, t)^3 = 1.000000\cdot Ka(T)$

The common ion did not suppress solubility very much; this is because the added ionic strength is increasing the solubility and counteracting the common-ion effect. Of course, adding more sodium sulfate would decrease the silver solubility more, but the calculation becomes suspect for ionic strength greater than 0.1 because of the DHG approximation. Vary *mx* to see the effect of a common ion.

Acid/Base Solutions

Example 8.4 Dissociation and pH of a weak acid.

The dissociation of a weak acid (HA) has the following material balance (assuming no added common ions):

$$\text{HA(ao)} = \text{H}^+\text{(ao)} + \text{A}^-\text{(ao)}$$

$$m_0\,(1 - \alpha) \qquad \alpha m_0 \qquad \alpha m_0$$

m_0 is the formal molality of the acid and α is the degree of dissociation. The equilibrium expression is:

$$K_a = \frac{a_+ a_-}{a_{\text{HA}}} \approx \frac{m_+ m_- \gamma_\pm^2}{m_{\text{HA}}} = \frac{\alpha^2 m_0 \gamma_\pm^2}{1-\alpha}$$

We take our example for acetic acid: $A^- = CH_3COO^-$.

---

kJ := 1000　　Tref := 298.15　　R := 8.31451

DHref := (- 486.01 + 485.76)·kJ　　DHref = -0.25·kJ

DGref := (- 369.31 + 396.46)·kJ　　DGref = 27.15·kJ

$K_a := \exp\left(-\frac{DGref}{R \cdot Tref}\right)$　　$K_a = 1.752 \cdot 10^{-5}$

Because *DHref* (ΔH°) is so small, we do not expect very much change with temperature; we will do the calculation for 25 °C.

Calculate the degree of dissociation and pH of a solution 0.15 mol/kg acetic acid with 0.05 mole/kg KCl. The salt has no common ion so it merely adds to the ionic strength (*ix*). The molalities of the hydrogen and acetate ions is αm_0 so the total ionic strength is $I = ix + \alpha m_0$. Assuming ideal solution and neglecting α compared to 1, we can approximate the degree of dissociation as:

$$\alpha \approx \sqrt{\frac{K_a}{m_0}}$$

This is used in the box below to get an estimate for use in a solve block. Having a good estimate (and resetting *TOL* appropriately) is important for achieving accurate solutions.

$m_0 := 0.15$　　$\alpha := \sqrt{\frac{K_a}{m_0}}$　　$\alpha = 1.081 \cdot \%$　　$TOL := 10^{-8}$

$ix := 0.05$

Given

$$K_a = \frac{\alpha^2 \cdot m_0 \cdot gpm(ix + \alpha \cdot m_0, 1, 25)^2}{1 - \alpha}$$

$\alpha := \text{Find}(\alpha)$　　$\alpha = 1.336 \cdot \%$　　$gpm(ix + \alpha \cdot m_0, 1, 25) = 0.804$

$pH := -\log(\alpha \cdot m_0 \cdot gpm(ix + \alpha \cdot m_0, 1, 25))$　　$pH = 2.793$

$$\frac{\alpha^2 \cdot m_0 \cdot gpm(ix + \alpha \cdot m_0, 1, 25)^2}{1 - \alpha} = 1.000000 \cdot K_a$$

Explore the effect of the added ionic strength (*ix*) on the pH. How accurate is the ideal-solution approximation in this case (you can check deleting *gpm* in the equilibrium statement)?

Example 8.5 pH of a buffer.

A buffer is a mixture of a weak acid and a salt of that acid, acetic acid and sodium acetate, for example. Buffers are useful for preparing solutions of predictable pH. The pH is given approximately by the equation

$$\text{pH} = \text{pK} + \log\left[\frac{m_{\text{A}^-}}{m_{\text{HA}}}\right] \tag{8.4}$$

where pK = $-\log_{10}K_a$. We will compare this result for acetic acid to the result using the DHG approximation for the activity coefficient. We will do the calculation for 25° only, so it is simplest to just enter the equilibrium constant and *gpm* directly.

$K_a := 1.752 \cdot 10^{-5}$ $\quad pK := -\log(K_a)$ $\quad pK = 4.756$ $\quad gpm(I) := \exp\left(\frac{-1.177\cdot\sqrt{I}}{1+\sqrt{I}}\right)$

$mx := 0.05$ $\quad m_0 := 0.25$

$pHa := pK + \log\left(\frac{mx}{m_0}\right)$ $\quad pHa = 4.057$

We have denoted the pH calculated with Eq. (8.4) as *pHa*. The equilibrium expression for the dissociation of a weak acid (molality m_0) with added anion (A^-, molality *mx*) is:

$$K_a = \frac{a_+a_-}{a_{\text{HA}}} \approx \frac{m_+m_-\gamma_\pm^2}{m_{\text{HA}}} = \frac{\alpha m_0(mx+\alpha m_0)\gamma_\pm^2}{(1-\alpha)m_0}$$

The ionic strength (*is*) is equal to $mx + \alpha m_0$. We set *TOL* to several orders of magnitude less than K_a and display *ERR* to ensure that the answer is correct.

$\alpha := 0$ $\quad TOL := 10^{-8}$

Given

$$K_a = \frac{\alpha\cdot(mx+\alpha\cdot m_0)\cdot gpm(mx+\alpha\cdot m_0)^2}{(1-\alpha)}$$

$\alpha := \text{Find}(\alpha)$ $\quad \alpha = 5.373\cdot10^{-4}$ $\quad ERR = 0$

Because the common-ion effect suppressed dissociation an initial guess of 0 (zero) for α should be reasonable for most cases. The results are summarized in the box to right. Try other values for the parameters *mx* and m_0. What is the most important factor for the accuracy of Eq. (8.4)?

$mx = 0.05$ $\quad m_0 = 0.25$

$aH := \alpha\cdot m_0\cdot gpm(mx+\alpha\cdot m_0)$

$pH := -\log(aH)$

$pH = 3.97$ $\quad pHa = 4.06$

$$\frac{\alpha\cdot\left(mx+\alpha\cdot m_0\right)\cdot gpm\left(mx+\alpha\cdot m_0\right)^2}{(1-\alpha)}=1.000000\cdot K_a$$

Copy and paste the right-hand side of the equilibrium expression in order to display the check (box to left).

Example 8.6 Base hydrolysis

Start a new work sheet and include or insert *gpm.mcd*. We use the hydrolysis of ammonia for our example. The reaction is

$$NH_3(ao) + H_2O(liq) = NH_4^+(ao) + OH^-(ao)$$

with equilibrium constant (assuming no ammonium or hydroxyl ions except from the dissociation):

$$K_a = \frac{a_- a_+}{a_{NH_3} a_{H_2O}} \approx \frac{m_- m_+ \gamma_\pm^2}{m_{NH_3} X_{H_2O}} \approx \frac{m_0 \alpha^2 \gamma_\pm^2}{1-\alpha}$$

Because the water is the solvent, its standard state is the pure liquid and its ideal activity is the mole fraction. A kg of water contains 55.508 moles so the mole fraction for an acid molality of 0.1 mol/kg is 55.508/55.608 = 0.99820, which we approximate as 1. The equilibrium is calculated in the usual manner data from thermodynamic data (e.g. Tables 6.1 and 8.3, Noggle).

$Tref := 298.15 \quad R := 8.31451 \quad kJ := 1000$

$DHref := (-132.51 - 229.994 + 80.29 + 285.830)\cdot kJ \qquad DHref = 3.616\cdot 10^3$

$DGref := (-79.31 - 157.244 + 26.50 + 237.129)\cdot kJ \qquad DGref = 2.707\cdot 10^4$

$DSref := 113.4 - 10.75 - 111.3 - 69.91 \qquad DSref = -78.56$

$$Kcalc(t) := \exp\left[\frac{DSref}{R} - \frac{DHref}{R\cdot(t+273.15)}\right] \qquad Kcalc(25) = 1.833\cdot 10^{-5}$$

As before we use the global definition (≡) so the parameters can be set near where the results are viewed. The values of m_0, *ix* and *t* are displayed at the beginning of the next box for information only; the actual global definitions are later in the worksheet.

$m_0 = 0.05 \quad ix = 0.05 \quad t = 25 \quad T := 273.15 + t$

$\alpha := 0 \quad TOL := 10^{-8}$ (m_0, ix and t set below)

Given

$$Kcalc(t) = \frac{\alpha^2\cdot m_0\cdot gpm\left(ix+\alpha\cdot m_0, 1, t\right)^2}{1-\alpha}$$

$\alpha := Find(\alpha) \quad \alpha = 2.351\cdot\% \quad gpm\left(ix+\alpha\cdot m_0, 1, t\right) = 0.805$

What happens if you use the default *TOL*? (Try a more accurate guess for α with the default *TOL*.) As always, check back to be sure the answer is correct.

$$\frac{\alpha^2 \cdot m_0 \cdot gpm(ix + \alpha \cdot m_0, 1, t)^2}{1-\alpha} = 1.000000 \cdot Kcalc(t) \qquad ERR = 0$$

The activity of the OH⁻ is the molality times the activity coefficient; that is $\alpha m_0 \gamma_\pm$. With that we calculate the hydrogen-ion activity from the ion product of water

$$K_w = a_{H^+} a_{OH^-} = 10^{-14}$$

and the pH.

$$a_{OH} := gpm(ix + \alpha \cdot m_0, 1, t) \cdot m_0 \cdot \alpha \qquad a_H := \frac{10^{-14}}{a_{OH}} \qquad pH := -\log(a_H)$$

$t \equiv 25$ $\quad ix \equiv 0.05$ $\quad m_0 \equiv .05$
$Kcalc(t) = 1.833 \cdot 10^{-5}$
$\alpha = 2.351 \cdot \%$
$pH = 10.976$

Finally we display the results (along with the global definitions mentioned above); see box to left. Vary the conditions and observe the results. How is pH affected by changes in temperature, ammonia concentration (m_0) or the concentration of the added salt (ix)?

Multiple Equilibria

Multiple equilibria, cases where several reactions occur simultaneously, as among the most difficult calculations a student encounters in undergraduate chemistry. Having a program like Mathcad helps — it can't help you if you don't know how to set up such a problem, but it does take away much of the drudgery.

Example 8.7 Multiple equilibria: the solubility of silver chloride in chloride solution.

We explore the solubility of AgCl in water in the presence of dissolved NaCl. Normally you would expect the common ion (chloride) to suppress solubility, but because of the formation of the complex ion $AgCl_2^-$, the added chloride can actually increase the solubility. In addition, silver chloride can exist as an undissociated neutral species in solution: AgCl(ao). The equilibria are:

$$AgCl(s) = Ag^+(ao) + Cl^-(ao) \qquad K_1 = m_{Ag^+} m_{Cl^-} \gamma_\pm^2$$

$$AgCl(s) = AgCl(ao) \qquad K_2 = m_{AgCl}$$

$$AgCl(s) + Cl^-(ao) = AgCl_2^-(ao) \qquad K_3 = m_{AgCl_2^-} / m_{Cl^-}$$

In writing the equilibrium expressions we assumed that the activity of all solids is 1 and ideal solution for the neutral AgCl. In the last expression, we have canceled the activity coefficients; such a cancellation is valid to the approximation of the DHG equation.

We denote the concentrations (actually molalities) of the species as follows: *cNa*, sodium cation; *cCl*, chlorine anion; *cAg*, silver cation; *cAgCl2* silver dichloride anion; *cAgCl* for AgCl(ao) (in solution, not solid). The concentration of the added NaCl is just *cNa*.

As before, we use a global assignment so the key variable (*cNa*) can be set where the results are viewed; you need to enter this variable before the equations to follow — do this now at the bottom of the worksheet — then enter the statements in the box below.

$zz := 1 \qquad \alpha_{DH} := 1.177$

$$gpm(is) := \exp\left(\frac{-\alpha_{DH} \cdot zz \cdot \sqrt{is}}{1+\sqrt{is}}\right)$$

Given quantities:

$K_1 := 1.777 \cdot 10^{-10} \qquad K_2 := 3.249 \cdot 10^{-7}$

$K_3 := 3.324 \cdot 10^{-5} \qquad cAgCl := K_2 \qquad cNa = 0.005$

cNa made by global assignment (below)

The calculation of *cAgCl* is simple since it doesn't interact with the other equilibria, so it is done here.

In problems like this it is very important to start with good estimates of the unknowns. When a lot of NaCl is added, it is accurate to assume that the chloride concentration is equal to the concentration of the added salt (*cNa*), but when no salt is added, the chloride concentration is closer to that calculated from equilibrium 1 in isolation — for an ideal solution, this is the square root of K_1. To account for the full range of possibilities, we add these estimates to get a starting value that should work for any value for *cNa* (including zero). The other two can be estimated by considering the 1st and 3rd equilibria in isolation: $cAg = K_1/cCl$ and $cAgCl2 = K_3\ cCl$ — see box below:

$cCl := \sqrt{K_1} + cNa \qquad cAg := \dfrac{K_1}{cCl} \qquad cAgCl2 := K_3 \cdot cCl$

$TOL := 10^{-8} \qquad cAg = 3.545 \cdot 10^{-8} \qquad cAgCl2 = 1.666 \cdot 10^{-7}$

There are 5 species, but *cNa* and *cAgCl* are fixed, so there are 3 unknowns. Therefore we need three equations, which are the 1st and 3rd equilibrium expressions and the charge balance:

$$cAg + cNa = cCl + cAgCl2$$

The ionic strength is:

$$I = \tfrac{1}{2}(cNa + cCl + cAg + cAgCl2)$$

The calculation is shown in the box below.

Given

$$K_1 = cAg \cdot cCl \cdot gpm\left[\frac{1}{2}\cdot(cNa + cCl + cAg + cAgCl2)\right]^2$$

$$cCl \cdot K_3 = cAgCl2$$

$$(cNa + cAg) - (cCl + cAgCl2) = 0$$ charge balance

$$\begin{pmatrix} cAg \\ cCl \\ cAgCl2 \end{pmatrix} := Find(cAg, cCl, cAgCl2)$$ $ERR = 2.585\cdot 10^{-26}$

$solubility := cAg + cAgCl + cAgCl2$	
Results for $cNa \equiv 5\cdot 10^{-3}$	(global assignment)
$cAg = 4.152\cdot 10^{-8}$	$cCl = 4.999875\cdot 10^{-3}$
$cAgCl = 3.249\cdot 10^{-7}$	$cAgCl2 = 1.662\cdot 10^{-7}$
$solubility = 5.326\cdot 10^{-7}$	

The solubility, the amount of solid AgCl that dissolves in 1 kg water, is the sum of all the species that result from that process: *cAg* + *cAgCl* + *cAgCl2*. The results are displayed in the box to the left. Vary the concentration of added salt (*cNa*) and observe the effect on the various species and on the total solubility.

As always, check to be sure the answer is correct.

$$(cNa + cAg) - (cCl + cAgCl2) = 0 \qquad \frac{cAgCl2}{cCl} = 1.000000000\cdot K_3$$

$$cAg \cdot cCl \cdot gpm\left[\frac{1}{2}\cdot(cNa + cCl + cAg + cAgCl2)\right]^2 = 1.000000000\cdot K_1$$

(Select, from Math-menu Numerical Format, displayed precision 9, trailing zeros on, zero tolerance 99.)

8.2 Electrochemistry

Example 8.8 Equivalent conductivity at infinite dilution.

The box below gives data for the equivalent conductivity (Λ) of NaBr in methanol (25 °C) as a function of concentration (mmol/liter). The objective is to determine the equivalent conductivity at infinite dilution by extrapolating these data to zero concentration.

$i := 0..4$ $conc_i :=$ $\Lambda_i :=$

$conc_i$	Λ_i
0.1	99.19
0.2	98.11
0.5	96.04
1.0	93.80
2.0	90.86

$vs := cspline(conc, \Lambda)$

$f1(c) := interp(vs, conc, \Lambda, c)$ $c := 0, 0.1..2$

$f1(0) = 100.577$

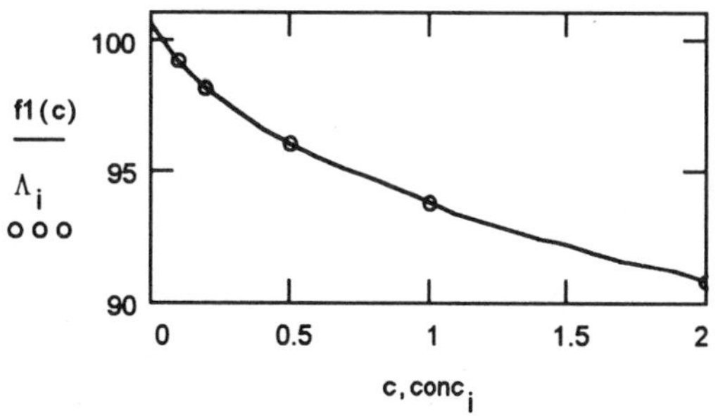

The analysis above does the obvious thing: fit the data by interpolation and calculate the intercept — *f1*(0). The graph, however, is troubling: the curve bends rather sharply between the 2nd and 3rd points and is rising sharply between the lowest concentration and the intercept. Compare the results for the other types of interpolation (**pspline, lspline**).

It is known theoretically and experimentally that conductivity in solution varies smoothly with the square root of the concentration: in fact, it is nearly linear. Perhaps that type of fit would be better (box below, xv_4 is displayed to find out how to set the plot range variable *sc*).

$xv_i := \sqrt{conc_i}$ $vs := cspline(xv, \Lambda)$ $f2(c) := interp(vs, xv, \Lambda, c)$

$sc := 0, .1..1.5$ $xv_4 = 1.414$

$f2(0) = 101.935$

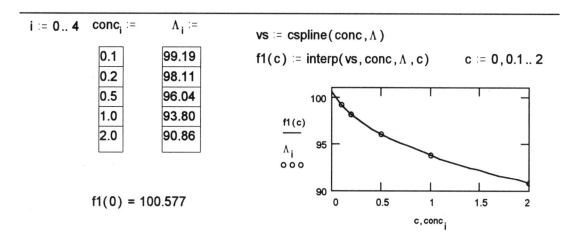

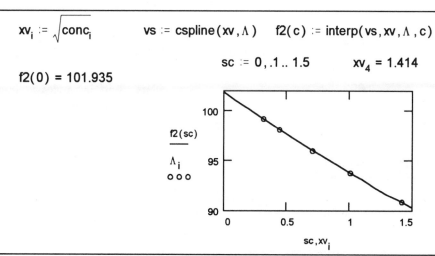

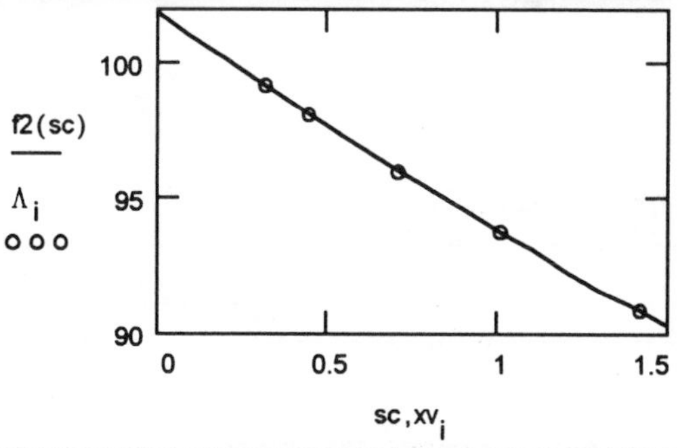

The curve is now very close to linear, increasing our confidence in the extrapolation. This is the value you would accept at the correct answer.

Linear regression has the advantage over interpolation that random variations due to experimental error may be smoothed out. (Indeed, if the data have a lot of random scatter, interpolation is the not an effective method.) The box below shows the fit of *xv* (square root of *c*) to a quadratic function.

$$F(x) := \begin{pmatrix} 1 \\ x \\ x^2 \end{pmatrix} \qquad \text{ans} := \text{linfit}(xv, \Lambda, F) \qquad f3(x) := \text{ans} \cdot F(x) \qquad \text{ans} = \begin{pmatrix} 101.901 \\ -8.788 \\ 0.692 \end{pmatrix}$$

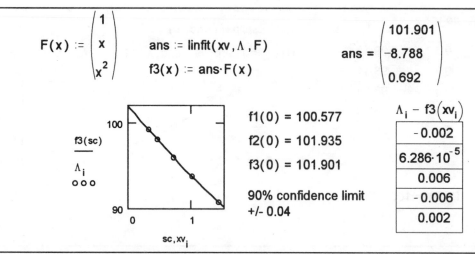

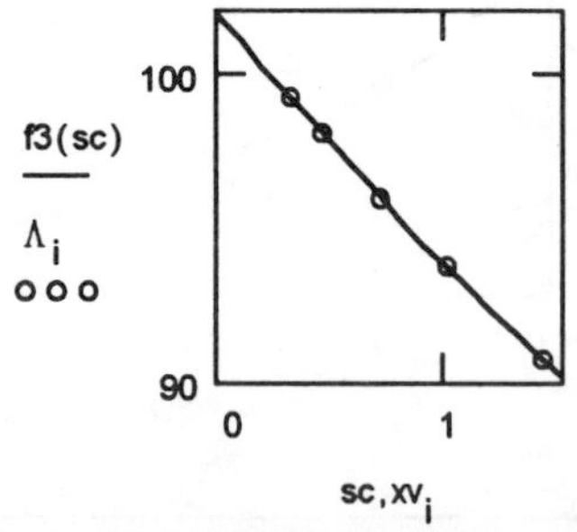

$f1(0) = 100.577$

$f2(0) = 101.935$

$f3(0) = 101.901$

90% confidence limit
+/- 0.04

$\Lambda_i - f3(xv_i)$
-0.002
$6.286 \cdot 10^{-5}$
0.006
-0.006
0.002

The calculation to the right in the box above shows the residuals, which vary randomly as desired. Mathcad cannot determine the errors of the coefficients for such analyses, but another program was used to determine the confidence limits shown. The interpolation result does fall within the 90% confidence interval of the linear regression, but it is clear that linear regression vs. $\sqrt{c}$ is the best method for such problems.

$$\text{regress}(xv, \Lambda, 2) = \begin{bmatrix} 3 \\ 3 \\ 2 \\ 101.901 \\ -8.788 \\ 0.692 \end{bmatrix} \qquad \text{ans} = \begin{pmatrix} 101.901 \\ -8.788 \\ 0.692 \end{pmatrix}$$

The functions we used with **linfit** constitute a polynomial. Mathcad provides another command, **regress,** that uses polynomials exclusively; its use is illustrated in the box to the left (with the same data). It also provides the coefficients, but in a less direct way (comparison to the previous answer, vector **ans**, should show you where the coefficients are). The last argument of **regress** is the order of the polynomial, so it is easier to change that order with **regress** than it is with **linfit**. The output of this function is designed to be used with **interp** as illustrated below:

$$f4(x) := \text{interp}(\text{regress}(xv, \Lambda, 3), xv, \Lambda, x)$$

Compare *f4* to the other functions used earlier.

Example 8.9 Thermodynamic equilibrium constants from conductivity.

The degree of dissociation of a weak acid is related to conductivity as:

$$\alpha = \frac{\Lambda}{\lambda_+ + \lambda_-} \tag{8.5}$$

The single-ion conductivities (in the denominator) are often known only at infinite dilution, so the easiest thing to calculate is the apparent degree of dissociation:

$$\alpha' = \frac{\Lambda}{\Lambda^\circ} \tag{8.6}$$

(Λ° is the equivalent conductivity at infinite dilution.) This can be used to obtain an approximation to the equilibrium constant:

$$K_a = \frac{\alpha^2 c_0 \gamma_\pm^2}{1-\alpha} \approx \frac{(\alpha')^2 c_0}{1-\alpha'} \tag{8.7}$$

There are two approximations in this equation: the use of the apparent degree of dissociation in place of the true value, and the assumption of ideal solution. At infinite dilution, both of these approximations go away so the apparent equilibrium constant

$$K_a'' \approx \frac{(\alpha')^2 c_0}{1-\alpha'}$$

(*Kaa* in the Mathcad document below) approaches the true equilibrium constant as the concentration of the solution (c_0) goes to zero.

$i := 0..5$ $\quad Lz := 390.7$

$tc_i :=$	$\Lambda_i :=$
11.135	127.75
21.844	96.493
136.34	42.227
344.065	27.199
591.153	20.962
984.21	16.371

$$c := \frac{tc}{10^5}$$

$$\alpha := \frac{\Lambda}{Lz}$$

$$Kaa_i := \frac{(\alpha_i)^2 \cdot c_i}{1-\alpha_i}$$

We take our example for acetic acid for which data are given in the box to the left. The original concentration data (**tc**) actually have unit 10^{-5} mol/kg; the correction to mol/kg is made by dividing these numbers by 10^5 giving the array **c**. The conductivity of acetic acid at infinite dilution is denoted *Lz* and this is used to calculate the apparent degree of dissociation (α) and the apparent equilibrium constant (*Kaa*). The data are listed and plotted in the box below. (The graph vs. the square root of *c* seems smoother; try both and see what you think.)

α_i	$10^5 \cdot Kaa_i$
0.327	1.769
0.247	1.769
0.108	1.786
0.07	1.792
0.054	1.798
0.042	1.804

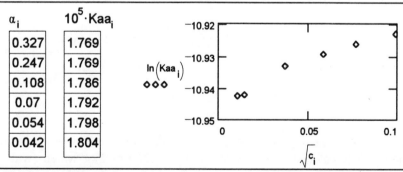

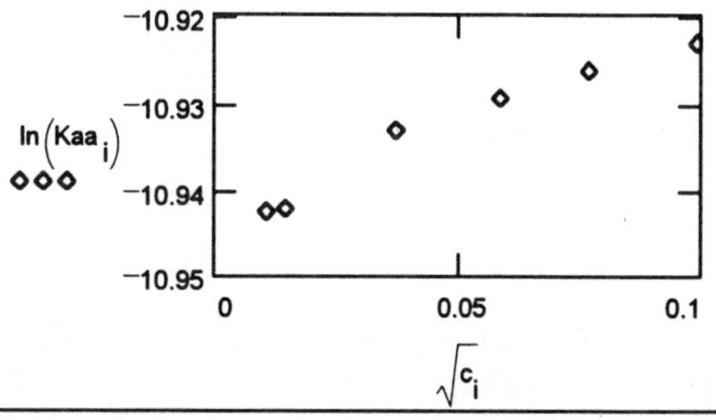

This looks like it should be fit by a low-order power series but, as so often for ionic phenomena, a series in the square root of *c* is probably best. (These data are also an example of a case for which interpolation should *not* be used.) This analysis is shown in the box below.

$$F(c) := \begin{pmatrix} 1 \\ \sqrt{c} \\ c \end{pmatrix}$$

$y_i := \ln(Kaa_i)$

$ans := \text{linfit}(c, y, F)$

$\exp(ans_0) = 1.761 \cdot 10^{-5}$

$fit(c) := ans \cdot F(c)$

$$ans = \begin{pmatrix} -10.947 \\ 0.411 \\ -1.734 \end{pmatrix}$$

$conc := 0, .001 .. .01$

$\ln(Kaa_i) - fit(c_i)$
$3.663 \cdot 10^{-4}$
$-8.807 \cdot 10^{-4}$
0.001
$-4.91 \cdot 10^{-4}$
$-4.007 \cdot 10^{-4}$
$2.704 \cdot 10^{-4}$

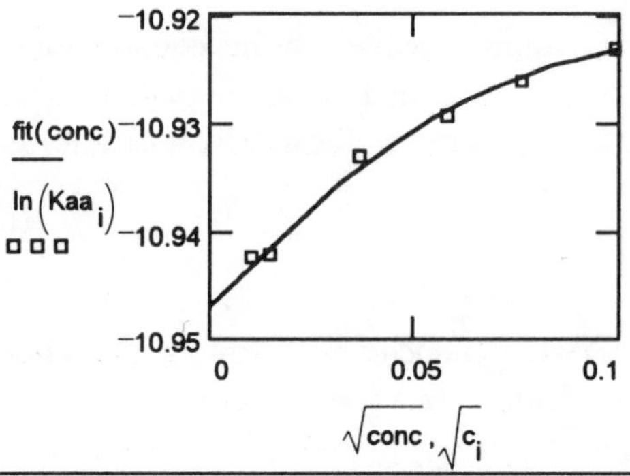

The intercept is $\ln(K_a)$, the logarithm of the true (thermodynamic) equilibrium constant, whose value is seen to be 1.761×10^{-5}. (Note that this is for concentration-scale activity.)

8.3 Electrochemical Cells

Example 8.10 Cell emf and the Nernst equation.

Calculate the emf of the cell:

$$Zn(s) \mid ZnCl_2(ai,\ m = 0.200 \text{ mol/kg}) \mid AgCl(s) \mid Ag(s)$$

(The symbol ai indicates that the salt is referenced to the 100% dissociated state.) The cell reaction is

$$Zn(s) + 2\,AgCl(s) = 2\,Ag(s) + Zn^{2+}(ao) + 2\,Cl^{-}(ao)$$

for which the Nernst equation is:

$$E = E^\circ - \frac{RT}{2F}\ln(4m^3\gamma_\pm^3)$$

(*E* denotes emf, *F* denotes Faraday's constant, and E° is the standard emf — *Es* in the Mathcad calculation below.) The calculation below is for $m = 0.200$ mol/kg which (with $I = 0.600$ mol/kg) is too concentrated for DHG to be effective; therefore we use the experimental value for the mean ionic activity coefficient (e.g. Table 8.1, Noggle).

$F := 96485 \cdot \text{coul}$ $\quad R := 8.31451 \cdot \frac{\text{joule}}{K}$ $\quad T := 298.15 \cdot K$

$Es := (0.2225 - (-.7628)) \cdot \text{volt}$ $\quad n := 2$ $\quad m := 0.200$ $\quad \gamma := 0.448$

$E := Es - \frac{R \cdot T}{n \cdot F} \cdot \ln(4 \cdot m^3 \cdot \gamma^3)$ $\quad E = 1.0605 \cdot \text{volt}$

Compare this to the ideal-solution value (which is easily obtained by simply setting the activity coefficient equal to 1).

Example 8.11 Standard emf and activity coefficients from cell emf.

Determine the standard emf of the cell

$$\text{Pt}, H_2(P = 1 \text{ atm}) \mid \text{HCl(ai}, m) \mid \text{AgCl(s)} \mid \text{Ag}$$

from data for emf vs. concentration. The cell reaction (for 1 electron) is

$$\tfrac{1}{2} H_2(g) + AgCl(s) = Ag(s) + H^+(ao) + Cl^-(ao)$$

for which the Nernst equation is:

$$E = E^\circ - \frac{RT}{F}\ln(m^2\gamma_\pm^2)$$

Approximating the activity coefficient with DHG, we get an estimate of the standard emf (denoted *Ep* below) which becomes the exact value at infinite dilution (where DHG becomes exact).

$F := 96485 \cdot \text{coul}$ $\quad R := 8.31451 \cdot \frac{\text{joule}}{\text{K}}$ $\quad \alpha_{DH} := 1.177$ $\quad \text{gpm}(m) := \exp\left(\frac{-\alpha_{DH} \cdot \sqrt{m}}{1 + \sqrt{m}}\right)$

$i := 0..4$ $\quad n := 1$ $\quad kJ := 10^3 \cdot \text{joule}$ $\quad T := 298.15 \cdot K$

$m_i :=$ $\quad E_i :=$ $\quad Ep_i := E_i + \frac{R \cdot T}{n \cdot F} \cdot \ln\left[(m_i)^2 \cdot \text{gpm}(m_i)^2\right]$

m_i	E_i
0.003215	0.52053·volt
0.005619	0.49257·volt
0.009138	0.46860·volt
0.013407	0.44974·volt
0.02563	0.41824·volt

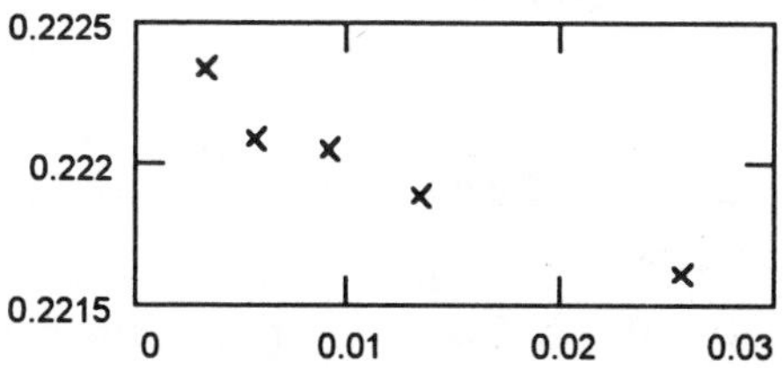

The graph (above) suggests an extrapolation using a low-order power series will be effective. We have seen that power series in the square root of molality are generally useful for ionic solutions, but our use of the DHG formula has removed the first ($m^{1/2}$) term, so the series should begin with the first power (box below).

$$\text{Fn}(m) := \begin{pmatrix} 1 \\ m \\ m^{1.5} \end{pmatrix} \quad \text{ans} := \text{linfit}\left(m, \frac{Ep}{\text{volt}}, \text{Fn}\right) \quad \text{ans} = \begin{pmatrix} 0.2225 \\ -0.0757 \\ 0.2621 \end{pmatrix}$$

Apparently **linfit** cannot handle quantities with units so we must divide *Ep* by the unit. The standard emf is the intercept (ans_0), which must be multiplied by the unit (volt) previously removed; similarly, the unit is restored to the fitted function, *Efit*.

$Es := ans_0 \cdot volt$ $\qquad Efit(m) := ans \cdot Fn(m) \cdot volt$ $\qquad mv := 0, .001 .. .0299$

$\dfrac{Efit(m_i) - Ep_i}{10^{-6} \cdot volt}$

-43.8261
78.9737
-27.5867
-11.7011
4.1401

$Es = 0.22249 \cdot volt$

(accepted 0.2225)

$DGx := -n \cdot F \cdot Es$

$DGx = -21.467 \cdot kJ$

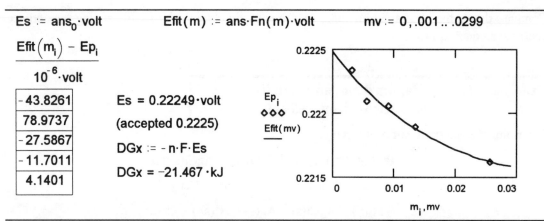

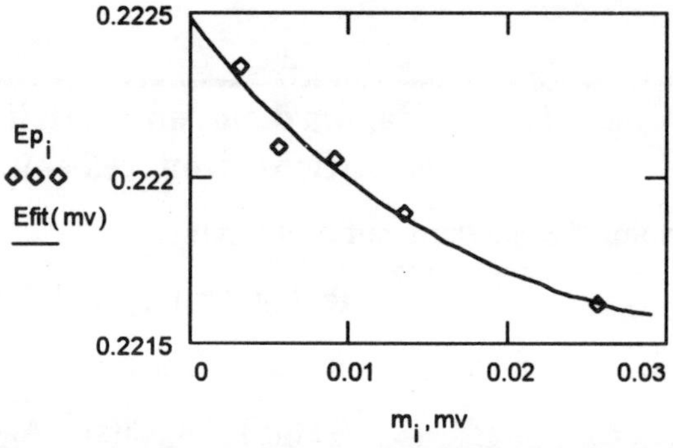

The graph and residuals look reasonably good (except for the 2nd point, which looks out of line) and the answer is exactly the accepted value (0.2225 volt).

Next we use the standard emf to calculate the activity coefficients of each of the solutions. You need to solve the Nernst equation for $\gamma_\pm$ (*g* in boxes below); Mathcad will do this for you: enter the Nernst equation as shown below; then place the cursor next to *g* and select Symbolic-Menu, Solve for Variable.

$$E = Es - \frac{R \cdot T}{n \cdot F} \cdot \ln\left(m^2 \cdot g^2\right) \quad \text{has solution(s)} \quad \begin{bmatrix} \dfrac{-1}{m} \cdot \sqrt{\exp\left[\dfrac{-(E \cdot n \cdot F - Es \cdot n \cdot F)}{(R \cdot T)}\right]} \\ \dfrac{1}{m} \cdot \sqrt{\exp\left[\dfrac{-(E \cdot n \cdot F - Es \cdot n \cdot F)}{(R \cdot T)}\right]} \end{bmatrix}$$

$$g_i := \frac{1}{m_i} \cdot \sqrt{\exp\left[\frac{-\left(E_i \cdot n \cdot F - Es \cdot n \cdot F\right)}{(R \cdot T)}\right]}$$

The positive root is clearly the one we want. Copy the equation to the clipboard and type `"g[i:"` and paste the equation into the placeholder (box above). You need to edit the right-hand side to add the subscripts.

$10^3 \cdot m_i$	g_i	$gpm(m_i)$
3.215	0.942	0.939
5.619	0.928	0.921
9.138	0.910	0.902
13.407	0.895	0.885
25.63	0.865	0.850

The box to the left shows the array of calculated activity coefficients (**g**) compared to the DHG approximation (*gpm*). The DHG equation clearly does a good job for this solution (at least some of the difference is due to experimental error in the original data).

For an easier comparison, we interpolate **g** so as to calculate values at other molalities (box to right). Compare these to the DHG predictions and data (e.g. Noggle Table 8.1).

$gx(mv) := interp(cspline(m, g), m, g, mv)$

$mv := 0.02$ (molality)

$gpm(mv) = 0.864$

$gx(mv) = 0.881$ Table 8.1 gives 0.875

Example 8.12 Entropy from cell emf.

The entropy of the cell reaction is related to the cell emf as

$$\Delta_{rxn} S = nF \frac{dE}{dT} \tag{8.8}$$

where E is the emf and F is Faraday's constant.

Data and calculations for the Ag/AgCl electrode (vs. the standard hydrogen electrode) are shown in the box to the right. Data are entered in vectors (using the Matrix palette) to facilitate adding units and converting from Celsius to kelvin; the vector **emf** contains the standard emfs of the cell at the temperatures in **T**. With only 3 data points, the best estimate of the derivative of the emf with respect to temperature (*dedt*) at the center point is calculated from the points above and below. The entropy (*DScell*) is the standard entropy of the cell reaction. The free energy and enthalpy of the cell reaction are calculated as shown in the box below.

$$F := 96485 \cdot \text{coul} \qquad kJ := 1000 \cdot \text{joule}$$

$$T := \left[273.15 + \begin{pmatrix} 20 \\ 25 \\ 30 \end{pmatrix}\right] \cdot K \qquad emf := \begin{pmatrix} 0.22557 \\ 0.22234 \\ 0.21904 \end{pmatrix} \cdot \text{volt}$$

$$dedt := \frac{emf_2 - emf_0}{T_2 - T_0} \qquad dedt = -6.53 \cdot 10^{-4} \cdot \frac{\text{volt}}{K}$$

$$DScell := F \cdot dedt \qquad DScell = -63.005 \cdot \frac{\text{joule}}{K}$$

$$DGcell := F \cdot emf_1 \qquad DHcell := DGcell + T_1 \cdot DScell$$

$$DGcell = 21.452 \cdot kJ \qquad DHcell = 2.668 \cdot kJ$$

Since the emfs used in this calculation are standard emfs, the quantities calculated above are $\Delta S°$, $\Delta G°$, and $\Delta H°$ for the cell reaction.

Problems

8.1 Create a function (gpm) for the mean ionic activity coefficient (DHG approximation) as a function of temperature in water. (a) Calculate the activity coefficients of a 1:1 electrolyte at 0.05 mol/kg and temperatures 0, 25 and 100 °C. (b) Calculate the mean ionic activity coefficient of $La_2(SO_4)_3$ at 0.0025 mol/kg, 25 °C. (c) Calculate the mean ionic activity coefficient of Na_2SO_4 at 0.01 mol/kg in a mixture with 0.033 mol/kg NaCl at 0 °C. Use the function gpm for the remainder of the problems.

8.2 Calculate the solubility of PbI_2 in water at 0, 25 and 100 °C. Use the DHG approximation and $\Delta H° = 63.4$ kJ/mol, $\Delta S° = 58.25$ J/(K mol).

8.3 For the acid dissociation of chloroacetic acid, $\Delta H° = -4.845$ kJ/mol and $\Delta S° = -71.1$ J/(K mol). Calculate the degree of dissociation and pH of a solution 0.17 mol/kg in water with 0.072 mol/kg KCl at (a) 0 °C, (b) 25 °C, (d) 100 °C.

8.4 Butyric acid has pK = 4.82 (25 °C) for acid dissociation. Calculate the pH of a solution 0.025 mol/kg acid with 0.044 mol/kg sodium butyrate in water at 25 C using (a) the buffer equation and (b) using the DHG approximation. (c) Calculate the degree of dissociation for the same conditions.

8.5 The following are data for the solubility of TlCl in water (25 °C).

$$TlCl(s) = Tl^{+}(ao) + Cl^{-}(ao) \qquad K_1 = 1.86 \times 10^{-4}$$

$$TlCl(s) = TlCl(ao) \qquad K_2 = 7.17\times10^{-4}$$

$$TlCl(s) + Cl^-(ao) = TlCl_2^-\ (ao) \qquad K_3 = 2.72\times10^{-4}$$

Calculate the solubility of TlCl in (a) water (b) water with 0.005 mol/kg NaCl (c) water with 0.05 mol/kg NaCl. Also report the percent of dissolved thallium present as Tl^+ in each case.

Conductivity (S/cm^2) of solutions of propionic acid vs. concentration.

$c\times10^3$	Λ	$c\times10^3$	Λ
0.56685	55.320	4.8026	20.099
0.87116	45.348	8.8839	14.903
1.865	31.657	15.401	11.373

Conductivity (S/cm^2) of KCl in water at 25 °C vs. concentration.

c	Λ	c	Λ
0.0005	147.81	0.0200	138.34
0.0010	146.95	0.0500	133.37
0.0050	143.55	0.1000	128.96
0.0100	141.27		

8.6 Use the data for the conductivity of KCl in water (table) to calculate the infinite-dilution conductivity of this salt.

8.7 Use data from the table for the conductivity of propionic acid (25 °C) to calculate the thermodynamic equilibrium constant for the dissociation constant. Use DHG to calculate the apparent equilibrium constant at each concentration and extrapolate to infinite dilution using linear regression.

8.8 Use emf data (table) for the cell

$$Zn \mid ZnSO_4(ai, m) \mid PbSO_4(s) \mid Pb(Hg)$$

to calculate the standard emf.

Emf of the Zn, $PbSO_4$ cell.

m	emf/V
0.0005	0.61144
0.001	0.59714
0.002	0.58319
0.005	0.56598
0.01	0.55353

Answers

8.1 (a) 0.813, 0.806, 0.778 (b) 0.318 (c) 0.635

8.2 (a) 6.5×10^{-4} (b) 1.5×10^{-3} (c) 1.1×10^{-2} mol/kg

8.3 (a) $\alpha = 0.12$, pH = 1.806 (b) $\alpha = 0.11$, pH = 1.843 (c) $\alpha = 0.096$, pH = 1.924

8.4 (a) 5.066 (b) 4.977 (c) $\alpha = 5.17\times10^{-4}$

8.5 (a) 1.63×10^{-2}, 95.6% (b) 1.41×10^{-2}, 94.9% (c) 6.00×10^{-3}, 87.8%

8.6 149.957 S/cm^2 (using **cspline** on $\sqrt{c}$)

8.7 $K_a = 1.336\times10^{-5}$

8.8 0. 41249 V with series in m, $m^{1.5}$ and 0.41057 adding m^2.

CHAPTER 9

TRANSPORT PROPERTIES

9.1 Molecular Collisions

The formulas for intermolecular collision frequencies and related quantities are given in most texts and in the Mathcad worksheets below and, therefore, will not be repeated here.

Example 9.1 Intermolecular collisions and mean free path.

For this calculation we need Avogadro's number (L) and the gas constant, and data for the diameter (σ) and molecular weight of nitrogen. For the diameter, we use the Lennard-Jones diameter.

$$L := \frac{6.0221367 \cdot 10^{23}}{\text{mole}} \qquad R := 8.31451 \cdot \frac{\text{joule}}{\text{K} \cdot \text{mole}} \qquad \text{nm} := 10^{-9} \cdot \text{m}$$

$$\sigma := 0.3698 \cdot \text{nm} \qquad \text{mw} := (2 \cdot 14.0067) \cdot \frac{\text{gm}}{\text{mole}}$$

The number density (n^*, called *ns* in Mathcad) is approximated using the ideal-gas law:

$$n^* \equiv \frac{N}{V} \approx \frac{PL}{RT} \tag{9.1}$$

The results for nitrogen are shown in the box below. We first calculate the mean velocity (v) and collision frequency (z) and, from these, the mean free path, λ.

$$T := 300 \cdot \text{K} \qquad P := 1 \cdot \text{atm} \qquad \text{ns} := \frac{P \cdot L}{R \cdot T} \qquad v := \sqrt{\frac{8 \cdot R \cdot T}{\pi \cdot \text{mw}}} \qquad z := \sqrt{2} \cdot v \cdot \pi \cdot (\sigma)^2 \cdot \text{ns} \qquad \lambda := \frac{v}{z}$$

$$\text{ns} = 2.446 \cdot 10^{25} \cdot \text{m}^{-3} \qquad v = 476.2 \cdot \text{m} \cdot \text{sec}^{-1} \qquad z = 7.077 \cdot 10^{9} \cdot \text{sec}^{-1} \qquad \lambda = 67.281 \cdot \text{nm}$$

Try different values for temperature and pressure, observing how the parameters change. Try other gases (changing molecular weight and diameter). When you are finished exploring, restore the values above and save this worksheet (*mfp.mcd*) for later use.

Example 9.2 Collisions of hydrogen and carbon monoxide.

The H_2-CO system is very important since reactions of these molecules are involved in the gasification of coal. The box below sets up a calculation for the temperature, pressure and mole fraction as given (X_1 for H_2, CO is component 2).

$$L := \frac{6.0221367 \cdot 10^{23}}{mole} \qquad R := 8.31451 \cdot \frac{joule}{K \cdot mole} \qquad nm := 10^{-9} \cdot m \qquad k_b := \frac{R}{L}$$

$$mw1 := 2 \cdot 1.00794 \cdot \frac{gm}{mole} \qquad mw2 := (12.011 + 15.9994) \cdot \frac{gm}{mole}$$

$$\sigma_1 := 0.287 \cdot nm \qquad \sigma_2 := 0.3763 \cdot nm \qquad \sigma_{12} := \frac{\sigma_1 + \sigma_2}{2}$$

$$X_1 := 0.5 \qquad T := 500 \cdot K \qquad P := 5 \cdot atm$$

The calculation of the molecular masses (molecular weight divided by Avogadro's number), reduced mass (μ), average velocities and average relative velocity is shown next.

$$m_1 := \frac{mw1}{L} \qquad m_2 := \frac{mw2}{L} \qquad \mu := \frac{m_1 \cdot m_2}{m_1 + m_2} \qquad v_1 := \sqrt{\frac{8 \cdot R \cdot T}{\pi \cdot mw1}}$$

$$ns1 := \frac{X_1 \cdot P \cdot L}{R \cdot T} \qquad ns2 := \frac{(1 - X_1) \cdot P \cdot L}{R \cdot T} \qquad v_2 := \sqrt{\frac{8 \cdot R \cdot T}{\pi \cdot mw2}} \qquad v_{12} := \sqrt{\frac{8 \cdot k_b \cdot T}{\pi \cdot \mu}}$$

$$v_1 = 2.292 \cdot 10^3 \cdot m \cdot sec^{-1} \qquad v_2 = 614.772 \cdot m \cdot sec^{-1} \qquad v_{12} = 2.373 \cdot 10^3 \cdot m \cdot sec^{-1}$$

Note that the CO-H_2 relative velocity (v_{12}) is closer to the H_2 velocity than that of CO; the fastest (smallest) molecule dominates the relative velocity. The number densities ($n^* = N/V$) are denoted *ns1* for H_2 and *ns2* for CO, and calculated using the ideal-gas law: $n^* = PL/RT$.

$$z_{11} := \sqrt{2} \cdot v_1 \cdot \pi \cdot (\sigma_1)^2 \cdot ns1 \qquad z_{11} = 3.077 \cdot 10^{10} \cdot sec^{-1}$$

$$z_{22} := \sqrt{2} \cdot v_2 \cdot \pi \cdot (\sigma_2)^2 \cdot ns2 \qquad z_{22} = 1.419 \cdot 10^{10} \cdot sec^{-1}$$

$$z_{12} := \pi \cdot \sigma_{12}^2 \cdot v_{12} \cdot ns2 \qquad z_{12} = 3.008 \cdot 10^{10} \cdot sec^{-1}$$

$$z_{21} := \pi \cdot \sigma_{12}^2 \cdot v_{12} \cdot ns1 \qquad z_{21} = 3.008 \cdot 10^{10} \cdot sec^{-1}$$

The calculation of the collision frequencies is shown in the box to the left. The quantities are: z_{11}, H_2-H_2 collisions; z_{22}, CO-CO; z_{12}, collisions of H_2 with CO; z_{21}, collisions of CO with H_2. The last two are equal in this case because our example is for equal numbers of molecules; but notice that, although the opportunities are equal, CO has more collisions with H_2 than with its own ilk.

$$Z_{11} := \frac{z_{11} \cdot ns1}{2} \qquad Z_{11} = 5.646 \cdot 10^{35} \cdot m^{-3} \cdot sec^{-1}$$

$$Z_{22} := \frac{z_{22} \cdot ns2}{2} \qquad Z_{22} = 2.604 \cdot 10^{35} \cdot m^{-3} \cdot sec^{-1}$$

$$Z_{12} := z_{12} \cdot ns1 \qquad Z_{12} = 1.104 \cdot 10^{36} \cdot m^{-3} \cdot sec^{-1}$$

In reaction kinetics we usually measure reactions per unit volume, so the interesting collision frequency is that per unit volume (Z). These calculations are shown in the box to the right. You may find it surprising (given the equal numbers of each type of molecule) that there are more CO-H_2 collisions than any other type. The reason is simple: collisions are favored by large cross sections and high velocity, but large molecules tend to move slowly and small molecules have a small cross section. For CO-H_2 we have a combination of a large target with a fast projectile, and collisions are very frequent.

9.2 Random Walks

The theory of random walks (e.g. Section 9.2 Noggle) is a remarkably simple model having widespread application in physical science. It postulates a position (for any object, including a person or a molecule) that changes randomly, moving in the positive or negative direction depending on the result of a coin flip. Applications range from diffusion to signal averaging and polymer conformation. For a walk of n steps, the probability (W) of being on step m is

$$W(n,m) = \frac{1}{2^n} C\left(n, \frac{n+m}{2}\right) \mathrm{P}_{n,m} \tag{9.2}$$

where C is the binomial coefficient and P is the parity factor: equal to 1 of n and m have the same parity, zero otherwise. The parity factor accounts for the fact that a walk of n steps where n is even, must end on an even-number step (try it).

Example 9.3 The binomial coefficients.

The binomial coefficients are given by:

$$C(n,p) = \frac{n!}{p!(n-p)!} \tag{9.3}$$

As an initial exercise, explore the nature of this function. Because the maximum factorial possible in Mathcad is $170! = 7.257\times10^{306}$, direct calculations using Eq. (9.3) are limited to 170 steps. An alternate equation for the binomial coefficient, which takes advantage of cancellation, can be used for much larger numbers. It is:

$$C(n,p) = \prod_{j=p+1}^{n} \frac{j}{j-p} \tag{9.4}$$

The two methods of calculation are illustrated in the box below.

$$\mathrm{binom}(n,p) := \frac{n!}{p!\cdot(n-p)!} \qquad C(n,p) := \mathrm{if}\left(p<n, \prod_{j=p+1}^{n} \frac{j}{j-p}, 1\right)$$

$$\mathrm{binom}(100,50) = 1.009\cdot10^{29} \qquad C(100,50) = 1.009\cdot10^{29}$$

An exception for $p = n$: $C(n, n) = 1$ is made using the Mathcad function **if**. The syntax of this statement is:

if(condition, value if true, value if false)

Thus, in C, if $p<n$, the product is calculated, otherwise ($p = n$) the value is 1 (which can be deduced by inspection of Eq. (9.3)).

The box below illustrates the binomial function and its use.

$n := 6 \qquad p := 0..n$

$\sum_{p} C(n,p) = 64$

$2^n = 64$

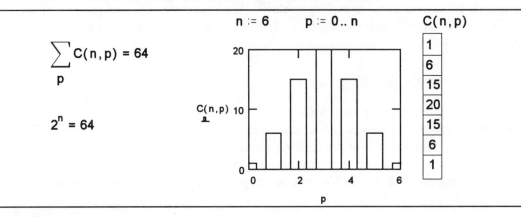

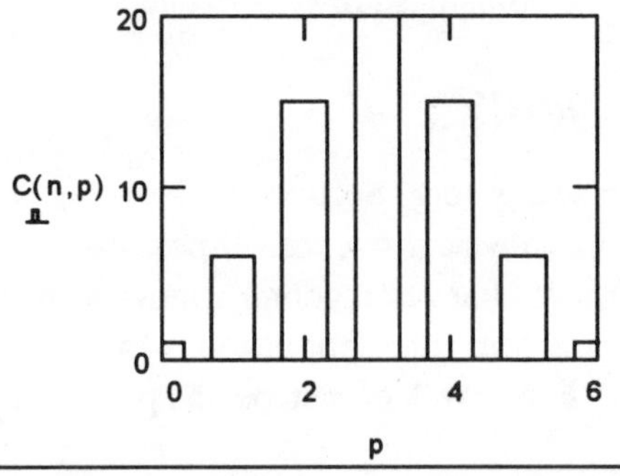

C(n,p)

1
6
15
20
15
6
1

To create a bar graph, double-click on the graphic to bring up the Graph Format menu; select Traces, trace 1, and set the type to bar. These calculations also demonstrate that the sum of the binomial coefficients of order n is 2^n. Try this calculation for various values of n. For the smaller n, you may find the numbers familiar, as coefficients of the expansion $(1 + x)^n$ or rows of Pascal's triangle (Example 5.3). For our present application, the most important significance it is the number of distinct sequences possible for n objects, p of one type (e.g. heads) and $(n-p)$ of another type (e.g. tails).

Example 9.4 Random walk in one dimension.

Continuing on the same worksheet, we can use the function *binom* to implement Eq. (9.2) for the random-walk probability function. (The equality in the **mod** statement is a logical equals: ctrl+=.)

$$W(n,m) := \text{if}\left(\text{mod}(n+m,2)=0, \frac{1}{2^n}\cdot C\left(n, \frac{m+n}{2}\right), 0\right)$$

$W(5,5) = 0.031$

$W(5,4) = 0$

The parity factor is created using the Mathcad function **if**. The **mod** function calculates the value of the first argument modulus the second; for example:

mod(7,4) = 3 mod(8,3) = 2 mod(9,3) = 0 mod(10,3) = 1

A number modulus 2 is equal to 1 for odd numbers, and 0 for even numbers:

mod(9,2) = 1 mod(10,2) = 0 mod(11,2) = 1 mod(12,2) = 0

Thus W returns zero unless $n + m$ is an even number, which happens when n and m are both odd or both even.

Make a bar graph of the probabilities, and calculate their sum (which should equal 1, since the walk must end on some step, $-n < m < n$.

$n := 36 \qquad m := -n .. n$

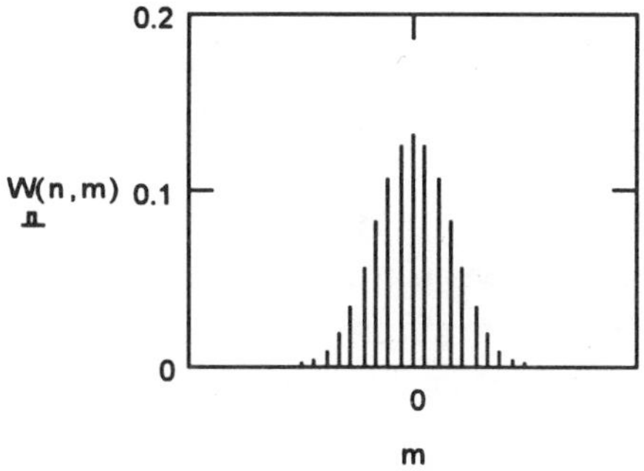

$$\sum_{m=-n}^{n} W(n,m) = 1$$

$$\sum_{m=-6}^{6} W(n,m) = 75.702 \cdot \%$$

The last calculation shows that there is a 75.7% probability that a 36-step walk ends less than 7 steps from the origin (m = -6 to 6 inclusive). Try other numbers (may be slow for very large n).

$$n := 30^2 \qquad \sum_{m=-\sqrt{n}}^{\sqrt{n}} W(n,m) = 69.856 \cdot \%$$

It is shown below that the standard deviation of the distribution for large n is $\sqrt{n}$. For the normal distribution, it is well known that the area inside $\pm\sigma$ is 68.3%. Do the example above for various values of n that are perfect squares, and calculate the area between $\pm\sqrt{n}$. (You can't go much beyond n = 900, example shown above left, without encountering problems with numeric overflow.)

The probability W is, of course, the probability for the outcomes of flipping a coin. Note that, while equal head and tails (m = 0) is always the most probable outcome, it is not the only one with significant probability.

What is the average distance moved in n steps? Since positive and negative moves have equal probability, it may be obvious that the average position is zero; this is demonstrated by the calculation below.

$$n := 25 \qquad m_{ave} := \sum_{m=-n}^{n} m \cdot W(n,m) \qquad m_{ave} = 0$$

The rms distance is not zero and is a good answer to the "how far?" question.

$$n := 81 \qquad m_{rms} := \left(\sum_{m=-n}^{n} m^2 \cdot W(n,m) \right)^{\frac{1}{2}} \qquad m_{rms} = 9 \qquad \sqrt{n} = 9$$

It can be demonstrated theoretically that the rms distance is the square root of the number of steps; demonstrate this by trying various n in the example above.

The variance of the distribution for m is

$$\sigma^2 = \langle m^2 \rangle - \langle m \rangle^2$$

We have demonstrated that $\langle m\rangle = 0$ and $\langle m^2\rangle = N$, so the standard deviation is, therefore, $\sigma = \sqrt{N}$.

Example 9.5 Net distance traveled by a molecule in a gas.

A molecule diffusing in air with velocity v has z collisions per unit time. The distance traveled between collisions is the *mean free path*: $\lambda = v/z$. This is effectively a random walk with $n = zt$ steps, each with length λ. The rms distance traveled is equal to the square root of the number of steps times the length of step:

$$x_{rms} = \sqrt{zt}\,\lambda \tag{9.5}$$

Calculate this quantity for nitrogen gas. Recover the file (*mfp.mcd*) used for Example 9.1.

$T = 300\cdot K$	$v = 476.174\cdot m\cdot sec^{-1}$
$P = 1\cdot atm$	$z = 7.077\cdot 10^{9}\cdot sec^{-1}$
$mw = 28.013\cdot gm$	$\lambda = 6.728\cdot 10^{-8}\cdot m$
$t := 1\cdot sec$	$x_{rms} := \sqrt{z\cdot t}\cdot\lambda$
$x_{rms} = 5.66\cdot mm$	

The box to the left shows a sample calculation. The molecules are traveling very fast, 476 m/s, but colliding frequently, 7 billion times per second, so the mean free path is quite small. The net distance traveled is likewise surprisingly small. Repeat the calculation for 1 min, 1 hr and 1 day (Mathcad knows these units so you can enter them directly). Compare them to the results for a pressure of 1 Pa. Try a heavier or lighter molecule.

Diffusion Limit

For a large number of very small steps, the *diffusion limit*, the probability of Eq. (9.2) becomes the distribution function $W(x, t)$: the probability that a random walk in some particular direction (x) ends between x and $x + dx$ in time t. For z steps per unit time with length λ, the *Gaussian approximation* to Eq. (9.2) is

$$W(x,t)\,dx = \frac{1}{\sqrt{4\pi Dt}}\exp(-x^2/4Dt)\,dx \tag{9.6}$$

where $D = z\lambda^2/2$ is the *diffusion coefficient*. (We call this function *wg* in Mathcad, below.) Combining the definition of the diffusion coefficient with Eq. (9.5) gives, for the mean distance:

$$x_{rms} = \sqrt{2Dt} \tag{9.7}$$

The box below sets up the calculation. The diffusion coefficient is a typical magnitude for a small molecule in a nonviscous liquid. The quantities *xmax* and *inc* are for calculations to follow; you should set *xmax* to about 5 times the rms distance.

$D := 2.5\cdot10^{-5}\cdot\frac{cm^2}{sec}$ $wg(x,t) := \frac{1}{\sqrt{4\cdot\pi\cdot D\cdot t}}\cdot\exp\left(-\frac{x^2}{4\cdot D\cdot t}\right)$

$t := 6\cdot hr$ $xmax := 4.99\cdot cm$ $incr := .01\cdot cm$

$x_{rms} := \sqrt{2\cdot D\cdot t}$ $x_{rms} = 1.039\cdot cm$

For this example, the rms distance traveled in 6 hours is about 1 cm.

The box below shows a graph of the distribution function. The first integral demonstrates that there is a probability of 66% that, after 6 hours, the particle has moved less than 1 cm in any direction. (The integration limits are displayed on the graph by selecting Show Markers.)

$x := -xmax, -xmax + incr .. xmax - incr$

$\int_{-1\cdot cm}^{1\cdot cm} wg(x,t)\,dx = 0.664$

$TOL := 10^{-6}$

$\left(\int_{-2\cdot xmax}^{2\cdot xmax} x^2\cdot wg(x,t)\,dx\right)^{\frac{1}{2}} = 1.039\cdot cm$

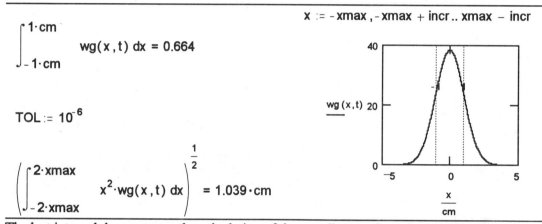

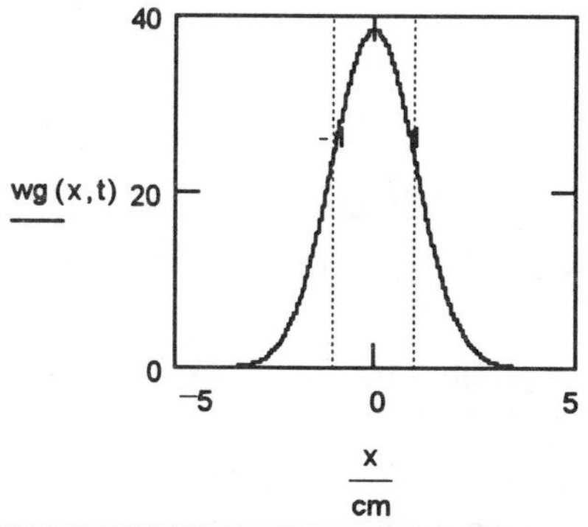

The last integral demonstrates the calculation of the rms distance from the mean square:

$$<x^2>= \int_{-\infty}^{\infty} x^2 W(x,t)dx$$

We approximate the infinity as 2 *xmax* (about 10 cm in this example). This should give the same result as before (x_{rms}) but may not in all cases because of approximations in the numerical integral. What do you get with the default value of *TOL* (0.001)? Save this worksheet for later use (*rwdiff.mcd*).

Example 9.6 The radial distribution function and average distance from origin.

The one dimensional distribution of the previous examples refers to motion along any axis — that is, in a particular direction. In some applications we are interested in how far a particle moves from the origin, regardless of the direction of travel. This involves the *radial distribution function*, $W(r, t)$, the probability of a position between r and $r + dr$ after time t in any direction. When motion is possible in 3 dimensions:

$$W(r,t)\,dr = \frac{4\pi}{(4\pi Dt)^{3/2}}\exp(-r^2 / 4Dt)\,r^2\,dr \qquad (9.8)$$

This is called *wr3* in the Mathcad example below. Since $r = \sqrt{x^2 + y^2 + z^2}$, its range is $0 < r < \infty$. The average distance moved in time *t* is given by:

$$<r>= \int_0^\infty rW(r,t)dr$$

The box below continues the previous example (same *D* and time).

$$wr3(r,t) := \frac{4\cdot\pi}{(4\cdot\pi\cdot D\cdot t)^{1.5}}\cdot \exp\left(-\frac{r^2}{4\cdot D\cdot t}\right)\cdot r^2 \qquad TOL = 1\cdot 10^{-6} \qquad r := 0, incr .. xmax$$

$$r_{ave} := \int_0^{10\cdot cm} r\cdot wr3(r,t)\, dr$$

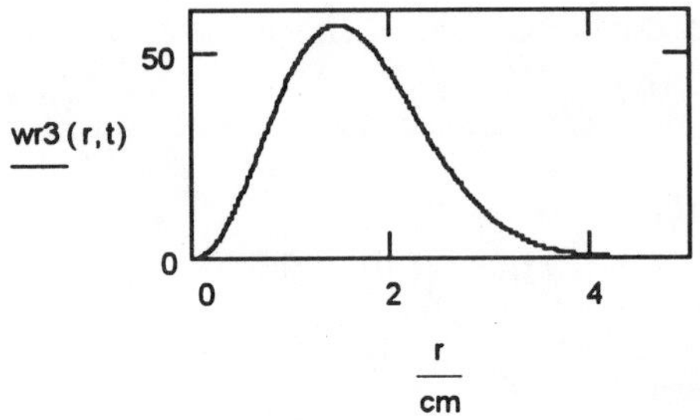

$$r_{rms} := \left(\int_0^{10\cdot cm} r^2\cdot wr3(r,t)\, dr\right)^{\frac{1}{2}} \qquad r_{ave} = 1.658372\cdot cm \qquad r_{rms} = 1.800000\cdot cm$$

The average and rms distances could be calculated with integrals, or with formulas (Noggle, Problem 9.26 and Example 9.9). It is worthwhile to do them both ways for comparison; if the answers are not the same you must improve accuracy by either increasing the upper limit or decreasing *TOL*.

Check the average distance: actual value = $\sqrt{\frac{16\cdot D\cdot t}{\pi}} = 1.658372\cdot cm$

Check the rms distance: actual value = $\sqrt{6\cdot D\cdot t} = 1.800000\cdot cm$

$$\int_0^{2\cdot cm} wr3(r,t)\, dr = 0.705$$

What is the probability that, after 6 hours, the particle is still within 2 cm of the origin? The result, shown in the box to the left, is about 70%.

Effect of a Barrier

The calculations of the preceding examples presume that the particle can move forever in space without encountering a barrier. If a barrier is present, and the molecule encounters it, it could be either reflected or absorbed. The probabilities for these events can be written simply in terms of the probability function *W* for an unrestricted walk. For a barrier at x_1, the probability distribution function for a reflecting wall (W_r) is :

$$W_r(x, x_1, t) = W(x,t) + W(2x_1 - x, t) \tag{9.9}$$

For an absorbing wall, the probability function is W_a:

$$W_a(x, x_1, t) = W(x, t) - W(2x_1 - x, t) \tag{9.10}$$

The probability function W could be either the random-walk function of Eq. (9.2) (implemented as *W(n, m)*) or the Gaussian approximation of Eq. (9.6) (implemented as *wg*).

Example 9.7 Diffusion of a particle away from a wall.

Suppose a particle is produced next to a wall, perhaps at an electrode in solution. How does it move away from the wall? Recover the worksheet *rwdiff.mcd* saved earlier (which defines the function *wg*).

$D := 2.5\cdot 10^{-5}\cdot\frac{cm^2}{sec}$ $\quad wg(x,t) := \frac{1}{\sqrt{4\cdot\pi\cdot D\cdot t}}\cdot\exp\left(-\frac{x^2}{4\cdot D\cdot t}\right)$

$t := 6\cdot hr$ $\quad xmax := 4.99\cdot cm$ $\quad incr := .01\cdot cm$

$x_{rms} := \sqrt{2\cdot D\cdot t}$ $\quad x_{rms} = 1.039\cdot cm$

The work to follow assumes the same parameters as before, so if you have changed them, they must be returned to the original (box to left). Now it is simple to define the function of a reflecting wall (*Wr*): box below. This function is valid only in the accessible area, so we use **if** to restrict it, presuming that the barrier is to the left of the starting position ($x = 0$). The graph shows the probability distribution (which is also the concentration profile for a series of molecules so produced) compared to the unrestricted function (*wg*).

$Wr(x, x1, t) := if(x>x1, wg(x,t) + wg(2\cdot x1 - x, t), 0)$ $\quad x1 := 0\cdot cm$

$TOL := 10^{-3}$

$$\int_{x1}^{2\cdot xmax} Wr(x, x1, t)\,dx = 1$$

(May not converge with smaller TOL.)

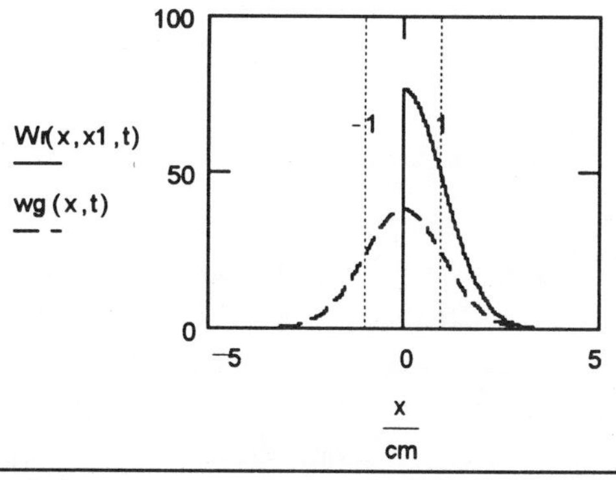

The integral above demonstrates that the reflected function is still normalized — that is, its integral over all accessible spaces ($x1 < x < \infty$) is equal to 1. (Mathcad has difficulty with this integral, especially if *TOL* is set too small.)

How do the probabilities of moving more than 1 cm from the initial position compare?

$$\int_{1\cdot cm}^{10\cdot cm} wg(x,t)\,dx = 0.168 \qquad \int_{1\cdot cm}^{10\cdot cm} Wr(x, x1, t)\,dx = 0.336$$

Try placing the barrier at other positions (but always in the negative-x region, unless you change the **if** statement), observing the distribution function.

Example 9.8 The effect of an absorbing wall on the diffusion of a molecule.

Continuing with the same parameters, we define a distribution function (*Wa*) for an absorbing wall, this time placing the wall to the right of the starting position. The box below shows the distribution function compared to that for an unrestricted walk (*wg*). The graph shows clearly the difference in area, which indicated the amount absorbed.

$$Wa(x,x1,t) := \text{if}(x<x1, wg(x,t) - wg(2\cdot x1 - x,t), 0) \qquad x1 := 1\cdot cm$$

$$P_{surv} := \int_{-xmax}^{x1} Wa(x,x1,t)\,dx$$

$$P_{abs} := 1 - P_{surv} \qquad P_{abs} = 0.336$$

$$2\cdot\int_{x1}^{2\cdot xmax} wg(x,t)\,dx = 0.336$$

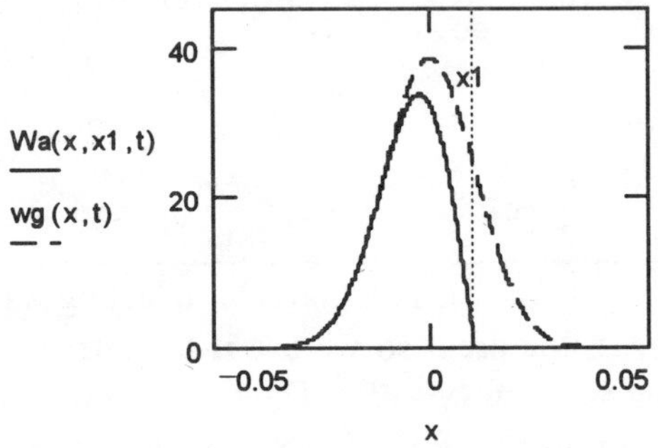

The quantity P_{surv} is the area under the curve and represents the probability of survival; since the original area was 1, $P_{abs} = 1 - P_{surv}$ is the probability of absorption. The last calculation demonstrates the fact (which can be proven rigorously) that the probability of absorption is exactly twice the probability of the walk ending outside the location of the wall if it were not there. (In this calculation, 2 *xmax* approximates infinity for the integral).

9.3 Diffusion

The previous section, on random walks, was largely about diffusion. If a group of molecules is located at a point source, and each molecule moves from that source by a random walk, then the distribution functions developed above (*wg* for example) describe the distribution of the molecules after some time. In this section we discuss diffusion from a step-function source: the molecules are initially uniformly distributed on one side of a boundary with pure solvent on the other side. There is a simple "random walk" type model that describes such diffusion, the *diffusion game* of Example 9.10. This will be discussed after a detour to discuss programming. (If you do not have the PLUS version, or prefer to omit the programming examples, proceed to Example 9.11.)

Example 9.9 Introduction to programming. ⊕

This example requires the PLUS version of Mathcad, and is used to discuss diffusion in the next example. All of the examples can be done by a simpler method, available in the regular version, and are given only to illustrate the techniques of Mathcad programming.

If you know any programming language, you probably have already noticed that Mathcad functions are very limited: they must be complete in a single statement. The programming features of Mathcad PLUS overcome this limitation and permit functions of considerable capability.

```
test(n) :=  | ▪
            | ▪
            | ▪
```

Locate and open the programming palette. On a new worksheet, type "`test(n):`"; then click on the "Add Line" button of the palette 3 times. You should see 3 placeholders to the right of a vertical line (box to right). The placeholders are where the statements of the function will be entered; you can delete any by clicking on it and backspacing, or add at any point with the "Add line" button.

```
test(n) :=  | sum ← 0
            | while  n > 0
            |     | sum ← sum + n
            |     | n ← n − 1
            | sum

test(5) = 15       test(0) = 0
test(10) = 55      test(−5) = 0
```

You will be creating the program shown in box to left, which adds the integers between 1 and some number (the argument, *n*). Click on the first placeholder and type "`sum`"; then click on the ← button and type 0 into the placeholder that appears; this statement gives *sum* and initial value of zero. Click on the second placeholder and click the **while** button; this creates two new placeholders, beside and below (indented) the word while. In the placeholder beside while, type "`n>0`". Click on the placeholder below and then the "Add line" button; enter the statements shown in the two indented placeholders. The first of these statements replaces the value of *sum* by *sum* (previous value) plus *n*; the second decrements the value of *n*. In operation these statements are repeated as long as *n* remains greater than zero. In the last placeholder, type "`sum`"; this statement determines what the function returns as a value when used: the value in *sum*. The statements below the function definition show its results. For $n = 5$ the result is

$$1 + 2 + 3 + 4 + 5 = 15$$

Note that this function returns zero for negative arguments since the $n > 0$ condition is never met; hence *sum* retains its initial value of zero and that is returned as the value of the function.

Variables like *sum* that are introduced and assigned values within a program function are *local* to that function: that is, they have no meaning outside the function. To test this, in an area of the worksheet below the function, enter "`sum=`".

```
test(n) :=  | sum ← 0
            | for  k ∈ 0..n
            |     sum ← sum + k
            | sum
```

The box to the right demonstrates a different way to do this sum. Start as before by typing "`test(n):`" and adding 3 lines. Enter the first line as before. In the second line, click on the "for" button; this creates 3 placeholders which should be filled as shown (recall that "0..n" is entered as "`0;n`"). Fill the last line as before.

```
test(5) = 15     test(0) = 0
test(10) = 55    test(−5) = −15
test(4.7) = 10   test(4) = 10
```

The sample calculations (box left) are as before *except* for the negative number. Clearly the **for** statement can work forwards or backwards. The last line demonstrates how this function deals with noninteger arguments.

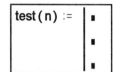

The preceding example demonstrated two levels of statements. You can add lines at either level, so the action repeated by **for** could be any number of statements (click on the single placeholder and "Add line"). If you need to add lines to such a function, use the up-arrow key to select a statement after which you want to add the line, at the level that you want to add. A little experimentation here is worth a page full of words, so I'll stop.

```
test(n) := | sum ← 0
           | break  if  n<1
           | for  k ∈ 1..n
           |   sum ← sum + k
           | sum

test(5) = 15        test(0) = 0
test(10) = 55       test(-5) = 0
```

What if you wanted to exclude negative numbers? (Of course, that happened automatically when we used **while**, but we seek a more general method.) The box to left demonstrates one way to do this; the **break** command exits the routine if the condition on that line is met (n negative, in this case). Note that you do not type **break**, **if** or **for**, but insert them from the programming palette. What happens if you reverse the order of the first two statements? (Try it!) If no value is assigned before exiting the function an "invalid" error message is given. The statement below **for** replaces the value of *sum* by its previous value plus k, and this is repeated for successive values of k between 1 and n, yielding the desired sum of integers.

The box to the right gives an example for which it is preferred to have an error message to a meaningless result; it calculates the factorial of a number. The first two lines are as before, but on the third line, click the **for** and **if** buttons while on that line. Fill in placeholders as shown. In this function, *prod*, with an initial value of 1, is successively replaced by its current value times the value of k which, in turn, takes on all the values in the range 1 to n.

```
fac(n) := | break  if  n<0
          | prod ← 1
          | for  k ∈ 1..n    if  n>0
          |   prod ← prod·k
          | prod

fac(5) = 120    fac(1) = 1    fac(-5) =
fac(6) = 720    fac(0) = 1    [invalid]
```

```
fac(n) := | break  if  n<0
          | 1  if  n=0
          | prod ← n·fac(n - 1)  otherwise

fac(5) = 120    fac(1) = 1    fac(-5) =
fac(6) = 720    fac(0) = 1    [invalid]
```

The box to the left shows a more elegant way to do the factorial function. The second line is made by clicking the **if** button and placing 1 and "n=0" (use ctrl+= for a logical equals) in the placeholders that appear. The number in the first placeholder is the value of the function if the **if**-condition is true (1 in this case). For the third line, click on **otherwise**; a placeholder appears to the left of the word; this is where you type a statement to be executed if the preceding **if** condition is false (you can place any number of statements here by clicking on the placeholder and then "Add line"). The **otherwise** action in this case involves a call to the same function we're using: *fac*. This is a *recursive* function. Recursive functions are elegant but harder to understand. It may help you understand this routine to look at the successive assignments to *prod* for $n = 3$:

$$prod = 3 \times fac(2)$$

$$prod = 3 \times 2 \times fac(1)$$

$$prod = 3 \times 2 \times 1 \times fac(0)$$

$$prod = 3 \times 2 \times 1 \times 1 \qquad \text{(finished).}$$

Some of the things we've learned in this example are used in the next example.

Example 9.10 The diffusion game. ⊕

(This example requires Mathcad PLUS.) Imagine a series of slots, in line from left to right. The slots on the left are filled with balls and those on the right are empty. Now the balls start moving, with the restriction that they can only move to an adjacent slot, with equal probability to go each way. If we follow the random walk model, we would make the moves based on a coin flip, with probability 50:50 each way. It is slightly more interesting to make the probability for each move 25% each way, with 50% for staying put. If each ball is moving randomly with these probabilities, then for each slot 25% move left while 25% move right on each move. At the same time, the slot gains population from its neighbors so, if a slot is surrounded by slots with the same population (as, at the beginning, are all except those at the boundary), there is no net change in population.

We begin with an array, *pop*, containing the populations (as a percent). The parameter *max* determines the number of slots: there will be 2 *max* + 1 slots.

$max := 19$ $min := -max$ $ORIGIN := min$ $i := max .. min$

$pop_i := if(i<0, 100, 0)$ Initialize population array

Create a bar graph for the populations.

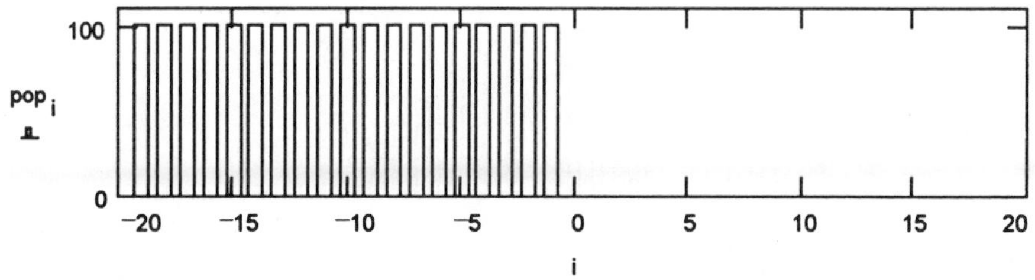

After creating the graph, double-click on it to bring up the Graph Format menu; select Trace, Type and set to bar.

The box to the right shows a function to update the populations. Note that the end slots are treated differently (since the population can move only one direction). Recall that

$$update(pp) := \left| \begin{array}{l} new_{max} \leftarrow 0.75 \cdot pp_{max} + 0.25 \cdot pp_{max-1} \\ new_{min} \leftarrow 0.75 \cdot pp_{min} + 0.25 \cdot pp_{min+1} \\ \text{for } m \in min+1 .. max-1 \\ \quad new_m \leftarrow 0.25 \cdot pp_{m-1} + 0.50 \cdot pp_m + 0.25 \cdot pp_{m+1} \\ new \end{array} \right.$$

for and ← are created with buttons from the program palette. This function is used to update the *pop* array with syntax "`pop:update(pop)`".

Move the graph to the bottom of the screen so the *update* function and some space is above it. Enter an update command (between the function and the graph) and observe the effect. Then enter another one, effectively updating the updated *pop*. This is what you will see after 3 updates.

pop := update(pop)   **Make graph (below) before entering these statements, then add them one at a time.**

pop := update(pop)

pop := update(pop)

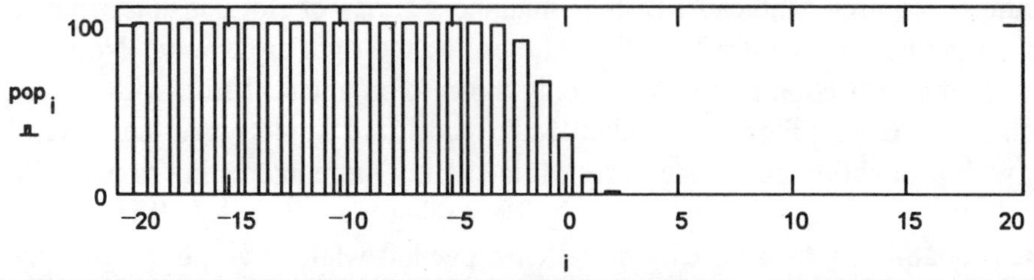

As you continue to update *pop,* things start moving more slowly — that is, you need more and more updates to get an observable effect. Well before you reach equilibrium (all slots equally populated) you will surely tire of this game.

The box to the right gives a function that can be used to update the arrays repeatedly (the first argument, *reps*, determines the number of repetitions). Now we can move along a bit faster as demonstrated below.

```
repeat(reps, pp) :=  | for j ∈ 1 .. reps
                     |    pp ← update(pp)
                     | pp
```

pop := repeat(20, pop)

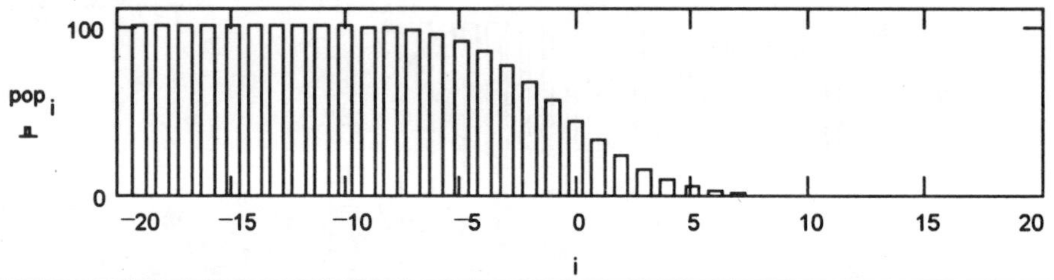

(The graph is actually for 23 cycles: the 20 here and the 3 above; your graph may be different if you have a different total number of cycles.) The changes are cumulative unless you reinitialize *pop*. How many repetitions does it take to reach an apparently uniform population?

pop := repeat(200, pop)   (223 total repetitions)

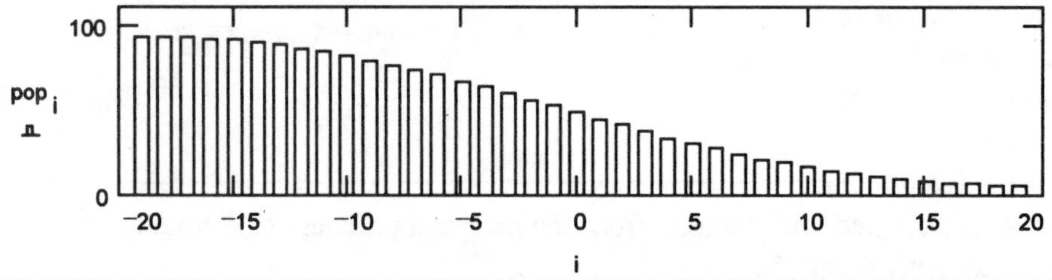

It takes quite a few actually; for speed, you may want to do this example with a smaller number of slots.

Experimentation with the model will give you a feeling for why diffusion is so slow (relative to how fast the molecules are moving). It also gives us insight into the nature of diffusion. If we layer a solvent over a solution, the solute moves into the solvent not (necessarily) because it "likes" it better there, or because there is some force driving it, but simply because of mass action. That is, more molecules move up than down because there are more of them below than above. Each molecule individually has an equal probability of moving in any direction. This example is actually a finite-element solution to the classical diffusion equations (Fick's laws) as will be demonstrated in the next example.

Example 9.11 Diffusion from a step-function source.

Fick's second law of diffusion

$$\frac{\partial c}{\partial t} = D\frac{\partial^2 c}{\partial x^2}$$

is a partial differential equation that gives the concentration as a function of position (x) and time (t). The solution to this equation depends on the initial conditions (boundary conditions). For the case of a step-function initial distribution — a layer of solvent over the solution (with the x axis in the vertical direction), $c = c_0$ for $x < 0$ and $c = 0$ for $x > 0$ at $t = 0$ — the concentration function $c(x, t)$ is given by:

$$c(x,t) = c_0\left(\frac{1}{2} - \frac{1}{\sqrt{\pi}}\int_0^{\xi} e^{-y^2}dy\right) \text{ with } \xi = \frac{x}{\sqrt{4Dt}} \tag{9.11}$$

Here, c_0 is the initial concentration of the solution layer and D is the diffusion constant (y is a dummy variable of integration).

The example below assumes unit concentration for the solution, and a diffusion coefficient that is typical for small molecules in a nonviscous solvent.

$c_0 := 1 \qquad D := 2.5\cdot10^{-5}\cdot\frac{cm^2}{sec} \qquad TOL := 10^{-6}$

$$conc(x,t,D) := c_0\cdot\left[\frac{1}{2} - \frac{1}{\sqrt{\pi}}\cdot\int_0^{\frac{x}{\sqrt{4\cdot D\cdot t}}} exp\left(-y^2\right) dy\right]$$

$conc(1\cdot mm, 1\cdot min, D) = 0.034$

$conc(1\cdot mm, 1\cdot hr, D) = 0.407$

$conc(1\cdot cm, 1\cdot day, D) = 0.315$

This is the solution, and you should use it to explore and learn. (Calculations for short times or large distances, that is, large values of ξ, can be very time consuming.) What happens for negative values of x (into the solution layer)? How are the concentrations at flanking points, x and $-x$, related? Make graphs of concentration profiles (box below).

xmax := 10·mm xinc := 0.1·mm t := 15·min x := - xmax , - xmax + xinc .. xmax

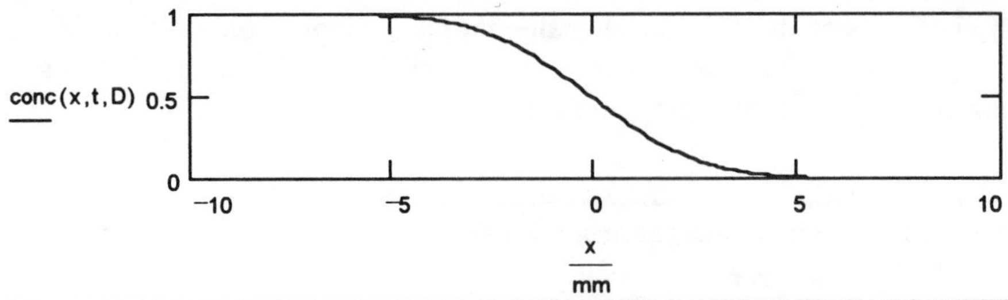

Make the graphs for a variety of times, including very long and very short. For short times, *conc* should approach a step function, but such calculations could be very slow.

Try a series of calculations, increasing time with constant increment.

conc(1·cm ,5·hr ,D) = 0.146 conc(1·cm ,10·hr ,D) = 0.228
conc(1·cm ,15·hr ,D) = 0.271 conc(1·cm ,20·hr ,D) = 0.299

You are seeing here the phenomenon we observed with the diffusion game — the longer you wait the more slowly things go. A graph (for a constant distance of 1 cm ,box right) makes this point vividly. (The value must go to 0.5 eventually.)

t := 2·hr ,4·hr .. 300·hr x := 1·cm

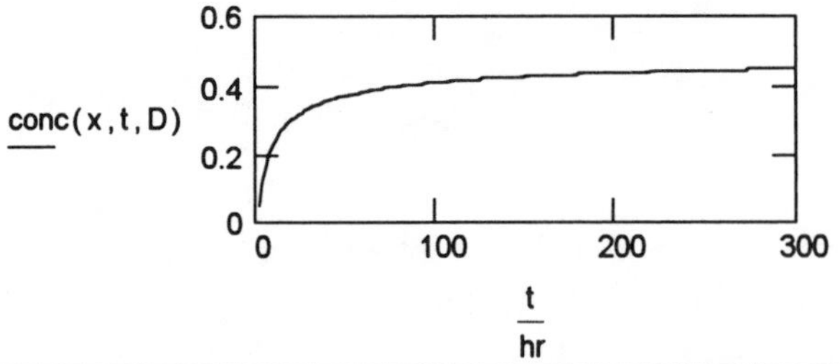

Equation (9.11), as with most equations relating to diffusion, is derived assuming a container of infinite length. Real containers, of course, are finite in length, but the equations apply as long as the diffusion does not proceed to an extent that the concentrations at the ends of the container change significantly. A typical experiment for measuring diffusion constants consists of an apparatus in which a cylinder of solution (length *len*) is brought into contact with a cylinder of solvent (same length) for a period of time. Then they are separated, and the contents of the "solvent" container are analyzed to determine the fraction of material that has diffused across the interface. The box below establishes parameters for such a calculation.

$D := 2.5\cdot 10^{-5}\cdot cm^{2}\cdot sec^{-1}$ t := 1·hr len := 5·cm

xinc := .04·cm x := - len , - len + xinc .. len − xinc

$\sqrt{2\cdot D\cdot t} = 0.424\cdot cm$

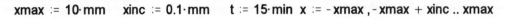

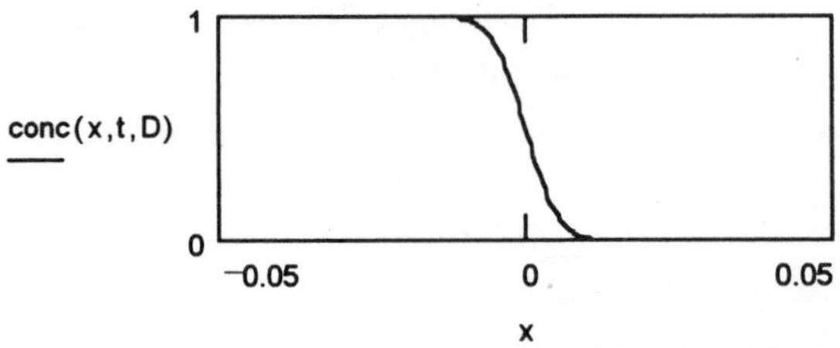

The calculations above demonstrate that, for this time, the infinite-length approximation is valid.

The function *conc* gives the fraction of material between x and $x + dx$; to get the amount in some finite interval, you integrate this function over the interval. The calculation below shows the calculation of the fraction of material in the "solvent" layer after 1 hour.

$$\frac{\int_{0}^{len} conc(x,t,D)\,dx}{\int_{-len}^{len} conc(x,t,D)\,dx} = 3.385\cdot\% \qquad \frac{1}{len}\cdot\sqrt{\frac{D\cdot t}{\pi}} = 3.385\cdot\%$$

The right-most calculation (box above) uses a formula that can be derived by doing the symbolic integral. It is used with such an experiment to calculate the diffusion coefficient.

9.4 Viscosity

Viscosity has dimensions mass/(length time). Mathcad recognizes the cgs unit (poise) for viscosity; there is no name for the SI unit.

$$poise = 0.1\cdot kg\cdot m^{-1}\cdot sec^{-1}$$

More practical units, such as millipoise (mp) for nonviscous liquids or micropoise (μp) for gases, need to be defined by the user.

Example 9.12 Flow of an incompressible fluid through a tube.

Calculate the rate of flow of an incompressible fluid through a tube due to a fluid head of constant height using Poiseuille's formula (below). Enter data for water.

$mp := 0.001\cdot poise$ $\qquad \eta := 10.050\cdot mp$ $\qquad \rho := 1\cdot\frac{gm}{cm^3}$ $\qquad$ water at 20 C

Consider a water tank with the water level 15 m above ground; we assume that the capacity is large enough that this height is reasonably constant as water is drawn. You connect a 2 cm pipe (pipes are usually specified by diameter, hence the radius is 1 cm) for delivery of water to your cabin at ground level, 2 km away. Calculate the flow rate. (The keystroke for the Greek letter η, eta, is h ctrl+g)

$T := (273.15 + 20)\cdot K$ $\qquad h := 15\cdot m$

$\Delta P := \rho\cdot g\cdot h$ $\qquad \Delta P = 1.471\cdot 10^{5}\cdot Pa$

$length := 2\cdot km$ $\qquad r := 1\cdot cm$

$$flow\_rate := \frac{\pi\cdot r^4\cdot\Delta P}{8\cdot\eta\cdot length} \qquad flow\_rate = 4.555\cdot\frac{gal}{min} \qquad flow\_rate = 0.287\cdot\frac{liter}{sec}$$

The formula we are using assumes laminar (nonturbulent) flow. Assuming you can't move the water tower or the cabin, the only way to get more water is to increase the pipe diameter. With the 4th power dependence of flow rate on radius this is an effective course: what is the flow rate for a 2-inch (diameter) pipe?

Example 9.13 Flow of a compressible fluid through a tube.

Nitrogen is withdrawn from a tank, where it is compressed at 10 atm, through a 5 m length of 2 mm diameter tubing. Calculate the flow rate assuming laminar flow and an outlet pressure of 1 atm.

$r := 1\cdot mm$ $\quad\eta := 178.6\cdot 10^{-6}\cdot poise$ $\quad length := 5\cdot m$ $\quad$ Nitrogen at 300 K

$P_f := 1\cdot atm$ $\quad P_0 := 1\cdot atm$ $\quad P_i := 10\cdot atm$

$$flow\_rate := \frac{\pi\cdot r^4}{16\cdot\eta\cdot length}\cdot\left(\frac{P_i^{\,2} - P_f^{\,2}}{P_0}\right) \qquad flow\_rate = 22.056\cdot\frac{liter}{sec}$$

The 22 liter delivered in 1 sec is the gas volume measured at 1 atm 300 K.

Example 9.14 Stokes law.

A half-inch (diameter) lead ball is dropped into a cylinder of a fluid. On the cylinder there are marks 12 in apart, and the time required for the ball to pass between the marks is measured. The densities are 1.26 gm/cm^3 for the fluid and 11.35 gm/cm^3 for lead. Calculate the viscosity of the fluid.

$length := 12\cdot in$ $\quad time := 25\cdot sec$ $\quad d := 0.5\cdot in$

$$velocity := \frac{length}{time} \qquad r := \frac{d}{2}$$

$$\rho := 11.35\cdot\frac{gm}{cm^3} \qquad \rho_0 := 1.26\cdot\frac{gm}{cm^3} \qquad \eta := \frac{2\cdot r^2\cdot(\rho - \rho_0)\cdot g}{9\cdot velocity} \qquad \eta = 727.23\cdot poise$$

The first mark cannot be at the top of the fluid since the ball requires a brief time to reach its steady velocity. Also, the diameter is the cylinder must be substantially greater than the diameter of the ball for the formula to be accurate.

Example 9.15 Viscosity of a gas.

Recover the file *mfp.mcd* saved earlier (Example 9.1). To this we need only add a calculation for density ($\rho = PM/RT$, where M is the molecular weight, called *mw* in Mathcad) and viscosity. The box below shows the calculation for nitrogen at 300 K, 1 atm (the example used before).

$mw = 28.013 \cdot gm$ $\lambda = 67.281 \cdot nm$ $v = 476.174 \cdot m \cdot sec^{-1}$ $T = 300 \cdot K$

<u>viscosity</u> $\rho := \dfrac{P \cdot mw}{R \cdot T}$ $\mu p := 10^{-6} \cdot poise$ $P = 1 \cdot atm$

$\eta := 0.5 \cdot v \cdot \rho \cdot \lambda$ $\eta = 182.286 \cdot \mu p$ <u>Noggle, Table 9.2 gives 178.6</u>

What happens to the viscosity if you change the pressure? What happens if you raise the temperature? The answers to these questions are counterintuitive but reasonably correct: the viscosity of a gas is independent of pressure at least in the low-pressure range, and increases with temperatures. If the formula for gas viscosity is simplified (cf. Example 9.19 Noggle) you should get:

$$\eta = \frac{\sqrt{MRT}}{L\pi^{3/2}\sigma^2} \tag{9.12}$$

As you can see, the pressure has canceled, and the viscosity is proportional to $\sqrt{T}$ — or is it? Example 9.16 examines this question.

Example 9.16 The Sutherland equation: nonlinear regression.

The Sutherland equation for viscosity takes into account the attractive forces between the molecules. It is

$$\eta = \frac{k_s\sqrt{T}}{1+\dfrac{S}{T}} \tag{9.13}$$

where S is a parameter and

$$k_s = \frac{\sqrt{RM}}{L\pi^{3/2}\sigma^2} \tag{9.14}$$

Note that if S = 0, Eq. (9.13) reduces to Eq. (9.12).

The table to the right gives the viscosity of carbon dioxide at various temperatures. Enter these data using any convenient method. The example below assumes that the data are in an array, **M**.

$Tx := M^{<0>}$ $\eta := M^{<1>}$

$i := 0 .. last(Tx)$

Table 9.1 Viscosity of CO_2 (micropoise) vs. temperature (kelvin).

t	$\eta/\mu p$	*T*	$\eta/\mu p$	*T*	$\eta/\mu p$
175.35	89.6	288.15	145.7	575.15	268.2
194.95	97.2	303.15	153.0	763.15	330.0
213.15	106.1	313.15	157.0	958.15	380.0
232.95	115.5	372.25	186.1	1123.15	435.8
252.15	129.4	377.15	188.9	1325.15	478.6
273.15	139.0	455.55	222.1		

Before beginning the analysis with the Sutherland equation let's examine the accuracy of Eq. (9.12) (the Sutherland equation with S = 0). This equation is widely quoted and used for gas viscosities, and implies a square root of T dependence. We can estimate the constant k_s with any of the data points, calling this quantity *kss*. Then compare the prediction of Eq. (9.12) using a graph.

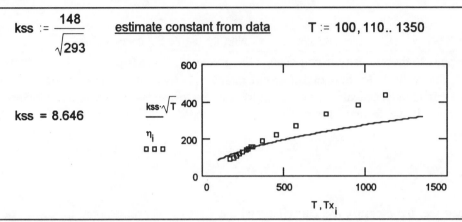

$kss := \frac{148}{\sqrt{293}}$ estimate constant from data $T := 100, 110 .. 1350$

$kss = 8.646$

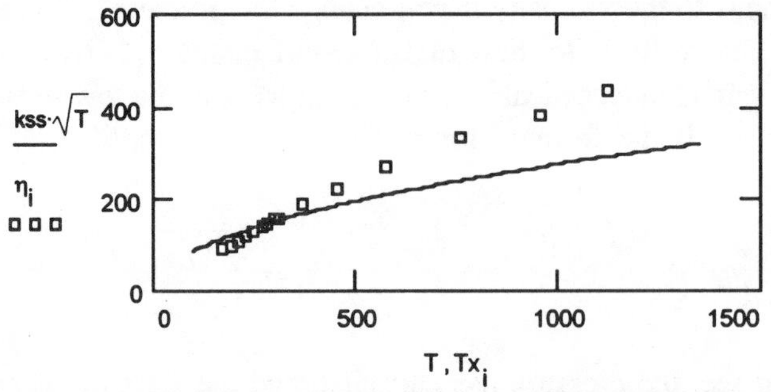

Clearly this formula works only at the temperature whose value we used to determine the constant: this equation for viscosity is no more than a crude approximation. Furthermore, there is no value of *kss* that will work for more than one temperature. (It is not acceptable to consider σ, the molecular diameter, to be changing with temperature; molecules may not be exactly like billiard balls, but a rigid sphere is a much better approximation than a balloon.)

We use nonlinear regression to determine the constants of the Sutherland equation. This technique is implemented in the PLUS version as **genfit**, which has a syntax similar to **linfit**. But you can do nonlinear regression without this function, and this is what we will do.

$$f(T, k_s, S) := \frac{k_s \cdot \sqrt{T}}{1 + \frac{S}{T}}$$

$$SSE(k_s, S) := \sum_i \left(\eta_i - f(Tx_i, k_s, S)\right)^2$$

The box to the left uses Eq. (9.13) to define a function (f) of the variable (T) and the parameters (S and k_s). This function would be equal to the viscosity data if we had the correct parameters and if there were no experimental error in the measured viscosities (the array η). *SSE* is the sum of the squares of the deviations of the model (f) from the data (η). Ideally, *SSE* should be zero with correct parameters; because of experimental error it will not be zero, so we shall seek a minimum (which is just what all regression techniques do).

The solution is shown in the box to the right. Effectively this is a solve block with **Minerr** in place of **Find**. With **Find**, a solve block will return an answer only if an exact solution is found (within the tolerance, *TOL*). **Minerr** will always return the best answer it can find, so it is up to the user to decide whether this represents a reasonable answer. As always, you must provide some initial estimate for the parameters. In this case, S was chosen to be of the same magnitude as the temperatures in the data set (otherwise the term in the denominator would have no effect) and k_s was chosen to be of the magnitude of *kss* (calculated above). Better guesses

$S := 500$ $k_s := 9$

Given

$S > 0$ $k_s > 0$

$SSE(k_s, S) = 0$

$$\begin{pmatrix} k_s \\ S \end{pmatrix} := \text{Minerr}(k_s, S)$$

$k_s = 15.519$ $S = 231.591$

will converge faster, and worse ones may not converge at all. If such a calculation does not converge, just keep trying different guesses for the parameters.

To find out if this is a reasonable answer, we compare the graphs of the data and the fitted function (*f*).

T := 150.. 1350

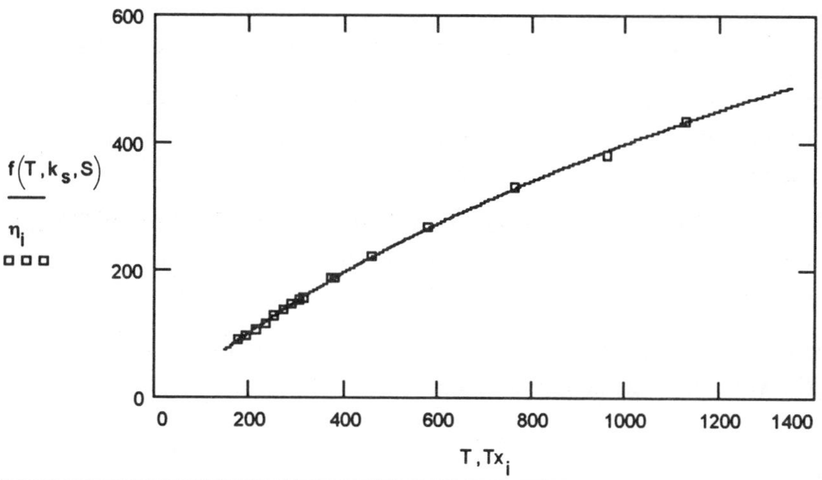

The fit is extraordinarily good over a very wide range of temperature. The Sutherland model for gas viscosity is a good one.

Problems

9.1 For argon at 20 °C, 1 torr, calculate (a) the average speed (b) the collision frequency and (c) the mean free path. Use $\sigma = 0.3405$ nm (the Lennard-Jones value). (d) Calculate the rms distance traveled (in any one direction) in 1 second, 1 minute and 1 hour.

9.2 Calculate (a) the relative velocity and (b) the number of CO-H_2 collisions per unit volume, in a mixture 1/3 hydrogen at $P = 16$ torr, $T = 453$ K.

9.3 For an random walk of 25 steps, calculate the probability that it will end more than 10 steps from the origin.

9.4 For ribonuclease in water at 20 °C, $D = 11.9\times10^{-7}$ cm^2/s. If a molecule of ribonuclease is 7.8 mm away from an absorbing surface, what is the probability that it will be absorbed in 24 hours? Make a graph of the probability distribution function at 24 hours.

9.5 A molecule in solution has $D = 5.6\times10^{-5}$ cm^2/s. (a) Calculate the probability that, after 25 minutes, it is still within a 1-cm radiuus from its initial position. (b) Calculate the time at which that probability is 10%.

Viscosity of argon.		Viscosity of methane.	
t/°C	η/μp	t/°C	η/μp
0	209.6	-181.6	34.8
20	221.7	-78.5	76
100	269.5	0	102.6
200	322.3	20	108.7
302	368.5	100	133.1
401	411.5	200.5	160.5
493	448.4	284	181.3
584	481.5	380	202.6
714	525.7	499	226.4

9.6 Pure solvent is layered over a solution, each with a depth of 6 cm. The solute has $D = 5.65\times10^{-5}$ cm^2/s. (a) Calculate the relative concentration 1 cm into the solvent after 1 hour, 1 day, 1 week. What is the limit for infinite time? (b) At what time is the concentration at 1 cm equal to 10% of the initial concentration of the solution? (c) Calculate the fraction of the solute that has diffused into the solvent after 1.5 hour.

9.7 You need to move gasoline through a 2-in diameter tube, 100 ft long. Using $\eta = 5.42$ mp and $\rho = 0.70$ gm/cm3 (data for octane at 20 °C), calculate the pressure required to obtain a flow rate of 40 gal/min. To what fluid height does this pressure correspond?

9.8 Calculate the viscosity of argon at 20 °C using data from problem 9.1. Compare to the experimental value (221.7 μp) and discuss the discrepancy (if any). Calculate the molecular diameter (σ) implied by the experimental viscosity.

9.9 Fit the viscosity data for argon from the table to the Sutherland equation. Use the Sutherland constant to calculate the molecular diameter (σ) and compare to the result of the previous problem. Make a graph showing the data and the fitted line.

9.10 Use the viscosity data for methane (table) to determine its Sutherland parameters. Make a graph showing the data and the fitted line. Calculate the diameter (σ) of this molecule.

Answers

9.1 (a) 394.172 m/s (b) 6.688×10^6 sec^{-1} (c) 58.9 μm. (d) 15.2 cm, 118 cm, 914 cm

9.2 (a) $v_{12} = 2.373\times10^3$ m/s (b) $Z_{12} = 1.74\times10^{31}$ /(m^3 s)

9:3 4.33%

9.4 8.542%

9.5 (a) 88.6% (b) 4.244 hours

9.6 (a) 0.058, 0.374, 0.452 ... limit 0.5 (b) 1.497 hours

9.7 255.1 Pa, 3.7 cm

9.8 253.806 μp, 0.3642 nm

9.9 $k_s = 19.1$, $S = 138.0$, $\sigma = 0.3000$ nm

9.10 $k_s = 9.84$, $S = 159.0$, $\sigma = 0.3326$ nm

CHAPTER 10

CHEMICAL KINETICS

10.1 Analysis of Kinetic Data

The analysis of kinetic data to obtain rate constants and other kinetic parameters offers many lessons in data analysis and curve fitting that have utility well beyond the immediate subject. This is the first of several sections in this chapter that feature these techniques.

A typical technique for determining rate constants from rate data (concentration vs. time) is to arrange the integrated rate law into a linear form. For example, the first-order rate law

$$\frac{dC}{dt} = -kC$$

can be integrated (from $t = 0$, concentration C_0) to give:

$$C = C_0 \exp(-kt) \tag{10.1}$$

This equation can be linearized by taking its logarithm:

$$\ln C = \ln C_0 - kt \tag{10.2}$$

Thus a graph or regression of ln C vs. t is linear with slope $-k$.

The second-order rate law

$$\frac{dC}{dt} = -kC^2$$

integrates to:

$$C = \frac{C_0}{1 + C_0 kt} \quad \text{or} \quad \frac{1}{C} = \frac{1}{C_0} + kt \tag{10.3}$$

In this case a graph or regression of $1/C$ vs. t is linear with slope k.

Example 10.1 First-order reaction.

The decomposition of ethylene oxide

$$C_2H_4O \rightarrow CH_4 + CO$$

Table 10.1 Decomposition of Ethylene Oxide			
t/min	*P*/torr	*t*/min	*P*/torr
0	115.30	10	129.10
6	122.91	11	130.57
7	124.51	12	132.02
8	126.18	13	133.49
9	127.53	18	140.16

(all gases) was studied by measuring the total pressure of the reaction vs. time; the data are given in Table 10.1. This is a first-order reaction. The rate of the reaction is proportional to the concentration of the reactant (C_2H_4O), so we must calculate this quantity from the data. Since concentration is proportional to the partial pressure, it is sufficient to determine this quantity. The material balance for partial pressure is (denoting the reactant as A and the products as B and C):

$$A \rightarrow B + C$$

pressure: $P_0 - x \quad x \quad x$

The total pressure thus is: $P = P_0 + x$. The partial pressure of the reactant is $P_A = P_0 - x$ which, after eliminating x gives:

$$P_A = 2P_0 - P$$

In this manner the partial pressure of the ethylene oxide (A) is calculated from the total pressure, and the logarithm of this quantity should be linear with time with slope $-k$.

Enter the data of Table 10.1 in any manner you find convenient. The data analysis is simple, as shown in the box below. The pressure of ethylene oxide is calculated into the vector **pa**, whose logarithm is denoted y. The rate constant is denoted *kx*.

$tx := M^{<0>}$ $px := M^{<1>}$ $i := 0..\,last(tx)$

$pa_i := 2 \cdot px_0 - px_i$ $y_i := \ln(pa_i)$ $incp := intercept(tx, y)$ $kx := -slope(tx, y)$

$yfit(t) := incp - kx \cdot t$ $kx = 0.014$ $r := corr(tx, y)$ $r = -0.997944$

When you display the correlation coefficient by entering "r=", the default display (3 figures) suggests that we have a perfect fit: the correlation coefficient is -1. You must increase the number of displayed figures to see its value (double-click on the number to bring up the Numerical Format menu and change the displayed precision to 6). Even so r is respectably close to the ideal (-1), and it might seem justifiable to declare the problem solved and the rate constant determined — but that would be wrong. Correlation coefficients are very deceptive, and one should never base an assessment of the quality of fit on it alone. A graph is much more helpful, and really essential in any such curve-fitting exercise.

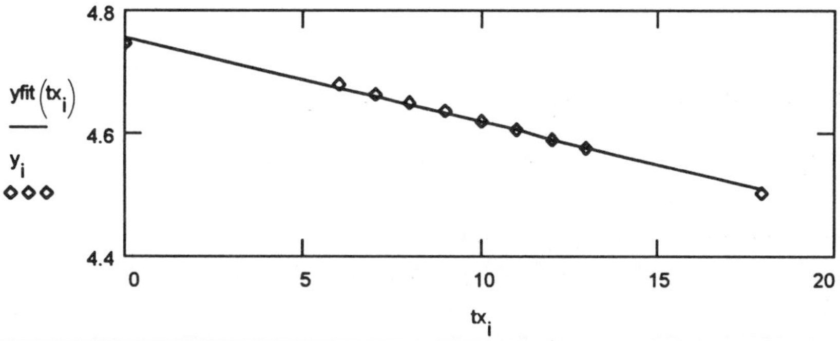

Even so a casual glance may suggest a good fit, but careful examination reveals a problem. The first point is well below the line and the latter points seem to form a line of their own, going (left to right) from above to below the line.

$resid_i := y_i - yfit(tx_i)$

$DF := length(tx) - 2$

$\sigma_{fit} = 4.45 \cdot 10^{-3}$

$$\sigma_{fit} := \sqrt{\frac{\sum_i (resid_i)^2}{DF}}$$

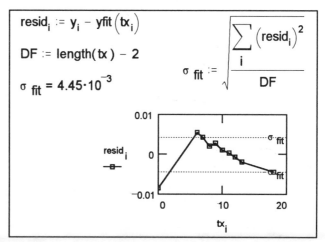

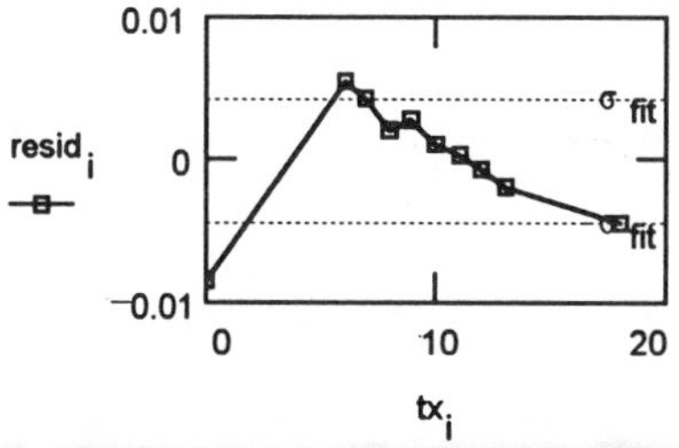

The box to the right illustrates the calculation of the *standard deviation of the fit* (σ_{fit}); this quantity is generally a better indication of the quality of fit than the correlation coefficient. Also, a commonly used criterion for eliminating "bad points" is that a point can be eliminated if it is more than two standard deviations from the line; but this criterion is problematical because the possibly bad point has contributed to determining the fitted line that forms the criterion. Examine the graph of the residuals. You can display σ_{fit} on this graph by double clicking on the graph (to display graph format menu) and clicking Show Markers for the *y* axis; this action displays two new place holders into which you type σ_{fit} and $-\sigma_{fit}$ (result shown above). As you can see, no point is outside two standard deviations, but the first and second point are outside one standard deviation. Nonetheless it is hard to escape the impression that the first point is the deviant one and that eliminating it will improve the fit.

In chemical kinetics, initial points are often suspect. It is often difficult to know the initial time ($t = 0$) exactly, or the rate law may apply only after an initial transient. The latter case is exemplified in Example 10.8 (see discussion page 215).

$j := 0 .. length(tx) - 2$

$paa_j := pa_{j+1} \quad txx_j := tx_{j+1} \quad yy_j := \ln(paa_j)$

Mathcad does not make it easy to eliminate points from arrays,[1] but doing the first point is fairly easy (box left). First define a new index variable (j), shorter by 1 than the previous index (i). Then use it to shift the data down into new vectors

[1] Actually this is fairly easy when the data are entered directly into Mathcad — just click on the point and backspace over it — but when data are entered from a disk file or pasted from another program it is simpler to eliminate the point from the source file and read or paste again.

(**txx** and **paa** in this example). To see what this procedure has accomplished, display the **y** and **yy** vectors.

The new analysis (box right) shows that r has improved considerably but, as noted before, this quantity can be deceptive.

$$incp := \mathrm{intercept}(txx, yy) \qquad kx := -\mathrm{slope}(txx, yy)$$

$$kx = 0.0145 \qquad r := \mathrm{corr}(txx, yy) \qquad r = -0.999923$$

The graph (below) looks much better than before. (Previously we used the times in **tx** for the argument of *yfit(t)*; this time we define a new range variable, t, so that the line can be graphed down to $t = 0$.)

$$yfit(t) := incp - kx \cdot t \qquad t := 0 .. \max(tx)$$

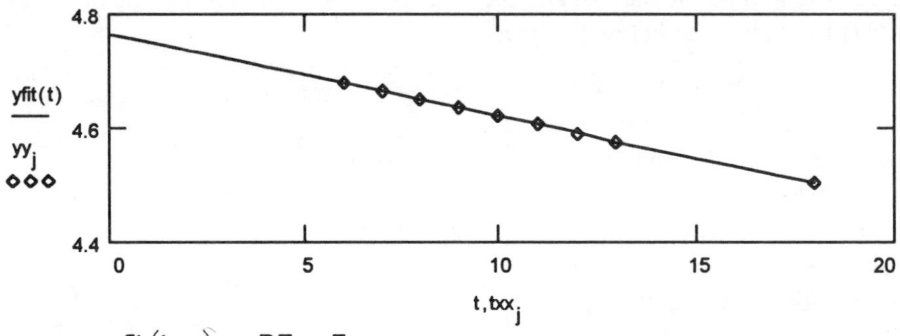

$$resid_j := yy_j - yfit\left(txx_j\right) \qquad DF := 7$$

$$\sigma_{fit} := \sqrt{\frac{\sum_j \left(resid_j\right)^2}{DF}}$$

$$\sigma_{fit} = 7.036 \cdot 10^{-4}$$

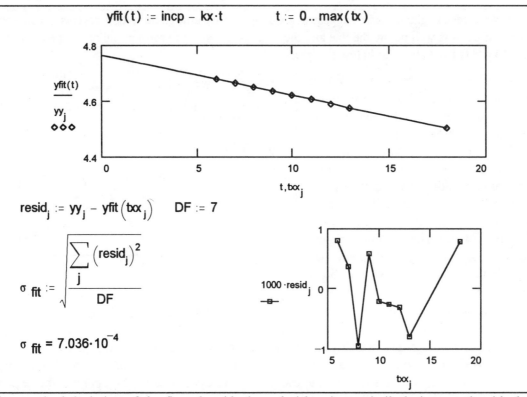

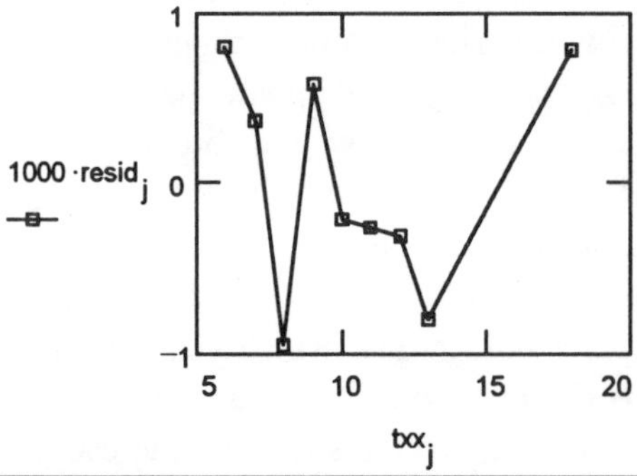

The standard deviation of the fit and residual graph (above) are similarly improved, with the latter showing no trend or unusual deviations at all. (Why is *resid* by multiplied by 1000 for graphing? What happens if you don't do this?)

Finally we need to calculate the error of the rate constant and display the answer with an appropriate number of decimals. The standard error (σ) is a very conservative error estimate. It is better to report the confidence limit, calculated as $t_c\sigma$, where t_c is the critical t factor (listed in many books, including Noggle, Appendix I, Table AI.1). We will usually use 90% confidence limits.

$$tc := 1.90 \qquad err := -\frac{tc \cdot kx}{r} \cdot \sqrt{\frac{1 - r^2}{DF}} \qquad kx = 1.4546 \cdot 10^{-2} \qquad err = 1.297 \cdot 10^{-4}$$

The answer is $k = (1.45 \pm 0.01) \times 10^{-2}\ \mathrm{min}^{-1}$, for 90% confidence. (To get the display for *kx* above, open the numerical-format menu and enter 1 for the Exponential Threshold.)

What happens if you analyze with the wrong order? It is fairly simple to take what you have done and analyze it as if it were second order; do this using the **paa** and **txx** arrays (with the $t = 0$ point eliminated).

$$yy_j := \frac{1}{paa_j} \qquad incp := intercept(txx, yy) \quad m := slope(txx, yy)$$

$$r := corr(txx, yy) \qquad r = 0.999748$$

The correlation coefficient (r) is not much worse than before. Moreover, the graph (below) looks fairly linear.

$$yfit(t) := incp + m \cdot t \qquad resid_j := yfit(txx_j) - yy_j$$

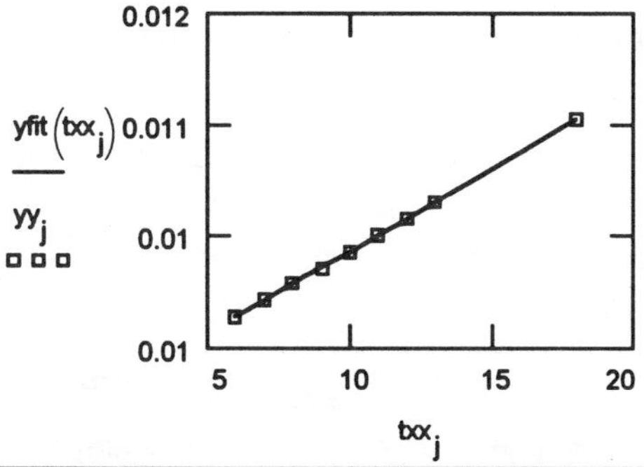

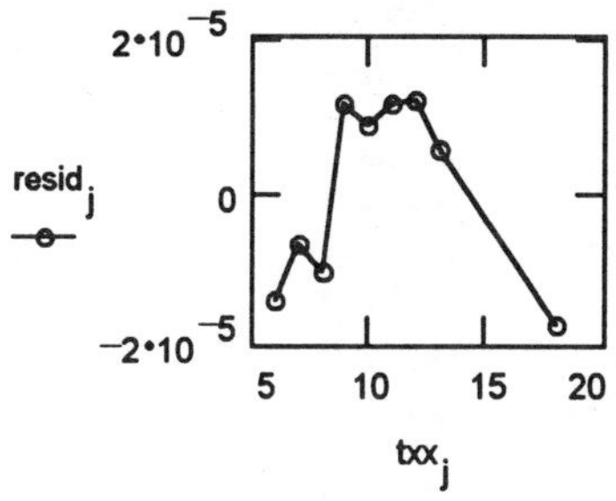

The residual graph (above, right) does show a definite systematic trend, indicating that first order is better (this is, in fact, a first-order reaction), but the evidence is not overwhelming.

Ordinarily, analysis with the wrong order would produce a definite curvature in the graph of y vs. t, which can be seen more clearly in the residual plot. The problem with this particular data set is that the original data span less than the half-life of the reaction, with the pressure of the reactant declining only from 115 torr to 90 torr. To make a definitive determination of order you should have data for at least one and preferably two half lives.

Example 10.2 Second-order reaction.

For second-order kinetics, the integrated rate law gives

$$\frac{1}{C} = \frac{1}{C_0} + kt \tag{10.4}$$

Thus the slope of a graph of $1/C$ vs. t is equal to the rate constant.

In many cases the concentration of the reactants or product is not measured directly; rather, some quantity proportional to the extent of reaction is measured. We call this quantity λ. It could represent conductivity (for an ionic reaction in solution), absorbence, volume (as in a dilatometry experiment), or any number of physical properties. Generally there is a background value, λ_∞, the value at $t = \infty$, which must be subtracted from the values λ. (If λ is increasing, indicating that it is sensitive to the product concentration, it is better to subtract λ from the background, thus giving a positive quantity.) Given $C = p(\lambda - \lambda_\infty)$, the proportionality factor p is evaluated from the initial concentration as $C_0 = p(\lambda_0 - \lambda_\infty)$. For first-order kinetics, the proportionality factor cancels so it need not be evaluated, but for second-order rate law substitution into Eq. (10.4) gives:

$$\frac{1}{\lambda - \lambda_\infty} = \frac{1}{\lambda_0 - \lambda_\infty} + \frac{C_0 kt}{\lambda_0 - \lambda_\infty} \qquad (10.5)$$

$R_{inf} := 24.5 \quad C_0 := 0.1$

$N := 9 \quad i := 0..N-1$

$t_i :=$	$R_i :=$
2	128.5
6	108.4
10	95.9
14	85.5
18	76.2
22	72.0
26	66.7
30	63.9
42	54.1

The data shown in the box to the left represent readings (R) of some instrument measuring the extent of a second-order reaction. Note that there is no reading for $t = 0$, thus we do not know R_0 (i.e. λ_0). There are a number of reasons that the initial reading may not be known: for example, the instrument may not be able to respond that rapidly, or the mixing may not be complete. However, the initial concentration is needed to determine the rate constant; in this case $C_0 = 0.1$ mol/liter.

Although we have stated that these are data for a second-order reaction, let's try first order to see how it works. In such a case, you would make a regression of $\ln(\lambda - \lambda_\infty)$ vs. t: see box, below right.

$y_i := \ln(R_i - R_{inf}) \quad r := \mathrm{corr}(t, y)$

$a := \mathrm{intercept}(t, y) \quad m := \mathrm{slope}(t, y)$

$y_{fit}(t) := a + m \cdot t \quad r = -0.984767$

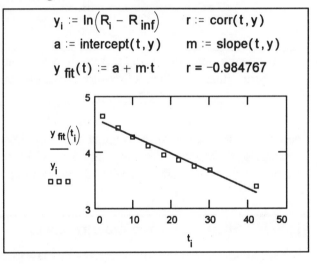

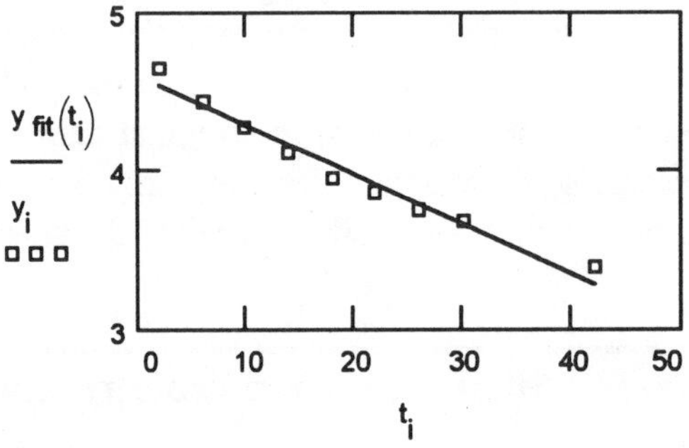

It is difficult to draw any conclusion from the correlation coefficient (r) alone since we don't know whether its deviation from the ideal value (-1) is due to experimental error or model deficiency (i.e., because we used the wrong rate law). But looking at the graph carefully, it is apparent that the points lie along a curve, and systematically deviate from the best-fit straight line. A residual graph would make this even more apparent, but an educated look at this graph is sufficient.

Now let's try second order.

$y_i := \frac{1}{R_i - R_{inf}} \quad a := \mathrm{intercept}(t, y) \quad m := \mathrm{slope}(t, y) \quad r := \mathrm{corr}(t, y)$

$a = 0.008 \quad m = 5.962 \cdot 10^{-4} \quad r = 0.998733$

$y_{fit}(t) := a + m \cdot t$

The correlation coefficient is clearly much better than before.

$$k := \frac{m}{a \cdot C_0}$$

$$k = 0.727$$

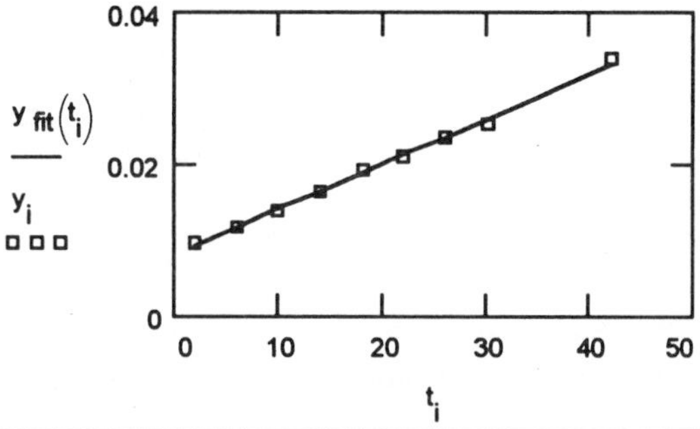

The graph (box left) shows no apparent systematic deviation from the straight line. The box also shows the calculation of the rate constant: from Eq. (10.5) we see that the slope is aC_0k, where a is the intercept (the reciprocal of $\lambda_0 - \lambda_\infty$)

$$resid_i := y_i - y_{fit}(t_i)$$

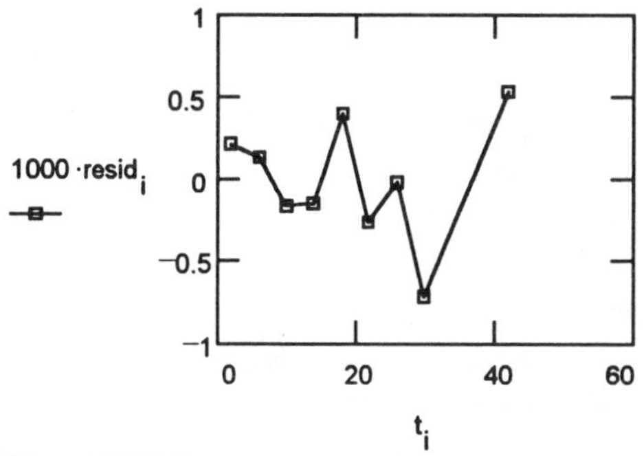

The residual graph (box right) makes the point even clearer: the random scatter is just what we seek. (Actually, the clear increase in scatter with time suggests that we should be doing weighted regression, but since this is difficult with Mathcad, we will avoid that subject for now.)

The error analysis for the slope and intercept is as before; however, since the rate constant is calculated as a ratio of slope/intercept, we must calculate the error of the rate constant from the errors of the slope and intercept as illustrated below. (This topic, "propagation of error", is covered in most physical chemistry lab texts, and many analytical chemistry texts.)

$$sxx := \sum_i (t_i)^2 \qquad \sigma_m := \frac{m}{r} \cdot \sqrt{\frac{1-r^2}{N-2}} \qquad \sigma_a := \sigma_m \cdot \sqrt{\frac{sxx}{N}}$$

$$\sigma_k := k \cdot \sqrt{\frac{\sigma_a^2}{a^2} + \frac{\sigma_m^2}{m^2}} \qquad k = 0.727 \qquad \sigma_k = 0.026$$

The standard error of the slope is 0.026, but the critical t factor for this case is $t_c = 1.90$, so the result should be reported as $k = (0.73 \pm 0.05)$ mol liter^{-1} min^{-1}.

Example 10.3 Nonlinear regression.

Table 10.2 displays data for the hydration of isobutene as measured by the dilatometer method. In this method, the volume of the reacting solution is measured by observing the height of a liquid column in a capillary (h), and it is this quantity that is given (in mm, the unit is irrelevant). The height h is a property proportional to extent of reaction as discussed in Example 10.2 (where it was denoted λ).

Table 10.2 Hydration of isobutene by the dilatometer method.

t/min	h/mm	t/min	h/mm
0	18.84	120	13.5
10	17.91	140	13.19
20	17.19	160	12.92
30	16.56	180	12.75
40	16.00	240	12.43
50	15.53	260	12.36
60	15.13	280	12.31
70	14.76	300	12.27

Since the values for h vary in time, it is clear that they are reflecting the extent of reaction. The value when the reaction is complete (h_∞) is not zero (nor is there any reason to expect it to be so), so this quantity (the *background*) must be subtracted from the readings to get a quantity that is directly proportional to the reactant concentration. (In cases where the measured quantity increases with time, subtract the values from the background rather than, as in this case, the background from the value; in any case, you want positive numbers.) Now the concentrations in Eq. (10.1) can be evaluated as $C \propto (h - h_\infty)$ and $C_0 \propto (h_0 - h_\infty)$ giving (since the proportionality factor cancels):

$$h(t) = h_\infty + (h_0 - h_\infty)\exp(-kt)$$

Of course, this equation can be linearized by subtracting h_∞ from each side and taking the logarithm, but first we must determine the value of h_∞. As you can see from the data in the table, after 5 hours the readings have still not reached a steady value, and even if the experimenter had waited 10 hours there would still be an uncertainty as the whether the last change was a random error or a systematic decrease. Also, when the infinity value is subtracted from all points, it is given excessive weight: that is, any error in its measurement is reflected in all of the data points. A better method is to use nonlinear regression to determine the rate constant without any presumptions about the infinity value, which is determined independently as part of the procedure.

Enter the data by any convenient method, placing the dilatometer readings in the vector **hx** and the times in **tx**.

$M := \mathrm{READPRN}(ord1data)$ $\quad tx := M^{<0>}$ $\quad hx := M^{<1>}$ $\quad i := 0 .. \mathrm{last}(tx)$

For nonlinear regression, we first define a function (f, box to right) whose arguments are the independent variable (t) and the parameters. Then we define a function (SSE) for the sum of squares of the errors — the deviations of the observed value (h) from the calculated values (f). If we knew the parameter values exactly and if there were no error in the measurements, SSE would be zero. We seek a best fit by finding a minimum in this quantity. Before iterating, we need good estimates for the parameters. The ini-

$$f(t, h_0, h_{inf}, k) := h_{inf} + (h_0 - h_{inf}) \cdot e^{-k \cdot t}$$

$$SSE(h_0, h_{inf}, k) := \sum_i \left(hx_i - f(tx_i, h_0, h_{inf}, k)\right)^2$$

$h_0 := 19$

$h_{inf} := 12$

$k := \dfrac{1}{100}$

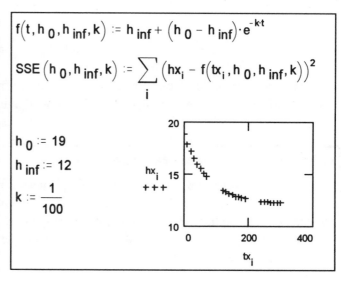

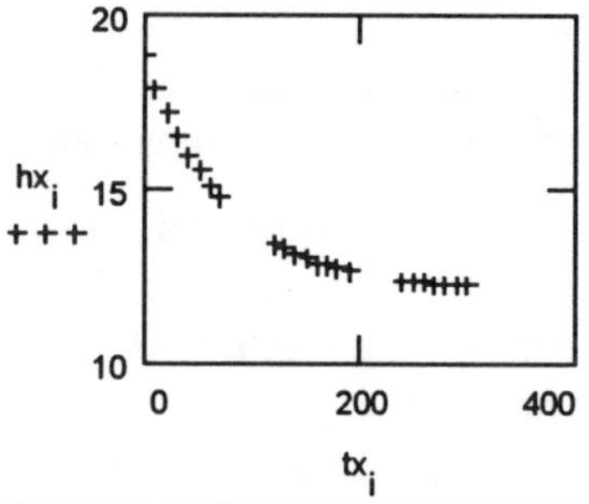

tial and final heights are readily estimated from the graph; the value of k is approximately the reciprocal of the time it takes for the height to change 2/3 of the way between the initial and final values.

Given

$$k>0 \qquad h_0>0 \qquad h_{inf}>0$$

$$SSE(h_0, h_{inf}, k)=0$$

$$\begin{pmatrix} h_0 \\ h_{inf} \\ k \end{pmatrix} := \text{Minerr}(h_0, h_{inf}, k)$$

$$\begin{pmatrix} h_0 \\ h_{inf} \\ 100 \cdot k \end{pmatrix} = \begin{pmatrix} 18.78 \\ 12.171 \\ 1.348 \end{pmatrix} \qquad ERR = 0.01$$

The solution is shown in the box to the left. This is effectively a solve block with **Minerr** replacing **Find**; the distinction is that the **Find** returns a result only if it can find an exact solution (within the tolerance, *TOL*) whereas **Minerr** does the best it can, finding a minimum but not necessarily a zero for *SSE*. At least two additional conditions are required because 3 parameters are sought; this is a somewhat artificial requirement of Mathcad, but in fact it's not a bad idea to restrict the variable search to positive numbers since it is certain that all parameters are positive. The results are shown at the bottom (k is multiplied by 100 so an adequate number of figures are displayed). *ERR* is an internal Mathcad variable that measures the quality of the fit; in this case it is just the value of *SSE* for the best-fit parameters.

One of the problems with nonlinear regression is that it is difficult to estimate the errors, but we can at least reassure ourselves of the quality of fit by examining the graph of the fitted line and data and the residuals.

$$t := 0..400 \qquad resid_i := hx_i - f(tx_i, h_0, h_{inf}, k)$$

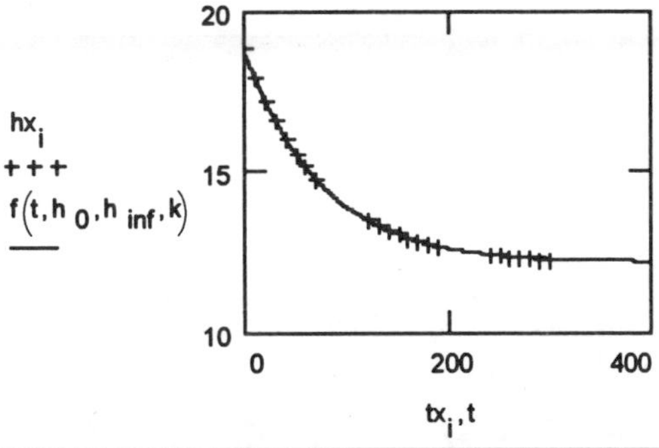

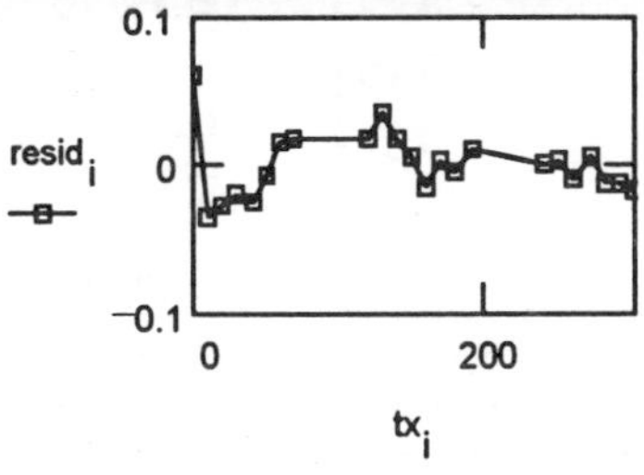

The residual graph suggests that the first point is suspect and, in fact, you could get a somewhat improved fit without it.

If you have the PLUS version of Mathcad, you can use their procedure (**genfit**) to solve this problem, but you will find this is be scarcely less trouble than the procedure outlined above.

10.2 Temperature Dependence of Rate Constants

The temperature dependence of rate constants is often analyzed using the Arrhenius equation:

$$k = A\exp\left(-\frac{E_a}{RT}\right) \tag{10.6}$$

Sometimes other models such as that due to Eyring (Noggle, Section 10.4) are used. The Arrhenius equation works about a well as any other so we shall examine it first.

Example 10.4 Arrhenius analysis of rate-constant data.

Equation (10.6) can be linearized by taking the logarithm:

$$\ln k = \ln A - \frac{E_a}{RT} \tag{10.7}$$

Thus $y = \ln k$ vs. $x = 1/T$ would be linear with slope $-E_a/R$ and intercept $\ln A$ (called *lnA* in Mathcad, below).

Rate constants for the decomposition of HI vs. temperature (K) are given in the box below. These change so rapidly with temperature that a graph is unrewarding unless a log scale is used; the graph below can be used to check for errors in data entry.

$i := 0..8$

$T_i :=$	$k_i :=$
556	$3.53 \cdot 10^{-7}$
575	$1.22 \cdot 10^{-6}$
629	$3.02 \cdot 10^{-5}$
647	$8.59 \cdot 10^{-5}$
666	$2.19 \cdot 10^{-4}$
683	$5.12 \cdot 10^{-4}$
700	$1.16 \cdot 10^{-3}$
716	$2.50 \cdot 10^{-3}$
781	$3.95 \cdot 10^{-2}$

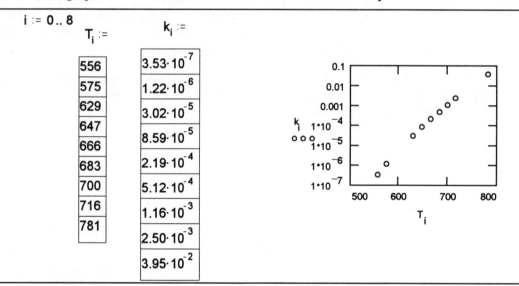

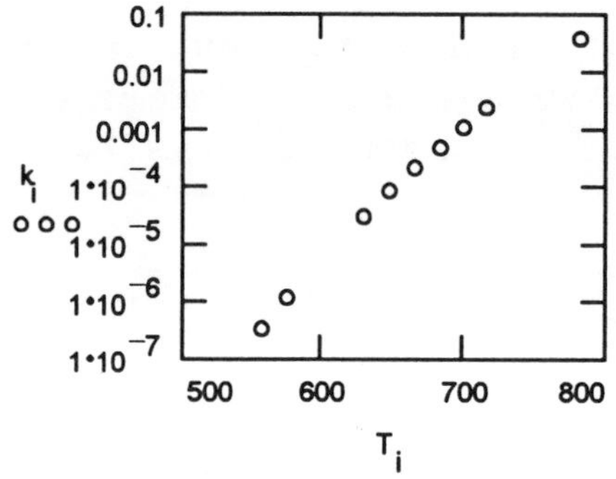

The analysis of these data is straightforward as shown below.

$y_i := \ln(k_i)$ $\quad x_i := \frac{1}{T_i}$ $\quad lnA := \text{intercept}(x, y)$ $\quad R := 8.31451$

$E_a := -R \cdot \text{slope}(x, y)$ $\quad E_a = 1.857 \cdot 10^5$

As always, you should look at a graph of the fitted curve and data (box below). There is no problem apparent on the graph, but the residual graph (box below, right) tells a different story. Clearly there is a systematic deviation, though the problem is not very serious. Nonetheless for accurate work you may want a better model. (Using $1000/T$ on the x axis rather than $1/T$ (i.e. x) makes the axis labeling more readable, but has no effect on our analysis.)

$$Tv := \min(T)..\max(T) \qquad y_{fit}(T) := \ln A - \frac{E_a}{R \cdot T} \qquad resid_i := y_{fit}(T_i) - y_i$$

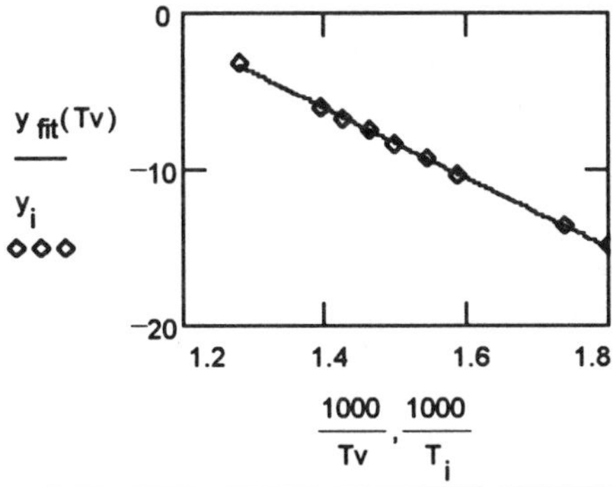

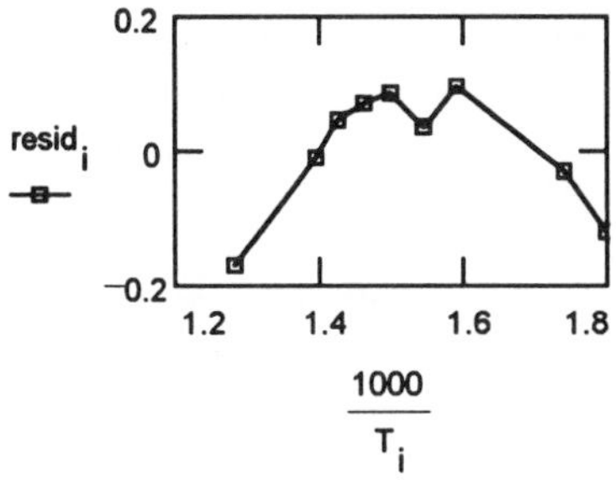

The equation

$$k = aT^n \exp\left(-\frac{E}{RT}\right) \tag{10.8}$$

can be used for an improved fit. Various theories of reaction rates give equations of this sort with various values for the exponent n (Eyring, for example, gives $n = 1$), but we shall simply treat it a another parameter. Taking the logarithm of Eq. (10.8) gives:

$$\ln k = \ln a - \frac{E_a}{RT} + n \ln T \tag{10.9}$$

With the same data, we determine the parameters of this equation by generalized linear regression (**linfit**) as shown below. (We include *-R* in the function so that the parameter, the second element of *ans*, is the value of *E* directly.)

$$F(T) := \begin{bmatrix} 1 \\ \dfrac{-1}{R \cdot T} \\ \ln(T) \end{bmatrix} \qquad ans := \mathrm{linfit}(T, y, F) \qquad y_{fit}(T) := ans \cdot F(T) \qquad ans = \begin{pmatrix} -91.174 \\ 1.018 \cdot 10^5 \\ 15.557 \end{pmatrix}$$

$$resid_i := y_{fit}(T_i) - y_i$$

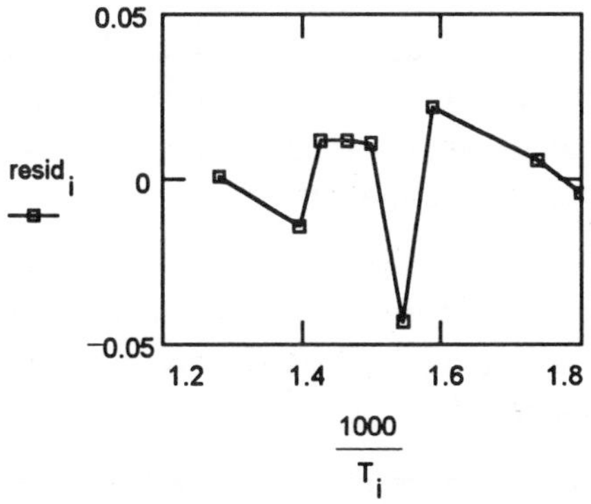

To judge from the residuals, this procedure is very successful. Not only are the residuals reduced substantially, but there is no sign of a systematic trend.

The value of n calculated by this analysis (15) is far from any value predicted by theory. On the other hand, Eq. (10.9) with these parameters is very successful as a practical equation for predicting rate constants for this reaction. Make a graph of the fitted line (y_{fit}) and data: do you see any improvement on the simple Arrhenius treatment?

10.3 Differential Equations and Mechanisms

The rate laws that arise in chemical kinetics are, of course, differential equations. Some are easily solved (by separation of variables) by anyone versed in calculus. Others can be solved by standard methods of differential equations. In general, however, the rate laws must be solved by numerical methods. Numerical solution of differential equations is implemented in the PLUS version of Mathcad, which is needed for all of the examples of this section except 10.8.

Example 10.5 Solving differential equations with Mathcad. ⊕

We begin with a simple, nonchemical example: the damped oscillator. The differential equations for this system are

$$\frac{du}{dt} = \omega v - \frac{v}{\tau}; \quad \frac{dv}{dt} = -\omega u - \frac{v}{\tau} \tag{10.10}$$

where ω is the radial frequency (radians per second, 2π times the frequency in cycles per second) and τ is the relaxation time. The meaning of the variables depends on the physical application, but typically *u* represents a displacement and *v* is the velocity (*du/dt*).

In Mathcad, the dependent variables (*u* and *v* in the above equation) must initially be elements of a vector; we shall denote the vector as **y** with *u* as y_0 and *v* as y_1. The box below defines values for the parameters, the maximum time (to which *t* is run) and the number of points in the numerical solution (*npts*) (actually, we enter the period, *p*, and calculate the frequency, ω, from it). Be careful to distinguish between label-type subscripts, e.g. "`t.max`" and indexing subscripts, e.g. "`y[1`".

$p := 1 \qquad \omega := \frac{2\cdot\pi}{p} \qquad \tau := 2 \qquad t_{max} := 6 \qquad npts := 500$

$y := \begin{pmatrix} 1 \\ 0 \end{pmatrix} \qquad D(t,y) := \begin{bmatrix} \omega\cdot y_1 - \frac{y_0}{\tau} \\ -\omega\cdot y_0 - \frac{y_1}{\tau} \end{bmatrix} \qquad s := \mathrm{rkfixed}(y, 0, t_{max}, npts, D)$

The vector **y** is given values equal to the initial values of the variables; in this case, at $t = 0$, $u = 1$ and $v = 0$. The vector function **D** contains the right-hand sides of the differential equations for the variables — Eq. (10.10) in this case. The solution is calculated using the Mathcad function **rkfixed**; this is one of several methods available, and uses the Runge-Kutta method with a fixed interval (the interval is $h = t_{max}/npts$ — more about this shortly).

The solution matrix, called **s** in this example, contains the answers. Column 0 contains the times, column 1 contains the values of y_0 and column 2 contains y_1; this renumbering of the variables is a potential source of confusion which we will avoid by immediately renaming the variables to something more meaningful than y_0, y_1 and so forth.

The box below demonstrates how the solution matrix is separated into the solution vectors. (The superscripts are made with ctrl+6).

$t := s^{\langle 0 \rangle}$ $u := s^{\langle 1 \rangle}$ $v := s^{\langle 2 \rangle}$ $i := 0..\, npts - 1$

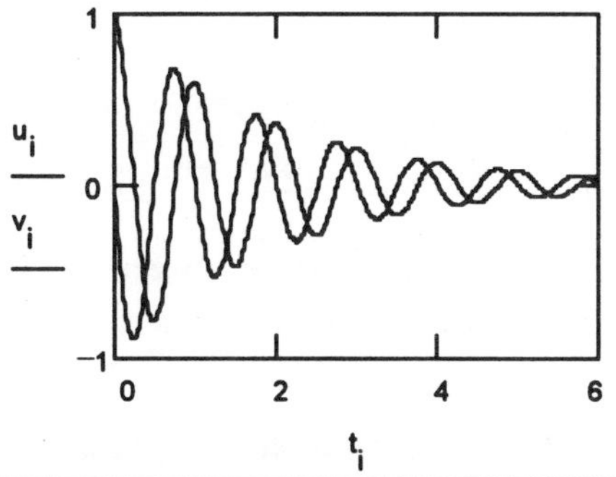

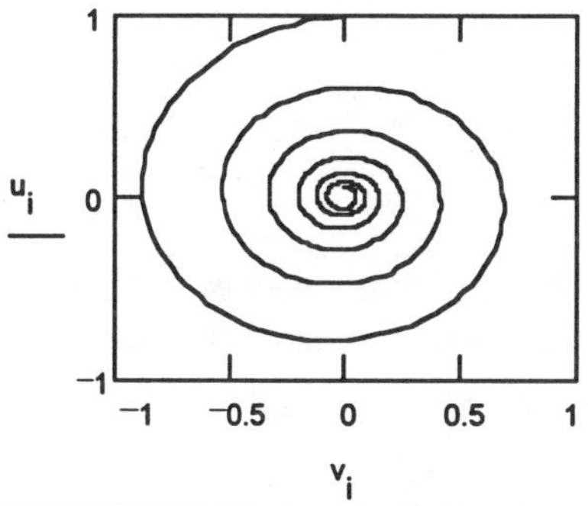

The first graph shows *u* and *v* as a function of time. The second shows *u* vs. *v;* this graph is given a variety of names depending on the field of application — one name is *phase graph.*

$h := t_1 - t_0$ $\quad \frac{t_{max}}{npts} = 0.012$

$h = 0.012$

A very important parameter for the numerical solution of differential equations is the solution interval (called *h*, above). This is the time difference between adjacent points of the solution vector (box to right). If this quantity is too large, one of two things can happen: the solution curve may be "steppy" (not smooth) or the solutions may be incorrect. You can demonstrate these phenomena by systematically reducing *npts* in this example. With 50 points, the graphs are not smooth but the solutions are still accurate. At 5 points, the solutions are entirely inaccurate. Commonly, if *h* is small enough to produce a smooth curve, it is small enough to produce accurate solutions. There are, however, exceptions: systems of equations characterized as *stiff.* Stiff equations usually result when a series of fast processes combine to produce a slow overall change. In kinetics this may happen if, for a series of reactions, the rate constants differ by an order of magnitude or more. Mathcad has a special functions for solving such equation: **stiffb** and **stiffr** (see manual for details).

In any case, you must pay very close attention to the value of *h* (unfortunately, not directly an input in Mathcad). Too small a value and the solution is very time consuming and may suffer from the accumulation of roundoff errors. Too large a value and the solutions may be poorly defined (curves not smooth) or even inaccurate. The appropriate value depends on the parameters of the problem: in this example, *h* should be an order of magnitude shorter than the period or the relaxation time (whichever is smaller).

Example 10.6 The autocatalytic reaction. ⊕

If the rate of a reaction A → P depends on the concentration of the product, the reaction is called *autocatalytic*. The equations for such a system, including a first-order reaction to get it started, are:

$$\frac{d[\mathrm{A}]}{dt} = -k_1[\mathrm{A}] - k_2[\mathrm{A}][\mathrm{P}]$$
$$\frac{d[\mathrm{P}]}{dt} = k_1[\mathrm{A}] + k_2[\mathrm{A}][\mathrm{P}] \qquad (10.11)$$

The second term is the autocatalytic term, but it is zero at the beginning of the reaction when [P] = 0, which is why the first term is needed.

$k2 := 1.234 \qquad k1 := 0.003$

$$y := \begin{pmatrix} 1 \\ 0 \end{pmatrix} \qquad D(t,y) := \begin{pmatrix} -k2 \cdot y_0 \cdot y_1 - k1 \cdot y_0 \\ k2 \cdot y_0 \cdot y_1 + k1 \cdot y_0 \end{pmatrix} \qquad \begin{matrix} tmax := 10 \\ npts := 200 \quad i := 0 .. npts - 1 \end{matrix}$$

The first component of **y** is [A], whose initial concentration is 1, and the second is [P] with initial concentration 0. The rate constants used determine that the autocatalytic mechanism will be dominant once it gets started.

All that remains is to solve the equations (giving a solution matrix **ans**), disassemble the answer into properly named vectors, and make a graph.

$ans := rkfixed(y, 0, tmax, npts, D) \qquad t := ans^{<0>} \qquad A := ans^{<1>} \qquad P := ans^{<2>}$

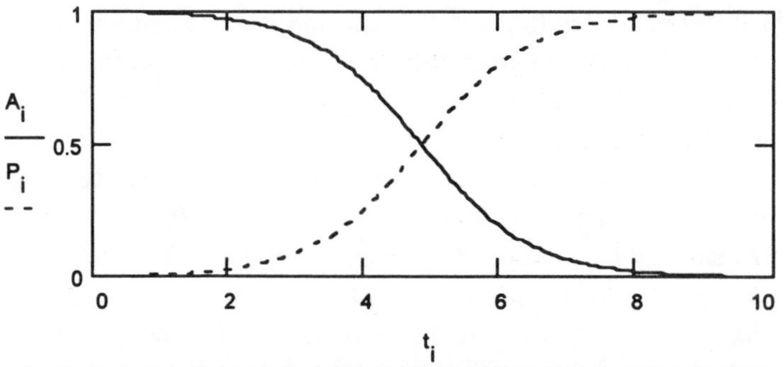

The characteristics of this graph, for example the induction period (period at the beginning when nothing seems to be happening), the rate of rise, and time to completion are controlled by the rate constants. Vary these to explore the variety of responses this system is capable of.

Example 10.7 Consecutive first-order reactions.

⊕

The symbolic solution for two consecutive first-order reactions

$$A \rightarrow B \rightarrow C$$

is given in most texts, for example Noggle Eqs. (10.34). Here we shall demonstrate the numeric solution for 4 reactions

$$A \rightarrow B \rightarrow C \rightarrow D \rightarrow E$$

(rate constants $k_1 \ldots k_4$, from left to right).

For the setup we use only 4 variables, representing A, B, C and D; we can solve for E by difference. The ratio *npts/tmax* is displayed; this number (the reciprocal of the solution interval *h*) should be larger than the largest rate constant.

$$y := \begin{bmatrix} 1 \\ 0 \\ 0 \\ 0 \end{bmatrix} \qquad npts := 200 \qquad tmax := 5 \qquad k_1 := 5 \qquad k_2 := 1$$

$$\frac{npts}{tmax} = 40 \qquad \textit{maximum } k \qquad k_3 := 3 \qquad k_4 := 2$$

$$i := 0..\, npts - 1$$

The box below shows the solution. It appears to be necessary that the positive terms of the latter 3 equations be entered first — otherwise some combinations of rate constants may give erroneous solutions (e.g. negative concentrations for B, C and D).

$$D(t,y) := \begin{bmatrix} -k_1 \cdot y_0 \\ k_1 \cdot y_0 - k_2 \cdot y_1 \\ k_2 \cdot y_1 - k_3 \cdot y_2 \\ k_3 \cdot y_2 - k_4 \cdot y_3 \end{bmatrix} \qquad ans := \text{rkfixed}(y, 0, tmax, npts, D)$$

$$t := ans^{<0>} \qquad A := ans^{<1>} \qquad B := ans^{<2>} \qquad C := ans^{<3>}$$

$$D := ans^{<4>} \qquad E := y_0 - A - B - C - D$$

The initial concentration of A, y_0, is used to calculate the concentration of E (last equation above). Finally we make a graph.

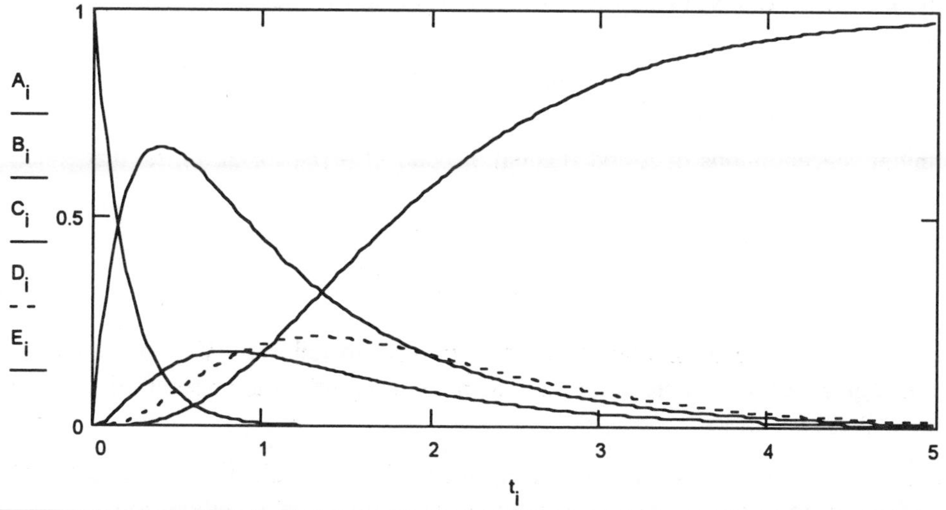

(This graph is much clearer in color, as you will see on your own screen.) Try different combinations of rate constants, observing and trying to understand the results. Which rate constant is most important for the rate of formation of the product? (Hint: keep the time scale and the value of the smallest rate constant fixed — any rate constant could be the smallest, but it is the "small value" you want to keep the same.)

Example 10.8 Testing the steady-state approximation. ⊕

The steady-state approximation contains an apparent contradiction: we set the time derivative of the concentration of some species (a reaction intermediate) equal to zero — implying that it is a constant — and then derive a formula showing how it changes with time. Actually, there is no contradiction since all that is required is that the rate of change of the "steady" species be slow compared to the rate of reaction (as measured by the rate of disappearance of the reactant or appearance of the product). But exactly when (in a practical sense) is this approximation appropriate? It is often applied as a matter of convenience and justified *ex post facto* — that is, if the resulting rate law fits the data then the approximation is considered justified. But as this example demonstrates, such reasoning is dangerous and possible erroneous.

We examine the mechanism

$$\begin{aligned} &\mathrm{A+B} \xrightarrow{1} \mathrm{C} \\ &\mathrm{C} \xrightarrow{2} \mathrm{A+B} \\ &\mathrm{C} \xrightarrow{3} \mathrm{P} \end{aligned} \tag{10.12}$$

(Note that the second reaction is the reverse of the first, so we have a reversible second-order reaction followed by an irreversible first-order reaction.) The rate constants are k_1 for the forward reaction of the first step, k_2 for the reverse of the first step, and k_3 for the second step. This mechanism is readily solved with the steady-state approximation to give

$$\frac{d[\mathrm{A}]}{dt} = -k_e[\mathrm{A}][\mathrm{B}] \quad \text{with} \quad k_e = \frac{k_1 k_3}{k_2 + k_3} \tag{10.13}$$

With initial concentrations of A and B equal, hence [A] = [B] for all times, this equation integrates to

$$\frac{1}{[\mathrm{A}]} = \frac{1}{A_0} + k_e t \tag{10.14}$$

where A_0 is the initial concentration (equal to 1 in work to follow). We can use this as a diagnostic: if a graph of the reciprocal of the reactant concentration is linear, then the steady-state law, Eq. (10.13) is correct.

In this example we shall solve the equations for this mechanism numerically in order to test the limits of the steady-state approximation. The differential equations are:

$$\frac{d[\mathrm{A}]}{dt} = -k_1[\mathrm{A}][\mathrm{B}] + k_2[\mathrm{C}]$$

$$\frac{d[\mathrm{C}]}{dt} = k_1[\mathrm{A}][\mathrm{B}] - k_2[\mathrm{C}] - k_3[\mathrm{C}]$$

$$\frac{d[P]}{dt} = k_3[\mathrm{C}]$$

For simplicity we assume [A] = [B] and designate these quantities as the first variable, y_0. The second variable is $[C] = y_1$ and the third is $[D] = y_2$. Be sure you understand how the equations in the vector **D** follow from the differential equations above.

A + B ⇌ C -> P $k_1 := 5$ $k_2 := 10$ $k_3 := 0.2$ $k_e := \frac{k_1 \cdot k_3}{k_2 + k_3}$

$$y := \begin{pmatrix} 1 \\ 0 \\ 0 \end{pmatrix} \qquad D(t,y) := \begin{bmatrix} -k_1 \cdot (y_0)^2 + k_2 \cdot y_1 \\ k_1 \cdot (y_0)^2 - k_2 \cdot y_1 - k_3 \cdot y_1 \\ k_3 \cdot y_1 \end{bmatrix}$$

$tmax := 10$ $npts := 100$ $\frac{1}{k_e} = 10.2$ $\frac{npts}{tmax} = 10$

The numbers above use rate constants with the same order of magnitude, but be careful: with rate constants of greatly different magnitude, these equations can easily become "stiff". Keep an eye on the ratio *npts/tmax*: it should be larger than k_e and any individual rate constant. If the steady-state law, Eq. (10.13) is correct, then $1/k_e$ is the half life of the reaction; this calculation (above) can be used to determine *tmax* but, again, you must be careful: it is not appropriate in all circumstances.

The solution is shown below. The steady-state solution is calculated as *ss* for comparison (later); *ss* represents 1/[A] as predicted by the steady-state solution, Eq. (10.14).

$ans := rkfixed(y, 0, tmax, npts, D)$ $i := 0 .. npts - 1$ $mult := 1$

$t := ans^{<0>}$ $A := ans^{<1>}$ $C := ans^{<2>}$ $P := ans^{<3>}$ $ss_i := 1 + k_e \cdot t_i$

The box below shows the concentrations vs. time (left) and the reciprocal of [A] vs. time. (The intermediate, [C] is multiplied by *mult*:, defined above. Since *mult* = 1, there is no effect, but other combinations of rate constants may give [C] too small to be seen on the same graph with the others, and increasing *mult* is a simple way to make it visible.)

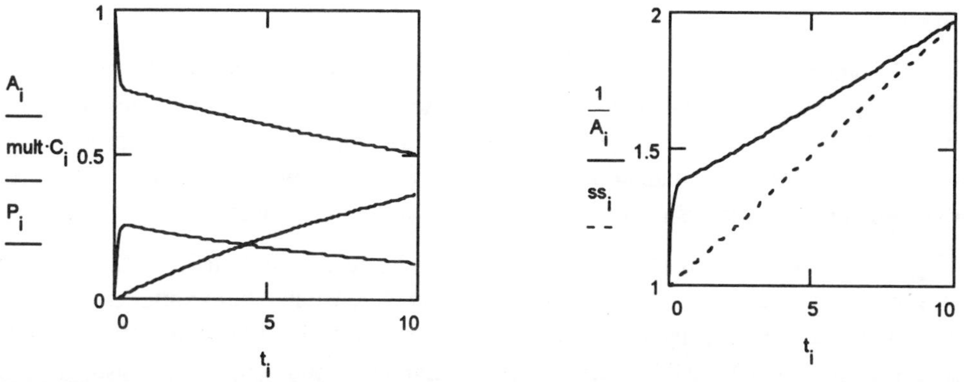

Comparison to the steady-state solution (*ss*, dashed line, above) makes it clear that the steady-state solution is not correct in this case, but would you realize that if you were dealing with real data? The calculated line (solid) is quite close to linear after the initial transient. Experimental considerations may prohibit you from obtaining measurements in the region of the transient — for example, mixing may be incomplete. Also, initial points are often deviant, and may be dropped from the analysis; we did exactly that in Example 10.1. Indeed, this example illustrates one reason that initial points may be deviant: a rate law may apply only after an initial transient.

Next, we will treat the calculated [A] as a data set, selecting points for analysis. We want to avoid the initial point since our objective is to see how well the second-order law works without that point.

$$k := 0..\frac{npts}{10} - 1 \qquad y_k := \frac{1}{A_{10\cdot k+10}} \qquad tx_k := t_{10\cdot k+10}$$

$$k_x := \text{slope}(tx, y) \qquad k_x = 0.062 \qquad k_e = 0.098$$

The box to the left demonstrates how to select every 10th point, starting with number 10, to be used as a data set for linear regression. Display the new arrays with "tx=" and "y=" to see what you have and to be certain it is what you want. The slope is the rate constant (*kx*) which is compared to the prediction, *ke*. The comparison is not good, but would we know that if we didn't know the answer? In the box below we calculate the error of the slope and compare the fitted line to the data with a graph.

$$time := 0..tmax \qquad y_{fit}(t) := \text{intercept}(tx, y) + k_x\cdot t$$

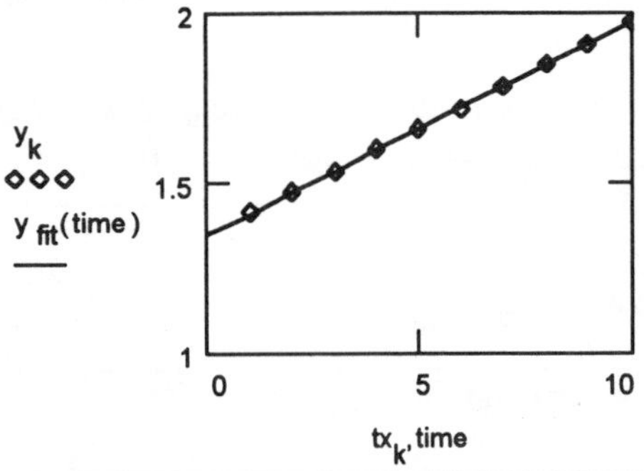

$$r := \text{corr}(tx, y) \qquad DF := 8$$

$$r = 0.999853$$

$$\sigma_k := \frac{k_x}{|r|}\cdot\sqrt{\frac{1 - r^2}{DF}}$$

$$k_e = 0.0980 \qquad k_x = 0.0622 \qquad \sigma_k = 0.0004$$

The graph looks very good; the residual graph (not shown) would show a clear systematic deviation, but with real data this could easily be obscured by experimental error (random scatter). The correlation coefficient (r) and standard deviation of the calculated rate constant (σ_k) are very good.

On one sense, this model is successful: it predicted a second-order rate law and, after the initial transient, that is what we find. For practical purposes, calling this a second-order rate with rate constant 0.0622 is quite correct. On the other hand, the relationship of the rate constant to the rates of the individual reactions is not at all what Eq. (10.13) predicts. The steady-state approximation is not correct for this set of rate constants.

Try different rate constants; since there are 3 rate constants to vary (k_1, k_2, and k_3), to get meaningful comparisons it is best to keep something constant. For example, fix one of them and adjust the others, keeping k_e constant. Find conditions for which the steady-state law is exact: that is, it could not be distinguished from a simple second-order mechanism ($A + B \rightarrow P$) with any reasonable accuracy of the experimental data for [A]. Are there any conditions that give data that no reasonable person would ever mistake for a second order reaction?. What controls the length of the initial transient? In the end, you should be able to state in explicit, operational terms exactly what the conditions are for the steady-state approximation to be valid.

Example 10.9 The Lotka-Volterra mechanism. ⊕

One of the most exciting developments in chemical kinetics in recent years has been the discovery of reactions for which the intermediates, rather than reaching a steady state, show oscillatory variations in either time or space. Most of these reactions are quite complicated. This example examines a very simple mechanism, the Lotka-Volterra mechanism, which exhibits temporal oscillations.

The mechanism is:

$$\begin{aligned} A + X &\xrightarrow{1} 2X \\ X + Y &\xrightarrow{2} 2Y \\ Y &\xrightarrow{3} P \end{aligned} \tag{10.15}$$

The rate laws for the intermediates are:

$$\begin{aligned} \frac{d[X]}{dt} &= k_1[A][X] - k_2[X][Y] \\ \frac{d[Y]}{dt} &= k_2[X][Y] - k_3[Y] \end{aligned} \tag{10.16}$$

The concentration of A is kept constant in this reaction by adding it steadily to the reacting mixture. Because of this, we only need to know the product k_1[A], which we treat (below) as a parameter *k1A*. The other two parameters are k_2 for the second reaction and k_2 for the third. The setup is shown below; all subscripts in this box are "decorative" — for example, you would enter "`X.0:1.5`".

$X_0 := 1.5 \quad Y_0 := 1 \quad npts := 200 \quad tmax := 10 \quad \frac{npts}{tmax} = 20$

$k1A := 2.4 \quad k_2 := 4.2 \quad k_3 := 5.1$

As always, we must make the variables into elements of a vector (y, below); this requires the use of true subscripts created with the left bracket ([).

$$y := \begin{pmatrix} X_0 \\ Y_0 \end{pmatrix} \quad D(t,y) := \begin{pmatrix} k1A \cdot y_0 - k_2 \cdot y_0 \cdot y_1 \\ k_2 \cdot y_0 \cdot y_1 - k_3 \cdot y_1 \end{pmatrix} \quad s := \text{rkfixed}(y, 0, tmax, npts, D)$$

$t := s^{<0>} \quad X := s^{<1>} \quad Y := s^{<2>} \quad i := 0 .. npts - 1$

Graph the concentrations, [X] and [Y].

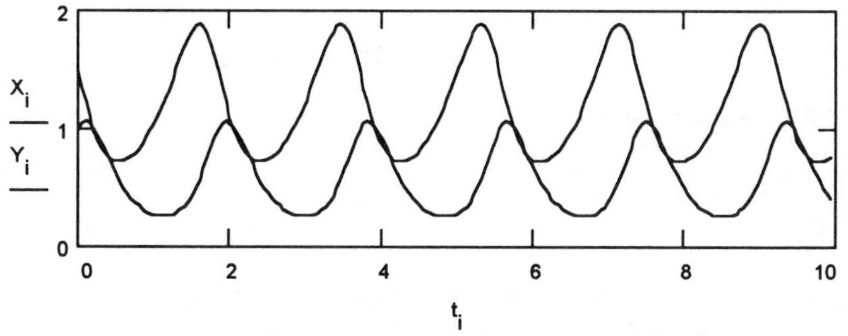

(Your graph should be in color so the species can be distinguished easily.)

Another presentation of these data is the phase graph shown in the box to the right, except in this application it is called the *limit cycle* plot.

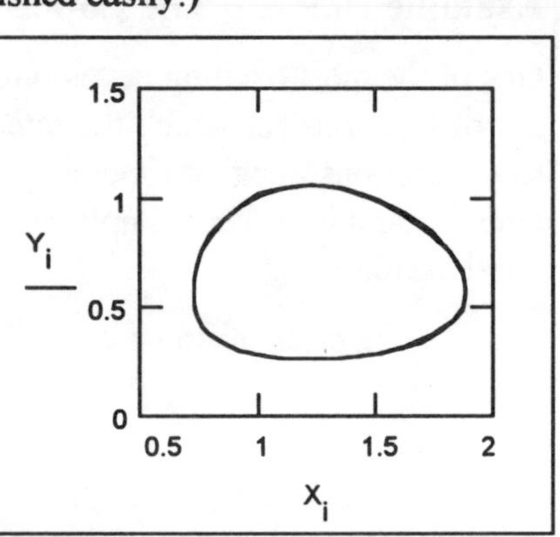

This system shows an immense variety depending on the constants used, and you should explore it thoroughly. Vary not only the rate constants but the initial concentrations as well.

An interesting variation is shown in the box below. (The complete calculation is not shown — it's just like the one above — but with the constants displayed.) The limit cycle plot (below, right) is very different this time.

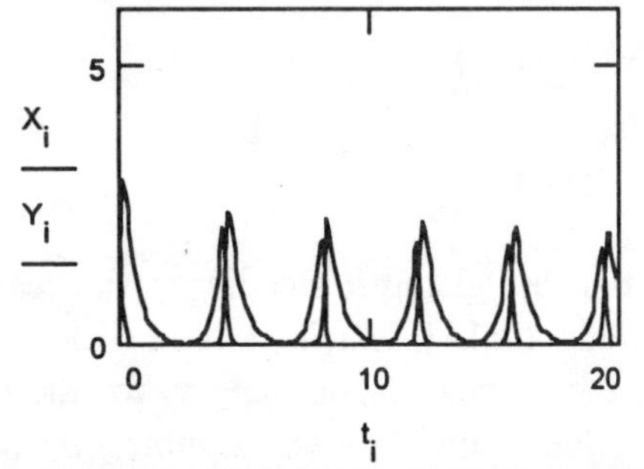

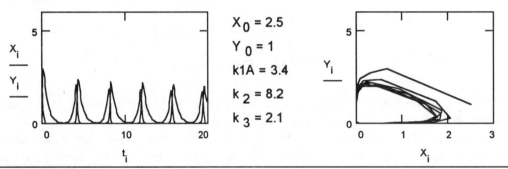

$X_0 = 2.5$

$Y_0 = 1$

$k1A = 3.4$

$k_2 = 8.2$

$k_3 = 2.1$

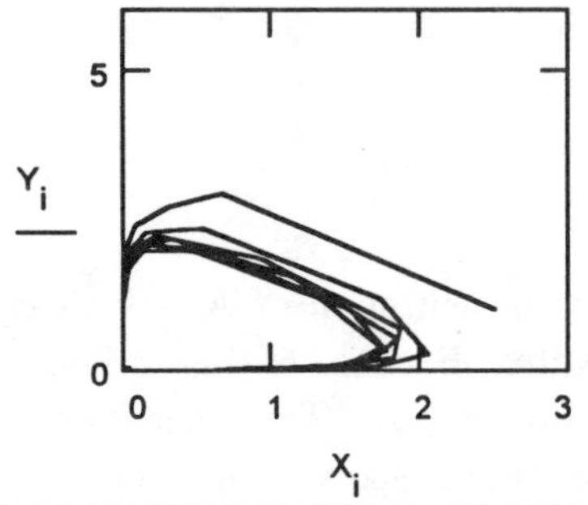

The reason for the odd limit-cycle plot, which may be apparent on close examination of the time plot (increase *tmax* by an order of magnitude, and *npts* in proportion), is that the oscillations are slowing dying. Are we dealing with an irreversible decay or a transient?

Example 10.10 The chaos game.

We have seen examples of reactions that decay irreversibly (Example 10.1, 10.2), reach a steady state (Example 10.6) or oscillate (Example 10.7). Another possibility is that the concentrations may vary chaotically. While chaotic reactions have been observed, we treat this subject with a nonchemical example: the *logistic equation*. This equation, depending on the value of a single parameter, shows all of these behaviors: decay, steady state, oscillation and chaos.

The logistic equation is a *difference* equation in which the value of some quantity (the *population*, *p*) is calculated from the previous value with

$$p_j = rp_{j-1}(1 - p_{j-1}) \tag{10.17}$$

where $0 < p < 1$ and the parameter r (called the *fecundity*) takes values from 0 to 4. This equation has been used to describe population growth in many applications, but the discovery that it can behave chaotically was an important advance in the field. These developments are well described in the easily read book by Gleick.[2] The significance of this equation goes far beyond

[2] James Gleick, *Chaos: The Making of a New Science*, Penguin Books, New York, 1987. The logistic equation is discussed on pp 59-90.

our present subject: That such a simple equation can show such a wide variety of behaviors, some of them unpredictable (chaotic) is a lesson and a warning to all scientists and engineers. (Engineers above all, we don't want our bridges doing this do we?)

The box below shows how to do the calculation with Mathcad: not at all difficult. Also we see a graph of the population; for various types of behavior, this graph may be clearer using either lines, points. The example below is shown with both points and lines; this is accomplished on the Graph Format menu by selecting, traces, line type = line, symbol = o. In order to get a consistent picture as we vary the conditions, you want to manually set the axis limits. To do this, click on the graph so placeholders appear at the axis ends. For the *y* axis, enter 0 and 1 in the bottom and top placeholders; for the *x* axis enter 0 and *npts* in the left- and rightmost placeholders.

npts := 32 $p_0 := 0.7$ r := 1 j := 1 .. npts $p_j := r \cdot p_{j-1} \cdot (1 - p_{j-1})$

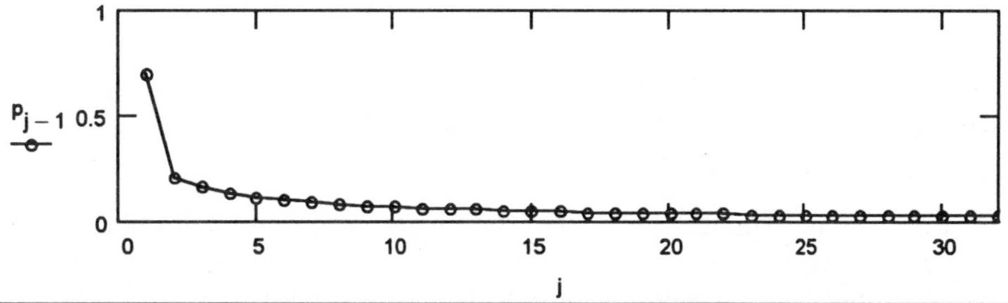

Now all you need to do is to increase *r* (but always less than 4) and observe the result (the initial population, p_0, is less important, but you can vary it too). Initially you will want to increase rapidly (perhaps by 0.5); later you will need to increase *r* slowly (0.01 or less) in order to catch all of the variations. You should see the following (as these progress, you will need to increase *npts* to see the full picture):

- The population decays to zero (example above).
- The population goes to a steady state.
- The population goes to a steady state after an initial oscillation (long or short).
- The population oscillates between two values.
- The oscillation period doubles, so the population alternates among 4 levels. With care you may see doublings to 8, 16, 32, 64, or more.
- The population behaves chaotically, with no apparent pattern. The box below, for *r* = 3.8, shows an apparently random variation.

npts := 128 $p_0 := .7$ r := 3.8 j := 1 .. npts $p_j := r \cdot p_{j-1} \cdot (1 - p_{j-1})$

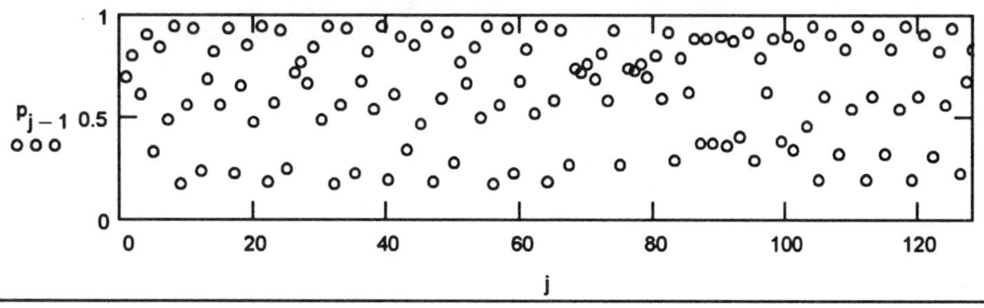

To see if this variation is truly random (chaotic is a more precise term), as opposed to merely complicated (an oscillation with a high frequency) we need to extent the calculation to see if there is any repetition. You can do this by increasing *npts* or by continuing the calculation (with the last population calculated). The box below demonstrates how to continue the calculation.

$j := npts - 1 .. 2 \cdot npts - 1 \qquad p_j := r \cdot p_{j-1} \cdot (1 - p_{j-1})$

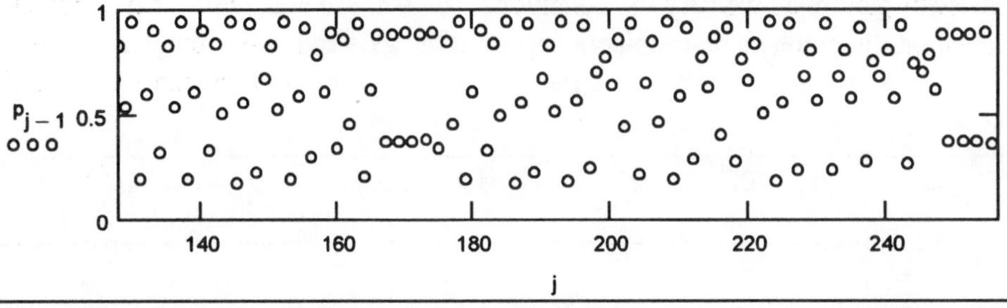

Even after the onset of chaotic behavior, careful exploration is rewarding. You will find small regions where the fluctuations are again steadily oscillating, including oscillations with odd frequencies such as 3 or 7.

Is there any order in the chaos? For a different picture, we will utilize a lag graph: a graph of each point vs. the previous point. We use an example that is in an extreme of chaos. Before collecting the data, we "burn" some calculations to get into a region of steady behavior. Then the array is initialized with the last value (p_0 = last calculation) and the calculation is continued.

$npts := 4 \qquad p_0 := .7 \qquad r := 3.987 \qquad j := 1 .. npts - 1 \qquad p_j := r \cdot p_{j-1} \cdot (1 - p_{j-1})$

$p_0 := p_{npts-1} \qquad npts := 256 \qquad j := 1 .. npts - 1 \qquad p_j := r \cdot p_{j-1} \cdot (1 - p_{j-1})$

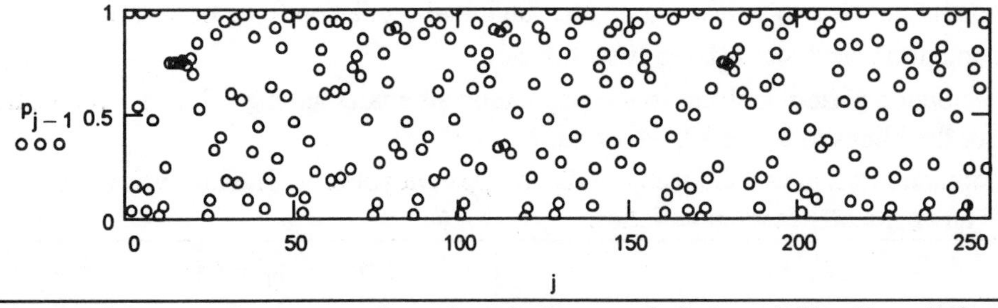

There is certainly no order apparent here, but the lag graph (below, left) tells a different story, showing a definite pattern for the variation. What does the lag graph look like for smaller values of *r*?

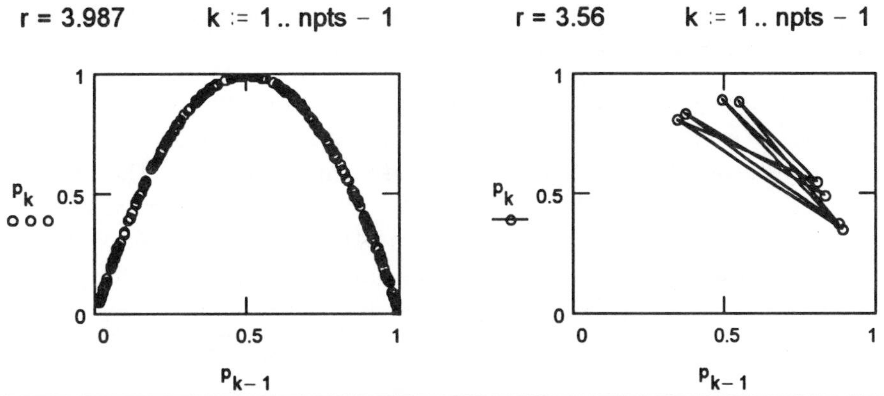

With oscillations, it is somewhat more revealing to show the lines, thus revealing how the points are connected. The example above right is for an oscillation among 8 values: that is, an oscillation at quadruple the fundamental frequency. Make a lag graph for other values of *r*. A different view of such oscillations is seen in the next example.

Example 10.11 Fourier transform. ⊕

Continuing the previous example with the logistic equation, it is natural to think of the number of repetitions as time, and, hence, the oscillations as frequency. The relationship between a time dependence and the frequencies contained in it is made by the *Fourier transform* (FT). For example, in FT NMR (nuclear magnetic resonance), a transient signal is collected in the time interval between pulses of electromagnetic radiation. The Fourier transform of this transient reveals the frequencies contained in it — the NMR spectrum. This technique has widespread utility in science and engineering, and in this example we use the oscillating behavior of the logistic equation to illustrate it.

We start with an array of points representing a variation in the time domain: perhaps experimental data or, in this example, the successive calculations with the logistic equation. The time between these points is the *sampling interval* (τ). Since it takes a minimum of two points to specify an oscillation, the maximum frequency that can be represented by a series of discrete points is $1/2\tau$. This is also called the *Nyquist frequency*. In the examples above in which the population alternated between two values on alternate steps, the system was oscillating at the maximum frequency — the Nyquist frequency.

The Fourier transform changes a signal in the time domain, $s(t)$, into a spectrum in the frequency domain, $f(\omega)$, as:

$$f(\omega) = \frac{1}{2\pi}\int_0^\infty s(t)\exp(i\omega t)\,dt \tag{10.18}$$

($\omega = 2\pi f$, where f is the frequency in cycles per second and ω is the radial frequency in radians per second.) The specific formulas for the discrete Fourier transform (for a limited series of discrete time-domain values) are not needed to understand what follows, but they may be found in the Mathcad manual and in many texts on numerical analysis.

The fastest method for calculating Fourier transforms is the fast Fourier transform, or *fft*. The *fft* technique requires that the number of points in the time domain array be a power of two; this explains our preference in the examples presented for arrays sizes of 32, 64, 128, and so forth. The Mathcad function for doing this is called **fft**.

Before analyzing the logistic equation with the Fourier transform, we will present an example designed to explain the technique. We create an artificial signal that consists of three oscillating, exponentially damped functions with different amplitudes. The decay constant is called T_2 (the relaxation time, an NMR convention). In entering the statements below, note that the subscripts for the frequencies (*f*) and amplitudes (*A*) are true (index) subscripts (made with left bracket) while those on T_2 and f_N are decorative subscripts, made using the period.

$f_1 := 20$ $f_2 := 50$ $f_3 := 60$ frequencies $i := 1..3$

$A_1 := 2$ $A_2 := 4$ $A_3 := 1$ amplitudes $T_2 := 0.5$ Relaxation time

$$F(t) := \left(\sum_{i=1}^{3} A_i \cdot \cos(2\cdot\pi\cdot f_i \cdot t)\right)\cdot \exp\left(-\frac{t}{T_2}\right)$$

$f_N := 100$ Nyquist frequency

The frequency f_N is the Nyquist frequency, which sets the scale for the other frequencies. Next we generate an array of times (t_i) and signals (sig_i) and graph them.

$\tau := \frac{1}{2\cdot f_N}$ npts := 512 $i := 0..\text{npts} - 1$ $t_i := i\cdot\tau$ $\text{signal}_i := F(t_i)$

spec := fft(signal)

length(spec) = 257

k := 0.. length(spec) − 1

$$\text{freq}_k := k\cdot\frac{f_N}{\text{length(spec)}}$$

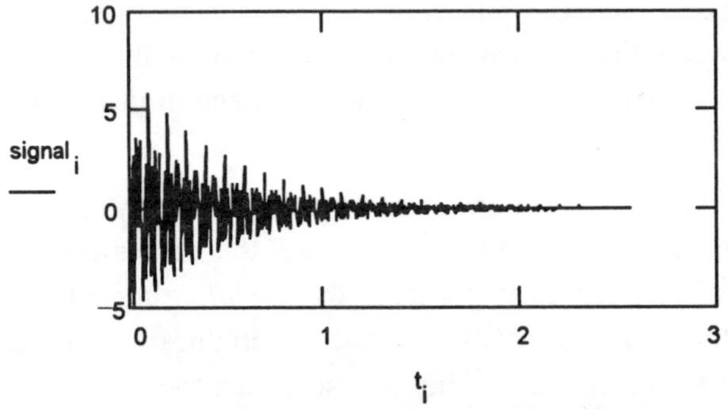

Looking at the signal, one would be hard put to identify the frequencies contained in it. But this information is made immediately plain by the Fourier transform. This operation creates a new array, **spec** (of half the length of the original array, **signal**), which represents the amplitudes of the frequencies of the spectrum. Those frequencies are generated as shown in the last step.

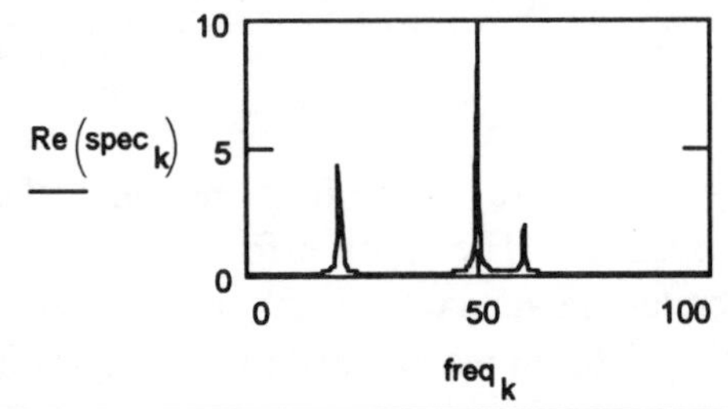

The box to the right displays the spectrum calculated above. Looking at the original frequencies and amplitudes we can see that this is correct. However if we did not know that information, it is apparent that the frequency-domain spectrum gives clear information that was not apparent in the time-domain signal. The amplitudes are not exact; this may be an effect of limited digital resolution. Generate the spectrum again with more points to test this hypothesis. What is the effect on the spectrum of a larger or smaller relaxation time (T_2)? What happens if you include a frequency greater than the Nyquist frequency? (This phenomenon is called *folding* or *aliasing*.)

Now, let's return to the logistic equation. As you will have discovered in your explorations, it is not always easy to discern what frequencies are present in the population variation. The Fourier transform should make this clearer. Before doing the Fourier transform, we want an array that has reached steady behavior. For that reason, in the box below, we "burn" 64 points and then reinitialize the populations before generating the final array (of 256 points, in this example).

$npts := 64 \qquad p_0 := .7 \qquad r := 3.57 \qquad j := 1 .. npts - 1 \qquad p_j := r \cdot p_{j-1} \cdot (1 - p_{j-1})$

$p_0 := p_{npts-1} \qquad npts := 256 \qquad j := 1 .. npts - 1 \qquad p_j := r \cdot p_{j-1} \cdot (1 - p_{j-1})$

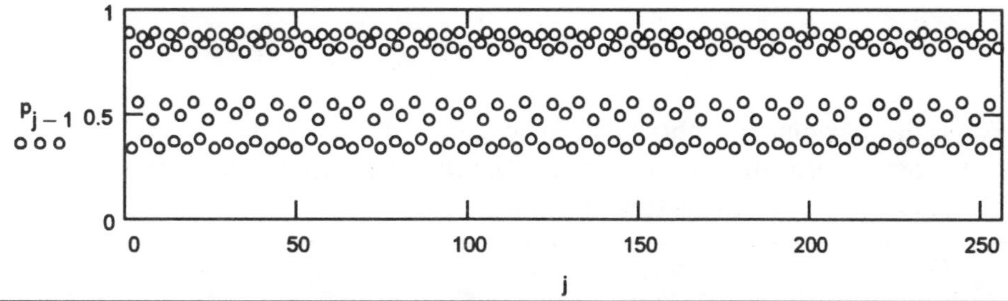

There appear to be 8 levels, implying an oscillation at 8 times the fundamental period (1/8 the fundamental frequency). Check this with **fft**. In contrast to the previous example, the graph of the frequency spectrum is not always clear because the amplitudes vary a lot. Therefore we will use a log-power spectrum. The power is $|v_i|^2$; taking a logarithm emphasizes the smaller components, but since the smallest component is noise (roundoff error of the calculation), we add a constant, *offset* to the power before taking the logarithm. This graph is shown below.

$offset := .001 \qquad v := \mathrm{fft}(p) \qquad i := 0 .. \mathrm{length}(v) - 1$

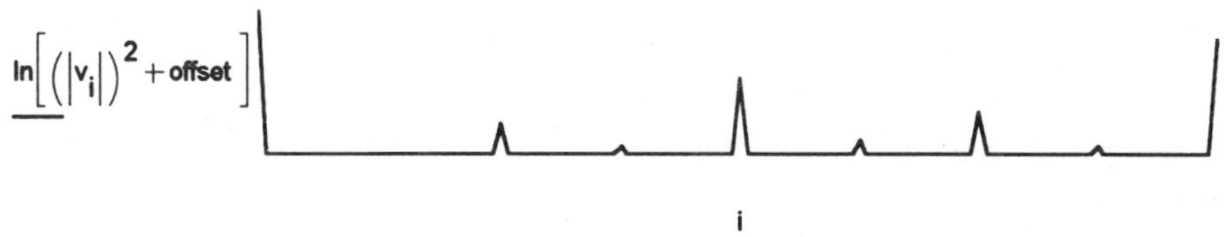

For this graph the axes tend to obscure essential features; to see this graph as it appears above, open the graph-format menu and select axes style, none. (Experiment with *offset* to see its effect, and why it's there.)

The horizontal axis of the graph above is frequency, with zero on the left and the fundamental (Nyquist) frequency on the right. The peak at the left is simply the DC offset (constant level) of the signal; the term DC offset is from electronics, and this component could be removed by subtracting the mean of the population array (**p**) before making the transform. The peak at the right represents the fundamental frequency: an alteration between two levels in each interval. Try a value of *r* for which you found this oscillation and observe the effect. The peak at the center represents an oscillation among 4 levels; doubling the repetition interval and halving the frequency. The peak at 1/4 represents an oscillation among 8 levels, which is what we saw in the time domain signal. However there is a hint of another doubling in the Fourier spectrum. We do not really have enough points to characterize such a variation clearly. Try 1024 points. What do you see? What do you conclude? Try FFT on other interesting examples you have found.

10.4 Surface Adsorption and Catalysis

Example 10.12 Data analysis of Langmuir adsorption.

According to the Langmuir theory of adsorption, the quantity of gas adsorbed on a surface (V_{ads}, measured as volume adsorbed per gram of adsorbent) is given by

$$V_{ads} = \frac{V_{max} bP}{1 + bP} \tag{10.19}$$

where V_{max} is the maximum quantity that can be adsorbed and b is the adsorption constant. The adsorption constant measures the strength of the attraction between the adsorbent and the surface and V_{max} can be related to the surface area.

$$px := \begin{bmatrix} 47 \\ 136 \\ 250 \\ 364 \\ 473 \\ 577 \\ 680 \end{bmatrix} \quad Vads := \begin{bmatrix} 0.531 \\ 1.114 \\ 1.518 \\ 1.757 \\ 1.903 \\ 2.022 \\ 2.121 \end{bmatrix} \quad \begin{matrix} N := \text{length}(px) & i := 0..N-1 \\ DF := N-2 & t_c := 2.01 \quad (90\%) \end{matrix}$$

The degree of freedom (DF) and critical t constant (t_c) are for later use.

The data are shown on the graph to the right. The volume adsorbed approaches V_{max} asymptotically, corresponding to the surface being completely covered and unable to adsorb more.

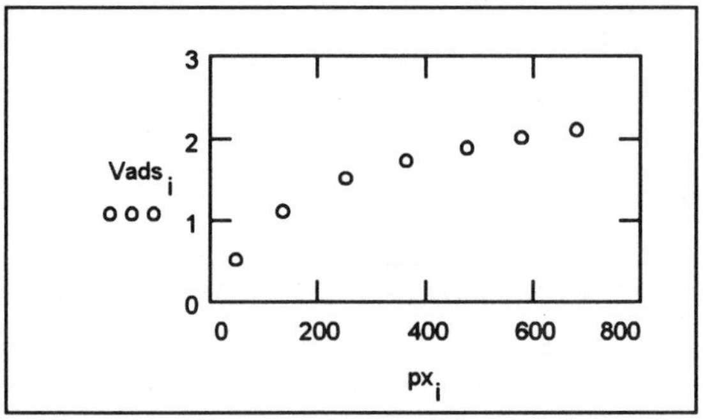

Data can be analyzed using Eq. (10.19) by nonlinear regression or by linearizing the equation and using linear regression. Nonlinear regression has be illustrated elsewhere; here we shall explore two methods for using linear regression on data of this sort.

Equation (10.19) can be rearranged as

$$\frac{1}{V_{ads}} = \frac{1}{V_{max}} + \frac{1}{bV_{max}} \frac{1}{P} \tag{10.20}$$

which is linear with variables $y = 1/V_{ads}$ vs. $x = 1/P$. With this method the parameters are calculated as

$$b = \text{intercept/slope}; \quad V_{max} = 1/\text{intercept}$$

The box below shows this calculation (denoting the intercept as *a* and the slope as *m*).

$$y_i := \frac{1}{Vads_i} \qquad x_i := \frac{1}{px_i} \qquad a := \text{intercept}(x, y) \qquad m := \text{slope}(x, y)$$

$$r := \text{corr}(x, y) \qquad b := \frac{a}{m} \qquad V_{max} := \frac{1}{a} \qquad 10^3 \cdot b = 5.246$$

$$r = 0.999982 \qquad y_{fit}(x) := a + m \cdot x \qquad V_{max} = 2.683$$

The linear graph, below, is a bit bothersome; most of the data, which were originally had near-equal spacing on *P*, is clumped to the left, and if the first point (the rightmost one, because we took reciprocals) were in error it could have an undue influence on the slope.

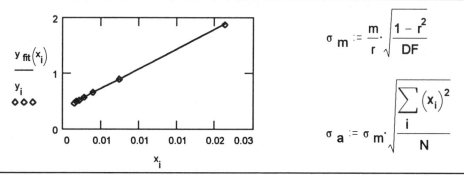

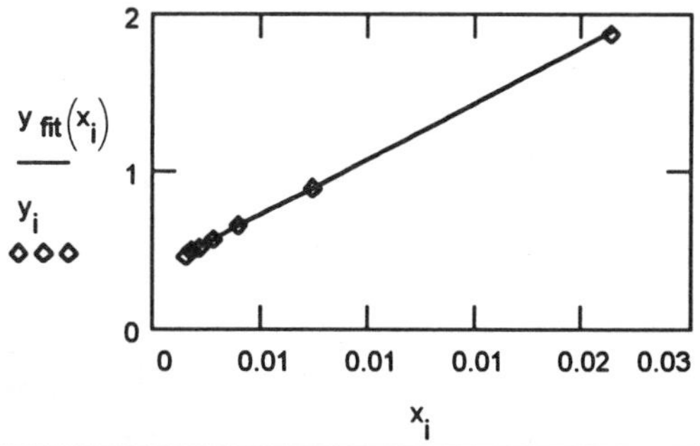

$$\sigma_m := \frac{m}{r} \cdot \sqrt{\frac{1 - r^2}{DF}}$$

$$\sigma_a := \sigma_m \cdot \sqrt{\frac{\sum_i (x_i)^2}{N}}$$

The box above also shows the calculation of the standard deviations for the slope (σ_m) and intercept (σ_a). But we want to know the error of the parameters which are calculated from the slope and intercept as described above. The box below demonstrates how the standard deviation of *b* and V_{max} (denoted σ_b and σ_V respectively) are calculated. (This topic, "propagation of error", is covered in most physical chemistry lab texts, and many analytical chemistry texts.)

$$\sigma_b := b \cdot \sqrt{\frac{\sigma_a^2}{a^2} + \frac{\sigma_m^2}{m^2}} \qquad \sigma_b = 2.71 \cdot 10^{-5} \qquad \sigma_V := \frac{\sigma_a}{a^2} \qquad \sigma_V = 0.012$$

$$\text{ans1} := \left(10^3 \cdot b \quad t_c \cdot \sigma_b \cdot 10^3 \quad V_{max} \quad t_c \cdot \sigma_V\right)$$

Results with 90% confidence limits:

$$\text{ans1} = (\,5.246 \quad 0.054 \quad 2.683 \quad 0.024\,)$$

The results are placed in a vector, **ans1**, for comparison to other methods described below.

Another way Eq. (10.19) can be arranged is

$$\frac{P}{V_{ads}} = \frac{1}{bV_{max}} + \frac{P}{V_{max}} \tag{10.21}$$

which is linear with $y = P/V_{ads}$ vs. $x = P$; the parameters in this case are:

$$b = \text{slope/intercept}; \quad V_{max} = 1/\text{slope}$$

This analysis is shown in the box below.

$$y_i := \frac{px_i}{Vads_i} \qquad x_i := px_i \qquad a := \text{intercept}(x, y) \qquad m := \text{slope}(x, y)$$

$$r := \text{corr}(x, y) \qquad b := \frac{m}{a} \qquad V_{max} := \frac{1}{m} \qquad 10^3 \cdot b = 5.098$$

$$r = 0.999873 \qquad y_{fit}(x) := a + m \cdot x \qquad V_{max} = 2.714$$

Note that r is not as good for this method as for the preceding one; this fact proves to be totally irrelevant as we shall shortly discover that the second method is the more reliable. This is another illustration of the fact that the correlation coefficient by itself is generally useless in judging the quality of a linear analysis. (It is useful, but only for calculating other quantities.)

The graph for this method, below, is more attractive and reassuring than that for the previous analysis, with the points evenly distributed along the x axis. (This, however, depends on how the original data were distributed and does not prove that the second method is generally superior.)

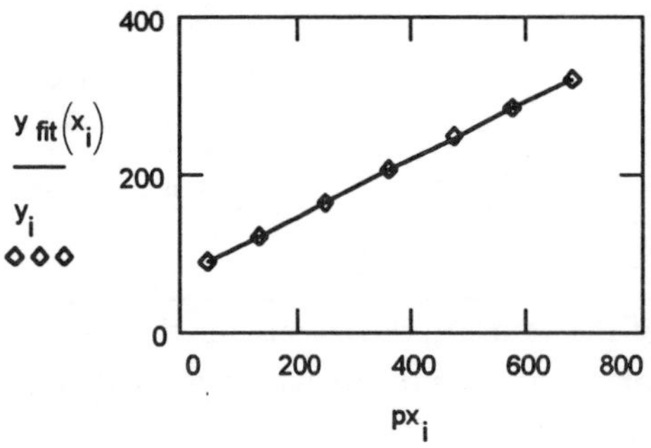

$$\sigma_m := \frac{m}{r} \cdot \sqrt{\frac{1 - r^2}{DF}}$$

$$\sigma_a := \sigma_m \cdot \sqrt{\frac{\sum_i (x_i)^2}{N}}$$

$$\sigma_V := \frac{\sigma_m}{m^2} \qquad \sigma_b := b \cdot \sqrt{\left(\frac{\sigma_a}{a}\right)^2 + \left(\frac{\sigma_m}{m}\right)^2}$$

$$ans2 := \left(10^3 \cdot b \quad t_c \cdot \sigma_b \cdot 10^3 \quad V_{max} \quad t_c \cdot \sigma_V\right)$$

Results with 90% confidence limits:

ans1 = (5.246 0.054 2.683 0.024)

ans2 = (5.098 0.173 2.714 0.039)

The error analysis (box above and to the left) is similar to the previous one, with the roles of slope and intercept being exchanged.

The results, summarized to the left, show that these methods give somewhat different answers; in particular, the value of b from the second method is outside the 90% confidence region of the first value. What is the problem?

The equations we have been using to calculate the parameters and their errors make certain assumptions about the data; in particular, the assume that the error is in the y variable and not in x, and that the error of y is uniform (independent of x). It is probable, in this case, that the error in V_{ads} is reasonably constant, but if this is true, it is certainly not true for the reciprocal of that quantity. That is, the errors of the data have been distorted by the transformations we made to linearize the equation. This problem can be avoided by either analyzing the original data without transformation (with nonlinear regression) or by using weighted linear regression (cf. Example 10.17).

The weights required are given in Table 10.3 for several common cases (see references[3] for further discussion and weights for other cases). The weights are appropriate if the errors are uniform in the original data. (Lineweaver-Burk and Hanes refer to the analysis of enzyme data, discussed in Section 10.5.)

Table 10.3 Weighting factors for common kinetic analyses.

Example	new y	new x	weight
1st order	$\ln C$	t	C^2
2nd order	$1/C$	t	C^4
Langmuir 1	$1/V_{ads}$	$1/P$	V_{ads}^4
Langmuir 2	P/V_{ads}	P	V_{ads}^4/P^2
Lineweaver-Burk	$1/v$	$1/S$	v^4
Hanes	S/v	S	v^4/S^2

Mathcad does not implement weighted linear regression, but it does have the tools required. If you are doing much of this type of analysis you can probably find a more convenient program to use, but for now we continue the analysis to illustrate what weighted linear regression is and how it affects the results.

Since your worksheet is now set up for method 2, we shall use it; however, with weighted regression both methods should give exactly the same answer. The calculations required are shown in the box below.

$$w_i := \frac{(Vads_i)^4}{(px_i)^2} \qquad Sw := \sum_i w_i \qquad Sx := \sum_i w_i \cdot x_i \qquad Sy := \sum_i w_i \cdot y_i$$

$$Sxy := \sum_i w_i \cdot x_i \cdot y_i \qquad Sxx := \sum_i w_i \cdot (x_i)^2 \qquad D := Sw \cdot Sxx - Sx^2$$

$$m := \frac{Sw \cdot Sxy - Sx \cdot Sy}{D} \qquad a := \frac{Sy \cdot Sxx - Sxy \cdot Sx}{D}$$

The results are summarized in the box to the right, with the weighted analysis in the vector **ans3**. (The errors for the weighted regression were calculated with another program and are included here only for comparison.) This box also includes the results of a nonlinear regression. (This analysis was done with another program; it is difficult to get error estimates with nonlinear regression, so these are given as zero in the answer vector only as placeholders.) You can see that the weighted and nonlinear results are virtually identical. Also, for these data at least, the second method of analysis is closer to the correct answer than the first (despite the fact that the first method gave smaller error limits). Which method gives the better answer depends on the distribution of the original data; the weighted method is always appropriate.

$$V_{max} := \frac{1}{m} \qquad b := \frac{m}{a}$$

$$ans3 := \begin{pmatrix} 10^3 \cdot b & 0.163 & V_{max} & 0.039 \end{pmatrix}$$

ans1 = (5.246 0.054 2.683 0.024)

ans2 = (5.098 0.173 2.714 0.039)

ans3 = (5.097 0.163 2.712 0.039)

ansNL = (5.096 0 2.712 0)

[3]Robert de Levie, *J. Chem. Ed.*, **63**, 10 (1986); D. E. Sands, *J. Chem. Ed.*, **51**, 473 (1974).

Example 10.13 Decomposition on a surface ⊕

The Langmuir model can be used to discuss reactions that occur on a surface. For a decomposition reaction

$$A \rightarrow B + C$$

we assume a mechanism where A is adsorbed on the surface, decomposes, and the products are subsequently desorbed. We expect the velocity of reaction to be proportional to the amount of A adsorbed; thus

$$v = k\, S_0\, \theta_A$$

where S_0 is the total surface area and θ_A is the fraction of that area occupied by A molecules. Using the Langmuir equation for the fraction adsorbed we get:

$$v = \frac{kS_0 b_A P_A}{1 + b_A P_A + b_B P_B + b_C P_C} \tag{10.22}$$

If only A is strongly adsorbed, this becomes:

$$v = \frac{kS_0 b_A P_A}{1 + b_A P_A} \tag{10.23}$$

Furthermore, at the beginning of the reaction, the second term of the denominator may dominate, giving a velocity $v = kS_0$ — a *zero-order* reaction. For a zero-order reaction, the velocity, $-dP_A/dt$ is a constant and P_A would vary linearly in time.

If you have the PLUS version of Mathcad, it is simple enough to solve Eq. (10.22); assuming a 1:1 stoichiometry as suggested above, $P_A = P_0 - x$, $P_B = x$ and $P_C = x$ where P_0 is the initial pressure (all A). The differential equation (using velocity $v = dx/dt$ in Eq. (10.22) is

$$\frac{dx}{dt} = \frac{kS_0 b_A (P_0 - x)}{1 + b_A (P_0 - x) + b_B x + b_C x}$$

It is solved as shown in the box below. The unknown x must be presented as a vector despite the fact that there is only one unknown; the symbol x_0 is implemented as "`x[0:0`"; all other subscripts in this box are labels, implemented as, for example "`b.A:20`" and "`P.0:100`". (Remember: do not type the quotes.)

$npts := 200 \qquad tmax := 15 \qquad kS := 10 \qquad P_0 := 100$

$b_A := 20 \qquad b_B := 1 \qquad b_C := 2 \qquad x_0 := 0$

$$D(t,x) := \frac{kS \cdot b_A \cdot (P_0 - x_0)}{1 + b_A \cdot (P_0 - x_0) + b_B \cdot x_0 + b_C \cdot x_0} \qquad ans := rkfixed(x, 0, tmax, npts, D)$$

With these constants, the reaction is effectively zero order for short times. This is demonstrated by the graph (box right) (we denote x as *xval* since the symbol x was used earlier). The ammonia line (solid line, decreasing) is nearly linear at first, are the products (solid line, increasing). The straight line (dashed) shows the course of a hypothetical zero-order reaction.

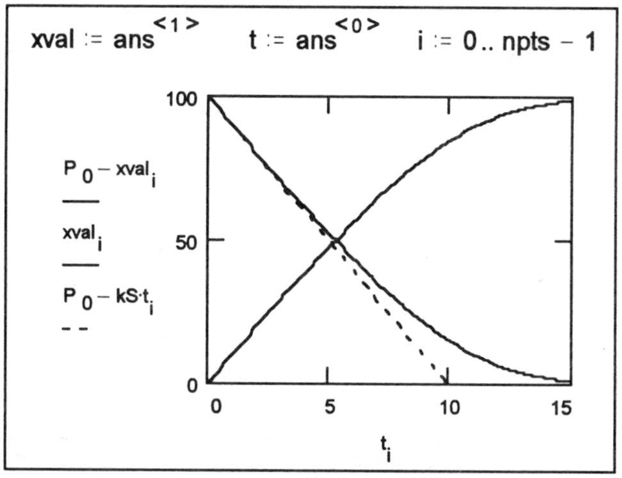

This is an excellent opportunity to explore: try a variety of constants, including cases for which one of the products is strongly adsorbed. If a product is strongly adsorbed, it inhibits the reaction by occupying surface area needed for the reaction to proceed. Can it stop the reaction completely before completion?

Example 10.14 Decomposition of ammonia on tungsten.

This example presents data for a surface decomposition for which the theory was discussed in the previous example. Table 10.4 gives data for the decomposition of ammonia on tungsten (W). The reaction is:

$$NH_3 \rightarrow {}^1/_2\, N_2 + {}^3/_2\, H_2$$

except for the stoichiometry, this is just like the hypothetical case discussed in the preceding example. Since the ammonia is strongly adsorbed compared to the hydrogen and nitrogen, we shall use Eq. (10.23) to analyze the data, and the stoichiometry will not matter.

Table 10.4 Decomposition of ammonia on tungsten.

t/sec	*P*/torr	*t*/sec	*P*/torr
0	200	800	292
100	214	1000	312
200	227	1200	332
300	238	1400	349
400	248.5	1800	378
500	259	2000	387
600	270		

The pressures in the table are total pressure:

$$P = P_A + P_B + P_C$$

(with A, B and C representing ammonia, nitrogen and hydrogen, respectively). Material balance gives $P_A = P_0 - x$, $P_B = x/2$ and $P_C = 3x/2$. Thus $P = P_0 + x$. With a little algebra, demonstrate that the pressure of the ammonia is $P_A = 2P_0 - P$.

Enter these data using any method you prefer; the example below assumes the data are in the matrix **M**. The ammonia pressure is calculated into the array **pA** using the first element of the pressure array (px_0) as the initial pressure. A graph of the pressure of the ammonia is nearly linear for early times, confirming our suggestion of strong reactant adsorption.

$tx := M^{<0>}$ $px := M^{<1>}$ $i := 0 .. last(px)$ $pA_i := 2 \cdot px_0 - px_i$

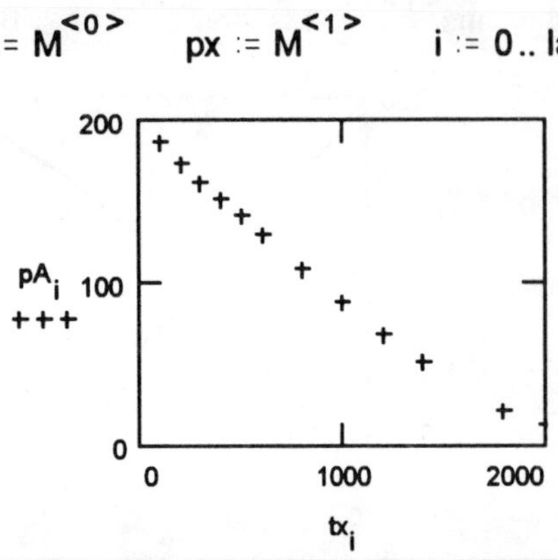

$j := 0 .. last(px) - 1$

$$vel_j := -\frac{pA_{j+1} - pA_j}{tx_{j+1} - tx_j}$$

$$pa_j := \frac{pA_{j+1} + pA_j}{2}$$

To analyze the data using Eq. (10.23) it is simplest to differentiate the data numerically; we use a simple 2-point method to calculate the velocity ($-dP_A/dt$, in vector **vel**); the vector **pa** represents the average pressure of ammonia for the intervals represented by **vel**.

Equation (10.23) has the form of the Langmuir isotherm, Eq. (10.19), and so can be made linear as P/v vs. P. This is done in the box below, where the slope and intercept are calculated.

$y_j := \frac{pa_j}{vel_j}$ $x_j := pa_j$ $a := intercept(x, y)$ $m := slope(x, y)$

$yfit(x) := a + m \cdot x$ $r := corr(x, y)$ $r = 0.968$

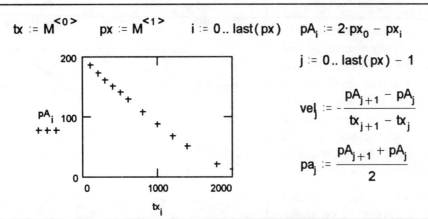

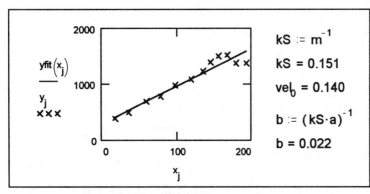

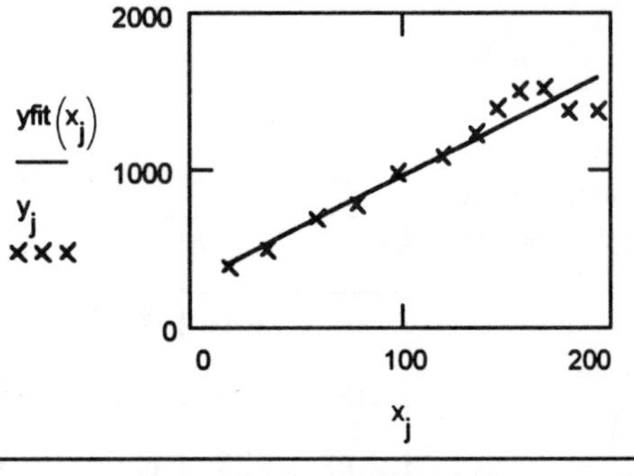

$kS := m^{-1}$

$kS = 0.151$

$vel_0 = 0.140$

$b := (kS \cdot a)^{-1}$

$b = 0.022$

The graph (box left) shows a pretty good fit — the latter points deviate quite a bit, but in a way that suggests that they would not influence the calculated slope enough to make it worthwhile eliminating them. The product of the rate constant times the surface area (kS_0, denoted kS in Mathcad) is the reciprocal of the slope; its value, 0.151, is fairly close to the more reliable value calculated with nonlinear regression, 0.148 (this was calculated with another program, so details are not given here). The box above also displays the initial velocity, vel_0, which, as demonstrated earlier, is approximately equal to kS_0 for the case of strong reactant adsorption; you can see that this approximation is quite good.

10.5 Enzyme Catalysis

The kinetics of reactions catalyzed by enzymes are usually interpreted in terms of the Michaelis-Menten mechanism; this mechanism gives the reaction velocity as a function of substrate concentration, [S] as

$$v = \frac{v_{max}[S]}{K_m + [S]} \tag{10.24}$$

where K_m is the Michaelis constant and v_{max} is the maximum velocity (at high substrate concentration). If you note the similarity of this equation to the Langmuir equation, (10.19), you will be able to anticipate the two methods we will use for linear analysis.

Example 10.15 Lineweaver-Burk analysis.

Taking the reciprocal of Eq. (10.24) gives

$$\frac{1}{v} = \frac{1}{v_{max}} + \frac{K_m}{v_{max}} \frac{1}{[S]} \tag{10.25}$$

Thus graphs of $1/v$ vs. $1/[S]$ (called Lineweaver-Burk plot) are linear. The slope and intercept of this graph yield:

$$v_{max} = 1/\text{intercept}; \quad K_m = \text{slope/intercept}$$

The box below gives data for reaction velocity (vector **vel**) vs. substrate concentration (**S**) for the formation of maltose from starch, catalyzed by the enzyme amylase.

$N := 9 \qquad DF := N - 2 \qquad i := 0..N-1$

$S_i :=$	$vel_i :=$
0.03	0.14
0.04	0.165
0.05	0.18
0.0863	0.26
0.129	0.305
0.216	0.345
0.431	0.400
0.647	0.435
1.078	0.445

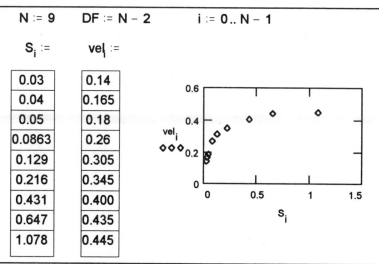

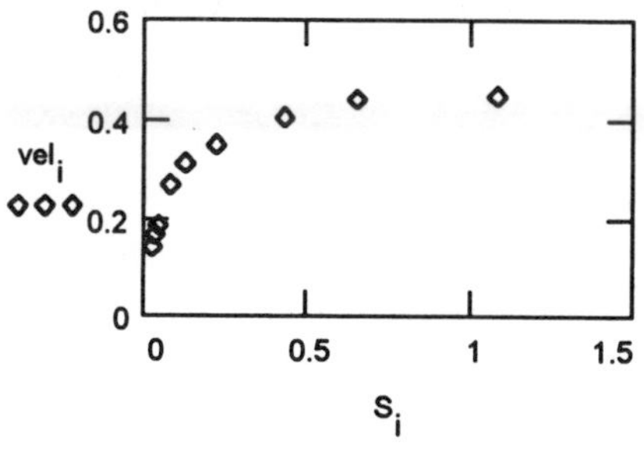

Forming the x and y variables from the reciprocals, the calculation of the linear parameters is as before —box below.

$x_i := \frac{1}{S_i} \qquad y_i := \frac{1}{vel_i} \qquad a := intercept(x, y) \qquad m := slope(x, y) \qquad r := corr(x, y)$

$y_{fit}(x) := a + m \cdot x \qquad a = 2.127 \qquad m = 0.156 \qquad r = 0.997181$

The graph (below) looks reasonably linear, but the grouping of a lot of points to the left, a symptom of double-reciprocal methods, is a bit worrisome. The box below also shows the calculation of the standard deviations of the slope and intercept: σ_m and σ_a.

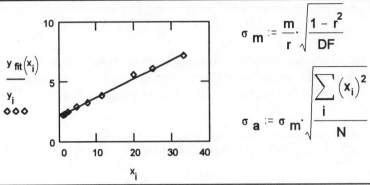

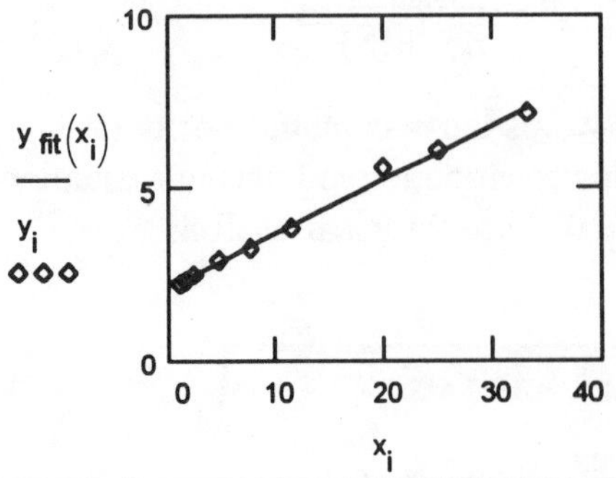

$$\sigma_m := \frac{m}{r} \cdot \sqrt{\frac{1 - r^2}{DF}}$$

$$\sigma_a := \sigma_m \cdot \sqrt{\frac{\sum_i (x_i)^2}{N}}$$

Calculation of the Michaelis constant and maximum velocity (denoted *vmax*) is simple, but calculating their errors is a bit more trouble. The calculation of error is analogous to method used for Langmuir adsorption above (page 225).

$$K_m := \frac{m}{a} \qquad \sigma_K := K_m \cdot \sqrt{\frac{\sigma_a^2}{a^2} + \frac{\sigma_m^2}{m^2}} \qquad vmax := \frac{1}{a} \qquad \sigma_{vx} := \frac{\sigma_a}{a^2}$$

$$K_m = 0.0732 \qquad \sigma_K = 0.0032 \qquad vmax = 0.47 \qquad \sigma_{vx} = 0.016$$

$$ans1 := (K_m \ \ \sigma_K \ \ vmax \ \ \sigma_{vx}) \cdot 1000$$

The answers are summarized in a vector **ans1** for comparison to other methods.

Save this worksheet — it is used for the next two examples.

Example 10.16 Hanes analysis.

Another method by which Eq. (10.24) can be linearized is called the Hanes plot:

$$\frac{[S]}{v} = \frac{K_m}{v_{max}} + \frac{[S]}{v_{max}} \tag{10.26}$$

In this case the parameters are calculated as:

$$v_{max} = 1/\text{slope}; \ K_m = \text{intercept/slope}$$

This differs from the Lineweaver-Burk method by a simple exchange of slope and intercept, so you might expect the result to be the same. Not so: both methods use nonlinear transformations that distort the experimental errors, and they rarely give the same answers. The methods are perfectly equivalent only for data containing no error. (The two methods do give the same answer when weighted regression is used — see Example 10.17, below.)

Continuing with the same worksheet as before, create the x and y variables as shown in the box below.

$x_i := S_i \qquad y_i := \dfrac{S_i}{vel_i}$ $\qquad a := \text{intercept}(x, y) \qquad m := \text{slope}(x, y) \qquad r := \text{corr}(x, y)$

$y_{fit}(x) := a + m \cdot x \qquad a = 0.16 \qquad m = 2.092 \qquad r = 0.999827$

The correlation coefficient for these data with this method is better than for Lineweaver-Burk, but this really doesn't tell us much. The graph is shown below.

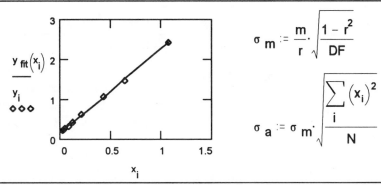

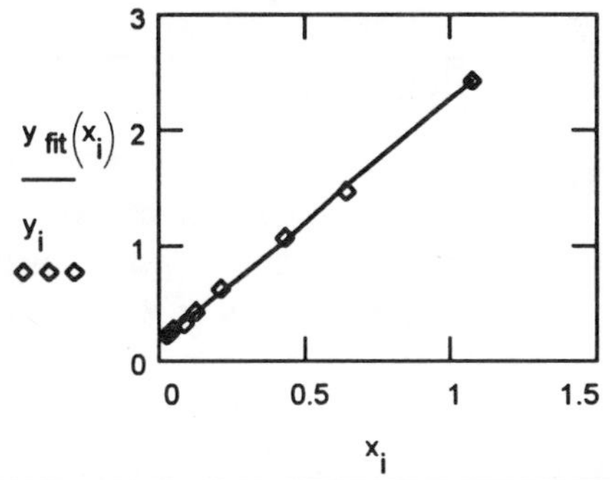

$$\sigma_m := \frac{m}{r} \cdot \sqrt{\frac{1 - r^2}{DF}}$$

$$\sigma_a := \sigma_m \cdot \sqrt{\frac{\sum_i (x_i)^2}{N}}$$

The error analysis is similar to the preceding one, but the roles of slope and intercept are reversed.

$K_m := \dfrac{a}{m} \qquad \sigma_K := K_m \cdot \sqrt{\left(\dfrac{\sigma_a}{a}\right)^2 + \left(\dfrac{\sigma_m}{m}\right)^2} \qquad vmax := \dfrac{1}{m} \qquad \sigma_{vx} := \dfrac{\sigma_m}{m^2}$

$K_m = 0.0765 \qquad \sigma_K = 0.0032 \qquad vmax = 0.478 \qquad \sigma_{vx} = 0.003$

$ans2 := (K_m \;\; \sigma_K \;\; vmax \;\; \sigma_{vx}) \cdot 1000$

The results for this analysis are summarized in the vector **ans2**; by displaying them you can compare. They are not greatly different, but it's not clear which is better.

Example 10.17 Weighted Linear regression.

If we can assume that the errors in the original data were uniformly distributed — that is, they have the same average size regardless of the [S] at which the measurement was made — then either nonlinear analysis, using Eq. (10.24) directly with no transformation of the data, or weighted linear regression should be used. Since nonlinear regression has been illustrated already in a number of examples, we shall analyze these data (from Examples 10.15 and 10.16) by weighted linear regression.

Unfortunately Mathcad in its current version does not implement weighted linear regression. However the tools needed for this method are present and with a bit of trouble we can enter the necessary equations.

With weighted linear regression, the Hanes and Lineweaver-Burk methods should give identical results; since the *x* and *y* variables in your current worksheet are set for the Hanes method, it is simplest to use it. The weights required are calculated as indicated in Table 10.3.

$$w_i := \frac{(vel_i)^4}{(s_i)^2} \qquad Sw := \sum_i w_i \qquad Sx := \sum_i w_i \cdot x_i \qquad Sy := \sum_i w_i \cdot y_i$$

$$Sxy := \sum_i w_i \cdot x_i \cdot y_i \qquad Sxx := \sum_i w_i \cdot (x_i)^2 \qquad D := Sw \cdot Sxx - Sx^2$$

$$m := \frac{Sw \cdot Sxy - Sx \cdot Sy}{D} \qquad a := \frac{Sy \cdot Sxx - Sxy \cdot Sx}{D} \qquad vmax := \frac{1}{m} \qquad K_m := \frac{a}{m}$$

Because of the complications involved, the error analysis is omitted.

$10^3 \cdot K_m = 75.618 \qquad 10^3 \cdot vmax = 477.127$

ans1 = (73.248 3.232 470.144 15.86)

ans2 = (76.465 3.23 478.051 3.365)

The results for weighted linear regression are displayed in the box to the left together with the earlier results. In this case the correct answer (the weighted method) are closest to the Hanes method, but such is not always the case (it depends on how the original data were distributed). Try weighted regression using the Lineweaver-Burk method; it should give exactly the same results.

For serious work, weighted linear regression is mandatory for such data analyses; however if you did this very often you would certainly want a program that made it easier than does Mathcad.

Problems

10.1 The decomposition of oxalic acid in concentrated sulfuric acid was studied by titration with potassium permanganate. The table gives volume of titrant required vs. time. Assume first-order kinetics to determine the rate constant for this reaction. Give the error limits for 90% confidence, and make a graph of the data and fitted line.

Oxalic acid decomposition		2nd-order kinetics		Inversion of sucrose		Hydrolysis of methyl acetate	
t/min	*C*	*t*/s	*C*	*t*/hr	α	*t*/min	*x*
0	11.45	1	2.341	0	78.0	200	0.08455
120	9.63	2	1.85	2	71.0	280	0.1171
240	8.11	3	1.548	4	65.1	445	0.1727
420	6.22	4	1.305	12	44.6	620	0.2311
600	4.79	5	1.143	18	32.40	1515	0.4299
900	2.97	6	1.036	24	22.45	1705	0.4588
1440	1.44	7	0.893	42	2.30		
		8	0.823	48	-1.96		
		9	0.775	61	-9.0		
		10	0.712	86	-15.8		
				95	-17.25		

10.2 Use data for "2nd order" (table above) (concentration (mmol/liter) vs. time) to determine the rate constant and its 90% confidence limits. Make graphs showing the linear fit and concentration as a function of time — fitted and experimental.

10.3 Use data from the table above for the inversion of sucrose (optical rotation, α, vs. time) to determine the rate constant. Use nonlinear regression with the initial and infinite-time optical rotation as undetermined constants.

10.4 Use data from the table above for the hydrolysis of methyl acetate in water (extent of reaction vs. time)

$$CH_3COOCH_3(aq) + H_2O(liq) \rightarrow CH_3COOH(aq) + CH_3OH(aq)$$

to determine the rate constant. Since the water concentration does not change significantly in the course of the reaction, you can assume that this is a pseudo-first-order reaction. The initial concentration of ester was 0.7013 mol/liter, and x is moles per liter reacted.

10.5 Use data from the table for the adsorption of a gas (volume adsorbed vs. pressure) to determine the Langmuir constants.

10.6 Use data from the table for the velocity of an enzyme-catalyzed reaction vs. substrate concentration to determine the maximum velocity and Michaelis constant using nonlinear regression.

Langmuir adsorption *P* in torr, *V* in mL		Enzyme catalysis *v* in mmol/liter/s *S* in mmol/liter	
P	*V*	*S*	*v*
1	4.12	0.25	0.035
10	26.40	0.5	0.065
25	41.18	1	0.109
50	50.68	2	0.151
75	54.75	3	0.173
100	57.13	4	0.189

10.7 ⊕ For the reversible reaction

$$A + B \underset{2}{\overset{1}{\leftrightarrow}} C$$

solve the differential equations for arbitrary starting concentrations of all species. Show numerically the relationship between the rate constants and the equilibrium constant.

10.8 ⊕ Many reactions of the type 2A + B = products are 3rd order. The proposed mechanism is:

$$A + B \underset{2}{\overset{1}{\leftrightarrow}} C; \quad A + C \overset{3}{\rightarrow} P$$

Solve the differential equations for this system. Find sets of rate constants for which this mechanism is apparently 3rd order or apparently 2nd order. (Demonstrate the order's validity with appropriate "linear" plots; the function *corr* will quantitatively assess the linearity of a set of points.)

10.9 ⊕ For the mechanism

$$A + B \underset{2}{\overset{1}{\leftrightarrow}} C \overset{3}{\rightarrow} P$$

(example 10.8), find sets of constants giving k_e = 1 (or as assigned by your instructor), looking for cases for which steady-state does and does not work. Try to find a simple operational criterion for the validity of the steady state approximation.

Answers

10.1 $k = (1.45 \pm 0.03) \times 10^{-3}\ \text{min}^{-1}$

10.2 $k = (0.109 \pm 0.003)$ (liter/mmol) s^{-1}

10.3 $\alpha_0 = 77.81$, $\alpha_\infty = -21.11$, $k = 3.422 \times 10^{-2}\ \text{hr}^{-1}$

10.4 $k = (6.20 \pm 0.07) \times 10^{-4}\ \text{min}^{-1}$ (90% confidence)

10.5 $V_{max} = 65.64$ $\sigma = 0.05$ (mL), $b = 6.73 \times 10^{-2}$ $\sigma = 0.02 \times 10^{-2}$ (torr^{-1}) (for P/V vs. P)

10.6 v_{max} = 0.258 mmol/liter/sec, K_m = 1.439 mmol/liter.

CHAPTER 11

QUANTUM THEORY

11.1 Bohr Theory

Although based on an incorrect model, the Bohr theory does give the correct formula for the energy of a one-electron atom or ion, and we can use this result to compare to experiment and introduce some basic concepts.

The energy of a state characterized by a quantum number N is

$$E_n = -\frac{Z^2}{N^2}\frac{e^4 m_e}{2\hbar^2(4\pi\varepsilon_0)^2} \tag{11.1}$$

with $N = 1, 2, 3, \ldots$ (positive integers up to infinity). The constants in this formula are used to define other quantities including the Bohr radius (a_0) and the atomic unit of energy (hartree), E_{h} so:

$$E_n = -\frac{Z^2}{N^2}\frac{E_{\mathrm{h}}}{2}; \quad a_0 = 4\pi\varepsilon_0\frac{\hbar^2}{m_e e^2}; \quad E_{\mathrm{h}} = \frac{\hbar^2}{m_e a_0^2}$$

Example 11.1 Constants and sample calculations.

For these calculations, and others to come, we need a lot of constants that are a nuisance to enter. For that reason, create a special document containing them (*qconst.mcd*), which can be inserted as needed into other work sheets. Since there are many small numbers involved, you will first want to change the zero tolerance (Math-menu, Numerical Format) to its maximum value. If you have not done so already, make this the default by saving the configuration (File-menu, Save Configuration). Then carefully enter the constants below.

$$L := 6.0221367 \cdot 10^{23} \qquad e := 1.60217733 \cdot 10^{-19} \cdot coul$$

$$a_0 := 5.2917725 \cdot 10^{-11} \cdot m \qquad m_e := 9.1093897 \cdot 10^{-31} \cdot kg$$

$$k_b := 1.380658 \cdot 10^{-23} \cdot \frac{joule}{K} \qquad E_h := 4.3597482 \cdot 10^{-18} \cdot joule$$

$$c := 2.99792458 \cdot 10^{8} \cdot \frac{m}{sec} \qquad \varepsilon_0 := 8.8541878 \cdot 10^{-12} \cdot \frac{coul^2}{joule \cdot m}$$

$$h := 6.6260755 \cdot 10^{-34} \cdot joule \cdot sec \qquad hbar := \frac{h}{2 \cdot \pi} \qquad m_p := 1.672623 \cdot 10^{-27} \cdot kg$$

As a check (of your typing, as well as the accuracy of the constants involved), enter the formulas for E_h and a_0.

$$4 \cdot \pi \cdot \varepsilon_0 \cdot \frac{hbar^2}{m_e \cdot e^2} = 1.00000001 \cdot a_0 \qquad \frac{hbar^2}{m_e \cdot a_0^2} = 1.00000001 \cdot E_h$$

After typing the left-hand sides of these equations, enter a_0 or E_h in the unit place holder. In effect, these are the units for length (called the bohr) and energy (called the hartree). Increase the displayed precision to 8 to see how accurate the constants are.

$$eV := e \cdot volt$$

$$E_h = 27.2114 \cdot eV$$

We have seen how fundamental constants can be used to define units. Another useful unit of energy is the electron volt (eV) — the energy required to move an electron charge (e) through a potential of 1 volt. This is defined as in the box to the left, and, with it, the unit conversion, hartree = 27.2114 eV is easily calculated. Several other units will be useful (box below); enter these and then save the worksheet (you can delete the sample calculations).

$$\mu m := 10^{-6} \cdot m \qquad nm := 10^{-9} \cdot m \qquad pm := 10^{-12} \cdot m$$

Save this file; it will be inserted at the beginning of most worksheets of this and subsequent chapters. As an alternative to inserting the file, you can *include* it in a worksheet. To do this, start a new worksheet, and also open the file to be included (*qconst.mcd*, in this case). Then (while the new file is active) select Edit-menu, Include. A box will appear with all other open files shown. Select the one you want. Now your new worksheet looks like this:

Include:C:\MCAD6\BOOK\QCONST.MCD

$$m_e \cdot c^2 = 5.11 \cdot 10^5 \cdot eV$$

The calculation above is only to show that the current worksheet knows values for the constants in *qconst.mcd*. (The path for *qconst.mcd* will, of course, be different on your machine.) You can now close *qconst.mcd*. You can use the new file in the future without opening *qconst.mcd* or repeating this procedure (so long as the included file remains in the same directory).

Example 11.2 Ionization potential.

For comparison to experiment, we use the energy required to ionize the atom; i.e. the energy of the process $H \rightarrow H^+ + e$, or $He^+ \rightarrow He^{2+} + e$, and so forth. This is called the *ionization energy* (IE) or *ionization potential* (IP), the latter because the measured unit of energy is typically the electron volt.

The energy required to remove an electron is the energy to raise the quantum number N of Eq. (11.1) from 1 to infinity:

$$\text{IE} = E_\infty - E_1 = -E_1$$

The calculation follows for the hydrogen atom ($Z = 1$). (The simple formula, IE = $E_h/2$ is not used because we will need the full formula of Eq. (11.1) shortly.)

$$Z := 1 \qquad E(N) := \frac{-Z^2}{N^2} \cdot \frac{m_e \cdot e^4}{2 \cdot \text{hbar}^2 \cdot (4 \cdot \pi \cdot \varepsilon_0)^2} \qquad -E(1) = 13.606 \cdot \text{eV}$$

$obs = 13.5983$ eV

While the accuracy is not bad, it is clearly less accurate than the constants involved. The problem is the use of the electron mass in Eq. (11.1), which implies that the electron is orbiting about a nucleus in a fixed position. Actually they are both rotating about their center of mass. This problem is easily fixed by editing the expression above, changing m_e to the reduced mass (μ).

$$\mu := \frac{m_e \cdot m_p}{m_e + m_p} \qquad E(N) := \frac{-Z^2}{N^2} \cdot \frac{\mu \cdot e^4}{2 \cdot \text{hbar}^2 \cdot (4 \cdot \pi \cdot \varepsilon_0)^2} \qquad -E(1) = 13.5983 \cdot \text{eV}$$

Now the value is correct. Regardless of this, the fundamental constants such as the hartree (E_h) are defined from Eq. (11.1), which is for a hypothetical ion with infinite nuclear mass, and not a directly measured quantity.

Example 11.3 The Rydberg series.

Another experimental phenomenon that can be used to test the Bohr theory is the absorption and emission of light. Rydberg noted that the emitted light from the hydrogen atom (helium ion, etc.) fell into series that the wavelengths (λ), actually, their reciprocals $\tilde{\nu} = 1/\lambda$ (the wave-number frequency) could be fit by the empirical formula

$$\tilde{\nu} = \frac{1}{\lambda} = Z^2 \Re \left[\frac{1}{N_1^2} - \frac{1}{N_2^2} \right] \tag{11.2}$$

where N_1 is an integer characteristic of the series and $N_2 = N_1 + 1, N_1 + 2, \ldots$ to infinity. The constant $\Re$ is called the *Rydberg constant*. The series are the Lyman series ($N_1 = 1$, in the infrared), the Balmer series ($N_1 = 2$, in the visible region of the spectrum), the Paschen ($N_1 = 3$), Brackett ($N_1 = 4$) and Pfund ($N_1 = 5$) series, all in the ultraviolet. Bohr realized that these discrete absorptions were a result of the atom's changing between the energy levels of Eq. (11.1), with frequency:

$$\Delta E = h\nu = hc\tilde{\nu} = \frac{hc}{\lambda}$$

The first line of the Balmer series is (using the correct $E(N)$ above, that is, the one with the reduced mass):

$nu := \frac{E(3) - E(2)}{h \cdot c}$ $\quad nu = 15232.997 \cdot cm^{-1}$ $\quad$ *visible* 13333-25000 cm^{-1}

$\lambda := \frac{1}{nu}$ $\quad \lambda = 656.47 \cdot nm$ $\quad$ *visible* 400-750 nm

The series of lines can be calculated using range variables as shown in the box to the right. Note that the lines are converging to a limit ($N_2 = \infty$). How many are in the visible region? Are there any lines from the other series in the visible?

$lambda(N) := \frac{h \cdot c}{E(N) - E(2)}$ $\quad i := 3..12 \quad j := 13..20$

lambda(i) nm
656.47
486.274
434.173
410.294
397.124
389.019
383.651
379.901
377.174
375.125

lambda(j) nm
373.547
372.303
371.306
370.494
369.824
369.264
368.792
368.389

Combining Eq. (11.2) with Eq. (11.1) will demonstrate that the Rydberg constant should be just $E_h/(2hc)$:

$\frac{E_h}{2 \cdot h \cdot c} = 109737.315 \cdot cm^{-1}$

observed = 109677.581 cm^{-1}

Once again the accuracy is good, but not as good as it should be. (Many references list the Rydberg constant as 109737 cm^{-1}, in effect the limit for infinite mass.) If we use the correct formula for the energy (i.e. using reduced mass), we get the correct answer (box below).

$Ry := \frac{\mu \cdot e^4}{2 \cdot hbar^2 \cdot (4 \cdot \pi \cdot \varepsilon_0)^2} \cdot \frac{1}{h \cdot c}$

$Ry = 109677.581 \cdot cm^{-1}$

Doing other ions requires knowing the mass of the nucleus. This can be obtained from the isotopic mass (do not use the atomic weight, which is an average of the various isotopes), subtracting the mass of the electrons. For He, the mass of the nucleus (the α particle) is well known. Let's compare the calculated mass and the literature value for the mass of the alpha particle.

$Z := 2$ $\quad m_{He} := \frac{4.00260324gm}{L} - 2 \cdot m_e$ $\quad m_{alpha} := 4.001506170\frac{gm}{L}$

$\mu := \frac{m_e \cdot m_{He}}{m_e + m_{He}}$ $\quad R := \frac{\mu \cdot e^4}{2 \cdot hbar^2 \cdot (4 \cdot \pi \cdot \varepsilon_0)^2} \cdot \frac{1}{h \cdot c}$ $\quad R = 109722.271 \cdot cm^{-1}$

obs 109722.263

$\mu := \frac{m_e \cdot m_{alpha}}{m_e + m_{alpha}}$ $\quad R := \frac{\mu \cdot e^4}{2 \cdot hbar^2 \cdot (4 \cdot \pi \cdot \varepsilon_0)^2} \cdot \frac{1}{h \cdot c}$ $\quad R = 109722.271 \cdot cm^{-1}$

Although the results are the same to experimental error, the masses are not exactly the same.

$m_{He} = 6.64466165 \cdot 10^{-27} \cdot kg$ $\qquad$ $m_{alpha} = 6.64466180 \cdot 10^{-27} \cdot kg$

One possible source of this difference is the energy mass (Einstein's $E = mc^2$) — the mass equivalence of the energy required to remove the two electrons from a helium atom. The calculation to the right shows that this difference is largely accounted for by this phenomenon. However, for calculating the Rydberg constant, the difference is insignificant.

$ip1 := 24.46 \cdot eV \qquad ip2 := 54.41 \cdot eV$

$ip1 + ip2 = 78.87 \cdot eV$

$(m_{alpha} - m_{He}) \cdot c^2 = 83.649 \cdot eV$

$$\mu := \frac{m_e \cdot m_{alpha}}{m_e + m_{alpha}} \qquad Z := 2$$

$$\frac{Z^2 \cdot \mu \cdot e^4}{2 \cdot hbar^2 \cdot (4 \cdot \pi \cdot \varepsilon_0)^2} = 54.4153 \cdot eV$$

obs 54.41 eV

Only a little more is required to calculate the 2nd ionization potential for helium (i.e. the energy for $He^+ \rightarrow He^{2+} + e$, the formula does not apply to 2-electron atoms, and so cannot be used to calculate the first ionization potential). The result is shown in the box to the left.

11.2 Particle in a Box

The formulas for the particle in a box are given in most texts and will be repeated here only as part of the Mathcad work.

Example 11.4 Wave functions and probability.

The probability in quantum mechanics is given by $\psi\psi^*$ which, in the case (like the present one) where the wave function is real, by ψ^2. Calculate the probability that the particle is in the middle third of the box. Below we define the wave function (for unit length, which does not effect the results). The first integral demonstrates that the wave function as entered is normalized.

$$len := 1 \qquad n := 1 \qquad psi(n,x) := \sqrt{\frac{2}{len}} \cdot \sin\left(\frac{n \cdot \pi \cdot x}{len}\right) \qquad x1 := \frac{1}{3} \qquad x2 := \frac{2}{3}$$

$$\int_0^1 psi(n,x)^2 \, dx = 1 \qquad \int_{x1}^{x2} psi(n,x)^2 \, dx = 0.609$$

The second integral shows that the particle has a 60.9% probability of being in the center third; the classical expectation is 1/3. Try this for other values of *n*. Keep an eye on what you are doing by showing the graph (below).

x := 0, 0.001 .. 1

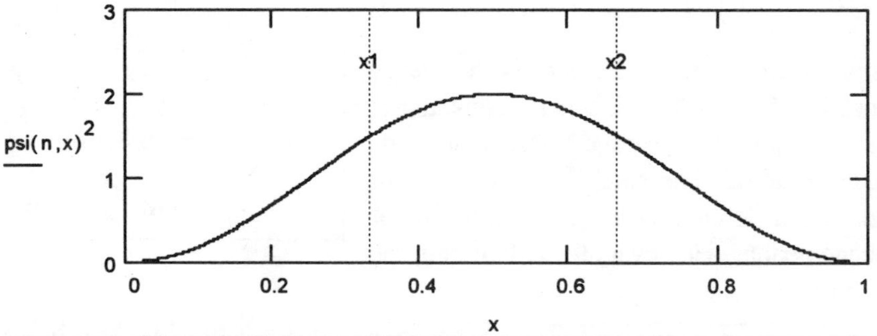

You will note that when $n = 3$ (or any multiple of 3) the result is exactly 1/3; this is a result of symmetry. More significant, as n gets larger all states approach the classical limit: 1/3. To plot the higher values you may need to reduce the step size (0.001, above).

Example 11.5 Is translational motion quantized?

For discussion of the classical limits, it is better to use the more realistic 3-dimensional, cubic box. In 3 dimensions, the particle in a box obeys the Bohr correspondence principle (quantum mechanics approaches classical mechanics in the limit of large quantum numbers), whereas the 1-dimensional box does not.

First, let's examine a macroscopic situation: a 1-gram mass in a 1 cm^3 box.

$len := 1 \cdot cm \qquad mass := 1 \cdot gm \qquad box := \dfrac{h^2}{8 \cdot mass \cdot len^2}$

$E(n_1, n_2, n_3) := (n_1^2 + n_2^2 + n_3^2) \cdot box$

The spacing between the first two levels is very small.

$space := E(2,1,1) - E(1,1,1) \qquad space \cdot L = 9.915 \cdot 10^{-37} \cdot \dfrac{joule}{mole}$

One of the peculiarities of the quantum particle is that it cannot have zero energy: it cannot be stationary. But we know that objects apparently sit still for length periods. The box to the right illustrates the calculation of the minimum velocity. Since atomic sizes are ~ 100 nm, the calculation means it would take millions of millennia for the mass to move the width of an atom.

$E_{min} := E(1,1,1)$

$v_{min} := \sqrt{\dfrac{2 \cdot E_{min}}{mass}}$

$v_{min} = 1.811 \cdot 10^{-6} \cdot \dfrac{pm}{1000 \cdot yr}$

More realistically, can be assume that atoms and molecules in gases obey classical mechanics? This, implicitly, the basic assumption of kinetic theory (Chapter 1), so we are testing the validity of that theory.

Consider a helium atom is a 1-mm cube box at 4.2 K. Its average energy is 1.5 k_bT, so this must equal the particle-in-a-box energy:

$$(n_x^2 + n_y^2 + n_z^2)\, box = \tfrac{3}{2} k_b T$$

where *box* is the collection of constants shown below. On the average, the three quantum numbers will be the same, which leads to the calculation below:

$$\mathrm{mass} := \frac{4\cdot \mathrm{gm}}{L} \qquad \mathrm{len} := 1\cdot \mathrm{mm} \qquad \mathrm{box} := \frac{h^2}{8\cdot \mathrm{mass}\cdot \mathrm{len}^2} \qquad T := 4.2\cdot K$$

$$n_{ave} := \sqrt{\frac{1.5\cdot k_b\cdot T}{3\cdot \mathrm{box}}} \qquad n_{ave} = 1.873\cdot 10^6$$

This is a very large number, suggesting that the classical limit is valid.

$$E_{min} := 3\cdot \mathrm{box}$$

$$v_{min} := \sqrt{\frac{2\cdot E_{min}}{\mathrm{mass}}}$$

$$v_{min} = 5.184\cdot \frac{\mathrm{mm}}{\mathrm{min}}$$

Another approach to this problem is to consider the minimum speed of a helium atom. The calculation (box to left) shows it to be a snail-like pace, but the more relevant comparison here is with the average velocity (below).

$$R := 8.31451\cdot \frac{\mathrm{joule}}{K\cdot \mathrm{mole}} \qquad \mathrm{mw} := 4\cdot \frac{\mathrm{gm}}{\mathrm{mole}}$$

$$v_{ave} := \sqrt{\frac{8\cdot R\cdot T}{\pi\cdot \mathrm{mw}}} \qquad v_{min} = 8.639\cdot 10^{-5}\cdot \mathrm{m}\cdot \mathrm{sec}^{-1} \qquad v_{ave} = 149.102\cdot \mathrm{m}\cdot \mathrm{sec}^{-1}$$

The smallness of the minimum velocity tells us that what we did in Chapter 1, extend the Maxwell-Boltzmann distribution to zero speed, is reasonable. Also since the difference in speeds is of the same magnitude, the assumption that speed is a continuous variable is also valid. This is a worst case: a very light molecule, at low temperature, in a small container. For all practical purposes, molecular translation can be considered to be classical: that is, velocity is a continuous variable ranging from 0 to infinity.

Example 11.6 The blue electron.

When lithium reacts with liquid ammonia a deep blue color is observed (the Birch reduction). The color appears to be due to the absorption of light by solvated electrons. We will test this idea to see if an electron, confined to a "molecule size" hole, would absorb light in this region. We use the particle in a box as the model. A blue solution absorbs red light, which we take to have a wavelength of 700 nm.

We begin with the box formula for an electron mass, with the length of side (*len,* for a cube) undefined.

$$\mathrm{mass} := m_e \qquad E(\mathrm{len}, n_1, n_2, n_3) := \left(n_1^2 + n_2^2 + n_3^2\right)\cdot \frac{h^2}{8\cdot \mathrm{mass}\cdot \mathrm{len}^2}$$

Next we calculate the energy of the photon, and define a formula for the difference between the energies of the two lowest levels as a function of the length.

$$\lambda := 700\cdot \mathrm{nm} \qquad E_{photon} := \frac{h\cdot c}{\lambda} \qquad \Delta E(\mathrm{len}) := E(\mathrm{len},2,1,1) - E(\mathrm{len},1,1,1)$$

The solution is shown in the box to the right. We need to give an estimate for *len*, but, within reason, this should not effect the answer. The calculated value is certainly reasonable.

The requirement of a cubic box, when we are dealing with the interstitial space of a solution, may seem too restrictive, but if we interpret *len* as the cube-root of the volume, the method may not be too far from wrong so long as the volume is unconstricted (e.g. as for a sphere).

$len := 1 \cdot nm$

Given

$\Delta E(len) = E_{photon}$

$len := Find(len)$

$len = 0.798 \cdot nm$

11.3 Harmonic Oscillator

The harmonic oscillator model, effectively a spring obeying Hookes' law, is widely used in science. In chemistry its most common application is to molecular vibration. The energy of a harmonic oscillator is quantized with

$$E_n = (n + \tfrac{1}{2})h\nu_0\,; \quad \nu_0 = \frac{1}{2\pi}\sqrt{\frac{k}{\mu}} \tag{11.3}$$

where k is the force constant and μ is the reduced mass (in the case of a diatomic oscillator). The collection of constants called ν_0 is the same as the classical frequency of oscillation, and is often interpreted as such.

Example 11.7 How fast do molecules vibrate? How stiff is a chemical bond?

The vibrational constant ν_0 is more commonly found in wavenumber units and called ω_e; these are simply related as $\nu_0 = c\,\omega_e$, where c is the speed of light. The calculation is shown for nitrogen (N_2) in the box to the right. The reciprocal of the frequency is the period of the oscillation; for this molecule the period is 14 femtoseconds — very short. While there is a lot of variation among molecules, the general conclusion that molecular vibration is very rapid is correct. Try some others (data, for example, Noggle Table 13.1).

$\omega_e := 2360 \cdot cm^{-1}$ *Nitrogen:* N_2

$\nu_0 := c \cdot \omega_e$ $\nu_0 = 7.075 \cdot 10^{13} \cdot sec^{-1}$

$fs := 10^{-15} \cdot sec$ *femtosecond* $\frac{1}{\nu_0} = 14.134 \cdot fs$

The nuclear mass is used to calculate the reduced mass as shown below, and this in turn is used to calculate the force constant (k) of the bond. Note that the reduced mass is for one molecule, so using (as we have) 14 gm/mole, it is necessary to divide by Avogadro's number (L). To get an expression for k, the definition of ν_0 of Eq. (11.3) is entered (using ctrl+=) as shown below. Then, placing the cursor on k, use Symbolic Solve. This gives an expression for k that can be cut and pasted into a definition (below).

$$\nu_0 = \frac{1}{2\cdot\pi}\cdot\sqrt{\frac{k}{\mu}}$$

use Symbolic Solve to solve for k, giving $4\cdot\mu\cdot\nu_0^{\,2}\cdot\pi^2$

$$\mu := \frac{14\cdot 14}{14+14}\cdot\frac{gm}{L}$$

$\mu = 1.162\cdot 10^{-26}\ \cdot kg$

$k := 4\cdot\mu\cdot\nu_0^{\,2}\cdot\pi^2$

$k = 2.297\cdot 10^{3}\ \cdot kg\cdot sec^{-2}$

$g = 9.807\cdot m\cdot sec^{-2}$	
$force := 1\cdot lb\cdot g$	$force = 4.448\cdot newton$
$x := \frac{force}{k}$	$x = 1.9365\cdot mm$
$force := 1\cdot kg\cdot g$	$force = 9.807\cdot newton$
$x := \frac{force}{k}$	$x = 4.2692\cdot mm$

To assess the stiffness of the bond, consider a spring with the same force constant. From this spring we hang a mass, which exerts a force *mg* (*g*, the acceleration of gravity, is displayed in box to left); the spring stretches until the restoring force equals the force of gravitation. The box to left shows this calculation for masses of 1 lb and 1 kg. The extension of a few millimeters suggests a fairly stiff spring.

Example 11.8 Wave functions; the classical turning point.

The wave functions of the harmonic oscillator are:

$$\psi_n = A_n H_n(y)\exp(-y^2/2) \tag{11.4}$$

where H_n is the Hermite polynomial of order n and $y = x/\alpha$ with

$$\alpha = \left(\frac{\hbar^2}{k\mu}\right)^{1/4} \tag{11.5}$$

The variable $x = R - R_e$, where R is the length of the spring (or bond) and R_e is the length at equilibrium (that is, when there is no force). α is a convenient measure of length when considering vibrations, so we first calculate it for the example of nitrogen. (Continue with the same worksheet as for the preceding example).

$\alpha := \left(\frac{hbar^2}{k\cdot\mu}\right)^{\frac{1}{4}}$	$\alpha = 4.518\cdot pm$	
$R_e := 1.094\cdot 10^{-8}\cdot cm$	$R_e = 109.4\cdot pm$	$R_e = 24.216\cdot\alpha$

The box to the right shows the calculation of α for nitrogen. The value, 4.5 pm (picometer = 10^{-12} m must be defined earlier), is small by atomic dimensions. The bond length if this molecule is over 100 pm, or about 24 times α. As we shall see in the examples to follow, this means that the vibration of a bond in, at least, the lower vibrational state (small *n*) changes the bond length by only a small fraction.

To enter formulas for the wave functions you need a table of Hermite polynomials. The are found in many references including Noggle, Table 11.2. The box below shows the first 5 harmonic oscillator wave functions.

$$\psi_0(y) := \exp\left(-\frac{y^2}{2}\right) \qquad \psi_1(y) := (2\cdot y)\cdot\exp\left(-\frac{y^2}{2}\right) \qquad \psi_2(y) := \left(4\cdot y^2 - 2\right)\cdot\exp\left(-\frac{y^2}{2}\right)$$

$$\psi_3(y) := \left(8\cdot y^3 - 12\cdot y\right)\cdot\exp\left(-\frac{y^2}{2}\right) \qquad \psi_4(y) := \left(16\cdot y^4 - 48\cdot y^2 + 12\right)\cdot\exp\left(-\frac{y^2}{2}\right)$$

(These functions are not normalized.) The graphs of these functions are shown below. The scale used for these plots corresponds to changing the bond length by $\pm 5\alpha$ or about 20%.

$$y := -5, -4.99 .. 5 \qquad 5\cdot\alpha = 22.588\cdot pm \qquad \frac{5\cdot\alpha}{(R_e)} = 20.647\cdot\%$$

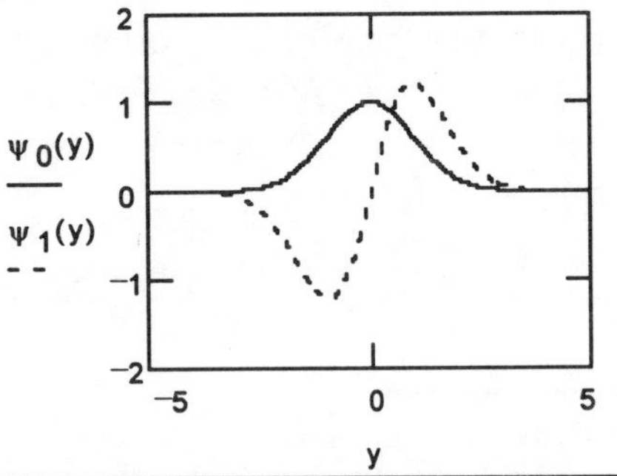

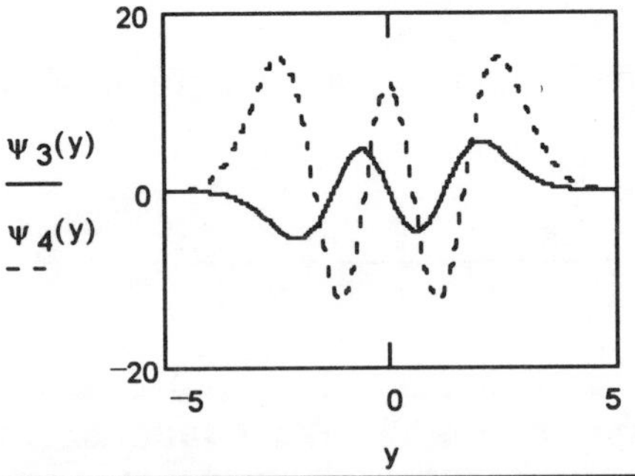

Continue your explorations by trying higher *n* values and by plotting the squares of the wave functions, which is proportional to the probability of finding the vibration at a certain extension.

The turning point of a classical oscillator is the extension for which the total energy is equal to the potential energy (therefore the kinetic energy is zero). Equating these gives:

$$E_n = V(x)$$

$$(n+\tfrac{1}{2})\hbar\sqrt{\frac{k}{\mu}} = \tfrac{1}{2}kx^2$$

$$(n+\tfrac{1}{2})\hbar\sqrt{\frac{k}{\mu}} = \tfrac{1}{2}k\alpha^2 y^2$$

Substituting α to remove $k\mu$ and solving for y gives the turning points as:

$$y = \pm\sqrt{2n+1} \qquad (11.6)$$

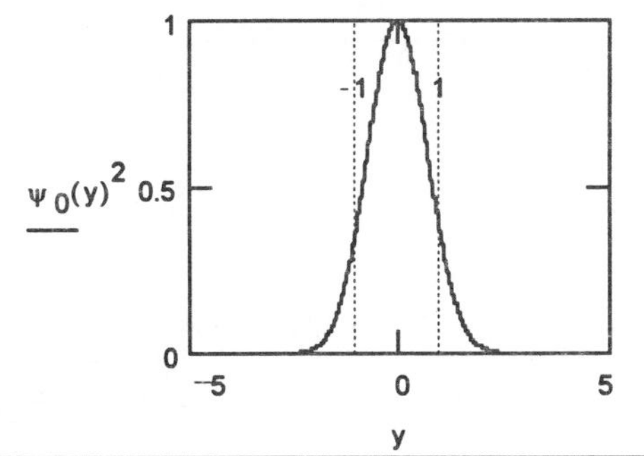

The graph to the right for the $n = 0$ state shows the turning points (±1) using "Show markers" (Graph-format menu) and the probability. Clearly there is considerable probability that the quantum harmonic oscillator will be found outside the turning points — a region forbidden by classical mechanics. To calculate the probability, we must integrate ψ^2 over the forbidden region. Since the integral's limits go to infinity, it is simpler to calculate the probability of the oscillator's *not* being outside the limits.

$$P_{in} := \frac{\int_{-1}^{1} \psi_0(y)^2\, dy}{\int_{-5}^{5} \psi_0(y)^2\, dy}$$

$$P_{in} = 84.27 \cdot \%$$

$$1 - P_{in} = 15.73 \cdot \%$$

The calculation is shown in the box to left. Since the functions as given above are not normalized, it is necessary to divide by the normalization integral. The limits of this integral infinity, but, as we can see from the graph, there is not much area outside ±5, so these values are used for the limits.

The probability that the quantum oscillator is outside the classical turning points is about 16%. Try the calculation for some higher states. You should find that, for larger quantum numbers, the probability of being outside the classical limits is less, so quantum oscillator approaches the classical limit as required by the Bohr correspondence principle.

Example 11.9 Populations of vibrational energy levels.

Continuing with the same example (nitrogen) we calculate the population of the vibrational states using Boltzmann's law. The equation below gives only the relative population, which is proportional to exp($-E/k_bT$).

$$E(n) := \left(n + \frac{1}{2}\right) \cdot h \cdot \nu_0 \qquad T := 3000 \cdot K \qquad P(n) := \exp\left(\frac{-E(n)}{k_b \cdot T}\right)$$

$j := 0..5$

$$norm := \sum_{n=0}^{10} P(n)$$

$P(j)$	$\frac{P(j)}{norm}$
0.568	0.678
0.183	0.218
0.059	0.07
0.019	0.023
0.006	0.007
0.002	0.002

The results for 3000 K are shown in the box to left. The left columns give the relative populations; by calculation the sum (*norm*) we can convert this to the fractional populations (right column). You can see that, even at 3000 K, there are not many molecules in the excited vibrational states. Try lower temperatures to see the effect. Make a bar graph of the populations (below):

n := 0.. 10

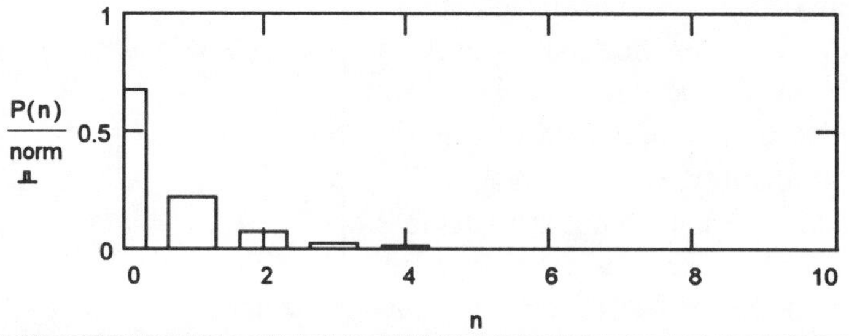

Example 11.10 Hermite polynomials by recursion. ⊕

As Example 11.8 demonstrates, it is a bit tedious to type in the Hermite polynomials for the higher quantum numbers. Wouldn't it be nice if we could enter two and calculate the rest? This can be done using the recursion relationship:

$$H_n(y) = 2yH_{n-1} - 2(n-1)H_{n-2} \tag{11.7}$$

The first two must be given; they are $H_0 = 1$ and $H_1 = 2y$. To implement this calculation with Mathcad, you need the PLUS version (6.0 or higher). Start a new worksheet and enter "`H(n,y):`" (do not type quotes or plus). Then open the programming palette and click "add line". In the first placeholder, type "`1`" and click "if" on the palette; in the new placeholder, type "`n ctrl+= 0`" (do not type spaces or quotes). Go to the second placeholder and click "otherwise" on the palette. In the new placeholder, click "add line". In the first placeholder, type "`2*y`", click "if" and, in the placeholder to the right, type "n ctrl+= 1. Click on the placeholder below this line and click "otherwise". In the placeholder to the left of "otherwise" enter the right-hand side of Eq. (11.7). You should get the result shown in the box below.

```
H(n,y) := | 1  if  n=0
          | otherwise
          |   | 2·y  if  n=1
          |   | 2·y·H(n - 1,y) - 2·(n - 1)·H(n - 2,y)  otherwise
```

Run a few tests.

H(3,1) = -4 H(3,-1) = 4 H(4,0) = 12 H(5,0) = 0

We use this function to define the harmonic oscillator wave function.

$$\text{psi}(n,y) := \frac{H(n,y)}{\sqrt{2^n \cdot (n)! \cdot \sqrt{\pi}}} \cdot \exp\left(-\frac{y^2}{2}\right)$$ *n! (factorial) in denominator*

This wave function is normalized, as we shall show shortly. It can be used to make the sort of graphs we did earlier. Start with $n = 0$ and work your way up.

$n := 6 \qquad yinc := 0.01 \qquad ymax := 5 \qquad y := -ymax, -ymax + yinc .. ymax$

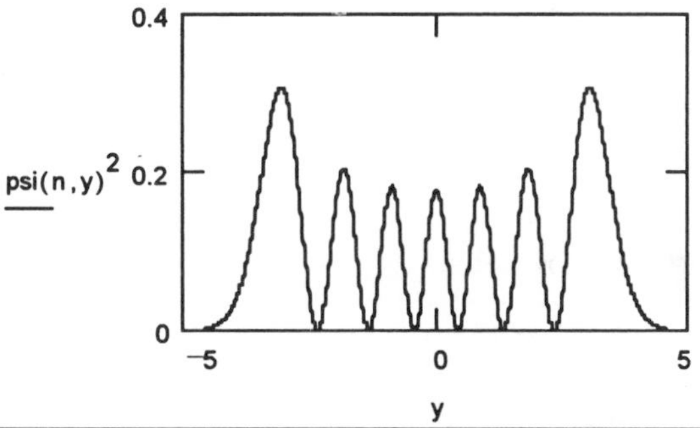

$$\frac{2 \cdot ymax}{yinc} = 1000 \quad \textit{points}$$

$n = 6 \qquad$ *nodes*

The downside of this method, as you will soon learn, is its speed. Each point requires a calculation with n - 2 recursions of the function. Also, for higher n, more points are need to resolve the increasingly rapid oscillations and this, too, increases computation time.

Demonstrate that these functions are normalized (again, starting with $n = 0$ and working your way up). The calculation (box to right) truncates the infinite integral at 2 *ymax*. Also demonstrate that they are orthogonal.

$$\int_{-2 \cdot ymax}^{2 \cdot ymax} psi(2,y)^2 \, dy = 1$$

$$\int_{-3 \cdot ymax}^{3 \cdot ymax} psi(2,y) \cdot psi(4,y) \, dy = 5.695834 \cdot 10^{-11}$$

Since the product of an odd and even function is odd, and the integral of an odd function is zero, it may be evident that such products have zero integral. Demonstrate this for the other cases (box above: in this case the integral is not quite zero because of the approximations made in truncating the integral and using numerical integration).

11.4 Rigid Rotor

Example 11.11 Complex numbers.

In the quantum theory of angular momentum we encounter, for the first time, complex numbers. Although we will be doing little here that will use this feature, this is a good place to learn how Mathcad handles complex numbers.

The letter i, as we have seen many times, can represent an ordinary variable, but in Mathcad it can also represent the imaginary $i = \sqrt{-1}$. (Mathcad also permits you to use j — a notation favored by electrical engineers). The difference is in how it is entered. If you were to enter "`3+4*i`" you would get an expression equal to $3+4i$ where i is an ordinary variable, but if you enter "`3+4i`", with no operation between 4 and i, the i is interpreted as the imaginary.

$z := 3 + 4i$

$\bar{z} = 3 - 4i$

Enter "`z:3+4i`" (do not type quotes) (see box to left), thus defining the complex number z. The complex conjugate, z^*, displayed by Mathcad as z with a bar above, is implemented with the quote key. To get the second expression shown to left, enter "`z"=`" (type the quote in the middle, but not the ones on the end).

The box to the right illustrates the multiplication of z times its complex conjugate (multiplication is done with an asterisk as usual), the magnitude (vertical bar on keyboard), and the functions for extracting the real and imaginary parts of a complex number.

$$z \cdot \bar{z} = 25 \qquad |z| = 5$$
$$\mathrm{Re}(z) = 3 \qquad \mathrm{Im}(z) = 4$$

Having defined complex numbers, the arithmetic operations are implemented in the usual fashion. The first number ($z1$, below) is entered as "`z1:31+1i`"; the 1 is not displayed but is essential to distinguish i from an ordinary variable.

$$z1 := 31 + i \qquad z2 := 4 - 5i \qquad z1 + z2 = 35 - 4i$$
$$z1 \cdot z2 = 129 - 151i \qquad \frac{z2}{z1} = 0.124 - 0.165i \qquad \frac{z2 \cdot \overline{z1}}{(|z1|)^2} = 0.124 - 0.165i$$

The rightmost expression above demonstrates the method for calculating a quotient, but this is implemented by Mathcad without your needing to do anything.

Complex numbers can also be expressed in exponential notation:

$$z = a + bi = A\exp(i\phi)$$
$$z^* = a - bi = A\exp(-i\phi) \tag{11.8}$$

where $A = |z|$ and the angle $\phi = \tan^{-1}(b/a)$. The box below demonstrates the identity of these forms.

$$\mathrm{ang} := \mathrm{atan}\left(\frac{\mathrm{Im}(z)}{\mathrm{Re}(z)}\right) \qquad \mathrm{ang} = 0.927 \qquad \mathrm{ang} = 53.13 \cdot \mathrm{deg}$$
$$zp := |z| \cdot \exp(i \cdot \mathrm{ang}) \qquad zp \cdot \overline{zp} = 25 \qquad |zp| = 5$$

The last equation to the left of the box above is entered as "`zp:z|*exp(1i*ang)`".

Eulers' equation relates complex exponentials to sines and cosines:

$$\exp(i\phi) = \cos(\phi) + i\sin(\phi) \tag{11.9}$$

The box to the right illustrates that the real and imaginary parts of the variable zp (or z for that matter, for they are identical) are related to the cosine and sine of the angle.

$$|zp| \cdot \cos(\mathrm{ang}) = 3 \qquad \mathrm{Re}(zp) = 3$$
$$|zp| \cdot \sin(\mathrm{ang}) = 4 \qquad \mathrm{Im}(zp) = 4$$

$$\mathrm{ang} := 1.68 \qquad \exp(i \cdot \mathrm{ang}) = -0.109 + 0.994i$$
$$\cos(\mathrm{ang}) = -0.109$$
$$\sin(\mathrm{ang}) = 0.994$$
$$zn := \exp(i \cdot \pi) \qquad zn = -1$$

The box to the left shows that complex numbers can be entered in exponential form, but they are immediately interpreted by Mathcad as in the right-hand side of Eq. (11.9). The last line illustrates the remarkable fact that $e^{i\pi} = -1$.

The archetypal function by which complex functions enter quantum mechanics is

$$\psi = A\exp(im\phi), \ \psi^* = A\exp(-im\phi) \tag{11.10}$$

where m is typically an integer. The box below shows the definition for such a function, and its normalization integral. (Enter the exponential as "`exp(m,1i*m*f ctrl+g)`".)

$$\psi(m,\phi) := \frac{1}{\sqrt{2\cdot\pi}}\cdot\exp(i\cdot m\cdot\phi) \qquad \int_0^{2\cdot\pi} \overline{\psi(2,\phi)}\cdot\psi(2,\phi)\,d\phi = 1$$

This integral is really quite simple, and you should work it out by hand if the point is not obvious.

$$\int_0^{2\cdot\pi} \psi(2,\phi)\cdot\overline{\psi(3,\phi)}\,d\phi = -1.352\cdot10^{-9}$$

These functions are also orthogonal (box left). This integral is done numerically, so the answer is a small number rather than exactly zero, as it ought to be. Symbolic integration will give zero, but because we are integrating a defined function, you need the PLUS version to do this (box to right). The orthogonality integral is less obvious than the normalization integral, but it may be clearer if you combine the exponentials and expand them with Euler's equation, Eq. (11.9).

$$\int_0^{2\cdot\pi} \psi(2,\phi)\cdot\overline{\psi(3,\phi)}\,d\phi \rightarrow 0$$

Example 11.10 How fast do molecules rotate?

The energy of rotation of an object with moment of inertia I is:

$$E_J = J(J+1)\frac{h^2}{8\pi^2 I} \qquad (11.11)$$

where the quantum number J is a positive integer. For a diatomic molecule, the moment of inertia is calculated from the bond length (R_e) and reduced mass (μ) as $I = \mu R_e^2$.

What numbers can we expect for J? This question can be answered with the average rotational energy which, according to equipartition theory, is k_bT (for a linear molecule). Start a new worksheet by inserting or including *qconst.mcd* and setting the zero tolerance to 307. We take carbon monoxide (CO) as an example, using the nominal mass numbers (12 and 16) to calculate the moment of inertia (using the accurate isotopic masses would, in this case, give no better accuracy).

$$M1 := 12\cdot\frac{gm}{mole} \qquad M2 := 16\cdot\frac{gm}{mole} \qquad \mu := \frac{M1\cdot M2}{M1+M2}\cdot\frac{1}{L} \qquad \mu = 1.139\cdot10^{-26}\cdot kg$$

As mentioned before, Mathcad does not keep track of the mole as a unit, so you must remember to divide the reduced molar mass by Avogadro's number (L) to get the reduced molecular mass. Now we can calculate the moment of inertia.

$$R_e := 1.1282\cdot10^{-8}\cdot cm \qquad I := \mu\cdot R_e^{\,2} \qquad I = 1.449\cdot10^{-46}\cdot kg\cdot m^2$$

Use a solve block to calculate the J-value for the average energy:

$J := 1$ *start for iteration* $T := 300 \cdot K$ $E(J) := J \cdot (J+1) \cdot \frac{h^2}{8 \cdot \pi^2 \cdot I}$

Given

$E(J) = k_b \cdot T$

$aveJ := Find(J)$ $aveJ = 9.902$ $J_{ave} := 10$

The average J is 9.9, but this is not a possible state since J must be an integer. Therefore we define the quantum number for the average state, J_{ave} as the nearest integer. (Mathcad version 6.0 does not have a round-off function.)

How fast is the molecule rotating? The classical kinetic energy of a body with moment of inertia I and radial frequency ω (radians per second, or 2π time the frequency in cycles per second), is $\frac{1}{2}I\omega^2$. Equate this quantity to the quantum mechanical energy, $E(J)$ to get the frequency.

$\omega := \sqrt{2 \cdot \frac{E(J_{ave})}{I}}$ $\frac{\omega}{2 \cdot \pi} = 1.215 \cdot 10^{12} \cdot sec^{-1}$ $\frac{2 \cdot \pi}{\omega} = 8.233 \cdot 10^{-13} \cdot sec$

The last calculation above gives the period of the rotation. While this is very fast, it is much slower than vibration (see Example 11.7, page 244).

Example 11.12 Populations of rotational energy levels.

Continuing with the same example as for 11.11, we inquire about the thermal populations of the rotational levels. The energy level characterized by the quantum number J has a degeneracy $g = 2J + 1$. The Boltzmann law for levels with degeneracy g gives the relative populations as:

$$P_i \propto g_i \exp(-E_i / k_b T)$$

This is easily implement with the material developed above. The graph is best as a bar graph.

$T := 1000 \cdot K$ $P(J) := (2 \cdot J + 1) \cdot \exp\left(\frac{-E(J)}{k_b \cdot T}\right)$

$J := 0 .. 50$

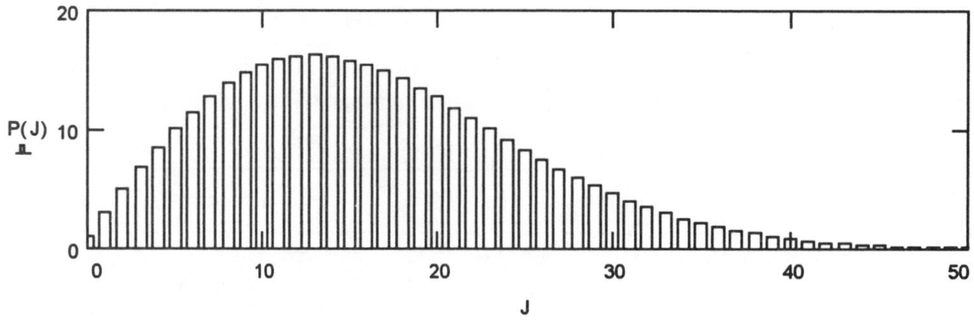

Try other temperatures and other molecules. In general, a sizable number of rotational states are occupied at room temperature. This is in contrast to the vibrational case where, typically, most molecules are in the lowest-energy (ground) state at room temperature.

Problems

11.1 Calculate the minimum velocity of a nitrogen molecule in a cubic box which measures 1 cm on a side.

11.2 Calculate the probability at the particle in a box is in the left 1/4 of the box for the n=7 state.

11.3 An F-center occurs when an anion vacancy in a crystal is replaced by a free electron. The light absorbed by the electron is often in the visible region, giving the crystal color (F is from the German word *Farben*, meaning color). In NaCl, the F-center absorption is at 3.6 eV (29000 cm^{-1}). Assuming the particle in a cubic box model to be valid, calculate the box size that would give rise to this absorption. Compare your result to the diameter of the chloride ion, 0.362 nm.

11.4 The vibration constant of Cl_2 is $\omega_e = 564.9\ cm^{-1}$, and the bond length is $R_e = 198.8$ pm. Calculate the force constant and α. Make graph of probability (ψ^2) vs. R (not $x = R - R_e$ or $y = \alpha x$) for the $n = 0$ state. How far would a spring with the force constant stretch if a 1 kg mass were suspended from it?

11.5 Calculate the probability of being inside the classical turning point for the harmonic oscillator in the n=6 state.

11.6 For the chlorine molecule (data problem 11.4) calculate the fraction of molecules that are in the $n = 0$ vibrational state at 400 K.

11.7 HCl has a bond length $R_e = 127.6$ pm. Use the accurate isotopic masses for $^1H^{35}Cl$ to calculate the reduced mass and the moment of inertia. What J state has the maximum population at 300 K? What is the average J at that temperature? Make a bar graph of the populations for 300 K.

Answers

11.1 1.234×10^{-6} m/s

11.2 0.273

11.3 0.560 nm

11.4 $k = 328.9$ kg /s^2, $\alpha = 5.84$ pm, $x = 29.8$ mm.

11.5 92.982%

11.6 86.9%

11.7 $\mu = 1.62665\times10^{-27}$ kg, $I = 2.64848\times10^{-47}$ kg m^2, max. pop. at $J = 3$, ave. $J = 3.98$

CHAPTER 12

ATOMS AND MOLECULES

12.1 Atomic Orbitals

The wave functions of the hydrogen atom form the basis for much of atomic and molecular theory, so understanding them is an important step in understanding chemical theory. Mathcad can help this understanding with its graphics, and this chapter will introduce you to additional graphics features of the program.

The wave function, with quantum numbers *n, l, m*, can be written:

$$\Psi_{nlm} = R_{nl}(r)Y_{lm}(\theta,\phi) \tag{12.1}$$

where *R* is the radial wave function and *Y* is a spherical harmonic. The wave function can also be written in Cartesian coordinates, with $r = (x^2 + y^2 + z^2)^{1/2}$, but either way, the problem of picturing the wave function remains the same: with 3 variables, we would need a 4-dimensional graph to picture the function fully. In the next group of examples, we will show various views of this wave function, varying two coordinates while holding the third constant. Taken together, these views should give you a good picture of these functions.

For simplicity we shall consider only the hydrogen atom with $Z = 1$, and use atomic units throughout — measuring distances in units of the Bohr radius a_0. Thus, the exponential part of the radial function, $\exp(-Zr/na_0)$ will be written simply as $\exp(-r/n)$. Also we will not bother normalizing the functions.

Example 12.1 Polar plots.

To make a polar graph, you first define a range variable for the angle and then the function to be plotted.

$n := 120 \qquad \phi := 0, \frac{2\cdot\pi}{n} .. 2\cdot\pi \qquad N := 5 \qquad f(\phi) := \cos(N\cdot\phi)$

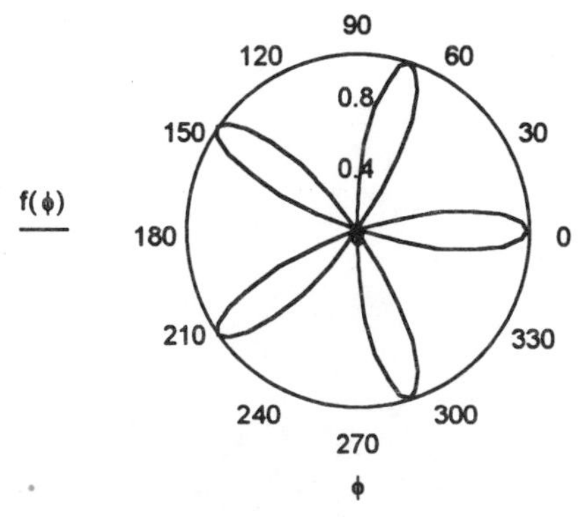

Next, select Graphics-menu, Polar Plot. On the frame that appears, fill in the lower placeholder with the variable name and the left placeholder with the function. (The other 2 are for the radial range and will not be used here.). The graph (box right) has a lot of axis numbers which are often more of a distraction than information. They can be removed by double-clicking on the graph to bring up the graph format menu; then unset the "Numbered" boxes as desired.

Try this graph with other values of N, including nonintegers. Try half integers like 2.5; repeat after increasing the plot range to 4π. What do you make of this? This example is closely related to the occurrence of integers in the quantum theory of angular momentum. Only integer values of N give a single-valued function; that is, a function that has a unique value for each ϕ in the range $0 < \phi < 2\pi$. Half-integers are double-valued. Nonintegers do not repeat after one cycle, and may never repeat if they are not rational numbers.

Example 12.2 Surface and contour plots.

Surface and contour plots are effectively the same procedure. First you define a grid of points for 2 Cartesian axes (among x, y and z, however, Mathcad always calls them x and y).

$nx := 30 \qquad xmax := 3 \qquad xinc := \frac{2 \cdot xmax}{nx} \qquad i := 0..\, nx \qquad x_i := -xmax + i \cdot xinc$

$ny := 30 \qquad ymax := 2 \qquad yinc := \frac{2 \cdot ymax}{ny} \qquad j := 0..\, ny \qquad y_j := -ymax + j \cdot yinc$

Next you use the function to be plotted to calculate a grid of points (matrix **M**, below). Select from the Graphics Menu, either Surface Plot or Contour Plot, and enter the matrix name in the lone placeholder. (Surface and Contour are the same, differing only by the selection of an option box on the Graph Format menu; thus it is simple to change from one to the other.)

$M_{i,j} := \sin\left(\frac{\pi \cdot x_i}{3}\right) \cdot \cos\left(\frac{\pi \cdot y_j}{3}\right)$ xmax = 3   ymax = 2

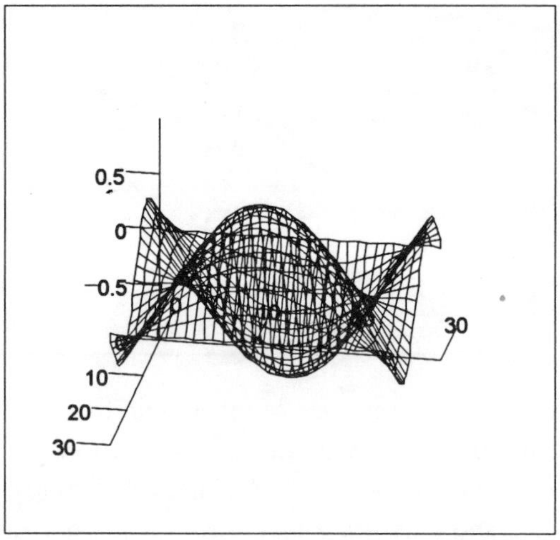

M

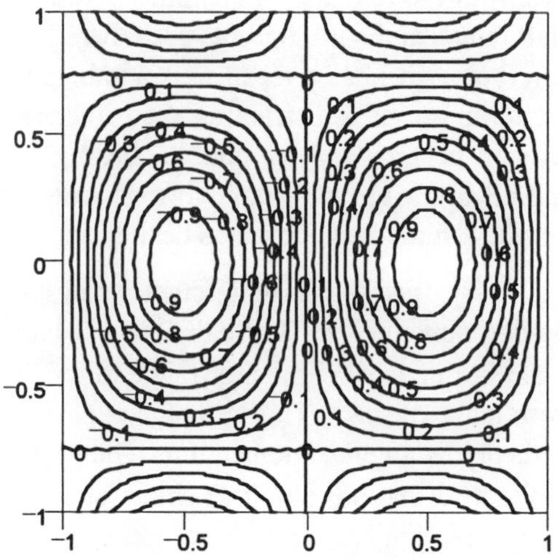

M

The numbers on these plots are, for most of our examples, a useless distraction Also, note that they have nothing to do with the actual plot limits (*xmax* and *ymax*, displayed above for information only). For the surface plot, the *x* and *y* axes are labeled by the index numbers (*nx* and *ny* in this example); for the contour plot they are arbitrarily labeled from -1 to 1. It is possible (from the Graph Format menu) to change these to the actual axis range, but since this quantity cannot be a variable but only numbers, it would have to be changed for each example. Since we are interested in exploring a variety of functions in succession, it is simplest just to turn off the axis numbering, and we shall do this from now on.

Example 12.3 Surface plots of atomic orbitals.

We will graph some wave functions in the *xy* plane, for $z = 0$. Thus we start by defining a grid of points in that plane.

$nx := 40$ $xmax := 10$ $xinc := \frac{2 \cdot xmax}{nx}$ $i := 0 .. nx$ $x_i := -xmax + i \cdot xinc$

$ny := 40$ $ymax := 10$ $yinc := \frac{2 \cdot ymax}{ny}$ $j := 0 .. ny$ $y_j := -ymax + j \cdot yinc$

Next, enter a series of wave functions in Cartesian coordinates. (We omit the $2p_z$ function since it is zero in the plane we are plotting.)

$$f_{1s}(x,y,z) := \exp\left(-\sqrt{x^2+y^2+z^2}\right) \qquad f_{2s}(x,y,z) := \left(2-\sqrt{x^2+y^2+z^2}\right)\cdot\exp\left(-\frac{\sqrt{x^2+y^2+z}}{2}\right)$$

$$f_{2px}(x,y,z) := x\cdot\exp\left(-\frac{\sqrt{x^2+y^2+z^2}}{2}\right) \qquad f_{2py}(x,y,z) := y\cdot\exp\left(-\frac{\sqrt{x^2+y^2+z^2}}{2}\right)$$

These are used to make surface and/or contour plots. (Since we reuse the matrix **M**, it's a good idea to set this symbol equal to zero before redefining it. This gets rid of any previous information in the matrix. Otherwise, if you made a graph with a smaller grid than before, the old points would still be there.)

$M := 0 \qquad M_{i,j} := f_{2py}\left(x_i, y_j, 0\right)$

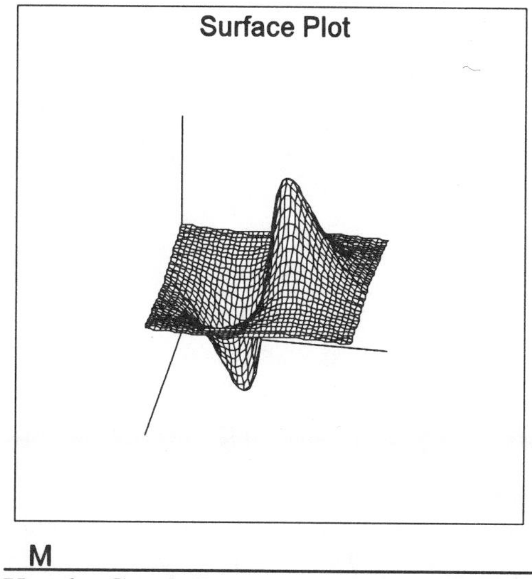

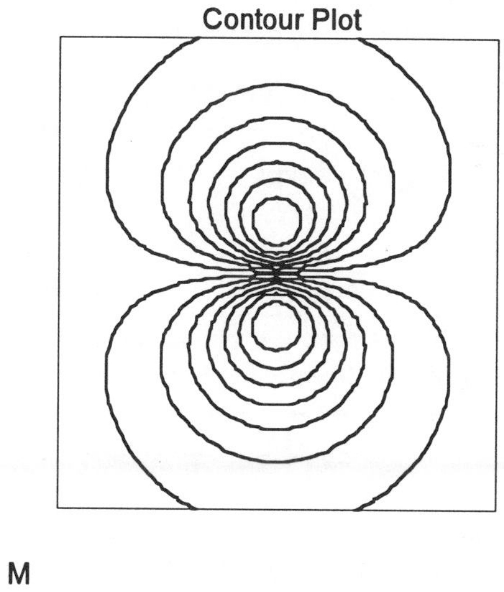

Use the Graph-Format menu to select Hidden Lines and to turn off axis numbering. Try each function in turn. Try different plot limits. Make graphs of $\psi\psi^*$ (equal to ψ^2, since these are real functions), which displays the electron density. Vary the rotation of the surface plot, and the number of grids for the contour plot. The $2p_z$ function is similar to $2p_x$, replacing x by z; to view it you need to do an xz or yz cross section. It will look much the same at the others, but Mathcad always calls the axes x and y.

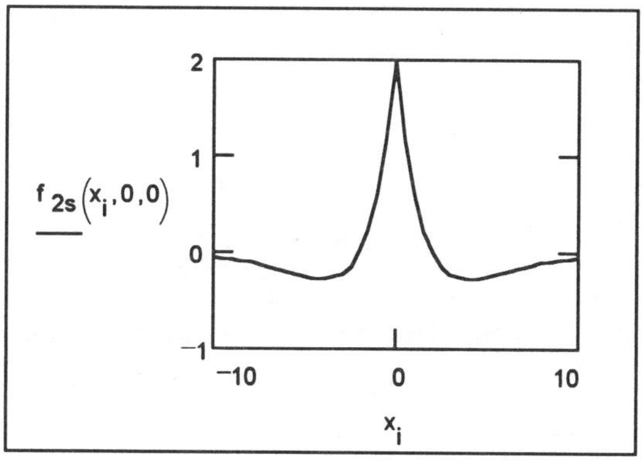

Take particular note of the $2s$ function. It is obvious that there is a negative portion? This may be clearer with a 1D plot (varying x with y and z equal to zero): see box to left. It looks as if most of the electron density is near the nucleus ($x = 0$), but this is not true, as is explained in the next section.

Example 12.4 The radial distribution function.

The function $\psi\psi^*$ gives the probability that the electron will be found in a volume element

$$d\tau = dx\,dy\,dx$$

But is discussing how far the electron is from the nucleus it is somewhat more relevant to ask the probability that it lies between radius r and $r + dr$; that is, in an annulus at some distance from the nucleus. The volume of this annulus is $4\pi r^2\,dr$, so its size increases as the radius increases. The volume element is:

$$d\tau = 4\pi r^2 dr$$

The *radial distribution function* —

$$f(r) = R^2 r^2 \qquad (12.2)$$

gives the probability that the electron will be found in the annulus between r and $r + dr$. (The 4π is omitted since the functions are not normalized in any case.)

The box below defines several radial functions and the radial distribution function (f).

$R_{1s}(r) := \exp(-r) \qquad R_{2s}(r) := (2 - r)\cdot\exp\left(-\frac{r}{2}\right) \qquad R_{2p}(r) := r\cdot\exp\left(-\frac{r}{2}\right)$

$f(r) := R_{1s}(r)^2\cdot r^2 \qquad r_{max} := 5 \qquad r_{inc} := .01 \qquad r := 0, r_{inc} .. r_{max}$

$f(r)$ is defined only once; to do another orbital, change the statement above left. For the 1*s* function, $f(r)$ has a maximum (box below).

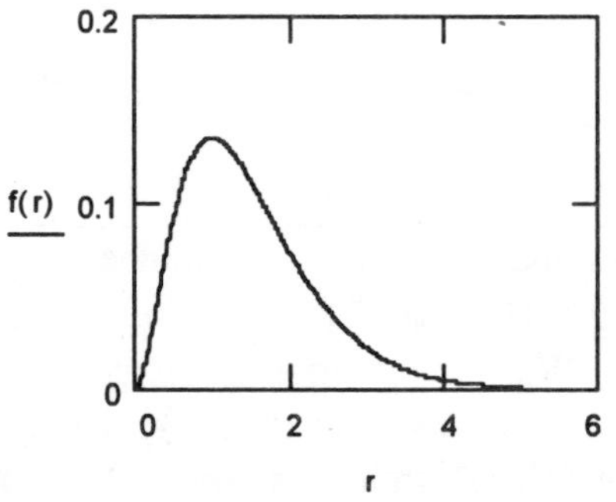

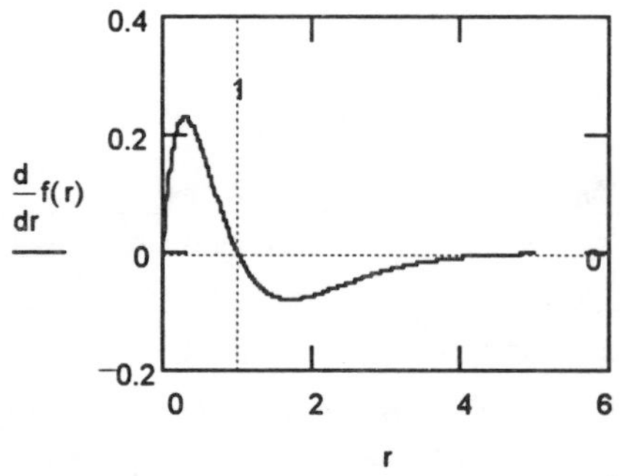

In this case it may be obvious that the maximum is at $r = 1$ (that is, 1 bohr), but you can use the symbolic capabilities of Mathcad to prove this.

$\exp(-r)^2\cdot r^2$ *by differentiation, yields*

$-2\cdot\exp(-r)^2\cdot r^2 + 2\cdot\exp(-r)^2\cdot r$ *which has solution(s)* $\begin{pmatrix}0\\1\end{pmatrix}$

(It should be obvious from inspection that the $r = 0$ solution is a minimum while the $r = 1$ solution is a maximum.) To make this calculation, enter the expression shown (f for 1*s*); place the cursor next to r and select Symbolic-menu, Differentiate. In the resulting expression, place the cursor next to r and select Symbolic-menu, Solve.

The radial distribution function for $2s$, shown next, has two maxima with a node (zero) in between.

$f(r) := R_{2s}(r)^2 \cdot r^2 \qquad r_{max} := 15 \qquad r_{inc} := .01 \qquad r := 0, r_{inc} .. r_{max}$

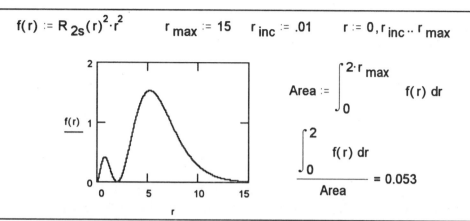

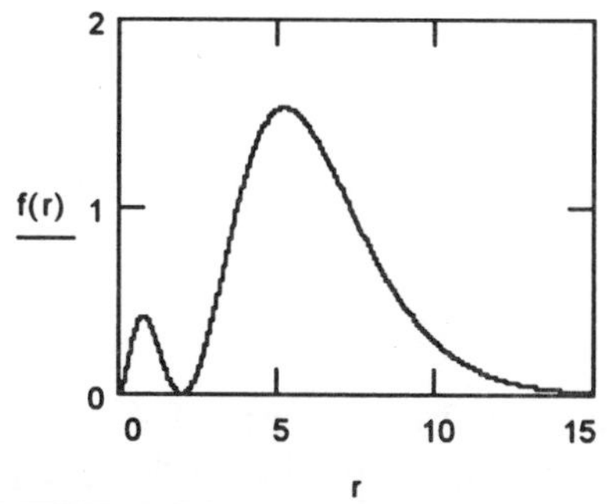

$$\text{Area} := \int_0^{2 \cdot r_{max}} f(r)\, dr$$

$$\frac{\int_0^2 f(r)\, dr}{\text{Area}} = 0.053$$

It may be evident from inspection of R_{2s} that the node is at $r = 2$ (that is, 2 bohr = 0.1058 nm), and that most of the electron density is outside the node. The fraction of the electron probability inside the node is the ratio of the areas of the first hump to the total area (if the function were normalized, the total area would be 1, but it is not normalized). This calculation is shown above right; the integral for the total area should extend to infinity, but, as the graph shows, there is not much area outside r_{max} so the integral to 2 r_{max} should be sufficiently accurate. As the calculation shows, only 5% of the probability is inside the node. Thus the earlier picture (the 2D surface plots) were misleading because they did not take into account that there is more space available for the electron as r increases. It is certainly true that the electron density per unit volume is higher inside the node, but the electron is much more likely to be outside the node.

$$\text{ave} := \frac{\int_0^{2 \cdot r_{max}} r \cdot f(r)\, dr}{\text{Area}}$$

$$\text{ave} = 6$$

The numerical evaluation of the average value of r is shown in the box to the left. As before we approximate the integral to infinity with a large but finite value (which should always be confirmed by observing the graph, as we have done). Try the integral to $4r_{max}$ — is there any difference? The average is in units of bohr; in meters $\langle r \rangle = 6a_0 =$ 0.3175 nm.

Your version of Mathcad may be able to evaluate this integral symbolically. Enter the expression shown to right; then click in the expression and press space or up-arrow until the entire expression is selected. Then select Symbolic-menu, Evaluate, Symbolically.

$$\frac{\int_0^{\infty} r \cdot \left[(2-r)\cdot \exp\left(-\frac{r}{2}\right)\right]^2 \cdot r^2\, dr}{\int_0^{\infty} \left[(2-r)\cdot \exp\left(-\frac{r}{2}\right)\right]^2 \cdot r^2\, dr} \quad \textit{symbolic evaluation yields} \quad 6$$

Repeat these calculations and graphs for the other functions given above.

Example 12.5 Polar plots and the shape of atomic orbitals.

For seeing the shapes of atomic orbitals, it is best to look at just the angular dependence, for r = constant. This means the spherical harmonics of Eq. (12.1). The spherical harmonics can be written as

$$Y_{l,m}(\theta,\phi) = P_l^{|m|}(\theta)\exp(im\phi) \qquad (12.3)$$

where $P_l^{\{m\}}$ is the associated Legendre polynomial; we will also call it $P_{l,m}$, because superscript indexes are not supported by Mathcad.

Since $\psi\psi^*$ does not depend on ϕ, it is the θ dependence of the Legendre polynomials that is most interesting. Mathcad does not permit the definition of functions with true (index) subscripts, but we can work around that limitation by defining the polynomials in a matrix.

$$P(\theta) := \begin{bmatrix} \frac{1}{\sqrt{4\cdot\pi}} & 0 & 0 \\ \sqrt{\frac{3}{4\cdot\pi}}\cdot\cos(\theta) & \sqrt{\frac{3}{8\cdot\pi}}\cdot\sin(\theta) & 0 \\ \sqrt{\frac{5}{16\cdot\pi}}\cdot\left(3\cdot\cos(\theta)^2 - 1\right) & \sqrt{\frac{15}{8\cdot\pi}}\cdot\sin(\theta)\cdot\cos(\theta) & \sqrt{\frac{15}{32\cdot\pi}}\cdot\sin(\theta)^2 \end{bmatrix}$$

Order
0,0 -- --
1,0 1,1 --
2,0 2,1 2,2

The text to the right shows how the elements are indexed. Thus, the element $P_{2,0}$, the Legendre polynomial for l = 2, m = 0, is the lower left function in the matrix. These functions are normalized as given:

$$\int_0^{2\cdot\pi}\int_0^{\pi} P(\theta)_{2,1}\cdot P(\theta)_{2,1}\cdot\sin(\theta)\,d\theta\,d\phi = 1$$

Check this integral for the others. Also, they are orthogonal, so the integral of the product of any two different Legendre polynomials is zero. Demonstrate this for a few examples:

$$\int_0^{2\cdot\pi}\int_0^{\pi} P(\theta)_{2,1}\cdot P(\theta)_{2,0}\cdot\sin(\theta)\,d\theta\,d\phi = 0$$

First, let's look at some polar plots of the Legendre polynomials. The box to right defines an angle range variable for plotting. The box below shows the graph for l = 2, m = 0.

$$\text{theta} := 0, \frac{2\cdot\pi}{60} .. 2\cdot\pi$$

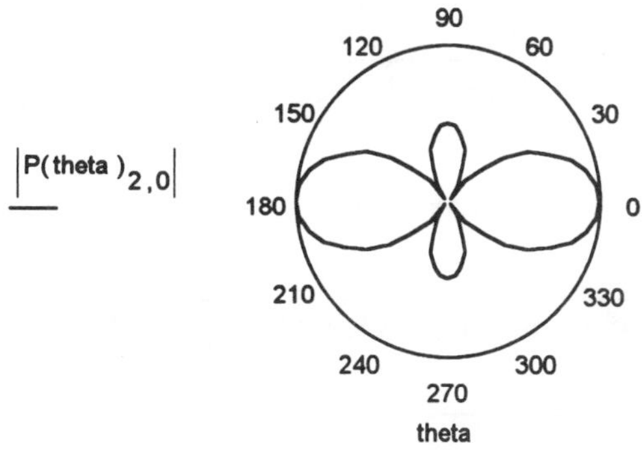

<------ *z axis*

The usual convention in physical chemistry is that the theta (θ) angle measures the declination from the *z* axis, which is taken to be 0 and drawn vertically. Mathcad's polar plots puts zero angle on the horizontal, which is rotated by 90° from the usual way they are pictured. (Parametric surface plots, as we shall see, do place the *z* axis vertically.)

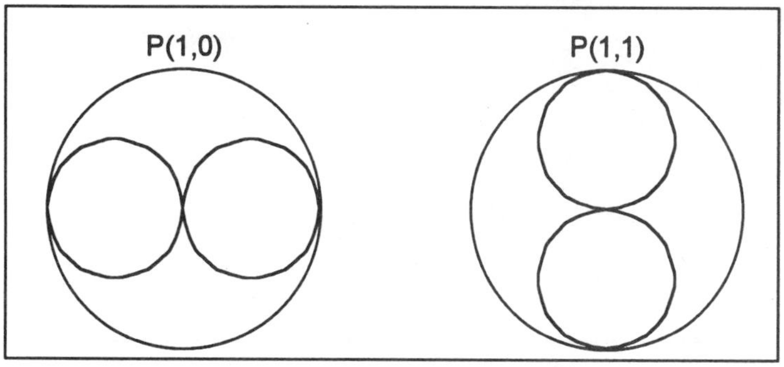

Make graphs for the other Legendre polynomials, noting, for example, the distinction between the $l = 1$, $m = 0$ and 1, functions (box to left, remembering that the *z* axis is horizontal).

Example 12.6 Parametric surface plots.

Spherical harmonics, of course, are complex, so we have 3 choices for plotting them. We could plot the real part, the imaginary part, or the magnitude (whose square is the electron density). Since $|\exp(im\phi)| = 1$, the magnitude is simply the Legendre polynomial: $|Y_{l,\,m}| = |P_{l,\,m}|$. We'll look at it first.

To view functions of two angles, we use the parametric surface plot feature of Mathcad. This involves creating 3 matrices with grid points, which we call **X**, **Y** and **Z**. The box below starts by setting these equal to zero (in case they are used repeatedly, as we plan to do). Also, we define two range variables for the angles (*theta* and *phi*).

$npts := 60 \qquad X := 0 \qquad Y := 0 \qquad Z := 0$

$m := 0 .. npts \qquad n := 0 .. npts \qquad phi_m := \frac{2\cdot\pi\cdot m}{npts} \qquad theta_n := \frac{2\cdot\pi\cdot n}{npts}$

Doing 60 points can be time consuming, depending, of course, on the speed of your computer (we need 3 $npts^2$ calculations of the function). If you find it too slow, try using fewer points.

Now we need to place the x, y and z projections of the functions in the arrays **X**, **Y**, and **Z**, respectively.

$$f(\theta,\phi) := \left|P(\theta)_{2,1}\right| \qquad X_{m,n} := \sin(theta_n)\cdot\cos(phi_m)\cdot f(theta_n, phi_m)$$

$$Y_{m,n} := \sin(theta_n)\cdot\sin(phi_m)\cdot f(theta_n, phi_m) \qquad Z_{m,n} := \cos(theta_n)\cdot f(theta_n, phi_m)$$

We these arrays, the graph is created by Graphics-menu, Surface plot, typing "`X,Y,Z`" into the placeholder. The result is shown below for $P_{2,1}$.

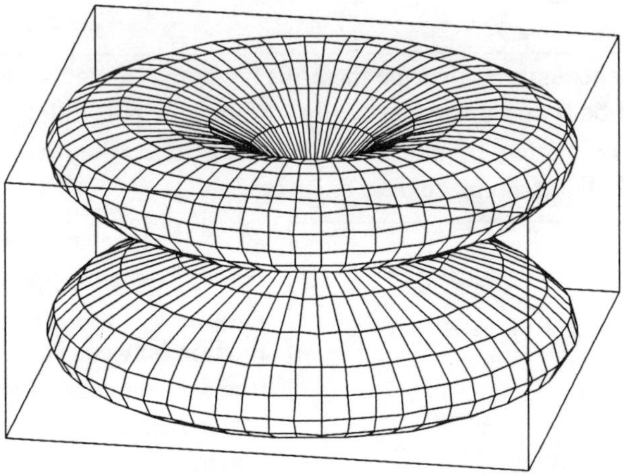

Hidden lines,
numbers none
axes none
show box yes
show border no

X,Y,Z

Try the others. The $P_{0,0}$ function is, of course, a constant. What shape do you get in that case?

The alternative is to plot the real and imaginary parts; this gives the more conventional Cartesian representation of the orbitals seen in many chemistry texts. To this end, recall the relationship of the Cartesian coordinates to spherical polar coordinates:

$$x = r\sin(\theta)\cos(\phi)$$
$$y = r\sin(\theta)\sin(\phi)$$
$$z = r\cos(\theta)$$

For the case $l = 1$, we have three functions for $m = 0, \pm 1$. For $m = 0$:

$$P_{1,0} \propto \cos(\theta) \propto z$$

Hence, this function is called p_z.. (The $2p$ and $3p$ functions have the same angular parts, differing only in the radial part.) Recalling the Euler relationship:

$$\exp(im\phi) = \cos(m\phi) + i\sin(m\phi)$$

we see that the real and imaginary parts of the $m = 1$ (or -1) functions give:

$$\mathrm{Re}(P_{1,1}) \propto \sin(\theta)\cos(\phi) \propto x$$
$$\mathrm{Im}(P_{1,1}) \propto \sin(\theta)\sin(\phi) \propto y$$

Thus, these functions are called p_x and p_y respectively. Similar relationships apply to the d (l = 2) functions.

The box below shows the definitions of the Cartesian orbitals. Of course, *px* means p_z (and so forth); *dz2* is usually called d_{z^2} and *dx2y2* is usually called $d_{x^2-y^2}$.

$s(\theta,\phi) := 1$	$dz2(\theta,\phi) := P(\theta)_{2,0}$
$pz(\theta,\phi) := P(\theta)_{1,0}$	$dxz(\theta,\phi) := P(\theta)_{2,1}\cdot\cos(\phi)$
$px(\theta,\phi) := P(\theta)_{1,1}\cdot\cos(\phi)$	$dyz(\theta,\phi) := P(\theta)_{2,1}\cdot\sin(\phi)$
$py(\theta,\phi) := P(\theta)_{1,1}\cdot\sin(\phi)$	$dxy(\theta,\phi) := P(\theta)_{2,2}\cdot\sin(2\cdot\phi)$
	$dx2y2(\theta,\phi) := P(\theta)_{2,2}\cdot\cos(2\cdot\phi)$

These graphs are made using the same procedure as above.

$f(\theta,\phi) := |pz(\theta,\phi)|$ $\quad X_{m,n} := \sin(theta_n)\cdot\cos(phi_m)\cdot f(theta_n, phi_m)$

$Y_{m,n} := \sin(theta_n)\cdot\sin(phi_m)\cdot f(theta_n, phi_m)$ $\quad Z_{m,n} := \cos(theta_n)\cdot f(theta_n, phi_m)$

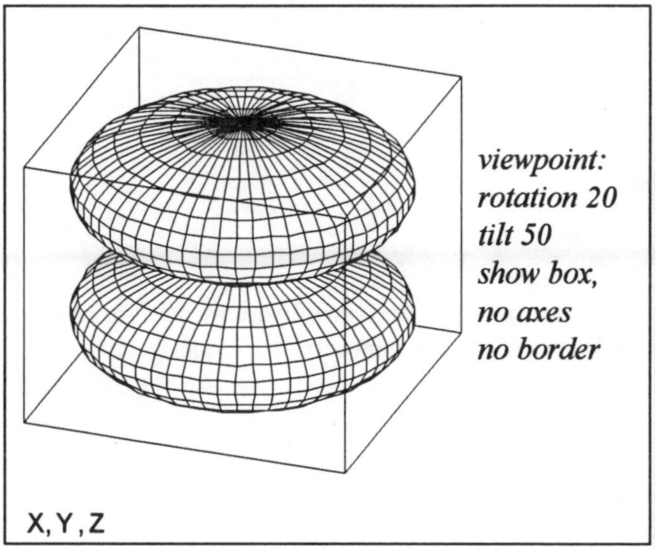

viewpoint:
rotation 20
tilt 50
show box,
no axes
no border

The box to the left shows the p_z orbital, while that below shows d_{z^2}.

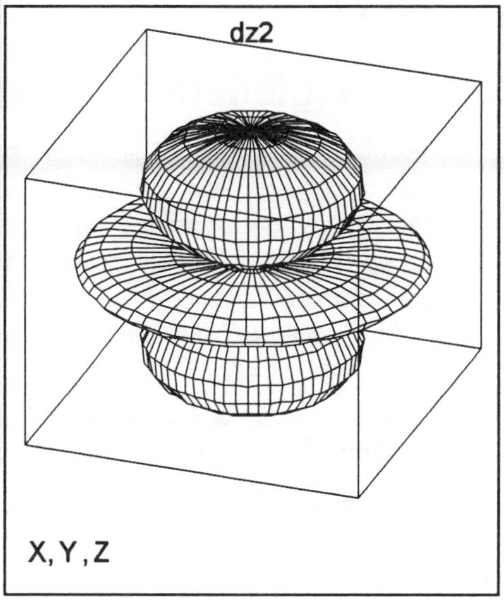

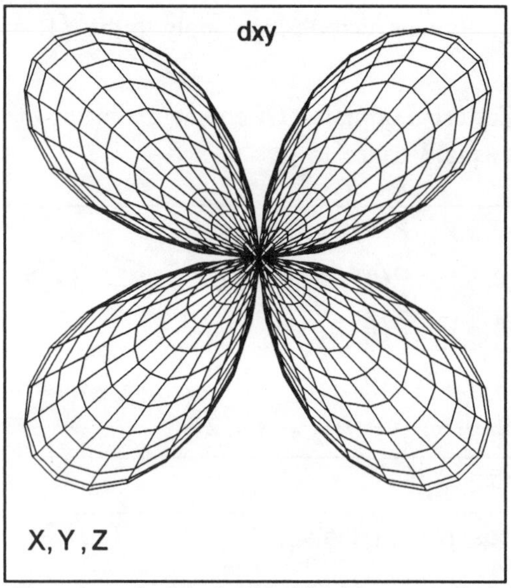

To get a better view of p_x and p_y, d_{xy} and $d_{x^2-y^2}$, you may want to change the tilt. The box to left shows the d_{xy} orbital with rotation 0 degrees, tilt 90 degrees. How does this compare to $d_{x^2-y^2}$? Look at the p_x and p_y functions to establish where the x and y axes are in this view.

Make graphs for all of the orbitals defined above. Vary the viewing angle as needed. What does the s function look like?

Try some f orbitals ($l = 3$); the $m = 0$ function (box to right) is especially interesting. The Legendre polynomial for $l = 3$, $m = 0$, is

$$f(\theta, \phi) := \left|\cos(\theta)\cdot\left(5\cdot\cos(\theta)^2 - 3\right)\right|$$

(The others can be found, for example, in Noggle, Table 11.7.)

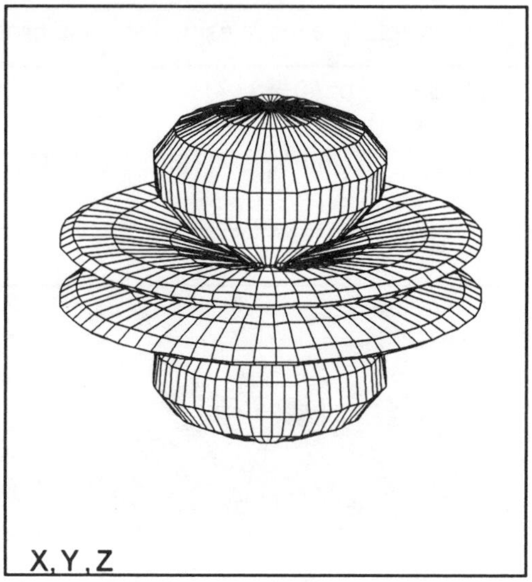

12.2 Molecular Orbitals

Molecular orbitals (MOs) serve the same role for the theory of molecular structure as do the atomic orbitals (AOs) do for atomic structure. They are one-electron wave functions that are used to build up (German: *aufbau*) many-electron functions. A common method of constructing MOs is by linear combination of atomic orbitals: LCAO. The simplest case is the one-electron molecule, H_2^+, whose LCAO functions we now examine.

Example 12.7 The sigma MOs

Consider two nuclei (A and B), lying on the z axis, separated by a distance R. Each has a set of AOs, which are:

$$f_{1s}(x,y,z) := \exp\left(-\sqrt{x^2+y^2+z^2}\right) \qquad f_{2pz}(x,y,z) := z\cdot\exp\left(-\frac{\sqrt{x^2+y^2+z^2}}{2}\right)$$

$$f_{2s}(x,y,z) := \left(2-\sqrt{x^2+y^2+z^2}\right)\cdot\exp\left(-\frac{\sqrt{x^2+y^2+z^2}}{2\cdot}\right)$$

$$f_{2px}(x,y,z) := x\cdot\exp\left(-\frac{\sqrt{x^2+y^2+z^2}}{2}\right) \qquad f_{2py}(x,y,z) := y\cdot\exp\left(-\frac{\sqrt{x^2+y^2+z^2}}{2}\right)$$

The distinction between the A and B AOs lies in the z coordinate, the AOs being centered at (respectively) $z = -R/2$ and $z = R/2$. Thus the LCAO $1s_A + 1s_B$ can be formed as:

$$f_{1s}\left(x,y,z-\frac{R}{2}\right) + f_{1s}\left(x,y,z+\frac{R}{2}\right)$$

We will look at surface and contour plots of these functions in the xz plane (with, usually, $y = 0$). We begin by setting up the range variables:

$$nx := 30 \qquad xmax := 4 \qquad xinc := \frac{2\cdot xmax}{nx} \qquad i := 0..nx \qquad x_i := -xmax + i\cdot xinc$$

$$nz := 40 \qquad zmax := 10 \qquad zinc := \frac{2\cdot zmax}{nz} \qquad j := 0..nz \qquad z_j := -zmax + j\cdot zinc$$

We use different ranges for x and z since the figure generally has greater extension in the z direction. Then we define the function desired and calculate a grid of points (in matrix **M**, which is initialized to zero, as usual, to prevent problems in case you change the number of grid points).

$$R := 6 \qquad F(x,z) := f_{1s}\left(x,0,z-\frac{R}{2}\right) + f_{1s}\left(x,0,z+\frac{R}{2}\right)$$

Do 1s, 2s, 2pz for various R, and BO and ABO

$$M := 0 \qquad M_{i,j} := F\left(x_i, z_j\right)$$

The contour graph is shown below (z is the vertical axis). (As before, we are working in atomic units, so $R = 8a_0 = 0.423$ nm.)

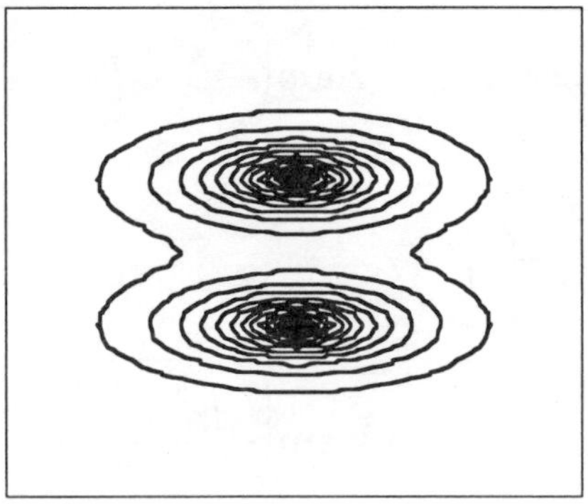

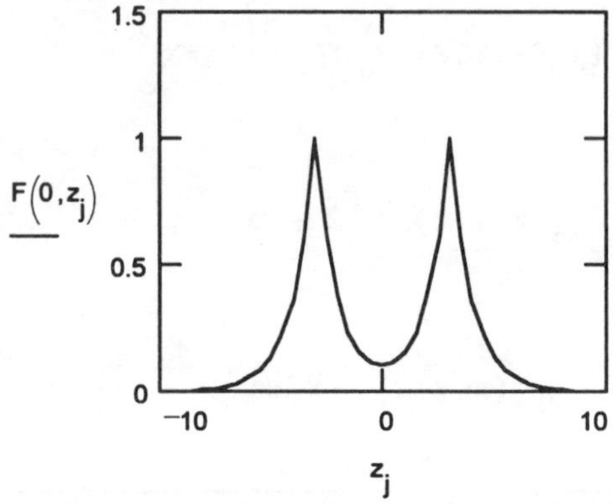

M

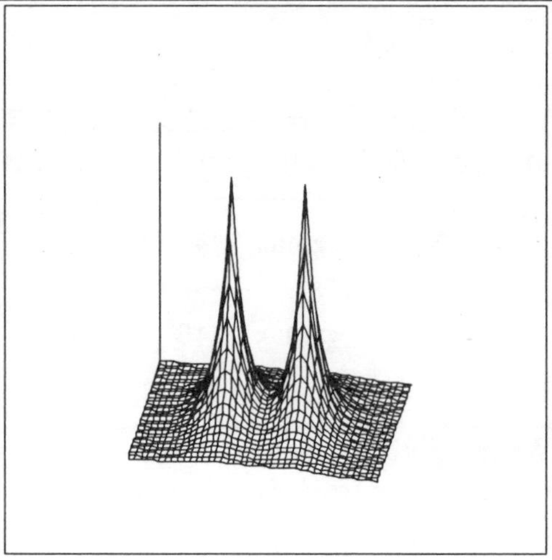

M

The profile along the x axis is informative (above, right). You may find it helpful to color the contours. The surface plot (box right) gives a different perspective.

Vary the distance R and observe the effect. Then do the antibonding combination: $1s_A$-$1s_B$. (Edit the expression above to make similar plots for this combination.) Can you see why the antibonding combination does not make a stable bond?

Continue the same procedure for the $2s$ and $2p_z$ orbitals. How does $2s$ differ from $1s$? Which combination, $p_{zA} + p_{zB}$ or $p_{zA} - p_{zB}$ is the bonding combination? Also, make graphs of the electron density ($\psi\psi^*$) for each of these.

Example 12.8 The pi MOs

The combinations in the previous example were all σ-type MOs. The p_x and p_y AOs form π-type MOs; these are a degenerate pair, and the pictures we will make for the x combinations are essentially identical to those you would get for the y combinations.

For the π orbital, we want a somewhat different axis scale.

$nx := 30 \qquad xmax := 8 \qquad xinc := \dfrac{2 \cdot xmax}{nx} \qquad i := 0 .. nx \qquad x_i := -xmax + i \cdot xinc$

$nz := 40 \qquad zmax := 12 \qquad zinc := \dfrac{2 \cdot zmax}{nz} \qquad j := 0 .. nz \qquad z_j := -zmax + j \cdot zinc$

For the antibonding combination at $R = 8$:

$$R := 8 \qquad F(x,z) := f_{2px}\left(x,0,z-\frac{R}{2}\right) - f_{2px}\left(x,0,z+\frac{R}{2}\right)$$

$$M := 0 \qquad M_{i,j} := F\left(x_i, z_j\right)$$

we get:

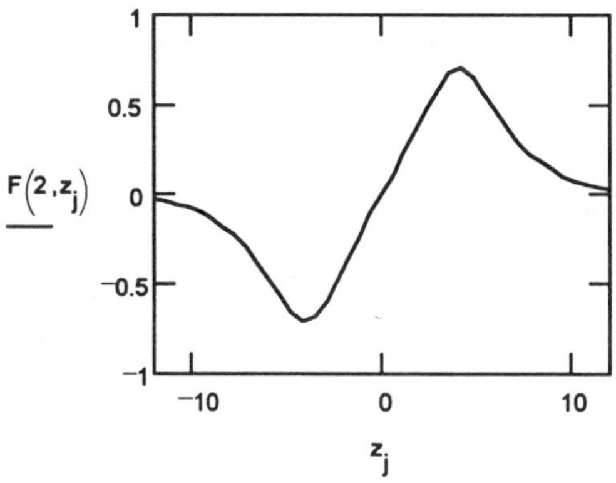

M

Note that the 1-dimension plot is for $x = 2$: why? (Hint: try $x = 0$.) As before, vary R and observe the effect. Repeat for the bonding combination. Try plotting the squares. The surface plots for these functions will make the phase relationships clearer.

12.3 Molecular Spectroscopy

The next 3 examples will be for carbon monoxide (CO) whose spectroscopic constants are:

$$\omega_e := 2170.21\cdot cm^{-1} \qquad wex := 13.461\cdot cm^{-1} \qquad B_e := 1.9314\cdot cm^{-1}$$

$$R_e := 1.1281\cdot 10^{-8}\cdot cm \qquad D_0 := 11.108\cdot eV \qquad \alpha_e := 0.01748\cdot cm^{-1}$$

These are standard notation (which will be explained as needed) except for *wex*, which denotes the anharmonicity constant, $\omega_e x_e$.

Insert or include the constants file (*qconst.mcd*).

Example 12.9 Vibrational spectroscopy.

The vibrational energy of a linear molecule is characterized by a quantum number $n = 0, 1, \ldots$ and has energy:

$$E_n = hc\left[(n+\tfrac{1}{2})\omega_e - (n+\tfrac{1}{2})^2\omega_e x_e\right] \tag{12.4}$$

This equation is implemented below with constants for CO.

$$E_{vib}(n) := h \cdot c \cdot \left[(n + 0.5) \cdot \omega_e - (n + 0.5)^2 \cdot wex \right]$$

$$ff := \frac{E_{vib}(1) - E_{vib}(0)}{h \cdot c} \qquad ff = 2.143 \cdot 10^3 \cdot cm^{-1} \qquad \frac{1}{ff} = 4.666 \cdot \mu m$$

The fundamental frequency (*ff*) is the principle absorption of the vibrational mode for the transition $n = 0$ to 1. As you can see from the wavenumber frequency or the wavelength, this is in the IR region of the spectrum. The overtone band, for $n = 0$ to 2, is weakly observed. As the calculation below shows, it is approximately twice the frequency of the fundamental.

$$ot := \frac{E_{vib}(2) - E_{vib}(0)}{h \cdot c} \qquad 2 \cdot ff = 4.287 \cdot 10^3 \cdot cm^{-1} \qquad ot = 4.260 \cdot 10^3 \cdot cm^{-1} \qquad \frac{1}{ot} = 2.348 \cdot \mu m$$

Of course, the spectroscopic constants given earlier were probably determined by measurement of the fundamental and first overtone frequencies, so we are effectively going backwards here.

Another band that can be observed in the IR is the *hot band (hb)*, for $n = 1$ to 2. It is strongly allowed, like the fundamental, but weaker because, except at high temperatures, there aren't many molecules in the $n = 1$ state. The calculation below of the relative populations of the $n = 0$ and 1 states (right) shows that the intensity of hot band will approximately 4% of the fundamental at 1000 K.

$$hb := \frac{E_{vib}(2) - E_{vib}(1)}{h \cdot c} \qquad ff = 2.143 \cdot 10^3 \cdot cm^{-1} \qquad hb = 2.116 \cdot 10^3 \cdot cm^{-1} \qquad \exp\left(\frac{-h \cdot c \cdot \omega_e}{k_b \cdot 1000 \cdot K} \right) = 0.044$$

This band is most prominent, of course, at high temperature, which is why it's called "hot".

Example 12.10 The Morse potential.

The intermolecular potential is not directly observable but can be deduced from observables such as the spectroscopic constants. Often it is useful to use approximate forms for this potential, the best known being the *Morse potential*:

$$E(R) = D_e[1 - \exp(-\beta(R - R_e)]^2 \tag{12.5}$$

Here, R_e is the distance at which the potential is the minimum (the bond length), and D_e is the well depth (closely related to the bond energy). The Morse constant β is calculated from the spectroscopic constants of the molecule as described below.

$$D_e := D_0 + E_{vib}(0) \qquad D_e = 11.242 \cdot eV$$

$$m_{O16} := 15.9949156 \frac{gm}{L} \qquad m_{C12} := 12 \cdot \frac{gm}{L}$$

$$\mu := \frac{m_{O16} \cdot m_{C12}}{m_{O16} + m_{C12}} \qquad \mu = 1.139 \cdot 10^{-26} \cdot kg$$

The quantity D_0, given above, is the bond energy: the energy required to dissociate a molecule in the $n = 0$ vibrational state. D_e differs from this by the vibrational energy of the $n = 0$ state (box to left). We also need the reduced mass, calculated as shown in box to left.

The calculation of the Morse constant is shown in the box to right. The first problem we have in plotting this function is deciding on a range for R. The box below displays R_e, which gives us some idea of where to start looking.

$$\beta := 2\cdot\pi\cdot c\cdot\omega_e\cdot\sqrt{\frac{\mu}{2\cdot D_e}} \qquad \beta = 2.298\cdot 10^{10}\cdot m^{-1}$$

$$E(R) := D_e\cdot\left[1 - \exp\left[-\beta\cdot\left(R - R_e\right)\right]\right]^2$$

$$R_e = 112.81\cdot pm$$
$$E(76\cdot pm) = 19.891\cdot eV$$
$$E(400\cdot pm) = 11.212\cdot eV$$
$$D_e = 11.242\cdot eV$$

The energy increases rapidly as R goes to zero; the calculation shows that at 76 pm, it is about twice D_e. At large distances, the energy approaches D_e; the sample calculation shows that it is close at 400 pm. This gives us a good idea of the range to plot. (It takes some experimentation to come up with these numbers.)

The graph of the Morse potential for CO is shown in the box to right. Even with a careful choice of the lower limit of R, you may need to manually set the upper limit on the y axis in order to see the interesting parts of the graph clearly.

$$R := 76\cdot pm, 77\cdot pm .. 400\cdot pm$$

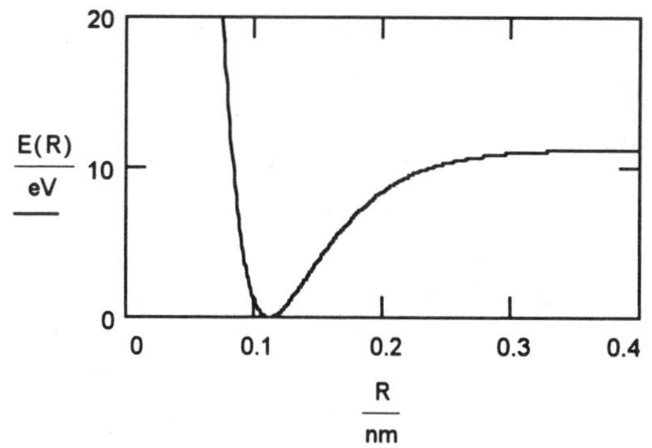

The force constant (k) of the vibration is actually defined as the second derivative of the potential at the minimum ($R = R_e$). The calculation below demonstrates this fact.

$$\omega_e = \frac{1}{2\cdot\pi\cdot c}\cdot\sqrt{\frac{k}{\mu}} \qquad \textit{use Symbolic Solve to get k} \qquad 4\cdot\mu\cdot\omega_e^{2}\cdot\pi^{2}\cdot c^{2}$$

$$k := 4\cdot\mu\cdot\omega_e^{2}\cdot\pi^{2}\cdot c^{2} \qquad k = 1.903\cdot 10^{3}\cdot kg\cdot sec^{-2}$$

$$R := R_e \qquad \frac{d^2}{dR^2}E(R) = 1.903\cdot 10^{3}\cdot kg\cdot sec^{-2}$$

Of course, this is a circular calculation since the Morse constant (β) and the force constant (k) were determined from the same datum (ω_e), but it does make the point about the meaning of k. Also, Mathcad does its differentials numerically, and numerical differentiation is a troublesome and error-prone procedure. The accuracy of the calculation shows how well Mathcad did in this application.

$$D_{em} := \frac{h\cdot c\cdot\omega_e^{2}}{4\cdot wex} \qquad D_e = 11.242\cdot eV \qquad D_{em} = 10.845\cdot eV$$

The calculation in the box to the left illustrates an equation relating the vibrational constants and the well depth, derived from the Morse potential. The formula can be used to estimate anharmonicities or, given an experimental anharmonicity, to estimate the bond strength. The difference between the calculated value (D_{em}) and the actual value (D_e) gives some impression of the accuracy of the Morse potential, which varies from molecule to molecule.

Example 12.11 Rotational spectroscopy.

The rotational energy of a molecule is characterized by the quantum number $J = 0, 1, 2, \ldots$ with the formula

$$E_J = hc\left[J(J+1)B_n - J^2(J+1)^2 D_c\right] \qquad (12.6)$$

where B_n is the rotational constant in the n vibrational state

$$B_n = B_e - (n + \tfrac{1}{2})\alpha_e \qquad (12.7)$$

α_e is the vibration-rotation interaction constant and D_c is the centrifugal stretching constant.

Taking our example for CO (with spectroscopic constants as above), we first estimate the centrifugal stretching constant (box right). As you can see, it is insignificant for as accurately as the rotational constant is given. Also we calculate B_0, the rotational constant for the $n = 0$ vibrational state. The does differ significantly from B_e. The equation for the rotational energy is implemented in the box below.

$$D_c := \frac{4 \cdot B_e^{\,3}}{\omega_e^{\,2}} \qquad D_c = 6.119 \cdot 10^{-6} \cdot cm^{-1}$$

$$B_e = 1.9314 \cdot cm^{-1}$$

$$B_0 := B_e - \frac{1}{2} \cdot \alpha_e \qquad B_0 = 1.9227 \cdot cm^{-1}$$

$$E_{rot}(J) := h \cdot c \cdot \left[J \cdot (J+1) \cdot B_0 - J^2 \cdot (J+1)^2 \cdot D_c \right] \qquad GHz := 10^9 \cdot Hz$$

$$nu(J) := \frac{E_{rot}(J+1) - E_{rot}(J)}{h} \qquad nu(0) = 115.279 \cdot GHz \qquad \lambda := \frac{c}{nu(0)} \qquad \lambda = 2.601 \cdot m$$

The rotational absorptions are from any occupied state J to $J + 1$. These frequencies are usually in the microwave region of the spectrum, as the calculation above illustrates. Note the wavelength, given in *millimeters*, is much longer than for the vibrational absorption.

Example 12.12 Bond length of a diatomic molecule.

Rotational absorptions, generally found in the microwave region of the spectrum, can be measured very accurately, and are the most accurate method for determining bond lengths. The calculation below shows the calculation of the moment of inertia; note that the rotational constant has 7 significant figures (Planck's constant, h, should have at least that many digits, and will if you are using *qconst.mcd*).

$$B_e := 15.48369 \cdot 10^9 \cdot Hz \qquad I := \frac{h}{8 \cdot \pi^2 \cdot B_e} \qquad I = 5.4199113 \cdot 10^{-46} \cdot kg \cdot m^2$$

To maintain accuracy, we need accurate isotopic masses; for example, Noggle, Table 13.2.

$$m_{F19} := 18.9984032 \cdot \frac{gm}{L} \qquad m_{Cl35} := 34.9688527 \cdot \frac{gm}{L} \qquad \mu := \frac{m_{F19} \cdot m_{Cl35}}{m_{F19} + m_{Cl35}}$$

$$\mu = 2.044172 \cdot 10^{-26} \cdot kg \qquad R_e := \sqrt{\frac{I}{\mu}} \qquad R_e = 162.8311 \cdot pm$$

The calculation above gives the bond length to 7 significant figures.

Problems

12.1 The 3*s* state of the hydrogen atom has a radial function

$$R_{3s}(r) := \left(3 - 2 \cdot r + \frac{2 \cdot r^2}{9}\right) \cdot \exp\left(-\frac{r}{3}\right)$$

Make a surface plot of this function and its square.

12.2 For the 3*s* function (problem 12.1), make a graph of the radial distribution function. (a) Determine the positions of the nodes. (b) Calculate the probability that the electron is in each of the 3 humps.

12.3 For the 3*s* function (problem 12.1), calculate $\langle r \rangle$ and $\langle r^2 \rangle$. Report results in nanometers.

12.4 The 3*p* function is

$$R_{3p}(r) := r \cdot \left(4 - \frac{2 \cdot r}{3}\right) \cdot \exp\left(-\frac{r}{3}\right)$$

(a) Calculate the probability that the electron is inside the node. (b) Calculate the average distance between the electron and the nucleus.

12.5 Make surface and contour plots for the $3p\pi$ MOs. How to they differ from the 2*p* examples given in text?

12.6 The observed bond length of H_2^+ is $R_e = 0.132$ nm. Make a contour graph of the electron density at this distance.

12.7 The fundamental and first overtone frequencies of $^1H^{35}Cl$ are 2885.9 and 5668.0 cm^{-1} respectively. Calculate the vibrational constant and anharmonicity from these data.

12.8 The rotational constant of $^{19}F^{37}Cl$ is $B_e = 15.18922$ GHz. Calculate the bond length of this molecule. Compare to the results of Example 12.12 for the ^{35}Cl isotope.

12.9 According to Bohr's theory, the electron is on an orbit with radius $N^2 a_0/Z$. For the 1*s* state we found that this corresponded to the maximum of the radial distribution function (i.e. at $r = a_0$ for the hydrogen atom), which gives an interesting interpretation for the meaning of the Bohr orbits. Is this generally true? Find the maxima for 2*s*, 2*p*, 3*s*, 3*p* and 3*d*. What generalization can you make?

Answers

12.2 nodes = $9/2 \pm 3\sqrt{3}/2$ (b) 1.435, 10.043, 88.522%

12.3 0.714 nm, 0.580 nm^2

12.4 (a) 11.067% (b) 0.661 nm

12.7 2989.7 and 51.9 cm^{-1}

12.8 162.83106 pm compared to 162.83109 pm. No difference to 7 figures.

12.9 The maxima are at the Bohr orbits for the max. *l* for each *n*; that is, 1*s*, 2*p*, 3*d* and 4*f*.

APPENDIX: MATHCAD KEYBOARD OPERATORS

Operators in Mathcad can be invoked in a number of ways including the palettes and menus. The keystroke method is usually faster and most convenient, but only if you remember it. Generally, the ones you use the most will be remembered, but this list may help.. With one exception (the " key) the operators below behave the same way in blank space as they do in an equation.

- `!` Factorial
- `"` In equation, complex conjugate
- `"` In blank space, create text region.
- `#` Range product
- `$` Range sum
- `&` Integral
- `'` Matched pair of parentheses
- `(` Left parenthesis
- `)` Right parenthesis
- `*` Multiplication
- `+` Addition
- `,` Separates arguments in a function
- `,` Separates entries in plot placeholders.
- `,` Precedes 2nd number in range
- `;` Precedes last number in range
- `-` Negation or Subtraction
- `/` Division
- `<` Less than
- `>` Greater than

- `?` Derivative
- `[` Subscript
- `\` Square root
- `^` Power
- `|` Absolute value
- Ctrl+1 Transpose
- Ctrl+3 Not equal to
- Ctrl+4 Vector sum
- Ctrl+9 Less than or equal
- Ctrl+0 Greater than or equal
- Ctrl+8 Cross product
- Ctrl+- Vectorize
- Ctrl+= Equal to
- Ctrl+6 Superscript
- Ctrl+Shift+4 Summation
- Ctrl+Shift+3 Product
- Ctrl+Shift+? nth Derivative
- Ctrl+Enter Addition with line break
- Ctrl+Period Symbolic equal sign

INDEX

Entries in **bold face** are Mathcad commands.